Communications
in Computer and Information Science   1158

More information about this series at http://www.springer.com/series/7899

Sergii Babichev · Dmytro Peleshko ·
Olena Vynokurova (Eds.)

Data Stream Mining & Processing

Third International Conference, DSMP 2020
Lviv, Ukraine, August 21–25, 2020
Proceedings

Springer

Editors
Sergii Babichev 🆔
Department of Informatics
Univerzita Jana Evangelisty
Purkyně v Ústí nad Labem
Ústí nad Labem, Czech Republic

Dmytro Peleshko 🆔
GeoGuard
Kharkiv, Ukraine

Olena Vynokurova 🆔
Kharkiv National University
of Radio Electronics
Kharkiv, Ukraine

ISSN 1865-0929   ISSN 1865-0937 (electronic)
Communications in Computer and Information Science
ISBN 978-3-030-61655-7   ISBN 978-3-030-61656-4   (eBook)
https://doi.org/10.1007/978-3-030-61656-4

This Springer imprint is published by the registered company Springer Nature Switzerland AG
The registered company address is: Gewerbestrasse 11, 6330 Cham, Switzerland

Preface

Collecting, analyzing, and processing information, including big data, are one of the current directions of modern computer science. Many areas of current existence generate a wealth of information which should be stored in a structured manner, analyzed, and processed appropriately in order to gain the knowledge concerning investigated process or object. Creating new modern information and computer technologies for data analysis, and processing in various fields of data mining and machine learning, create the conditions for increasing effectiveness of the information processing by both the decrease of time and the increase of accuracy of the data processing.

The IEEE International Scientific Conference on Data Stream Mining & Processing (DSMP) is a series of conferences performed in East Europe. They are very important for this geographic region since the topics of the conference cover the modern directions in the field of artificial and computational intelligence, data mining, machine learning, and decision making. The aim of the conference is the reflection of the most recent developments in the fields of artificial and computational intelligence used for solving problems in a variety of areas of scientific researches related to data mining, machine learning, big data processing, and decision making.

The third edition of the IEEE DSMP 2020 conference was held in Lviv, Ukraine, during August 21–25, 2020. The conference was held virtually due to the COVID-19 pandemic. DSMP 2020 was a continuation of the highly successful DSMP conference series started in 2016. The last DSMP 2016 and 2018 conferences had attracted hundreds and possibly thousands of researchers and professionals working in the field of artificial intelligence and decision making.

This volume consists of 36 carefully selected papers out of 134 submissions, that were assigned to four thematic sections:

Section 1. Hybrid Systems of Computational Intelligence
Information processing systems which combine different approaches of computational intelligence, for example, artificial neural networks which are learnt by evolutionary algorithms, neuro-fuzzy systems, wavelet-neuro-fuzzy systems, neuro-neo-fuzzy systems, particle swarm algorithms, evolving systems, deep learning, etc.

Section 2. Machine Vision and Pattern Recognition
Video streams that are fed from video cameras in an online mode under environment uncertainty and variability conditions.

Section 3. Dynamic Data Mining & Data Stream Mining
Data mining problems (classification, clustering, prediction, identification, etc.) occur when information is fed in an online mode in the form of data streams.

Section 4. Big Data & Data Science Using Intelligent Approaches
Systems of computational intelligence (artificial neural networks, fuzzy reasoning systems, evolutionary algorithms) in the tasks of big data processing (high-dimensional

data) where data are stored in VLDB or fed in an unlimited data stream. Natural language processing (using machine learning) to get the semantic objects from natural language; the deep learning methods for natural language understanding.

We hope that the broad scope of topics related to the fields of artificial intelligence and decision making, covered in this proceedings volume, will help the reader to understand that the methods of data mining and machine learning have become an important element of modern computer science.

September 2020   Yuriy Rashkevych
                                                        Yevgeniy Bodyanskiy
                                                            Igor Aizenberg

Organization

DSMP 2020 conference was organized by:
- IEEE Ukraine Section, Ukraine
- IEEE Ukraine Section (West) AP/ED/MTT/CPMT/SSC Societies Joint Chapter, Ukraine
- IEEE Ukraine Section IM/CIS Societies Joint Chapter, Ukraine
- Kharkiv National University of Radio Electronics, Ukraine
- Manhattan College, USA
- Ukrainian Catholic University, Ukraine

Executive Committee

Honorary Chairpersons

Yuriy Rashkevych   Lviv Polytechnic National University, Ukraine
Yevgeniy Bodyanskiy   Kharkiv National University of Radio Electronics, Ukraine
Igor Aizenberg   Manhattan College, USA

General Chairs

Dmytro Peleshko   IEEE Ukraine Section (West), Lviv, Ukraine
Olena Vynokurova   IEEE Ukraine Section, Kharkiv, Ukraine
Yaroslav Prytula   Ukrainian Catholic University, Ukraine

Technical Program Committee Chair

Dmytro Peleshko   IEEE Ukraine Section (West), Lviv, Ukraine

Publication Chair and Conference Treasurer

Olena Vynokurova   IEEE Ukraine Section, Kharkiv, Ukraine

Local Organizing Committee Chair

Tetyana Sviridova   EPAM, Lviv, Ukraine

Workshop

Sergii Babichev   University of Jan Evangelista Purkyně in Ústí nad Labem, Czech Republic

Technical Program Committee Members

Ankur Agrawal	Manhattan College, USA
Svitlana Antoshchuk	Odessa National Polytechnic University, Ukraine
Sergii Babichev	University of Jan Evangelista Purkyně in Ústí nad Labem, Czech Republic
Jayaram Balasubramaniam	Indian Institute of Technology, Hyderabad, India
Oleksandr Baiev	Samsung R&D Institute, Kyiv, Ukraine
Oleg Berezkiy	Ternopil National Economic University, Ukraine
Petro Bidyuk	National Technical University of Ukraine "Ighor Sikorsky Kyiv Polytechnic Institute", Ukraine
Sergii Bogomolov	The Australian National University, Australia
Vilalii Boyun	V.M. Glushkov Institute of Cybernetic, NAS, Ukraine
Gennadii Churyumov	Kharkiv National University of Radio Electronics, Ukraine
Ibraim Didmanidze	Batumi Shota Rustaveli State University, Georgia
Kai Du	Penn State University, USA
Mykola Dyvak	Ternopil National Economic University, Ukraine
Oleksandr Dumin	IEEE Ukraine Section, Kharkiv, Ukraine
Andrey Fisunenko	Samsung R&D Institute, Ukraine
Mohammed Gabsi	École normale supérieure Paris-Saclay, France
Mounir Gabsi	Higher Institute of Technological Studies of Sousse, Tunisia
Oleksandr Gozhiy	Petro Mohyla Black Sea National University, Ukraine
Rostyslav Gryniv	Ukrainian Catholic University, Ukraine
Volodymyr Hnatushenko	Dnipro University of Technology, Ukraine
Wen Bin Hu	Shanghai Jiao Tong University, China
Zhengbing Hu	Shanghai Jiao Tong University, China
Kareem Kamal A. Ghany	Beni-Suef University, Egypt
Bekir Karlik	Neurosurgical Simulation Research and Training Centre, Canada
Ghédira Khaled	Ecole Nationale des Sciences de l'Informatique, Tunis
Vyacheslav Kharchenko	National Aerospace University, Kharkiv Aviation Institute, Ukraine
Frank Klawonn	Helmholtz Centre for Infection Research, Germany
Illya Kokshenev	TYPI Ltda R&D, Brazil
Viktor Krylov	Odessa National Polytechnic University, Ukraine
Yurii Krak	Taras Shevchenko National University of Kyiv, Ukraine
Yurii Kondratenko	Petro Mohyla Black Sea National University, Ukraine
ChuiWei Lu	HuangShi Institute of Technology, China
Volodymyr Lytvynenko	Kherson National Technical University, Ukraine
Leonid Lyubchik	National Technical University, Kharkiv Polytechnic Institute, Ukraine
Yaroslav Lubinets	SoftServe, Ukraine
Mykola Malyar	Uzhhorod National University, Ukraine

Krassimir Markov — Institute for Information Theories and Applications, Bulgaria

Viktor Mashkov — University of Jan Evangelista Purkyně in Ústí nad Labem, Czech Republic

Volodymyr Mashtalir — Kharkiv National University of Radio Electronics, Ukraine

Sergii Mashtalir — Kharkiv National University of Radio Electronics, Ukraine

Andrian Nakonechny — Lviv Polytechnic National University, Ukraine

Eduard Petlenkov — Tallinn University of Technology, Estonia

Shao-Cheng Qu — Central China Normal University, China

Taras Panchenko — ACM Ukrainian Chapter, Kyiv, Ukraine

Nataliya Pankratova — National Technical University of Ukraine "Ighor Sikorsky Kyiv Polytechnic Institute", Ukraine

Bohdan Pavlyshenko — SoftServe, Ukraine

Ievgen Pichkalov — IEEE Ukraine Section, Ukraine

Kashifuddin Qazi — Manhattan College, USA

Olga Radyvonenko — Samsung R&D Institute, Ukraine

Ali Rekik — Sfax University, Tunisia

Yurii Romanyshyn — Lviv Polytechnic National University, Ukraine

Bohdan Rusyn — Lviv Institute of Physics and Mechanics, Ukraine

Anatolii Sachenko — Ternopil National Economic University, Ukraine

Galina Setlak — Rzeszow University of Technology, Poland

Nataliya Sharonova — Kharkiv National University of Radio Electronics, Ukraine

Igor Shelevytsky — Kryvyi Rih Economic Institute, Ukraine

Aleksandr Slipchenko — Booking.com BV, The Netherlands

Andrzej Smolarz — Lublin University of Technology, Poland

Vitalii Snytyuk — Taras Shevchenko National University of Kyiv, Ukraine

Oleksandr Sokolov — Nicolaus Copernicus University, Poland

Yaroslav Sokolovsky — Ukrainian National Forestry University, Ukraine

Makram Souii — University of Gabes, Tunisia

Volodymyr Stepashko — National Academy of Sciences of Ukraine, Ukraine

Martin Štěpnička — Institute for Research and Applications of Fuzzy Modeling, CEIT Innovations, University of Ostrava, Czech Republic

Sergii Subbotin — Zaporizhia National Technical University, Ukraine

Jun Su — Hubei University of Technology, China

Zdislav Szymanski — Społeczna Akademia Nauk, Poland

Moncef Temani — University of Sfax, Tunisia

Oleksii Tyshchenko — Institute for Research and Applications of Fuzzy Modeling, CEIT Innovations, University of Ostrava, Czech Republic

Roman Tkachenko — Lviv Polytechnic National University, Ukraine

Ivan Tsmots — Lviv Polytechnic National University, Ukraine

Kristina Vassiljeva   Tallinn University of Technology, Estonia
Valentyna Volkova   Samsung R&D Institute, Ukraine
Roman Vorobel   Institute of the National Academy of Sciences of
                              Ukraine, Ukraine
Sergii Vorobyov   IEEE Member, Finland
Waldemar Wójcik   Lublin University of Technology, Poland
J. Q. Wu   Hubei University of Technology, China
Felix Yanovsky   IEEE Ukraine Section, Kyiv, Ukraine
Myhailo Yatsymirskyy   Lodz University of Technology, Poland
Zhi Wei Ye   Hubei University of Technology, China
Elena Yegorova   London Media Exchange, UK
Yevhenii Yakishyn   Samsung R&D Institute, Ukraine

Local Organizing Committee Members

Iryna Perova   Kharkiv National University of Radio Electronics,
                              Ukraine
Polina Zhernova   Kharkiv National University of Radio Electronics,
                              Ukraine
Vlad Alekseyev   Lviv Polytechnic National University, Ukraine
Mykhailo Andriychuk   IEEE Ukraine Section (West), Lviv, Ukraine
Yuriy Borzov   Lviv Polytechnic National University, Ukraine
Anastasia Doroshenko   Lviv Polytechnic National University, Ukraine
Roman Figura   University of Social Sciences, Poland
Diana Kndzera   Lviv Polytechnic National University, Ukraine
Igor Malets   Lviv State University of Life Safety, Ukraine
Roman Martsyshyn   Lviv Polytechnic National University, Ukraine
Yulia Miyushkovych   Lviv Polytechnic National University, Ukraine
Nadiia Tsiura   IT Step University, Ukraine
Victoriia Lutsko   Intellias, Ukraine
Viktoria Vysotska   Lviv Polytechnic National University, Ukraine

Sponsoring Institutions

IEEE Ukrainian Section (Technical Co-sponsor)

Contents

Hybrid Systems of Computational Intelligence

Machine Vision and Pattern Recognition

Hybrid Systems of Computational Intelligence

On-Line Relaxation Versus Off-Line Spectral Algorithm in the Learning of Polynomial Neural Units

Vladyslav Kotsovsky[1](✉) and Anatoliy Batyuk[2]

[1] Uzhhorod National University, Uzhhorod, Ukraine
kotsavlad@gmail.com
[2] Lviv Polytechnic National University, Lviv, Ukraine
abatyuk@gmail.com

Abstract. The problem of the learning of polynomial threshold units over a fixed set of polynomials is treated in the paper. We consider two approaches in the supervised learning: off-line relaxation-like algorithms and spectral off-line algorithms. Our research is focused on answering the question: what values of the learning rate provide the fast convergence of the learning algorithm? We propose and justify a new adaptive rule of the choice of learning rates, which ensures that on-line relaxation-like algorithms produce a desired weight vector of polynomial neural unit after a finite number of learning steps. Then, we deal with the spectral off-line learning algorithm and give the reasons that the extension of the range of acceptable values for the learning rate preserves the convergence and the finiteness of learning. The relaxation-like learning algorithm with margin is also considered. Its advantage is the finite learning time in the case when a constant learning rate belongs to $(0, 2]$. Next, we propose a new rule of the choice of initial approximation significantly accelerating the convergence both for on-line and for off-line learning. Finally, the simulation results are given for quadratic neural units, which confirm the validity and the advantage of the proposed approaches.

Keywords: Polynomial neural unit · Neural network · On-line learning · Off-line learning · Relaxation

1 Introduction

Neural networks find applications in such important fields as intensive data processing [11], time series analysis [6,10], classification [2], pattern recognition [12], signal processing [22,24], information security [23], natural language processing [16], decision making [18,19], and control [20] by virtue of an important property: the ability to learn from input data [9]. First neural networks used the threshold activation function and linear input operator [1]. Somewhat later, many kinds of more sophisticated models of neural units were proposed in order to increase the computational power and the capability of the networks [9,21].

© Springer Nature Switzerland AG 2020
S. Babichev et al. (Eds.): DSMP 2020, CCIS 1158, pp. 3–21, 2020.
https://doi.org/10.1007/978-3-030-61656-4_1

For example, neurons with more complicated activation functions were introduced. Multithreshold-like activations were studied in [13,15], continuous ones were described in [9]. Another approach deals with a non-linear input operator of neurons. One of the most popular in this direction is a model of polynomial threshold unit (PTU), which is a powerful generalization of the linear threshold unit [1]. PTUs use the threshold activation function and are applied in the design of effective classifiers based on the separation in Euclidean space using a polynomial decision hypersurface [1,9]. The theoretical foundation of the representational power of PTUs is the well-known Cover's theorem on the separability of patterns [9].

The most important issue concerning the polynomial units is the problem of their learning. Let us consider some prominent works in the field. First, the perceptron learning algorithm was used (see [1] for details). Next, the relaxation method of Motzkin and Schoenberg [17] was applied [8]. The batch generalization of the relaxation with margin was proposed in [4]. The linear programming approach was also considered [1]. Kotsovsky et al. developed the off-line learning algorithm [14], which stemmed from Dertouzos' synthesis iterative procedure based on the use of characteristic vectors of Boolean functions [3].

The key question concerning learning algorithms based on the use of relaxation-like rules is the choice of the learning rate. These algorithms were proved to be convergent but can have an infinite learning time and produce the unacceptable vectors lying on the boundary of the solution region [4,9]. Therefore, the theoretical results concerning the conditions ensuring the finiteness of learning are very important.

The classical version of Relaxation for solving a system of linear inequalities was proved finite only when the learning rate is equal to 2 [17]. Goffin established that finite convergence occurs for any value of learning rate between one and two in the case of obtuse polyhedrons [7]. Hampson and Kibler claimed [8] that a slightly larger learning rate (namely, 2.001) improves performance and leads to the finite learning time. Notice that their consequence was based only on empirical results and was not supported by any proof or theoretical reasons. The finiteness of the learning procedure for PTU in the case of both batch and off-line learning was unknown for a long time. For the first time the conditions on the learning rate ensuring the finite convergence of the off-line spectral learning appeared in [14], where the wide range of admissible values for learning rate was established. But similar conditions are unknown in the case of the PTU learning using relaxation-like algorithms. The important question also remains unclear regarding the efficient choice of an initial approximation for such algorithms.

The aim of the research is the study of on-line and off-line methods for learning PTUs, finding the learning rate values ensuring the finite convergence and the comparison of the efficiency of on-line and off-line approaches in the learning of PTU.

The paper has the following structure: first, the model of PTU is defined and the notion of P-threshold function is introduced. Then, the off-line Relaxation-like learning algorithm is described and the rule of the choice of learning coefficients is proposed ensuring the Fejér condition and the finiteness of learning. In the next subsection the off-line spectral learning algorithm is considered. Then, we deal with the off-line learning with margin. Thereafter, we treat the question concerning the initial approximation both for on-line and for off-line learning. Finally, we give simulation results, compare the performance of learning algorithms and discuss their efficiency.

2 Materials and Methods

2.1 Model of a Polynomial Threshold Unit

A computation unit with n inputs $x_1, \ldots, x_n$ and one output $y \in \{-1, 1\}$ is a polynomial threshold unit (PTU) with the weight vector $\mathbf{w} = (w_1, \ldots, w_m)$ if

$$y = \mathrm{sgn} \left(\sum_{k=1}^{m} w_k \prod_{i=1}^{n} x_i^{j_{ki}} \right), \quad j_{ki} \in \{0, 1, \ldots\}, \quad k = 1, \ldots, m, \ i = 1, \ldots, n,$$

where

$$\mathrm{sgn}\,(x) = \begin{cases} 1 & \text{if } x > 0, \\ 0 & \text{if } x = 0, \\ -1 & \text{if } x > 0, \end{cases}$$

is the activation function of the PTU.

We pay our attention on the important subtask concerning the application of PTUs—namely, the separation of binary patterns of the length n, i.e., all considered patterns are vertices of a n-dimensional Boolean hypercube. For many reason it is more convenient to deal with data in the bipolar base $E_2 = \{-1, 1\}$ [1]. Then we can simplify the polynomial to the weighted sum of the terms $x_{i_1} \ldots x_{i_k}$ [14].

We shall treat a Boolean function as a mapping $f : E_2^n \to E_2$, where $E_2^n = \underbrace{E_2 \times \ldots \times E_2}_{n \text{ times}}$.

Let us to consider monomials $p : E_2^n \to E_2$ of the form $p(\mathbf{x}) = x_1^{j_1} \cdot \ldots \cdot x_n^{j_n}$, where $\mathbf{x} = (x_1, \ldots, x_n) \in E_2^n$, $j_i \in \{0, 1\}$, $(i = 1, \ldots n)$, that is, $p(\mathbf{x}) = \prod_{i:\ j_i=1} x_i$. The total number of all possible monomials whose degree does not exceed k is $\binom{n+k}{k}$ in the general case and $\sum_{i=0}^{k} \binom{n}{i}$ in the binary case [1], where $\binom{n}{i}$ are binomial coefficients. Thus, the weight vector of PTU, which contains all possible monomials of degree k, can be very large. For this reason relatively small numbers of k are used in practice. Another approach consists in the use of a predefined set of m polynomials, where m is a number chosen with respect to a specific task. Let $P = \{p_1, \ldots, p_m\}$ be an arbitrary set of monomials. After fixing the set P and selecting the weight vector $\mathbf{w} = (w_1, \ldots, w_m)$ we can consider the following simplified model of PTU:

$$f(\mathbf{x}) = \mathrm{sgn} \left(\sum_{j=1}^{m} w_j p_j(\mathbf{x}) \right), \tag{1}$$

where $f(\mathbf{x})$ is the output function of PTU. Let $\mathbf{p}(\mathbf{x}) = (p_1(\mathbf{x}), \ldots, p_m(\mathbf{x}))$. We can rewrite (1) in the form $f(\mathbf{x}) = \operatorname{sgn}(\mathbf{w} \cdot \mathbf{p}(\mathbf{x}))$, where $\mathbf{w} \cdot \mathbf{p}(\mathbf{x})$ is the dot product of vectors $\mathbf{w}$ and $\mathbf{p}(\mathbf{x})$. Furthermore, we demand that the weight vector $\mathbf{w}$ obey: for all $\mathbf{x} \in E_2^n$ $\mathbf{w} \cdot \mathbf{p}(\mathbf{x}) \neq 0$. We call such weight vectors P-acceptable. Every PTU with the P-acceptable weight vector $\mathbf{w}$ induces the corresponding Boolean function $f(\mathbf{x})$ defined according to (1). We say that $f(\mathbf{x})$ is a P-threshold function. We denotes the set of all weight vectors satisfying (1) for the given P-threshold function f as $W_P(f)$.

2.2   Relaxation Learning

We shall consider two supervised learning algorithms to train a PTU to realize a given P-threshold Boolean function $f(\mathbf{x})$ of n variables, where $P = \{p_1, \ldots, p_m\}$ is the fixed set of monomials. First, we consider on-line learning algorithm based on the relaxation procedure. Let k denotes a current step of learning algorithm (we shall write it in the superscript of vectors and in the subscript of scalar values), $\mathbf{w}^k$ is a weight vector of PTU in step k, $X_k = \{\mathbf{x} \in E_2^n | \operatorname{sgn}(\mathbf{w}^k \cdot \mathbf{p}(\mathbf{x})) \neq f(\mathbf{x})\}$ is a set of misclassified patterns, $\mathbf{p}^k = \mathbf{p}(\mathbf{x}^k)$, $t_k > 0$ is a learning rate depending on $\mathbf{w}^k, \mathbf{x}^k, P, f, t_k^{(1)}, t_k^{(2)}$, where $t_k^{(1)}, t_k^{(2)}$ are two additional sequences. In greater detail, then, the algorithm is as follows:

Algorithms 1 (Single-Sample Relaxation):

1 initialize $\mathbf{w}^0, \left\{t_k^{(1)}\right\}, \left\{t_k^{(2)}\right\}$
2 $k \leftarrow 0$
3 while $X^k \neq \varnothing$:
4   select randomly $\mathbf{x}^k \in X^k$
5      $t_k \leftarrow t\left(\mathbf{w}^k, \mathbf{x}^k, P, f, t_k^{(1)}, t_k^{(2)}\right)$
6      $\mathbf{w}^{k+1} \leftarrow \mathbf{w}^k - t_k \dfrac{\mathbf{w}^k \cdot \mathbf{p}^k}{m}\mathbf{p}^k$
7      $k \leftarrow k + 1$
8 return $\mathbf{w}^k$

Single-Sample Relaxation is based on the use of the decrement vector

$$\Delta \mathbf{w}^k = t_k \frac{\mathbf{w}^k \cdot \mathbf{p}^k}{m}\mathbf{p}^k \tag{2}$$

in kth iteration of learning and the correction $\mathbf{w}^{k+1} = \mathbf{w}^k - \Delta \mathbf{w}^k$, $(k = 0, 1, \ldots)$ in step 6, where the value of coefficient t_k is calculated in step 5 using a function $t\left(\mathbf{w}^k, \mathbf{x}^k, P, f, t_k^{(1)}, t_k^{(2)}\right)$, which will be specified later.

It is well known that the relaxation algorithm converges in the case $0 < t_k < 2$ [4]. Moreover, the relaxation learning is finite if $t_k = 2$ [17]. The relaxation method is based on the fact that if $0 < t_k \leq 2$, then the Fejér condition [17]:

$$\left\|\mathbf{w}^{k+1} - \mathbf{w}\right\| < \left\|\mathbf{w}^k - \mathbf{w}\right\| \tag{3}$$

holds for all $\mathbf{w} \in W_P(f)$, where $\|\mathbf{x}\| = \sqrt{\mathbf{x} \cdot \mathbf{x}}$ is the Euclidean norm in the space $\mathbb{R}^m$. Hampson and Kibler claimed in [8] that the use of $t_k = 2.001$ provides the finiteness of the learning and decreases the duration of the learning procedure. We justify the correctness of this "overrelaxation" approach shortly. Namely, we show that the relaxation algorithm is finite for a more wide range of values for the learning rate t_k.

First, let us to show that we can extend the admissible range for t_k if we want that (3) holds only for a given $\mathbf{w} \in W_P(f)$. Inequality (3) is equal to

$$\left\| \mathbf{w}^{k+1} - \mathbf{w} \right\|^2 - \left\| \mathbf{w}^k - \mathbf{w} \right\|^2 < 0.$$

Since

$$\left\| \mathbf{w}^{k+1} - \mathbf{w} \right\|^2 = \left\| \left(\mathbf{w}^{k+1} - \mathbf{w}^k \right) + \left(\mathbf{w}^k - \mathbf{w} \right) \right\|^2 =$$
$$\left\| \mathbf{w}^k - \mathbf{w} \right\|^2 - 2 \left(\mathbf{w}^k - \mathbf{w} \right) \cdot \Delta \mathbf{w}^k + \left\| \Delta \mathbf{w}^k \right\|^2,$$

Fejér condition (3) holds if the following inequality is true

$$\left\| \Delta \mathbf{w}^k \right\|^2 - 2 \left(\mathbf{w}^k - \mathbf{w} \right) \cdot \Delta \mathbf{w}^k < 0. \tag{4}$$

By using (2) and taking into account that $\|\mathbf{p}^k\|^2 = m$, we can rewrite (4) as

$$\frac{\left(\mathbf{w}^k \cdot \mathbf{p}^k \right)^2 t_k^2}{m} - 2 t_k \frac{\mathbf{w}^k \cdot \mathbf{p}^k}{m} \left(\mathbf{w}^k - \mathbf{w} \right) \cdot \mathbf{p}^k < 0.$$

The solution of the previous quadratic inequality is given by

$$0 < t_k < \frac{2 \left(\mathbf{w}^k - \mathbf{w} \right) \cdot \mathbf{p}^k}{\mathbf{w}^k \cdot \mathbf{p}^k}.$$

Thus, (3) is satisfied for a given $\mathbf{w}$ if

$$0 < t_k < 2 \left(1 - \frac{\mathbf{w} \cdot \mathbf{p}^k}{\mathbf{w}^k \cdot \mathbf{p}^k} \right). \tag{5}$$

Since $\mathbf{x}^k \in X_k$, $\mathrm{sgn}\left(\mathbf{w} \cdot \mathbf{p}^k \right) \neq \mathrm{sgn}\left(\mathbf{w}^k \cdot \mathbf{p}^k \right)$. Hence, the upper bound for t_k in (5) is greater than 2. Consider the set $W_P(f, \mathbb{Z}) = W_P(f) \cap \mathbb{Z}^m$. It was shown in [14] that $W_P(f, \mathbb{Z}) \neq \varnothing$. Let τ be an arbitrary positive real number. Since for all $\mathbf{w} \in \tau W_P(f, \mathbb{Z}) = \{\tau \mathbf{w} \mid \mathbf{w} \in W_P(f, \mathbb{Z})\} \mid \mathbf{w} \cdot p(\mathbf{x})| \geq \tau$, we can conclude that the weight vectors $\mathbf{w}^k$ satisfy Fejér condition (3) for the set $\tau W_P(f, \mathbb{Z})$ if

$$0 < t_k < 2 + \frac{2\tau}{|\mathbf{w}^k \cdot \mathbf{p}^k|}. \tag{6}$$

Now we can state our main result, which give sufficient conditions providing the finiteness of relaxation-like learning.

Proposition 1. *If f is an arbitrary P-threshold Boolean function and learning rates t_k are chosen according to the following adaptive rule:*

$$t_k = t_k^{(1)} - \frac{f\left(\mathbf{x}^k\right) t_k^{(2)}}{\mathbf{w}^k \cdot \mathbf{p}^k}, \tag{7}$$

where

$$0 \le t_k^{(1)} \le 2, \quad 0 < t_{\text{inf}}^{(2)} \le t_k^{(2)} \le t_{\text{sup}}^{(2)} < \infty \quad (k = 0, 1, \ldots), \tag{8}$$

then Algorithms 1 converges finitely to a weight vector of $W_P(f)$.

Proof. We need two additional lemmas from [14].

Lemma 1. *Let X be a set in Euclidean space. If for all $\mathbf{x} \in X$ $\|\mathbf{v} - \mathbf{x}\| < \|\mathbf{w} - \mathbf{x}\|$, then the inequality $\|\mathbf{v} - \mathbf{y}\| < \|\mathbf{w} - \mathbf{y}\|$ holds for all $\mathbf{y}$ belonging to the convex hull of the set X.*

Lemma 2. *Let $\{\mathbf{x}^n\}$ be a sequence of m-dimensional real vectors, $D \subset \mathbb{R}^m$ and the interior of the set D in non-empty. If for every $\mathbf{z} \in D$ $\|\mathbf{x}^{n+1} - \mathbf{z}\| < \|\mathbf{x}^n - \mathbf{z}\|$, then the sequence $\{\mathbf{x}^n\}$ is convergent.*

Suppose the contrary. Then the sequence of weight vectors $\{\mathbf{w}^k\}$ is infinite. Let $\mathbf{w} \in W_P(f, \mathbb{Z})$ and $\tau = \max\left\{\sup\left\{t_k^{(1)}\right\}, t_{\text{sup}}^{(2)}\right\}$. For all weight vectors from the set $\tau W_P(f, \mathbb{Z})$ the choice of the increment coefficients according to (7)–(8) ensures that condition (6) is satisfied. Thus, the use of decrements in the form (2) provides that the Fejér condition for the set $\tau W_P(f, \mathbb{Z})$ is true for every member of the sequence $\{\mathbf{w}^k\}$. It was shown in [14] that if $\mathbf{w} \in W_P(f, \mathbb{Z})$, then $2\mathbf{w} \pm \mathbf{e}_j \in W_P(f, \mathbb{Z})$, where $\mathbf{e}_j$ are m-dimensional unit vectors, $j = 1, \ldots, m$ (i.e., $\mathbf{e}_j = (0, \ldots, 0, 1, 0, \ldots, 0)$ is the unit vector along the jth direction). Let A be the convex hull of the set $\tau \{2\mathbf{w} + \mathbf{e}_1, \ldots, 2\mathbf{w} + \mathbf{e}_m, 2\mathbf{w} - \mathbf{e}_1, \ldots, 2\mathbf{w} - \mathbf{e}_m\}$. By applying Lemma 1 to the polytope A we obtain that if $\mathbf{z} \in A$, then for every $k \ge 0$ the following inequality is true: $\|\mathbf{w}^{k+1} - \mathbf{z}\| < \|\mathbf{w}^k - \mathbf{z}\|$. Since $B(2\tau\mathbf{w}, 1) \subset A$, where $B(2\tau\mathbf{w}, 1)$ is unit open ball with the center in the point $2\tau\mathbf{w}$, the condition of Lemma 2 is satisfied. Therefore, we can conclude that the convergence of the sequence $\{\mathbf{w}^k\}$ take place. Consider the decrement vector (2):

$$\Delta\mathbf{w}^k = t_k \frac{\mathbf{w}^k \cdot \mathbf{p}^k}{m} \mathbf{p}^k = \frac{t_k^{(1)}\left(\mathbf{w}^k \cdot \mathbf{p}^k\right) - t_k^{(2)} f\left(\mathbf{x}^k\right)}{m} \mathbf{p}^k.$$

Hence,

$$\left\|\Delta\mathbf{w}^k\right\| = \frac{t_k^{(1)}\left|\mathbf{w}^k \cdot \mathbf{p}^k\right| + t_k^{(2)}}{m} \left\|\mathbf{p}^k\right\| \ge \frac{t_k^{(2)}}{\sqrt{m}} \ge \frac{t_{\text{inf}}^{(2)}}{\sqrt{m}} > 0.$$

Consequently, the necessary condition of the convergence $\Delta\mathbf{w}^k \to 0$ is broken down. Therefore, the learning process terminates on some $k \ge 0$ yielding P-acceptable weight vector $\mathbf{w}^k \in W_P(f)$.

2.3 Off-Line Spectral Learning

Now we consider off-line learning algorithm, which was proposed in [14]. Let us define the spectral vector $\mathbf{s}(f)$ in the following way:

$$\mathbf{s}(f) = \sum_{\mathbf{x} \in E_2^n} \mathbf{p}(\mathbf{x}) f(\mathbf{x}).$$

Therefore, $\mathbf{s}(f) = (s_1, \ldots s_m)$, where

$$s_j = \sum_{\mathbf{x} \in E_2^n} p_j(\mathbf{x}) f(\mathbf{x}), \quad j = \overline{1, m}.$$

Note that spectral vector $\mathbf{s}(f)$ differs from the spectrum of the Boolean function f with respect to set P only by the constant coefficient 2^n (i.e., we do not divide all coordinates of $\mathbf{s}(f)$ by 2^n). In greater detail, then, our modification of the spectral algorithm is as follows:

Algorithms 2 (Off-line Spectral Learning):

1 initialize $\mathbf{w}^0, \left\{ t_k^{(1)} \right\}, \left\{ t_k^{(2)} \right\}$
2 compute $\mathbf{s}(f)$
3 compute $f^0 = \mathrm{sgn}\left(\mathbf{w}^0 \cdot \mathbf{p}(\mathbf{x}) \right)$
4 $k \leftarrow 0$
5 while $f^k \neq f$:
6   compute $\mathbf{s}\left(f^k \right)$
7      $t_k \leftarrow t\left(\mathbf{w}^k, \mathbf{s}(f), \mathbf{s}\left(f^k \right), t_k^{(1)}, t_k^{(2)} \right)$
8      $\mathbf{w}^{k+1} \leftarrow \mathbf{w}^k - t_k \dfrac{\left(\mathbf{s}(f) - \mathbf{s}\left(f^k \right) \right) \cdot \mathbf{w}^k}{\left\| \mathbf{s}(f) - \mathbf{s}(f^k) \right\|^2} \left(\mathbf{s}(f) - \mathbf{s}\left(f^k \right) \right)$
9      $k \leftarrow k + 1$
10   compute $f^k = \mathrm{sgn}\left(\mathbf{w}^k \cdot \mathbf{p}(\mathbf{x}) \right)$
11 return $\mathbf{w}^k$

Algorithm 2 is based on the use of decrements

$$\Delta \mathbf{w}^k = t_k \frac{\left(\mathbf{s}(f) - \mathbf{s}\left(f^k \right) \right) \cdot \mathbf{w}^k}{\left\| \mathbf{s}(f) - \mathbf{s}(f^k) \right\|^2} \left(\mathbf{s}(f) - \mathbf{s}\left(f^k \right) \right) \tag{9}$$

in step 8 instead of (2). Consider what values of the coefficients t_k ensure that Fejér condition (3) is true for a given $\mathbf{w} \in W_P(f)$ in the case of decrement (9). When we substitute (9) into (4), we obtain

$$\frac{\left(\mathbf{s}(f) - \mathbf{s}\left(f^k \right) \right) \cdot \mathbf{w}^k}{\left\| \mathbf{s}(f) - \mathbf{s}(f^k) \right\|^2} \left(2t_k \left(\mathbf{w}^k - \mathbf{w} \right) + t_k^2 \mathbf{w}^k \right) \cdot \left(\mathbf{s}(f) - \mathbf{s}\left(f^k \right) \right) < 0.$$

The last inequality is equivalent to

$$2t_k \left(\mathbf{w}^k - \mathbf{w} \right) \cdot \left(\mathbf{s}(f) - \mathbf{s}\left(f^k \right) \right) + t_k^2 \left(\mathbf{s}(f) - \mathbf{s}\left(f^k \right) \right) \cdot \mathbf{w}^k > 0, \tag{10}$$

since $(\mathbf{s}(f) - \mathbf{s}(f^k)) \cdot \mathbf{w}^k < 0$ in the case $f^k \neq f$ by the generalized Chow's theorem [14]. Inequality (10) is a quadratic inequality of the variable t_k with negative leading coefficient $(\mathbf{s}(f) - \mathbf{s}(f^k)) \cdot \mathbf{w}^k$. The roots of the corresponding quadratic trinomial are 0 and $2 + 2\mathbf{w} \cdot (\mathbf{s}(f) - \mathbf{s}(f^k)) (\mathbf{w}^k \cdot (\mathbf{s}(f^k) - \mathbf{s}(f)))^{-1}$. Therefore, inequality (3) holds for fixed $\mathbf{w} \in W_P(f)$ if the value of the learning rate t_k satisfies the following inequality:

$$0 < t_k < 2 + \frac{2\mathbf{w} \cdot (\mathbf{s}(f) - \mathbf{s}(f^k))}{\mathbf{w}^k \cdot (\mathbf{s}(f^k) - \mathbf{s}(f))}. \tag{11}$$

Notice that (11) appeared in [14] without a proof.

It should be noted that we require that for all $\mathbf{x} \in E_2^n$ $\mathbf{w}^{k+1} \cdot \mathbf{p}(\mathbf{x}) \neq 0$ if the decrement is chosen according either to (2) or to (9) (i.e., the weight vector $\mathbf{w}^{k+1}$ must be P-acceptable). This requirement is important, since P-acceptability ensures that $\Delta \mathbf{w}^k \neq \mathbf{0}$—that is, the relaxation-like process does not stop on some $\mathbf{w}^k \notin W_P(f)$. If P-acceptability is violated, then we always can regain it by small reduction of the coefficient t_k without losing (5) or (11), respectively. Let $\Delta \mathbf{w}^k$ be a decrement violating the P-acceptability of $\mathbf{w}^{k+1} = \mathbf{w}^k - \Delta \mathbf{w}^k$. It was shown in [14] that decrement

$$\Delta \tilde{\mathbf{w}}^k = (1 - \beta_k) \, \Delta \mathbf{w}^k, \tag{12}$$

where

$$\beta_k = \min \left\{ \frac{1}{2}, \frac{\min \{ |\mathbf{w}^{k+1} \cdot \mathbf{p}(\mathbf{x})| \, | \, \mathbf{x} \in E_2^n \backslash A_k \}}{2 \max \{ |\Delta \mathbf{w}^k \cdot \mathbf{p}(\mathbf{x})| \, | \, \mathbf{a} \in A_k \}} \right\},$$

$A_k = \{ \mathbf{x} \, | \, \mathbf{x} \in E_2^n, \, \mathbf{w}^{k+1} \cdot \mathbf{p}(\mathbf{x}) = 0 \}$, ensures that $\mathbf{w}^k + \Delta \tilde{\mathbf{w}}^k$ is P-acceptable. This reduction is valid in the case of either on-line or spectral learning. It was proved that if the learning rate is chosen in the form

$$t_k = t_k^{(1)} + \frac{t_k^{(2)}}{\mathbf{w}^k \cdot (\mathbf{s}(f^k) - \mathbf{s}(f))}, \tag{13}$$

where sequences $\{t_k^{(1)}\}$, $\{t_k^{(2)}\}$ satisfy (8), then Spectral Learning is finite [14].

2.4   Learning with Margin

We saw that (7) together with (8) ensure the finiteness of Algorithm 1. Consider the following modification of Algorithm 1, which uses a positive margin b and provides the finiteness for more wide range of learning rates:

Algorithm 3 (Single-Sample Relaxation with Margin):

1 initialize b, $\mathbf{w}^0$, $\{t_k^{(1)}\}$, $\{t_k^{(2)}\}$
2 $k \leftarrow 0$
3 while $X^k \neq \varnothing$:

4   select randomly $\mathbf{x}^k \in X^k$

5        $t_k \leftarrow t\left(\mathbf{w}^k, \mathbf{x}^k, P, f, b, t_k^{(1)}, t_k^{(2)}\right)$

6        $\mathbf{w}^{k+1} \leftarrow \mathbf{w}^k - t_k \dfrac{\mathbf{w}^k \cdot \mathbf{p}^k - bf\left(\mathbf{x}^k\right)}{m} \mathbf{p}^k$

7        $k \leftarrow k + 1$

8   return $\mathbf{w}^k$

Notice that our modification differs from the Relaxation with Margin from [4] by the termination condition of the loop. We do not request a strong separation of true and false points of the function f with the margin b, but only use this margin when performing the correction in step 6. The following result gives conditions providing the finiteness of learning:

Proposition 2. *If f is an arbitrary P-threshold Boolean function, $b > 0$ and the learning rates t_k are chosen as*

$$t_k = t_k^{(1)} + \frac{t_k^{(2)}}{|\mathbf{w}^k \cdot \mathbf{p}^k| + b},$$

where

$$0 < t_{\inf}^{(1)} \le t_k^{(1)} \le 2, \ \ 0 \le t_k^{(2)} \le t_{\sup}^{(2)} < \infty \ \ (k = 0,\, 1,\, \ldots), \tag{14}$$

then Algorithms 3 converges finitely to a weight vector belonging to $W_P\left(f\right)$.

The proof is omitted and can be obtained using the techniques similar to the ones employed in the proofs of Proposition 1. Notice that the use of margins ensures that decrement vectors $t_k m^{-1}\left(\mathbf{w}^k \cdot \mathbf{p}^k - bf\left(\mathbf{x}^k\right)\right)\mathbf{p}^k$ in step 6 are always non-zero. Thus, we can execute step 6 of Algorithm 3 without additional efforts to keep the P-acceptability of weight vectors by using decrement correction rules similar to (12). It should be also noted that (14) ensures the finiteness in the case of constant learning rates (i.e., $t_k = t \in (0, 2]$).

2.5   Choice of the Initial Approximation

Traditionally, the random initial approximation $\mathbf{w}^0$ for relaxation-like algorithms is used [4]. This approach has the only merit in the learning of PTU that it leads almost certainly to the sequence of P-acceptable weight vectors $\mathbf{w}^k$, $k = 0, 1, \ldots$. But the learning can be slow enough. In [14] we suggested to use

$$\mathbf{w}^0 = \mathbf{s}\left(f\right) \tag{15}$$

as the initial approximation for the spectral learning. The simulation results prove that for Single-Sample Relaxation approximation (15) can be even more profitable than in the case of off-line learning. We can explain such choice of $\mathbf{w}^0$ by the following properties of the spectral vector $\mathbf{s}\left(f\right) = (s_1, \ldots, s_m)$:

1) if f is a P-threshold function, then there exists $\mathbf{w} = (w_1, \ldots, w_m) \in W_P\left(f\right)$ such that $\mathrm{sgn}w_i = \mathrm{sgn}s_i$, $i = 1, \ldots m$;

2) if f is a P-threshold function, then there exists $\mathbf{w} = (w_1, \ldots, w_m) \in W_P(f)$ such that $\operatorname{sgn}(w_i - w_j) = \operatorname{sgn}(s_i - s_j)$, $i, j = 1, \ldots m$.

Properties 1, 2 are the generalization of the similar properties for linear threshold units from [3]. Therefore, the use of (15) ensures that the coefficients of $\mathbf{w}^0$ have the right sign and, in addition, they are ordered in a proper way. Thus, (15) allows omit the long sequence of corrections necessary to attain the obligatory conditions 1, 2. Note that the random $\mathbf{w}^0$ is unlikely to satisfy these conditions (the corresponding probability is less than $1/m!$). The only disadvantage of the initial approximation (15) is the possible violation of the P-acceptability. It can be overcome by adding a "small" random noise vector to $\mathbf{s}(f)$ without breaking down the properties 1, 2. Notice that $\mathbf{s}(f)$ is an integer vector with even components, which can have the magnitude 2^n. Hence, the use of a relatively "small" margin in Algorithm 3 together with (15) is somewhat inefficient.

It should be also mentioned that (15) requires the complete iteration across the entire training set. Therefore, Single-Sample Relaxation with the "off-line" initial approximation (15) could not be regarded as a genuine on-line algorithm.

3   Experiment, Results and Discussions

We performed numerous simulations on purpose to study the behavior of the learning algorithms in the case of different combinations of the algorithm parameters. Let us describe our results in the case of quadratic neural units.

We started with Algorithm 1 in the case of a constant learning rate $t_k = t$ and tried to learn quadratic PTU to recognize a given Boolean function. First, we considered complete quadratic PTUs in the case $n = 8$. Hence, $m = \binom{8}{0} + \binom{8}{1} + \binom{8}{2} = 1 + 8 + 28 = 37$. Then, we continued simulations with $n \in \{9, 10, 11, 12\}$. In last four cases we also used the same $m = 37$. We employed the complete training sets consisting of 2^n 37-dimensional patterns ($8 \leq n \leq 12$). The influence of the learning rate to the performance of Algorithm 1 was studied. We observed that if $t \notin [1.3, 2.3]$, then Algorithm 1 became slow enough. Moreover, in the case $t < 1.3$ the learning often failed to converge finitely. We ran the learning for 1,001 values of t spaced uniformly in $[1.3, 2.3]$, i.e., we used the set $T_1 = \{1.3 + 0.001\, i \mid i = 0, \ldots, 1000\}$ as a domain of the learning rate. In order to collect exhaustive statistics data, we repeated the learning for 1,000 different P-threshold functions with randomly generated weight vectors.

The simulation results in the case of random initial approximations are presented in Table 1. For every $n \in \{8, 9, 10, 11, 12\}$ the percentage of unsuccessful learning trials is shown and the optimal value of learning rate is given for which the average number of corrections was minimum. We also present the size of training set, minimum, maximum and average number of corrections corresponding to the optimal value of learning rate. Note that the size of training set remained the same in all our experiments and we do not show it further.

The graph of the average number of corrections in the case $n \in \{8, 9, 10, 11, 12\}$ is shown in Fig. 1. Only learning rates $t \geq 1.5$ are shown for

Table 1. Simulation results for Algorithm 1 in the case of learning a quadratic PTU with a random initial approximation

n	Size of training set	Fails, %	t_{opt}	Number of corrections		
				Max	Min	Average
8	256	0.047	1.985	147	79	113.871
9	512	0.123	1.807	216	129	164.953
10	1024	0.219	1.951	278	146	221.758
11	2048	2.582	1.918	370	202	273.875
12	4096	8.301	1.855	457	243	340.554

which the learning never failed. We can see that there exists a complex non-linear dependence between the learning rate and the average number of corrections. The optimal values of learning rate oscillate near 2 and the ratio of the corresponding maximum and minimum number of corrections lies in the interval $(1.8, 1.9)$. In our simulation this tendency also held in the case $n > 12$.

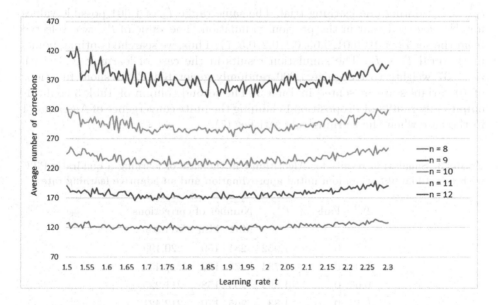

Fig. 1. Graph of the average number of corrections in the case $n \in \{8, 9, 10, 11, 12\}$

Next, we considered the behavior of Algorithm 1 in the case of optimized initial approximation (15). The simulation results are presented in Table 2.

In the last column we give the ratio between the numbers of average corrections with random and optimized initial approximations (15). Notice the significant improvement, which is providing by the use of optimized approximation. It

Table 2. Simulation results for Algorithm 1 in the case of learning a quadratic PTU with an optimized initial approximation

n	Fails, %	t_{opt}	Number of corrections			Ratio of corrections
			Max	Min	Average	
8	0	1.604	50	8	23.208	4.907
9	0	1.701	88	26	46.605	3.539
10	0.041	1.755	152	47	90.522	2.449
11	0.402	1.974	212	88	141.977	1.929
12	0.907	2.051	317	111	176.401	1.931

should be also mentioned that optimal values of learning rate for $n \in \{8, 9, 10\}$ is significantly less that the corresponding values in Table 1. Consequently, for such values of n Algorithm 1 with optimized initial approximation does not require so large correction step that the same algorithm with basic random approximation.

Then, we studied the performance of Algorithm 1 in the case of adaptive learning rates in the form (7). We considered the constant values of $t_k^{(1)} = t^{(1)}$ and $t_k^{(2)} = t^{(2)}$ during one learning trial. The same range T_1 of 1,001 possible values for $t^{(1)}$ was used that in the previous simulation. The value of $t^{(2)}$ was selected from the set $T_2 = \{0, 0.01, 0.05, 0.1, 0.2, 0.5, 1\}$. Thus, we searched optimal points in the grid $T_1 \times T_2$. The simulation results in the case of learning PTU with $m = 37$ weights to recognize 1,000 randomly generated P-threshold functions of 10 variables are presented in Table 3. The second column of Table 3 confirms empirically results of Proposition 1 claiming the finite convergence of Algorithm 1 in the case when the learning rate satisfies (7).

Table 3. Simulation results for Algorithm 1 in the case of learning a quadratic PTU with $n = 10$ inputs, a random initial approximation and an adaptive learning rate

$t^{(2)}$	Fails, %	$t_{opt}^{(1)}$	Number of corrections		
			Max	Min	Average
0	0	1.952	281	159	220.199
0.01	0	1.734	275	169	214.458
0.05	0	1.895	269	158	211.225
0.1	0	1.83	265	170	212.421
0.2	0	1.975	1999	169	248.204
0.5	0	1.889	3024	187	309.806
1.0	0	2.291	9623	346	1379.384

As shown in Table 3, the use of the adaptive rule improves the convergence for every $t^{(2)} \in \{0.01, 0.05, 0.1\}$. The maximum improvement is near 4.25%

compared to non-adaptive t. The very bad behavior of the learning in the case $t^{(2)} > 0.2$ is also remarkable. Notice also that values in the row corresponding to $t^{(2)} = 0$ differ slightly from the ones in Table 1. This difference can be explained by the use of a random initial approximation and the fact that the step 4 of Algorithm 1 is probabilistic.

The results presented in Table 4 confirm that adaptive learning rates can improve the learning speed when an initial approximation is closer to the solution set $W_P(f)$. As shown in Table 4, adaptive learning rates outperform the constant ones and the use of $t^{(2)} = 0.5$ decreases the corresponding number of corrections in the first row by about 3.81%. Note also that optimal values of $t^{(1)}$ in Table 4 are less than corresponding values in Table 3.

Table 4. Simulation results for Algorithm 1 in the case of learning a quadratic PTU with $n = 10$ inputs, an optimized initial approximation and an adaptive learning rate

$t^{(2)}$	Fails, %	$t^{(1)}_{opt}$	Number of corrections			Ratio of corrections
			Max	Min	Average	
0	0	1.732	164	58	86.751	2.538
0.01	0	1.815	140	35	86.001	2.494
0.05	0	1.772	186	32	85.708	2.464
0.1	0	1.689	162	42	84.902	2.502
0.2	0	1.885	140	43	85.277	2.916
0.5	0	1.736	196	41	84.051	3.686
1.0	0	2.011	212	67	91.252	15.117

Next, we considered the spectral off-line learning with adaptive rule (13) of the choice of learning rate. We observed that if $t^{(1)} < 1.7$ or $t^{(2)} > 0.2$, then learning speed was slow. For this reason, we concentrated on the study of the performance of Algorithm 2 in the case $T_1 = \{1.7 + 0.001\,i \mid i = 0, \ldots, 600\}$ and $T_2 = \{0, 0.01, 0.05, 0.1, 0.2\}$. Simulation results for a random initial approximation are presented in Table 5.

Table 5. Simulation results for Algorithm 2 in the case of learning a quadratic PTU with a random initial approximation

n	Fails, %	$t^{(1)}_{opt}$	$t^{(2)}_{opt}$	Number of corrections			Adaptive gains (%)
				Max	Min	Average	
8	0	2.073	0.1	11	3	5.981	0.503
9	0	2.241	0.01	13	4	7.289	0.819
10	0	2.26	0.01	16	5	9.014	1.108
11	0	2.242	0.01	21	7	11.155	0.232
12	0	2.201	0.01	23	8	14.294	1.074

The last column shows the performance gains of the use of adaptive learning rates (13) compared to the non-adaptive ones (calculated in percent). Notice that they are less than in the case of on-line learning. We can see that the number of corrections for Algorithm 2 is 19–24 times less compared to Algorithm 1. Generally speaking, it is caused by the off-line nature of Algorithm 2, which requires few corrections, but all patterns from the training set are involved in every correction. The other observations are following:

1) the relatively large values of $t^{(1)}$ lead to better convergence (the average number of corrections is less if $t^{(1)} > 2$);
2) the relatively small values of $t^{(2)}$ perform better ($t^{(2)} = 0.01$ was a winner in all cases except $n = 8$);
3) the growth rate of the number of corrections is close to the growth rate for on-line learning;
4) the use of adaptive learning rule (13) instead of the constant one does not provide any significant improvement.

Table 6 presents results of the performance of Algorithm 2 in the case of optimized initial approximation (15).

Table 6. Simulation results for Algorithm 2 in the case of learning a quadratic PTU with an optimized initial approximation

n	Fails, %	$t_{\text{opt}}^{(1)}$	$t_{\text{opt}}^{(2)}$	Number of corrections			Adaptive gains	Ratio of corrections
				Max	Min	Average		
8	0	2.035	0.1	9	2	3.808	0.552	1.571
9	0	2.224	0.05	12	3	5.69	0.718	1.281
10	0	2.161	0	15	3	7.506	0	1.201
11	0	2.26	0.01	16	5	9.275	0.164	1.203
12	0	2.27	0.2	22	7	13.101	0.197	1.099

By comparing data from Table 2 and Table 6, one can conclude that the optimized initial solution is not so important in the case of off-line learning. Moreover, its profit decreases when n increases. The above observation 1–4 are still actual, notably the observation 4.

Finally, let us consider our simulation results concerning the relaxation learning with margin. We tried the different margins b from the set $B = \{0.01, 0.02, 0.05, 0.1, 0.2, 0.5, 1, 2\}$ and looked for a set of parameters $(t^{(1)}, t^{(2)}, b)$ providing the optimal (that is, minimum) number of correction. Below we demonstrate results only in the case of random initial approximation.

Table 7. Simulation results for Algorithm 3 in the case of learning a quadratic PTU with a random initial approximation

n	$t_{opt}^{(1)}$	$t_{opt}^{(2)}$	b_{opt}	Number of corrections		
				Max	Min	Average
8	1.785	0.01	0	149	81	108.132
9	1.807	0.01	0	213	125	160.805
10	1.902	0.05	0	285	141	217.006
11	1.928	0.1	0	362	214	265.001
12	1.832	0.1	0	466	237	333.946

By comparing figures from Table 1 and Table 7, we can conclude that the use of the margin does not accelerate the learning process. Furthermore, the use of $b > 0.2$ can significantly slow down Algorithm 3. The only profit of the use of margins in relaxation-like learning is the impossibility of the convergence to points lying on the boundary of the solution region $W_P(f)$. It ensures the finiteness of learning. Hence, we have a trade-off between the speed in the average and the guaranteed finite convergence.

Now we can go to the main issue: which of the considered algorithms is the best in the case of PTU learning? Of course, the numbers of corrections in off-line case presented in Table 5 and Table 6 are significantly less than the ones from Table 1 and Table 2. But it was caused mainly by the difference in the on-line and off-line approaches. We claim that the best practical measure of the performance in the learning of PTUs is a learning time.

In order to compare Algorithm 1 and Algorithm 2 we performed series of simulations for different numbers of inputs of PTU. In our experiments we fixed $m = 30$ as the size of the set of polynomials P and for every $n \in \{5, \ldots, 24\}$ found the optimal set of parameters $(t^{(1)}, t^{(2)})$ providing the minimum average number of corrections, which is closely related to the learning time. Then, we measured and compared the average learning time for serial implementations of both algorithms. The obtained results for $n \geq 10$ are presented in Table 8. Note that we do not show the exact learning time, since it is hardware-dependent. Instead, in second and third rows we give the ratio of the learning times of off-line Algorithm 2 and on-line Algorithm 1 in the case of random (rnd) and optimized (opt) initial approximations, respectively.

Table 8. Comparison of learning times of algorithms

n	10	11	12	13	14	15	16	17	18	19	20	21	22	23	24
rnd	1.53	2.34	2.59	2.58	1.89	2.75	2.71	2.77	2.66	2.35	2.16	1.32	1.53	1.4	1.29
opt	1.51	2.15	2.57	2.6	2.07	2.26	2.25	2.64	2.46	2.07	2.04	1.63	1.82	1.5	1.35
rc1, %	7.23	1.26	0.84	9.94	9.66	0.98	4.04	4.43	3.43	5.39	1.07	29.09	28.71	7.42	23.04
rc2, %	8.44	9.28	1.61	9.24	1.06	18.62	20.33	8.92	9.77	16.66	6.57	12.44	15.20	0.81	19.46

We also show the reduction of the corrections number provided by the use of optimized initial approximation for both algorithms, which is expressed in percentage and presented in the rows entitled "rc1" and "rc2", respectively. Of course, optimized approximation requires significantly less corrections, but it does not mean automatically that its learning time is faster, since (15) requires a complete summation across the total training set. We can see in Table 8 that learning with optimized approximation is indeed faster but it does not provide so considerable decrease of the learning time as we could conclude from Table 2.

The graph of the ratio of algorithms learning times is shown in Fig. 2 both for random and for optimized initial approximations. The main observation is that the Single-Sample Relaxation is faster. The ratio of learning times increases to approximately 2.7 when $n = 14$–16 and decreases to 1.3 for larger n.

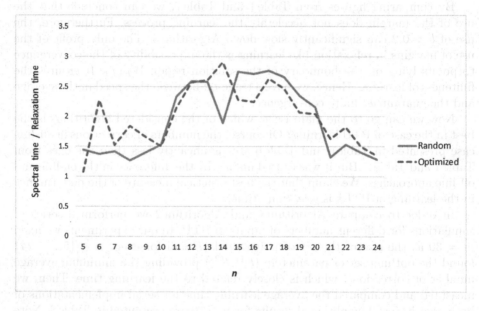

Fig. 2. A graph of the ratio of learning times

But despite the convincing arguments, which can be derived from Table 8 and Fig. 2, we cannot claim that the on-line approach in the learning of PTU is better. The above mentioned reasons concern only the case of the serial computing. But Algorithm 2 admits fairly simple parallel implementation, whereas on-line Algorithm 1 does not. In our simulation parallel version of Algorithm 2 outperformed its counterpart already on a quad-core architecture. Moreover, running on cluster or cloud, Algorithm 2 can be faster significantly.

Notice that many issues concerning learning of PTU are still open. We would be interesting to have bounds on the number of algorithm iterations and to know about the convergence rate in the case of the adaptive rules (7) and (13). The comparison of the performances of our algorithms and the synthesis procedure for integer weight vectors [5] would be also noteworthy.

4 Conclusions

We considered the issues concerning the learning of polynomial threshold units using two iterative approaches. The new adaptive rules (7) and (13) of the choice of the learning rate were proposed for on-line and off-line learning algorithms, respectively. The conditions ensuring the effectiveness and finite convergence of Single-Sample Relaxation with adaptive learning rate were stated in Proposition 1. We gave strict theoretical reasons confirming the suggestion of Hampson and Kibler [8] that the "overrelaxation" can be finite in the case when the learning rate is greater than 2. The modification of relaxation-like learning with margin was also considered. Unlike Duda et al. [4], we used the margin for ensuring the finiteness rather than for obtaining a strong separation. The sufficient conditions were given in Proposition 2 providing the finite learning time for both constant and adaptive learning rates. The new rule of the choice of initial approximation was considered. Despite its rather "off-line" nature, it provides a considerable reduction of the number of required corrections.

Numerous simulations were carried out in order to find the optimal parameter sets for our algorithms. Simulation results demonstrated that in the case of learning a quadratic PTU the use of adaptive learning rule provided the decrease of 4.25% and 1.11% in the number of corrections for Algorithm 1 and Algorithm 2, respectively. The use of the optimized initial approximation had the greater impact and allowed to decrease the learning time by 20–40% in comparison with the learning using the random approximation.

The serial implementation of on-line Algorithm 1 can be up to 3 times faster compared to off-line Algorithm 2. Thus, the on-line relaxation-like algorithm with an adaptive learning rate is a better choice in the case when the serial implementation of the learning algorithm is desired. On the other hand, in the case of learning on powerful hardware the parallel implementation of Off-line Spectral Learning algorithm has better performance.

References

1. Anthony, M.: Discrete Mathematics of Neural Networks: Selected Topics. SIAM, Philadelphia (2001). https://doi.org/10.1137/1.9780898718539
2. Bodyanskiy, Y., Dolotov, A., Peleshko, D., Rashkevych, Y., Vynokurova, O.: Associative probabilistic neuro-fuzzy system for data classification under short training set conditions. In: Zamojski, W., Mazurkiewicz, J., Sugier, J., Walkowiak, T., Kacprzyk, J. (eds.) DepCoS-RELCOMEX 2018. AISC, vol. 761, pp. 56–63. Springer, Cham (2019). https://doi.org/10.1007/978-3-319-91446-6_6

3. Dertouzos, M.L.: Threshold Logic: A Synthesis Approach. The MIT Press, Cambridge (1965)
4. Duda, R., Hart, P., Stork, D.: Pattern Classification, 2nd edn. Wiley-Interscience, New York (2001)
5. Geche, F., Kotsovsky, V., Batyuk, A.: Synthesis of the integer neural elements. In: 10th International Conference on Computer Sciences and Information Technologies, CSIT 2015, Lviv, pp. 63–66 (2015). https://doi.org/10.1109/STC-CSIT.2015.7325432
6. Geche, F., Kotsovsky, V., Batyuk, A., Geche, S., Vashkeba, M.: Synthesis of time series forecasting scheme based on forecasting models system. In: CEUR Workshop Proceedings, vol. 1356, pp. 121–136 (2015)
7. Goffin, J.L.: The relaxation method for solving systems of linear inequalities. Math. Oper. Res. **5**(3), 388–414 (1980)
8. Hampson, S., Kibler, D.: Minimum generalization via reflection: a fast linear threshold learner. Mach. Learn. **37**(1), 51–73 (1999). https://doi.org/10.1023/A:1007693109495
9. Haykin, S.: Neural Networks and Learning Machines, 3rd edn. Pearson Education, Upper Saddle River (2009)
10. Izonin, I., Kryvinska, N., Tkachenko, R., Zub, K., Vitynskyi, P.: An extended-input GRNN and its application. Procedia Comput. Sci. **160**, 578–583 (2019). https://doi.org/10.1016/j.procs.2019.11.044
11. Izonin, I., Tkachenko, R., Kryvinska, N., Zub, K., Mishchuk, O., Lisovych, T.: Recovery of incomplete IoT sensed data using high-performance extended-input neural-like structure. Procedia Comput. Sci. **160**, 521–526 (2019). https://doi.org/10.1016/j.procs.2019.11.054
12. Kazarian, A., Teslyuk, V., Tsmots, I., Tykhan, M.: Implementation of the face recognition module for the "smart" home using remote server. In: Shakhovska, N., Medykovskyy, M.O. (eds.) CSIT 2018. AISC, vol. 871, pp. 17–27. Springer, Cham (2019). https://doi.org/10.1007/978-3-030-01069-0_2
13. Kotsovsky, V., Geche, F., Batyuk, A.: Artificial complex neurons with half-plane-like and angle-like activation function. In: 10th International Conference on Computer Sciences and Information Technologies, CSIT 2015, Lviv, pp. 57–59 (2015). https://doi.org/10.1109/STC-CSIT.2015.7325430
14. Kotsovsky, V., Geche, F., Batyuk, A.: Finite generalization of the offline spectral learning. In: 2018 IEEE 2nd International Conference on Data Stream Mining and Processing, DSMP 2018, Lviv, pp. 356–360 (2018). https://doi.org/10.1109/DSMP.2018.8478584
15. Kotsovsky, V., Geche, F., Batyuk, A.: On the computational complexity of learning bithreshold neural units and networks. In: Lytvynenko, V., Babichev, S., Wójcik, W., Vynokurova, O., Vyshemyrskaya, S., Radetskaya, S. (eds.) ISDMCI 2019. AISC, vol. 1020, pp. 189–202. Springer, Cham (2020). https://doi.org/10.1007/978-3-030-26474-1_14
16. Lupei, M., Mitsa, A., Repariuk, V., Sharkan, V.: Identification of authorship of Ukrainian-language texts of journalistic style using neural networks. East. Eur. J. Enterp. Technol. **1**(2(103)), 30–36 (2020). https://doi.org/10.15587/1729-4061.2020.195041
17. Motzkin, T., Schoenberg, I.: The relaxation method for linear inequalities. Can. J. Math. **6**, 393–404 (1954). https://doi.org/10.4153/CJM-1954-037-2
18. Polishchuk, V.: Fuzzy method for evaluating commercial projects of different origin. J. Autom. Inf. Sci. **50**(5), 60–73 (2018). https://doi.org/10.1615/JAutomatInfScien.v51.i9.60

19. Polishchuk, V.: Technology to improve the safety of choosing alternatives by groups of goals. J. Autom. Inf. Sci. **51**(9), 66–76 (2019). https://doi.org/10.1615/JAutomatInfScien.v51.i9.60
20. Teslyuk, V., Beregovskyi, V., Denysyuk, P., Teslyuk, T., Lozynskyi, A.: Development and implementation of the technical accident prevention subsystem for the smart home system. Int. J. Intell. Syst. Appl. **10**(1), 1–8 (2018). https://doi.org/10.5815/ijisa.2018.01.01
21. Tkachenko, R., Izonin, I.: Model and principles for the implementation of neural-like structures based on geometric data transformations. In: Hu, Z., Petoukhov, S., Dychka, I., He, M. (eds.) ICCSEEA 2018. AISC, vol. 754, pp. 578–587. Springer, Cham (2019). https://doi.org/10.1007/978-3-319-91008-6_58
22. Tsmots, I., Teslyuk, V., Teslyuk, T., Ihnatyev, I.: Basic components of neuronetworks with parallel vertical group data real-time processing. In: Shakhovska, N., Stepashko, V. (eds.) CSIT 2017. AISC, vol. 689, pp. 558–576. Springer, Cham (2018). https://doi.org/10.1007/978-3-319-70581-1_39
23. Tsmots, I., Tsymbal, Y., Khavalko, V., Skorokhoda, O., Teslyuk, T.: Neural-like means for data streams encryption and decryption in real time. In: 2018 IEEE 2nd International Conference on Data Stream Mining and Processing, DSMP 2018, Lviv, pp. 438–443 (2018)
24. Vynokurova, O., Peleshko, D., Borzov, Y., Oskerko, S., Voloshyn, V.: Hybrid multidimensional wavelet-neuro-system and its learning using cross entropy cost function in pattern recognition. In: 2018 IEEE 2nd International Conference on Data Stream Mining and Processing, DSMP 2018, Lviv, pp. 305–309 (2018). https://doi.org/10.1109/DSMP.2018.8478608

The Principles of Organizing the Search for an Object in an Image, Tracking an Object and the Selection of Informative Features Based on the Visual Perception of a Person

Vitaliy Boyun[✉][iD]

National Academy of Sciences of Ukraine, Kyiv, Ukraine
vboyun@gmail.com

Abstract. A significant expansion of the scope of computer vision, in particular in real-time systems, places very high demands on them in terms of productivity and efficiency of information processing, and in feedback systems, it also requires information lag in it. Such requirements are not ensured by traditional approaches. The way out of the situation may be to use as a prototype the principles of organization of the human visual system, which has a very high selectivity of perception of video information. The paper presents a generalized dynamic model of the organization of these principles. It is proposed to use them to organize the search for an object in a coarse image of a scene, to track an object and, if necessary, to carry out its classification or recognition at a more detailed level.

Keywords: Retinal neural network · Receptive fields · Image preprocessing · Object search · Informative signs · Local (ring) organization of neurons · Adaptation mechanisms · Intelligent video systems

1 Introduction

Intelligent video cameras and real-time video systems play a large role in automation systems for production processes, visual quality control of products, robotics, security and military systems, automation systems for scientific and biomedical research, etc. Moreover, the range of their application, the requirements for them are constantly expanding. This is especially true for video systems with feedback, where the results of real-time information processing are used to control the process or for other actions. Such systems put forward increased demands not only on the performance of computing facilities, but also on the lag of information in the feedback loop, which are not provided within the framework of traditional approaches [7,9]. On the other hand, the human visual system has improved over millions of years and has reached an extremely

© Springer Nature Switzerland AG 2020
S. Babichev et al. (Eds.): DSMP 2020, CCIS 1158, pp. 22–44, 2020.
https://doi.org/10.1007/978-3-030-61656-4_2

high level of organization. Therefore, the phenomenon of vision provides an extremely many diverse solutions for computer vision systems. Despite the enormous amount of information in the image, and especially in the video sequence, the human visual-analyzing system very effectively and efficiently copes with these problems due to its extremely high selectivity [4, 8, 16, 18, 25].

There is a significant semantic gap in how a person perceives and describes an image and how the image is perceived by the video system. A person identifies the semantics of the image, and the video system represents the visual content of the image in the form of its low-level characteristics such as color, texture, orientation, shape, the presence of movement, etc. [22].

The second section briefly discusses the principles of organization of the human visual system, the third - the state of the problem, in the fourth - a generalized model of human perception in dynamics. The fifth section is devoted to the principles of organizing the search for an object in an image, tracking it and extracting informative features based on a person's visual perception.

2   The Principles of Organization of the Human Visual System

The following is a brief description of the structural features of the organization of the retina, the mechanisms and processes associated with the processing of video information in it [8, 15, 18, 22].

The scene image projected on the retina is inverted along two axes (top-bottom and left-right) and is a set of individual points obtained from rods and cones. These points represent, respectively, different light intensities in shades of gray and different wavelengths, perceived by the brain as three basic colors (red, blue and green with their shades). Moreover, dots in shades of gray are mainly located on the periphery of the retina with a low spatial resolution, and colored dots, more densely packed, are located in the central fossa (fovea zone). This representation of the environment is extremely redundant and not informative for the brain; it simply cannot cope with such huge flows of information. In the process of evolution, selective mechanisms have been developed in the human visual system to extract the most informative features for the perception of the environment, reducing the redundancy of scene images by many orders of magnitude. These mechanisms use the presence in the images of edges, borders of objects that differ in color, texture, shape, orientation, movement in space, which allows using different methods to distinguish between objects. The basic information in this case is the contrast, which, together with the retinal neurons (on- and off-centers) organized by the ring principle and lateral inhibition mechanisms, allows us to distinguish these primary signs of images of objects.

Although the rods and cones of the retina perceive absolute values of brightness and color, however, information is analyzed on the values of the differences between adjacent pixels in space (to detect the edges or borders of objects) or in time (between adjacent frames of a video sequence to detect movement or other changes in the scene). Therefore, color or brightness differences are a very important characteristic for extracting many informative features. There is evidence of the existence of spatial frequency detectors in the visual system. which are tuned to a limited frequency range. Spatial frequency analysis is a simple and reliable way to describe and generalize the structural details of visual objects. Such information is used by the brain to evaluate fragments of the image and to control the further process of perception of the image by the retina depending on the goal (search for a specific object in the scene, tracking it or recognizing it). In the case of contemplation of scenes without a goal (for example, from a car window), perception is carried out reflexively without the intense involvement of the brain, we only see an enlarged picture of flickering objects.

Similarly, perception in tracking mode of a fast-moving object works. In this case, shorter eye movements, with a previously determined scale of the object, carry out tracking. Visual information, before getting from the eye to the brain, passes through many layers of specialized retinal neurons on the retina. The retina is a complex network of photoreceptors (rods and cones) and nerve cells (neurons). The rods provide a perception of the brightness of achromatic light (in shades of gray), and cones - electromagnetic waves of different lengths, which are perceived by the human visual system as three basic colors (red, blue, green with their shades). The peripheral zone of the retina, on which the rods and partly cones are predominantly located, provides a wide field of view with a low spatial resolution. The dense placement of cones in the central fossa (fovea zone) provides clear color vision.

The peripheral retina and central fossa are organized according to the ring principle (the so-called on- and off-centers). In the on-center, the excitation zone occupies the central part, and around it there is an inhibition zone. In off-centers, the zones of excitation and inhibition are interchanged. Such centers of the peripheral retina are organized using horizontal and diffuse bipolar cells and extract larger spatial features. The centers of excitation-inhibition of the central fossa are organized using horizontal and small bipolar cells and extract more subtle features of the image. The sizes of receptive fields are controlled, respectively, by interplexiform and amacrine cells using horizontal cells. Such an organization allows you to extract spots or points that differ from the background in brightness, color, orientation, texture, etc.

The well-known phrase "the eye looks and the brain sees" quite accurately describes the process of perception, that is, thinking about stimulating our sensory receptors. In this case, ascending and descending processes are involved. Ascending processes are also called processes of transmitting information data from the receptors. And the descending processes, also called the processes of conceptualizing information data, are based on previously acquired knowledge, previous experience, understanding and expectations. To increase sensitivity in conditions of insufficient illumination, the rods of the peripheral retina are combined into groups with the sum of signals from larger receptive fields, i.e. there is an exchange of spatial resolution for increasing sensitivity in brightness.

At the level of the retina, a number of adaptation processes operate. In particular, it is the brightness adaptation to the level of illumination (10–12 orders of magnitude: from the threshold of sensitivity of night vision, which is ensured by the excitation of more sensitive rods of the retina, to the threshold of blinding brightness, which is limited by the level of perception of cones of color vision). The subjective brightness, which is perceived by the human visual analyzer, is a logarithmic function of the physical brightness of the light that has entered the eye. However, the range of brightness levels, which is simultaneously perceived by the eye, is about 3 orders of magnitude.

Excitation of retinal neurons in the presence of objects (spots) in the focused image on it, which differ from the background in brightness or color values, spatial frequencies, orientation, and the presence of movement, is used to quickly search for objects in the scene image. It consists in the fact that the place in the scene that caused the excitement, with the help of saccades, is refluxed (focused) into the central fossa for a more detailed analysis [1, 4, 21].

In this case, when the plasticity property of neurons is used, the formation of receptive fields of various sizes, the change in their shape, and the possibility of extracting informative features from an object that display various physical properties of the object [1]. Special (interlexiform and amacrine) cells control these processes by changing the sizes of receptive fields, the sizes of the excitation and inhibition zones of on- and off-centers, as well as neuron activation thresholds. In accordance with the theory of integration of the features of the object, the perception of the object is carried out in two stages [28]:

– previous attention - the quick extraction of simple visible features of an object (perceptual primitives), is carried out in parallel throughout the retina automatically without conscious effort and concentration;
– focused attention - requires the observer's efforts and close examination of the object, is carried out sequentially with the help of the central fossa.

Information from diffuse bipolar cells of the peripheral retina and small bipolar cells of the central fossa is transmitted using G_M- and G_P-type ganglion cells, respectively, to the magno- and parvocellular regions of the lateral geniculate body (LGB). In the parvocellular region, color information from the central fossa is also added. These areas, like the retina, are organized according to the concentric ring principle, but operate with larger receptive fields, thus increasing the level of abstractness of the presentation of information. LGB, in addition, performs the function of switching the received and processed information into the corresponding layers of the primary visual cortex of the brain.

Thus, a significant part of the preliminary processing of information is carried out already at the level of the retina. The peripheral zone of the retina is oriented toward a coarse spatial perception of the scene, with a high sensitivity to perception of brightness. The central zone of the retina is focused on clear vision both in spatial resolution and in color. Using the principles of organizing the retina of the eye allows us to more effectively organize the search for an object in the scene image and preliminary preparation of video data for recognition by extracting low-level informative features of the image.

3   Problem Statement

Quite often, the retina is considered as a structure with a logarithmic-polar organization [3], in the center of which is the central fossa (fovea zone), and the peripheral retina is located around. This provides a wide peripheral inspection and the possibility of a detailed perception of information in the central fossa. Attempts have been made to repeat this foveal organization of visual perception in technical and algorithmic models. One of the directions is the creation of foveal sensors with radial and hierarchical (pyramidal) organization of the receptive field [24]. The disadvantage of radial organization is the need to implement the management of the "look", i.e. direction of the optical axis of the sensor, which requires the use of a high-speed drive and its control system. In addition, the implementation of logarithmic-polar sensors and the subsequent processing of information on them also present significant difficulties.

To speed up the process of searching for an object in the scene, the most commonly used method is the pyramidal organization of the process of taking and processing information [14]. It consists in the fact that at first the image with the maximum resolution is read, and then, by smoothing and thinning, for example, using the Gauss or Laplace pyramids, the next layer of the pyramid is formed, whose dimensions are 4 times smaller than the original. This procedure is repeated several times until the desired level of coarsening is achieved. It is easier to find an object on a coarse image, and then, by applying the reverse procedure, it is possible to restore the original resolution of the image of the object for its recognition, measurement, etc. However, this approach, which was used to reduce the amount of information when transmitting images under conditions of limited channel capacity, does not fully meet the principles of organizing the human visual system and the requirements of real-time systems.

An important characteristic for texture analysis is spatial frequencies, for the evaluation of which the Fourier analysis methods are traditionally used, however, they require large computational costs [4]. In [23], models of the organization of the retina and central fossa are presented, the principles of the organization of connections on layers of neurons of different specializations, adaptive mechanisms for the perception of lighting and contrast, and the path of signals from receptors to ganglion cells are considered. In the process of modeling, the reliability of these models was confirmed to a large extent; therefore, in some parts of our work, we focus on their use. Close approaches to the principles of processing information on the retina, in terms of extracting informative features, are used in convolution neural networks, which are a further development of the cognitron and neocognitron [19]. They serve as the first layers of recognizing artificial neural networks (ANN). However, convolution neural networks realize only a small part of the arsenal of techniques developed in the process of evolution and embedded in the human visual analyzer. In particular, are not used:

- mechanisms of "attention" and techniques for quick search for an object on the coarse peripheral retina, followed by detailed analysis in the central fossa;
- adaptive mechanisms for controlling the dynamic range of perception of brightness, contrast and sensitivity in low light conditions.

This leads to a significant increase in the database of objects and scenes, as well as the training time of the ANN to improve the quality of classification and recognition. In addition, convolution neural networks are currently not designed to connect to real cameras and to work in real time with video sequences.

Neurophysiologists, neuropsychologists, gestalt psychologists, cognitive psychologists, cybernetics consider the human visual analyzer from different angles, from their fields of knowledge, but there is no generalized representation of the process of perceiving the environment, and especially in dynamics. The situation is aggravated by the use in different publications of different terminology of the same processes and the conflicting interpretation of the results, which makes it difficult to understand the complete process of perception.

4   Dynamic Model of the Processes of Searching for an Object in a Scene, Tracking It and Extracting Informative Features

The generalized model of the human visual system is multifunctional and consists of hundreds of local models that describe a number of structural, physical, biochemical, psychophysical mechanisms and processes. The process of perception of visual information by a person is dynamic, with many parameters that change in the process of perception, with many feedbacks. This is evidenced by a huge number of articles devoted to studies of specific properties, features, mechanisms, processes etc. in a human visual system [2,17,20,25–27,29]. However, there is practically no general idea and understanding of the process of perception by the visual system in dynamics for various modes.

In this work, a generalized model of the organization and functioning of the retina, as well as approaches to the implementation of its most important and fundamental principles, which could help increase the intelligence of computer vision systems, are considered from a general perspective. In accordance with this model, enlarged fields of receptors (rods) are created on the retina using horizontal cells, which create a center of excitation using diffuse bipolar cells. With the help of other horizontal cells from receptors adjacent to the receptors of the excitation zone, larger circular inhibition zones are formed, i.e. on- and off-centers are organized. This process is carried out along the entire periphery of the retina in parallel. The results of the work of these centers through Gm-type ganglion cells in parallel and topologically (i.e. with reference to the location on the retina) are transmitted to the LGB. At the same time, the dimensions of the center and surround gradually decrease, i.e. such centers work, as it were, on different scales of perception. In each center, a search is made for the maximum response of the on-center with the specification of the size of the region.

Amacrine cells control the outputs of on- and off-centers and control the change in the size of receptive fields, helping to search for the maximum response of these filters. It should also be noted that the search on the peripheral retina is carried out in parallel on many features: shades of gray, texture, orientation, movement, etc. The flows of this enlarged information through G_M-type ganglion cells enter the region of LGB magnocellular cells organized according to the same center-surround ring principle with local connections between neurons, but operating with larger receptive fields. Magnocellular cells work with fuzzy images; they are more sensitive to the difference in surface illumination (gray on gray), which contributes to the perception of the depth of the scene. In addition, they quickly respond to stimuli, but the reaction quickly dies away, which is well suited for detecting movement on the scene. The results of the generalization of information are transmitted from the LGB to the corresponding layers of the visual cortex. The visual cortex is organized on a linear basis, reacts to lines, stripes, rectangular segments. It contains simple cells, complex and hypercomplex, i.e. it also, according to the hierarchical principle, increases the level of abstractness of the features of an object for recognition [25].

If the results of the visual cortex using a coarse image of a fragment with additional fine information from the central fossa do not satisfy the search target, then the next image fragment detected on the retina is transferred to the central fossa to check if the searches target matches. This process is repeated for all identified fragments until a final positive or negative result is obtained. If a more detailed analysis is needed, similar to the above, a fragment is analyzed with additional color information for classification, recognition of an object, determination of its geometric dimensions, etc. Based on these coarse informative features, the visual cortex searches for their correspondence to some image of an object (model) from the ones in memory.

In the case of detecting an object when contemplating the environment or tracking a fast-moving object, this process is repeated many times. If it is necessary to search for an object in the scene for its classification, more detailed examination or recognition, a finer analysis of image fragments that have fallen on the retina is performed. It is possible that the visual cortex of the brain, controlling the response maxima throughout the retina, sets priorities for their sequential "transmission" to the central fossa (fovea zone). The process of "transmission" is carried out by saccades (rapid eye movements) by controlling the focusing system. In the central fossa, organized by the same principle of excitation-inhibition, due to the denser packing of cones, a more detailed analysis, including color, of the obtained image fragment is carried out in order to extract informative features from it. The results of the analysis in the central fossa through ganglion cells of the G_P type enter the region of parvocellular cells of the LGB, which is also organized on the principle of center-surround. These results are also parallel and topologically transmitted to the corresponding cortical layers of the visual cortex. In particular, layer V1 is responsible for frequency and orientation analysis, layers V2 and V3 process information about the shape and position in space, layer V4 is responsible for the perception of color information, layer V5 is for movement.

The presented work is not intended to accurately copy the functions of the retina and the processes occurring in it. The aim of the work is to understand the general structure and organization of the human visual system and use these principles to build specialized and problem-oriented video systems for various purposes, taking into account the state and capabilities of modern microelectronics. And, perhaps, at the same time to put before it those problems that will make it possible to more effectively solve the problems of finding an object in an image, tracking it, classifying, recognizing objects, scenes and situations in real time.

The advantage of this approach is the use of a number of adaptive mechanisms to increase sensitivity in low light conditions, increase contrast, attention mechanisms and coarse-accurate presentation of the scene, which will significantly reduce the amount of databases and time for training ANN, link them to the processes of shooting video sequences and use in computer vision systems.

4.1 Coarsening (Assumptions) Accepted in the Model to Ensure the Possibility of Its Technical Implementation at the Current Level of Microelectronics Development

Instead of a logarithmic-polar retina representation system, a Cartesian image representation system with a uniform grid is adopted. Accordingly, the ring organization of on- and off-centers has turned into a square-ring. Parallel processes of extracting all possible (or necessary for a given perception mode) features of an object at the level of the peripheral retina and central fossa, as well as the processes of their transmission to the higher layers of the brain, have been replaced by sequential or parallel-sequential ones.

The paper does not examine in detail the principles of organization of the primary visual cortex, since they are already actively used in the ANN. The results of the study can be used as the first layers of the ANN for preliminary preparation of information for recognition on them. This is an important point, since the analysis of large scenes is computationally significantly more expensive than recognizing the objects themselves, providing a reduction in the amount of information for recognition by many orders of magnitude, although the recognition process is more complicated in the logical sense.

5   Implementation of the Principles of Human Visual Perception for Building Computer Vision Systems and Their Interaction with the Outside World

The purpose of this section is to highlight the fundamental principles of the organization of the human retina and their implementation, taking into account the capabilities of the modern level of microelectronics and computer vision systems (CVS) requirements. These fundamental principles, which, in our opinion, will help create more advanced computer vision systems, are [5, 6]:

- the ability to change the resolution when working with the video sensor;
- implementation of methods for coarse-accurate search for an object in an image;
- the ability to expand the dynamic range of perception of brightness;

- the ability to implement various modes of perception of video information;
- the ability to use the differential presentation of information for image analysis;
- the ability to control in dynamics the parameters for reading information;
- organization of ascending and descending processes;
- ensuring the principle of ring organization of receptive fields;
- implementation of adaptation mechanisms to the level of lighting and contrast;
- the use of spatial frequencies, as an important principle of texture analysis;
- phased increase in the level of abstractness (generalization) of information.

The basis for the construction of CVSs can be modern CMOS video sensors, which are very complex devices and contain, in addition to the sensor matrix, about 10 specialized processors for preliminary (technological) image preparation organized in a conveyor, and several hundred registers for detailed programming of processes removal and preprocessing of the image. Thanks to the pipelined organization of the computing process, they provide the necessary rate of data output. In particular, the following operations are performed in the video sensor and conveyor:

- automatic exposure time control;
- the perception of light and converting it into analog signals of brightness or color;
- primary analog processing;
- automatic control of analog gain;
- conversion of analog signals into digital codes;
- determination of the level of "black";
- establishing a balance of "white" to adapt the sensor to different types of lighting;
- correction of the heterogeneity of the sensitivity of the elements of the sensor matrix;
- adaptation to the level of lighting;
- automatic focusing when using a lens with a servo drive;
- color correction due to imperfect characteristics of Bayer filters sprayed on each element of the sensor matrix;
- correction of defective pixels;
- the formation of all color components in each pixel (demosaicing or Color Filter Array (CFA) interpolation);
- gamma correction and saturation correction;
- conversion of presentation formats of the output RGB image to different formats (YCbCr, YUV, JPEG, MPEG, etc.).

Some of the above list of operations at the request of the user may be excluded. This organization of the video sensor is due to the task facing the video camera - providing high quality presentation of information for humans and the convenience of working with the camera. At the same time, the information captured by the camera is either stored in its memory or transmitted for storage and use by some information receivers. Given the enormous amount of information obtained from the video sequence, and the need for its storage and transmission, much attention was paid to the implementation of various image compression methods (JPEG, MPEG, etc.) when organizing the pipeline.

In modern video cameras, the principles of organizing the human visual system are already used to a large extent. In particular, these are:

- focusing the image by moving the objective lens (changing the shape of the lens);
- control of the perception of light by controlling the diaphragm and exposure (change in pupil diameter);
- expansion of the dynamic range due to the nonlinear conversion of signals from the sensor matrix (logarithmic characteristic of the perception of light by the rods and cones of the retina);
- the use of 3 Bayer demosaic filters, etc., sprayed onto the corresponding pixels (using the property of selective sensitivity of cones in 3 ranges of wavelengths of the spectrum interpreted by the brain as three basic colors);
- panning, tracking, etc. modes used in smart video cameras (different types of eye movements when searching for an object, tracking it, etc.).

Computer vision systems are mainly real-time systems and, in addition to registering a video sequence and its preliminary processing, should perform its functions of image segmentation, search for an object in an image, and selection of informative features for its classification, recognition, tracking, and other actions at the rate of information. Traditional video cameras and their approaches to the collection and processing of information, image compression do not always meet the high requirements of real-time systems and, in addition, require the use of additional computing tools to implement the above functions.

The main requirement for real-time systems is to ensure the rate of information retrieval and processing, and for real-time systems with feedback, it is also necessary to minimize the delay in the feedback loop. This is especially important for computer vision systems working with fast processes and high-speed objects. Detailed studies of video sensors and the organization of the pipeline for preliminary processing of information have shown that they have large reserves for increasing productivity in CVSs, but these reserves are practically not used in practice. Let us consider how the video sensor pipeline can be modified and what needs to be added to it in order to implement a computer vision system with the fundamental principles of the human visual analyzer, discussed at the beginning of this section.

The possibility of changing the resolution of the video sensor will allow, on the one hand, to provide a wide field of view, and on the other hand, the possibility of a detailed analysis of the selected object. Image coarsing is an effective method of reducing the amount of information when searching for an object in an image, tracking it, as well as in the mode of simple contemplation of the situation and panning of a scene. Unfortunately, the modern technology for the production of CMOS video sensors does not fully ensure such capabilities. An exception is the possibility of thinning the image into rows and columns when reading it, which allows 4 times to coarsen the representation of the image. In addition, it is possible to increase the resolution of a color image by 4 or more times compared to the original physical resolution due to linear or quadratic interpolation between adjacent image pixels. It is proposed to provide coarsening of the image by summing and then averaging the signals of neighboring pixels of the receptive fields, as it is the case in the peripheral retina of the human eye. Such summation can not only reduce image size, but also increase sensitivity in low light conditions. This process can be controlled (by analogy with amacrine cells) depending on the average or local brightness of the image by changing the sizes of the summed receptive fields and the gain of the on- and off-centers.

Summing and averaging the brightness values of the sensor matrix across rows and columns can be determine local levels of illumination. An analysis of these values allows us to identify local areas that differ significantly in the degree of illumination, and take measures to expand the dynamic range of perception of brightness.

The ability to change the resolution when working with a video sensor will allow, on the one hand, to provide a wide field of view, and on the other hand, the possibility of a detailed analysis of the selected object. Image coarsening is an effective method of reducing the amount of information when searching for an object in an image, tracking it, and also in the mode of simple contemplation of the situation.

The ability to change the resolution of the video sensor allows us to implement the method of coarse-accurate search for an object in the image, in which the search is performed on the coarse image for informative features of higher order, which significantly reduces the amount of processed information [6]. These features are transmitted in ascending channels to the central processor or to the recognition layers of the ANN, performing the functions of the primary visual cortex of the brain, where they are compared with the existing models of objects accumulated as a result of previous experience. If the comparison of the features of the object and the model was unsuccessful, then, in accordance with the priorities, the coarse features of the next object selected in the scene are compared. In the case of a successful comparison of features, depending on the purpose of the search, an object can be accompanied on a coarse image or, if necessary, a given image fragment with a higher resolution can be read for a more detailed examination, classification or recognition of an object. The center of the selected object and its overall dimensions has already been obtained when searching for the object. The central processor in descending channels controls these processes.

The expansion of the dynamic range of brightness perception can be provided by a nonlinear, for example, a logarithmic, scan of the reference voltage during parallel (throughout the matrix) analog-to-digital conversion (scanning method by parameter) [7,10]. If it is necessary to obtain a binarized image, it is also possible to use a nonlinear sweep of the reference voltage, but a threshold element and a trigger must be integrated in each element of the sensor matrix, which records the achievement of the threshold signal level by this matrix element [11].

The human visual system has in its arsenal a number of types of eye movements (saccades, mini-saccades, tremors, microtremors, tracking eye movements, vestibular-ocular movements to stabilize the image on the central fossa, vergent movements to reduce and dilate the axes of the eyes when they focus on the selected object). They contribute to a more efficient perception of video information in various modes (contemplation, panning when turning the head or observing a person, searching for an object in an image, detailed examination of an object for its classification/recognition).

When you turn the observer's head, for example, to the right on the retina, a part of the scene image is added on the right side and the part of the image on the left disappears. This feature can be effectively used to pan the scene, while eliminating the repeating part of previous frames and using only new information that arose when the camera was rotated. The transition from a dynamic image to a panoramic one can significantly reduce the amount of information that depends on the speed of head rotation or the movement of the observer. At the same time, it remains possible to restore a dynamic video sequence at any tempo in time and along an arbitrary trajectory of moving the gaze.

The amount of information in a video sequence can be estimated based on the amplitude-spatial and temporal resolution according to the formula

$$C_{v.seq} = \frac{X}{\Delta x} \cdot \frac{Y}{\Delta y} \cdot \log_2(\frac{Z}{\delta z} + 1) \cdot \frac{1}{\Delta t} \tag{1}$$

where X and Y are the sizes of the image field; Z is the brightness coordinate of the image; Δx, Δy, δz, Δt are discreteness of presentation of the corresponding image coordinates; $\frac{X}{\Delta x} \cdot \frac{Y}{\Delta y}$ is the number of pixels in the frame of the video sequence; $log_2(\frac{Z}{\delta z} + 1)$ is the bit depth representation of pixels; $\frac{1}{\Delta t}$ is the frame rate.

The values of X, Y and Z in a formula are usually fixed (maximum). The values Δx, Δy, δz, Δt are also fixed, therefore, this approach gives a (very high!) upper estimate of the amount of information and does not indicate ways to reduce the redundancy of the digital representation of images.

Providing the ability to dynamically change the parameters in the above formula (in accordance with the types of eye movements) will allow you to adapt the camcorder to the requirements and features of the tasks, as well as significantly reduce the redundancy of the representation of images and video sequences. In accordance with this approach, dynamic models of the processes of panning and editing of video sequences, automatic search for changes in the systems of circular and sector view, search and selection of objects or changes in the scene (movement, color, size) and tracking them were developed and studied [4,8,9].

Searching for an object by the visual system is carried out by identifying on the peripheral retina (coarse image) using special mechanisms of informative features of "suspicious" image fragments corresponding to the rough model of the object. Using saccades, moving and focusing in the central fossa of the image fragment with the supposed object is carried out. According to the principle of a hierarchical coarse-grained representation of information [4], a coarse image of the scene (thinned out and then further coarsened) is first read out, in which all fragments that differ from the background are highlighted. In accordance with priority, these fragments are analyzed, during which crude informative features characterizing the object are identified and compared with the model of the desired object. The process continues until information is received about the presence of an object in the scene or its absence. Such an approach when searching for "suspicious" fragments due to image coarsenining allows reducing the amount of information by a factor equal to the degree of roughening for each fragment. Image coarsening, i.e. increase in the sampling step over the space Δx and Δy in n times:

$$\Delta x' = n \cdot \Delta x, \quad \Delta y' = n \cdot \Delta y$$

$$C_{image} = \frac{X}{\Delta x'} \cdot \frac{Y}{\Delta y'} \cdot \log_2(\frac{Z}{\delta z} + 1) = \frac{1}{n^2} \cdot \frac{XY}{\Delta x \Delta y} \cdot \log_2(\frac{Z}{\delta z} + 1) \qquad (2)$$

reduces the amount of information by n^2 times.

Reading an arbitrary rectangle from an image ranging from X_1 to X_2 and from Y_1 to Y_2

$$C_{image} = \frac{\Delta X}{\Delta x} \cdot \frac{\Delta Y}{\Delta y} \cdot \log_2(\frac{Z}{\delta z} + 1) \qquad (3)$$

reduces the amount of information in the image representation in $\dfrac{XY}{\Delta x \Delta y}$ times, where

$$\Delta X = X_2 - X_1, \quad \Delta Y = Y_2 - Y_1$$

Tracking of an object can be carried out both by its rough features, and by more subtle ones. In this case, the trajectory of the object's movement, changes in its shape, color are tracked and the rest of the scene is ignored. When implementing this approach, the video camera, having information about the overall dimensions of the object and its location, reads only a fragment of the image with dimensions slightly exceeding (taking into account the speed of the object) the overall dimensions of the object. Moreover, the reduction in the amount of information is determined in accordance with formula (3). A coarse presentation of information may concern not only the resolution of the spatial representation of the image, but also the accuracy of the representation of brightness (color), i.e. bit depth. The brightness (color) picture of the image is not constant, but varies from pixel to pixel and from frame to frame. Therefore, the value Z in the formula (1) is not a constant, but a function of the image coordinates $Z_{ij} = f(x_i, y_j)$.

In [8], the concept of the entropy of a random variable value was

$$H_N = \sum_{i=1}^{k} p_i \log_2(N_i + 1)$$

introduced, which is a measure of the uncertainty of the random variable value itself and represents the average number of digits per one random variable value. Considering the matrix (m × n) of pixel brightness values as random values, we obtain an image entropy estimate [4]

$$H_{image} = \sum_{j=1}^{n} \sum_{i=1}^{m} p_{ij} \log_2 \left(\frac{z_{ij}}{\delta z} + 1 \right) \tag{4}$$

As for the Shannon statistical entropy, the logarithm base determines the unit of measurement of the entropy of a random variable. At the logarithm base of two, the unit of entropy of the value is a bit. Normalizing the H_{image} by the value of $\log_2(\frac{z_{max}}{\delta z} + 1)$, we obtain the reduced entropy of the image brightness characteristic,

$$h_z = \frac{H_{image}}{\log_2 \left(\frac{z_{max}}{\delta z} + 1 \right)} \tag{5}$$

The reduced entropy of the brightness characteristic of the image characterizes the spread in the bitness of the representation of the brightness of the image pixels and varies in the range (0 1). This characteristic will allow us to evaluate the effectiveness of using various methods for representing the variable bit depth of the brightness (color) parameter of the image. A decrease in bit depth leads, respectively, to a decrease in the amount of information in the image, however, in most cases it is rather difficult to use this decrease in the amount of information in full.

Conditionally, we can assume that the amount of information received from a color video camera increases by 3 times. However, in real-time systems, in a number of applications, it is possible to use only individual R-, G-, and B-components, or, going to the HSB model, for example, use only the color or brightness characteristics, which to a greater extent carry useful information for this task. Therefore, to increase the selectivity, it is advisable to provide the ability to read only the necessary information in this task. Change the frequency of video recording, i.e. an increase or decrease in the sampling step in time Δt, leads to a proportional decrease in the amount of information in the video sequence. Video frequency control can be organized taking into account the dynamism of the scene, i.e. the speed of ongoing processes or the speed of moving objects in the scene.

Thus, using the considered dynamic models for selecting the parameters for reading information from the video sensor and the principles of controlling its pipeline for processing this information, it is possible to significantly increase the performance of the camera by adapting it to the conditions of the current task. Further, we consider those computing operations that cannot be implemented on the pipelines of existing video sensors and require the use of additional computing tools (central processor, group of graphic processors, FPGAs, etc.) for their implementation.

It is known that the retina operates when analyzing images not with absolute values of brightness or color of pixels, but with their differences between adjacent pixels in a row, column or between frames. The differential representation of information on the retina is obtained due to special eye movements (tremor and microtremor). As studies have shown, the use of difference representations, which actually represent the contrast or changes between frames, is an effective way to highlight a number of useful properties in the image and video sequence. Taking into account the presence of correlation between neighboring elements in the row and column of the matrix, the image can be represented as a matrix of differences between neighboring elements (growth matrix). In this case, the entropy of the image is determined in this way:

$$H_{image} = \sum_{j=1}^{n} \sum_{i=1}^{m} p_{ij} \cdot log_2 \left(\left| \frac{\Delta z_{ij}}{\delta z} \right| + 1 \right) \tag{6}$$

where the differences Δz_{ij} can be determined both by rows ($\Delta z'_{ij}$), and columns (Δz_{ij}) of the matrix:

$$\Delta z'_{ij} = z_{i+1,j} - z_{ij}, \quad \Delta z''_{ij} = z_{i,j+1} - z_{ij}$$

Typically, fewer bits are required to encode differences in brightness, which will also reduce the amount of information in the image. Given the correlation between the corresponding pixels of two adjacent frames, we obtain a difference image matrix [4], the entropy of which is defined as

$$H_{dif} = \sum_{j=1}^{n} \sum_{i=1}^{m} p_{ij} \cdot \log_2 \left(\left| \frac{\Delta z_{ij}^k}{\delta z} \right| + 1 \right) \tag{7}$$

where $\Delta z_{ij}^k = \Delta z_{ij}^{k+1} - \Delta z_{ij}^k$, k is the frame number of the video sequence.

In the difference image, similarly to the previous one, useful information can also be distinguished, i.e. moving object or scene changes between frames. In this case, similarly to the previous one, a reduction in the amount of information in the image is also provided here. In contrast to the statistical measure of information by C. Shannon, developed to compress information during transmission and storage, a dynamic measure of information is proposed - δ-entropy. It is defined as the average value of the modulus of the video derivative and is a measure of the uncertainty of a random process change [25]:

$$H_\delta = \frac{\Delta t}{\delta_z} \cdot M[|f'(t)|] \tag{8}$$

δ-entropy allows you to extract useful (dynamic) information from signals, images, video sequences, iterative processes, etc., significantly reducing its redundancy, and can be the basis for evaluating the processes of conversion and processing of information in real-time systems.

In a discrete form, the estimate of the δ-entropy of the image is defined as

$$H_\delta = \sum_{j=1}^{n} \sum_{i=1}^{m} p_{ij} \cdot \left| \frac{\Delta z_{ij}}{\delta z} \right| \tag{9}$$

where Δz are the differences between the brightness of pixels in rows or columns; δ-entropy is a measure of the dynamism of an image, characterizes its contrast and can be used to assess the information content of an image, the amount of useful (dynamic) information in it, spatial frequencies, search and evaluate the characteristics of textures and objects, as well as to control the level of contrast.

The known method of averaging transverse slices of the image brightness profile over rows and columns [16] allows you to determine the location of an object in the image that differs from the background, but does not allow you to select objects of the texture type. To determine the location of such objects, it is proposed to average (modulo) the transverse sections of the image according to dynamic signs, i.e. by differences in brightness between adjacent pixels in rows and columns [20]:

$$H_{\delta_j} = \frac{1}{M} \cdot \sum_{i=1}^{M} \left| \frac{\Delta z_{ij}}{\delta z} \right|, \quad H_{\delta_i} = \frac{1}{N} \cdot \sum_{j=1}^{N} \left| \frac{\Delta z_{ij}}{\delta z} \right| \tag{10}$$

An important characteristic for texture analysis and a number of other applications are spatial frequencies, for the analysis of which the Fourier analysis is most often used. In this paper, instead of the Fourier analysis, it is proposed to use δ-entropy, which is calculated much easier. Such a dynamic measure of information can be effectively used for a number of applications. In particular, for:

- image segmentation into high and low dynamic sections;
- segmentation of text information in the image;
- search and classification of textures;
- search for barcodes, DMX codes, fingerprints, car numbers, etc.;
- extracting movement, changes in brightness or color;
- control the frequency of shooting a video camera, etc.

Estimating the contrast level of the scene image by rows and columns, we can select areas with significantly different values and take measures to correct it. In addition, you can classify textures as irregular and regular (Fig. 1), determine the step of the texture, its contrast, identify changes in the texture (defect), etc.

According to the graphs of δ-entropy (Fig. 1), we can distinguish between rows and columns: a) - irregular texture; b), c), d) - regular textures.

From the distances between the maxima or minima, you can determine the step of regular textures, by the magnitude of the signal amplitude - the value of the contrast of the texture; if the regularity of the texture is violated, a defect can be detected - c). Contrast control can be carried out by changing the size of the masks (filters on-and off-centers) and their gains. For example, a 3 × 3 mask provides maximum contrast enhancement of 4 or 8 times, a 5 × 5 mask - 16 or 32 times, etc. The gain is selected taking into account contrast by choosing a mask so that the result of its application is, for example, in the second half of the brightness representation scale (128–255 for an 8-bit scale). Masks are desirable to adjust so that their coefficients are multiples of the power of two in order to exclude the operation of multiplying by coefficients. This will replace

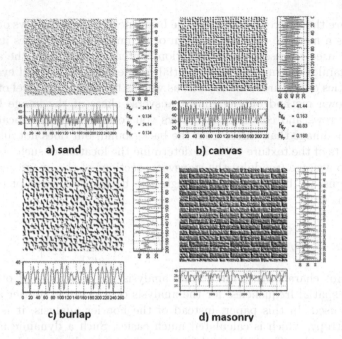

a) sand

b) canvas

c) burlap

d) masonry

Fig. 1. Assessment of texture parameters

the operations of multiplication by the operations of shift by the corresponding number of bits, which is especially effective in the hardware implementation of such procedures.

A very important point is the providing of the *principle of ring organization of receptive fields*, since it equally effectively works both on the model of the peripheral retina and on the model of the central fossa. In addition, on the basis of the *center-surround* principle, one can extract many informative features of a higher level on the retina model (spots that differ from the background in brightness, color, orientation, dynamic characteristics - spatial frequencies, the presence of motion in the video sequence, etc.) that provide the search for objects in the scene. The principle of *center-surround* in accordance with the three-component color theory is used by the visual system not only to extract individual colors, but also at a higher level of the visual system when extracting colors in accordance with the theory of opponent processes.

It is problematic to organize parallel processing of all signs and sequential on different scales, as is done on the retina, on modern video sensors. However, they can be implemented in parallel-serial or serial-parallel manner on a large number of GPU or on the FPGA. Although with large coarsening on the peripheral retina, it becomes necessary to repeatedly calculate the sums of square or rectangular fragments, this can be effectively solved using an integrated matrix [2]. The same principle can be applied to calculate the *center-surround* operator (with the same inhibition zone coefficients).

In this case, the total amount of the entire *center-surround* fragment is calculated from 4 points, and then the center area is determined from 4 points, i.e. it takes only 7 operations of addition/subtraction and one shift operation for several digits (using masks with a central coefficient multiple of degree 2). In the central fossa, according to the principle of *center-surround*, more detailed informative features are extracted (brighter/darker or different in color or orientation points that characterize the edges of areas or contours of objects, spatial frequencies of textures, etc. that stand out from the background). The *center-surround* principle is implemented in computer vision using appropriate masks (Laplace, Roberts, Sobel, Prewitt, etc.), which are already widely used in image processing techniques to extract the edges and boundaries of areas, object contours, orientation features, etc.

With an insufficient level of illumination, by analogy with the grouping of rods on the peripheral retina, the summation of signals from rods for larger receptive fields is performed, which can significantly increase the sensitivity to light perception, i.e. exchange spatial resolution for increased sensitivity.

In the case of insufficient light in the arsenal of the human visual system, there are techniques that can significantly increase the sensitivity to light perception in exchange for a decrease in spatial resolution. They consist in the possibility of combining and summing the signals of neighboring rods of the peripheral retina using horizontal cells, as well as the ring concentric organization of neurons, which allows to increase the contrast in the perception of the scene.

The sensitivity of light perception is controlled by changing the number of summed signals of the rods and by changing the number of concentric rings around the central excitation zone of on- and off-centers. Thus, the coefficient of sensitivity increase is directly proportional to the number of summed signals from neighboring retinal rods and the gain due to the ring organization of neurons. Examples of using this approach and the results of increasing the sensitivity are shown in Fig. 2.

However, with large degrees of coarsening, i.e. combining a large number of rods, the gain of sensitivity is very large (in the range from 1 to n^2) and they need to be adjusted. At the same time, large degrees of roughening can be effectively used to quickly search for "interesting" places in the scene image in accordance with the dynamic model of the visual analyzer. In this case, combining and summing the signals from the rods can be carried out with the averaging operation, i.e. with a coefficient of gain equal to the central element of the mask.

An increase in contrast can be achieved by building up the brake rings around the exciting center, i.e. by using masks of large sizes (for example, 5×5, 7×7, etc.). The principle of ring concentric organization, as noted above, can be used to extract a large number of coarse and subtle informative features not only in monochrome, but also in color images. Let's consider this issue in more detail on the example of the on-center. As you know, in the Bayer color representation

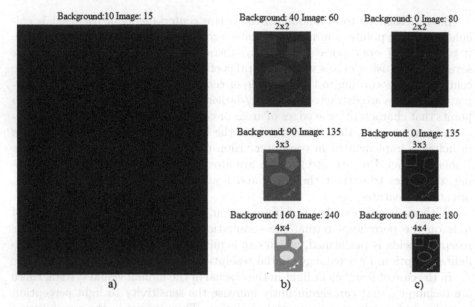

Fig. 2. Increasing the sensitivity of the peripheral retina by summing the signals from the rods and their ring organization: a) input image; b) the result of amplification due to the summation of the signals of fields of size 2×2, 3×3 and 4×4; c) the result of amplification due to the ring organization with a Laplace 3×3 mask

model, three basic colors are placed in the sensor matrix as follows:

$$
\begin{array}{l}
r\,g\,r\,g\,r\,g\,r\,g\,r\,g \\
g\,b\,g\,b\,g\,b\,g\,b\,g\,b \\
r\,g\,r\,g\,r\,g\,r\,g\,r\,g \\
g\,b\,g\,b\,g\,b\,g\,b\,g\,b \\
r\,g\,r\,g\,r\,g\,r\,g\,r\,g \\
g\,b\,g\,b\,g\,b\,g\,b\,g\,b
\end{array}
$$

If we consider 3×3 masks, we can see that to extract blue (exciting) color, you need to use an 8-connected mask h_1. Moreover, for color B, the colors r and g are inhibitory (opposing), and colors b and g are inhibitory for color R. For color G, the colors r and b are inhibitory, but this uses a 4-connected Laplace mask h_2.

$$
h_1 = \begin{vmatrix} -1 & -1 & -1 \\ -1 & 8 & -1 \\ -1 & -1 & -1 \end{vmatrix}, \quad h_2 = \begin{vmatrix} 0 & -1 & 0 \\ -1 & 4 & -1 \\ 0 & -1 & 0 \end{vmatrix}
$$

For the off-center, the signs in the masks are reversed, and with their help it is possible to identify color pixels that are smaller in magnitude of the corresponding opponent colors in the mask. This fully corresponds to the three-component theory of color vision [11]. In accordance with the theory of opponent processes in the human visual system, in the second stage, which takes place at higher levels (possibly in the LGB), according to the same principle, center-surround, differences in colors are revealed in larger receptive fields. As a result of the implementation of the three-component color theory, 3 color planes are obtained: R, G and B. Additionally, the Y plane is formed in accordance with the formula

$$Y = (r + g)/2 - |r - g|/2 - b$$

Further, negative values are zeroed, after that pairs of opponent colors RG and BY are considered, for example: R is the center, G is the surround; B is the center, and Y is the surround, or vice versa. In this case, the selection of colors can be performed at different scales of the presentation of information. To reduce the amount of information when roughening the color layer or implementing the *center-surround*, as for monochrome images, an integrating matrix can be used.

An important point in order to reduce the delay in the feedback circuit of the CVS is the combination of the processes of reading and processing information from the sensor matrix. This combination is implemented using 2–3 channels of direct access to memory. In this case, the first channel controls the input of information into memory, the second - reads information for processing, and the third - controls the recording of results in a new memory array. This approach reduces the processing processor's time spent working with several sources and receivers of information and allows obtaining information for controlling the reading parameters of the next frame of the video sequence with minimal time after reading data. Typically, the frequency of reading information in modern video sensors is about one and a half to two orders of magnitude lower than the frequency of the processing processor (for example, a digital signal processor or graphic processors), which allows up to hundreds of image processing operations to be performed during the reading of one data from a video sensor. Since the time diagram of the video sensor also contains additional losses of time for switching to reading the next line and for completing a frame, the delay in information in the CVS feedback circuit is reduced by approximately the processing time of one frame in comparison with the traditional approach.

Such approaches were used to create the first in Ukraine IVK-1 family of intelligent video cameras (2000) and a number of real-time video systems based on them. Among them:

- product quality control system for color, size, shape;
- control system for static and dynamic parameters of physical, chemical and biological objects;
- digital optical capillaroscope for non-invasive control of static and dynamic parameters of human blood microcirculation;
- MacroMicroPotok hemodynamic laboratory based on an advanced Dopplerograph and a digital optical capillaroscope for monitoring the human cardiovascular system at macro and micro levels;
- tracking device for the selected object, etc.

6   Conclusions

Using an arsenal of methods and mechanisms for processing information on the retina of a human visual analyzer made it possible to propose a number of original principles for organizing the search for an object in an image, tracking it and extracting informative features for recognition. In particular:

- the modernization of the video sensor conveyor based on dynamic models and the control of information reading parameters can significantly (by several orders of magnitude) reduce the amount of processed information. This is achieved due to the possibility of changing the resolution of the video sensor, coarse-accurate representation of the scene (coarse - when searching for an object or tracking it, and accurate representation of only fragments of the image of the object - during recognition) [9]. At the same time, the same video sensor is used for coarse and detailed processing, and the combination of image input and processing processes can significantly increase the efficiency of processing video information;
- the use of the proposed principles of the ring concentric organization of on- and off-centers and an integrating matrix for their implementation, adaptation mechanisms to the level of illumination and contrast, the method of determining spatial frequencies based on δ-entropy, the differential representation of images for their analysis can significantly simplify the implementation of these principles and accelerate the process of training ANN in the subsequent stages of classification/recognition of objects. The selection of informative features directly in CVS allows reducing the amount of information transmitted to higher levels of information processing (for example, in the ANN) by 3–4 orders of magnitude [9];
- the introduction of a processing processor into the CVS (DSP processor, a group of graphic processors, FPGAs, ANNs of convolution type, etc., depending on the characteristics of the task and performance requirements) to implement the above principles will significantly increase the productivity, efficiency and effectiveness of the CVS. A significant increase in productivity can be achieved by constructing a multilayer matrix that combines parallel reading, analog-to-digital conversion and information processing (suitable for specialized applications) [6,10–13].

Acknowledgments. This work was carried out in the framework of fundamental competitive topics (VFK 200.15 and VFK 200.19), which were funded by the Presidium of the National Academy of Sciences (NAS) of Ukraine.

I express my sincere gratitude to the employees of the Department of Intelligent Real-Time Video Systems of the Institute of Cybernetics named after V.M. Glushkov NAS of Ukraine, which took part in the creation of tools, modeling and verification of theoretical provisions.

References

1. Anderson, D.: Cognitive Psychology, 5th edn. Piter, St. Petersburg, Russia (2002). (Russian translation)

2. Bay, H., Ess, A., Tuytelaars, T., Van Gool, L.: Speeded-up robust features (surf). Comput. Vis. Image Underst. **110**(3), 346–359 (2008). https://doi.org/10.1016/j.cviu.2007.09.014
3. Benoit, A., Caplier, A., Durette, B., Herault, J.: Using human visual system modeling for bio-inspired low level image processing. Comput. Vis. Image Underst. **114**(7), 758–773 (2010). https://doi.org/10.1016/j.cviu.2010.01.011
4. Boyun, V.: Intelligent selective perception of visual information in vision systems. In: Proceedings of the 6th IEEE International Conference on Intelligent Data Acquisition and Advanced Computing Systems: Technology and Application, IDAACS 2011, Czech Republic, Prague, vol. 1, pp. 412–416 (2011)
5. Boyun, V.: Directions of development of intelligent real time video systems. Appl. Theor. Comput. Technol. [S.l.] **2**(3), 48–66 (2017)
6. Boyun, V.P., Voznenko, L.O., Malkush, I.F.: Principles of organization of the human eye retina and their use in computer vision systems. Cybern. Syst. Anal. **55**(5), 701–713 (2019). https://doi.org/10.1007/s10559-019-00181-0
7. Boyun, V.: The dynamic theory of information. Fundamentals and applications. Institute of Cybernetics of NASU, Kyiv, Ukraine (2001)
8. Boyun, V.: A human visual analyzer as a prototype for construction of the set of dedicated systems of machine vision. In: Proceedings of the International Science and Technology Conference on "Artificial Intelligence", Intelligent Systems II-2010, vol. 1, pp. 21–26 (2010)
9. Boyun, V.: Intelligent selective perception of visual information: informational aspects. Artif. Intell. **3**, 16–24 (2011). (in Ukrainian)
10. Boyun, V.: Device for determining the location and parameters of image objects, UA patent no. 76597, BI no. 6 (2013)
11. Boyun, V.: Sensor device for determination of location and center of gravity of an object, UA patent no. 106292, BI no. 12 (2014)
12. Boyun, V.: Sensor device for determining the location and moments of inertia of an object in an image, UA patent no. 106301, BI no. 15 (2014)
13. Boyun, V.: Sensor matrix with image processing, UA patent no. 109335, BI no. 6 (2015)
14. Burt, P.: Smart sensing within a pyramid vision machine. Proc. IEEE **76**(8), 175–185 (1988). https://doi.org/10.1109/5.5971
15. Gollisch, T., Meister, M.: Eye smarter than scientists believed: neural computations in circuits of the retina. Neuron **65**(2), 150–164 (2009). https://doi.org/10.1016/j.neuron.2009.12.009
16. Gonsales, R., Woods, R.: Digital Image Processing. Technosphere, Moscow, Russia (2005)
17. Hubel, D.H.: Eye, Brain and Vision. Scienceific American, New York (1988)
18. Kolb, H.: How the retina works: much of the construction of an image takes place in the retina itself through the use of specialized neural circuits. Am. Sci. **91**(1), 28–35 (2003). https://doi.org/10.1511/2003.1.28
19. Krizhevsky, A., Sutskever, I., Hinton, G.: ImageNet classification with deep convolutional neural networks. In: NIPS Proceedings. Advances in Neural Information Processing Systems, vol. 25 (2012). http://papers.nips.cc/paper/4824-imagenet-classification-with-deep-convolutional-neural-network
20. Marr, D.: Computational Investigation into Human Representation and Processing of Visual Information. W.H. Freeman and Company, New York (1987)
21. Podvigin, N., Makarov, F., Shelepin, Y.: Elements of Structural and Functional Organization of Visual Oculomotor System. Nauka, Leningrad, USSR (1986). (in Russian)

22. Schiffmann, H.: Sensation and Perception: An Integrated Approach. Piter, St. Peterburg (2003). (Russian translation)
23. Shah, S., Levine, M.: Visual information processing in primate cone pathway - part i: a model, part ii: experiments. IEEE Trans. Syst. Man Cybern. Syst. Part b Cybern. **26**(2), 259–289 (1996). https://doi.org/10.1109/3477.485837
24. Shelepin, Y., Bondarko, V., Danilova, M.: Foveola construction and visual system pyramidal organization model. Sens. Syst. **9**(1), 87–97 (1995). (in Russian)
25. Shevelev, I.: Neurons of Visual Cortex. Adaptability and Dynamics of Receptive Fields. Nauka, Moscow (1984). (in Russian)
26. Siagian, C., Itti, L.: Rapid biologically-inspired scene classification using features shared with visual attention. IEEE Trans. Pattern Anal. Mach. Intell. **29**(2), 300–312 (2007)
27. Supin, A.: Neuron Mechanisms of Visual Analysis. Nauka, Moscow, USSR (1974). (in Russian)
28. Tagare, H., Toyama, K., Wang, J.: A maximum-likelihood strategy for directing attention during visual search. IEEE Trans. Pattern Anal. Mach. Intell. **23**, 490–500 (2001)
29. Yamasaki, H., Shibata, T.: A real-time image-feature-extraction and vector-generation VLSI employing arrayed-shift-register architecture. IEEE J. Solid-State Circ. **42**(9), 2046–2053 (2007)

Software and Algorithmic Support for Finite-Element Analysis of Anisotropic Heat-and-Mass Transfer Using Parallel and Cloud Technologies

Yaroslav Sokolovskyy[1]([✉])(iD), Andriy Nechepurenko[1], Ivan Sokolovskyy[2](iD),
and Olha Mokrytska[1](iD)

[1] Ukrainian National Forestry University, Lviv, Ukraine
sokolowskyyyar@yahoo.com, andriy.nechepurenko@gmail.com,
mokrytska@nltu.edu.ua
[2] Lviv Polytechnic National University, Lviv, Ukraine
Sokolovskyy.vani@gmail.com

Abstract. The software was developed to perform finite element analysis of moisture transfer using Compute Unified Device Architecture technology. It was developed using the basis of a three-dimensional mathematical model of non-isothermal heat-and-mass transfer in capillary-porous materials, taking into account the anisotropy of thermophysical properties. The program database is divided into two parts. One part is located on the Azure server and the other part is on the local device where the application is installed. This solution made it possible to use CUDA parallelization software. It is done from Azure Cloud add-ons or from the local device where the program is located. The application of parallel technologies using the cuBLAS library made it possible to transfer all large-scale matrix computations to the graphics processor. That reduced resource consumption with increasing grid density.

Keywords: Software · Mathematical model · Heat-and-mass transfer · Finite element method · CUDA · cuBLAS · Azure

1 Introduction and Literature Review

We are working on improving the technologies which are related with the drying of wood now. Currently developed methods and research results are being tested in enterprises to identify the shortcomings of scientific approaches and all the new ad-vantages. Most of the methods are predominantly developed using the finite element method. Studies are being conducted on problems of heat-and-moisture transfer in capillary-porous materials. Since most software resources are spent on sampling and computing finite elements when running software, it is important to find the optimal technology to parallelize such processes. The construction of a three-dimensional mathematical model and the study of spatial case of

S. Babichev et al. (Eds.): DSMP 2020, CCIS 1158, pp. 45–61, 2020.
https://doi.org/10.1007/978-3-030-61656-4_3

non-isothermal heat-and-mass transfer are relevant. Therefore, the choice of an effective numerical method for implementing the 3D approach is important. That and the correct use of CUDA parallel computing technologies in conjunction with Azure cloud technologies can give impetus to the creation of an object-oriented software package. The software should provide for the implementation of a user-friendly interface with extensive graphical visualization of finite element partitioning. Also it is necessary to provide the results of simulations of moisture transfer process and to implement effective methods of working with data in cloud technologies.

Today, one-dimensional, two-dimensional linear and non-linear mathematical models of heat-and-mass transfer are built taking into account the anisotropy of thermophysical properties [9, 17, 24–26]. However, studies of the spatial case of nonisothermal mass transfer remains relevant. The practical implementation of such mathematical models is so complicated that the application of analytical and approximate methods is impossible, so we have to resort to searching for numerical methods. Over the past decades, numerical methods for solving non-stationary field theory problems, in particular finite- and boundary element methods, have been rapidly developing and successfully competing among themselves [11, 12]. The use of the finite element method has several advantages that are essential for solving real-life problems. A number of scientific studies [1, 12] are devoted to the improvement and extension of parallelization methods for finite element analysis using an object-oriented approach [16]. Methods for the decomposition of regions based on finite element approximation are given in [12, 13].

An important aspect in the implementation of parallel computing is the use of graphics processors (GPUs). According to the studies [7, 19], in this case, the efficiency of computing processes is significantly increased. However, this approach requires the development of new algorithms and appropriate software. In particular, the scientific works [3, 7] are devoted to the study of the use of graphic accelerators for parallelization of spatial finite-element analysis of physical processes using CUDA technologies. The experimental estimates of parallelization efficiency based on the use of CUDA technologies are presented in [8].

The development of modern information technologies for parallel finite element analysis also includes automation of the discretization of the computational region into a finite number of 2D or 3D elements. On the one hand, the automation of the region discretization significantly affects the computational complexity of the finite element method (FEM), and on the other hand, its solution requires the use of a different set of algorithms and methods than those used directly in the numerical implementation of the FEM. The use of adaptive discretization adjustment allows reducing the error in applying the FEM [13]. The choice of criteria for adaptation of the discretization region for the application of such procedures are considered in [14, 15]. The approximation properties of discretization elements are given, in particular, in [12, 14, 15]. The studies of software and algorithmic aspects with wide possibilities for graphical visualization of parallelization of finite element analysis using cloud technologies, effective programs for storing and importing data are the subject of works [1,12].

Thus, the development of efficient numerical algorithms and appropriate software should be based on modern methods of parallelization using graphics processors and sampling data representation structures that allow to optimize the computational process.

The aim of the research is to develop software and algorithmic support for finite element analysis of heat and mass transfer processes in anisotropic capillary-porous materials using parallel computing technologies CUDA and cloud services. It is important to conduct numerical experiments and evaluate the effectiveness of the parallelization of processes.

2 Materials and Methods

2.1 Formulation of a Mathematical Model

The three-dimensional mathematical model of heat and mass transfer is described by a system of differential equations (1)–(2) in partial derivatives in the drying process of capillary-porous materials, taking into account the anisotropy of thermo-physical properties:

$$\rho_0 \frac{\partial T(x,y,z,\tau)}{\partial \tau} = \frac{\partial}{\partial x}(\lambda_x \frac{\partial T(x,y,z,\tau)}{\partial x}) + \frac{\partial}{\partial y}(\lambda_y \frac{\partial T(x,y,z,\tau)}{\partial y}) +$$

$$\frac{\partial}{\partial z}(\lambda_z \frac{\partial T(x,y,z,\tau)}{\partial z}) + \varepsilon\rho_0 r((\frac{\partial U(x,y,z,\tau)}{\partial \tau}))) \tag{1}$$

$$\frac{\partial U(x,y,z,\tau)}{\partial \tau} = \frac{\partial}{\partial x}\left(a_{m_x}\frac{\partial U(x,y,z,\tau)}{\partial x}\right) + \frac{\partial}{\partial y}\left(a_{m_y}\frac{\partial U(x,y,z,\tau)}{\partial y}\right) +$$

$$\frac{\partial}{\partial z}\left(a_{m_z}\frac{\partial U(x,y,z,\tau)}{\partial z}\right) + \frac{\partial}{\partial x}\left(a_{m_x}\sigma\frac{\partial T(x,y,z,\tau)}{\partial x}\right) + \tag{2}$$

$$\frac{\partial}{\partial y}\left(a_{m_y}\sigma\frac{\partial T(x,y,z,\tau)}{\partial y}\right) + \frac{\partial}{\partial z}\left(a_{m_z}\sigma\frac{\partial T(x,y,z,\tau)}{\partial z}\right)$$

with boundary conditions:

$$\lambda_n \frac{\partial T}{\partial n}\Big|_{x=S} + \rho_0(1-\varepsilon)r\beta_n\left(U\mid_{x=S} - U_{p_n}\right) = \alpha_n\left(T_c - T\mid_{x=S}\right)$$

initial conditions with irregular release of moisture:

$$\left(a_{m_n}\frac{\partial U}{\partial n} + a_{m_n}\sigma\frac{\partial T}{\partial n}\right)\Big|_{x=S} = \beta_n\left(U_{p_n} - U\mid_{x=S}\right) \tag{3}$$

$$\left(a_{m_n}\frac{\partial U}{\partial n} + a_{m_n}\sigma\frac{\partial T}{\partial n}\right)\Big|_{x=0} = 0; \quad \frac{\partial T}{\partial n}\Big|_{x=0} = 0;$$

initial conditions with irregular release of moisture:

$$T|_{\tau=0} = T_0(x, y, z); U|_{\tau=0} = U_0(x, y, z), \tag{4}$$

where $T(x, y, z, \tau)$, $U(x, y, z, \tau)$ are required function of temperature and humidity in the region in accordance:

$$V = \{(x, y, z) : x\epsilon[0, R_1], y\epsilon[0, R_2], z\epsilon[0, R_3], \tau\epsilon[0, \tau^*]\};$$

FEM is finite element method; R_1, R_2, R_3 are geometric dimensions of lumber; S is the geometric surface of the region; τ^* is the time of the process; c is the heat capacity of wood; ρ_0 is the heat capacity and base density of wood; $\lambda_1, \lambda_2, \lambda_3$ are the coefficients of thermal conductivity in the directions of anisotropy; ε is the phase transition criterion; τ is the current time; ; r is the specific heat of vaporization; a_n is the heat exchange coefficient; a_{mx}, a_{my}, a_{mz} are the moisture conductivity coefficients in the directions of anisotropy; T_c is the ambient environment; U_p is the equilibrium humidity; β_a is the moisture exchange coefficient; σ is the thermo-gradient coefficient; n is the normal vector to the surface.

The initial conditions are given by spatial quadratic functions [21,29], for a regular regime characterized by the corresponding values of the Fourier number criterion F_0 and Bio (Bi). For numerical implementation of the algorithm and finite element analysis mathematical model of heat and moisture in capillary-porous materials [25,28] was developed software.

2.2   Algorithmic Aspects of Finite Element Analysis

From the finite element method follows a variable formulation of the mathematical model of heat transfer. Numerical implementation of the mathematical model (1)–(4) is also provided by the use of FEM. To establish the problem, it is assumed that the change in moisture content can be represented as the sum of values due to the gradients of humidity and temperature $\frac{\partial U}{\partial \tau} = \frac{\partial U_1}{\partial \tau} + \frac{\partial U_2}{\partial \tau}$. Then Eq. (2) takes the form:

$$\frac{\partial U_1}{\partial \tau} = \frac{\partial}{\partial x}\left(a_{m_x}\frac{\partial U_1}{\partial x}\right) + \frac{\partial}{\partial y}\left(a_{m_y}\frac{\partial U_1}{\partial y}\right) + \frac{\partial}{\partial z}\left(a_{m_z}\frac{\partial U_1}{\partial z}\right) \tag{5}$$

$$\frac{\partial U_2}{\partial \tau} = \frac{\partial}{\partial x}\left(a_{m_x}\sigma\frac{\partial U_2}{\partial x}\right) + \frac{\partial}{\partial y}\left(a_{m_y}\sigma\frac{\partial U_2}{\partial y}\right) + \frac{\partial}{\partial z}\left(a_{m_z}\sigma\frac{\partial U_2}{\partial z}\right) \tag{6}$$

The implementation of the mathematical model is reduced to solving an equivalent variational problem based on the minimization of functionals [12], taking into account the assumptions. To approximate continuous values of temperature T and moisture content in the wood U in the discrete model, the study region V is divided into a finite number of elements. Then the moisture content $\{U^{(e)}\}$ and the temperature $\{T^{(e)}\}$ are determined for each discretization element:

$$\frac{\partial U_2}{\partial \tau} = \frac{\partial}{\partial x}\left(a_{m_x}\sigma\frac{\partial U_2}{\partial x}\right) + \frac{\partial}{\partial y}\left(a_{m_y}\sigma\frac{\partial U_2}{\partial y}\right) + \frac{\partial}{\partial z}\left(a_{m_z}\sigma\frac{\partial U_2}{\partial z}\right) \tag{7}$$

We introduce the notation

$$\left\{g_T^{(e)}\right\}^T = \left\{\frac{\partial T}{\partial x}\frac{\partial T}{\partial y}\frac{\partial T}{\partial z}\right\}, \left\{g_U^{(e)}\right\}^U = \left\{\frac{\partial U}{\partial x}\frac{\partial U}{\partial y}\frac{\partial U}{\partial z}\right\}. \tag{8}$$

Then

$$\left\{g_T^{(e)}\right\}^T = \left[B^{(e)}\right]\{T\}, \left\{g_U^{(e)}\right\}^U = \left[B^{(e)}\right]\{U\} \tag{9}$$

where U is the vector of moisture content; T is temperature vector; $[N^{(e)}]$ are element shape functions, $[B^{(e)}]$ is gradient matrix. The first-order tetrahedron is a finite element [5]; therefore, taking into account the functions of shape and differentiation of functionals with respect to U and T, we obtain their minimum. After grouping the integrals and equating them to zero, the resulting system of matrix equations of FEM is obtained:

$$[C]\frac{\partial\{U\}}{\partial\tau} + [K]\{U\} + \{F\} = 0; [\bar{C}]\frac{\partial\{T\}}{\partial\tau} + [\bar{K}]\{T\} + \{\bar{F}\} - 0, \tag{10}$$

where:
$[C] = \int_V \rho_0 [N]^T [N] dV; [K] = \int_V [B]^T [D^*] [B] dV + \int_S \rho_0\beta_w [N]^T [N] dS;$
$\{F\} = \int_V [B]^T [H] [B] [T] dV - \int_S \rho_0\beta U_p [N]^T dS$ are damping and loading, according to the matrix of thermo-physical properties of material, $\{N\}$ is the matrix of form functions. $[\bar{C}], [\bar{K}], \{\bar{F}\}$ are those analogical matrices which related with the coefficient of heat conductivity and heat exchange.

To find the spatial functions of humidity and temperature at any point in the time interval, it is necessary to reduce them to finding the solution of the system of Eq. (10). It uses an algorithm predictor – corrector. For calculations the values of change of temperature T and humidity U in time the Finite difference method is used [26,27]. Then the numerical implementation of the mathematical model (7)–(8) is reduced to solving the type of system equations: $[A]\{U\}_{next} = \{R\}$; $[A_T]\{T\}_{next} = \{R_T\}$.

Thermo-physical descriptions of wood depend on a temperature and humidity. Equalization of model (5)–(6) are related with each other. The iteration process of equalizations realization (10) is carried out on every sentinel step. Considering the additional iteration procedure, which specifies influence of humidity on apportionment of temperature in material and vice versa. Completing of iterations for equalizations (10) are performed implementation of conditions: $\{U_n\} - \{U_n - 1\} \leq 10^{-4}$ and $\{T_n\} - \{T_n - 1\} \leq 10^{-4}$.

One of the main steps in solving the problem of moisture transfer using FEM is discretization of the study area. The task is accomplished through the construction of a three-dimensional finite-element grid. It is created by building up the layers of triangulations constructed at the initial stage [12,23]. This grid is constructed in such a way that the studied area consists only of finite elements - a tetrahedron. It meets the following requirements:

– the grid must be compatible. Namely, in the three-dimensional case, the tetrahedron face can be divided only between two elements;

- the quality of the shape of the elements should be optimized. This is necessary to reduce the sampling error. Specifically, degenerate elements are not allowed;
- the size and shape of the elements must correspond to the functions of the form of the corresponding nodes;
- the numbering of nodes and their orientation must be consistent;
- some nodes, ribs, and faces can be created in the specials, well defined locations.

The construction of tetrahedrons is carried out due to the establishment of connections between triangular faces. The data structure Tetrahedrons-Triangles-Nodes is using for the discretization [12,23]. The algorithm Direct construction of the Delaunay triangulation was chosen as the basis. In particular, a step-by-step algorithm with a k-d search tree. The important point is the quality assessment of the constructed tetrahedron in the three-dimensional region. This is especially true for a group of algorithms of direct construction. Their feature is the construction of immediately regular tetrahedrons without further restructuring [12]. The coefficient for assessing the quality of the constructed tetrahedron is performance index. It is calculated as the ratio of the volume of the tetrahedron to the sum of the areas of its faces: restructuring

$$\gamma = \frac{12\sqrt{3}(AB \times AC) \times AD}{(AB^2 + BC^2 + CA^2 + AD^2 + BD^2 + CD^2)^{\frac{3}{2}}} \tag{11}$$

where A, B. C. D are apices of the tetrahedron.

The maximum volume of an equilateral tetrahedron will be 1. The normalizing factor is $12\sqrt{3}$. If the coefficient of quality assessment of the tetrahedron is equal to 0, then it must be removed.

2.3 Software Implementation

The implementation of the finite element method in the moisture-transfer problem is represented by using object-oriented programming. Due to the use of the Microsoft Visual Studio programming environment, a finite-element calculation in the C# language is implemented using CUDA parallel computing technology [7,8]. The peculiarity of using the Graphics Processing Unit (GPU) in the calculations by the finite element method involves the application of CudaFY libraries. This is due to the fact that the calculations on the video adapter are performed using the language "C", so a kind of translator C# - C - C# is used. The process of solving the moisture transfer problem using the finite element method can be conditionally divided into three calculation modules. These are: discretization of the region, formation of system matrices and the solution of the system of equations.

A three-level architecture pattern was used to develop the software [6] (Fig. 1). It consists of three main components: the client, the application server, and the database server. For such software construction, the client is the user interface. In turn, the "Application Server" is located simultaneously in two places: "Azure Cloud" and the local server. The structure of the database is organized in the same way. The data-base is shared between the cloud and the local server. Communication with the database can be carried out simultaneously by several client terminals. The sequence of queries in such an architecture is shown in Fig. 1.

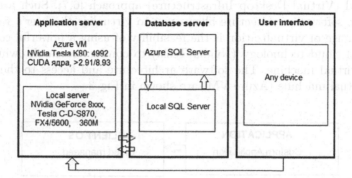

Fig. 1. Software architecture

To better understand the architecture, we give a detailed description of the soft-ware (Fig. 2). The first step is to enter the input data. At the same time, a request is actually received from the user interface regarding the ability of using CUDA in the local environment. After receiving data on the readiness of the video adapter for calculations and the possibility of using CUDA kernels, the user interface, using the simple logical operator "if (id.cudathread! = null)", determines the place where the calculations will be performed. If the local server is not able to parallelize the calculation, then the software sends a request to Azure Cloud with the input data. That is, in fact, the interface acts as the FrontEnd part, while the local server and cloud - as the BackEnd.

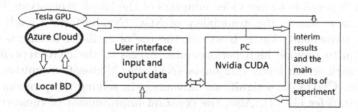

Fig. 2. Sequence of steps in executing the program requests.

The calculation results are stored in the database. It is located in the place where the calculations were carried out. That is, if the calculations were carried out on the local server, then the database will be local and vice versa. If there is an Internet connection with the databases, then synchronization is performed. The advantage of using this approach for software development is the ability for the user to access research data even with limited access to the Internet. Or, lacking the necessary computing power, you can conduct an experiment using cloud technologies and their capabilities.

It should be noted that the partial use of cloud technologies refers to the use of the VDI (Virtual Desktop Infrastructure) approach [6,7]. Such a construction of the software architecture allows you to virtualize the user's workplace. The advantage of virtualization is the feasibility of using a powerful computing resource of cloud technology (Nvidia Tesla) to conduct research owing to the AZURE virtual machine. The software architecture and access to the GPU in Azure Virtual machine (Azure VM) are shown in Fig. 3.

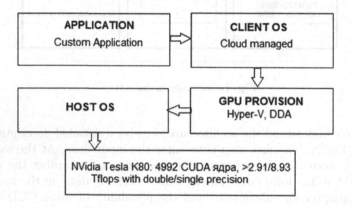

Fig. 3. The architecture of GPU operation in Azure VM.

The numerical implementation of the mathematical model of moisture transfer (1)–(4) involves the execution of calculations by the finite element method in the cloud. Owing to the use of Azure VM, on which part of the software is located, it is possible to use video adapters of the latest generations for calculations. This is due to the availability of NGC (Nvidia GPU Cloud) containers. Their implementation is based on the use of artificial intelligence, which allows them to provide high performance. Access to the NGC repository and the framework which holds containers (NVCaffe, Microsoft Cognitive Toolkit, TensorFlow, CUDA) is a significant advantage in solving the problem of heat-and-mass transfer (1)–(4). Also, the constant improvement of these containers expands opportunities of applying the latest approaches to machine learning. The description of the software architecture also indicates a similar construction of the database and its partial operation. Also important is to synchronize local database with the database in the cloud. This synchronization is done using the Web API. Application programming interface is an option for constructing ASP.NET software. This option is used specifically to work in the style of REST

(Representation State Transfer) [4,19]. The REST architecture, in turn, involves the use of methods or types of requests to interact with the server.

In most cases, using REST to form any user interface is very convenient. Therefore, special javascript-frameworks like Angular, React or Knockout are quite often used. One of the features of software applications is the ability to represent any technology and platform. From the description above, it is clear that the web application programming interface (Web API) is synchronized directly through the Entiti Framework with the database. The connection string located on the API looks like:

```
var connection = "Data Source=Context.db";
services.AddDbContext<DataContext>
(options => options.UseSqlite(connection));
```

The proposed dual model for using the database also has a negative component. This is a slow interface. But still, when developing the interface, one of the rules of User interface (UI) developers is that there should be less logic on the FrontEnd part. That is, actually, it is just the design itself that is responsible for the UI of the program. Therefore, due to cloud technologies, the program interface actually works as a kind of application, because the key algorithmic aspects of the numerical implementation of the mathematical model of heat-and-mass transfer (1)–(4) occur on the BackEnd part and on the cloud. In turn, the program uses the local location only in the absence of the Internet connection.

3   Results and Discussion

As was described hereinbefore, one of the successful components of the implementation of modelling the process of non-isothermal heat-and-moisture transfer (1)–(4) is the execution of a large number of matrix operations. Actions with matrices occur both in the triangulation of the region and in the calculations of moisture content and temperature in each finite element. Since the accuracy of the result depends on the density of the grid, and this, in turn, leads to an increase in the number and dimension of matrices, which is quite resource-intensive, it is customary to use the CUDA parallel computing technology, namely the Nvidia cuBLAS library [4]. Using the cuBLAS API, the speed of the software application will be 20 % higher (Fig. 4) compared to the standard calculation approach based on the CPU. Numerical experiments indicate that with an increase in the density of the triangulation grid, this percentage will increase. With the number of tetrahedrons >1000, the percentage can increase up to 40 %. This is primarily due to the ability of cuBLAS to accelerate operations on matrices by performing computational operations in a single GPU, or to effectively scale up and distribute computations in configurations of several GPUs. The key advantages are as follows: the ability to support standard BLAS procedures, API and error log for debugging and tracking, support for CUDA threads for simultaneous operations.

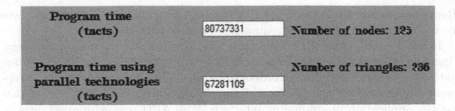

Fig. 4. CuBLAS performance indicators

Using the cuBLAS library has another advantage. For example, to implement matrix multiplication with the standard parallelization approach in CUDA, you need to make the GPU memory images. The BLAS and LAPACK APIs were created in such a way that you can specify the starting point, step length, length of leading dimensions, etc. and avoid copying CPU-GPU-CPU data. The following is code snippet (cuBLAS) from the developed software:

```
int M = N * P;
int K = N * P;
for (int i = 0; i < N; i++)
{
double *d_In = d_A + i * P;
double *d_Out = d_C + i * P;
cublasSetStream(streams[i]);
cublasDgemm(cublasHandle, CUBLAS_OP_N,
CUBLAS_OP_N, &alpha, d_In, M, d_B, M, &beta, d_Out, K);
}..
```

By parallelizing the most resource-intensive parts of the program, the GPU actually unloads the Central processing unit (CPU) and makes it a kind of software manager which forms the sequence of tasks and monitors their execution. A node is an important component for forming a data structure. To quickly find a node and check it against the Delaunay condition, a k-d tree is formed. Such a tree allows obtaining software acceleration. The essence of constructing an algorithm based on the k-d tree is to divide the plane into two half-planes using a straight line parallel to one of the coordinate axes, for example, the OY axis. Each of these half-planes can be further re-divided by a straight line parallel to another coordinate axis. These actions are repeated, changing at each step the direction of the dividing line. The lines dividing the plane are selected according to the dichotomy principle, that is, guided by receiving approximately equal number of nodes on each side of the dividing line. One of the main methods for working in a k-d tree is to add nodes to the tree structure in a balanced way. The path to the left or right branch depends on the parameters set when building the tree L = (x, y, LeftSide, RightSide). It is definitely necessary to take into account the balance in the tree, because in the future it will affect the quality of the tree traversal. This can reduce the search time for the nearest node. That is, with a positive balance, the number of nodes on the left side will be approximately equal to the number of nodes on the right (length Node leftSide = length Node rightSide). Formally, such a method can be represented in the following way: *algorithm AddNode:*

```
input:
algorithm AddNode
input:
Nb { base point;
Nt { a new point to add to the tree structure;
L {    a list of points with branch parameters (rightSide, leftSide);
tree { tree;
output:
k {d tree - regenerated list of nodes formed
in the structure of k {d tree using the List collection
begin
// Case No.1
if |L = null|
a dd Nb to L
return L
// Case No.2
else
addTo L new Nt
rebuilt L
return L
end if
```

In the existing pseudo-code, you can find two cases of adding nodes. In the first case, if the list of points with branch parameters is equal to "null" (that is, empty), then the base point is added to the parent or added to the list as a parent. In fact, this tree is without branches. In the second case, a new node is added to the list and the tree is rebuilt into a tree with branches. The parameter is a metric that indicates which side of the parent branch the node belongs to, after the k-d tree is constructed, discretization begins. When dividing the plane into finite elements (tetrahedrons), the "direct construction" algorithm is used. The essence of the algorithm is to construct a single iteration of triangles that are not subject to reconstruction. This algorithm is quite time consuming. But the decision to transfer multiple checks of the fulfillment of the Delaunay condition from the CPU to the GPU threads makes this method the most successful option for application in this field of research. When describing the parallelization of triangulation in the GPU, one can schematically depict the process itself (Fig. 5). Thus, the number of parallel threads used in the software implementation is equal to the number of operations that the algorithm for checking the Delaunay condition requires (calculating the center and the radius of the circle circumscribed around a triangle). Accordingly, each thread of the block is responsible for a certain operation necessary for calculating the Delaunay criterion of a triangle with vertices [2]. In particular, block (0; 0) is responsible for calculating (Fig. 5) the Delaunay criterion for a triangle, etc.

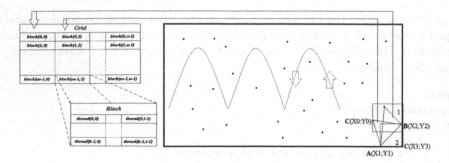

Fig. 5. The thread diagram of parallel execution of operations to verify the Delaunay condition

We studied the dynamics of spatial heat-and-moisture transfer in wood during the drying process. What based, on having examined the mathematical model (1)–(4) and the software. For this purpose, the following environmental parameters were used: $T_S = 80°C$; relative humidity $\varphi = 60\%$ [9,18]; characteristics of pine wood: $a_{m_x} = 0.97\,\mathrm{cm}^2/s$, $a_{m_y} = 1.3\,\mathrm{cm}^2/s$, $a_{m_z} = 1.8\,\mathrm{cm}^2/s$, $\rho_0 = 450\,\mathrm{kg/m}^3$; coefficients of thermal conductivity and moisture conductivity: $\alpha = 23\,\mathrm{W/\left(m^2 \cdot K\right)}, \beta = 2 \cdot 10^{-6}\,\mathrm{m/s}$ [2,10]. On the basis of experimental data were obtained other characteristics and necessary empirical dependencies [5,20,24].

Especially, dependence of coefficient of wood hydraulic conductivity as functions from a temperature and humidity is used. It is received on the basis of working of experimental data: am1(T,U) = amt(T) amu(U), am1/am2 = 1,25. For determination of coefficient of humidity exchange we use the dependence: $\alpha = 0.95\left(T/\varphi\varepsilon exp(-2\sigma Vp/rTR)\right)10^{-9}$, where V_p, σ – molar volume and superficial strain of liquid, φ– relative humidity of environment. Value $r = r(U)$ have been received on the basis of wood structure. Modeling of the system of inconstant capillaries of radius r, that depends on humidity was used [17,22]. The dynamics of changes in moisture content $U^* = (U - U_0)/U_0$ for different values of the time of wood drying is shown in Fig. 6–Fig. 7. The dynamics of temperature change with the same parameters is also shown in Fig. 8–Fig. 9. Figure 10 shows the indicator values of using parallelization in conjunction with Azure Cloud in modeling the heat-and-mass transfer problem. The CPU becomes more resource intensive compared to the GPU with an increase in load. But there is not so much difference between the indicator values. However, the difference in performance becomes much more noticeable with an increase in the density of the triangulation grid. The cause of this phenomenon is the structure of GPUs.

Information processing is performed in all cores of the GPU, when performing this task. This happens regardless of the load of all threads. Accordingly, the GPU handles small calculations more slowly. In turn that causes programmer to use all possible threads on the GPGPU. Therefore parallelization in the GPU is better to use for large calculations.

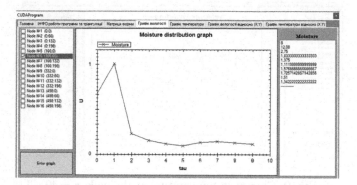

Fig. 6. Change in moisture content for $\tau = 10h$ $(R_1 = R_2; R_3 = 0)$

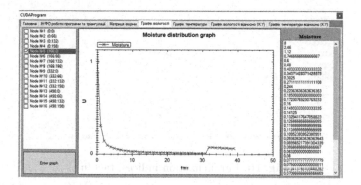

Fig. 7. Change in moisture content for $\tau = 40h$ $(R_1 = R_2; R_3 = 0)$

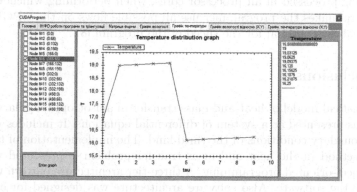

Fig. 8. Change in temperature at the node $\tau = 10$

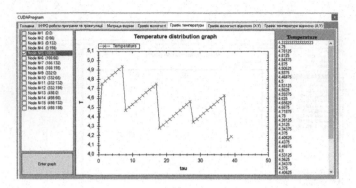

Fig. 9. Change in temperature at the node $\tau = 40$

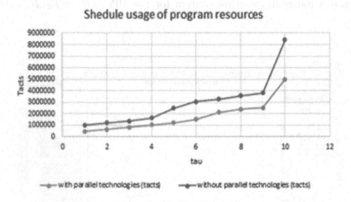

Fig. 10. Parallelization indices, tact/h

Hovewer, it should be noted that CUDA technology has its own negative aspects. In particular this is the design of graphics processors. Namely information is being processed in all processor cores, when performing whichever task. This in turn makes the programmer use all possible flows on the GPGPU. But that's not always optimal for the speed of the program [8].

4   Conclusions

A mathematical model of heat-and-mass transfer in anisotropic capillary-porous materials is presented as a system of differential equations. It includes with initial and boundary conditions of the third kind. The implementation of the finite element method in the heat and mass transfer problem is presented with the help of object-oriented programming. A three-tier architecture pattern was used to develop the software. Also software architecture was designed for exploring moisture transfer processes. It combines Azure cloud technology. The software contains the input and output data of the project, with a user interface. The

developed software uses a test of the possibility of using CUDA parallelization technologies. It is possible on the device where the software application is
installed. The database of the program is divided into two parts. One part is
located on the Azure server and the other part is on the local device where the
application is installed. This solution made it possible to use CUDA parallelization software from Azure Cloud add-ons or from the local device on which the
program is hosted. All parallel computing is performed using the Azure service,
if this is not possible according to the software settings. An algorithm based on
the initial plane triangulation is implemented to discretize the three-dimensional
domain. The three-dimensional grid is built by building layers similar to the triangulation that was built on the original layer. The data structure "Tetrahedra-
triangles-nodes" was chosen to represent the sampling.

The created graphical user interface allows to set parameters of decryption
of three-dimensional areas and to control changes of geometrical sizes of elements of partition for the purpose of condensation of a grid in the set places of
area. The matrix operations of the project were implemented using the cuBLAS
library. This allowed possible to accelerate the obtaining of the result, despite
the increase in the dimension of the matrices. The analysis of indicators of efficiency of parallelization of numerical research of processes of spatial heat and
mass transfer is given. In particular, the use of parallel technologies already at
sampling, can improve efficiency by 3.13 times. The software complex automates
all stages of the study full cycle of finite-element modeling processes heat mass
transfer in heterogeneous hygroscopic materials, provides efficient data manipulation, graphical display. The proposed object-oriented models, numerical algorithms can be used to improve processes heat mass transfer, intensification procedures for the development of technological solutions saving.

References

1. Badri, M.A., Jolivet, P., Rousseau, B., Favennec, Y.: High performance computation of radiative transfer equation using the finite element method. J. Comput.
Phys. **360**(6), 74–92 (2018). https://doi.org/10.1016/j.jcp.2018.01.027
2. Bodig, J., Jayne, B.A.: Mechanics of Wood and Wood Composites. Fla. Krieger,
Malabar (1993)
3. Boreskov, A.V.: Parallel GPU Computing. CUDA Architecture and Software
Model. Moscow University Publishing House (2012)
4. Cook, S.: CUDA Programming: A Developers Guide to Parallel Computing with
GPUs. Morgan Kaufmann Publishers Inc. (2013)
5. Duško, R.S., Dedić, A.D., Mujumdav, A.S., Ćuprić, N.L.: Two-dimensional mathematical model for simulation of the drying process of thick layers of natural materials in a conveyor-belt dryer. Thermal Sci. **21**(3), 1369–1378 (2017)
6. Farber, R.: CUDA Application Design and Development. Elsevier (2011)
7. Goldstein, S., Zurbalev, D., Flatow, I.: Optimization of Applications on the .NET
Platform Using the C# Language. DMK Press (2014). https://doi.org/10.1201/
b17713

8. Klimonov, I.A., Korneev, V.D., Sveshnikov, V.M.: Parallelization technologies for solving three-dimensional boundary value problems on quasi-structured grids using the CPU+GPU hybrid computing environment. Comput. Methods Program. **7**, 65–71 (2016). https://doi.org/10.26089/NumMet.v17r107

9. Kowalski, S., Banaszak, J.: Modeling and experimental identification of cracks in porous materials during drying. Drying Technol. **31**(12), 1388–1399 (2013). https://doi.org/10.1080/07373937.2013.796484

10. Laurindo, J.B., Prat, M.: Modeling of drying in capillary-porous media: a discrete approach. Drying Technol., 1769–1787 (2007). https://doi.org/10.1080/07373939808917495

11. Lewis, R.W., Nithiarasu, P., Seetharamu, K.N.: Fundamentals of the Finite Element Method for Heat and Fluid Flow. Wiley, Hoboken (2004). https://doi.org/10.1002/0470014164

12. Lo, S.H.: Finit Element Mesh Generation. CRC Press is an Imprint of Taylor & Francis Group (2014). https://doi.org/10.1201/b17713

13. Loeb, A., Earls, C.: Analysis of heterogeneous computing approaches to simulating heat transfer in heterogeneous material. J. Parallel Distrib. Comput. **133**, 1–17 (2019). https://doi.org/10.1016/j.jpdc.2019.06.004

14. Martínez, D., Velho, L., Carvalho, P.: Computing geodesics on triangular meshes. Comput. Graph. **29**, 667–675 (2005). https://doi.org/10.1016/j.cag.2005.08.003

15. Meyer, A., Marin, P.: Segmentation of 3D triangulated data points using edge constructed with a C1 discontinuous surface fitting. Comput. Aided Des. **36**, 1327–1336 (2004). https://doi.org/10.1016/j.cad.2004.02.002

16. Pantalé, O.: Parallelization of an object-oriented fem dynamics code: influence of the strategies on the speedup. Adv. Eng. Softw. **36**(6), 361–373 (2005). https://doi.org/10.1016/j.advengsoft.2005.01.003

17. Perré, P.: Coupled heat and mass transfer in wood and wood-based products: macroscopic formulation, upscaling and multiscale modelling. In: CompWood 2019. International Conference on Computational Methods in Wood Mechanics - from Material Properties to Timber Structures, p. 5 (2019)

18. Pinchevska, O., Spirochkin, A., Sedliačik, J., Oliynyk, R.: Quality assessment of lumber after low temperature drying from the view of stochastic process characteristics. Wood Res. **61**(6), 871–883 (2016)

19. Sanders, J., Kandrot, E.: CUDA by example: an introduction to general-purpose GPU programming. Concurr. Comput. Pract. Exp. **21**, 312 (2010)

20. Schnabel, T., Huber, H., Petutschnigg, A.: Modelling and simulation of deformation behaviour during drying using a concept of linear difference method. Wood Sci. Technol. **51**(3), 463–473 (2017). https://doi.org/10.1007/s00226-017-0897-6

21. Shymanskyi, V., Protsyk, Y.: Simulation of the heat conduction process in the claydite-block construction with taking into account the fractal structure of the material. In: XIII-th International Scientific and Technical Conference; Computer Science and Information Technologies, pp. 27–31 (2018). https://doi.org/10.1109/STC-CSIT.2018.8526747

22. Siau, J.F.: Wood Influence of Moisture on Physical Properties. Virginia State University (1995)

23. Skvortsov, A., Mirza, N.: Construction Algorithms and Analysis of Triangulation. Tomsk University (2006)

24. Sokolovskyy, Y., Boretska, I., Kroshnyy, I., Gayvas, B.: Mathematical models and analysis of the heat-mass-transfer in anisotropic materials taking into account the boundaries of phase transition. In: IEEE 15th International Conference on the Experience of Designing and Application of CAD Systems (CADSM), pp. 28–33 (2019)
25. Sokolovskyy, Y., Kroshnyy, I., Yarkun, V.: Mathematical modeling of visco-elastic-plastic deformation in capillary-porous materials in the drying process. In: IEEE 10th International Scientific and Technical Conference on Computer Sciences and Information Technologies (CSIT), pp. 52–56 (2015). https://doi.org/10.1109/STC-CSIT.2015.7325429
26. Sokolovskyy, Y., Levkovych, M., Mokrytska, O., Atamanvuk, V.: Mathematical modeling of two-dimensional deformation-relaxation processes in environments with fractal structure. In: IEEE 2nd International Conference on Data Stream Mining and Processing (DSMP), pp. 375–380 (2018)
27. Sokolovskyy, Y., Shymanskyi, V., Levkovych, M.: Mathematical modeling of non-isothermal moisture transfer and visco-elastic deformation in the materials with fractal structure. In: IEEE 11th International Scientific and Technical Conference on Computer Sciences and Information Technologies (CSIT), pp. 91–95 (2016). https://doi.org/10.1109/STC-CSIT.2016.7589877
28. Sokolovskyy, Y., Sinkevych, O.: Calculation of the drying agent in drying chambers. In: 14th International Conference The Experience of Designing and Application of CAD Systems in Microelectronics (CADSM), pp. 27–31 (2017). https://doi.org/10.1109/CADSM.2017.7916077
29. Trcala, M.: A 3D transient nonlinear modelling of coupled heat, mass and deformation fields in anisotropic material. Int. J. Heat Mass Transfer, 4588–4596 (2012). https://doi.org/10.1016/j.ijheatmasstransfer.2012.04.009

Hybrid Deep Convolutional Neural Network with Multimodal Fusion

Olena Vynokurova[1,2](✉) , Dmytro Peleshko[1] , and Marta Peleshko[3]

[1] GeoGuard, Kharkiv, Ukraine
vynokurova@gmail.com, dpeleshko@gmail.com
[2] Kharkiv National University of Radio Electronics, Kharkiv, Ukraine
[3] Lviv State University of Life Safety, Lviv, Ukraine
marta.peleshko@gmail.com

Abstract. The Hybrid Deep Convolutional Neural Network with Multimodal Fusion (HDCNNMF) topology for the multimodal recognition of the speech, the face, the lips, and human gestures behavior is proposed. Conducted researches relate to improving the understanding of complex dynamic scenes. The basic unit of the proposed hybrid system is deep neural network topology, which combines 2D and 3D convolutional neural network (CNN) for each modality with proposed intermediate-level feature fusion subsystem. Such a feature map fusion method is based on scaling procedure with a specific combination of pooling operation with non-square kernels and allows merging different type of modalities. Also, the method for forming the audio modality feature is proposed. This method is based on eigenvectors of Mel frequency cepstral coefficients (MFCC) and Mel frequency energy coefficients (MFEC) self-similarity matrix and allows increasing informativeness of modality feature. The specific characteristics of proposed fusion operation is that the data of the same dimension without regard to the modality type are fed to the input of fusion subsystem. During the experiments, the high recognition efficiency was obtained both in cases of individual modalities and their fusion. The distinctive feature of proposed HDCNNMF topology is that the input set can be extended by new modalities types. This extension of modalities set should improve the quality of identification, segmentation or recognition in complex ambiguous visual scenes and simplify the task of affordance detection.

Keywords: Multimodal fusion · Hybrid system · Deep learning · Video stream · Recognition

1 Introduction

By improving the quality of video semantic segmentation based on multimodal system we try to simplify affordance detection in cases of complex visual scenes. The essence of this simplification is the correct definition of the scene subjects and the actions classification in cases where the visual representation does not

© Springer Nature Switzerland AG 2020
S. Babichev et al. (Eds.): DSMP 2020, CCIS 1158, pp. 62–78, 2020.
https://doi.org/10.1007/978-3-030-61656-4_4

allow to correctly identify the functional interaction of objects and people. For example, in the case when

- it is not clear who of several people gave the instruction command.
- one and the same object of attention in different scenes can be identified by different modalities - in one scene, voice modality, and in another - only by visual one.
- there are several attention objects of one type. And only the accuracy of the pointer's trajectory or additional information in the voice stream (for example, the dish is large, and not small) allows identifying the attention object uniquely. For successful semantic segmentation in described cases, one or two modalities may not be sufficient.

Moreover, sometimes the physical parameters of the visual scene (changing illumination, point of view, etc.) require big datasets for acceptable recognition. In such cases, the addition of another modality makes it possible to avoid the use of a big dataset.

In order to improve a semantic segmentation, HDCNNMF topology is proposed that not only increases the accuracy of the segmentation of the visual scenes in the indicated cases, but also gives the opportunity to expand the set of necessary modalities specialized for cases of complex scenes.

In the developed HDCNNMF topology a set of most used standard modalities is used. But if necessary, the set can be completed by modalities for a particular case of affordance detection. In this case, the precision of semantic segmentation will not increase. The fusion procedure of modalities is one of the main parts in the HDCNNMF topology that was developed. The modern artificial intelligence systems are the systems with the integrated video stream data processing where each of the streams is a selected modality. The fusion of the several modalities in single processing is lead to additional informativeness. This informativeness should not only improve the quality of processing but also move the robotics systems closer to natural communication processes.

2   Related Works

The mainstream of understanding the dynamic scenes is the answer to the question "know what can be done with such objects?" [11,12]. That is, the category of the object is determined by the action, and not the visual appearance [4]. This means that semantic segmentation or recognition is a preprocessing stage in affordance detection. In the case of simple scenes, when the illumination is unchanged, the scale does not change, all projections of attention objects are separated, the pointing gestures is unique and the other, segmentation and recognition are high quality and affordance detection is quite successful [20]. In the case of complex scenes when the pointing gestures is ambiguous, projections of attention objects are not separated, the subjects of the scene are weakly identified and others, the quality of objects (processes) segmentation or recognition is weak. Accordingly, the definition of affordance detection is complicated or impossible at all.

In such cases, the segmentation and recognition systems should be a multi-modal using the fusion operation of the chosen type. This approach is due to three reasons. The first of these is to improve the solution quality of the segmentation, identification or recognition tasks. An additional modality has additional useful informativeness, which can increase the accuracy of classification tasks.

The second reason - the lack of a signal in one of the modalities can be neglected by the presence of a signal in other modalities. An appropriate classification problem with sufficient accuracy will be solved.

The third reason - when new tasks related to the scene understanding or the appearance of new scenes, there is a need to expand the set with new modalities. It should be noted here that the existing most used fusion approaches require re-training throughout the system. In the vast majority of modern researches, only two modalities have been considered. These modalities are obtained from audio and video streams. Sometimes three type of modalities are considered: audio, video, NLP [17].

Processing audio modality is a speech recognition. Processing video stream in multimodal systems in the vast majority focuses on gestures, lips, faces, bodies/poses.

Most modern multimodal systems are based on existing or modifications of existing models for individual modalities recognition. Among the results obtained in the field of recognition of gestures, it is should be noted researches based on the using shallow networks [1–3,5] and deep or 3D networks [10,13,24,29,32].

In [5], an approach based on a skins model is proposed. The basic idea of identification (estimation) of motion is a background model (in YUV space) and a Kalman filter on two next frames. In fact, due to the movement assessment, resistance to the color of the skin is achieved. Symptoms of speech recognition are Mel-scale Frequency Cepstral Coefficients (MFCC). The main advantage of the proposed approach is that a large number of states can be used to classify gestures. This means that the gesture can be described in great detail. And the accuracy of recognition is very high.

However, this number of states is also a problem - for the fusion it is necessary to reconcile the number of states of various modalities. The correspondence between the states obtains based on a threshold. Defining such threshold may also be a problem. One of the most successful models for recognizing gestures is described in [9].

One of the most successful models for recognizing gestures is described in [9]. The feature of proposed method is the use of two classifiers. The first of these is the classifier of motion, which is determined by normalized vectors in a given direction. And the second one is a classifier for trajectory that contains a skin detector, a normalized skeleton representation of one or two hands. The localization of the scene is performed by the threshold method in the space YCrCb.

The main advantages of the method are the following:

- gesture representation by a set of subgestures;
- defining the trajectory of the gesture movement by a special point of gesture ("centroid" of the ROI area). The direction and acceleration of the gesture motion are determined using such "centroid";
- simplicity of practical implementation and high performance and precision of method at acceptable conditions in which recognition takes place.

Typical approaches using Hidden Markov Model (HMM) and CNN are now being developed in various uses of LSTM or 3D networks. For example, such models are proposed in [8, 10, 13, 22, 24, 28, 31, 32].

In [28], a model for dynamic gesture recognition is presented based on Convolutional Long-Term Memory Recurrent Neural Network (CNNLSTM). In [13], the recognition of gestures is performed by means of a 3D separable convolutional neural network. The main idea of the research - at the network input data are grouped and each group is a separate array of inputs (a separate dimension). In this case, the convolution is carried out between groups.

In [29] multimodal emotion recognition (facial expressions) and speech are considered. The visual representation of emotions in different people is different. Therefore, the main problem of recognizing emotions is the lack of strict timelines for identifying emotions.

The system architecture in [29] consists of three networks: CNN for analysis of audio modality, ResNet for visual modalities analysis, and LSTM for fusion operations on outputs of audio and video modalities. The feature of the proposed methodology is that all networks are trained together.

The synchronization modalities task is also considered in [23]. The proposed multimodal fusion strategy is very effective for the identification of speakers. However, it is a closed system. Fusion pattern is specialized for these modalities. He does not provide the use of other modalities.

Summarizing the analysis of the selected existed approaches, one can formulate common general problems:

- orientation is exclusively on two modalities;
- missing or complicated addition of new modalities;
- use of relatively simple visual scenes;
- impossibility of full or partial effective functioning in cases of lack of input data from one of the modalities.

Contrary to these results, in [27], the authors have proposed multimodal architecture, which is partially devoid of these disadvantages.

The Aim of the Research. In the research, the main problem is the development of the HDCNNMF topology with specified intermediate-type fusion subsystem that is based on multidimensional modalities. The main purpose of this architecture is to increase the quality of segmentation and recognition of objects and actions in complex dynamic scenes.

3   Hybrid Deep Convolutional Neural Network with Multimodal Fusion

3.1   HDCNNMF Topology

HDCNNMF topology is a hybridization of 2D and 3D deep convolutional neural networks which are coupled by proposed fusion subsystem for processing multimodal data streams.

The proposed HDCNNMF consists of five sequential processes of multimodal data stream processing. The first process is the generation of data tensors from audio and video modalities streams. The second process is a parallelized subsystem for generation of feature map for each modality stream. Such subsystem consists of 2D or 3D convolution and pooling operation. The proposed network topology is presented in Fig. 1.

In the HDCNNMF, the size of the input, output, kernel, and stride of operations in Sequential models 1–4 are shown in Table 1 for video modalities and Table 2 for audio modality.

The feature map of each modality (the necessary condition is the same dimension of the feature map of each modality) is fed to the input of the process of feature matching and fusion, which will be described in detail in Subsect. 4.3. Tables 3, 4 and 5 show the size of the input, output, kernel, and stride of operations in the fusion subsystem for different number of modalities. Feature Map Unions is a block for modalities feature concatenation. Feature Fusion Union is a block for modalities feature concatenation after fusion operation. Fusion Polling is a fusion operation which is based on 2D pooling operation with non-square kernels.

Table 1. Size of operations in network topology for video modality processing (generating video modalities feature map)

Layer	Input-size	Output-size	Kernel	Stride
Conv1	$27 \times 64 \times 64 \times 1$	$24 \times 62 \times 62 \times 64$	$4 \times 3 \times 3$	1
Pool1	$24 \times 62 \times 62 \times 64$	$12 \times 31 \times 31 \times 64$	$2 \times 2 \times 2$	$2 \times 2 \times 2$
Conv2	$12 \times 31 \times 31 \times 64$	$10 \times 28 \times 30 \times 128$	$3 \times 4 \times 2$	1
Pool2	$10 \times 28 \times 30 \times 128$	$5 \times 14 \times 15 \times 128$	$2 \times 2 \times 2$	$2 \times 2 \times 2$
Conv3	$5 \times 14 \times 15 \times 128$	$4 \times 12 \times 14 \times 256$	$2 \times 3 \times 2$	1
Pool3	$4 \times 12 \times 14 \times 256$	$2 \times 6 \times 7 \times 256$	$2 \times 2 \times 2$	$2 \times 2 \times 2$
Conv4	$2 \times 6 \times 7 \times 256$	$1 \times 2 \times 7 \times 512$	$2 \times 5 \times 1$	1

In Tables 3, 4 and 5, the spatial size of the 2D or 3D convolution kernel for audio and video modalities has the following dimension $C_d \times H_d \times W_d \times K_d$, where C_d is the kernel size in the time dimension (channels), H_d and W_d are the kernel dimensions of the modality frame in height and width respectively, and K_d is the number of kernels (filters).

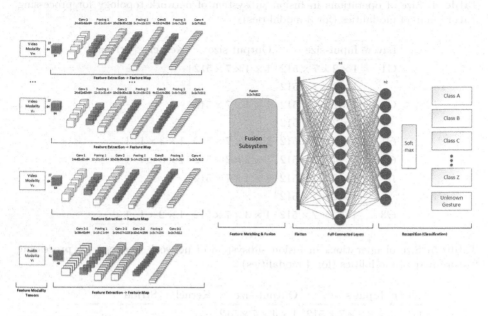

Fig. 1. Hybrid deep convolutional neural network with multimodal fusion topology

Table 2. Size of operations in network topology for audio modalities (generating audio modality feature map)

Layer	Input-size	Output-size	Kernel	Stride
Conv1	$1 \times 40 \times 45 \times 1$	$1 \times 36 \times 42 \times 64$	$1 \times 5 \times 4$	1
Pool1	$1 \times 36 \times 42 \times 64$	$1 \times 18 \times 21 \times 64$	$1 \times 2 \times 2$	$1 \times 2 \times 2$
Conv2-1	$1 \times 18 \times 21 \times 64$	$1 \times 14 \times 17 \times 128$	$1 \times 5 \times 5$	1
Conv2-2	$1 \times 14 \times 17 \times 128$	$1 \times 10 \times 14 \times 256$	$1 \times 5 \times 4$	1
Pool2	$1 \times 10 \times 14 \times 256$	$1 \times 5 \times 7 \times 256$	$1 \times 2 \times 2$	$1 \times 2 \times 2$
Conv3	$1 \times 5 \times 7 \times 256$	$1 \times 2 \times 7 \times 512$	$1 \times 4 \times 1$	1

Table 3. Size of operations in fusion subsystem of network topology for processing feature map of modalities (for 2 modalities)

Layer	Input-size	Output-size	Kernel	Stride
G1	$1 \times 2 \times 7 \times 512$	$1 \times 4 \times 7 \times 512$	–	–
	$1 \times 2 \times 7 \times 512$			
Θ1	$1 \times 4 \times 7 \times 512$	$1 \times 3 \times 7 \times 512$	$1 \times 2 \times 1$	1

Table 4. Size of operations in fusion subsystem of network topology for processing feature map of modalities (for 3 modalities)

Layer	Input-size	Output-size	Kernel	Stride
G1	$1 \times 2 \times 7 \times 512$ $1 \times 2 \times 7 \times 512$	$1 \times 4 \times 7 \times 512$	–	–
G2	$1 \times 2 \times 7 \times 512$ $1 \times 2 \times 7 \times 512$	$1 \times 4 \times 7 \times 512$	–	–
$\Theta 1$	$1 \times 4 \times 7 \times 512$	$1 \times 2 \times 7 \times 512$	$1 \times 3 \times 1$	1
$\Theta 2$	$1 \times 4 \times 7 \times 512$	$1 \times 2 \times 7 \times 512$	$1 \times 3 \times 1$	1
Ω	$1 \times 2 \times 7 \times 512$ $1 \times 2 \times 7 \times 512$	$1 \times 4 \times 7 \times 512$	–	–
$\Theta 3$	$1 \times 4 \times 7 \times 512$	$1 \times 3 \times 7 \times 512$	$1 \times 2 \times 1$	1

Table 5. Size of operations in fusion subsystem of network topology for processing feature map of modalities (for 4 modalities)

Layer	Input-size	Output-size	Kernel	Stride
G1	$1 \times 2 \times 7 \times 512$ $1 \times 2 \times 7 \times 512$	$1 \times 4 \times 7 \times 512$	–	–
G2	$1 \times 2 \times 7 \times 512$ $1 \times 2 \times 7 \times 512$	$1 \times 4 \times 7 \times 512$	–	–
G3	$1 \times 2 \times 7 \times 512$ $1 \times 2 \times 7 \times 512$	$1 \times 4 \times 7 \times 512$	–	–
$\Theta 1$	$1 \times 4 \times 7 \times 512$	$1 \times 2 \times 7 \times 512$	$1 \times 3 \times 1$	1
$\Theta 2$	$1 \times 4 \times 7 \times 512$	$1 \times 2 \times 7 \times 512$	$1 \times 3 \times 1$	1
$\Theta 3$	$1 \times 4 \times 7 \times 512$	$1 \times 2 \times 7 \times 512$	$1 \times 3 \times 1$	1
Ω	$1 \times 2 \times 7 \times 512$ $1 \times 2 \times 7 \times 512$ $1 \times 2 \times 7 \times 512$	$1 \times 6 \times 7 \times 512$	–	–
$\Theta 4$	$1 \times 6 \times 7 \times 512$	$1 \times 3 \times 7 \times 512$	$1 \times 2 \times 1$	$1 \times 2 \times 1$

Θ_j - Fusion Polling; Ω_j - Feature Fusion Union; G_j - Feature Map Union

An important feature of the network for streaming video modality is its 3D pooling operation with the parameter pooling stride equal two in three dimensions in order to increase robustness to the moving ROI effect and to maintain ROI movement features in the neighborhood of the pooling kernel. The 3D convolutional operations are performed to find the correlation between high-level temporal and spatial information by fusion among them. No zero-padding is used in the network topology.

By geometric shape the extracted features were close both to the square (a head, a gesture, the eyes) as to the rectangle (lips, gesture, palm). Therefore, in the developed network topology in the process of formation feature map of each modality for the 2D and 3D convolution operation both square and non-square filters were used. At the stage of the formation of the modalities feature map, square filters were used for the pooling operation, which completely corresponds to the methodology of images sub-sampling.

It should be noted that the fusion subsystem combines the features of the selected modalities to each other. And the sub-sampling operation of the dimension of the features in the middle of the modality does not occur. Therefore, the pooling operation is used in the fusion subsystem with non-square filters. Since a convolutional neural network with non-square kernels provides a transition from low-level attributes to higher-level attributes, this fact is lead to extraction and processing temporal features at the lower level that are connected with speech functions. Thus, at the output of the process of generating feature map for each modality stream, we have a unique set of features of the same dimension (in our case, the shape $= 1 \times 2 \times 7 \times 512$). Batch normalization and Dropout operation were used for all layers. Except for the last layer, all layers used the activation function Parametric ReLU (PReLU) [16]

$$\psi(o^{[i]}) = max(0, o^{[i]}) + a_i min(0, o^{[i]}) \tag{1}$$

where $o^{[i]}$ is the network layer output; a_i is the parameter of the steepness of the negative part of the function.

The activation function of PReLU is a synthesis of the ReLU function and in comparison with the activation function of ReLU, PReLU has demonstrated better data stream processing. After that, the results are fed to the last process, which corresponds to the recognition (classification) of gestures. Optimizing tuned parameters of the 3DDCNN is based on cross entropy criterion optimization:

$$E(k) = -\sum_{j=1}^{Z} y_j(k) log(\hat{y}_j(k)) \tag{2}$$

where $y_j(k)$ is label of class j for k observation; $\hat{y}_j(k)$ is predicted label of class j for k observation.

To tune the parameters, we will use the root mean square propagation (rmsProp) learning algorithm [21], which can be written in the form

$$W(k+1) = W(k) - \frac{\eta}{\sqrt{S[g^2](k) + \epsilon}} g(k) \tag{3}$$

where $W(k)$ is the tuned parameters of network, k is instant of discrete time or number of observation, η - learning rate ($0 < \eta < 1$), $S[g^2](k)$ is the moving average at k discrete time

$$S[g^2](k) = \gamma S[g^2](k-1) + (1-\gamma)g^2(k). \tag{4}$$

Here, $g(k) = \nabla_W E(k)$ is the gradient of the optimization criterion by the tuned parameters W, $0 \le \gamma \le 1$.

3.2   Feature Extraction of Modalities

The stage of preprocessing is generation of the features for each modality which is shown in Fig. 2. Input features are formed in the tensor form. The sizes of data tensors of each modality are shown in Fig. 1 and Tables 1, 2, 3, 4 and 5.

Audio Modality. The input signal of audio modality V_1 is a discrete mono speech signal in the format of WAV with a sampling frequency of 16 kHz–40 kHz and a length of T ms. Such a signal may be obtained from the input device or extracted from the video. The voice region in the speech signal had a different start point. Therefore, a speech detector [19] was used to reduce noise in the input set of features.

The discrete speech signal $x = x(t), t = 0, 1, \ldots, T$ splits into frames x_j of length $l(x_j) = 20$ ms:

$$x_j = x(t), t \in I_{t,j} \tag{5}$$

where $I_{t,j}$ is j-th time section of length 20 ms in $[0, T]$.

These sections are the basis of a sample of audio modality features. The length of section is 20 ms because the speech signal in this interval has the pseudo-stationary property. The basic characteristic for forming the features of audio-modalities is MFEC [19] $C_{j,i}$ of the speech signal, which can be determined by the formula

$$S_{j,i} = \sum_{k=0}^{I_{t,j}-1} ln\|X_i(k)\|^2 H_j(k), 0 \leq i \leq I_{t,j} \tag{6}$$

where M is a coefficients number; $X_i(k)$ is a specter of speech signal in interval $I_{t,j}$ using the FFT and Hemming window; $H_j(k)$ is a set of filters for frame x_j.

Using $C_{j,i} = C_{j,1}, C_{j,2}, \ldots, C_{j,M}$ for each x_j we can obtain the self-similarity matrix

$$C_j = [c_{j,(m,n)}]_{m=1,\ldots,M}^{n=1,\ldots,M} \tag{7}$$

the elements of which can be written in the following way:

$$c_{j,(m,n)} = \frac{C_{j,n}}{C_{j,m}}, m = 1, \ldots, M, n = 1, \ldots, M \tag{8}$$

where M is a count of filters.

The matrix C_j is square matrix with dimension $M \times M$. Based this matrix we can define $a_{j,i}$ eigenvectors

$$C_j a_{j,i} = \lambda_{j,i} a_{j,i} \tag{9}$$

where $\lambda_{j,i}$ is the eigenvalues of the matrix C_j. In our case we take $M = 40$.

For further formation of the "cube" features we take the first vectors $a_{j,1}$. Based on the vectors $a_{j,i} = a_{j,(i,1)'},\ldots,a_{j,(i,M)}$ we can obtain matrix of frame features x_j

$$a_j = [a_{j,(m,n)}]_{m=1,\ldots,M}^{n=1,\ldots,N_a}. \tag{10}$$

Here, $a_{j,(m,n)}$ is a normalized value $a'_{j,(m,n)}$. In our case we take $N_a = 48$. The total length of the time span which is considered is $Na \times 20\,\text{ms}$. If the specified duration was not enough, then the matrices a_j can be interpolated or extrapolated.

Video Modalities. For solving practical tasks, we use two topologies of proposed network, which is shown on Fig. 1. The first topology of network (TP_1) consists of two modalities: V_1 (the audio modality) and V_3 (the video modality for lips detection). The second topology of network (TP_2) consists of four modalities: V_1 and V_2, V_3, V_4 (V_2 - video modality for face detection, V_4 – video modality for gestures detection. Such types of modalities are the most widespread).

In the general network topology, which is shown in Fig. 1, three video modalities are considered. The first of these is V_2 - video modality for face detection, the second modality V_3 - video modality for lips detection and the third modality V_4 – video modality for gestures detection. Such types of modalities are the most widespread. Motion detection was performed using algorithm from [14]. Video streams were selected and processed by OpenCV. The feature extraction for V_2 was performed in accordance with the following algorithm:

1. Detecting a motion.
2. Using a background model based on a Gaussian set, we separate the background [15, 26].
3. Selecting frames and converting them to grayscale using skvideo and OpenCV libraries.
4. Cropping an excessive part of the image in the frame.
5. Extracting ROI using the algorithm from [27] which is based on the dlib library.
6. Using the bicubic interpolation for forming ROI with size 64×64 pixels.

Features for modality V_3 were selected based on a known proportion: the region of the human lip is the third bottom part of the human head region. This approach allows detecting faces along with the extraction of ROI for V_2 modality.

Since this proportion may be slightly different for each person, using the Haar detector and Viola-Jones method [30], ROI of faces are periodically verified. The combined detection of the face and lips gives the opportunity to get the full synchronization of the two modalities. Using 27 sequential frames the tensors of input features for the modalities V_2 and V_3 (with dimensions of $27 \times 64 \times 64$ pixels) are formed. This dimension determines the existence a set of 27 frames. Very often it is difficult to provide such a set. The reasons for this may be short stream or inadequate performance of the feature detector.

To solve this problem, it is suggested to interpolate or extrapolate the required number of frames (that is, the number that is missing) based on the optical stream model. For this model, the value of brightness in each pixel is considered as the discrete value of some function. Accordingly, using the resampling operation based on the discrete Fourier transform [18], we obtain the function of

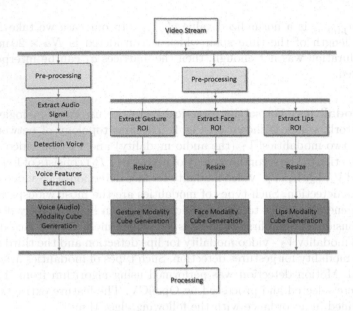

Fig. 2. Modality preprocessing

brightness in pixels of those frames that are missing. In the used dataset, 90% of
the video streams were supposed to have one to six frames. Using this approach
is satisfactory for a case where at least three ROIs in three different frames were
detected in the video stream. In the absence of such frames, a zero data will be
specified in the input set of attributes, which will be noise and will negatively
affect the quality of work in the system. The features extraction for V_4 modality
was performed in accordance with the following algorithm:

1. Detecting a motion.
2. Using a background model based on a Gaussian set, we separate the background [26].
3. Selecting frames and converting them to grayscale using skvideo and OpenCV
   libraries.
4. Cropping an excessive part of the image in the frame.
5. Increasing FPS up to 55 frames per second based on ffmpeg codec. In the
   case of the good-quality detection of ROI this operation can be omitted.
6. Extracting ROI for right and left hands based on algorithm from [7].
7. Concatenating the extracted regions into one array.
8. Using the bicubic interpolation for forming ROI with dimension 64×64 pixels.
9. In the case when the number of extracted ROIs were less than 27, the interpolation like for modalities V_2 and V_3 is used.

In the case that only one or two ROIs are detected for all modalities, you
can select ROI on the other frames using the geometric characteristics of the
detected ROI. This approach is possible when there is a sufficient number of

frames in the video stream and the spatial shift of the object of attention is not very large. If the frames in the video stream are not enough, then they can be extrapolated according to the method described above.

4 Experiments, Results and Discussion

4.1 Preprocessing

The input tensors of audio and video modalities have been standardized and in addition, the input tensors of audio modality have been normalized in the interval $[0, 1]$.

4.2 Metric for Performance Evaluation

The main metrics that have been used for performance evaluation are Equal Error Rate (ERR) (which is the point when false acceptance rate (FAR) and false recognition rate (FRR) are equal), Area Under Curve (AUC), Accuracy (Precision), Recall, F1 score. Also, the Micro and Macro Averaged metrics have been used for evaluation accuracy for multi-classes classification.

4.3 Evaluation on LWR Dataset

To confirm effectiveness and compare the proposed approach with known approaches, it was chosen the Oxford-BBC Lip Reading in the Wild (LRW) Dataset described in [6].

For comparison of the proposed approach with known ones, the HDCNNMF topology was adapted for two modalities – the audio (extracted MFCC) and video (features of lips motion) modalities, where the proposed fusion subsystem is used for the coupling modalities.

The dataset consists of up to 1000 occurrences per target word for training, 50 occurrences per word for testing and 50 occurrences per word for validating of 500 different words, spoken by hundreds of different speakers. All videos are 29 frames in length, and the word occurs in the middle of the video. The word duration is given in the metadata, from which you can determine the start and end frames. Thus, the features tensors of the modalities were generated based on the dataset. For video modality, the tensor dimension was $27 \times 64 \times 64$ (27 channel visual feature tensor with size 64×64 pixels) and, accordingly, an audio modality has $1 \times 40 \times 45$ dimension, which corresponds to 40 MFCCs, which were calculated on sections 20 ms without overlap on a full audio signal with a length of 900 ms. Then, a matrix of eigenvectors with a dimension of $1 \times \times 45$ was generated based on matrix with MFEC coefficients.

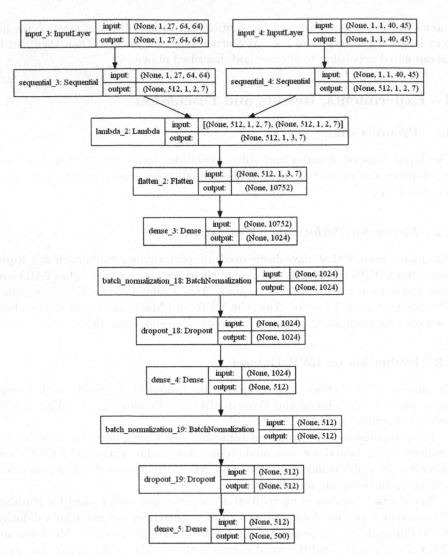

Fig. 3. Hybrid deep convolutional neural network with multimodal fusion topology (layer's dimensions)

Figure 3 and Tables 1, 2 and 3 show layer's dimensions of Hybrid Multidimensional Deep Convolutional Neural Network for solving recognition task based on Oxford-BBC Lip Reading in the Wild (LRW) Dataset.

The rmsProp training algorithm had the following parameters: learning step 0.0001 with decay parameter 10^{-6}. The number of epochs was about 15. Dropout parameters in the sequential models were taken 0.1.

In the paper [25], the authors have presented the main results for processing Oxford-BBC Lip Reading in the Wild (LRW) dataset based on different approaches. These approaches contain 7 type of deep networks:

- Baseline - the multi-tower VGG-M;
- N1 - the 2D convolution ResNet, while the back-end is based on temporal convolution;
- N2 - the same model as N1, but with 3D convolution;
- N3 - Deep Neural Network (DNN) of approximately the same number of parameters (20M);
- N4 - the same model as N1 based on a single-layer Bi-LSTM instead of temporal convolution;
- N5 - the same model as N1 based on a double-layer Bi-LSTM instead of temporal convolution;
- N6 - the same model as N5, but trained end-to-end, using the weights of N5 as starting point;
- N7 - is also trained end-to-end and the sole difference with N6 is that the outputs of the two directional LSTMs are concatenated together instead of added together.

All models trained from 15 to 20 epochs. All networks have approximately the same number of parameters (20M).

Table 6 shows the results of Oxford-BBC Lip Reading in the Wild (LRW) data set processing based on different approaches.

Table 6. Size of operations in fusion subsystem of network topology for processing feature map of modalities (for 3 modalities)

Network	Accuracy
Baseline (VGG-M)	61.1%
N1 CNN with 2D conv (Res Net)	69.6%
N2 CNN with 3D conv (Res Net)	74.6%
N3 DNN 3D conv	69.7%
N4 Network based on LSTM	78.4%
N5 Network based on Bi-LSTM	79.6%
N6 The same as N5, but trained end-to-end, using the weights of N5 as starting point	81.5%
N7 It is also trained end-to-end and the sole difference with N6 is that the outputs of the two directional LSTMs are concatenated together instead of added together	83.%
Proposed HDCNNMF	86%

The accuracy of the proposed model is 86.0%, which corresponds to the improvement of the result relative to the baseline VGG-M network by 25.1%

and an increase in accuracy relative to the state-of-the art by 3%. It should be noted that the provided network contains almost 2 times less configurable parameters.

5   Conclusions

As already mentioned the proposed HDCNNMF is intended to improve the understanding of the robot systems of various complex dynamic scenes. That is, in cases where the identification of action or subject is not unambiguous.

The developed HDCNNMF topology and fusion method give an opportunity to expand the set of new modalities without restrictions (the limitations are only computing resources of the operating environment). In this case, the processing of these modalities can be both in 3D and in 2D dimension. The level of data preprocessing can be different: from convolution operation sequences to deep network processing. It should be noticed that HDCNNMF topology allows using the different patterns of fusion. In the process of developing HDCNNMF, several variants of the fusion operation have been developed. The presented fusion procedure in the paper is chosen according to the criterion of the highest accuracy of the classification problem based on the selected datasets. The question of the choice of fusion procedure demands the individual research and in this paper has not been considered. The results of experiments and their comparison with the existed approaches confirmed the high accuracy of HDCNNMF both in the case of individual modalities and in the case of their fusion. This fact allows using HDCNNMF in cases where some of the modalities are inaccessible or the modality stream has unsatisfactory quality.

Acknowledgments. This research was supported by Samsung R&D Institute Ukraine, which kindly provided computing power for practical experiments. We are very grateful to Rob Cooper at BBC Research for help in obtaining the LRW.

References

1. Bodyanskiy, Y., Dolotov, A., Vynokurova, O.: Evolving spiking wavelet-neuro-fuzzy self-learning system. Appl. Soft Comput. J. **14**(B), 252–258 (2014). https://doi.org/10.1016/j.asoc.2013.05.020
2. Bodyanskiy, Y., Setlak, G., Peleshko, D., Vynokurova, O.: Hybrid generalized additive neuro-fuzzy system and its adaptive learning algorithms. In: Proceedings of the 2015 IEEE 8th International Conference on Intelligent Data Acquisition and Advanced Computing Systems: Technology and Applications, IDAACS 2015, vol. 1, pp. 328–333 (2015). https://doi.org/10.1109/IDAACS.2015.7340753
3. Bodyanskiy, Y., Vynokurova, O., Pliss, I., Peleshko, D., Rashkevych, Y.: Hybrid generalized additive wavelet-neuro-fuzzy-system and its adaptive learning. In: Zamojski, W., Mazurkiewicz, J., Sugier, J., Walkowiak, T., Kacprzyk, J. (eds.) Dependability Engineering and Complex Systems. AISC, vol. 470, pp. 51–61. Springer, Cham (2016). https://doi.org/10.1007/978-3-319-39639-2_5

4. Castellini, C., Tommasi, T., Noceti, N., Odone, F., Caputo, B.: Using object affordances to improve object recognition. IEEE Trans. Auton. Ment. Dev. **3**(3), 207–215 (2011). https://doi.org/10.1109/TAMD.2011.2106782

5. Cheng, S.T., Hsu, C.W., Li, J.P.: Combined hand gesture-speech model for human action recognition. Sensors **13**, 17098–17129 (2013). https://doi.org/10.3390/s131217098

6. Chung, J.S., Zisserman, A.: Lip reading in the wild. In: Lai, S.-H., Lepetit, V., Nishino, K., Sato, Y. (eds.) ACCV 2016. LNCS, vol. 10112, pp. 87–103. Springer, Cham (2017). https://doi.org/10.1007/978-3-319-54184-6_6. http://www.robots.ox.ac.uk/ vgg/data/lipreading/lrw1.html

7. Dibia, V.: Handtrack: A library for prototyping real-time hand tracking interfaces using convolutional neural networks (2017). https://github.com/victordibia/handtracking

8. Ding, R., Pang, C., Liu, H.: Audio-visual keyword spotting based on multidimensional convolution neural network. In: Proceedings of the 2018 IEEE International Conference on Image Processing, Athens, Greece, pp. 4138–4142 (2018). https://doi.org/10.1109/ICIP.2018.8451096

9. Favorskaya, M., Nosov, A., Popov, A.: Localization and recognition of dynamic hand gesture based on hierarchy of manifold classifiers. Int. Arch. Photogram. Remote Sens. Spat. Inf. Sci. **XL-5/W6**, 151–161 (2015). https://www.int-arch-photogramm-remote-sens-spatial-inf-sci.net/XL-5-W6/1/2015/isprsarchives-XL-5-W6-1-2015.pdf

10. Feichtenhofer, C., Pinz, A., Zisserman, A.: Convolutional two-stream network fusion for video action recognition. In: Proceedings of the IEEE Conference on Computer Vision and Pattern Recognition, pp. 1933–1941 (2016). arXiv:1604.06573

11. Gibson, J.: The Theory of Affordances. Erlbaum, Hillsdale (1977)

12. Gibson, J.: The Ecological Approach to Visual Perception. Erlbaum, Hillsdale (1986)

13. Hu, Z., Youmin, H., Liu, J., Wu, B., Han, D., Kurfess, T.: 3D separable convolutional neural network for dynamic hand gesture recognition. Neurocomputing **318**, 151–161 (2018). https://doi.org/10.1016/j.neucom.2018.08.042

14. Jackson, L.: Motion-detection-python (2017). https://github.com/ic0n/Motion-Detection-Python

15. KaewTraKulPong, P., Bowden, R.: An improved adaptive background mixture model for real-time tracking with shadow detection. In: Remagnino, P., Jones, G.A., Paragios, N., Regazzoni, C.S. (eds.) Video-Based Surveillance Systems, pp. 135–144. Springer, Boston (2001). https://doi.org/10.1007/978-1-4615-0913-4_11. http://personal.ee.surrey.ac.uk/Personal/R.Bowden/publications/avbs01/avbs01.pdf

16. Kaiming, H., Xiangyu, Z., Shaoqing, R., Sun, J.: Delving deep into rectifiers: surpassing human-level performance on ImageNet classification. In: Computer Vision and Pattern Recognition (2015). arXiv:1502.01852

17. Kampman, O., Barezi, E., Bertero, D., Fung, P.: Investigating audio, video, and text fusion methods for end-to-end automatic personality prediction. In: Proceedings of the 56th Annual Meeting of the Association for Computational Linguistics, Melbourne, Australia, pp. 606–611. Springer (2018). https://doi.org/10.1007/978-981-10-7560-5118

18. Lyons, R.: FFT interpolation based on FFT samples: a detective story with a surprise ending (2018). https://www.dsprelated.com/showarticle/1156.php

19. Majeed, S., Husain, H., Samad, S., Idbeaa, T.: Mel frequency cepstral coefficients (MFCC) feature extraction enhancement in the application of speech recognition: a comparison study. J. Theoret. Appl. Inf. Technol. **79**(1), 38–56 (2015)
20. Nguyen, A.: Scene understanding for autonomous manipulation with deep learning (2019). arXiv:1903.09761
21. RMSProp (2020). http://ruder.io/optimizing-gradient-descent/index.html#rmsprop
22. Rua, E., Bredin, H., Mateo, C., Chollet, A., Jimenez, D.: Audio-visual speech asynchrony detection using co-inertia analysis and coupled hidden Markov models. Pattern Anal. Appl. **12**, 271–284 (2009). https://doi.org/10.1007/s10044-008-0121-2
23. Sargin, M., Yemez, Y., Erzin, E., Tekalp, A.: Audiovisual synchronization and fusion using canonical correlation analysis. IEEE Trans. Multimedia **9**, 1396–1403 (2007). https://doi.org/10.1109/TMM.2007.906583
24. Simonyan, K., Zisserman, A.: Two-stream convolutional networks for action recognition in videos. In: Advances in Neural Information Processing Systems, vol. 1, pp. 568–576 (2014). arXiv:1406.21998
25. Stafylakis, T., Tzimiropoulos, G.: Combining residual networks with LSTMs for lipreading. In: INTERSPEECH, pp. 3652–3656 (2017)
26. Stauffer, C., Grimson, W.: Adaptive background mixture models for real-time tracking. In: Proceedings of IEEE Computer Society Conference on Computer Vision and Pattern Recognition, pp. 246–252 (1999). https://doi.org/10.1109/CVPR.1999.784637
27. Torfi, A., Iranmanesh, S., Nasrabadi, N., Dawson, J.: 3D convolutional neural networks for cross audio-visual matching recognition. Comput. Vis. Pattern Recogn. **PP**, 1396–1403 (2017). https://doi.org/10.1109/ACCESS.2017.2761539
28. Tsironi, E., Barros, P., Weber, C., Wermter, S.: An analysis of convolutional long short-term memory recurrent neural networks for gesture recognition. Neurocomputing **268**, 76–86 (2017). https://doi.org/10.1016/j.neucom.2016.12.088
29. Tzirakis, P., Trigeorgis, G., Nicolaou, M.A., Schuller, B., Zafeiriou, S.: End-to-end multimodal emotion recognition using deep neural networks. IEEE J. Sel. Top. Signal Process. **11**(8), 1301–1309 (2017). https://doi.org/10.1109/JSTSP.2017.2764438
30. Viola, P., Jones, M.: Robust real-time face detection. Int. J. Comput. Vis. **57**(2), 137–154 (2004). https://doi.org/10.1109/CVPR.1999.784637
31. Wu, P., Liu, H., Li, X., Fan, T., Zhang, X.: A novel lip descriptor for audio-visual keyword spotting based on adaptive decision fusion. IEEE Trans. Multimedia **18**(3), 326–338 (2016). https://doi.org/10.1109/TMM.2016.2520091
32. Yue-Hei Ng, J., Hausknecht, M., Vijayanarasimhan, S., et al.: Beyond short snippets: deep networks for video classification. In: Proceedings of the IEEE Conference on Computer Vision and Pattern Recognition, pp. 4694–4702 (2015). https://doi.org/10.1109/CVPR.2015.7299101

Modeling and Forecasting of Innovative, Scientific and Technical Activity Indicators Under Unstable Economic Situation in the Country: Case of Ukraine

Liubov Halkiv⊙, Oleh Karyy⊙, Ihor Kulyniak(✉)⊙, and Solomiya Ohinok⊙

Lviv Polytechnic National University, Lviv, Ukraine
{liubov.i.halkiv,oleh.i.karyi,ihor.y.kulyniak,solomiia.v.ohinok}@lpnu.ua

Abstract. The indicated range of problems at the level of countries with developed scientific and innovative potential and unstable economic situation to which Ukraine belongs has a particular interest. The authors verify the hypothesis of the expected upward dynamics of Ukraine's GDP under the influence of trends in the development of indicators of innovative and scientific and technical activity. The research is based on the official materials of Ukraine's state institutions, for whose elaboration content analysis, methods of logic, comparison, and analogies are used. The fractal theory is applied to test the hypothesis, in particular, parametric methods of R/S-analysis (the nature of dynamic changes in the indicators of innovative and scientific and technical activity and the GDP of Ukraine are investigated and trends are identified) and the method of correlation-regression analysis (the nature, density, and direction of Ukraine's GDP dependence on specific indicators of innovative and scientific and technical activity are evaluated). The research proves public demand, evaluates current trends, and makes forecasts of the indicators of innovative and scientific and technical activity and the GDP of Ukraine. It is revealed that the GDP of Ukraine correlates with the results of innovative and scientific and technical activity and will gradually increase under their influence. All the forecasting results point to the upward dynamics of Ukraine's GDP. Despite the asymmetry of the trends of individual indicators of innovative and scientific and technical activity, the prospect of a generalized assessment of the effectiveness of this activity is evaluated positively.

Keywords: Innovative activity · Scientific and technical activity · Indicators · Unstable economic situation · Trend · Modeling · Forecasting

1 Introduction

In the system of drivers of public well-being growth, the role of innovative and scientific and technical activity is increasing. The modern era has been marked by a

© Springer Nature Switzerland AG 2020
S. Babichev et al. (Eds.): DSMP 2020, CCIS 1158, pp. 79–97, 2020.
https://doi.org/10.1007/978-3-030-61656-4_5

significant strengthening of the role of intellectual products (scientific knowledge, advanced technologies, socially useful innovations) in the system of activators of the competitiveness of territorial social systems. The institutional environment of research and innovation plays a fundamental role in ensuring high productivity in the spheres of intellectual potential capitalization. Consequently, the field of the activity of social progress paradigms is enriched by the results of scientific research on various aspects of this environment. Given that the world has stopped on the threshold of the fourth industrial revolution that has already begun, innovative and scientific and technological activity is an important factor in the transition of enterprises to Industry 4.0 [35].

However, it should be noted that innovative activity depends on the conditions of the unstable economic situation in the country and significantly increases the uncertainty of the dynamics of the organization's activity results [9]. The innovation development of the economic system at the present stage, in addition to stimulating the innovative activity of existing entities, deals with the formation of network structures and the researches [32,33] address the indicators for networks modeling by developing and testing a series of points indicating how networks affect economic growth. Therefore, it is important to study new trends in the indicators of innovative and scientific and technical activity and assess their impact on the national economy. However, the latest research on this topic in Ukraine is fragmented, while the complex studies of past years have lost their relevance.

Based on the above-mentioned fact, the authors aim to carry out modeling and forecasting of the indicators of innovative and scientific and technical activity on the example of Ukraine, as well as to confirm the hypotheses that the dynamics of Ukraine's GDP correlates with the dynamics of indicators of innovative and scientific and technical activity (share of innovatively active enterprises in the total number of enterprises; the volume of innovative activity financing; the number of new technological processes implemented; the number of the names of innovative products introduced; the specific weight of the volume of sold innovative products in the total volume of products sold; the number of new technologies purchased; the number of producers of scientific and technical works; the number of specialists performing scientific and technical works; amount of funding for research and development) and is determined by their effect.

The content analysis of scientific published works makes it possible not only to get acquainted with the heritage of the scientific thought but also to outline niches for further research. The usage of an electronic array of scientific periodicals as an information base allows systematizing the published results of the latest scientific research, in the title of which the terms "innovative activity" and/or "scientific and technical activity" are found. The results of the analysis of the received array of scientific published works make it possible to state that the topic of innovative and scientific and technical activity is permanently in the field of scientists' view, the interest in this topic does not disappear, and the most recent research published over the last five years focuses on the following four aspects:

1. Policy and legal basis of the country's scientific and technical activity. Because further research results will be presented on the example of Ukraine, the authors will mention some achievements of the Ukrainian scientific schools in this research area. In the developments of the scientific school of the State Institution "Institute of Economics and Forecasting of NAS of Ukraine" under the leadership of I. Yehorov, there is information about the formation of state policy in the field of scientific and technical and innovative activity based on the extended model of a "triple helix" (state-science-industry) [46] and substantiation of approaches to the construction of a system of complex indicators for evaluating this policy effectiveness [45]. At the same time, it emphasizes the need to use the indicators that reflect the effectiveness of the functioning of all subsystems of the national economy as indicators of the effectiveness of the state's political measures. The legal basis for the scientific and technological activity of Ukraine is studied in several contexts: a historical view on current legislation [41]; information support as an element of quality management [36]; administrative and legal regulation [37]; legal foundations for intellectual property protection [6]; corporate culture of the cybersecurity of entities of scientific and technical activity [13] and its entities in the field of judicial expertise [40], international legal regulation of scientific and technical activity [38].

2. Characteristic aspects of scientific and technical and innovative activity. The scientists are studying the peculiarities of manifestations of scientific and technical and innovative activity in various spheres of economic activity, in particular, Daron and Gorska [12] present management trends in metal market enterprises in Poland in the context of innovative activity. They characterize this sector, presenting its importance for the Polish economy, and analyze the innovative activity of enterprises producing metals and metal products. Samukdjanovna [34] analyzes the problems of ensuring innovation development of the credit activities of commercial banks in Uzbekistan and offers recommendations for their elimination. Pazilov et al. [29] present the results of studies of integration processes in Kazakhstan, the purpose of which is to form a mechanism of innovative activity of the hotel enterprise. The analysis and conclusions are based on the activity of the textile industry, which has significant potential for the development of the innovative activity. Parfentieva et al. [28] research the formation of new scientific solutions regarding the assessment of the impact of stimulating innovative activity on ensuring the strategic development of enterprises in the motor transport sector of transport industries in the key countries of the post-Soviet economic space (Ukraine, Russia, Belarus, Kazakhstan).

3. Commercialization of the results of scientific and technical and innovative activity. In particular, Butko and Popelo [7] characterize the stages of this commercialization, its factors, methods, principles, subjects, and describe the organizational and economic mechanism. Chukhray et al. [10] develop the

methodical approach to assessing the readiness level of technologies for the transfer as the stage of commercialization of the R&D. The hypothesis of Kato-Vidal and Occhipinti [21] states that higher innovative activity offers more business opportunities, creating groups of entrepreneurs who will positively contribute to local economies. The GMM estimation was conducted by a dynamic panel with the data from the 32 Mexican states during 2005–2014. It was found that innovative activity, measured based on patenting and FDI fosters the emergence of business-to-business (B2B) entrepreneurs. A significant innovation impact was not found when grouping all the entrepreneurs (consumers and industrial B2B markets). However, all the entrepreneurs contributed positively as entrepreneurial capital to a higher GDP per capita. Ceci et al. [8] investigate the role of different means of interactions to support innovative activity rather than a strategic or operational activity for cooperating internally and externally at the company. The research design is based on the exploitation of a case study in the aerospace sector. Three significant results on the role of face-to-face interactions are described; the interaction through ICT tools for communication; different types of support provided by ICT tools in the company's activity. The authors extend the state of the art with new evidence in the field of relationship management for sustaining innovation. Mura and Mazák [27] explore the innovative activity of small and medium enterprises having a character of family businesses in the regions of Slovakia in their research, and also identify those important determinants that influence the innovative ability of family businesses. In the book chapter of Perez-de-Lema et al. [22] the effect which the entrepreneurial culture has on production processes and development of micro-, small and medium businesses (SMEs) over innovation is analyzed. An empirical study was conducted with over 600 firms from Spain. The data processed through linear regressions by ordinary least squares (OLS), which indicates that all the factors associated with entrepreneurship have positive effects on innovative activity in SMEs, especially those which are a bit larger.

4. Evaluation of the results of scientific and technical and innovative activity. Melnik et al. [26] based on the activity analysis of the largest Russian companies estimate that innovation development indicators are not always aimed at achieving strategic outcomes. For this reason, to solve it, the mechanism for the adjustment of innovation development indicators to the company's strategic guidelines is worked out. Its design is based on the groundwork of the demand to necessarily provide increasing payoff from innovative activity. To implement it, a certain procedure is suggested for maintaining the ratio between individual indicators of the company's innovative activity effectiveness and its strategic development indicators, reflected in the devised dynamical model. Ziyadin et al. [50] model successful effects in evaluating the innovative activity of hotel organizations. Voitsekhovska [42] investigates the effect of innovative technology parameters on the renovation of fixed assets. Zavidna et al. [48] analyze the practice and assessment of the innovative activity of companies to form an innovation development strategy. To achieve this, the authors compare a theoretical opinion with empirical testing methods. In their

study, the methods of statistical studies, expert assessments are used, which allows determining the system of coefficients for the assessment of innovative activity in justifying the choice of innovation development strategies. From the perspective of ranking firms or industries according to their innovation intensity, Hollenstein [16] develops a composite measure of the firm's innovativeness by using factor analysis of a whole set of innovation variables. The resulting aggregate indicator is based on the extraction of two factors depicting the technical and market dimension in the case of product innovations; for new production techniques, the two factors refer to the input and output side of innovation generation.

The problems of innovative activity are studied from the standpoint of theoretical and methodological approaches, in particular within the framework of innovation. Instead, scientific studies of analytical direction focus mainly on the nano-scale – the individual (most often the teaching staff), the micro-level – the enterprise, meso-level – the economic sector. The analysis of the meaningful content of the latest published works, whose titles cover the issues of trends of Ukraine's innovative activity at the macro-level, reveals the following research aspects: the position of Ukraine in the international ratings of innovation and innovativeness of the economy during 2013–2015 [15]; comparison of dynamic changes in the GDP intensity and the number of scientists for the period 1996–2015 [44]; comparison of the dynamics of the share of enterprises introducing innovations and the dynamics of the share of the volume of realized innovative products for the period 2000–2016, as well as analyzing structural changes in the state financing of innovative activity for the period 2010–2016 [47]; analyzing the rate of change in 2017 relative to 2012 of individual pairs of indicators (investment volumes and sales of innovative products; the number of organizations performing scientific and technical works and the number of employees involved in the implementation of scientific research; the number of patents for inventions and the number useful models) [31].

According to the findings of the analysis of the array of published results of the latest research on the problems of innovative and scientific and technical activity, despite the recognition of the topic relevance, the poly-aspect of scientific research, the presence of fragmentary analytical materials, including using some characteristics of dynamic changes, today there is a niche which remains vacant and concerns the parametric estimation of trends and development of forecasts according to modern realities. Analytical modeling is one of the methods of retrospective unbiased analysis with a possible extension of the results to the future.

2   Materials and Methods

2.1   Data

The authors propose to use the indicators whose quantitative values are publicly available on the website of the State Statistics Service of Ukraine [1], for the construction of models of the dynamics of innovative and scientific and technical activity, namely:

1. Indicators of the innovative activity of Ukraine:
   - x_{11} is the share of innovatively active enterprises in the total number of the surveyed industrial enterprises, %;
   - x_{12} is the total amount of innovative activity financing, thousand UAH;
   - x_{13} is the number of new technological processes implemented at industrial enterprises, processes;
   - x_{14} is the number of the names of introduced innovative types of products at industrial enterprises, units;
   - x_{15} is the specific weight of the volume of realized innovative products in the total volume of industrial products sold, %;
   - x_{16} is the number of new technologies (technical achievements) acquired, units;
2. Indicators of the scientific and technical activity of Ukraine:
   - x_{21} is the number of organizations performing scientific and technical works, units;
   - x_{22} is the number of specialists who perform scientific and technical works (at the end of the year, people);
   - x_{23} is the amount of financing of internal expenses for the implementation of research and development, thousand UAH.

Taking into account the fact that the data for 2018 are missing in Ukraine since the periodicity of the state statistical observation "Innovative Activity of the Industrial Enterprise" was changed by the state regulator from "annual" to "once every two years", starting with the report for 2015, the period from 2005 to 2017 was selected for analysis. The numerical values of the indicators until 2015 were collected based on the state statistical observation of Form 1-innovation (annual) "Inspection of Innovative Activity of the Industrial Enterprise", which covered the enterprises of economic activity of sections B, C, D, E by the Classification of Types of Economic Activity (CTEA). The information for 2016 is formed based on the data of the state statistical observation of form No. INN "Inspection of Innovative Activity of Enterprises for the Period 2014–2016" (by the international metrology) according to the following separate reporting units: enterprises by the types of economic activity of sections B, C, D, by CTEA.

To assess the efficiency and effectiveness of innovative and scientific and technical activity in Ukraine, the authors propose to use the main indicator of economic development, which most fully reflects the aggregate economic performance of units-residents of the national economy that are involved in the production of goods and services – the Gross Domestic Product (GDP). The basic data for further studies are presented in Table 1.

2.2 Methodology

It is known that undetermined phenomena in social systems, to which the indicators of scientific and innovative development of the economy belong, may be

Table 1. Basic data for assessing development trends and forecasting the indicators of innovative and scientific and technical activity of Ukraine

Years	The values of indicators									
	x_{11}	x_{12}	x_{13}	x_{14}	x_{15}	x_{16}	x_{21}	x_{22}	x_{23}	GBP
2005	11.9	5,751,563	1,808	3,152	6.5	237	1,510	105,512	5,160,399.8	441,452
2006	11.2	6,159,950	1,145	2,408	6.7	382	1,452	100,245	5,164,434.9	544,153
2007	14.2	10,850,898	1,419	2,526	6.7	1,141	1,404	96,820	6,149,231.5	720,731
2008	13.0	11,994,225	1,647	2,446	5.9	603	1,378	94,138	8,024,758.9	948,056
2009	12.8	7,949,908	1,893	2,685	4.7	631	1,340	92,403	7,822,209.8	913,345
2010	13.8	8,045,478	2,043	2,407	3.8	565	1,303	89,564	8,107,057.4	1,082,569
2011	16.2	14,333,892	2,510	3,238	3.8	672	1,255	84,969	9,591,349.5	1,302,079
2012	17.4	11,480,563	2,188	3,403	3.3	571	1,208	82,030	10,558,480	1,459,096
2013	16.8	9,562,626	1,576	3,138	3.3	512	1,143	77,853	11,161,064	1,522,657
2014	16.1	7,695,890	1,743	3,660	2.6	426	999	69,404	10,320,328	1,586,915
2015	17.3	13,813,674	1,217	3,136	1.4	1,131	978	63,864	11,001,890	1,988,544
2016	18.9	23,229,458	3,489	4,139	1.05	1,033	972	97,912	11,530,698	2,385,367
2017	16.2	9,117,537	2,037	2,387	0.7	935	963	94,274	13,379,292	2,983,882

Source: systematized by [1]

characterized by chaotic dynamics. The mathematical theory of fractals is used to investigate the nature of this kind of a dynamic change, identify trends, and further prediction. In the 60s Benoît Mandelbrot was the first one to use the notion of the "fractal" to name objects with complex geometry that could not be characterized by an integral dimension [25]. A major characteristic of fractal objects is the fact that metrically measured properties such as the length or area are dependent on the measurement scale. The fractal dimension is a measure of object complexity [2,23].

The fractal theory is the most commonly used in research in geography, physics, biology, mechanics, geology, but is rarely used in economic science. In the scientific environment, research works in economic topics on the fractal theory use can be found mainly in banking studies [43], modeling the behavior of financial time series of stock markets and forecasting stock indices [5,19,20], modeling the exchange rate behavior [3,39], analyzing prices in commodity markets [11]. The basis of this theory is R/S-analysis (the method of normalized span) – a set of statistical techniques and methods of the analysis of time series that allow determining some of their important characteristics, such as the availability and depth of long-term memory (non-periodic cycles). This method allows distinguishing a random series from a non-random one. The Hurst coefficient (H) and fractal dimension coefficient (D) are used to determine the nature of changes in the levels of a series of dynamics and their forecasting in R/S-analysis. The value of the fractal dimension coefficient (D) is two units higher than the Hurst coefficient H [14,17,18]. Indicator H takes the value from 0 to 1, characterizing the measure of a quantitative assessment of the level of the data "noisiness" presented in the form of a time series. The strength of the trend resistance (per-

sistence) of the behavior of a dynamics series increases with the Hurst coefficient
approaching 1 (Table 2).

Table 2. Characteristic of time series by the Hurst coefficient value

Hurst coefficient (H)	Characteristic of the time series
$H = 0$	The series is "dead". Dynamic changes are either absent or cyclic or have large amplitude of oscillation
$0 \leq H < 0.5$	The series is anti-persistent (unstable). The closer H is to zero, the more unstable the dynamics of the indicator is. In the future, the dynamic process will show a trend opposite to that which was characteristic of the previous period
$H = 0.5$	The series is random. Events are uncorrelated, "randomly walking". The current indicator's state is in no way related to its future state
$0.5 < H \leq 1$	The persistent (trend-resistant) series. The future values of series levels depend on the past ones. The trend, as evidenced by the time series, will be prolonged for a certain future period. The series is characterized by the presence of fractal properties

Source: drawn up according to [4, 24, 30]

The stepwise procedure to calculate the coefficient H is the following one
[30, 51]:

1. Calculation of the average value of numeric line ($\overline{X}$):

$$\overline{X} = \frac{1}{n} \sum_{i=1}^{n} x_i, \tag{1}$$

where n is the number of values of the time series; x_i is the value of i-indicator.

2. Calculation of the mean square deviation (S_n):

$$S_n = \sqrt{\frac{1}{n} \sum_{i=1}^{n} (x_i - \overline{X})^2}. \tag{2}$$

3. Calculation of the magnitude of accumulated deviation (R_n):

$$R_n = \max_{1 \leqslant k \leqslant n} \left(\sum_{i=1}^{k} x_i - \overline{X} \right) - \min_{1 \leqslant k \leqslant n} \left(\sum_{i=1}^{k} x_i - \overline{X} \right). \tag{3}$$

4. Calculation of the normalized span of accumulated sums ($(R/S)_n$):

$$(R/S)_n = \frac{R_n}{S_n}. \tag{4}$$

5. Calculation $\ln(n)$ and $\ln(R/S)_n$.
6. Formation of a sequence of points on plane $(x_n, y_n) = (\ln(n), \ln(R/S)_n)$.
7. Construction of regression line $\ln(R/S)_n = f(\ln(n))$.
8. Calculation of the Hurst coefficient as the value of the angular coefficient of linear regression.

3   Experiment, Results and Discussion

The graphical representation of regression lines of the indicators of innovative and scientific and technical activity of Ukraine, which are constructed by the method of normalized span, is given in Fig. 1 (a–j). The theoretical representation of linear regression equations, the values of the Hurst indicators and fractal dimension are presented in Table 3.

Table 3. Equations of linear regression, the value of the Hurst coefficient and fractal dimension of the indicators of the innovative and scientific and technical activity of Ukraine

Indicator's name	Linear regression equation	Hurst coefficient (H)	Fractal dimension (D)	Characteristic of the time series
x_{11}	$\ln(R/S) = 0.7815$ $\ln(n) - 0.0078$	0.7815	1.2185	Persistent
x_{12}	$\ln(R/S) = 0.7401$ $\ln(n) - 0.5738$	0.7401	1.2599	Persistent
x_{13}	$\ln(R/S) = 0.3339$ $\ln(n) + 0.5092$	0.3339	1.6661	Anti-Persistent
x_{14}	$\ln(R/S) = 0.6963$ $\ln(n) + 0.1486$	0.6963	1.3037	Persistent
x_{15}	$\ln(R/S) = 0.7507$ $\ln(n) - 0.132$	0.7507	1.2493	Persistent
x_{16}	$\ln(R/S) = 0.7626$ $\ln(n) - 0.8174$	0.7626	1.2374	Persistent
x_{21}	$\ln(R/S) = 0.8754$ $\ln(n) - 0.3905$	0.8754	1.1246	Persistent
x_{22}	$\ln(R/S) = 0.9111$ $\ln(n) - 0.599$	0.9111	1.0889	Persistent
x_{23}	$\ln(R/S) = 0.7928$ $\ln(n) - 0.2747$	0.7928	1.2072	Persistent
GDP	$\ln(R/S) = 0.8691$ $\ln(n) - 0.3425$	0.8691	1.1309	Persistent

Source. own calculations

As it can be seen from the analysis (Table 3), only indicator x_{13} ("Introduction of new technological processes at industrial enterprises") is characterized by unstable dynamics and the absence of a clear trend, which allows choosing a model of the random walk "one-dimensional Brownian motion". In this case, it is expedient to use exponential smoothing and moving average for forecasting. All the other indicators are characterized by a steady trend of their change, that is, trend dependence, which will be extended into the future.

Linear trend models (Table 4) are used to simulate development trends and forecast numerical values of the indicators selected by the authors. It should be noted that all the indicators used by the authors as indicators of innovative and scientific and technical activity are logically considered to be indicators that stimulate scientific and technical progress and economic innovation. Nevertheless, three indicators (x_{15} – the specific weight of the volume of realized innovative products in the total volume of industrial products sold, x_{21} –

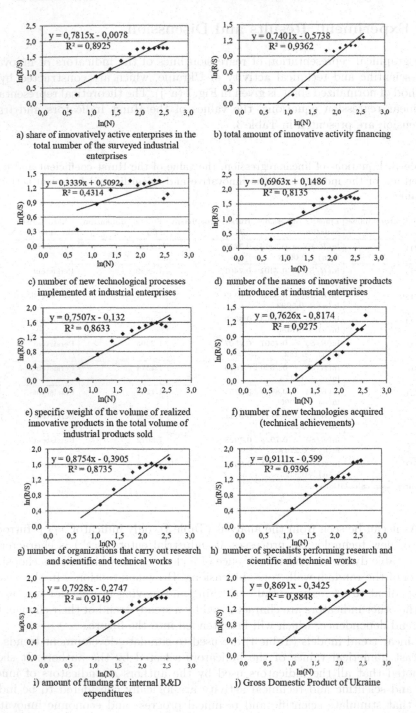

Fig. 1. Visualization of regression lines of the analyzed indicators of the innovative and scientific and technical activity of Ukraine, constructed by the method of normalized span

Table 4. Linear trend models and forecasting the indicators of innovative and scientific and technical activity of Ukraine for 2019–2021

Indicator's name	Trend line equation	Determination factor, R^2	Indicators' predicted values		
			2019	2020	2021
x_{11}	$x_{11} = 0.5363\ t +$ 11.308	0.76	19.4	19.9	20.4
x_{12}	$x_{12} = 610,769\ t +$ 6E+06	0.26	15,161,535	15,772,304	16,383,073
x_{13}	Forecasting by the exponential smoothing method		2,283	2,684	2,608
x_{14}	$x_{14} = 66.203\ t +$ 2,515.4	0.21	3,508	3,575	3,641
x_{15}	$x_{15} = -0.5354\ t +$ 7.6288	0.96	0.1	0	0
x_{16}	$x_{16} = 36.484\ t +$ 424.54	0.24	972	1,008	1,045
x_{21}	$x_{21} = -49.516\ t +$ 1,570.1	0.97	827	778	728
x_{22}	$x_{22} = -1,767.9\ t$ $\vert$ 100,759	0.32	74,241	72,473	70,704
x_{23}	$x_{23} = 640,501\ t +$ 5E+06	0.94	14,607,515	15,248,016	15,888,517
GDP	GDP $= 181,558\ t$ $+ 104,387$	0.92	2,827,757	3,009,315	3,190,873

Source: own calculations

number of organizations performing scientific and technical works, x_{22} – number of specialists performing scientific and technical works) show a downward trend. The differently vectored orientation of dynamic changes (the tendency of a decrease in the share of innovative products in their total volume against the background of an increase in the share of innovatively active enterprises, an increase in expenses for innovative activity, name extension and an increase in the number of innovations) cannot indicate the effective innovative development of Ukraine. Similarly, under conditions of a trendy decline in producers of scientific and technical developments, the outflow of human science capital, risks and threats for the research sphere progress is activated. This situation is partly explained by the existence of a discrepancy between the declared purpose and the actual implementation of the state scientific and technical and innovative policy.

The declaration of the necessity of innovative development of the Ukrainian economy, in the opinion of Yehorov [46], is not supported by specially designed policy measures, in particular, the use of effective mechanisms for the implementation of innovative activity results. Therefore, there are urgent societal goals including improving the institutional environment, reforming the research sector, developing and implementing a coherent science, technology, and innovation policy. The implementation of these tasks will lead to an improvement in the overall material well-being of the country and an increase in its GDP.

The method of correlation-regression analysis is used for parametric estimation of nature, density measure, and direction of Ukraine's GDP dependence (productive indicator) on specific indicators of innovative and scientific and technical activity (independent variables), as well as proving substantiality (non-randomness). For this purpose, correlation coefficients, determination coefficients, the F-criterion are calculated. The results are systematized and interpreted in Table 5.

Table 5. Characteristic of the parameters, density and nature of the relationship between innovative and scientific and technical indicators of Ukraine's GDP

Innovative activity of Ukraine						
Indicators	x_{11}	x_{12}	x_{13}	x_{14}	x_{15}	x_{16}
Relationship nature	Linear straight	Linear straight	Linear straight	Linear straight	Linear inverse	Linear straight
Correlation coefficient (r)	0.79	0.51	0.44	0.33	−0.94	0.55
Relationship density	Moderate	Weak	Weak	Very weak	Strong	Weak
Determination coefficient (R^2)	0.62	0.26	0.20	0.11	0.89	0.30
F-test at substantiality level $\alpha = 0.05$	$Fv > Fcr$	$Fv > Fcr$	$Fv > Fcr$	$Fv > Fcr$	$Fv > Fcr$	$Fv > Fcr$
Relationship substantiality	Significant	Significant	Significant	Significant	Significant	Significant
Scientific and technical activity of Ukraine						
Indicators	x_{21}		x_{22}		x_{23}	
Relationship nature	Linear inverse		Linear inverse		Linear straight	
Correlation coefficient (r)	−0.93		−0.35		0.94	
Relationship density	Strong		Very weak		Strong	
Determination coefficient (R^2)	0.86		0.12		0.88	
F-test at substantiality level $\alpha = 0.05$	$Fv > Fcr$		$Fv < Fcr$		$Fv > Fcr$	
Relationship substantiality	Significant		Not significant		Significant	

Source: own calculations

Multi-collinearity (relationships between independent variables) is known to distort a regression model. In the arsenal of testing instruments for the availability of mutual influence between independent variables, the leading role is given to the estimation of paired correlation coefficients. In statistics for this purpose, a correlation matrix with specified pairwise coefficients for all variables is constructed. The correlation matrixes of the two groups of indicators – innovative activity and scientific and technical activity – are summarized in Table 6.

As can be seen from Table 6, the absolute value of the correlation coefficient for the innovative activity indicators is more than 0.8, characteristic of the pair of variables x_{11} and x_{15}. The negative value of this coefficient (−0.843) indicates the inverse direction of the relationship between the share of innovative enterprises in the total number of the surveyed industrial enterprises and the share of the

Table 6. Correlation coefficients of the indicators of innovative and scientific and technical activity of Ukraine

Innovative activity							Scientific and technical activity			
Indicators	x_{11}	x_{12}	x_{13}	x_{14}	x_{15}	x_{16}	Indicators	x_{21}	x_{22}	x_{23}
x_{11}	1.000						x_{21}	1.000		
x_{12}	0.712	1.000								
x_{13}	0.533	0.709	1.000				x_{22}	0.617	1.000	
x_{14}	0.685	0.595	0.604	1.000						
x_{15}	−0.843	−0.504	−0.470	−0.474	1.000		x_{23}	−0.925	−0.543	1.000
x_{16}	0.528	0.635	0.184	0.045	−0.449	1.000				

Source: own calculations

Table 7. Regression equations of the influence of the innovative activity indicators on the GDP of Ukraine

Indicators	Regression equations and economic content
x_{11}	$243{,}616\,x_{11} - 2E{+}06$
	With the increase in the share of innovative enterprises in the total number of the surveyed industrial enterprises by 1%, the GDP of Ukraine will increase by UAH 243,616 million
x_{12}	$0.0817\,x_{12} + 495{,}553$
	With the increase in the volume of innovative activity financing by 1 thousand UAH, Ukraine's GDP will increase by UAH 81.7 thousand
x_{13}	$535.24\,x_{13} + 357{,}731$
	With the increase in the number of new technological processes implemented at industrial enterprises by 1, the GDP of Ukraine will increase by UAH 535.24 million
x_{14}	$441.48\,x_{14} + 60{,}203$
	With the increase in the number of names of innovative products introduced at industrial enterprises by 1 unit, Ukraine's GDP will increase by UAH 441.48 million
x_{15}	$-327{,}962\,x_{15} + 3E{+}06$
	With the increase in the specific weight of the volume of realized innovative products in the total volume of industrial products sold by 1%, Ukraine's GDP will decrease by UAH 327,962 million
x_{16}	$1{,}381.8\,x_{16} + 435{,}780$
	With the increase in the number of new technologies acquired by 1 unit, Ukraine's GDP will increase by UAH 1,381.8 million
$x_{12}, x_{13}, x_{14}, x_{15}, x_{16}$	$0.0036\,x_{12} + 89.9\,x_{13} - 227.9\,x_{14} - 323{,}522\,x_{15} + 271.2\,x_{16} + 2{,}915{,}817\ r = 0.96;\ R^2 = 0.920$ High relationship density
	The coefficients of this regression equation testify to the volume of Ukraine's GDP, which will change as each of indicators $x_{12}, x_{13}, x_{14}, x_{15}, x_{16}$ increases or decreases by unit of measure
$x_{11}, x_{12}, x_{13}, x_{14}, x_{16}$	$308{,}894\,x_{11} - 0.06\,x_{12} + 416.3\,x_{13} - 467{,}5\,x_{14} + 510.7\,x_{16} - 2{,}393{,}557.2\ r = 0.865;\ R^2 = 0.748$ High relationship density
	The coefficients of this regression equation testify to the volume of Ukraine's GDP, which will change as each of indicators $x_{11}, x_{12}, x_{13}, x_{14}, x_{16}$ increases or decreases by unit of measure

Source: own calculations

volume of realized innovative products in the total volume of industrial products sold. To eliminate the revealed multicollinearity for the construction of regression dependencies, indicators x_{11} and x_{15} were eliminated by turn from the model (see Table 7). Similarly, among the scientific and technical activity indicators,

Table 8. Regression equations of the influence of the scientific and technical activity indicators on the GDP of Ukraine

Indicators	Regression equations and economic content
x_{21}	$-3{,}488.8\ x_{21} + 6E{+}06$
	With the increase in the number of organizations that perform scientific and scientific and technical works by 1 unit, Ukraine's GDP will decrease by UAH 3,488.8 million
x_{22}	$-20.947\ x_{22} + 3E{+}06$
	With the increase in the number of specialists performing scientific and technical works per 1 person, the GDP of Ukraine will decrease by UAH 20.947 million
x_{23}	$0.2691\ x_{23} - 1E{+}06$
	With the increase in the amount of funding for internal research and development expenditures by 1 thousand UAH, Ukraine's GDP will increase by UAH 269.1 thousand
x_{22}, x_{23}	$13.75\ x_{22} + 0.3\ x_{23} - 2{,}605{,}532\ r = 0.958;\ R^2 = 0.917$ High relationship density
	With the increase in the number of specialists performing scientific and scientific-technical works by 1 person and the volume of financing of internal expenses for the implementation of research and development by 1 thousand UAH, Ukraine's GDP will increase by UAH 14.05 million
x_{21}, x_{22}	$-4{,}324.8\ x_{21} + 21.6\ x_{22} + 4{,}754{,}247\ r = 0.968;\ R^2 = 0.937$ High relationship density
	With the increase in the number of organizations that perform scientific and scientific-technical works by 1 unit and the number of specialists performing scientific and technical works by 1 person, the GDP of Ukraine will decrease by UAH 4,303.2 million

Source: own calculations

a high level of inverse relationship is available between variables x_{21} and x_{23}, that is, between the number of organizations performing scientific and technical works and the amount of financing for internal R&D expenditures. To eliminate the revealed multicollinearity for the construction of regression dependencies, indicators x_{21} and x_{23} were eliminated by turn from the model (Tables 7 and 8).

The illogicalness of economic interpretation of the regression models, which contain negative values of the regression coefficients, is explained by the opposite direction of the trend values of indicators x_{15}, x_{21}, x_{22} (trend decrease) and the GDP trend (trend increase). This asymmetry of dynamic changes is explained not only by the result of inflationary processes in cost macro indicators but also by the low knowledge capacity of domestic products, the weak role of scientific and innovative activity in the national production system. Therefore, there is a need to update the content of a scientific and technical and innovation policy, to update the current legislative framework by creating not only effective by-

Table 9. Forecasting Ukraine's GDP using regression equations

Indicators' names whose forecast value is taken into account in the GDP forecasting	GDP forecast value, mln. UAH			GDP trend
	2019	2020	2021	
x_{11}	2,726,150.4	2,847,958.4	2,969,766.4	↑
x_{12}	1,734,250.4	1,784,150.2	1,834,050.1	↑
x_{13}	1,579,683.9	1,794,300.1	1,753,636.9	–
x_{14}	1,608,914.8	1,638,494.0	1,667,631.7	↑
x_{15}	2,967,203.8	3,000,000.0	3,000,000.0	↑
x_{16}	1,778,889.6	1,828,634.4	1,879,761.0	↑
$x_{12}, x_{13}, x_{14}, x_{15}, x_{16}$	2,607,421.2	2,672,516.0	2,662,875.4	–
$x_{11}, x_{12}, x_{13}, x_{14}, x_{16}$	2,496,117.6	2,767,917.5	2,842,120.4	↑
x_{21}	3,114,762.4	3,285,713.6	3,460,153.6	↑
x_{22}	1,444,873.8	1,481,908.1	1,518,963.3	↑
x_{23}	2,930,882.3	3,103,241.1	3,275,599.9	↑
x_{22}, x_{23}	2,797,536.3	2,965,376.6	3,133,203.1	↑
x_{21}, x_{22}	2,781,243.0	2,954,969.4	3,132,999.0	↑
Maximum value	3,114,762.4	3,285,713.6	3,460,153.6	–
Minimum value	1,444,873.8	1,481,908.1	1,518,963.3	–
Average value	2,351,379.2	2,471,167.6	2,548,520.1	–
Standard deviation	593,926.2	626,744.7	676,486.9	–
Coefficient of variation, %	25.3	25.4	26.5	–

Source: own calculations

laws for the implementation of the Law of Ukraine "On Scientific and Technical Activity", but also effective mechanisms for increasing the role of science and its innovation potential [41]. To activate the innovative activity of the domestic business environment, it is advisable to implement the best practices of the world, including those related to the activity of spin-offs, start-ups, venture capital companies. It is important to combine financial and non-financial levers to stimulate business towards the need for research and developments. Based on the regression models presented in Tables 7 and 8, and the results of forecasting indicators using linear trend models (see Table 4), the authors forecast the GDP of Ukraine for 2019–2021 (Table 9).

4 Conclusions

The largest deviations of the GDP forecast values obtained by the regression model and the linear trend equation are observed in the cases of use of the indicators of innovative and scientific and technical activity, which in pairs the least correlate with the GDP volume – x_{14} and x_{22}. However, all the forecasting results point to an upward trend in the GDP. The quadratic coefficient of variation of the GDP forecast values obtained by the regression model does not exceed the critical value (in 2019, 2020, 2021 it is 25.3%, 25.4%, 26.5%, respectively). This allows arguing for the homogeneity of a set of the GDP forecast values obtained by regression models, including the indicators of innovative and scientific and technical activity, and the typicality of the average value of the GDP forecast indicator (in 2019, 2020, 2021 it is 2,351 billion UAH, 2,471 billion UAH, 2,548 billion UAH respectively). All the GDP estimates do not go beyond the deviation of one and half times of the range of variation from the average value. This indicates that there are no atypical values of the forecast indicators, so-called statistical "outliers".

Global shifts in the direction of informatization and knowledge-richness of social productions are contributing to the transnational scale of both resources and results of innovative and scientific and technical activity. Network effects in this activity development, according to Zhylinska [49], are provided by the acceleration of the development of the world market of industrial property objects, the mechanism of licensing agreements creates an economic platform for the intensification of scientific and technical cooperation, the economic realization of established scientific and technical knowledge and obtaining quasi-targeted income as a source financing of new research and developments. Therefore, the progress of science and innovatization of the Ukrainian economy is not possible without increasing the effects of complementarity from the world markets (educational services, scientific and technical information, high technology products, venture capital investments, etc.).

The innovative and scientific and technical activity in Ukraine has not taken the place of the systemic core of social progress. Despite the persistence of upward dynamics of the share of innovatively active enterprises, the volume of scientific and innovative activity financing, the number of new technological processes implemented and new technologies acquired, the time series of the list of names of innovative products is anti-persistent. Instead, these important indicators of scientific and innovation progress, which characterize the level of innovative product sales, the number of organizations, and the human capital of the research field, show a downward trend. The asymmetries found do not level the role of science and innovation in the national economy's development. The GDP correlates with the results of innovative and scientific and technical activity and, as the forecast calculations show, will gradually increase under their influence.

The ways of solving the identified problems lie in the actualization of the content of scientific and technical and innovation policy, updating the existing legislative framework in the direction of the effectiveness of socially acceptable mechanisms of increasing the role of scientific and innovative potential in the national complex, the implementation of the world's best practices.

References

1. Science, technology and innovation: official website of state statistics service of Ukraine (2019). http://www.ukrstat.gov.ua/druk/publicat
2. Agop, M., Colotin, M., Păun, V.: Haoticitate, fractalitate şi câmpuri. Editura ArsLonga, Iaşi (2009)
3. Amar, A., El Wahli, I., Guennou, Z., Laaroussi, Y.: Fractal analysis of Moroccan dirham exchange rate: theory and comparative results. J. Appl. Econ. Sci. **11**(3), 340–350 (2016)
4. Bartashevska, Y., Yavorsky, A.: Fractal analysis of other markets: theoretical and practical aspects of use. Eur. Vector Econ. Dev. Econ. Sci. **18**(1), 7–14 (2015)
5. Bayraci, S.: Testing for multi-fractality and efficiency in selected sovereign bond markets: a multi-fractal detrended moving average (MFDMA) analysis. Int. J. Comput. Econ. Econom. **8**(1), 95–120 (2018). https://doi.org/10.1504/IJCEE.2018.088324
6. Busol, O.: Methods of legal other intellectual property of subjects of scientific and scientific-technical activity. Scientific works of the National Library of Ukraine named after V.I. Vernadsky, no. 43, pp. 194–198 (2016)
7. Butko, M., Popelo, O.: Commercialization of scientific results and technical activity in conditions of integration deepening processes. Probl. Prospects Econ. Manag. **1**(1), 7–20 (2015)
8. Ceci, F., Lazoi, M., Mohammad, H., Corallo, A.: Collaborative relationships strengthening innovative activities: an industrial exploration. In: Proceedings of the European Conference on Intellectual Capital (2019)
9. Chukhrai, N., Lisovska, L.: Formation of innovation's consumer utility. Actual Probl. Econ. **11**(149), 27–34 (2013)
10. Chukhray, N., Shakhovska, N., Mrykhina, O., Bublyk, M., Lisovska, L.: Methodical approach to assessing the readiness level of technologies for the transfer. In: Shakhovska, N., Medykovskyy, M.O. (eds.) CSIT 2019. AISC, vol. 1080, pp. 259–282. Springer, Cham (2020). https://doi.org/10.1007/978-3-030-33695-0_19
11. Cromwell, J., Labys, W., Kouassi, E.: What color are commodity prices? A fractal analysis. Empirical Econ. **25**(4), 563–580 (2000). https://doi.org/10.1007/s001810000033
12. Daron, M., Gorska, M.: Management premises and barriers in the metal industry in Poland in the context of innovative activity. Sustainability **11**(23), 6761 (2019). https://doi.org/10.3390/su11236761
13. Dovgan, A., Tarasyuk, A.: Corporate culture of cybersecurity subjects of scientific and scientific-technical activity. Inf. Law **25**(2), 51–61 (2018)
14. Feder, E.: Fractals. Mir, Moscow (1991)
15. Hanechko, I., Afanasiev, K.: Innovative activity in Ukraine: tendencies and problems of development. Uzhgorod Univ. Sci. Bull. Ser.: Econ. **1**(1), 189–193 (2016)
16. Hollenstein, H.: A composite indicator of a firm's innovativeness. An empirical analysis based on survey data for Swiss manufacturing. Res. Policy **25**(4), 633–645 (1996). https://doi.org/10.1016/0048-7333(95)00874-8
17. Hurst, H.: Long-term storage capacity of reservoirs. Trans. Am. Soc. Civ. Eng. **116**, 770–808 (1951)
18. Hurst, H., Black, R., Simaika, Y.: Long-Term Storage: An Experimental Study. Constable, London (1965)
19. Ikeda, T.: A fractal analysis of world stock markets. Econ. Bull. **37**(3), 1514–1532 (2017)

20. Karaca, Y., Zhang, Y.D., Muhammad, K.: Characterizing complexity and self-similarity based on fractal and entropy analyses for stock market forecast modelling. Expert Syst. Appl. **144**(113098) (2020). https://doi.org/10.1016/j.eswa.2019.113098

21. Kato-Vidal, E., Occhipinti, C.: Innovative activity and entrepreneurial rates in Mexico. Contaduria y Administracion **64**(2), 4 (2019). https://doi.org/10.22201/fca.24488410e.2018.1429

22. Perez-de Lema, D., Galvez-Albarracin, E., Garcia-Solarte, M.: Effect of the intra-trepreneurial culture on the innovative activity of Spain's SMEs. In: Handbook of Research on Intrapreneurship and Organizational Sustainability in SMEs, pp. 50–72 (2018). https://doi.org/10.4018/978-1-5225-3543-0.ch003

23. Mandelbrot, B.: Fractals, Case and Finance (1959–1997). RC Dynamics, Izhevsk (2004)

24. Mandelbrot, B., Hudson, R.: (Non) Obedient Markets: The Fractal Revolution in Finance. Williams, Moscow (2006)

25. Mandelbrot, B.: How long is the coast of Britain? Statistical self-similarity and fractal dimension. Science **156**(155), 636–638 (1967). https://doi.org/10.1680/jmacr.17.00445

26. Melnik, A., Ermolaev, K., Kuzmin, M.: Mechanism for adjustment of the companies innovative activity control indicators to their strategic development goals. Glob. J. Flex. Syst. Manag. **20**(3), 189–218 (2019). https://doi.org/10.1007/s40171-019-00210-z

27. Mura, L., Mazák, M.: Innovative activities of family SMEs: case study of the Slovak regions. Online J. Model. New Eur. (27), 132–147 (2018). https://doi.org/10.24193/OJMNE.2018.27.06

28. Parfentieva, O., Grechan, P., Grechan, A.: Stimulating innovative activity as a tool for ensuring strategic development of motor transport enterprises. Manag. Sci. Lett. **9**(10), 1655–1668 (2019). https://doi.org/10.5267/j.msl.2019.5.022

29. Pazilov, G., Ivashchenko, K., Bimendiyeva, L., Kalmenova, M., Yessirkepova, A.: Management of innovative activity of the textile enterprises of Kazakhstan. Izvestiya Vysshikh Uchebnykh Zavedenii, Seriya Teknologiya Tekstil'noi Promyshlennosti **379**(1), 135–142 (2019)

30. Peters, E.: Fractal Analysis of Financial Markets: Application of Chaos Theory to Investment and Economy. Internet Trading, Moscow (2004)

31. Petryk, I.: Innovative activity in Ukraine: current trends, problems, measures for activation. Young Sci. (4), 510–516 (2019). https://doi.org/10.32839/2304-5809/2019-4-68-113

32. Prokopenko, O., Kudrina, O., Omelyanenko, V.: ICT support of higher education institutions participation in innovation networks. In: Proceedings of the 15th International Conference "ICT in Education, Research and Industrial Applications. Integration, Harmonization and Knowledge Transfer", pp. 482–487 (2019)

33. Prokopenko, O., Omelyanenko, V., Ponomarenko, T., Olshanska, O.: Innovation networks effects simulation models. Periodicals Eng. Nat. Sci. **7**(2), 752–762 (2019). https://doi.org/10.21533/pen.v7i2.574

34. Samukdjanovna, A.: Problems of ensuring innovative development of credit activities of commercial banks and ways of their solution. Int. J. Recent Technol. Eng. **8**(2(10)), 356–360 (2019). https://doi.org/10.35940/ijrte.B1058.0982S1019

35. Shpak, N., Odrekhivskyi, M., Doroshkevych, K., Sroka, W.: Simulation of innovative systems under Industry 4.0 conditions. Soc. Sci. **8**, 202 (2019). https://doi.org/10.3390/socsci8070202

36. Smernytskyi, D.: Scientific and technical activities: some issues of information support. Mod. Spec. Equip. **45**(2), 3–11 (2016)
37. Smernytskyi, D.: Scientific and technical activity as an object of administrative and legal support. Sci. Law Enforcement **38**(4), 110–119 (2017)
38. Smernytskyi, D., Bakal, V., Budzynskyi, M., Samus, Y., Tryhubenko, M.: International legal aspect of scientific (scientific and technical) activity regulation. Int. J. Innov. Technol. Explor. Eng. **8**(10), 1883–1888 (2019). https://doi.org/10.35940/ijitee.J9240.0881019
39. Soofi, A., Galka, A.: Measuring the complexity of currency markets by fractal dimension analysis. Int. J. Theoret. Appl. Finan. **6**(6), 553–563 (2003). https://doi.org/10.1142/S0219024903001955
40. Sviderskyi, O.: The notion of subjects of scientific and scientific-technical activity in the aspect of expert support of justice. Theory Pract. Forensic Sci. Forensic Sci. **17**, 191–197 (2017)
41. Vasylenko, M.: Scientific and technical activity in Ukraine: a historical and legal perspective on the new law. Legal Bull. (1), 91–97 (2016)
42. Voitsekhovska, Y.: Parameters of innovative technology and their influence on the renovation of fixed assets. J. Lviv Polytech. Nat. Univ. Ser. Econ. Manag. Issues **4**(2), 17–23 (2019). https://doi.org/10.23939/semi2019.04.017
43. Wang, W., Khan, M.: Analysis and numerical simulation of fractional model of bank data with fractal-fractional Atangana-Baleanu derivative. J. Comput. Appl. Math. **369**(112646) (2020). https://doi.org/10.1016/j.cam.2019.112646
44. Yegorov, I., Hryha, V.: Innovative and scientific-technical activity in Ukraine in the context of European integration policy: tendencies and problems. Scientific Notes of the Institute of Political and Ethnic Studies IF Kuras, NAS of Ukraine, no. 5–6, pp. 184–196 (2016)
45. Yegorov, I.: System of integrated indicators for the assessment of scientific-technical and innovation activity in the context of European integrations. Sci. Innov. **12**(4), 21–23 (2016). https://doi.org/10.15407/scin12.04.021
46. Yegorov, I.: The formation of national R&D and innovation policy based on "Triple Helix" (government-science-industry) extended model (brief information about the project). Sci. Innov. **14**(1), 87–89 (2018). https://doi.org/10.15407/scin14.01.086
47. Yershova, H.: Innovative activity in Ukraine: main trends and problems. Econ. Forecast. (4), 137–148 (2017). https://doi.org/10.15407/eip2017.04.137
48. Zavidna, L., Makarenko, P., Chepurda, G., Lyzunova, O., Shmygol, N.: Strategy of innovative development as an element to activate innovative activities of companies. Acad. Strateg. Manag. J. **18**(4), 6 (2019)
49. Zhylinska, O.: Complementary effects in activization of scientific and technical activities in the information society. Bull. Taras Shevchenko Nat. Univ. Kyiv Econ. **9**(186), 6–16 (2016). https://doi.org/10.17721/1728-2667.2016/186-9/1
50. Ziyadin, S., Shash, N., Levchenko, T., Khudaibergenova, S., Yessenova, G.: Modeling of resultant effects in assessment of innovative activity of the hotel organizations. Entrepreneurship Sustain. Issues **6**(4), 2180–2193 (2019). https://doi.org/10.9770/jesi.2019.6.4(43)
51. Zynenko, A.: R/S stock market analysis. Bus. Inform. **3**(21), 24–30 (2012)

The Issue of Efficient Generation of Generalized Features in Algorithmic Classification Tree Methods

Igor Povkhan$^{(\boxtimes)}$, Maksym Lupei , Mykhailo Kliap , and Vasyl Laver

Uzhhorod National University, Uzhgorod, Ukraine
{igor.povkhan,mihaylo.klyap,vasyl.laver}@uzhnu.edu.ua,
maxim.lupey@gmail.com

Abstract. The paper studies the basic issue of methods of constructing models of algorithmic classification trees which is the problem of generating generalized features in their structure. There has been suggested a simple and efficient method of approximating the initial training dataset with the help of a set of generalized features of the type of geometric objects in feature space of the current application problem. This approach allows ensuring the necessary accuracy of classification trees, reducing the structural (constructional) complexity and achieving the appropriate performance indicators of the model. Based on the proposed algorithmic scheme of the training set coverage there has been developed the corresponding software which enables the work with a set of different-type applied problems of data processing. Hence, a simple, efficient and economical approximation of the initial training set provides the appropriate speed, level of complexity of the classification scheme, which ensures the simple and complete recognition (coverage) of sets of discrete objects.

Keywords: Discrete objects recognition · Approximation by means of geometric objects · Recognition function · Generalized feature · Classification trees

1 Introduction

The research offers a solution to the problem of pattern recognition in the deterministic variant based on the use of the methodology (concept) of the logical (algorithmic) tree method [2,6,7,15,18–23,31,32]. The specificity of methods of classification trees (decision trees) enables creating on its basis software systems for automating the process of constructing new algorithms and recognition systems in general. And within the approach of an algorithmic classification tree (ACT) [18], whose main idea is to approximate the initial training dataset with the help of a set of independent classification algorithms, there arises the central question regarding the issue of generating generalized features (the vertices of the classification tree structure) [20]. In this way an opportunity to effectively

© Springer Nature Switzerland AG 2020
S. Babichev et al. (Eds.): DSMP 2020, CCIS 1158, pp. 98–113, 2020.
https://doi.org/10.1007/978-3-030-61656-4_6

use the long-term experience, accumulated in the theory and practice of pattern recognition, giving already known algorithms and recognition programs a second life, is fulfilled. In this respect, the tree method completes the branch feature selection methodology [12]. Therefore, a simple and efficient method of approximating a training set (or part of it) by means of geometric objects is proposed. The idea of the developed algorithm for generating generalized features (GFs) [20] still lies in the approximation of a certain class by means of the sequence of certain generalized features [30] (hyperparallelepipeds). With regard to its algorithmic implementation, it should be noted that it develops the work [29] that was not devoid of certain systemic constraints (fixed orientation in space, the impossibility of adaptation, etc.).

The use of a set of geometric objects (in the sense of generalized features of the ACT structure) for the approximation of discrete sets enables building a relatively simple classification model (scheme) provided several approaches are used jointly (for example, the links of the hypersphere and hypercube algorithms), which ensures a complete classification even with weak separation of classes (or their number, and the character of arrangement). It should be stressed here that each of the geometric implementations has its own fixed efficiency with regard to the training set and in the worst case will fail to carry out the complete approximation of the training set (this does not apply to the hypersphere algorithm which enables recognition even if the separation hypothesis is not fulfilled) that is, to construct the sequence of GFs.

It should be emphasized that constructing a set of GFs (in the form of approximating the dataset with the help of the sequence of hyperparallelepipeds) has certain peculiarities due to the additional verification of the constructed hyperparallelepipeds (the impossibility of touching the area of another class) and the general scheme of constructing all possible hyperparallelepipeds in the fixed class. In our case, an important peculiarity of the hyperparallelepiped algorithm in comparison with other geometric approaches is that for storing a constructed generalized feature by the information system (a hyperparallelepiped) it is sufficient to remember two opposite diagonal vertices.

2   Formal Problem Statement

Suppose that in the beginning there is given some training dataset of the general type (1) – in the form of a sequence of training pairs (A_j, Ω_{i_j}), with the m power, the n-dimensional feature space and a fixed set of heterogeneous classification algorithms $(\alpha_1, \alpha_2, \ldots, \alpha_s)$.

$$(A_1, \Omega_{i_1}), (A_2, \Omega_{i_2}), \ldots, (A_m, \Omega_{i_m}). \tag{1}$$

It should be noted that here the data of the initial training set specify some partitioning of U into classes $(\Omega_0, \Omega_1, \ldots, \Omega_k)$, and the corresponding α_i algorithms are not necessarily related by a single recognition concept, but they implement various classification methods and algorithms (for example, these can be conventional geometric algorithms whose principle of work is to approximate the training set with the help of appropriate geometric objects, algorithms for calculating estimates, potential functions, etc.) [3–5,8,9,11,26,28].

Let us note that A_j are objects (vectors) of some n-dimensional space of $\mathbb{R}^n$ features, and Ω_{i_j} is the numbers of classes, which contain A_j objects, and here $(j \in 1,\dots,m; i \in 1,\dots,k)$.

Suppose that Ω_0 is a class of objects and none of them is found in any of the classes $\Omega_1, \Omega_2, \dots, \Omega_k$, then the true equation is $\Omega_1 \cup \Omega_2 \cup \cdots \cup \Omega_k = \mathbb{R}^n$. The central task of recognizing patterns (discrete objects) is the construction of such a system (model), which for each object provided at the input would output a class number containing this object [1,10,13,14,16,17,24,25,27]. Obviously, the training set itself (1) is a system of a selected type that recognizes objects, but only those listed in the set. The more objects the training dataset includes, the more objects with $\mathbb{R}^n$ can be recognized by such a system. Due to the finiteness of the training set and the computer memory that will process it, this approach is not the best option.

One of the ways to significantly increase the number of objects with $\mathbb{R}^n$ which, according to the present finite training set, that will be correctly classified by the recognition system (RS) is the geometric approximation of the Ω_i classes. An example of such methods is the partition of $\mathbb{R}^n$ space by hyperspheres. Here are the principles that will be adhered to in the following approximation of the initial training dataset by hyperparallelepipeds:

1. Since the training set is usually the only initial information in the statement of the recognition problem, it is necessary to make a start mainly from this information when constructing the RS.
2. Since the training set is finite, and therefore – restricted, the approximation elements, in our opinion, should be bounded, that is, in the n-dimensional space the approximation elements are closed hypersurfaces.
3. Suppose ξ is some neighbourhood (a hypersphere, a hypercube, a hyperellipse, a hyperparallelepiped). Let us consider the possible assumptions:
   a) in ξ neighbourhood of each point A_i (a discrete object) from the training set there is no object with $\mathbb{R}^n$;
   b) in ξ neighbourhood of point A_i there are objects with $\mathbb{R}^n$, but all of them together with point A_i belong to the same class;
   c) in ξ neighbourhood of point A_i there are objects with $\mathbb{R}^n$, but they can be from different classes.

Assumption (a) is not the best one since this option is unlikely and there is no approximation which will be better than the training set itself. Assumption (c) is most feasible but in this case in the whole neighbourhood the ξ neighbourhood of point A_i we possess information only about point (object) A_i. Based on these considerations principle (b) is formulated – each point A_i belongs to the class Ω_{i_j} together with ξ neighbourhood.

3   Literature Review

The study continues a series of works devoted to a complex of issues (the construction, minimization, selection of vertices, generation of features and classification rules) of tree schemes of recognizing (classifying) discrete objects [2,7,12,15,18–20,23,30–32]. The central issues they raise are related to building, using, and optimizing logical trees. It is known from [32] that the resulting classification rule (scheme), which is constructed by means of an arbitrary method or an algorithm or the branched feature selection method, has a tree-like logical structure and belongs to the class of models of logical classification trees (LCTs).

An arbitrary logical tree (the logical classification tree model) consists of vertices (features, algorithms) that are grouped by tiers (levels) and which are obtained at a certain step (stage) of building a recognition tree (a decision tree) [18]. Moreover, an important problem arising from [20] is the problem of synthesis of recognition trees, which will actually be represented by a tree (graph) of algorithms – a class of algorithmic classification trees.

In contrast to the existing methods, the main peculiarity of tree-based recognition systems (LCT/ACT models) is that the importance of separate features (a group of features or algorithms) is determined regarding the function which specifies the division of objects into classes [31]. Thus, in work [28], the fundamental issues with regard to generating decision trees for the case of low-data features are raised. So the ability of classification tree structures to perform one-dimensional branching in order to analyze the influence (importance, quality) of individual variables makes it possible to work with variables of different types in the form of predicates (in the case of ACTs, with the corresponding autonomous classification and recognition algorithms). This concept of classification trees is actively employed in intellectual analysis of data, where the ultimate goal is to synthesize a model which predicts the value of the target variable based on the initial dataset at the input of the system [6].

The important elements of branched feature selection methods are described in [32] which provides the scheme of constructing a classification tree on the basis of a logical tree algorithm with the step by step estimation of importance of discrete features according to the training dataset. Work [19] focuses on a modified branched feature selection algorithm with one-time evaluation of a set of features, and [18] proposes the description of an algorithm for generating a set of random logical classification trees with the final stage of selecting the optimal one. So, as the main idea of branched feature selection methods and algorithms can be defined as an optimal approximation of some initial training dataset by means of a set of elementary features (attributes of objects), then their central problem is the issue of choosing an effective branching criterion (selecting vertices, attributes, features of discrete objects). These fundamental problems are considered in [30], where the talk is about the issues of qualitative evaluation of individual discrete features, their sets and fixed combinations, which enables the introduction of an efficient mechanism of the realization of branching. The structure (LCT/ACT) is characterized by compactness on the one hand, and the unevenness of filling (dis-charging) the tiers on the other hand in comparison with regular trees (the algorithm with one-time estimation of the value of the features) [31]. It should be noted that the important issues which still remain are related to the convergence of the model building process (LCT/ACT) in view of branched feature selection methods as well as the choice of the criterion of stopping the process of synthesizing a logical tree (for example, limitations in terms of the depth or complexity of the tree, limitations in terms of the accuracy or the number of errors of the structure which is being constructed) [15].

It must be underlined that the concept of logical trees does not contradict the ability to use as features (vertices) of LCTs not only the individual attributes (features) of the objects of their combination (the idea of a generalized feature was considered in work [30]) and sets; but if we go further and the attributes of objects (features) are not considered as branching – and if we select separate independent recognition algorithms (estimated with regard to the training dataset), then a new structure (an ACT) will be obtained at the output [20]. It is the issue of generating the generalized features in the ACT methods that is studied in this work.

4   The Issue of Generating the Generalized Features

Let us to describe the essence of hyperparallelepiped E-approximation algorithm of the training set, which is used to generate generalized features in the methods of constructing an ACT. Suppose, in n-dimensional space the training dataset is specified in the following way (1). Suppose that there is given the number $0 < E \leq 1$. Let us construct such a system of hyperparallelepipeds that do not intersect $\{P_j\}$, each of them meeting the next basic condition:

$$\max_i \frac{M_j^i \cdot V_\xi}{V_j} \geq E > 0. \tag{2}$$

It must be stressed that here M_j^i is the number of vectors (objects) of the initial training set, which are in hyperparallelepiped P_j and belong to class Ω_i. And yet V_j is the volume of hyperparallelepiped P_j, V_ξ is the volume of the hyperpparallelepiped whose ribs are determined by vector $\xi = (\xi_1, \xi_2, \ldots, \xi_n)$, where:

$$\xi_l = \min_{i,j \in \{i_1, i_2, \ldots, i_m\}} \mid x_l^i - x_l^j \mid, i = 1, 2, \ldots, n. \tag{3}$$

Condition (2) determines the class number, whose objects belong to hyperparallelepiped P_j, and the total volume ξ neighbourhoods of these objects in relation to volume P_j, (not less than the specified figure E); ξ is a neighbourhood, in this case it is a hyperparallelepiped whose ribs are the shortest distance between orthogonal projections of objects of the training set on all coordinates of n-space $\mathbb{R}^n$ is the condition (3).

Let us to present a step-by-step description of the basic algorithm.

Step 1. Given a hyperparallelepiped P_0^0 which contains all vectors (objects) of the training set and whose faces are the planes described by the following equations:

$$\begin{cases} x_i = x_i^0, \\ x_i = x_i^1 \end{cases} \quad \text{here} (i = 1, 2, \ldots, n).$$

Step 2. Let us check condition (2). Provided it is met, the algorithm ends, otherwise step 3 is taken.

Step 3. We divide P_0^0 into two halves by the plane, parallel $x_1 = x_i^0$. We receive two hyperparallelepipeds P_1^1 and P_1^2. We do the checking of condition (2) for each of them. Those hyperparallelepipeds for which condition (2) is met, are remembered and are not taken into account in the following steps of the algorithm. If we deal with the situation:

$$\max_i \frac{M_j^i \cdot V_\xi}{V_j} = 0, \tag{4}$$

then the hyperparallelepiped is screened out or considered to be empty. Within $i+1^{st}$ step of the algorithm hyperparallelepipeds $P_{i_1}, P_{i_2}, \ldots, P_{i_t}$ obtained during the previous steps are divided by hyperplanes in the form: $x_j = x_j^0$. Those of the hyperparallelepipeds which meet condition (2) are remembered by the system and are not taken into account further, then those ones meeting condition (4) are screened out. Those that remain are provided at the input of the next step.

Step 4. Condition (2) is met for all hyperparallelepipeds which enter the current step.

To analyze the main characteristics of the algorithm we offer a number of propositions.

Proposition 1. *The hyperparallelepiped E-approximation algorithm of the training dataset converges with the arbitrary one E, $(0 < E \geq 1)$ and ends within the finite number of steps. It should be mentioned that the proof is obvious.*

Proposition 2. *Suppose, $\{P_j, j = 1, 2, \ldots, t\}$ is the result of the hyperparallelepiped E-approximation algorithm. Then $\{P_j\}$ is the recognition system which makes no more $m(1 - E)$ errors in response to the training set, where m is the number of training pairs of the training dataset.*

Proposition 3. *Suppose the E-approximation algorithm of the training set terminates after t-operations with hyperplanes and K_i is the number of those hyperparallelepipeds which are screened out at i step as such that do not contain any point (object) from the training dataset. Then the number of hyperparallelepipeds at the input of the E-approximation algorithm is equal to the number:*

$$S = 2^t \left(1 - \sum_{i=1}^t \frac{k_i}{2^i}\right).$$

Proof. The figure S is received from the expression:

$$(\ldots(((2 - K_1) \cdot 2 - K_2) \cdot 2 - K_3) \ldots) \cdot 2 - K_t.$$

Proposition 4. *Assume, $\bar{p}$ is the average number of objects of the training set which get into each of the hyperparallelepipeds of $\{P_i\}$ coverage, m is the size of the training dataset , n is the space dimension of the current application task. Then we have the compression of the initial training dataset by $\frac{n+1}{2n+1} \cdot \bar{p}$ times.*

Proof. An arbitrary hyperparallelepiped of n-dimensional space is uniquely determined by its diagonal. Then only $2n$ numbers are required to encode a hyperparallelepiped. At the same time only $(m \cdot (n+1))$ numbers are required to encode the training set. After approximation $\frac{m}{\bar{p}} \cdot (2n+1)$ numbers are necessary to memorize $\frac{m}{p}$ hyperparallelepipeds. Then the data compression ratio is:

$$\frac{m(n+1)}{\frac{m}{\bar{p}}(2n+1)} = \frac{n+1}{2n+1} \cdot \bar{p}.$$

Hence, the statement has been proved.

5   Experiment

Let us to compare the method proposed in the work with the similar hyperplane clipping method.

1. The main aim of the clipping methods is to construct some planes which optimally separate classes from each other. In this case only objects of the training set are divided, but what is meant is the division of the entire initial training set, which is unknown to us. On the contrary, in the E-approximation method, the limited nature of the training set is taken into account and the approximation is carried out with the specified E accuracy.
2. For the problem of finding the optimal clipping planes, a complex mathematical apparatus is used, which, when processing large amounts of data, is a serious drawback, even in modern conditions. The E-approximation method features mathematical simplicity: we use a hyperparallelepiped, which can be described by its one diagonal and its division into two parts by one of the planes which are parallel to its faces.
3. The clipping planes method often requires the a priori assumption of the possibility of separating the training set objects. It should be noted that in the proposed method, the objects of the training set can always be divided.
4. The result of the E-approximation algorithm makes it possible to easily construct a classification rule for objects which are recognized.
   It is clear that application of the hyperparallelepiped E-approximation method to the training set enables obtaining a set of $\{P_i\}$ hyperparallelepipeds. Each hyperparallelepied P_j contains the optimal sets of the objects of the training set which belong to class Ω. Then it is quite natural to assume that such a classification rule for recognizing objects can exist: Suppose that c is an arbitrary object provided at the input of the recognition system. If c is in any of the P_r hyperparallelepipeds, then c is recognized as an object of class Ω_{i_r}. Otherwise, the answer given is "unknown" (a classification error). A less stringent condition can be assumed: object c refers to class Ω_{i_r}, if $\min_i \rho(c, P_j) = \rho(c, P_{i_r}) < \rho_0$, where ρ is some metric in $\mathbb{R}^n$ and ρ_0 is a given number. The number ρ_0 can also be calculated as the shortest distance between the objects of the training set. It must be underscored that the

calculation of the estimates will be made not with the regard to the objects of the training set, but its E-approximation.

This, first of all, will greatly speed up the algorithm of recognizing, and, secondly, it will dump the computer ram memory (information system).

5. Admittedly, the recognition system can be built with the previously known accuracy E.
6. Using the method of hyperparallelepipeds different transformation can be easily made on the training dataset. In the case of images or scenes such transformations may be geometric transformations. In this way it is sufficient to have only the diagonals of hyperparallelepipeds to work the algorithms.
7. The hyperparallelepiped E-approximation algorithm takes into account the conditions under which it is possible to distinguish two different objects using the given training set.

5.1   The Issue of Modification of the Basic Algorithm

We propose modifications of the E-approximation algorithm, which make it possible to quickly approximate the training dataset obtaining fewer hyperparallelepipeds, to take into account the human factor and so on.

1. Choosing the best direction. In the proposed algorithm of hyperparallelepiped E- approximation of the training dataset, the choice of the direction of clipping by planes is made cyclically according to the coordinates, namely: parallelly to the planes specified by the equations $x_i = 0 (i = 1, 2, \ldots, n)$.
   We now propose dividing the hyperparallelepiped not one time, but n-possible times into halves. Then we have to choose the one method of clipping, in which the sum of the values shown on the left in the formula for each of the two obtained parts will be the largest:

$$\max_i \frac{M_{j_1}^i}{V_\xi} V_{j_1} + \max_i \frac{M_{j_2}^i}{V_\xi} V_{j_2}$$

2. The choice of the proportion of division. In the E-approximation algorithm the hyperparallelepipeds are divided into two halves. This is the simplest operation among other clippings, but the peculiarity of the current part of the training dataset is not taken into account. Hence, the suggestion is that the hyperparallelepiped P be divided into two (P_1 and P_2), so that the maximum number of the training dataset objects from one class of objects might appear in one of the hyperparallelepipeds.
3. The problem of the low threshold of approximation. This modification lies in the fact that along with condition (2) the condition with some value η is introduced:

$$\max_i \frac{M_j^i}{V_\xi} V_j < \eta. \tag{5}$$

Hyperparallelepipeds that do not meet condition (5) should be discarded. The main idea here is that the threshold η determines the minimum number of points in a given object, based on which it can be judged to what class the objects belong.

4. Specifying the smallest neighbourhood of objects of the training dataset. In
   the previous E- approximation of the training set the essential point is calculating of the smallest E-neighbourhood within which no two objects can be
   separated. In this case, information is taken only from the training dataset.

   Given the E-neighborhood a priori, we modify the initial algorithm in the
   following way. Based on common sense, it is necessary to assume that the
   E-neighborhood given a priori cannot be larger than that calculated in
   the hyperparallelepiped E-approximation algorithm, since in this case either
   redundancy of the training dataset or contradictions occur – two objects from
   the same E-neighborhood belong to different classes.
5. Limiting the number of algorithm steps. Given the processor time and computer memory are limited resources, it is appropriate to introduce the finite
   number of algorithm steps after which the approximation process is considered complete.
6. Interactive mode. It can be seen from Proposition 3 that the number of steps
   of the hyperparallelepiped E-approximation algorithm depends majorily on
   the initial clippings. However, a person within the first steps of the algorithm
   may turn out to be more efficient in this respect (the choice of clipping planes)
   than a rigid computer programme (script constraint). Therefore, it is advisable (especially it concerns the case of 2- and 3-dimensional space) to take
   the first steps of the algorithm in the interactive mode.
7. The use of the known recognition methods in the hyperparallelepiped E-
   approximation method. The E-approximation algorithm functions faster
   based on large homogeneous parts of the training dataset and much longer
   there where the objects of the training dataset are sufficiently scattered in
   space (discharge condition). Therefore, the following modification can be suggested.
   A certain number of algorithms of approximating (separating) the training
   dataset are fixed. The hyperparallelepiped E-approximation algorithm is the
   basis of the proposed algorithm. The algorithm scheme remains the same,
   only fixed methods are used at every step. If, as a result of their application, the separation of the dataset in the current hyperparallelepiped has
   taken place with the corresponding accuracy, then clipping this hyperparallelepiped terminates, otherwise the hyperparallelepiped E-approximation
   scheme is employed. Obviously, such an algorithm is more flexible than the
   previously proposed.

5.2   An Algorithmic Scheme of Approximation
by Hyperparallelepipeds

The idea behind this modification is again to approximate a certain class by the
sequence of hyperparallelepipeds. With regard to its algorithmic implementation,
it is noteworthy that it has become slightly complicated compared to the previous
geometric algorithms due to the additional checking of constructed hyperparallelepipeds for correctness (the impossibility to capture space of another class)

and the general scheme of constructing all possible hyperparallelepipeds in the fixed class.

Again, to simplify the introduction of the steps of the algorithm, let us suppose that the training dataset determines the partition into two classes H_0, H_1, and the task is to approximate class H_0 by hyperparallelepipeds, whose general scheme of constructing is similar to class H_1. It should be mentioned that by the definition, a hyperparallelepiped in n-dimensional space is a geometric set of points $P(x_1, x_2, \ldots, x_n)$ which satisfies the inequalities: $a_1 \leq x_1 \leq b_1$, $\ldots$, $a_n \leq x_n \leq b_n$, where $a_i < b_i$ are real numbers. To simplify the general scheme of the algorithm, we impose such an important condition that all the faces of the hyperparallelepipeds to be constructed will be parallel to the directional axes of coordinates, which will greatly simplify the general scheme of the algorithm.

In this case, an important peculiarity of the algorithm of hyperparallelepipeds in comparison with other geometric algorithms is that in order to store the constructed generalized feature (a hyperparallelepiped) it is sufficient to remember two opposite diagonal vertices, which by their economical efficiency can be compared to the algorithm of the hyperspheres (where in memory the center of the sphere and its radius were stored). That is, given the definition of a hyperparallelepiped, it is sufficient to remember the vertices $V_1(a_1, \ldots, a_n)$ and $V_2(b_1, \ldots, b_n)$ to store it, and so an arbitrary hyperparallalepiped in n-dimensional space is definitely determined by its diagonal and for its encoding (memorizing) $2n$ variables are sufficient, which immediately influences the complexity and efficiency of the scheme of the given algorithm.

Let us to describe the algorithm of approximation of the training dataset by means of the hyperparallelepiped sequence and consider its main implementation elements.

Step 1. The main fundamental problem that must be solved in the implementation of this algorithm is the problem of constructing all possible hyperparallelepipeds on a fixed set of points in order to approximate it efficiently. The simplest, but also the worst way to solve this problem is to directly go over all possible combinations of points (to construct hyperparallelepipeds). The second option is the initial processing of a set of points for the sake of determining a group of the so-called "boundary" points, for which one of n coordinates will be the largest or smallest compared to the same coordinate of all other points. It is clear that for any set, the number of such points will be equal to $2n$, that is, they will be points that actually lie on the top of that set (i. e., actually cover it).

Based on the identified group of points (boundary points) it is possible to construct a sequence of hyperparallelepipeds that approximate this set of points in the most efficient way. It is clear that all that has been said above will again be true with the compact arrangement of class domains in space, otherwise a brute-force search can be much more efficient.

In this algorithm of hyperparallelepipeds, the stage of determining the boundary points is carried out in two steps, that is, after constructing the first group and constructing all possible hyperparallelepipeds, the process of detecting the boundary points is repeated with the remaining points in the initial set. In fact, this resembles the process of the double peeling of the apple, when after peeling the skin we again, let us say, repeat the whole process of peeling.

Such double processing of the training dataset in order to construct a sequence of hyperparallelepipeds in some cases enables overcoming the problem of complex (connected) arrangement of domains of classes in space and reducing significantly the time of operating in comparison with a complete search of points (objects) in the set. We denote the set of all constructed hyperparallelepipeds on a fixed set of points (objects) of the training dataset by E.

Step 2. The calculation of the capacities of the found hyperparallelepipeds completely repeats a similar stage in the algorithms of hyperspheres and hyperellipses defining the capacity as the number of occurrences of the training dataset objects in the domain of the corresponding hyperparallelepiped []. Selecting from the set E the hyperparallelepiped, which has the highest capacity, it is necessary to test it for correctness – it means that no points of another class occur in its domain. If this step is successful, it will mean that the first element of the sequence of approximating hyperparallelepipeds (generalized features) has been found by us. In this case, first, changes must be introduced into the training dataset: all points (objects) that are absorbed by the found hyperparallelepiped are to be excluded from it, —secondly, the same should be done with it in the set E. Then it is necessary to return cyclically to the second step in order to construct the next generalized feature and continue this process unless the set E or all objects w_i of training dataset for which $f_R(w_i) = 0$ are exhausted, where f_R is a recognition function.

In the case when the highest-capacity hyperparallelepiped of the set E absorbs objects of class H_1 (that is, it will be rejected), then after its exclusion from E it is necessary to return to the second step again.

5.3   Model Selection

It should be noted that the proposed scheme of construction (generation) of GFs enables providing an effective mechanism for constructing tree-based models of classification, where the scheme of approximation by hyperparallelepipeds makes it possible to perform a stepwise coverage of the training dataset, to generate vertices of the classification tree model being built or to build a model with the predetermined accuracy. With this the task of estimating and selecting the model of the classification tree among a set of constructed classification trees (models based on other types of approximation) for a particular problem becomes relevant. Its solution is determined by a set of parameters (models), which are of decisive importance in relation to the current application task (the dataset of the initial training set).

It is fundamentally important to highlight their most important parameters (the dimension of feature space, the number of vertices, the number, capacity and the parametric complexity of the set of constructed GFs, etc.) and to determine their error with respect to the array of input data (the training dataset). It should be noted that in order to evaluate the constructed models (related structures of

GFs), it is important to consider the quality criteria of the obtained information models which depend on the error of the model, the power of the initial array data of the training set (the number of training pairs (the capacities of the training dataset and test set), and the dimension of feature space of the problem), the number of parameters of the model, and so on. It is evident that the critically important parameters of the constructed LCT model that need to be minimized are the total model errors respectively on the array data of the training dataset, test set (classification errors of all types) and for each of the classes of the initial partition which are determined by the initial condition (the training dataset) of the current application problem.

At the stage of optimization of the constructed models, the fundamental issue which remains is connected with reducing the complexity of the structure of classification trees – this refers to the number of attributes (elementary features, generalized features) in the tree structure, the total number of vertices of the ACT model and the total number of transitions in the structure of the classification tree), the parameters of the hardware resources of the information system. An important indicator of the quality of the constructed model in the form of a classification tree, taking into account the parameters of the structure of the LCT model is the general integral quality indicator in the following form:

$$Q_{Main} = \frac{U_{All}}{V_{All} A_{All} P_{All}} \cdot e^{-\frac{E_{N_S} + E_{T_S}}{M_{All}}} \tag{6}$$

For functional (6) the parameters E_{N_S}, E_{T_S} are the total number of errors of the classification tree model on the array data of the training and test sets, respectively M_{All} is the power of these two data arrays. Parameter U_{All} characterizes the number of vertices of the obtained ACT model with the resulting values f_R (recognition function), i.e. leaves of the classification tree or the values of the classes where they belong. Parameter V_{All} represents the total number of all types of vertices in the structure of the classification tree model, parameter A_{All} is the number of classification algorithms used in the classification tree model (ACT structure), parameter P_{All} is the number of transitions between vertices, tiers of the classification tree.

It must be admitted that this integral indicator of the quality of the model of the constructed classification tree can range from zero to one. The lower it is, the worse the quality of the constructed ACT is, and the higher the indicator is, the better the obtained model is.

6   Results and Discussion

It should be emphasized that based on the methods of classification trees, the principle of modularity, at Uzhhorod National University there was developed the software complex "Orion III" for generating autonomous recognition systems. The algorithm library of the system has 12 algorithms of recognition and classification (among which there are basic geometric algorithmic realizations – hypespheres, hyperellipses, hypercubes, hyperparallelepipeds and hyperplanes), among them proposed above in this work is the algorithmic realization of constructing GFs in the ACT structure.

A test example for checking the proposed approximation by a set of hyperparallelepipeds was a problem based on geological data (the problem of separating oil-bearing strata). For recognizing the objects there were employed 22 elementary features (the dimension of feature space of the problem) and the initial training set contains information about the objects of the two classes. Further, at the examination stage, there was constructed the classification model (ACT) which should ensure the efficient recognition of objects of the unknown classification with regard to these two classes. It must be stressed that the training set was automatically tested for correctness (searching for and removing the identical objects belonging to different classes – first-order errors) and the duplication of objects belonging to one class (coding errors, bad selection of feature space)).

The training set of this application problem contained 1250 objects (of which 756 objects were oil-bearing), and the efficiency of the constructed recognition system (the classification tree model) was evaluated with the help of the test set (objects of known classification) with the volume of 240 elements. It should be underscored that the data of the training and test sets were obtained on the basis of the geological exploration in the territory of Zakarpattia oblast from 2001 to 2011. Based on the training dataset, the ACT models with different-type GFs were constructed in the tree structure (only one geometric approximation algorithm was fixed for each of the classification trees when constructing the model).

Thus, a fragment of the main results (the comparison of ACT models based on different-type geometric approximations) presented above the experiments can be found in (Table 1). We stress that the constructed models of classification trees have provided the appropriate level of accuracy determined by the problem, speed of operation and the amount of working memory of the information system.

Table 1. Comparative table of classification tree models/methods

No	Logical tree structure synthesis method	Integral model quality index Q_{Main}	Total number of errors of the model at the TS and ST
1	ACT model based on hyperspheres algorithm	0,003451	0
2	ACT model based on hyperellipses algorithm	0,002832	1
3	ACT model based on hypercubes algorithm	0,002489	1
4	ACT model based on hyperparallelepipeds algorithm	0,003378	0

We underline that the proposed estimates of the quality of the model of classification trees (sets of GFs) fix the most important characteristics of algorithmic trees and can be used as a criterion for optimality in the procedure of constructing ACTs. It should be noted that approximation by means of hyper-parallelepipeds shown in the work was compared with other geometric methods of generating GFs and demonstrated an acceptable result in general with the main idea of ACTs being the approximation by means of a set of algorithms of the initial training set. The obtained ACT structure is characterized by its high universality and relatively compact structure of the model itself, but it requires some hardware costs for storing sets of generalized features of the initial evaluation of the quality (efficiency) of classification algorithms using the training dataset.

7   Conclusions

It should be highlighted that the research provides the solution to the problem of efficient generation of GFs in the methods of classification trees (ACTs) on the basis of the approximation of the training dataset by means of a set of hyperparallelepipeds in feature space of the problem. The novelty of the obtained results is that for the first time a simple method of constructing sets of GFs has been proposed based on the constructing the corresponding geometric objects within each step of generating a classification tree (ACT structures). Admittedly, at each step of branching (the stage of constructing GFs) a certain part (subset) of the training dataset is approximated, and the functional proposed in this work can be employed not only to evaluate the information content of separate GFs of the classification tree structure, but also to calculate the importance of sets of features (vertices, attributes of the classification tree) and their combinations, which in the long run enables the achievement of a more optimal structure of the synthesized algorithmic-logical classification tree using the initial training dataset. The paper also puts forth a set of general indicators (parameters of the classification tree) which enables the efficient representation of the general characteristics of the ACT model, and it can be used for selecting the most optimal classification tree structure out of the set of the constructed ones.

The practical value of the obtained results is that the proposed method of constructing sets of GFs for the ACT methods was implemented in the algorithm library of the universal software system "ORION III" (within a subset of other algorithms of geometric approximation) for solving different practical problems of classification (recognition) of array data of discrete objects. Note that the practical tests have confirmed the feasibility of the proposed ADC models based on the sets of appropriate UOs and software, which makes a recommendation on the use of this type of approximation and its software implementation for a wide range of applied problems of classification and recognition of discrete objects. of objects.

It should be underscored that the practical experiments confirmed the workability of the proposed ACT models on the basis of sets of the corresponding GFs and software, which enables producing a recommendation on the use of this type of approximation and its software implementation for a wide range of applied problems of classification and recognition of discrete objects.

The prospects for further research can be related to the development of methods of geometric approximation for algorithmic classification trees, efficient optimization of software implementations of the method of constructing ACTs as well as its practical testing with the help of solving many real world classification and recognition problems.

References

1. Alpaydin, E.: Introduction to Machine Learning. The MIT Press, Cambridge (2010)
2. Amit, Y., Wilder, K.: Joint induction of shape features and tree classifiers. IEEE Trans. Pattern Anal. Mach. Intell. **19**(11), 1300–1305 (1997). https://doi.org/10.1109/34.632990
3. Bodyanskiy, Y., Vynokurova, O., Setlak, G., Pliss, I.: Hybrid neuro-neo-fuzzy system and its adaptive learning algorithm. In: 2015 Xth International Scientific and Technical Conference "Computer Sciences and Information Technologies" (CSIT), pp. 111–114 (2015)
4. Breiman, L., Friedman, J., Olshen, R., Stone, C.: (1984)
5. Deng, Houtao, Runger, George, Tuv, Eugene: Bias of importance measures for multi-valued attributes and solutions. In: Honkela, Timo, Duch, Włodzisław, Girolami, Mark, Kaski, Samuel (eds.) ICANN 2011. LNCS, vol. 6792, pp. 293–300. Springer, Heidelberg (2011). https://doi.org/10.1007/978-3-642-21738-8_38
6. Hastie, Trevor, Tibshirani, Robert, Friedman, Jerome: The Elements of Statistical Learning. SSS. Springer, New York (2009). https://doi.org/10.1007/978-0-387-84858-7
7. Hyunjoong, K., Wei-Yin, L.: Classification trees with unbiased multiway splits. J. Am. Stat. Assoc. **96**(454), 589–604 (2001). https://doi.org/10.1198/016214501753168271
8. Kaminski, B., Jakubczyk, M., Szufel, P.: A framework for sensitivity analysis of decision trees. Cent. Eur. J. Oper. Res. **26**(1), 135–159 (2018). https://doi.org/10.1007/s10100-017-0479-6
9. Karimi, K., Hamilton, H.: Generation and interpretation of temporal decision rules. Int. J. Comput. Inf. Syst. Ind. Manag. Appl. **3**, 314–323 (2011)
10. Koskimaki, H., Juutilainen, I., Laurinen, P., Roning, J.: Two-level clustering approach to training data instance selection: a case study for the steel industry. In: 2008 IEEE International Joint Conference on Neural Networks (IEEE World Congress on Computational Intelligence), pp. 3044–3049 (2008)
11. Kotsiantis, S.: Supervised machine learning: a review of classification techniques. Informatica. Int. J. Comput. Inform. **31**(3), 249–268 (2007)
12. Laver, V., Povkhan, I.: The algorithms for constructing a logical tree of classification in pattern recognition problems. In: Scientific Notes of the Tauride National University. Series: Technical Sciences 4, pp. 100–106 (2019)
13. Lupei, M., Mitsa, A., Repariuk, V., Sharkan, V.: Identification of authorship of Ukrainian-language texts of journalistic style using neural networks. East.-Eur. J. Enterp. Technol. **1**, 30–36 (2020). https://doi.org/10.15587/1729-4061.2020.195041
14. Lopez de Mantaras, R.: A distance-based attribute selection measure for decision tree induction. Mach. Learn. 6, 81–92 (1991). https://doi.org/10.1023/A:1022694001379

15. Mingers, J.: An empirical comparison of selection measures for decision-tree induction. Mach. Learn. **3**(4), 319–342 (1989). https://doi.org/10.1007/BF00116837
16. Miyakawa, M.: Criteria for selecting a variable in the construction of efficient decision trees. Trans. Comput. **38**(1), 130–141 (1989). https://doi.org/10.1109/12.8736
17. Painsky, A., Rosset, S.: Cross-validated variable selection in tree-based methods improves predictive performance. IEEE Trans. Pattern Anal. Mach. Intell. **39**, 2142–2153 (2017)
18. Povhan, I.: Designing of recognition system of discrete objects. In: IEEE First International Conference on Data Stream Mining and Processing (DSMP), Lviv, Ukraine, pp. 226—231 (2016)
19. Povhan, I.: General scheme for constructing the most complex logical tree of classification in pattern recognition discrete objects. In: Electronics and information technologies. Collection of Scientific Papers, vol. 11, pp. 112–117. Ivan Franko National University of Lviv (2019). https://doi.org/10.30970/eli.11.7
20. Povkhan, I.: Features of synthesis of generalized features in the construction of recognition systems using the logical tree method. In: Proceeding of the International Scientific and Practical Conference "Information Technologies and Computer Modeling ITKM-2019", pp. 169–174 (2019)
21. Quinlan, J.: Induction of decision trees. Mach. Learn. **1**(1), 81–106 (1986). https://doi.org/10.1023/A:1022643204877
22. Srikant, R., Agrawal, R.: Mining generalized association rules. In: Proceedings of the 21th International Conference on Very Large Data Bases, pp. 407—419. Morgan Kaufmann Publishers Inc. (1995)
23. Strobl, C., Boulesteix, A.L., Augustin, T.: Unbiased split selection for classification trees based on the gini index. Comput. Stat. Data Anal. **52**, 483–501 (2007). https://doi.org/10.1016/j.csda.2006.12.030
24. Subbotin, S.: Methods of sampling based on exhaustive and evolutionary search. Autom. Control Comput. Sci. **47**, 113–121 (2013)
25. Subbotin, S.: The neuro-fuzzy network synthesis and simplification on precedents in problems of diagnosis and pattern recognition. Opt. Mem. Neural Notw. **22**, 97–103 (2013)
26. Subbotin, Sergey A., Oliinyk, Andrii A.: The dimensionality reduction methods based on computational intelligence in problems of object classification and diagnosis. In: Szewczyk, Roman, Kaliczyńska, Małgorzata (eds.) SCIT 2016. AISC, vol. 543, pp. 11–19. Springer, Cham (2017). https://doi.org/10.1007/978-3-319-48923-0_2
27. Subbotin, S.: Methods and characteristics of localitypreserving transformations in the problems of computational intelligence. Radio Electron. Comput. Sci. Control **1**, 120–128 (2014)
28. Subbotin, S.: Construction of decision trees for the case of low-information features. Radio Electron. Comput. Sci. Control **1**, 121–130 (2019)
29. Vasilenko, Y., Povkhan, I.: Approximation of the training. Sci. J. 9–17 (1998). UzhIIEL
30. Vasilenko, Y., Vasilenko, E., Povkhan, I.: Defining the concept of a feature in pattern recognition theory. Artif. Intell. **4**, 512–517 (2002)
31. Vasilenko, Y., Vasilenko, E., Povkhan, I.: Branched feature selection method in mathematical modeling of multi-level image recognition systems. Artif. Intell. **7**, 246–249 (2003)
32. Vasilenko, Y., Vasilenko, E., Povkhan, I.: Conceptual basis of image recognition systems based on the branched feature selection method. Eur. J. Enterp. Technol. **7**(1), 13–15 (2004)

Technique of Metals Strength Properties Diagnostics Based on the Complex Use of Fuzzy Inference System and Hybrid Neural Network

Sergii Babichev[1,2]([✉]) [iD], Bohdan Durnyak[3] [iD], Oleksandr Sharko[4] [iD],
and Artem Sharko[5] [iD]

[1] Jan Evangelista Purkyně University in Ústí nad Labem,
Ústí nad Labem, Czech Republic
sergii.babichev@ujep.cz
[2] Kherson State University, Kherson, Ukraine
[3] Ukrainian Academy of Printing, Lviv, Ukraine
durnyak@uad.lviv.ua
[4] Kherson State Maritime Academy, Kherson, Ukraine
avsharko@ukr.net
[5] Kherson National Technical University, Kherson, Ukraine
sharko_artem@ukr.net

Abstract. The results of the research concerning development of the technique of metals strength properties diagnostics using combination of the methods of non-destructive control based on the complex use of fuzzy inference system and hybrid neural network are presented in the paper. The acoustic non-destructive control method, the electromagnetic method and hardness control were used as the control methods within the framework of the proposed technique. The selection of the optimal combination of the methods was performed using fuzzy inference system, in which, the final solution was taken applying Harrington desirability function. The metal strength properties were determined using hybrid neural network the basis of which are fuzzy neurons. The simulation results with the use of samples of Y8 steel have shown that the combination of acoustic and electromegnetic methods of non-destructive testing is an optimal in terms of maximum value of heneral Harrington desiribility index and the hybrid neural network with two layers of neurons and triangular membership functions with combine algorithm of network training is an optimal one in terms of relative error of metals strength properties evaluation. To our mind, the proposed technique may allow us to increase the exactness of metals strength properties determination when the non-destructive methods of control are applied.

Keywords: Non-destructive control · Fuzzy inference system · Harrington desirability function · Metals strength properties · Hybrid neural network

© Springer Nature Switzerland AG 2020
S. Babichev et al. (Eds.): DSMP 2020, CCIS 1158, pp. 114–126, 2020.
https://doi.org/10.1007/978-3-030-61656-4_7

1 Introduction

The improvement of technological processes for the metal products making increases the requirements for the process of metals quality control during its production. Moreover, during exploitation process, the strength characteristics of the metal can be changed. This fact can lead to cracks appearing and, as a result, product destruction. The use of bursting tests for each group of products is not effective due to high economic costs on the one hand and the high labor intensity on the other hand. For this reason, at the stage of the metal products making, the non-destructive methods of technical diagnostics of the metals strength properties are used such as acoustic method [18,22,25], electro-magnetic method [14,22], X-ray method [5,8,23], optical method [8,15], etc.

Each of the methods has its advantages and shortcoming and decision making based on the use of a single method is not reasonable due to high probability of making incorrect decision. The use of a combination of non-destructive testing methods increases the testing reliability, however, the applying this approach leads to a sharp increasing the costs of the experiment performing and processing the obtained results. Moreover, in this case, it is appeared the problem of choice of the used methods optimal combination. The solution of this problem can be achieved on the basis of the use of modern techniques of complex data processing which are used successfully nowadays in various fields of artificial intelligence [9, 12,16,17]. Hereinbefore described indicates the relevance of the solved problem.

In this research, we propose the solution of this problem based on the complex use of fuzzy inference system and hybrid neural network. The use of fuzzy inference system allows us to select the optimal combination of non-destructive technical diagnostics methods. The hybrid neural network is applied at the final step to evaluate the metal strength properties using results of selected non-destructive technical diagnostics methods.

2 Problem Statement

Within the framework of our research, the initial data is presented as a subset of testing products. Each of the products was tested by various methods of non-destructive testing, after which, this sample was exposed to brushing tests to determine the required strength characteristics. Thus, the initial matrix of experimental data was represented as the results of testing by various methods of non-destructive control including the results of bursting tests at the last stage of the experiment performing for each of the investigated samples.

Evaluating strength characteristics by non-destructive testing methods assumes the following:

- development of stepwise procedure of the experimental data processing based on the use of both the fuzzy inference system for selection of optimal combination of the non-destructive testing methods and hybrid neural network to evaluate the metal strength properties;

- setup of fuzzy inference system. Choice of the membership functions for input and output variables, choice of fuzzy inference algorithm, formation of fuzzy rules agreed between input variables and output parameter;
- setup of hybrid neural network, choice of both the neurons membership functions and neural network training algorithm.

These tasks are solved within the framework of our research.

3 Literature Review

Many works are devoted to testing strength properties of various types of materials nowadays. So, in [11], the authors presents the results of the research concerning investigation and forecasting of strength properties of optimized recycled rubber concrete. In this work, the design of optimized rubber concrete composite containing silica fume and zeolite was investigated using destructive and non-destructive testing methods. The authors carried out the comprehensive comparative simulation using various predictive models based on regressions and machine-learning (ML) techniques.

The paper [19] dedicated to the development of technique of estimation of mechanical properties of both two-stage concrete and conventional concrete using non-destructive testing methods. The authors performed the uniaxial compression, tensile strength, and point load tests as destructive testing. As non-destructive testing, Schmidt hammer and ultrasonic pulse velocity tests were carried out during the experiment performing. As the results of the simulation, It was concluded that non-destructive testing of engineering materials, including concrete, considerably increases the speed and decreases the cost of evaluating the mechanical properties.

In [5, 8, 14, 18, 22, 23, 25] the authors considered applying the acoustic, electro-magnetic and X-ray non-destructive testing methods in various fields of scientific research. The analysis of the authors' research allows concluding that each of the method has its advantages and shortcoming, and complex use of them can decrease the testing error.

In [4, 20] the authors proposed the system of metals strength properties testing based on complex use of various non-destructive testing methods. They proposed the stepwise testing procedure with removing samples which are identified as defective product in terms of one of the used methods. The main disadvantage of the proposed technique is the high labor intensity of experimental research and processing of the results.

The issues concerning applying the fuzzy inference system in various fields of decision making are described in [1, 13, 24]. An analysis of the results presented by the authors shows that the successful implementation of models based on fuzzy logic depends on the correct setting of the model, which includes the choice of membership functions for input and output parameters, the choice of a fuzzy inference algorithm and the formation of a knowledge database used during the fuzzy inference procedure.

Papers [2,6,10,21] describe machine learning techniques based on hybrid neural networks which are widely used in various areas of scientific research nowadays. Within the framework of our research, we apply the hybrid neural network to determine the strength properties of metal at final step of the data processing. The main problem in this case consist of optimizing both the network structure and parameters including network training algorithm.

The objective of the paper is the development of technique of metals strength properties evaluation using non-destructive testing methods based on the complex use of fuzzy inference system and hybrid neural network.

4   Materials and Methods

Figure 1 shows the structure block-chart of technique of the hybrid model optimal parameters determination.

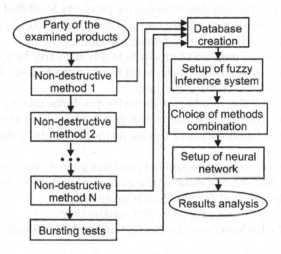

Fig. 1. A structural block-chart of technique of the hybrid model optimal parameters determination

Its implementation assumes the following. In beginning, formation of a set of products from a party of examined metal for subsequent control. At the second step, sequential control of the obtained products by each of the non-destructive testing methods with bursting tests of these products at the last step of this procedure implementation. Then, formation of a database containing information concerning the results of non-destructive testing and bursting tests for each of the examined products. The next step is to compare the number of defective samples with reduced strength properties (d) with the maximum allowable number of defective samples for a given type of metal (c) according to the relevant standards with following calculation of errors of both the first and the second kinds for each of the used non-descructive testing methods. Both the pass of defective products and the classification of non-defective products as defective ones are a disturbance of the normal testing regime determining the control quality. The first of these distributions is directly related to the operational dependability of manufactured products, expressing the "consumer's risk". The second distribution is associated with additional material costs, leading to an increase of the control cost and expressing the "supplier's risk".

When assessing the desirability of testing by a combination of non-destructive testing methods, the object of research is testing methods, which are considered as the factors affecting the quality of the assessment. Each of the factors can take two values corresponding to the presence $(+)$ or absence $(-)$ of this method during the control result assessing. The effectiveness of the current combination of testing methods is determined by the optimization parameters, which are a reaction (response) to the impact of the current combination of factors. Within the framework of the proposed technique, we proposed the following optimization parameters:

- Y_1 is the ratio of the number of defective products identified by appropriate combination of testing methods to the total number of defective products identified by all non-destructive testing methods;
- Y_2 is the ratio of the number of products falsely defective by appropriate combination of testing methods to the total number of products falsely defective by all non-destructive testing methods;
- Y_3 is the ratio of the number of defective products missed by appropriate combination of testing methods to the number of missed defective products identified by the combination of testing methods for which this number is the maximal one;
- Y_4 is the error of each of the applied combinations of non-destructive testing methods. In this case, the error of the combination of methods is taken to be the error of the method for which it is maximal one;
- Y_5 is the level of testing procedure automatization;
- Y_6 is the ability to determine the material properties, averaged over the entire product.

For a quantitative assessment of the parameters Y_5 and Y_6, we used a rank approach, while the value of the parameter Y_5 was varied from 0 to 5, and the parameter Y_6 from 0 to 4. To evaluate the general response of the model, we used the Harrington desirability function, which is used to solve multicriterial tasks in various areas of scientific research nowadays [3]. Here, the numbers correspond to some points on the curve (Fig. 2) [7] defined by the equation:

$$d = exp[-exp(-Y)]$$

Desirability index values which are plotted on the ordinate axes are varied within the range from 0 to 1. The abscissa axes shows the response values presented in a conditional scale. A value of 0 on this axis corresponds to a desirability of 0.37. The choice of this point is determined by the fact that it is an bending point, which creates convenience during the calculation procedure. Standard scores on the desirability scale are presented in Table 1.

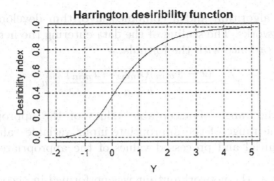

Fig. 2. An example of Harrington desirability function

Table 1. Standard scores on the desirability scale

Values of Desirability index	Quality of procedure
0,80 ... 1,00	Very good
0,63 ... 0,80	Good
0,37 ... 0,63	Satisfactory
0,20 ... 0,37	Bad
0,00 ... 0,20	Very bad

Within the framework of our research, we used the values of Harrington desirability index to create the fuzzy rules which are the basis of fuzzy inference system. To determine the fuzzy inference system optimal parameters, we carried out the simulation process using Mamdani and Sugeno fuzzy inference algorithms. As the membership functions for input parameters we used gaussian, double gaussian and triangular membership functions. To assess the quality of the fuzzy inference system operation, the value of the general desirability index was determined both as a result of the defuzzification process performing and algebraically as the geometric mean of the particular desirabilities d_i:

$$D = \sqrt[n]{\prod_{i=1}^{n} d_i}$$

An optimal combination of the non-destructive testing methods corresponds to a smaller deviation of the result of the fuzzy inference system operation from algebraic calculations.

The next stage of the proposed technique implementation involves determining the examined samples strength characteristics by a hybrid neural network, which contains fuzzy neurons with corresponding membership functions. To determine the optimal parameters of the neural network, the simulation procedure was carried out using Gaussian, triangular, trapezoidal, and Pi membership functions. The neuron weights were adjusted using both an error backpropagation algorithm and a combined algorithm developed for training hybrid neural networks. The scaling of the data entering the network input was carried out in accordance with the formula:

$$x' = \frac{(x - x_{min})(x_{max} - x_{min})}{b - a} + a \tag{1}$$

where: $[a, b]$ is the range of acceptable values of the appropriate variable; $[x_{min}, x_{max}]$ is the range of the appropriate input variable values variation; x and x' are the initial and processed values of the appropriate input variable respectively.

Data recovery at the network output was performed in accordance with the reverse formula:

$$y = \frac{(y' - a)(y_{max} - y_{min})}{b - a} + y_{min} \tag{2}$$

An effectiveness of the neural network operation was assessed by the relative error in determining the ultimate strength:

$$\varepsilon = \frac{|\sigma - \sigma_{exp}|}{\sigma_{exp}} \tag{3}$$

5   Experiment, Results and Discussion

Approbation of the proposed technique was carried out on the example of testing the ultimate strength of products made of Y8A steel in accordance with the experiment, the results of which are presented in [4,20]. Electromagnetic, acoustic and hardness testing were selected as non-destructive testing methods during the simulation process. This choice is determined by the fact that these methods provide the best correlation of the measured parameters with the ultimate strength. The tests were carried out on cylindrical specimens 90 mm long and 22 mm in diameter. All samples were sequentially controlled by the selected testing methods with determining the ultimate strength by each of the used methods. At the last stage, the products were exposed to bursting tests. The matrix of the full factor experiment, which implements all possible combinations of the factors and which contains the values of all parameters, is presented in Table 2.

The selected parameter values which correspond to the basic marks on the desirability scale are presented in Table 3. Analysis of the data in Table 3 allowed us to formulate a set of fuzzy rules which are the basis of the fuzzy inference system:

Rule 1: if Y1 = 0.98 and Y2 = 0.2 and y3 = 0.1 and Y4 = 0.3 and Y5 = 4 and Y6 = 3, when D = 0.8;

Rule 2: if Y1 = 0.89 and Y2 = 0.39 and y3 = 0.38 and Y4 = 0.64 and Y5 = 2.54 and Y6 = 3, when D = 0.63;

Rule 3: if Y1 = 0.8 and Y2 = 0.6 and y3 = 0.7 and Y4 = 0.1 and Y5 = 1 and Y6 = 1, when D = 0.37;

Table 2. Matrix of a full factor experiment to determine the strength properties of steel by non-destructive testing methods

Number	Factors			Parameters					
	X1	X2	X3	Y1, %	Y2, %	Y3, %	Y4, MPa	Y5, rank	Y6, rank
1	+	+	+	100	100	100	80	5	4
2	−	+	+	91	58	50	80	3	2
3	+	−	+	89	54	58	70	2	2
4	−	−	+	82	42	100	50	0	0
5	+	+	−	98	32	16	80	5	4
6	−	+	−	89	23	58	80	3	2
7	+	−	−	92	29	42	70	2	2

Table 3. Parameter values in the basic points of the Harrington desirability function

Optimization parameters	Parameter values in basic points of the desirability function			
	0.2	0.37	0.63	0.80
Y1, %	74	80	89	98
Y2, %	73	60	39	20
Y3, %	89	70	38	10
Y4, *100 MPa	1.2	1	0.64	0.3
Y5, rank	0.15	1	2.54	4
Y6, rank	0.35	1	2	3

Rule 1: if Y1 = 0.74 and Y2 = 0.73 and y3 = 0.89 and Y4 = 1.2 and Y5 = 0.15 and Y6 = 0.35, when D = 0.2.

Table 4 presents the result of the fuzzy inference system operation including the algebraic calculation of the general desirability index.

The analysis of the obtained results has shown that the highest value of the general desirability index is achieved when the combination of acoustic and electromagnetic methods of non-destructive testing and gaussian membership function for both the input and output parameters is applied. In this case, the values of general desirability index are equal to 0.702, 0.703 and 0.985 in the case of the use of algebraical calculation, Mamdani and Sugeno fuzzy inference algorithms respectively. The expediency of using a combination of acoustic and electromagnetic methods of non-destructive testing is determined by the physical nature of these methods. Each of the methods is based on the analysis of the average acoustic and electromagnetic characteristics of the entire metal as a whole and, therefore, is more stable in comparison with the method of determining the hardness from the indentation of the indenter.

Table 4. Simulation results concerning assessment of the generalized desirability index values by both the fuzzy inference system and the algebraically

Number	Factors			Gauss		Gauss2		Gauss+Tri		Algebraically
	X1	X2	X3	Mamdani	Sugeno	Mamdani	Sugeno	Mamdani	Sugeno	
1	+	+	+	0.504	0.667	0.500	0.665	0.500	0.572	0.603
2	−	+	+	0.619	0.666	0.626	0.663	0.627	0.613	0.642
3	+	−	+	0.591	0.651	0.565	0.668	0.533	0.592	0.593
4	−	−	+	0.383	0.211	0.500	0.634	0.500	0.588	0.575
5	+	+	−	**0.703**	**0.985**	0.500	0.637	0.500	0.611	**0.702**
6	−	+	−	0.619	0.667	0.625	0.658	0.627	0.614	0.619
7	+	−	−	0.627	0.667	0.628	0.661	0.602	0.609	0.623

Gauss - gaussian functions for both the input and output variables; Gauss2 - double gaussian functions for both the input and output variables; Gauss+Tri - gaussian functions for input and triangular for output variables

Figure 3 shows the results of hybrid neural network operation of determining the relative error in assessing the ultimate strength of steel in comparison with the values obtained during bursting tests. In accordance with technique described in the Sect. 2, we used to train the hybrid neural network Mamdani inference algorithm with triangular (tri), trapezoidal (trap), Pi (Pi) and gaussian (gauss) membership functions. The adjustment of the neurons weights of the network was carried out using both a hybrid algorithm (hybrid) and an error backpropagation algorithm (backpropagation).

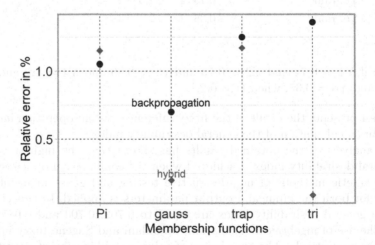

Fig. 3. Results of hybrid neural network operation

As it can be seen from Fig. 3, the smallest error in determining the hardness strength of U8A steel is achieved using triangular membership functions and a hybrid algorithm for adjusting the weights of neurons in the network.

The conducted research has allowed us to improve the version of the expert system of metals strength properties technical diagnostics, described in [4, 20] by automatizing the experimental data processing procedure. The structure block chart of the improved version is shown in Fig. 4. Practical implementation of this system assumes the following stages:

1. formation of a subset of products n_1 from a party of received metal;
2. sequential control of samples by non-destructive testing methods selected using a fuzzy inference system;
3. neural network control with the determination of the strength characteristics of the examined products. Analysis of the obtained results;
4. comparison of the number of defective products d_1 with reduced strength properties with the permissible value c_1 according to the technical condition (acceptance number). The party of products is accepted if the following condition is true: $d_1 \leq c_1$;
5. if the condition $d_1 \geq c_1$ is true, then, another subset n_2 is created and passed to burst testing. In this case, the decisive condition for the acceptance of all party of the products is the fulfillment of the condition: $d_2 \leq c_2$.

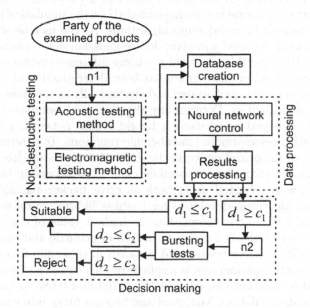

Fig. 4. A structural block-chart of expert system of metals strength properties technical diagnostics

To our mind, the implementation of the proposed technique for determining the strength properties of metals by non-destructive methods of technical diagnostics can allow us to increase both the dependability and efficiency of testing due to a reasonable choice of testing methods on the one hand and automatization of the experimental data processing and the determination of metals strength properties on the other hand.

6   Conclusions

The results of the research concerning development of hybrid model of metal strength properties evaluation by non-destructive testing methods based on the complex use of fuzzy inference system and hybrid neural network have been presented. The products from steel Y8A have been used within the framework of experimental research. In accordance with proposed stepwise procedure of the experiment performing and obtained results processing, sequential control of the examined products by acoustic, electromagnetic and hardness non-destructive testing methods with bursting tests of these products at the last step has been performed. It has allowed us to form a matrix of complete factor experiments, where factors are the used non-destructive testing methods. The analysis of the obtained results has allowed us to formulate a set of fuzzy rules which are the basis of the fuzzy inference system. To evaluate the general response of the model, we have used the Harrington desirability function. To determine the fuzzy inference system optimal parameters, we have carried out the simulation process using Mamdani and Sugeno fuzzy inference algorithms. As the membership functions for input parameters we used gaussian, double gaussian and triangular membership functions. To assess the quality of the fuzzy inference system operation, the value of the general desirability index has been determined both as a result of the defuzzification process performing and algebraically as the geometric mean of the particular desirabilities. Determining the examined samples strength characteristics has been performed using a hybrid neural network, which contains fuzzy neurons with corresponding membership functions. To determine the optimal parameters of the neural network, the simulation procedure has been carried out using Gaussian, triangular, trapezoidal, and Pi membership functions. The neuron weights were adjusted using both an error backpropagation algorithm and a combined algorithm developed for training hybrid neural networks. The results of the simulation has shown that the highest value of the general desirability index is achieved when the combination of acoustic and electromagnetic methods of non-destructive testing and gaussian membership function for both the input and output parameters is applied. In this case, the values of general desirability index have been equal to 0.702, 0.703 and 0.985 in the case of the use of algebraical calculation, Mamdani and Sugeno fuzzy inference algorithms respectively. The result of the hybrin neural network operation has shown that the smallest error in determining the hardness strength of U8A steel is achieved using triangular membership functions and a hybrid algorithm for adjusting the weights of neurons in the network.

The conducted research has allowed us to propose the improved version of the expert system of metals strength properties technical diagnostics, which is presented as a structural block chart. To our mind, the implementation of the proposed technique for determining the strength properties of metals by nondestructive methods of technical diagnostics can allow us to increase both the dependability and efficiency of testing due to a reasonable choice of testing methods on the one hand and automatization of the experimental data processing and the determination of metals strength properties on the other hand.

References

1. Alakhras, M., Oussalah, M., Hussein, M.: A survey of fuzzy logic in wireless localization. EURASIP J. Wirel. Commun. Netw. 1, art. no. 89 (2020). https://doi.org/10.1186/s13638-020-01703-7
2. Ardjmand, E., Ghalehkhondabi, I., et al.: A hybrid artificial neural network, genetic algorithm and column generation heuristic for minimizing makespan in manual order picking operations. Expert Syst. Appl. **159**, 113566 (2020). https://doi.org/10.1016/j.eswa.2020.113566
3. Babichev, S., Lytvynenko, V., Skvor, J., Fiser, J.: Model of the objective clustering inductive technology of gene expression profiles based on SOTA and DBSCAN clustering algorithms. In: Shakhovska, N., Stepashko, V. (eds.) CSIT 2017. AISC, vol. 689, pp. 21–39. Springer, Cham (2018). https://doi.org/10.1007/978-3-319-70581-1_2
4. Buhay, N., Lebedev, A., Sharko, A.: Comprehensive control of 12KH1MF steel during technical diagnostics of power equipment metals. Russ. J. Nondestr. Test. **5**, 47–53 (1992)
5. Ceballos-Francisco, D., García-Carrillo, N., Cuesta, A., Esteban, M.: Radiological characterization of gilthead seabream (Sparus aurata) fat by x-ray microcomputed tomography. Sci. Rep. 10(1), art. no. 10527 (2020). https://doi.org/10.1038/s41598-020-67435-2
6. Ghiasi, B., Sheikhian, H., Zeynolabedin, A., Niksokhan, M.: Granular computing-neural network model for prediction of longitudinal dispersion coefficients in rivers. Water Sci. Technolol. **80**(10), 1880–1892 (2020). https://doi.org/10.2166/wst.2020.006
7. Harrington, J.: The desirability function. Ind. Qual. Control **21**(8), 494–498 (1965)
8. Imashuku, S., Wagatsuma, K.: X-ray-excited optical luminescence imaging for on-site analysis of alumina scale. Oxid. Met. **94**(1), 27–36 (2020). https://doi.org/10.1007/s11085-020-09976-5
9. Izonin, I., Kryvinska, N., Vitynskyi, P., Tkachenko, R., Zub, K.: GRNN approach towards missing data recovery between IoT systems. In: Barolli, L., Nishino, H., Miwa, H. (eds.) INCoS 2019. AISC, vol. 1035, pp. 445–453. Springer, Cham (2020). https://doi.org/10.1007/978-3-030-29035-1_43
10. Jain, D., Kumar, A., Sharma, V.: Tweet recommender model using adaptive neuro-fuzzy inference system. Future Gener. Comput. Syst. **112**, 996–1009 (2020). https://doi.org/10.1016/j.future.2020.04.001
11. Jalal, M., Grasley, Z., Gurganus, C., Bullard, J.: Experimental investigation and comparative machine-learning prediction of strength behavior of optimized recycled rubber concrete. Constr. Build. Mater. **256**, 119478 (2020)
12. Kanishcheva, O., Vysotska, V., Chyrun, L., Gozhyj, A.: Method of integration and content management of the information resources network. In: Shakhovska, N., Stepashko, V. (eds.) CSIT 2017. AISC, vol. 689, pp. 204–216. Springer, Cham (2018). https://doi.org/10.1007/978-3-319-70581-1_14

13. Kluska, J.: Adaptive fuzzy control of state-feedback time-delay systems with uncertain parameters. Inf. Sci. **540**, 202–220 (2020). https://doi.org/10.1016/j.ins.2020.06.015

14. Lefebvre, T., et al.: Prospective comparison of transient, point shear wave, and magnetic resonance elastography for staging liver fibrosis. Eur. Radiol. **29**(12), 6477–6488 (2019). https://doi.org/10.1007/s00330-019-06331-4

15. Liang, J., Gu, X.: Development and application of a non-destructive pavement testing system based on linear structured light three-dimensional measurement. Constr. Build. Mater. **260**, 119919 (2020)

16. Mishchuk, O., Tkachenko, R., Izonin, I.: Missing data imputation through SGTM neural-like structure for environmental monitoring tasks. In: Hu, Z., Petoukhov, S., Dychka, I., He, M. (eds.) ICCSEEA 2019. AISC, vol. 938, pp. 142–151. Springer, Cham (2020). https://doi.org/10.1007/978-3-030-16621-2_13

17. Naum, O., Chyrun, L., Vysotska, V., Kanishcheva, O.: Intellectual system design for content formation. In: Proceedings of the 12th International Scientific and Technical Conference on Computer Sciences and Information Technologies, CSIT 2017, vol. 1, pp. 131–138. Institute of Electrical and Electronics Engineers Inc. (2017). https://doi.org/10.1109/STC-CSIT.2017.8098753

18. Pasternak, M., Jasek, K., Grabka, M.: Surface acoustic waves application for gas leakage detection. Diagnostyka **21**(1), 35–39 (2020). https://doi.org/10.29354/diag/116078

19. Rajabi, A., Omidi Moaf, F., Abdelgader, H.: Evaluation of mechanical properties of two-stage concrete and conventional concrete using nondestructive tests. J. Mater. Civil Eng. 32(7), art. no. 04020185 (2020). https://doi.org/10.1061/(ASCE)MT.1943-5533.0003247

20. Sharko, A., Buhay, N.: System for complex non-destructive testing of metals mechanical properties. Reliab. Durab. Mach. Struct. **8**, 104–106 (1985)

21. Shirgan, S.S., Bombale, U.L.: Hybrid neural network based wideband spectrum behavior sensing predictor for cognitive radio application. Sens. Imaging **21**(1), 1–21 (2020). https://doi.org/10.1007/s11220-020-00293-4

22. Sutin, A., Salloum, H.: Interaction of acoustic and EM waves in NDE and medical applications. In: Proceedings of the 26th International Congress on Sound and Vibration, ICSV 2019 (2019)

23. Vásárhelyi, L., Kónya, Z., Kukovecz, A., Vajtai, R.: Microcomputed tomography-based characterization of advanced materials: a review. Mater. Today Adv. 8, art. no. 100084 (2020). https://doi.org/10.1016/j.mtadv.2020.100084

24. Zadeh, L.A., Abbasov, A.M., Shahbazova, S.N.: Fuzzy-based techniques in human-like processing of social network data. Int. J. Uncertainty Fuzziness Knowl.-Based Syst. **23**, 14–17 (2015)

25. Łyżwa, P., Kłaczyński, M., Kazana, P.: Vibroacoustic methods of imaging in selected temporomandibular joint disorders during movement. Diagnostyka **19**(3), 109–117 (2018). https://doi.org/10.29354/diag/94264

Noise-Resistant Non-equidistant Data Conversion

Oleg Riznyk$^{(\boxtimes)}$, Olga Myaus , Yurii Kynash , Roman Martsyshyn ,
and Yuliya Miyushkovych

Lviv Polytechnic National University, Lviv, Ukraine
riznykoleg@gmail.com, myausolya2016@gmail.com, yuk.itvs@gmail.com,
mrs.nulp@gmail.com, jmiyushk@gmail.com

Abstract. The purpose of this article is to investigate and improve the algorithm for the syn-thesis of noise-resistant code-sequences. To achieve this goal, the following tasks have been solved: investigation of algorithms for the synthesis of noise-resistant code-sequences has been carried out; investigation and implementation in practice of the algorithm for the synthesis of noise-resistant code-sequences have been carried out; investigation and implementation in practice of the algorithm for finding and correcting errors (in the obtained noise-resistant code-sequences). The problem of improving the characteristics of noise-resistant code-sequences was solved by using ideal ring bundles.

Keywords: Noise-resistant code-sequence · Ideal ring bundle · Non-equidistant code-sequence component

1 Introduction

Technology for information noise immunity are becoming more and more important. This is due to the ever-increasing volume of information that is accumulated in all spheres of human activity. The "information distortion" should be understood as some form of information storage, which allows finding and correcting a certain number of errors. Any physical substance (human brain, computer memory or simple piece of paper) can be a carrier of information.

Very often it is said that the information carrier contains information as a certain real object. In fact, the information is an attribute of the information environment [8]. The information does not exist separately from information carrier. The information is a product of information carriers. "To receive the information" means "to read" a condition of the information carrier.

The information is an abstraction. When it comes to methods of distorting information (in fact, ways of changing its state) - it is not the information itself, but its carrier. The method of obtaining a noise-resistant presentation of information is called noise-resistant coding [1].

In real conditions, binary code reception always occurs with errors (instead of "1" it is "0" and vice versa). Errors occur due to interference in the communication channel (especially impulse interference), changes during transmission of

© Springer Nature Switzerland AG 2020
S. Babichev et al. (Eds.): DSMP 2020, CCIS 1158, pp. 127–139, 2020.
https://doi.org/10.1007/978-3-030-61656-4_8

channel characteristics (e.g. fading), reduction in transmission level, instability of amplitude and phase frequency characteristics of the channel, etc.

The generally accepted criterion for evaluating the quality of transmission in discrete channels is normalized to a sign (or symbol) of the acceptable error probability for this message type.

The probability of an error in data transmission is limited to 10^{-6} (per bit). For optical communication, these requirements are more stringent and are $10^{-9}...10^{-12}$ (per bit).

Special methods are used to provide such probability values. They improve the quality of receiving transmitted information. These methods can be divided into two groups. The first group includes methods to increase noise immunity of individual elements (symbols) of discrete information. These methods are related to the choice of signal level, signal/noise ratio (energy characteristics), channel bandwidth, reception methods, etc. The second group includes methods for error detection and correction. They are based on artificial introduction of redundancy into the transmitted message. It is possible to increase the redundancy of the transmitted signal in various ways.

Three main methods are used to improve the quality of receiving transmitted information:

- resend sent message;
- transmission of a code-sequence over several communication channels simultaneously;
- noise-resistant encoding (with correction).

"Resending an already sent message" is the easiest way to improve connection quality. To do this, additional bits are built into the information bits that are used to verify that the message is correct. If the message is not received correctly, it is resent.

The main disadvantage of this method is the low connection speed. This is due to the need to transmit signals about the correctness/incorrectness of the received message (and its retransmission if necessary).

2   Review of the Literature

To solve the tasks, it is necessary to generate code-sequences with correlation properties (which provide unambiguous measurement and high resolution) [13]. The code-sequences (which satisfy this condition) are sequences with the property "no more than R-coincidences" [17]. Modern development of information technologies is connected with studying methods of improving information coding systems. The actual task is to study methods of data coding with the use of new mathematical models (created on combinatorial configurations) and the use of a complex approach to the study of combinatorial structures of different types [14].

The importance of studying combinatorial structures is particularly evident in coding theory for the synthesis of code-sequences with high noise immunity. It is also important in the synthesis of discrete code-sequences with good correlation properties. Such sequences find practical application in radio engineering and data processing [5].

The purpose of this article is to investigate and improve the algorithm for the synthesis of code-sequences that will be noise-immunity. The object of investigation is non-equidistant code-sequences. The object of investigation is the algorithms for the synthesis of noise-resistant code-sequences [19]. To achieve this goal, the following problems have been solved:

- the algorithms for the synthesis of noise-resistant code-sequences have been investigated;
- the algorithm for the synthesis of noise-resistant code-sequences has been studied and implemented in practice;
- the algorithm of finding and correction of errors of received noise-resistant code-sequences is investigated and realized in practice.

When transmitting code-sequences over wireless channels, various types of interference may occur and data may be distorted. This problem must be solved by using noise-resistant code-sequences. Noise-like code-sequences allow data transmission (and reception) systems to find and correct errors. The proposed code-sequences are resistant to interference. They have practical value, because the resulting code-sequence can find up to 50% and correct up to 25% of distorted characters (from the length of the code-sequence, resistant to interference) [6].

It is necessary to find a fault-tolerant code-sequence that is capable of finding and correcting errors as much as possible (depending on the length of the resulting code sequence). The algorithms of fault-tolerant code-sequence synthesis are based on the redundancy principle. It allows finding and correcting errors due to the peculiarities of these sequences' structures [10].

3   Problem Statement

A noise-resistant code-sequence consists of a set of "0" and "1" (which convert the characters for subsequent transceiver operations). The main features of these noise-resistant code-sequences are improved error detection and correction functions. The stability of the system depends on these code-sequences. The properties of noise-resistant code-sequences may vary (with the same length of the sequences). The immunity to interference depends on both the length of the code-sequences and some other characteristics (e.g. mutual correlation of sequences). The choice of the best noise-resistant code-sequences is reduced to the search algorithm of such code-sequences [14].

Existing methods of code-sequence conversion do not fully improve coding/decoding systems. One of the important tasks is to investigate effective models to improve information encoding/decoding. This can be done using indicators such as data rate, interference in the code sequence, ease of correction and error detection. Such models can be non-equidistant code-sequences. They consist of numbers (or sequences of numbers) defined as their values and values of all sequential sums of adjacent elements [20].

To solve this problem, we will consider non-equidistant code-sequences. By the term "non-equidistant code-sequences" we mean sequences in which permissible code combinations form sequences with different distances between "1" and "0" [3]. These non-equidistant code-sequences have some advantages over other non-equidistant sequences. It is easy to find and correct errors on the receiver side because the appearance of the symbol "1" and/or symbol "0" in an unresolved position indicates an error (since the number of allowed distances has changed).

The error will not be detected only when the number of error codes equals (or exceeds) the code distance. If erroneous characters appear in this non-equidistant code sequence, they will be detected (which is facilitated by the high noise resistance of the code). The problem of improving the noise-resistance of non-equidistant code-sequences should be solved by using ideal ring bundles (IRB) [7].

4   Noise-Resistant Non-equidistant Code-Sequences

An ideal ring bundle is a sequence in which the set of all numbers exhausts values that are proportional to the elements of the natural series with a given number of repetitions for each element of this series [13]. A non-equidistant code sequence is called the sequence $K_n = (k_1, k_2, ..., k_i, ..., k_n)$ of elements, where all possible adjacent elements in the form of circular sums give the value of all numbers in the natural series $1, 2, ..., S_n = n^2 - (n - 1)$ [4].

Based on the definition, we construct a table of circular sums of the model of non-equidistant code sequence K_n. The total number of all ring sums of elements of a non-equidistant code sequence having different meanings:

$$S_n = n^2 - (n - 1) \tag{1}$$

For the values of $p_j = 1$, $q_j = n$, as well as for the values of $p_j \neq 1$, $q_j = p_j - 1$ the ring sums of the weights of the elements of the non-equidistant code sequence are equal to S_n. Figure 1 represents allowed circular sums of noise-resistant non-equidistant code sequence.

The number S_n^* of ring sums on the sequence of the weights of the elements is determined by the following dependence [9]:

$$S_n^* = n(n - 1) \tag{2}$$

Consider building a noise-resistant code sequence. As an example, we will take a non-equidistant code sequence constructed according to the weights of the elements of the 8th order of the 4th order of multiplicity: 1, 1, 1, 2, 2, 1, 3, 4.

Since these values of the weights of the elements are the numbers of the 8th order of the 4th multiplicity, each of these numbers of the natural series from 1 to $n(n - 1)/r = 15$ will be represented in different four ways, and the number of all methods is equal to the number of obtained numbers.

p_j	q_j					
	1	2	l-1	l	n-1	n
1	k_1	$\sum_{i=1}^{2}k_i$	$\sum_{i=1}^{l-1}k_i$	$\sum_{i=1}^{l}k_i$	$\sum_{i=1}^{n-1}k_i$	$\sum_{i=1}^{n}k_i$
2	$\sum_{i=1}^{n}k_i$	k_2	$\sum_{i=2}^{l-1}k_i$	$\sum_{i=2}^{l}k_i$	$\sum_{i=2}^{n-1}k_i$	$\sum_{i=2}^{n}k_i$
l-1	$\sum_{i=l-1}^{n}k_i+\sum_{i=1}^{1}k_i$	$\sum_{i=l-1}^{n}k_i+\sum_{i=1}^{2}k_i$	k_{l-1}	$\sum_{i=l-1}^{l}k_i$	$\sum_{i=l-1}^{n-1}k_i$	$\sum_{i=l-1}^{n}k_i$
l	$\sum_{i=1}^{n}k_i+\sum_{i=1}^{1}k_i$	$\sum_{i=1}^{n}k_i+\sum_{i=1}^{2}k_i$	$\sum_{i=1}^{n}k_i$	k_l	$\sum_{i=l}^{n-1}k_i$	$\sum_{i=l}^{n}k_i$
n-1	$\sum_{i=n-1}^{n}k_i+\sum_{i=1}^{1}k_i$	$\sum_{i=n-1}^{n}k_i+\sum_{i=1}^{2}k_i$	$\sum_{i=n-1}^{n}k_i+\sum_{i=1}^{l-1}k_i$	$\sum_{i=n-1}^{n}k_i+\sum_{i=1}^{l}k_i$	k_{n-1}	$\sum_{i=n-1}^{n}k_i$
n	$\sum_{i=n}^{n}k_i+\sum_{i=1}^{1}k_i$	$\sum_{i=n}^{n}k_i+\sum_{i=1}^{2}k_i$	$\sum_{i=n}^{n}k_i+\sum_{i=1}^{l-1}k_i$	$\sum_{i=n}^{n}k_i+\sum_{i=1}^{l}k_i$	$\sum_{i=1}^{n}k_i$	k_n

Fig. 1. Allowed circular sums of noise-resistant non-equidistant code sequence

For a non-equidistant code sequence with a number n of knitting elements, our algorithm provides the ability to encode any numbers from 1 to $S_n = n(n-1)/r + 1$ [18].

Code combinations of non-equidistant code sequence 00000100, 00100000, 01000000, 10000000 represent four ways of encoding the number 1. The number 2 is encoded as follows 00001000, 00010000, 01100000, 11000000. The number 3 is encoded respectively 00000010, 00001100, 00110000, 11100010, 00 4 - 00000000 , 00011000, 01110000, etc., number 14 - 10111111, 11111011, 11011111, 01111111, number 15 - 11111111.

Table 1 shows the synthesized noise immunity code sequence based on the ICW weights. Each numerical combination of a non-equidistant code-sequence corresponds to a set of units and zeros constructed according to the following rules: 1 is 1, 2 - 10, 3 - 100, 4 - 1000, and so on.

The number of different $S_n(S_n - 1)/2$ code-sequences contains exactly of single characters in the corresponding digits, which follows from the properties of the IRB. The other characters of any two non-equidistant code-sequences are different from the characters represented in the bits of the same name [21].

Thus, the minimum coding distance of any interfering non-equidistant coding sequence constructed using IRB will be defined as the ratio of IRB order and multiplicity [2]:

$$d_{min} = 2(n - r) \tag{3}$$

Table 1. Noise-resistant code sequence based on IRB weights of with $n = 8$, $r = 4$:1,1,1,2,2,1,3,4

1	1	1	1	0	1	0	1	1	0	0	1	0	0	0
0	1	1	1	1	0	1	0	1	1	0	0	1	0	0
0	0	1	1	1	1	0	1	0	1	1	0	0	1	0
0	0	0	1	1	1	1	0	1	0	1	1	0	0	1
1	0	0	0	1	1	1	1	0	1	0	1	1	0	0
0	1	0	0	0	1	1	1	1	0	1	0	1	1	0
0	0	1	0	0	0	1	1	1	1	0	1	0	1	1
1	0	0	1	0	0	0	1	1	1	1	0	1	0	1
1	1	0	0	1	0	0	0	1	1	1	1	0	1	0
0	1	1	0	0	1	0	0	0	1	1	1	1	0	1
1	0	1	1	0	0	1	0	0	0	1	1	1	1	0
0	1	0	1	1	0	0	1	0	0	0	1	1	1	1
1	0	1	0	1	1	0	0	1	0	0	0	1	1	1
1	1	0	1	0	1	1	0	0	1	0	0	0	1	1
1	1	1	0	1	0	1	1	0	0	1	0	0	0	1

We build a mirror noise-proof non-equidistant code-sequence with IRB weights, where we change "1" and "0" in the encoding [3]. This allows us to increase the number of allowed combinations of non-equidistant code-sequences using IRB..

Code combinations 01111111, 10111111, 11011111, 11111011 correspond to the 4 methods of coding the number 1. The coding of the number 2 correspond to 00111111, 10011111, 11101111, 11110111. The number 3 correspond to 00011111, 11001111, 11110011, 11111101, the number 4 to 10011111, 111111111 11111110, etc., number 14 - 10000000, 01000000, 00100000, 00000100, number 15 - 00000000.

Table 2 shows the implemented mirror non-equidistant code-sequence with IRB weights. The number of permitted combinations of master and mirror noise-resistant code-sequences [15]:

$$P = 2S_n^r \tag{4}$$

The number of errors t_1 detected by a noise-resistant code-sequence is determined by the minimum code distance d_{min} :

$$t_1 \leq d_{min} - 1 \tag{5}$$

The number of errors t_2 that are corrected by a noise-resistant code-sequence is determined by the number of errors detected by t_1:

$$t_2 \leq (t_1 - 1)/2 \tag{6}$$

Table 2. Mirror noise-resistant code-sequence based on IRB weights with $n = 8$, $r = 4$:$_{1,1,1,2,2,1,3,4}$

0	0	0	0	1	0	1	0	0	1	1	0	1	1	1
1	0	0	0	0	1	0	1	0	0	1	1	0	1	1
1	1	0	0	0	0	1	0	1	0	0	1	1	0	1
1	1	1	0	0	0	0	1	0	1	0	0	1	1	0
0	1	1	1	0	0	0	0	1	0	1	0	0	1	1
1	0	1	1	1	0	0	0	0	1	0	1	0	0	1
1	1	0	1	1	1	0	0	0	0	1	0	1	0	0
0	1	1	0	1	1	1	0	0	0	0	1	0	1	0
0	0	1	1	0	1	1	1	0	0	0	0	1	0	1
1	0	0	1	1	0	1	1	0	0	0	0	0	1	0
0	1	0	0	1	1	0	1	1	1	0	0	0	0	1
1	0	1	0	0	1	1	0	1	1	1	0	0	0	0
0	1	0	1	0	0	1	1	0	1	1	1	0	0	0
0	0	1	0	1	0	0	1	1	0	1	1	1	0	0
0	0	0	1	0	1	0	0	1	1	0	1	1	1	0

We define a dependency that determines the number of errors that can be detected by t_1 noise-resistant code-sequence:

$$t_1 \leq 2(n - r) - 1 \tag{7}$$

We define a dependency that determines the number of errors that can be corrected by t_2 noise-resistant code-sequence:

$$t_2 \leq n - r - 1 \tag{8}$$

We define the minimum code distance for a noise-resistant code-sequence as

$$d_{1,2} = S_n - 2(n - r) \tag{9}$$

Let's find dependencies to determine the number of errors that can be detected by a noise-resistant code-sequence:

$$t_1 \leq 2(n - r) - 1, \text{if } S_n \geq 4(n - r); \tag{10}$$

$$t_1 \leq S_n - 2(n - r) - 1, \text{if } S_n < 4(n - r); \tag{11}$$

Let's find dependencies to determine the number of bugs that can be corrected with a noise-resistant code-sequence:

$$t_2 \leq n - r - 1, \text{if } S_n \geq 4(n - r); \tag{12}$$

$$t_2 \leq \frac{S_n - 2(n - r + 1)}{2}, \text{if } S_n < 4(n - r); \tag{13}$$

We find the optimal correlation between the values of the parameters and in terms of the best corrective ability of a fault-tolerant code-sequence. The noise immunity of this code-sequence increases with increasing $l = n - r$ difference [16]. The largest value of l will be provided:

$$S_n = 2n \tag{14}$$

Here is a correlation between the parameters n and r , when a faulty code sequence detects and corrects most errors [12]:

$$l = \begin{cases} n/2, n - even \\ (n-1)/2, n - odd \end{cases} \tag{15}$$

The resulting code-sequences, derived from perfect ring bindings, can find up to $n - 1$ and correct up to $n/2 - 1$ errors for even values of n. They can also find up to n and correct up to $(n - 1)/2$ errors for odd values of n. This is possible because the number of acceptable combinations of code-sequences is theoretically doubled by the introduction of mirror interference-resistant code-sequences [11].

5   Results and Discussion

To verify the described method, a software product was created (in the Delphi 7 development environment). The developed program does not need a powerful computer and has all the capabilities to perform the task. The software is easy to use and has an intuitive interface. Let us describe the elements of the software:

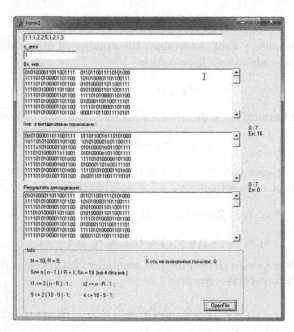

Fig. 2. Carry out coding, interference generation, and single error correction operations

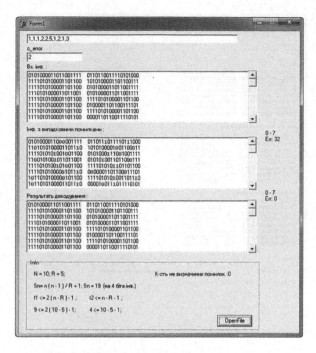

Fig. 3. Perform coding, interference generation, and double error correction operations

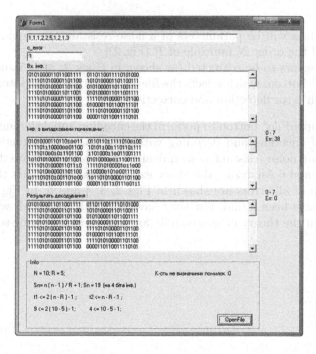

Fig. 4. Performing coding, interference generation, and decoding operations with a 3x error correction

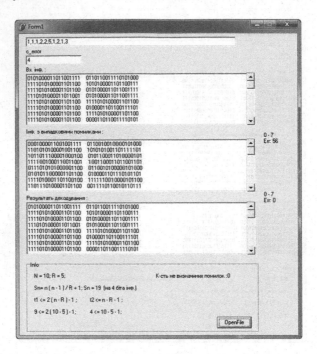

Fig. 5. Performing coding, interference generation, and decoding operations with a 4x error correction

- the input data will be parameters of a noise-resistant non-equidistant code-sequence of the order N multiple of R (Fig. 2);
- number of errors to be corrected (as shown in (Figs. 2, 3, 4, 5 and 6));
- "OpenFile" button, which selects the file to encode, generate interference and decode with error detection and correction.

Use the "OpenFile" button to perform the encoding and decoding operations. The results of encoding and decoding with detection and correction of up to five errors using noise resistant non-equivalent code-sequences are illustrated in Figs. 2, 3, 4, 5 and 6 Analyzing the above experiments, we see that the detection and correction of all errors are shown in Figs. 2, 3, 4 and 5. In Fig. 6 - quite a lot of errors have been found, but they have not been corrected, which is fully consistent with the theory of non-equidistant noise-resistant code-sequences.

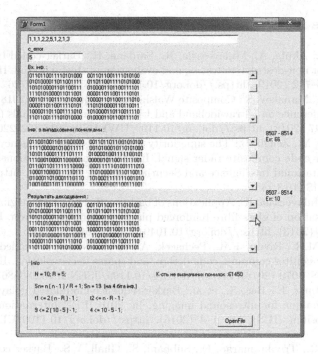

Fig. 6. Performing coding, interference generation, and decoding operations with a fivefold error

6   Conclusions

Known methods of transforming information (and code) sequences, algorithms and methods (using classical combinatorial structures) do not always fully reveal the possibilities of data encoding systems. Therefore, the process of investigating and applying new models to improve data encoding/decoding systems (in terms of noise immunity, number of detected and corrected errors, message rate, etc.) is of great practical importance.

The advantage of the proposed algorithm for the synthesis of non-equidistant noise-resistant sequences using ideal ring bindings is the greater noise-resistance of the resulting sequences. Comparison with other methods of building noise-like code-sequences shows that the use of ideal ring bindings significantly simplifies the synthesis of these sequences.

Application of data encoding and decoding algorithm on the basis of non-equidistant noise-resistant sequences allows increasing noise-resistance of received sequences. The prospect of further research is to reduce quite a large redundancy. For this purpose, the article suggests using mirror-like non-equidistant noise-like code-sequences.

References

1. Ahmad, J., Akula, A., Mulaveesala, R., Sardana, H.: Barker-coded thermal wave imaging for non-destructive testing and evaluation of steel material. IEEE Sens. J. **19**(2), 735–742 (2019). https://doi.org/10.1109/JSEN.2018.2877726
2. Banket, V., Manakov, S.: Composite Walsh-barker sequences. In: 2018 9th International Conference on Ultrawideband and Ultrashort Impulse Signals (UWBUSIS), pp. 343–347 (2018). https://doi.org/10.1109/UWBUSIS.2018.8520220
3. Chunhong, Y., Zengli, L.: The superiority analysis of linear frequency modulation and barker code composite radar signal. In: 2013 Ninth International Conference on Computational Intelligence and Security, pp. 182–184 (2013). https://doi.org/10.1109/CIS.2013.45
4. Dua, G., Mulaveesala, R.: Applications of barker coded infrared imaging method for characterisation of glass fibre reinforced plastic materials. Electron. Lett. **49**(17), 1071–1073 (2013). https://doi.org/10.1049/el.2013.1661
5. Kellman, M.R., Rivest, F.R., Pechacek, A., et al.: Node-pore coded coincidence correction: coulter counters, code design, and sparse deconvolution. IEEE Sens. J. **18**(8), 3068–3079 (2018). https://doi.org/10.1109/JSEN.2018.2805865
6. Kim, P., Jung, E., Bae, S., et al.: Barker-sequence-modulated golay coded excitation technique for ultrasound imaging. In: 2016 IEEE International Ultrasonics Symposium (IUS), pp. 1–4 (2016). https://doi.org/10.1109/ULTSYM.2016.7728737
7. Lakshmi, R., Trivikramarao, D., Subhani, S., Ghali, V.S.: Barker coded thermal wave imaging for anomaly detection. In: 2018 Conference on Signal Processing and Communication Engineering Systems (SPACES), pp. 198–201 (2018). https://doi.org/10.1109/SPACES.2018.8316345
8. Nazarkevych, M., Riznyk, O., Samotyy, V., Dzelendzyak, U.: Detection of regularities in the parameters of the Ateb-Gabor method for biometric image filtration. East.-Eur. J. Enterp. Technol. **1**, 57–65 (2019). https://doi.org/10.15587/1729-4061.2019.154862
9. Nilawar, R.C., Bhalerao, D.M.: Reduction of SFD bits of Wifi OFDM frame using wobbulation echo signal and barker code. In: 2015 International Conference on Pervasive Computing (ICPC), pp. 1–3 (2015). https://doi.org/10.1109/PERVASIVE.2015.7087095
10. Omar, S., Kassem, F., Mitri, R., et al.: A novel barker code algorithm for resolving range ambiguity in high PRF radars. In: 2015 European Radar Conference (EuRAD), pp. 81–84 (2015). https://doi.org/10.1109/EuRAD.2015.7346242
11. Riznik, O., Yurchak, I., Vdovenko, E., Korchagina, A.: Model of stegosystem images on the basis of pseudonoise codes. In: 2010 Proceedings of VIth International Conference on Perspective Technologies and Methods in MEMS Design, pp. 51–52 (2010)
12. Riznyk, O., Balych, B., Yurchak, I.: A synthesis of barker sequences is by means of numerical bundles. In: 2017 14th International Conference on the Experience of Designing and Application of CAD Systems in Microelectronics (CADSM), pp. 82–84 (2017). https://doi.org/10.1109/CADSM.2017.7916090
13. Riznyk, O., Kynash, Y., Povshuk, O., Kovalyk, V.: Recovery schemes for distributed computing based on bib-schemes. In: 2016 IEEE First International Conference on Data Stream Mining Processing (DSMP), pp. 134–137 (2016). https://doi.org/10.1109/DSMP.2016.7583524

14. Riznyk, O., Kynash, Y., Povshuk, O., Noga, Y.: The method of encoding information in the images using numerical line bundles. In: 2018 IEEE 13th International Scientific and Technical Conference on Computer Sciences and Information Technologies (CSIT), pp. 80–83 (2018). https://doi.org/10.1109/STC-CSIT.2018.8526751
15. Riznyk, O., Povshuk, O., Kynash, Y., Yurchak, I.: Composing method of anti-interference codes based on non-equidistant structures. In: 2017 XIIIth International Conference on Perspective Technologies and Methods in MEMS Design (MEMSTECH), pp. 15–17 (2017). https://doi.org/10.1109/MEMSTECH.2017.7937522
16. Riznyk, V., Riznyk, O., Balych, B., Parubchak, V.: Information encoding method of combinatorial optimization. In: 2006 International Conference - Modern Problems of Radio Engineering, Telecommunications, and Computer Science, p. 357 (2006). https://doi.org/10.1109/TCSET.2006.4404550
17. Rosli, S., Rahim, H., Ngadiran, R., et al.: Design of binary coded pulse trains with good autocorrelation properties for radar communications. In: MATEC Web of Conferences, vol. 150, 06016 (2018). https://doi.org/10.1051/matecconf/201815006016
18. Sekhar, S., Pillai, S.S.: Comparative analysis of offset estimation capabilities in mathematical sequences for WLAN. In: 2016 International Conference on Communication Systems and Networks (ComNet), pp. 127–131 (2016). https://doi.org/10.1109/CSN.2016.7824000
19. Wang, H., Cong, S., Zhang, S.: Pseudo Chirp-Barker-Golay coded excitation in ultrasound imaging. In: 2018 Chinese Control And Decision Conference (CCDC), pp. 4035–4039 (2018). https://doi.org/10.1109/CCDC.2018.8407824
20. Wang, S., He, H.: Research on low intercepting radar waveform based on LFM and barker code composite modulation. In: 2018 International Conference on Sensor Networks and Signal Processing (SNSP), pp. 297–301 (2018). https://doi.org/10.1109/SNSP.2018.00064
21. Xia, S., Li, Z., Jiang, C., et al.: Application of pulse compression technology in electromagnetic ultrasonic thickness measurement. In: 2018 IEEE Far East NDT New Technology Application Forum (FENDT), pp. 37–41 (2018). https://doi.org/10.1109/FENDT.2018.8681975

An Empirical Mode Decomposition Based Method to Synthesize Ensemble Multidimensional Gaussian Neuro-Fuzzy Models in Financial Forecasting

Alexander Vlasenko[1]($\boxtimes$) [iD], Nataliia Vlasenko[2] [iD], Olena Vynokurova[1,3] [iD], and Dmytro Peleshko[3] [iD]

[1] Kharkiv National University of Radio Electronics, Kharkiv, Ukraine
alexander.vlasenko86@gmail.com, vynokurova@gmail.com
[2] Simon Kuznets Kharkiv National University of Economics, Kharkiv, Ukraine
gorohovatskaja@gmail.com
[3] GeoGuard, Kharkiv/Lviv, Ukraine

Abstract. Time series arise in different fields of the economy and forecasting of them is important part of decision making. However, their intrinsic complexity and nonlinear behavior makes prediction in that field a challenging task. Hybrid artificial intelligence models are among the most powerful tools in handling such complex dynamics. This paper introduces a novel model which uses the empirical mode decomposition as a denoising and decomposition framework for the ensemble multidimensional Gaussian based neuro-fuzzy model in order to achieve better accuracy. The computational experimental results show clear advantages of the proposed approach - better prediction accuracy, faster error decay with preserving of the generalization abilities and reasonable computational overhead.

Keywords: Time series forecasting · Empirical mode decomposition · Neuro-fuzzy · Multidimensional Gaussian

1 Introduction

Technical time series analysis is an important field in modern finance, especially in currency, stock, derivatives and other markets. Nonlinear and non-stationary nature of the real-life data has paved a way to complex mathematical models development to handle it.

A plethora of statistical methods have dominated the field of analysis and forecasting in the financial domain for decades. Some of their limitations directed the scientific search into the field of the various artificial intelligence techniques.

The most popular field in artificial intelligence research are Artificial Neural Networks (ANN). They have been extensively used in forecasting different time series like the FOREX price trend using Long Short-term Memory (LSTM) [6],

© Springer Nature Switzerland AG 2020
S. Babichev et al. (Eds.): DSMP 2020, CCIS 1158, pp. 140–149, 2020.
https://doi.org/10.1007/978-3-030-61656-4_9

the direction of the SPDR S&P 500 ETF daily return by means of Deep Neural Networks (DNN) [24] and other.

Fuzzy logic is a proven instrument of handling uncertainty including financial data. Its abilities were applied to one of the most challenging tasks - trading strategies [12].

Neuro-fuzzy models inherently combine the advantages of fuzzy logic inference systems and neural networks and have been successfully applied in business tasks - works [15] and [2] provide a review of many cases.

The history of neuro-fuzzy models started in 1993 when Adaptive Network Fuzzy Inference System (ANFIS) was proposed by Jang [10]. Since then they have shown their efficacy in various domains including financial time series prediction. Among successful examples are work [16] where an interpretable neuro-fuzzy method to forecasting of stock prices is proposed, day closing price of Dhaka Stock Exchange prediction by a neuro-fuzzy model with Levenberg–Marquardt learning algorithm [1], price direction prediction in DAX-30 index by a hybrid fuzzy neural network [7]. In many cases neuro-fuzzy systems are combined with modeling techniques - for instance in order to exploit representative capabilities of wavelets [4].

Works [22] and [21] introduced a neuro-fuzzy model which displayed good performance through utilizing the representational power of the multidimensional Gaussian function in the consequent layer and combination of a stochastic gradient descent learning and a Kaczmarz method optimization. As a further development an ensemble model was proposed in [20] which simplified the hyperparameters tuning and benefited from differences in each components original random initialization. A modification of the original model [19] showed outstanding results on the prediction of synthetic time series generated by Mackey-Glass chaotic equation with added white noise. This means that signal decomposition and denoising technique may be used in neuro-fuzzy model training.

Hilbert-Huang transform was proposed in [9] and has been applied as a method to model nonstationary and nonlinear time series in various domains. It consists of Empirical Mode Decomposition (EMD) and Hilbert spectral transform. EMD, known also as Huang transform, decomposes signal into a set of simple Intrinsic Mode Functions (IMF), which are useful components for further analysis. Currently EMD lacks a solid theoretical background and considered to be an empirical method, but research is active in this direction, for instance [8] proves validity and robustness of EMD. Work [13] shows that it competitiveness as a denoising tool in financial data.

Using EMD as a signal decomposition and denoising tool, instead of Fourier and Wavelet transform, together with artificial intelligence models is a nascent, but a promising field of research. EMD combined with deep LSTM networks was used for Taiwan's CSR index forecasting [14]. Ensemble EMD (EEMD) together with other decomposition methods was used with ANNs and support vector machines (SVM) for stock market prediction [11]. In [3] complete ensemble empirical mode decomposition with adaptive noise (CEEMDAN) was utilized with LSTM and displayed better performance compared with sole LSTM

networks and other modern models. Among noteworthy examples of the mutually beneficial hybrid models are EEMD - independent component analysis (ICA)
in the task of factor analysis [23], EMD - BP neural network and principal component analysis (PCA) in Asia Pacific stock markets analysis [5].

The aim of the research is the development of a model which combines
the strengths of EMD with predictive abilities of the Neuro-Fuzzy model and
benefits of the ensemble.

2   Proposed Model

The main steps to build the proposed model are depicted in Fig. 1.

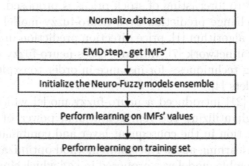

Fig. 1. The high-level structure of the proposed model.

On the first step, we normalize dataset, then EMD transform is applied in
order to obtain the IMFs. They represent simple harmonic motion components
of the time series and used as a basis to build a predictor.

The IMF extraction is called sifting and has the following structure:

1. local extrema identification in the set;
2. produce upper envelope $e_u(t)$ from all local maxima by applying cubic spline;
3. repeat the process for the local minima in order to obtain the lower envelope
   $e_l(t)$. Now all data should be in between the envelopes;
4. calculate the local mean $m_1(t) = \frac{e_u - e_l}{2}$;
5. the contrast between the data points and $m_1(t)$ is calculated by the following
   condition:

$$h_1(t) = x(t) - m(t)$$

6. in the subsequent sifting process, $h_1(t)$ described as follows:

$$h_{1k}(t) = h_{1(k-1)}(t) - m_{1k}(t)$$

7. repeat k times, until $h_{1k}(t)$ is an IMF. Now

$$h_{1k}(t) = c_1$$

is the primary IMF part obtained from the data.

To determine the number of sifting steps, standard deviation criterion is used [9]:

$$SD_k = \sum_{t=1}^{T} \frac{|h_{k-1}(t) - h_k(t)|^2}{h_k^2(t)} \tag{1}$$

An illustration of applied EMD decomposition is shown in Fig. 2.

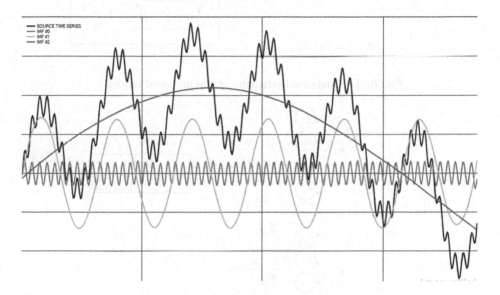

Fig. 2. The example of time series decomposition into IMFs.

Then we use the obtained IMFs to synthesize an ensemble of neuro-fuzzy models by the method from [20]. Figure 3 shows the high-level architecture of the ensemble.

On the fourth step, we train the forth layer receptive fields in each model as is shown at the example displayed in Fig. 4. Finally, the whole ensemble is trained on the original training set Fig. 5. The vectors of MDG centers $c_{ejl}^{\phi} \in C^e$ and receptive fields matrices $Q_{ejl} \in Q^e$ are tuned in the following way as in [22]:

$$\begin{cases} c_{ejl}^{\phi}(k+1) = c_{ejl}^{\phi}(k) + \lambda_c \frac{\tau_{ejl}^c(k)e(k)}{\eta_c(k)} \\ \eta_{ec}(k+1) = \beta_c \eta_{ec}(k) + \tau_{ejl}^{c}{}^T \tau_{ejl}^c \\ Q_{ejl}(k+1) = Q_{ejl}(k) + \lambda_Q \frac{\tau_{ejl}^Q(k)e(k)}{\eta_{eq}(k)} \\ \eta_{eQ}(k+1) = \beta_{Qe} \eta_{eQ}(k) + Tr\left(\tau_{ejl}^{Q}{}^T \tau_{ejl}^Q\right) \end{cases} \tag{2}$$

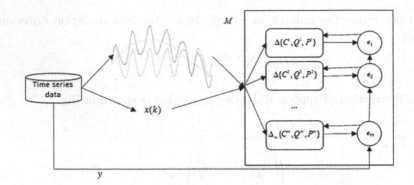

Fig. 3. The high-level structure of the proposed model.

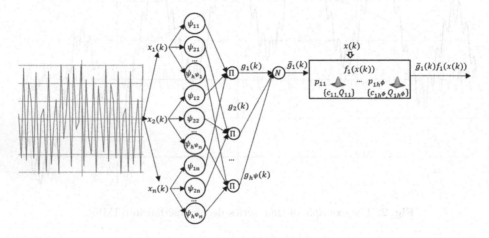

Fig. 4. The illustration of the forth layer learning on an IMF component in a single model.

where λ_c and λ_Q are the learning steps; β_{ce} and β_{Qe} are the memory parameters for the current ensemble member model; vector τ_{ajl}^c and matrix τ_{ejl}^Q of back propagated error gradient values with respect to c_{ejl}^ϕ and Q_{ejl}. The vectors η_{ec} and matrices η_{eQ} are the averages of the previous learning steps.

Then we train the whole model on the real original training set. Weights optimization is performed by Kaczmarz iterative method [22]:

$$p_e\left(k+1\right) = p_e\left(k\right) + \frac{e_a}{f_e{}^T\left(x\left(k\right)\right) f_e\left(x\left(k\right)\right)} f_e\left(x\left(k\right)\right) \tag{3}$$

where $p_e\left(k\right)$ is the fourth layer weights.

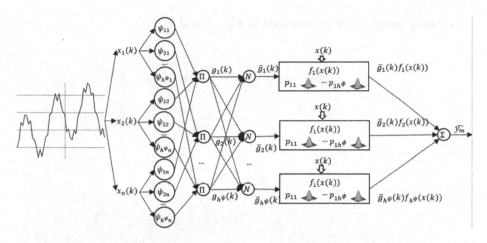

Fig. 5. The general single neuro-fuzzy model architecture with learning on the original dataset.

3   Experiment, Results and Discussion

The proposed ensemble model performance was verified on the real life daily log returns of IBM and Cisco stock datasets with 2528 records. Forecasting accuracy estimate is based on Symmetric Mean Absolute Percent Error (SMAPE) and Root Mean Square Error (RMSE) measures:

$$SMAPE = \frac{2}{N} \sum_{k=1}^{N} \frac{|\hat{y}(k) - y(k)|}{\hat{y}(k) + y(k)} \tag{4}$$

$$RMSE = \sqrt{\frac{\sum_{k=1}^{N} (y(k) - \hat{y}(k))^2}{N}} \tag{5}$$

where $y(k)$ represents the original signal value, $\hat{y}(k)$ is the forecast, and N is the size of the training set.

The computational simulations are implemented on Microsoft .Net Framework platform. Math.NET Numerics package [17] was used for the linear algebra operations and Accord.NET package [18] - for the reference neural networks implementation. The computational experiments were ran on a PC with two-core Intel Core i7 central processor unit and 8 GB of RAM.

Learning process plot is presented in Figs. 6 and 7.

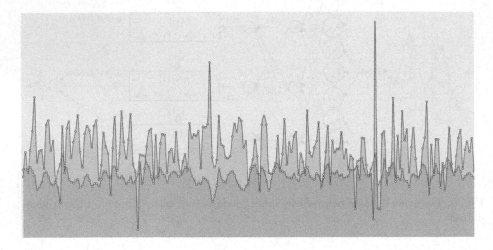

Fig. 6. The experiments on Cisco daily returns plot.

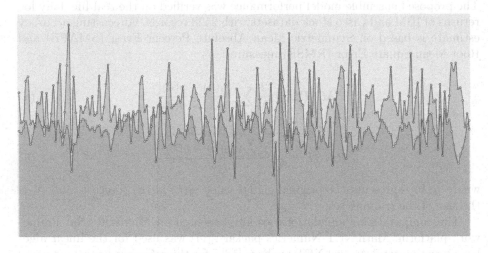

Fig. 7. The experiments on IBM daily returns plot.

Training of the competing bipolar sigmoid model was performed with alpha value 0.4, learning rate 0.55 and 80 epochs.

Results in the tables below indicate that introduced model has better prediction accuracy than the original neuro-fuzzy model and its ensemble variation but requires more computational resources (Tables 1 and 2).

Table 1. Results on IBM dataset

Model	Execution time, ms	RMSE, %	SMAPE, %
Proposed model	970	2.67	2.98
Simple MDG based neuro-fuzzy model	495	3.12	3.41
Ensemble MDG based neuro-fuzzy model	900	3.01	3.09
Bipolar Sigmoid Network	2215	3.32	3.67

Table 2. Results on Cisco dataset

Model	Execution time, ms	RMSE, %	SMAPE, %
Proposed model	1005	2.88	3.11
Simple MDG based neuro-fuzzy model	467	3.19	3.42
Ensemble MDG based neuro-fuzzy model	940	3.12	3.29
Bipolar Sigmoid Network	2645	3.29	3.63

4   Conclusions

This work proposes a novel hybrid approach to build a neuro-fuzzy financial time series forecasting model. Empirical mode decomposition is applied to produce intrinsic mode functions which amount determines the number of the first layer membership functions and fourth layer computational units. Then the retrieved signal components are used separately to optimize the multidimensional Gaussian functions of the consequent layer in each ensemble member model. After that the whole ensemble is trained on the original training set. In this way we combine denoising and signal decomposition power of EMD and learning and representational capabilities of the multidimensional Gaussian neuro-fuzzy ensemble model.

Software experiments on the real life time series have shown the good prediction accuracy of the proposed model, which has been compared to artificial neural networks, a single neuro-fuzzy model and a neuro-fuzzy ensemble. The combination of denoising performed by EMD and ensemble structure with variation in the original hyperparameters selection leads to a better error decay in stochastic gradient descent learning without harming its generalization abilities. The only drawback is a slightly higher computational costs in comparison to the simple neuro-fuzzy model and the neuro-fuzzy ensemble, but the performance is still highly competitive, and a small loss of it can be justified by the advantages provided by the model.

Applying EMD significantly simplifies the ensemble synthesis and hyperparameters selection, also it improves the forecasting precision by providing the neuro-fuzzy model with denoised signals for learning. The further research in this direction may include utilizing the ensemble EMD and more advanced stacking techniques in ensemble composition.

References

1. Billah, M., Waheed, S., Hanifa, A.: Stock market prediction using an improved training algorithm of neural network. In: 2016 2nd International Conference on Electrical, Computer and Telecommunication Engineering (ICECTE), pp. 1–4. IEEE (2016). https://doi.org/10.1109/ICECTE.2016.7879611
2. de Campos, S., Paulo, V.: Fuzzy neural networks and neuro-fuzzy networks: a review the main techniques and applications used in the literature. Appl. Soft Comput., Article no. 106275 (2020). https://doi.org/10.1016/j.asoc.2020.106275
3. Cao, J., Li, S., Li, J.: Financial time series forecasting model based on CEEMDAN and LSTM. Phys. A **519**, 127–139 (2019). https://doi.org/10.1016/j.physa.2018.11.061
4. Chandar, S.: Fusion model of wavelet transform and adaptive neuro fuzzy inference system for stock market prediction. J. Ambient Intell. Hum. Comput. 1–9 (2019). https://doi.org/10.1007/s12652-019-01224-2
5. Chengzhao, Z., Heping, Yu, M., Xun, H.: Analysis of Asia Pacific stock markets with a novel multiscale model. Phys. A: Stat. Mech. Appl. **534**, Article no. 120939 (2019). https://doi.org/10.1016/j.physa.2019.04.175
6. Dobrovolny, M., Soukal, I., Lim, K., et al.: Forecasting of FOREX price trend using recurrent neural network-long short-term memory (2020). https://doi.org/10.36689/uhk/hed/2020-01-011
7. Garcia, F., Guijarro, J., Oliver, J., et al.: Hybrid fuzzy neural network to predict price direction in the German DAX-30 index. Technol. Econ. Dev. Econ. **24**(6), 2161–2178 (2018). https://doi.org/10.3846/tede.2018.6394
8. Ge, H., Chen, G., Yu, H., et al.: Theoretical analysis of empirical mode decomposition. Symmetry **10**(11), 623 (2018). https://doi.org/10.3390/sym10110623
9. Huang, N., Shen, Z., Long, S., et al.: The empirical mode decomposition and the Hilbert spectrum for nonlinear and non-stationary time series analysis. Proc. R. Soc. Lond. Ser. A: Math. Phys. Eng. Sci. **454**(1971), 903–995 (1998). https://doi.org/10.1098/rspa.1998.0193
10. Jang, J.S.: ANFIS: adaptive-network-based fuzzy inference system. IEEE Trans. Syst. Man Cybern. **23**(3), 665–685 (1993)
11. Jothimani, D., Başar, A.: Stock index forecasting using time series decomposition-based and machine learning models. In: Bramer, M., Petridis, M. (eds.) SGAI 2019. LNCS (LNAI), vol. 11927, pp. 283–292. Springer, Cham (2019). https://doi.org/10.1007/978-3-030-34885-4_22
12. Lauguico, S., Ronnie, A., Macasaet, D., et al.: A fuzzy logic-based stock market trading algorithm using bollinger bands, pp. 1–6. IEEE (2019). https://doi.org/10.1109/HNICEM48295.2019.9072734
13. Li, Y., Han, H., Li, Y.: A new HHT-based denoising algorithm for financial time series data mining. In: 2019 IEEE 8th Joint International Information Technology and Artificial Intelligence Conference (ITAIC), pp. 397–401. IEEE (2019). https://doi.org/10.1109/ITAIC.2019.8785616
14. Lin, S., Huang, H.W.: Improving deep learning for forecasting accuracy in financial data. Discrete Dyn. Nat. Soc. **2020**, 1–12 (2020). https://doi.org/10.1155/2020/5803407

15. Rajab, S., Sharma, V.: A review on the applications of neuro-fuzzy systems in business. Artif. Intell. Rev. **49**(4), 481–510 (2017). https://doi.org/10.1007/s10462-016-9536-0
16. Rajab, S., Sharma, V.: An interpretable neuro-fuzzy approach to stock price forecasting. Soft. Comput. **23**(3), 921–936 (2017). https://doi.org/10.1007/s00500-017-2800-7
17. Ruegg, C., Cuda, M., Van Gael, J.: Math.net numerics (2016). http://numerics.mathdotnet.com
18. Souza, C.: The accord.net framework (2014). http://accord-framework.net
19. Vlasenko, A., Vlasenko, N., Vynokurova, O., Bodyanskiy, Y.: An enhancement of a learning procedure in neuro-fuzzy model. In: 2018 IEEE First International Conference on System Analysis and Intelligent Computing (SAIC), pp. 1–4. IEEE (2018). https://doi.org/10.1109/DSMP.2018.8478494
20. Vlasenko, A., Vlasenko, N., Vynokurova, O., Bodyanskiy, Y., Peleshko, D.: A novel ensemble neuro-fuzzy model for financial time series forecasting. Data **4**(3), Article no. 126 (2019). https://doi.org/10.3390/data4030126
21. Vlasenko, A., Vlasenko, N., Vynokurova, O., Peleshko, D.: A novel neuro-fuzzy model for multivariate time-series prediction. Data **3**(4), Article no. 62 (2018). https://doi.org/10.3390/data3040062
22. Vlasenko, A., Vynokurova, O., Vlasenko, N., Peleshko, M.: A hybrid neuro-fuzzy model for stock market time-series prediction. In: 2018 IEEE Second International Conference on Data Stream Mining and Processing (DSMP), pp. 352–355. IEEE (2018). https://doi.org/10.1109/DSMP.2018.8478494
23. Xian, L., He, K., Wang, C., Lai, K.: Factor analysis of financial time series using EEMD-ICA based approach. Sustain. Futures **2**, Article no. 100003 (2020). https://doi.org/10.1016/j.sftr.2019.100003
24. Zhong, X., Enke, D.: Predicting the daily return direction of the stock market using hybrid machine learning algorithms. Financ. Innov. **5**(1), Article no. 4 (2019). https://doi.org/10.1186/s40854-019-0138-0

Comparison Analysis of Clustering Quality Criteria Using Inductive Methods of Objective Clustering

Sergii Babichev[1,2]([envelope]) [ORCID], Aleksander Spivakovskiy[2] [ORCID], and Jiří Škvor[1] [ORCID]

[1] Jan Evangelista Purkyně University in Ústí nad Labem,
Ústí nad Labem, Czech Republic
{sergii.babichev,Jiri.Skvor}@ujep.cz
[2] Kherson State University, Kherson, Ukraine
spivakovsky@ksu.kherson.ua

Abstract. In this paper, we present the results of the research concerning comparison analysis of both the internal and external clustering quality criteria for clustering various types of datasets using density-based DBSCAN clustering algorithm implemented based on Inductive Methods of Objective Clustering (IMOC). Implementation of the IMOC technique assumes division of the initial dataset into two similar subsets contained the same number of pairwise similar objects at the first step of this procedure implementation. Then, we have executed the data clustering on the obtained subsets concurrently within the range of the appropriate algorithm parameters variation with estimation of various types of clustering quality criteria (internal (IQC) and external (EQC)) at each step of this procedure implementation. The final solution concerning algorithm optimal parameters determination was made based on the maximum values of the complex balance criterion (CBC) which contains both the ICQ and ECQ as the components. The analysis of the simulation results has allowed us to evaluate the effectiveness of both the internal and external clustering quality criteria to determine the optimal parameters of clustering algorithm using various type of data. To our mind, the obtained results can allow us to increase the clustering procedure exactness and to decrease the reproducibility error.

Keywords: Internal and external clustering quality criteria · Complex balance criterion · DBSCAN clustering algorithm · Inductive methods of objective clustering · Reproducibility error

1 Introduction

The problem of data clustering is relevant in various areas of scientific research nowadays [9,26,27]. The solution of this problem assumes division of objects or/and attributes into clusters considering their similarity. In the most cases, an optimal clustering matches to higher concentration of the objects within the

S. Babichev et al. (Eds.): DSMP 2020, CCIS 1158, pp. 150–166, 2020.
https://doi.org/10.1007/978-3-030-61656-4_10

clusters on the one hand and less concentration of the clusters in the feature space on the other hand. The quality of this procedure implementation depends on various factors. Firstly, it is necessary to choose the affinity function which determine the proximity level between objects, clusters and between objects and clusters. Very important step also is choice of the clustering quality criteria which allow us to evaluate the adequacy of the clustering procedure. Finally, it is necessary to select the clustering algorithm and to determine its optimal parameters considering the type of the studied data.

The next problem which has no solution nowadays is the reproducibility error. In other word, successful clustering results on one dataset do not repeat when we use another similar dataset. This shortcoming is common for all clustering algorithms. The main idea for this problem solution was presented in [17,21] and it was further developed in [1,2,4]. In [17,21], the authors proposed to verify the model using "fresh" information. This is the dataset which is similar to training data but they were not used during the model creation. To evaluate the model effectiveness, the authors proposed using the internal, external and balance clustering quality criteria. In [1,2,4], the authors proposed to use the multiplicative combination of Calinski Harabasz [6] and WB index [28] as the internal clustering quality criterion. The external clustering quality criterion was calculated as normalized difference of the internal criteria estimated on equal power subsets (contains the same quantity of pairwise similar objects). The balance clustering quality criterion contained as the components both the internal and external criteria and it was calculated based on the use of Harrington desirability function [14].

However, it should be noted that effectiveness of both the internal criteria and clustering algorithm operation depends on type of the examined data and this choice should be done in each of the cases separately. This fact indicates the relevance of the problem. In this research, we present the comparison analysis of various clustering quality criteria implemented based on the use of IMOC for clustering various types of two dimensional synthetic datasets contained clusters different shapes.

2   Problem Statement

Let the initial data are presented as a matrix: $A = \{x_{ij}\}, i = \overline{1,n}; j = \overline{1,m}$, where n is the number of the examined objects; m is the number of the features characterizing the objects. The goal of the clustering procedure is a partition of the objects into non-empty subsets of pairwise non-intersecting (in ideal case) clusters, herewith, a surface which distinguished the clusters from each other can take any shape:

$$K = \{K_s\}, s = \overline{1,k}; K_1 \cup K_2 \cup \cdots \cup K_k = A; K_i \cap K_j = \emptyset, i \neq j,$$

where k is the number of clusters, $i, j = \overline{1,k}$.

Let W is a set of all admissible clustering for initial dataset A. We will consider that clustering is an optimal in terms of quality criteria $QC(K)$ if it is performed the following condition:

$$K_{opt} = \arg \min_{K \subseteq W} CQ(K) \; or \; K_{opt} = \arg \max_{K \subseteq W} CQ(K) \qquad (1)$$

Clustering $K_{opt} \subseteq W$ is an objective one if there is the least difference of the clustering results obtained on the similar datasets. In this case, the value of the external clustering quality criterion achieved its extremum (maximum or minimum value) [21].

Thus, within the framework of our research, we compared the effectiveness of various types of the internal clustering quality criteria, external criterion and complex balance criterion implemented based on the apply of DBSCAN clustering algorithms for clustering various types of two dimensional synthetic data using techniques of IMOC considering the condition (1).

3   Literature Review

As was noted in Introduction section, the data clustering as a method of unsupervised learning is relevant in various fields of scientific research nowadays. A lot of scientific works are devoted to development of various types of data clustering techniques. So, in review [8], the authors study the issues concerning formation and growth of small clusters into aerosol particles which are one of the largest uncertainties in global climate forecasting. This paper reviews the present state-of-the-art quantum chemical methods and cluster distribution dynamics models that are applied to study the formation and growth of atmospheric molecular clusters.

Survey [25] considered the clustering as an important control mechanism in high-mobility networks. The authors provided a thorough review of clustering algorithms in Vehicular ad hoc networks (VANETs). They proposed a new taxonomy that categorizes clustering algorithms in VANETs on the basis of various design aspects and provides a description of the algorithms in each of the categories. They also provided a comparison analysis of different clustering algorithms in accordance with selected key parameters.

Papers [12, 20, 24] present the results of the research concerning application of different clustering algorithms in various areas of scientific studies. However, the analysis of works in this subject area allows us to conclude that in the most cases the authors' research are focused to the development of new clustering algorithms or to the improvement of the existing algorithms. The issues concerning evaluation of the optimal algorithm parameters in terms of quantitative clustering quality criteria are not considered in the works. Moreover, the authors do not consider the possibilities to decrease the reproducibility error during the clustering algorithm operation.

The idea of increasing the clustering objectivity was proposed in [21] and further developed in [1, 2, 4]. This idea is the basis of the Inductive Methods of Objective Clustering (IMOC). The authors proposed to execute the data clustering on two equal power subsets concurrently within the range of the algorithm parameters change with calculation of both the internal and external clustering quality criteria at each step of this procedure implementation. In [5], the issues concerning evaluation of some of the internal and external clustering quality criteria effectiveness using synthetic datasets are considered.

However, despite on achievements in this subject area, the problem of the clustering algorithm optimal parameters evaluation considering the used data based on the use of quantitative clustering quality criteria has not solved nowadays. The solution of this problem can be achieved based on the use of current techniques of data mining which are successfully applied in various areas of scientific research nowadays [15,18,19,22,23].

The objective of the research is to compare various internal clustering quality criteria calculated based on the use of IMOC technique with following calculation of both the external and balance criteria for clustering various types of two dimensional synthetic datsets applying density based DBSCAN clustering algorithm.

4 Stepwise Procedure of the Data Clustering and Criteria Calculation

As was noted hereinbefore, to reduce the reproducibility error, we carry out the clustering procedure on two equal power subsets (included the same quantity of pairwise similar objects) concurrently with calculation of both the internal clustering quality criteria for each of the subsets and external clustering quality criterion which should be minimal in terms of condition of the objective clustering. Thus, the first step of the data processing is the division of the initial dataset into two equal power subsets. Presented below Algorithm 1 describes the stepwise procedure of this stage implementation.

The Internal clustering Quality Criteria (IQC) were calculated using *cluster-Crit* package [7] of R software [16]. We used the IQC which allow determining the optimal clustering based on the extrema (min or max) values. As the first IQC, we have applied also Within-Between index (WB) which has been proposed in [28] and further evaluated in [1,3,5]. Below, we present the IQC which were used within the framework of our research (Table 1).

Table 1. The IQC used to evaluate the quality of the data clustering for each of the data subsets

No	Index	Rule	Abbr.	No	Index	Rule	Abbr.
1	Within-Between	min	WB	7	PBM	max	PBM
2	C index	min	CI	8	G +	min	GP
3	Calinski-Harabasz	max	CH	9	Ray-Turi	min	RT
4	Davies-Bouldin	min	DB	10	Ratkowsky-Lance	max	RL
5	Dunn	max	DN	11	McClain-Rao	min	MCR
6	Gamma	max	GM	12	Silhouette	max	SL

Algorithm 1: Equal power subsets formation

Initialization:
set: distance metric (Euclidean or correlation in the case of the use of
  low-dimensional or high-dimensional data respectively); iteration counter $t = 1$;
create the empty subsets A and B;
estimate the number of the examined objects n;
calculate the $\dfrac{n \times (n-2)}{2}$ pairwise distances between the examined objects.
while $t \leq round(n/2, digits = 0)$ **do**
  $\quad$ allocation of pair of objects s and p, the distance between which is minimal;
  $\quad$ distribution the objects s and p into the subsets A and B respectively;
  $\quad$ $t = t + 1$;
end
if $(n\%\%2)! = 0$ **then**
  $\quad$ distribution of the last object into both the subsets A and B;
end
Return the subsets A and B.

To calculate the external clustering quality criteria, we assumed that in the case of reproducibility error minimum value, the clustering results on equal power subsets should be maximally similar and, the difference of the IQC calculated for the clustering obtained on the equal power subsets should be minimal ones. For this reason, the External clustering Quality Criterion (EQC) was calculated as the normalized difference of the IQC obtained for equal power subsets at appropriate step of the clustering procedure implementation:

$$EQC = \frac{IQC(A) - IQC(B)}{IQC(A) + IQC(B)} \tag{2}$$

Minimum value of the criterion (2) corresponds to the best clustering in terms of the reproducibility error.

It is obvious that optimal clustering corresponds to extreme values of both the IQC and EQC. However, it should be noted that these criteria can disagree between each other. For example, the clustering results obtained on two equal power subsets can be no optimal in terms of IQC but, the difference of the clustering results can be minimal one and the EQC value in this case is minimal too. To solve this problem, it is necessary to calculate the Complex Balance Criterion (CBC) which should include both the IQC and EQC as the components. The idea of balance criterion calculation was proposed in [21] and follow developed in [1,2,4]. Below, we present the algorithm (Algorithm 2) to calculate the CBC based on the use of Harrington desirability function [14] presented by the equation:

$$d = exp(-exp(-Y)) \tag{3}$$

where Y is non-dimensional parameter, values of which is varied linearly within the range from -2 to 5; d is the private desirability, values of which is changed from 0 to 1 respectively. Within the framework of our research, we assumed the

IQC and EQC values are changed from its minimum to maximum values or back linearly too.

Algorithm 2: CBC values calculation

Initialization:

calculate: the vectors of both the IQC and EQC for each of the obtained clustering within the range of the clustering algorithm parameters change;

create the empty vector of CBC;

set: iteration counter $t = 1$; iteration counter of the used criteria $m = 1$; length of the IQC or EQC vectors n;

while $t \leq n$ **do**

Transforming the scales of both the IQC and EQC into Y scale considering the type of appropriate dependence as follows:

$$\begin{cases} Y = a \pm b \cdot IQC; \\ Y = a - b \cdot EQC. \end{cases} \quad (4)$$

while $m \leq 3$ **do**

Calculation of Y_m value for each of the used criteria by equation (4);

Calculation of the partial desirabilities for each of the criteria:

$$d_m = exp(-exp(-Y_m))$$

m = m + 1;

end

Calculation of the CBC as geometric average of all partial desirabilities:

$$CBC_t = \sqrt[3]{\prod_{m=1}^{3} d_m}$$

t = t + 1;

end

Return the vector of CBC values.

---

where: signs $+$ and $-$ correspond to positive and negative correlation between appropriate quality criterion and Y values respectively; parameters a and b are determined empirically considering the appropriate criterion boundary values:

$$Y_{max} = a - b \cdot IQC_{min} \ or \ Y_{max} = a + b \cdot IQC_{max}$$
$$Y_{min} = a - b \cdot IQC_{max} \ or \ Y_{min} = a + b \cdot IQC_{min}$$
$$Y_{max} = a - b \cdot EQC_{min}$$
$$Y_{min} = a - b \cdot EQC_{max}$$

Algorithm 3 presents the stepwise procedure of data processing based on the use of DBSCAN clustering algorithm.

Algorithm 3: General stepwise procedure of data processing based on the use of DBSCAN clustering algorithm

---

Initialization:
select the IQC considering the type of the examined data;
division of the dataset into two equal power subsets A and B using
   Algorithm 1;
set: range $(MinPts_{min}, MinPts_{max})$; iteration counter $k = p_{min}$;
create the empty array of EPS, IQC, EQC and CBC;
while $k \leq p_{max}$ **do**
    evaluate the range (eps_{min}, eps_{max}) and step the EPS-neighborhood
    value variation $(dEPS)$ using k-dist graph;
    set the eps value iteration counter $t = eps_{min}$;
    while $t \leq eps_{max}$ **do**
        Apply the clustering algorithm to equal power subsets A and B.
        Clusters formation;
        calculate the number of clusters in the obtained clustering n_A and
        n_B;
        if $n_A == n_B$ **then**
            calculation of the IQC for equal power subsets A and B in
            accordance with Table 1;
            calculation of the EQC by equation (2);
            $t = t + dEPS$
        else
            continue;
        end
    end
    $k = k + 1$;
end
calculation of the CBC in accordance with Algorithm 2;
creation of the charts of IQC, EQC and CBC criteria versus the
   algorithm parameters;
results analysis, select the optimal parameters of the algorithm operation
   considering the research objective.

---

5   Experiment, Results and Discussion

Simulation procedure was carried out based on R software [16] using packages: *clusterCrit* [7] and *dbscan* [13]. The DBSCAN clustering algorithm was proposed as a solution of the problem to divide the objects into clusters of arbitrary shapes [10,13]. This algorithm successfully recognize the clusters of complex form including noise. As was shown in [1,13], the result of this algorithm operation is determined by two parameters: ε-neighborhood (eps) and minimal number of points inside the *eps* (*minpts*). We evaluate these parameters within the framework of our research.

5.1   Experimental Datasets

We used the two dimensional synthetic datasets which are free available at website of the School of Computing, University of Eastern Finland [11]. The examined data are presented in Fig. 1.

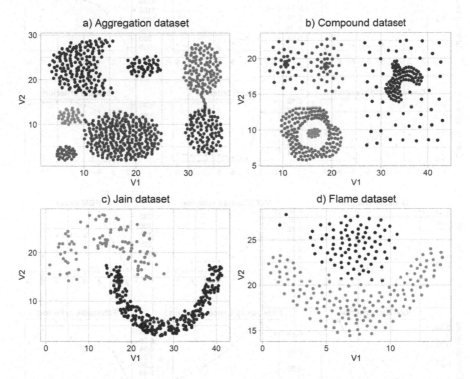

Fig. 1. Two dimensional synthetic datasets: a) Aggregation; b) Compound; c) Jain; d) Flame (Color figure online)

An analysis of the examined datasets description allows concluding that Aggregation and Compound data contain seven and six of non-intersection clusters respectively. In the case of Compound dataset use, some of the points can be identified as noise since the density of their distribution is significantly less in comparison with density of other points distribution. Datasets Jain and Flame contain two of clusters. Moreover, in the case of Jain data, the cluster in blue color can be divided into two subclusters considering the density of the points distribution.

5.2   Simulation Results and Discussion

Figures 2 and 3 show the results of the simulation concerning selection of the optimal *IQC* for *Aggregation* and *Compound* datasets respectively. Previously, we have divided the data into clusters from two to nine for *Aggregation* data and from two to eight for *Compound* dataset.

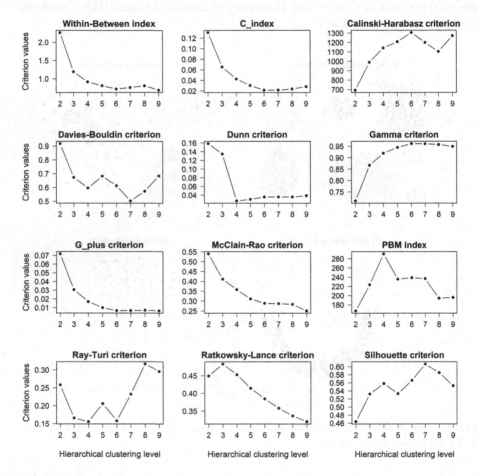

Fig. 2. Results of the simulation concerning selection of the optimal *IQC* for *Aggregation* dataset

The analysis of the charts presented in Fig. 2 allows concluding that only *Davies-Bouldin* and *Silhouette* criteria are effective ones for this type of data since, these criteria achieved its minimum and maximum values respectively at the seventh hierarchical level. Moreover, as it can be seen from the charts, *Davies-Bouldin* criterion is more reasonable in comparison with *Silhouette* criterion due to larger range of the criterion value variation during the hierarchical clustering level variation. As can be seen from Fig. 1, this dataset contains seven of clusters. Thus, the dendrogram was cut at hierarchical clustering levels from 2 to 9. The extreme values of the *IQC* (*max* or *min*) should correspond to the seventh hierarchical clustering level.

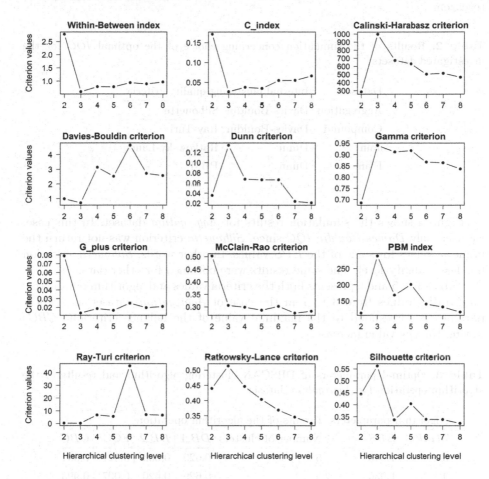

Fig. 3. Results of the simulation concerning selection of the optimal *IQC* for *Compound* dataset

In the case of *Compound* data use (Fig. 3), the result is more complex. So, three clusters are identified by most criteria. Really, the points can be divided into three separated groups. As it can be seen from Fig. 1, the centers of two clusters are differ and, the centers of other two pairs of clusters almost coincide. For this reason, the criteria which contain as the component the distance between clusters' centers should have local extremum at the sixth hierarchical level. As it can be seen from Fig. 3, *Davies-Bouldin* criterion allows us to identify both the third and sixth hierarchical clustering levels. Thus, to our mind, this criterion is more preferable one in comparison with other IQC.

The same results were obtained for other types of the examined datasets. The analysis of the simulation results has allowed us to choose the optimal IQC considering the type of the examined datasets. Table 2 presents the results of this stage implementation. These criteria were applied at the next stage of our research.

Table 2. Results of the simulation concerning choice of the optimal IQC for the investigated datasets

Datasets	Internal clustering quality criteria	
Aggregation	Davies-Bouldin	Silhouette
Compound	Davies-Bouldin	Ray-Turi
Jain	Dunn	Ratkowsky-Lance
Flame	Dunn	PBM

Figure 4 shows the simulation results for *Aggregation* dataset. In this case, we used only *Davies-Bouldin IQC* since, *Silhouette* criterion was not return the numeric values for some of the *EPS* values. In other words, *Silhouette* criterion has less stability level. The same results were obtained for other datasets.

Tables 3, 4, 5 and 6 presents both the criteria values and algorithm parameters for MinPts values from 3 to 7 in the case of *Aggregation* dataset use. These parameters correspond to the maximal value of the balance criterion (CBC) during the *eps* value increase.

Table 3. Optimal parameters of DBSCAN clustering algorithm and results of the algorithm operation for *Aggregation* dataset

Algorithm parameters		Results of the algorithm operation				
MinPts	*EPS*	Number of clusters	DB_1	DB_2	EQC	CBC
3	1.640	5	0.629	0.603	0.021	0.991
4	1.936	5	0.629	0.620	0.007	0.993
5	1.810	6	0.543	0.563	0.017	0.992
6	1.970	6	0.543	0.563	0.017	0.993
7	**2.019**	**7**	**0.509**	**0.498**	**0.011**	**0.994**

The analysis of both Fig. 4 and Tables 3, 4, 5 and 6 allows us to conclude the following:

– the internal clustering quality criteria (IQC) are not effective in terms of the reproducibility error since, the extreme values of these criteria disagree between each other for equal power subsets A and B for the same EPS value;

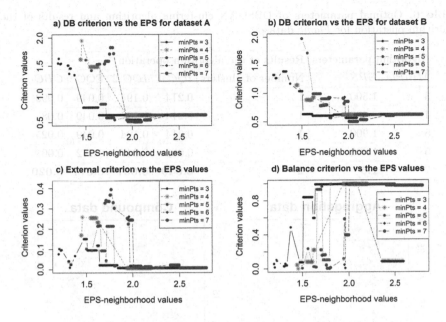

Fig. 4. Results of the simulation for *Aggregation* dataset

Table 4. Optimal parameters of DBSCAN clustering algorithm and results of the algorithm operation for *Compound* dataset

Algorithm parameters		Results of the algorithm operation				
MinPts	*EPS*	Number of clusters	*DB_1*	*DB_2*	EQC	*CBC*
3	1.220	5	4.059	3.455	0.080	0.600
4	**1.560**	**5**	**3.846**	**3.463**	**0.052**	**0.630**
5	2.370	4	1.817	2.812	0.295	0.653
6	2.400	4	1.687	2.378	0.170	0.448
7	2.540	4	1.692	3.025	0.283	0.415

Table 5. Optimal parameters of DBSCAN clustering algorithm and results of the algorithm operation for *Jain* dataset

Algorithm parameters		Results of the algorithm operation				
MinPts	*EPS*	Number of clusters	*DN_1*	*DN_2*	EQC	*CBC*
3	**2.865**	**3**	**0.107**	**0.119**	**0.056**	**0.993**
4	3.224	2	0.076	0.096	0.118	0.493
5	2.845	3	0.055	0.086	0.220	0.809
6	2.875	3	0.082	0.046	0.274	0.524
7	3.831	2	0.039	0.067	0.262	0.480

Table 6. Optimal parameters of DBSCAN clustering algorithm and results of the algorithm operation for *Flame* dataset

Algorithm parameters		Results of the algorithm operation				
MinPts	*EPS*	Number of clusters	*IQC_1*	*IQC_2*	EQC	*CBC*
3	1.500	1	0.214	0.194	0.049	0.993
4	1.496	1	0.214	0.194	0.049	0.085
5	1.900	1	0.214	0.194	0.049	0.025
6	1.600	2	0.066	0.047	0.172	0.008
7	**1.5**	**2**	**0.049**	**0.057**	**0.077**	**0.020**

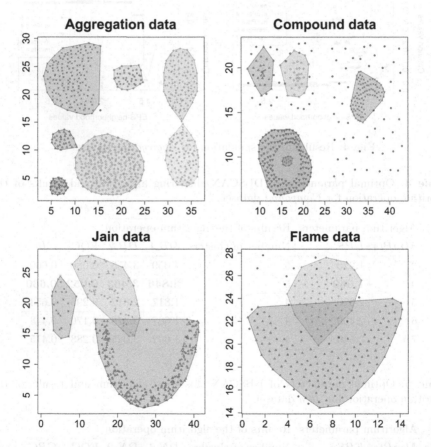

Fig. 5. Results of the two dimensional data clustering

– the use of the external clustering quality criterion (*EQC*) also do not allow finding the optimal solution. The minimum value of this criterion does not correspond to the optimal clustering. Moreover, the *IQC* and the *EQC* can be disagreed between each other;

– the complex balance clustering quality criterion (CBC) allows fixing the optimal clustering for appropriate combination of the DBSCAN algorithm parameters. Choice of the minpts and eps values combination in this case depends on goal of the clustering procedure.

Figure 5 presents the results of data clustering based on the apply of DBSCAN clustering algorithm with determined optimal parameters for each of the used datasets. The optimal parameters in each of the cases corresponded to maximum value of the CBC considering the clustering objectivity (number of clusters).

The analysis of the obtained results allows concluding that in all cases the data were distributed into clusters adequately. So, in the case of Aggregation data use, the clustering was done perfectly. Only one point was identified as noise. In the case of Compound dataset use, five clusters were marked out adequately. Many points were identified as noise. It is reasonable since. The density of these points distribution is significantly less in comparison with density of clusters points distribution. In the cases of Jain and Flame datasets use, the algorithm identified three and two of clusters respectively. The analysis of the points distribution in two-dimensional space confirms the adequacy of these divisions.

6 Conclusions

The conducted research concerning evaluation of the internal clustering quality criteria effectiveness using various types of two-dimensional synthetic datasets has confirmed assumption about importance of choice of the internal clustering quality criteria considering the type of the examined data. Four type of synthetic dataset which are free available at website of the School of Computing, University of Eastern Finland has been used during the simulation process: Aggregation, Compound, Jain and Flame. Previous analysis of these data distribution has shown that they contain different number of various shapes clusters. The Internal clustering Quality Criteria (IQC) were calculated using **clusterCrit** package of R software. We have used only the IQC which allow determining the optimal clustering based on the extrema (min or max) values. The External clustering Quality Criterion (EQC) was calculated as the normalized difference of the IQC estimated on equal power subsets (contain the same quantity of pairwise similar objects). The final decision concerning clustering algorithm optimal parameters determination was done based on maximum value of the CBC which include both the IQC and EQC as the components.

Density based DBSCAN clustering algorithm has been used during the simulation process. In beginning, we have divided artificially the data into clusters within the range from 2 to 9 for Aggregation data; 8 for compound dataset; 6 for Jain and Flame data. Then, we have calculated the IQC, EQC and CBC at each of the hierarchical levels. The analysis of the obtained results has allowed us to conclude that various datasets need different combination of the IQC. Moreover, the results of the simulation using DBSCAN clustering algorithm has shown also that the IQC are not effective in terms of the reproducibility error since, the extreme values of these criteria disagree between each other for equal power subsets A and B for the same EPS value. The use of the EQC also do not allow finding the optimal solution. The minimum value of this criterion does not correspond to the optimal clustering. Moreover, the IQC and the EQC can be disagreed between each other. It is effective the CBC since this criterion allows fixing the optimal clustering for appropriate combination of the DBSCAN algorithm parameters. Choice of the minpts and eps values combination in this case depends on goal of the clustering procedure. The simulation results analysis has shown also that in all cases the data were distributed into clusters adequately.

The further perspectives of the authors' research are the implementation of the obtained results for the development of the complex data clustering technique based on inductive methods of objective clustering with the use of various clustering algorithms.

References

1. Babichev, S., Durnyak, B., Pikh, I., Senkivskyy, V.: An evaluation of the objective clustering inductive technology effectiveness implemented using density-based and agglomerative hierarchical clustering algorithms. In: Lytvynenko, V., Babichev, S., Wójcik, W., Vynokurova, O., Vyshemyrskaya, S., Radetskaya, S. (eds.) ISDMCI 2019. AISC, vol. 1020, pp. 532–553. Springer, Cham (2020). https://doi.org/10.1007/978-3-030-26474-1_37

2. Babichev, S., Lytvynenko, V., Korobchynskyi, M., Taiff, M.A.: Objective clustering inductive technology of gene expression sequences features. In: Kozielski, S., Mrozek, D., Kasprowski, P., Małysiak-Mrozek, B., Kostrzewa, D. (eds.) BDAS 2017. CCIS, vol. 716, pp. 359–372. Springer, Cham (2017). https://doi.org/10.1007/978-3-319-58274-0_29

3. Babichev, S., Lytvynenko, V., Skvor, J., Fiser, J.: Model of the objective clustering inductive technology of gene expression profiles based on SOTA and DBSCAN clustering algorithms. In: Shakhovska, N., Stepashko, V. (eds.) CSIT 2017. AISC, vol. 689, pp. 21–39. Springer, Cham (2018). https://doi.org/10.1007/978-3-319-70581-1_2

4. Babichev, S., Taif, M., Lytvynenko, V.: Estimation of the inductive model of objects clustering stability based on the k-means algorithm for different levels of data noise. Radio Electron. Comput. Sci. Control 4, 54–60 (2016). https://doi.org/10.15588/1607-3274-2016-4-7

5. Babichev, S., Taif, M., Lytvynenko, V., Osypenko, V.: Criterial analysis of gene expression sequences to create the objective clustering inductive technology. In: 2017 IEEE 37th International Conference on Electronics and Nanotechnology, pp. 244–248 (2017). https://doi.org/10.1109/ELNANO.2017.7939756

6. Calinski, T., Harabasz, J.: A dendrite method for cluster analysis. Commun. Stat. 3, 1–27 (1974)

7. Desgraupes, B.: Compute clustering validation indices (2018). https://cran.r-project.org/web/packages/clusterCrit

8. Elm, J., Kubečka, J., Besel, V., et al.: Modeling the formation and growth of atmospheric molecular clusters: a review. J. Aerosol Sci. 149, Article no. 105621 (2020). https://doi.org/10.1016/j.jaerosci.2020.105621

9. Esposito, A.M., Alaia, G., Giudicepietro, F., Pappalardo, L., D'Antonio, M.: Unsupervised geochemical analysis of the eruptive products of Ischia, Vesuvius and Campi Flegrei. In: Esposito, A., Faundez-Zanuy, M., Morabito, F.C., Pasero, E. (eds.) Progresses in Artificial Intelligence and Neural Systems. SIST, vol. 184, pp. 175–184. Springer, Singapore (2021). https://doi.org/10.1007/978-981-15-5093-5_17

10. Ester, M., Kriegel, H., Sander, J., Xu, X.: A density-based algorithm for discovering clusters in large spatial datasets with noise. In: Proceedings of the Second International Conference on Knowledge Discovery and Data Mining, pp. 226–231 (1996)

11. Fränti, P., Sieranoja, S.: K-means properties on six clustering benchmark datasets. Appl. Intell. 48(12), 4743–4759 (2018). https://doi.org/10.1007/s10489-018-1238-7

12. Guo, X., Lin, H., Wu, Y., Peng, M.: A new data clustering strategy for enhancing mutual privacy in healthcare IoT systems. Future Gener. Comput. Syst. 113, 407–417 (2020). https://doi.org/10.1016/j.future.2020.07.023

13. Hahsler, M., Piekenbrock, M., Arya, S., Mount, D.: Density based clustering of applications with noise (DBSCAN) and related algorithms (2019). https://github.com/mhahsler/dbscan

14. Harrington, J.: The desirability function. Ind. Qual. Control 21(10), 494–498 (1965). http://asq.org/qic/display-item/?item=4860

15. Hu, Z., Tyshchenko, O.K.: An approach to online fuzzy clustering based on the Mahalanobis distance measure. In: Hu, Z., Petoukhov, S., He, M. (eds.) CSDEIS 2019. AISC, vol. 1127, pp. 364–374. Springer, Cham (2020). https://doi.org/10.1007/978-3-030-39216-1_33

16. Ihaka, R., Gentleman, R.: R: a language for data analysis and graphics. J. Comput. Graph. Stat. 5(3), 299–314 (1996)

17. Ivakhnenko, A.: Objective clustering based on the theory of self-organization models. Automatics 5, 6–15 (1987)

18. Izonin, I., Kryvinska, N., Vitynskyi, P., Tkachenko, R., Zub, K.: GRNN approach towards missing data recovery between IoT systems. In: Barolli, L., Nishino, H., Miwa, H. (eds.) INCoS 2019. AISC, vol. 1035, pp. 445–453. Springer, Cham (2020). https://doi.org/10.1007/978-3-030-29035-1_43

19. Kanishcheva, O., Vysotska, V., Chyrun, L., Gozhyj, A.: Method of integration and content management of the information resources network. In: Shakhovska, N., Stepashko, V. (eds.) CSIT 2017. AISC, vol. 689, pp. 204–216. Springer, Cham (2018). https://doi.org/10.1007/978-3-319-70581-1_14

20. Liu, Z., Barahona, M.: Graph-based data clustering via multiscale community detection. Appl. Netw. Sci. 5(1), Article no. 3 (2020). https://doi.org/10.1007/s41109-019-0248-7

21. Madala, H., Ivakhnenko, A.: Inductive Learning Algorithms for Complex Systems Modeling, p. 380. CRC Press, Boca Raton (1994). Chap. 5: Clusterization and Recognition

22. Mishchuk, O., Tkachenko, R., Izonin, I.: Missing data imputation through SGTM neural-like structure for environmental monitoring tasks. In: Hu, Z., Petoukhov, S., Dychka, I., He, M. (eds.) ICCSEEA 2019. AISC, vol. 938, pp. 142–151. Springer, Cham (2020). https://doi.org/10.1007/978-3-030-16621-2_13

23. Naum, O., Chyrun, L., Vysotska, V., Kanishcheva, O.: Intellectual system design for content formation. In: Proceedings of the 12th International Scientific and Technical Conference on Computer Sciences and Information Technologies, CSIT 2017, vol. 1, pp. 131–138. Institute of Electrical and Electronics Engineers Inc. (2017). https://doi.org/10.1109/STC-CSIT.2017.8098753

24. Ruiz, L., Pegalajar, M., Arcucci, R., Molina-Solana, M.: A time-series clustering methodology for knowledge extraction in energy consumption data. Expert Syst. Appl. **160**, Article no. 113731 (2020). https://doi.org/10.1016/j.eswa.2020.113731

25. Senouci, O., Harous, S., Aliouat, Z.: Survey on vehicular ad hoc networks clustering algorithms: overview, taxonomy, challenges, and open research issues. Int. J. Commun. Syst. **33**(11), Article no. e4402 (2020). https://doi.org/10.1002/dac.4402

26. Wang, F., Geng, Y., Zhang, H.: An improved fuzzy C-means clustering algorithm based on intuitionistic fuzzy sets. In: Liu, Q., Liu, X., Li, L., Zhou, H., Zhao, H.-H. (eds.) Proceedings of the 9th International Conference on Computer Engineering and Networks. AISC, vol. 1143, pp. 333–345. Springer, Singapore (2021). https://doi.org/10.1007/978-981-15-3753-0_32

27. Wang, S., Li, Q., Zhao, C., Zhu, X., Yuan, H., Dai, T.: Extreme clustering - a clustering method via density extreme points. Inf. Sci. **542**, 24–39 (2021). https://doi.org/10.1016/j.ins.2020.06.069

28. Zhao, Q., Xu, M., Fränti, P.: Sum-of-squares based cluster validity index and significance analysis. In: Kolehmainen, M., Toivanen, P., Beliczynski, B. (eds.) ICANNGA 2009. LNCS, vol. 5495, pp. 313–322. Springer, Heidelberg (2009). https://doi.org/10.1007/978-3-642-04921-7_32

Assessing the Investment Risk of Virtual IT Company Based on Machine Learning

Hrystyna Lipyanina[1]![ORCID], Valeriya Maksymovych[1]![ORCID], Anatoliy Sachenko[1]![ORCID], Taras Lendyuk[1(✉)]![ORCID], Andrii Fomenko[2]![ORCID], and Ivan Kit[1]

[1] Ternopil National Economic University, Lvivska Str., 11, Ternopil 46000, Ukraine
xrustya.com@gmail.com, maksymovych.lera@gmail.com, {as,tl}@tneu.edu.ua,
kitivan400@gmail.com
[2] Dnipropetrovsk State University of Internal Affairs,
Gagarin Avenue 26, Dnipro, Ukraine
mail@dduvs.in.ua

Abstract. A module for assessing the investment risks of a virtual IT company has been developed. It enables to reduce the time spent on assessing the inves-tor's risks of a virtual IT company. A detailed justification of each selected risk parameter that influences on the success of the investment project of the virtual IT Company has done. A developed algorithm for assessing the investment risk of the virtual IT company is based on machine learning and using the expert scoring method (10 experts from 20 implemented projects were involved) by 23 risk parameters. Forecasting of investment risk assess-ment modeling of the virtual IT company using machine learning is based on eight methods: Support Vector Classifier, Stochastic Gradient Decent Classifier, Random Forest Classifier, Decision Tree Classifier, Gaussian Na-ive Bayes, K-Neighbors Classifier, Ada Boost Classifier, Logistic Regression. In addition, a module was developed to support decision-making based on three methods with the best forecast, namely: Support Vector Classifier, Random Forest Classifier, K-Neighbors Classifier.

Keywords: Investment risk · Virtual enterprise · Support Vector Classifier · Random Forest Classifier · K-Neighbors Classifier · Machine learning

1 Introduction

In current business conditions, there is a need for a product (service), which requires an innovative approach to its manufacturing. All this creates a need for new forms of business, one of which is presented by virtual enterprises that are becoming increasingly popular nowadays. A virtual enterprise is created by selecting human, financial, material, organizational, technological and other resources from different enterprises and integrating them using computer networks [13, 26]. Effective risk management of a virtual enterprise allows increasing its profits.

© Springer Nature Switzerland AG 2020
S. Babichev et al. (Eds.): DSMP 2020, CCIS 1158, pp. 167–187, 2020.
https://doi.org/10.1007/978-3-030-61656-4_11

The investment project we consider as a set of certain elements and relations between them that ensures the achievement of investment goals within the time set and limited resources and contributes to the further development of economic processes. As the investment project is aimed at a long-term initial investment, which involves ensuring the processes of expanded reproduction, it must compensate not only the amount of investment for the investor, but also ensure the benefit of financing the further object development. At the same time, the external environment is characterized not only by a set of factors, but also by certain characteristics.

The reason for the risk is uncertainty and the lack of complete information, which makes it impossible to forecast economic phenomenon adequately. Thus, implementing an investment project, any entity faces a risk that is a subjective-objective category, which is associated with decision-making in a situation of uncertainty and conflict. It reflects the extent to which the expected result is achieved and the deviations from the goal, taking into account the controlled and uncontrolled factors, and virtual businesses are no exceptions.

In this regard, the development of a module for investment risks assessing of a virtual IT company based on machine learning is one of the promising areas in risk management for investment portfolio formation of a virtual company.

The paper is devoted to this topic, and the rest of paper is distributed in the following way: Sect. 2 discusses the analysis of related work, and Sect. 3 is devoted to data exploration. In Sect. 4, a cross-evaluation of classification methods based on machine learning was performed, and the three best methods were selected. Section 5 presents a decision-making module based on best practices. Section 6 summarizes the results of the study.

2 Related Work and Problem Statement

In references [17,18,20,35,39–41,52] conceptual models of virtual enterprises are offered and the innovative infrastructure of the information system and its network solution are presented. In References [5,31,49,50] recommendations for reducing the innovation and financial risks of a virtual enterprise are given.

In reference [14] the choice of partners is formulated as a type of fuzzy hybrid multicriteria group decision problem with degrees of fuzzy truth of alternatives comparisons presented as fuzzy numbers (TrFN). A reference [36] describes an INPR-based group decision-making algorithm that can be used to eliminate incomplete and inconsistent INPRs. In reference [47] the results of the study of cybernetic enterprise management based on the model and technology of the digital counterpart and the concept of intelligent enterprise management system are described. In references [2,10,24,32,34] risk management processes are discussed, which are established firmly in the context of project management task in general and are focused on efficiency improving. In references [4,9,23,24, 28,38] the strategy of risk management in IT projects is investigated on examples and it is established that the enterprises practicing in the IT industry, as a rule, are subjects to risk, who want to undertake risk management training.

A reference [51] presents the methodology and computer model developed by the International Energy Agency to quantify the effects for policy uncertainty of climate change on energy investment using the ROA approach. The reference [30] presents an innovative methodology for investments evaluating in ESS. The Reference [45] is a comparative study of modern and old investment tools, the reference [11] outlines the individuals who influence the investor investment structures.

The neural networks [19,43] were used in a number of following references. For example, the reference [3] presents a systematic survey of single-class support classifiers. The methods of support vector machines (SVM) and neural networks were used in reference [12], where the SVM model received the highest efficiency indicators among classifiers for each data set. The reference [22] highlights the stochastic gradient descent algorithms usage for big data applications, for example, to accelerate SVM or controlled regression on a large scale, or to improve the effectiveness of online learning or real-time prediction (control). In reference [6], the ensemble methods (Random Forest, AdaBoost and Kernel Factory) were compared with the models of single classifiers (Neural Networks, Logistic Regression, Vector Machine Support and K-Nearest Neighbor). In reference [44] the basic concepts of the multilevel classification strategy are presented and two methods of decision trees design are discussed. In reference [15], scenarios for decision tree classifier constructing are described. In [25] statistical methods were used to estimate nonparametric density. The reference [33] proposes a new solution for the k-nearest classification of neighbors based on Spark, and the reference [21] describes the choice of the parameter K in the algorithm of the k-nearest neighbor. In reference [42], the AdaBoost acceleration algorithm was analyzed, as well as its later versions Gentle and Real AdaBoost. The reference [48] proposes a new acceleration algorithm giving a smaller generalization error comparing to the mentioned algorithms due to a slightly larger learning error. The reference [27] describes the reasons for the logistics model popularity and its key features.

The vast majority of the above works clearly outline a specific area of applications, namely: risk management, virtual enterprise management, enterprise investment risk management, IT enterprises risk management, using of machine learning methods in socio-economic sphere. Some studies [5,9,24,28,30,50] partially combine several areas.

The reference [46] is the closest analogue in which machine learning methods were used to facilitate the process of government bonds artificial selection. The existing investment funds as well as income and expense were analyzed, and this simplifies decision-making.

The authors of this paper propose to up-date a work [46] exploring the investment risks of a virtual IT company based on machine learning. To do that, the analysis of machine learning methods must be carried out firstly Fig. 1. Secondly, authors are going to optimize the assessing result of the investment risks for the virtual IT company using machine learning methods and expert evaluation. Having such optimal result, the user can make management decisions regarding investing in a new virtual company.

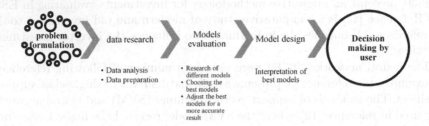

Fig. 1. Sequent analysis of evaluating the best models based on machine learning

3   Data Research

3.1   Data Analysis

The main problem in risk assessment is the analysis and forecast of possible losses. Losses are estimated by the amount and probability of their occurrence. This applies to material, financial, informational, labor, time and special types of losses. Sources of possible losses [5, 23, 28, 32, 37, 38, 49] are political factors, economic and social instability, growth rates of scientific and technological progress, goods and services aging, management methods imperfection, staff incompetence, clients dishonesty, imperfect monetary and legal policy.

Each country has its own risks legislation, it is very difficult to generalize them, so the authors consider the risks in accordance with the current Ukrainian legislation [1]: permits and licenses obtaining; demand and outlet; operational risks (supply and raw materials; costs underestimation; technology shortcomings); risks regulatory; financial and macroeconomic risks (financing availability; financial capacity of a private partner; interest rate; inflation; exchange rate of hryvnia to foreign currency); social and political risks, objections or resistance from key stakeholders; force majeure and other high-level contingencies.

If we consider the risks that apply to virtual enterprises, the general classification should include:

1. Risk of financial gain lost. These are the risks of indirect financial loss (lost profit) as a result of failure to take any action (for example, failure to achieve planned sales) or, if we consider the global option – the termination of economic activity of the enterprise.
2. Resource risk. It is connected with prices raising due to market fluctuations or deteriorating quality. In addition, this risk may arise as a result of labor costs increasing.

3. Implementation risk. This type of risk is due to the fact that during project implementation or company's strategy implementation the final forecast results are not achieved: experienced staff with the necessary qualifications, who would know the market specifics were not employed; inappropriate fulfill-ment or poor, untimely fulfillment of obligations by the company responsible for the provision of related services; design errors (not accurate calculations).
4. Bureaucratic and administrative risks. Such risks arise as a result of adoption of legally significant regulatory decisions by competent authority that directly or indirectly adversely affect the enterprise activities.
5. Financial risks. This category of risks includes risks that may lead to the possibility of non-return of borrowed capital in the planned time and at the investment planned cost. These include: the occurrence of uncertain circum-stances that may increase the project cost; increase of borrowed capital cost; change in the customers solvency, which may lead to the inability of timely and fully pay for their obligations; fluctuations in prices for manufactured products.
6. Reputational risk. Availability of an office for meetings with clients, branding, recognizability.
7. Staff work. Outflow of information, including using of unstable software.
8. Rapid development and changes in the technology market. Loss of product relevance.
9. Information accumulation and storage.

Taking into account the diversity and specificity of risks that arise in the process of investment project implementing, an important and mandatory com-ponent should be project risk management. With a sufficiently high degree of risk in alternative strategies a decision is often made that is less effective, but has a chance for timely and successful implementation. Analyzing the risk, the following models are used: a priori and empirical. The former ones are built using certain theoretical assumptions based on which recommendations on cer-tain decisions results are often given. The latter ones are based on the general-ization of past observations (statistical information).

Risk can be measured both in absolute and relative terms. In addition to the methods of risk measuring by the level of possible results deviations of activities from the average expected risks can be determined by the amount of possible losses. A 10-point and 5-point scale is used for qualitative risk assessment Table 1.

3.2   Data Preparation

For this study, 10 experts conducted an expert evaluation of 20 projects for the virtual IT companies' creation in the scoring system. The assessment is based on the above parameters. There was formed a database of characteristics for assessing the risk level of virtual IT enterprise, which is the product of the impact degree and risk probability (see Table 1).

The results obtained are given in Table 2.

Table 1. Risk components characteristics

Degree of influence – Q(R)		Degree of influence – I(R)		
5-point scale		10-point scale		
5	Very high 80-100% of investments	Always	Every day	10
		Practically inevitable	More than once a month	9
4	High 60-79% of investments	Very often	More often than once a year, and less than once a month	8
		Often	More often than once in 2 years, and less often than once a year	7
3	Average 40-59% of investments	Possible	More often than once in 3 years, and less often than once a year	6
		Randomness, often caused by human factors	1 time in 3 years, and more often than 1 time in 5 years	5
2	Low 20-39% of investments	Time to time	1 time in 5 years, and more often than 1 time in 7 years	4
		Rarely	1 time in 7 years, and less often than 1 time in 5 years	3
1	Very low 0-19% of investments	Practically impossible	Less than once every 7 years	2
		Impossible	Less than once every 10 years	1

4 Experimental Research

4.1 Data Evaluation

Data evaluation will be performed by machine learning methods, so the programming language for analysis is Python, because it works best with data analysis based on machine learning. The following libraries were used for analysis: pandas, numpy, traintestsplit, SVC, GridSearchCV, SGDClassifier, RandomForestClassifier, DecisionTreeClassifier, GaussianNB KNeighborsClassifier, AdaBoostClassifier, LogisticRegressionKFold and cross. Before data studying, they should be divided into two groups: training set 80%, test set 20%. The training kit should be used to build machine learning models. The test kit should be used to see how well the built model works on unknown data. To determine the best project with minimal risks, we add the fit parameter. Of course, machine learning algorithms operate on numerical values, so we assign the corresponding discrete values 0 or 1. Considering the data in the statistical description (Table 3) and visual (Fig. 2) it is seen that all indicators are dense and have no gaps, which means that the data does not require pre-processing and cleaning, respectively.

Table 2. Data characteristics for assessing the investment risks of a virtual IT enterprise

No	Parameter	Denotation	Denotation
1	Company ID	ID_p	object
2	Expert ID	ID_exp	object
3	Demand and outlet	DM	int64
4	Supplies and raw materials	SIM	int64
5	Underestimation of costs	UC	int64
6	Disadvantages of technology	ST	int64
7	Regulatory risks	RegR	int64
8	Availability of funding	AF	int64
9	Financial capacity of a private partner	FCPP	int64
10	Interest rate	IR	int64
11	Inflation	inflation	int64
12	Exchange rate of hryvnia to foreign currency	ERHFC	int64
13	Force majeure	FM	int64
14	Risk of financial gain loss	RLFG	int64
15	Implementation risk	RSup	int64
16	It is impossible to find staff with the required qualifications	PS	int64
17	Non-fulfillment of obligations by the company	Failure	int64
18	Design errors	DE	int64
19	Changing the solvency of customers	CSC	int64
20	Fluctuations in prices for manufactured products	FPMP	int64
21	Reputation	Reputational	int64
22	Staff work	IS	int64
23	Loss of product relevance	LR	int64
24	Accumulation and storage of information	ISe	int64
25	Accounting	accounting	int64

Table 3 shows the number of values, the average value, the minimum and maximum value in the data set. The line std shows the standard deviation, which measures how scattered the values are – not significant for all parameters. To understand how each attribute is correlated with the risk assessment, a standard correlation coefficient is calculated. The table shows that all values are close to 0, which indicates a low dependence of the parameters on the attribute "fit". Also, most parameters have a negative impact on the attribute, which is logical, because the parameters are risks that have a negative impact by their nature.

Due to the fact that the data set does not contain missed values and features that do not provide useful information for the task, we can conclude that the data set is quite clean. Therefore, it is not needed to do any complex data preparation.

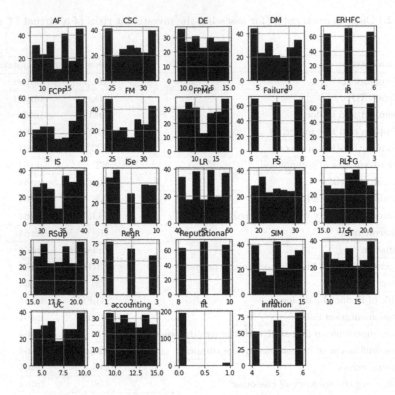

Fig. 2. Data visualization and statistical description

4.2   Cross-estimation of Models

Estimating a machine learning model can be quite complex. Usually the model is estimated on the basis of the error rate. This method is not very reliable, because the accuracy obtained for one test set can be very different from the accuracy obtained for another test set.

The key to a fair comparison of machine learning algorithms is to ensure that each algorithm is evaluated equally on the same data. K-multiple state cross-validation (CV) provides a solution to this problem by dividing the data into parts and ensuring that each part is used as a test set at some point.

We will cross-check on eight classical classification methods: Support Vector Classifier, Stochastic Gradient Decent Classifier, Random Forest Classifier, Decision Tree Classifier, Gaussian Naive Bayes, K-Neighbors Classifier, Ada Boost Classifier, Logistic Regression.

```
# prepare configuration for cross validation test harness
seed = 7
# prepare models
models = []
models.append(('SupportVectorClassifier', SVC()))
models.append(('StochasticGradientDecentC', SGDClassifier()))
models.append(('RandomForestClassifier', RandomForestClassifier()))
```

Table 3. Statistical data description

Parameter	Correlation to the "fit" value	Count	Mean	Std	Min	Max
fit	1,00	201	1	0	0	1
IS	-0,23	201	34	4	28	40
DM	-0,19	201	8	3	4	12
SIM	-0,18	201	11	3	6	15
ST	-0,17	201	14	3	9	18
RegR	-0,15	201	2	1	1	3
FPMP	-0,14	201	12	4	6	18
RLFG	-0,13	201	18	1	2	30
accounting	-0,12	201	12	2	9	15
PS	-0,12	201	25	4	18	32
ISe	-0,11	201	8	1	6	10
I8	0,10	201	2	1	1	3
Failure	-0,09	201	7	1	6	8
AF	-0,08	201	13	3	8	18
Reputational	-0,07	201	9	1	8	10
LR	-0,06	201	45	3	40	50
ERHFC	0,06	201	24	1	5	20
CSC	-0,05	201	28	2	24	32
inflation	-0,04	201	5	1	4	6
RSup	0,03	201	5	1	3	6
UC	0,02	201	7	2	4	10
DE	-0,02	201	12	2	9	15
FM	-0,02	201	8	1	4	12
FCPP	-0,02	201	7	2	3	10

```
models.append(('DecisionTreeClassifier', DecisionTreeClassifier()))
models.append(('GaussianNB', GaussianNB()))
models.append(('KNeighborsClassifier', KNeighborsClassifier()))
models.append(('AdaBoostClassifier', AdaBoostClassifier()))
models.append(('LogisticRegression', LogisticRegression()))
# evaluate each model in turn
results = []
names = []
scoring = 'accuracy'
for name, model in models:
kfold = model_selection.KFold(n_splits=10, random_state=seed)
cv_results = model_selection.cross_val_score(model, X_train, y_train, cv=kfold, scoring=scoring)
results.append(cv_results)
names.append(name)
msg = "%s: %f (%f)" % (name, cv_results.mean(), cv_results.std())
```

The results of cross-estimation (Table 4) show that the best methods are: Support Vector Classifier with a predicted score of 0.98 and a standard deviation close to 0.1; Random Forest Classifier with a predicted score of 0.98 and a standard deviation close to 0.2; K-Neighbors Classifier with a projected score of 0.98 and a standard deviation close to 0.3.

Table 4. Cross-validation results

No	Method	Forecast assessment	Standard deviation
1	SupportVectorClassifier	0.982	0.014
2	StochasticGradientDecentC	0.963	0.024
3	RandomForestClassifier	0.984	0.021
4	DecisionTreeClassifier	0.951	0.042
5	GaussianNB	0.962	0.023
6	KNeighborsClassifier	0.981	0.024
7	AdaBoostClassifier	0.953	0.044
8	LogisticRegression	0.984	0.027

For better evaluation by these methods, it is necessary to carry out their more detailed adjustment and interpretation, which will allow us to make more accurate conclusions.

4.3   Research of the Best Models

Support Vector Classifier. The main goal of Support Vector Classifier (SVC) as a classifier is to find the equation that divides the hyperplane [7] $w_1x_1+w_2x_2+\cdots+w_nx_n+w_0 = 0$ in the space Rn, which would divide the two classes optimally. General view of the transformation F of an object x into a label of class Y is as follows: $F(x) = sign(w^{Tx} - b)$. Then denote $w = (w_1, w_2, \ldots, w_n)$, $b = -w_0$. After adjusting the weights of the algorithm w and b, all objects that fall on one side of the constructed hyperplane will be defined as the first class, and objects that fall on the other side – the second class. In other words, the algorithm maximizes the margin between the hyperplane and the objects of the classes closest to it. Such objects are called reference vectors.

To evaluate the quality of the classifier output, the receiver operating characteristic (ROC) is used, which allows us to determine the class value relative to the method. This is a graph of the false positive learning rate (x-axis) versus the true positive rate (y-axis) for a number of different threshold values between 0.0 and 1.0. The area under the curve (AUC) can be used as a result of a model skill. The AUC function takes both the true results (0,1) from the test set and the predicted probability. The AUC is between 0 and 1. The higher the AUC is, the better the classifier is, and a value of 0.5 indicates the unsuitability of the chosen classification method.

Figure 3 shows that AUC = 0.91 and ROC curve acquires a positive value of 1 at 0.1 value false positive, which indicates a very good construction of the SVC algorithm on the data on investment risks to create a virtual IT company.

Therefore, we can classify on the basis of the SVC method with a test sample of 80% of the total set with a regularization parameter equal to 1 and a polynomial kernel with 4 degrees and equal weights for all parameters.

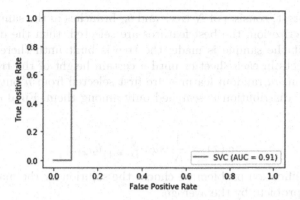

Fig. 3. Graph of the ROC curve for the SVC classifier on the data on investment risks for the creation of a virtual IT company

The next step is to display a text report with the main classification indicators and a confusion matrix to assess the classification accuracy, built on the basis of a test sample.

The main indicators of classification are: precision, recall, f1-score, support. Accuracy shows how precisely the model predicts the resulting class, according to the number of times it correctly defined the class. Completeness is also called sensitivity; it shows how often the relevant classes are selected. Class support shows the number of control instances that participated in grades calculation. Score F1 is the average harmonic in accuracy and completeness; this indicator is more informative than simple accuracy because it takes into account contribution of each class in the overall result.

Each row of the confusion matrix (Table 5) represents instances in the predicted class, and each column represents instances of the actual class (or vice versa).

At the end, we derive the best result using the GridSearchCV library, which allows us to search for the specified values of the parameters for the test sample.

Random Forest. Random Forest [8, 29] is a machine learning algorithm used for solving classification, regression and clustering problems. The main idea is to use a large ensemble of decision trees, each of which itself shows a very low quality of classification, but due to their large number they provide rather good result.

Table 5. Confusion matrix

		Actual class	
		P = Positive	N = Negative
Predicted class	P = Positive	TP = True Positive	FP = False Positive
	N = Negative	FN = False Negative	TN = True Negative

Random Forest, consists of N trees and b_n branches in the sample x: according to a given criterion, the best features are selected, then the division in the tree throughout the sample is made; the tree is built until there are no more than n_{min} objects in each sheet or until a certain height of the tree is reached; at each partition, m random features are first selected from n outputs, and the optimal sample distribution is searched only among them. Final classifier is as follows:

$$a\left(x\right) = \frac{1}{N}\ sum^N_{\{i\ =\ 1\}}b_{i(x)},$$

for the classification problem we choose the solution by the majority, and in the regression problem by the average.

During classification algorithm constructing on the basis of the Random Forest method, it is best to use 80% of the data for a training sample with random determination from the entire sample. The number of trees for analysis in the forest is 320. At visualizing the tree, the following indicators are displayed: feature names – from the list of features; node_ids – identification number on each node; criterion: gini – shows the evaluation of the quality of classification, it reaches its minimum (zero), when all cases in the node fall into one target category; samples; value; class_names – the names for each of the target classes in ascending order.

At the end of the method we get the best result for a test sample based on the Random Forest method.

k Nearest Neighbor. k Nearest Neighbor [16] is one of the simplest classification algorithms and is also sometimes used for solving regression problems. To classify each of the objects of the test sample, it is necessary to perform the following operations: calculate the distance to each of the objects of the training sample; select k objects of the training sample, the distance to which is minimal; assign each attribute to a separate class, which most often occurs among k nearest neighbors.

To determine the optimal k for the method k Nearest Neighbor, it is necessary to conduct a quick test (Fig. 4), which will show at which value of k the test score is stabilized. Testing is performed in the range from 1 to 9 values of k. For assessing the investment risks of creation a virtual IT company k = 2.

The next step is to build the Nearest Neighbor algorithm using 80% of the data in the entire sample. Weights are given by the method of 'distance': in this case, the closer neighbors will have a greater influence than the neighbors which are distant. Algorithm for calculating the nearest neighbors is 'auto' which will determine the most appropriate algorithm based on "fit" values.

Then, a text report is made with the main classification indicators and confusion matrix for assessing the classification accuracy, built on the basis of a test sample and the best project result.

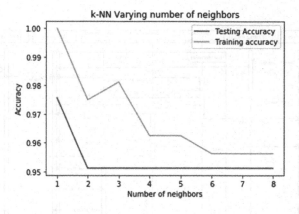

Fig. 4. k value for KNN

5   Obtained Results and Discussion

The developed module is in fact an information support system for decision-making, designed to operate in terms of determining investment risks for a virtual IT company (MLInvestRisks). The sequence diagram (Fig. 5) shows the messages exchange (i.e., methods calling) between different objects in a specific, time-limited situation. The sequence diagram specifically identifies the order and times of sending messages to objects. In sequence diagrams, objects are represented by vertical dashed lines with the object name at the top. Thus, messages sent from one object to another are displayed by arrows indicating the operation and parameters.

In the first stage, the performer (block 1) enters (1.1) test data into the MLInvestRisks interface (block 2), this is the project data for the creation of a virtual IT company that interests him with the appropriate risk assessment. The data is also output back (3.2) to the interface (block 2) so that the performer (block 1) can see it.

The data is transferred (2.1) to the database (block 3) with a test sample and entered (3.1) into the general database (block 7). Then the data enters (8.2) in the general database (block 7) of the training data (block 8). Training data is generated (8.1, 9.1) on the basis of expert assessment (block 9).

The next step is to process the data by three methods that have shown the best cross-evaluation – Support Vector Classifier (block 4), Random Forest Classifier (block 5), KNeighborsClassifier (block 6). Each block (block 4–6) submits a request for a training sample (4.1, 5.1, 6.1) to the general database (block 7) and a connection to it is obtained (7.1, 7.3, 7.5) (see Fig. 5). The simulation is performed on the basis of a training sample.

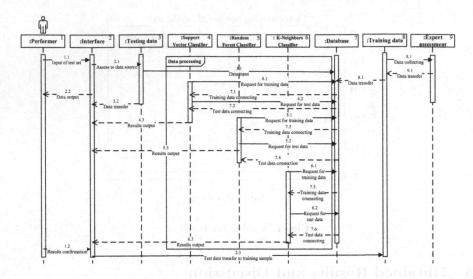

Fig. 5. Sequence diagram UML MLInvestRisks

Then the simulation is carried out based on a test sample, for which a request is first made to the general database (block 7) for test data (4.2, 5.2, 6.2) for each method separately and the connection to the data is obtained (7.2, 7.4, 7.6).

The obtained results for the test sample are displayed (4.3, 5.3, 6.3) in the interface (block 2). Then the performer (block 1) reviews the results obtained and on the basis of input data (2.2) confirms the result (1.2) with the appropriate decisions whether the module correctly presented the best result of investment risk assessment for a virtual IT company. This data is automatically transferred (2.3) to the training data (block 8), for further operation of the module) (see Fig. 5).

After input a new test sample in MLInvestRisks, we obtain the following results for the Support Vector Classifier method (Fig. 6).

The confusion matrix Support Vector Classifier identifies 47 projects in which the risks are optimal. Based on the algorithm, a prediction is made – three projects are the most profitable.

The algorithm evaluates the main indicators for the classification of the assessment of f1, when identifying projects that are not suitable for investment with the accuracy of 99%, and projects that should be accepted – with the accuracy of 86.

The overall estimate of the model accuracy is 98%, which is a pretty good value. According to the module results based on Support Vector Classifier, the most attractive investment project to create a virtual IT company is P8 project.

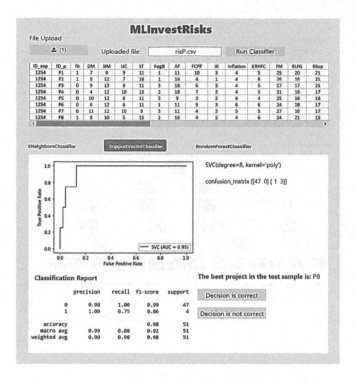

Fig. 6. Support Vector Classifier results window in MLInvestRisks

Due to the results (Fig. 7) of Random Forest Classifier, the average absolute simulation error is 0.05. Modeling score is 0.98, which is a good result. The tree shows that the results are correct for IR ¡= 0.7, ST ¡= −1.2, RLFG ¡= 0.8, which is 3% of all data. The best project in terms of the level of risk was P8 project that was presented by the module based on Random Forest Classifier, as well as by the method of Support Vector Classifier.

The confusion matrix KNeighborsClassifier (Fig. 8) identifies 39 projects to create a virtual IT company, in which the risks are optimal. According to the algorithm results, one project is the most profitable. Due to the main classification indicators it is seen that according to f1, when identifying projects that are not suitable for investment, the algorithm determines with an accuracy of 0.99 and projects that should be invested with an accuracy of 0.67. The overall accuracy estimate of the model is 0.98, which is a very good result. According to the module results based on KNeighborsClassifier, the P1 project was chosen.

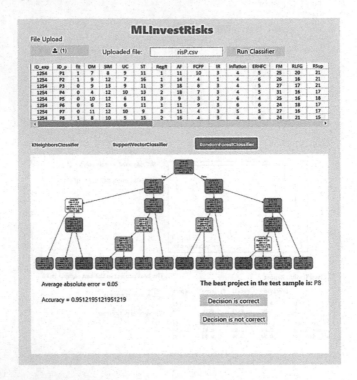

Fig. 7. Random Forest Classifier results window in MLInvestRisks

According to the module results based on Support Vector Classifier, the most attractive investment project to create a virtual IT company is the P8 project. If we consider this project from the expert assessment point of view, it falls into the risks category with project medium impact and with chance, which is more often caused by human factors and occurs once every 3 years. According to the results of the KNeighborsClassifier method we should select the P1 project. It falls into the risks category with project medium impact and with possible randomness of risks and frequency: more often than once every 3 years, and less often than once a year. The authors believe that both projects of virtual IT company creation may by invested, but P8 is less risky. The final decision is made by the user-investor.

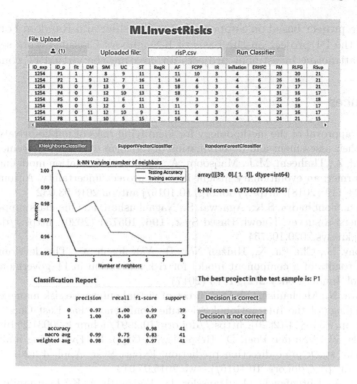

Fig. 8. KNeighborsClassifier results window in MLInvestRisks

6 Conclusions

The cross-assessment of investment risks for creating a virtual IT company is done. It's based on eight classification methods using machine learning, namely: Support Vector Classifier, Stochastic Gradient Decent Classifier, Random Forest Classifier, Decision Tree Classifier, Gaussian Naive Bayes, K-Neighbors Classifier, Ada Boost Classifier, Logistic Regression. From the evaluation results it was found that the best methods are Support Vector Classifier, Random Forest Classifier, K-Neighbors Classifier with estimates of forecasting accuracy at 0.98.

A more detailed refinement of the parameters of the best methods (Support Vector Classifier, Random Forest Classifier, K-Neighbors Classifier) was performed, which made it possible to partially increase the accuracy and reduce errors for these methods by an average of 1–2.

A software environment was developed based on Support Vector Classifier, Random Forest Classifier, K-Neighbors Classifier that enables to make decisions for potential investors. The results of the experiments in the developed module confirmed the effectiveness of using the methods selected in the cross-evaluation. Also, the results of this module make it possible to update the training sample for module further work.

The P8 project based on Support Vector Classifier and Random Forest Classifier and the P1 project on the basis of KNeighbors Classifier were selected as the most attractive investment projects for creating the virtual IT company.

References

1. About approval of the methodology for identifying risks of public-private partnership, their assessment and determination of the form of their management (2011)
2. Ahmad, Z., Thaheem, M.J., Maqsoom, A.: Building information modeling as a risk transformer: an evolutionary insight into the project uncertainty. Autom. Constr. **92**, 103–119 (2018). https://doi.org/10.1016/j.autcon.2018.03.032
3. Alam, S., Sonbhadra, S.K., Agarwal, S., Nagabhushan, P.: One-class support vector classifiers: a survey. Knowl.-Based Syst. **196**, 105754 (2020). https://doi.org/10.1016/j.knosys.2020.105754
4. Anthony, B., Che Pa, N., Haizan Nor, R., Yah Josoh, Y.: The development and initial results of a component model for risk mitigation in IT governance. J. Sci. Technol. Innov. Policy **2**(2), 1–13 (2017)
5. Apatova, N.: Mechanisms and resources of virtual enterprise risk management. In: Proceedings of the International Scientific Conference "Far East Con" (ISCFEC 2020), pp. 834–844 (2020). https://doi.org/10.2991/aebmr.k.200312.116
6. Ballings, M., Van den Poel, D., Hespeels, N., Gryp, R.: Evaluating multiple classifiers for stock price direction prediction. Expert Syst. Appl. **42**(20), 7046–7056 (2015). https://doi.org/10.1016/j.eswa.2015.05.013
7. Blumer, A., Ehrenfeucht, A., Haussler, D., Warmuth, M.K.: Learnability and the Vapnik-Chervonenkis dimension. J. ACM **36**(4), 929–965 (1989). https://doi.org/10.1145/76359.76371
8. Breiman, L.: Random forests. Mach. Learn. **45**(1), 5–32 (2001). https://doi.org/10.1023/a:1010933404324
9. Cabral, J.S.: Project risk management strategies for IT project managers. Ph.D. thesis, Walden University (2017)
10. Chapman, C., Ward, S.: Project Risk Management: Processes, Techniques and Insights. Wiley, Hoboken (1996)
11. Chen, T.H., Ho, R.J., Liu, Y.W.: Investigating the predictive power of investor personality in forecasting investment performance using machine learning models. Comput. Hum. Behav. **101** (2018). https://doi.org/10.1016/j.chb.2018.09.027
12. Costa, N.L., Llobodanin, L.A.G., Castro, I.A., Barbosa, R.: Using support vector machines and neural networks to classify merlot wines from South America. Inf. Process. Agric. **5**(2), 265–278 (2018). https://doi.org/10.1016/j.inpa.2018.10.003
13. Davidow, W.H.: The virtual corporation: Structuring and revitalizing the corporation for the 21st century. Harpercollins (1992)
14. Dong, J.Y., Wan, S.P.: Virtual enterprise partner selection integrating linmap and topsis. J. Oper. Res. Soc. **67**(10), 1288–1308 (2016). https://doi.org/10.1057/jors.2016.22
15. Du, W., Zhan, Z.: Building decision tree classifier on private data. In: Proceedings of the IEEE International Conference on Privacy, Security and Data Mining CRPIT 2002 (2002)
16. Dudani, S.A.: The distance-weighted k-nearest-neighbor rule. IEEE Trans. Syst. Man Cybern. **6**(4), 325–327 (1976). https://doi.org/10.1109/tsmc.1976.5408784

17. Esposito, E., Evangelista, P.: Investigating virtual enterprise models - literature review and empirical findings. Int. J. Prod. Econ. **148**, 145–157 (2014). https://doi.org/10.1016/j.ijpe.2013.10.003
18. Ferreira, L., Lopes, N., Avila, P.S., et al.: Virtual enterprise integration management based on a meta-enterprise - a PMBoK approach. Procedia Comput. Sci. **121**, 1112–1118 (2017). https://doi.org/10.1016/j.procs.2017.12.120
19. Golovko, V., Savitsky, Y., Laopoulos, T., Sachenko, A., Grandinetti, L.: Technique of learning rate estimation for efficient training of MLP. In: Proceedings of the International Joint Conference on Neural Networks, pp. 323–328 (2000)
20. Gou, H., Huang, B., Liu, W., Li, X.: A framework for virtual enterprise operation management. Comput. Ind. **50**(3), 333–352 (2003). https://doi.org/10.1016/s0166-3615(03)00021-6
21. Hassanat, A.B., Abbadi, M.A., Altarawneh, G.A., Alhasanat, A.A.: Solving the problem of the k parameter in the KNN classifier using an ensemble learning approach (2014). https://arxiv.org/abs/1409.0919
22. He, W., Liu, Y.: To regularize or not: revisiting SGD with simple algorithms and experimental studies. Expert Syst. Appl. **112**, 1–14 (2018). https://doi.org/10.1016/j.eswa.2018.06.026
23. Hwang, B.G., Chen, M.: Sustainable risk management in the construction industry: lessons learned from the IT industry. Technol. Econ. Dev. Econ. **21**(2), 216–231 (2015). https://doi.org/10.3846/20294913.2014.979455
24. Javani, B., Rwelamila, P.M.D.: Risk management in it projects - a case of the South African public sector. Int. J. Manag. Projects Bus. **9**(2), 389–413 (2016). https://doi.org/10.1108/ijmpb-07-2015-0055
25. John, G.H., Langley, P.: Estimating continuous distributions in Bayesian classifiers (2013). https://arxiv.org/abs/1302.4964
26. Kanovskyi, A., Sachenko, A., Kochan, V.: Virtual spatial displaying of dynamic graphic objects for IoT. In: Proceedings of the 2019 3rd International Conference on Advanced Information and Communications Technologies, AICT 2019, pp. 254–257 (2019)
27. Kleinbaum, D.G., Klein, M.: Introduction to logistic regression. In: Kleinbaum, D.G., Klein, M. (eds.) Logistic Regression. SBH, pp. 1–39. Springer, New York (2010). https://doi.org/10.1007/978-1-4419-1742-3_1
28. Kumsuprom, S., Corbitt, B., Pittayachawan, S.: ICT risk management in organizations: case studies in Thai business. In: Proceedings of the Australasian Conference on Information Systems ACIS 2008, p. artt. no. 98 (2008). https://doi.org/10.13140/2.1.2489.1689
29. Lipyanina, H., Sachenko, A., Lendyuk, T., Nadvynychny, S., Grodskyi, S.: Decision tree based targeting model of customer interaction with business page. In: Proceedings of the third International Workshop on Computer Modeling and Intelligent Systems (CMIS-2020), CEUR Workshop Proceedings, vol. 2608, pp. 1001–1012 (2020). http://ceur-ws.org/Vol-2608/paper75.pdf
30. Locatelli, G., Invernizzi, D.C., Mancini, M.: Investment and risk appraisal in energy storage systems: a real options approach. Energy **104**, 114–131 (2016). https://doi.org/10.1016/j.energy.2016.03.098
31. Lu, F., Bi, H., Huang, M., Wang, X.: Virtual enterprise risk management under asymmetric information. In: Proceedings of the 2013 10th International Conference on Service Systems and Service Management, pp. 202–207 (2013). https://doi.org/10.1109/icsssm.2013.6602655

32. Lytvyn, V., Vysotska, V., Veres, O., Rishnyak, I., Rishnyak, H.: The risk management modelling in multi project environment. In: Proceedings of the 2017 12th International Scientific and Technical Conference on Computer Sciences and Information Technologies (CSIT 2017), pp. 32–35 (2017). https://doi.org/10.1109/stccsit.2017.8098730

33. Maillo, J., Ramirez, S., Triguero, I., Herrera, F.: kNN-IS: an iterative spark-based design of the k-nearest neighbors classifier for big data. Knowl.-Based Syst. **117**, 3–15 (2017). https://doi.org/10.1016/j.knosys.2016.06.012

34. Marodin, G.A., Saurin, T.A., Tortorella, G.L., Fettermann, D.C.: Model of risk interactions hindering lean production implementation. Gestao Producao **25**(4), 696–712 (2018)

35. Martinez, M., Fouletier, P., Park, K., Favrel, J.: Virtual enterprise - organisation, evolution and control. Int. J. Prod. Econ. **74**(1–3), 225–238 (2001). https://doi.org/10.1016/s0925-5273(01)00129-3

36. Meng, F., Wang, N., Xu, Y.: Interval neutrosophic preference relations and their application in virtual enterprise partner selection. J. Ambient Intell. Hum. Comput. **10**, 5007–5036 (2019). https://doi.org/10.1007/s12652-019-01178-5

37. Noraini, C., Bokolo, A., et al.: A review on risk mitigation of IT governance. Inf. Technol. J. **14**(1), 1–9 (2015). https://doi.org/10.3923/itj.2015.1.9

38. Pa, N.C., Anthony, B.: A model of mitigating risk for it organisations. In: Proceedings of the IEEE 2015 4th International Conference on Software Engineering and Computer Systems (ICSECS), pp. 49–54 (2015). https://doi.org/10.1109/ICSECS.2015.7333082

39. Park, K.H., Favrel, J.: Virtual enterprise - information system and networking solution. Comput. Ind. Eng. **37**(1–2), 441–444 (1999). https://doi.org/10.1016/s0360-8352(99)00113-8

40. Sadigh, B.L., Nikghadam, S., Ozbayoglu, A.M., Unver, H.O., Dogdu, E., Kilic, S.E.: An ontology-based multi-agent virtual enterprise system (OMAVE): part 2: partner selection. Int. J. Comput. Integr. Manuf. **30**(10), 1072–1092 (2017). https://doi.org/10.1080/0951192x.2017.1285424

41. Sadigh, B.L., Unver, H.O., Nikghadam, S., Dogdu, E., Ozbayoglu, A.M., Kilic, S.E.: An ontology-based multi-agent virtual enterprise system (OMAVE): part 1: domain modelling and rule management. Int. J. Comput. Integr. Manuf. **30**(2–3), 320–343 (2016). https://doi.org/10.1080/0951192x.2016.1145811

42. Schapire, R.E.: Explaining adaboost. In: Scholkopf, B., Luo, Z., Vovk, V. (eds.) Empirical Inference, pp. 37–52. Springer, Heidelberg (2013). https://doi.org/10.1007/978-3-642-41136-6_5

43. Shu, C., Dosyn, D., Lytvyn, V., Vysotska, V., Sachenko, A., Jun, S.: Building of the predicate recognition system for the NLP ontology learning module. In: Proceedings of the 10th IEEE International Conference on Intelligent Data Acquisition and Advanced Computing Systems: Technology and Applications, IDAACS 2019, pp. 802–808 (2019). https://doi.org/10.1109/IDAACS.2019.8924410

44. Swain, P.H., Hauska, H.: The decision tree classifier: design and potential. IEEE Trans. Geosci. Electron. **15**(3), 142–147 (1977). https://doi.org/10.1109/tge.1977.6498972

45. Swami, R., Jain, T.K.: Managing investment risks: Modern vs traditional knowledge and practices (2019). https://doi.org/10.2139/ssrn.3310062, https://ssrn.com/abstract=3310062

46. Tao, T., Yan, K., Yang, S.: Classification of mutual fund investment types with advanced machine learning models. In: Proceedings of the 2019 IEEE International Conference on Big Data, Cloud Computing, Data Science and Engineering (BCD), pp. 84–89 (2019)
47. Tsvetkov, V.Y., Shaytura, S.V., Sultaeva, N.L.: Digital enterprise management in cyberspace. In: Proceedings of the 2nd International Scientific and Practical Conference "Modern Management Trends and the Digital Economy: from Regional Development to Global Economic Growth" (MTDE 2020), pp. 361–365 (2020). https://doi.org/10.2991/aebmr.k.200502.059
48. Vezhnevets, A., Vezhnevets, V.: Modest adaboost-teaching adaboost to generalize better. Graphicon **12**(5), 987–997 (2005)
49. Wan, J., Jiang, Q., Xie, L.: Research on risk factors of entrepreneurship in internet industry with the grounded theory. In: Proceedings of the Wuhan International Conference on e-Business, Association for Information Systems, pp. 99–107 (2017)
50. Wang, N.: Research on virtual enterprise risk control based on optimization. Adv. Mater. Res. **129–131**, 1267–1272 (2010). https://doi.org/10.4028/www.scientific.net/amr.129-131.1267
51. Yang, M., Blyth, W.: Modeling investment risks and uncertainties with real options approach. In: International Energy Agency Working Paper Series. p. Paper Number LTO/2007/WP01 (2007)
52. Yuan, M.Q., Li, Z.F., Li, L.: SI system housing virtual enterprise partners selection based on vector angle cosine. J. Civ. Eng. Manag. **35**, 117–122 (2018)

Methodological Support for the Management of Maintaining Financial Flows of External Tourism in Global Risky Conditions

Marharyta Sharko[1]([✉]) [iD], Olha Liubchuk[2] [iD], Vira Fomishyna[1] [iD],
Yuliia Yarchenko[2] [iD], Nadiia Fedorova[1] [iD], Natalia Petrushenko[1] [iD],
and Ruslan Ohorodnyk[1] [iD]

[1] Kherson National Technical University, Kherson, Ukraine
mvsharko@gmail.com, vfomi0709@gmail.com, fedorova-nadiia@ukr.net,
natalia.velikaya@gmail.com, ruslik77@meta.ua

[2] State Higher Educational Institution "Pryazovskyi State Technical University",
Mariupol, Ukraine
lyubchuk@ukr.net, july-248@ukr.net

Abstract. A solution to the problem of maintaining the dynamics of financial flows from the implementation of tourist offers in the context of global risks caused by COVID-19 is proposed. On the basis of graph theory, Ford-Fulkerson and Dinitz algorithms, a modified algorithm for determining the structure of a tourist product, based on the financial capabilities of consumers and the satisfaction of their preferences in the dynamics of compliance with restrictions in the implementation of tourist services has been developed. A feature of the algorithm is the synchronization of the throughput of financial flows of tourist services from the moment of the removal and introduction of restrictions on the onset of COVID-19. The novelty of the proposed algorithm is the possibility of adjusting travel offers in the process of monitoring the capabilities of manufacturers and travel preferences of consumers and transformation of services. The implementation of the algorithm ensures the effect of minimizing losses and the maximum financial flow from the sale of specific tourism services from the source, representing the components of manufacturers of tourism products before the outbreak of the pandemic, to the drain, representing consumer preferences.

Keywords: Tourism · Financial flows · Ford-Fulkerson and Dinitsa algorithms · Network modification · Service transformation · COVID-19 · Global risks

© Springer Nature Switzerland AG 2020
S. Babichev et al. (Eds.): DSMP 2020, CCIS 1158, pp. 188–201, 2020.
https://doi.org/10.1007/978-3-030-61656-4_12

1   Introduction

Tourist attraction is a complex, multifaceted and dynamic area of modern tourism. This sector directly provides an average of 4.4% of GDP and 21.5% of exports of services in OECD countries (Organization for Economic Co-operation and Development) [5]. For some OECD countries, these values are much higher. For example, tourism in Spain accounts for 11.8% of GDP, while travel accounts for 52.3% of total exports of services, in Mexico these figures are 8.7% and 78.3%, in Iceland 8.6% and 47.7%, in Portugal 8.0% and 51.1%, in France 7.4% and 22.2% [2] (Fig. 1).

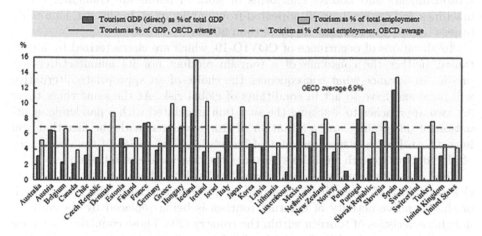

Fig. 1. Direct contribution of tourism to OECD countries

*Source: OECD Tourism Statistics (database) [3].

The coronavirus has redrawn the map of the tourist attraction of the countries of the world. Starting in December 2019 in the Chinese province of Hongbei, it continues to develop rapidly, covering more and more territories and acquiring the character of an international disaster, called a pandemic [17,18]. Despite a number of preventive measures in the summer months of 2020, a number of disease peaks were established on July 26, 2020 - 195496 diseases, July 5, 2020 - 196901 diseases. The negative statistics continues and is gaining momentum in Table 1.

Table 1. General world statistics

Infection cases	Dead	Recovered	Mortality	Recovery
11423689	534217	6451193	4,68%	56,47%

Based on information from international organizations and trade groups, the losses of European tourism due to the pandemic amounted to 275–400 million euros [4]. According to the World Association of Business Travel, the tourism industry has lost up to 300 million jobs, the aviation business has declined by 19% [1]. Travel demand in 2020 decreased by 25% in South America, by 10% in Europe and by 25% in the rest of the world. It is impossible to count on the full occupancy of hotels, since the volume of tourist flows has not been determined [11]. Many hotels do not make economic sense to open this year. It is assumed that about 30% of the room stock will be empty. In addition, the new requirements for certification of hotels will lead to higher costs and higher prices for certain services.

New safety standards are being introduced by airlines, airports, catering establishments and hotels. The forms of work of hotels are changing. Coffee machines and coolers have disappeared from public areas. In the spa, hammam, fitness rooms, you can stay no more than 30 min.

In situations of occurrence of COVID-19, which are characterized by uncertainty, neither the consumer of a tourism product nor its manufacturer can predict in advance what consequences the choice of an appropriate alternative will have and have to act in conditions of global risk. At the same time, there are two approaches to assessing the situation associated with a pandemic: a situation of uncertainty and a situation of risk associated with the fact that you have to work with a small amount of knowledge. The choice of the dominance of alternatives in such situations becomes the prerogative of intuition.

The current extreme situation caused by COVID-19 has dramatically reduced the possibility of external tourism due to travel restrictions. The globalization of the cognitive activity of external tourism is being replaced by the individual characteristics of tourism within the country [20]. Those countries that have opened their opportunities for visiting foreign tourists, taking into account their safety and possible restrictions such as the introduction of a mask regime, restrictions on groups, temperature measurements, observing the distances between clients, etc., are in dire need of the development and implementation of practical recommendations for maintaining their tourist financial flows under external constraints associated with the pandemic.

Due to the existence of a large number of factors that determine the effectiveness of tourism, methods for constructing mathematical models based on considering economic laws are not very effective. Therefore, it is promising to attract experimental identification methods based on the formalization of observation results and the analysis of the arrival of new information about changes in the current situation using new digital technologies [6–8, 26, 27, 29].

The identification of the market for tourism services offers is a set of methods for constructing mathematical models based on observation data, the adaptability of which to changes in the external environment is ensured in conditions of non-stationarity of processes [10, 19, 24, 25, 31]. The initial information on identifying the problems of unstable development of the tourism market is contained in the ratio of internal and external destabilizing factors and serves as a tool for the variation of the tourism management paradigm [21, 30, 32]. The implementation of social distancing forces people to limit activities outside the home, as a result of which, the turnover of sales of tourism services decreases sharply. Therefore, it is necessary to change the mindset when introducing the tourism business through technology transformations. In fact, in the context of COVID-19, only online businesses can make tourism sustainable.

In the problem of maintaining financial flows in the context of the coronavirus, the variables are the restrictions on the financial capabilities of consumers and their requirements for the quality of services offered, living conditions, food, excursion services, transfers, etc. An analogue of the analytical consideration of such a situation of uncertainty and unpredictability can be the theory of graphs [9], with the transport problem of the maximum flow along the edges under constraints on the capacity, solved using the algorithms of Ford L. R, Fulkerson D. R. and Dinitsa E. A. [33].

Recently, this line of research has been gaining the greatest popularity. For example, [23] presents an analysis of the bottlenecks of the Beijing-Hong Kong-Macau expressway with an analysis of the points of congestion in the network and the distribution of the schedule. In [16], an algorithm is presented to optimize the energy distribution of electrical infrastructures of data centers, aimed at reducing financial and environmental costs. In [15], the optimization of train routes based on neural-fuzzy modeling and genetic algorithms for controlling the throughput of the railway network in conditions of mass transportation of passengers and goods is presented. In [12], an implementation of the Ford-Fulkerson algorithm for finding the maximum flow with the smallest number of iterations by the breadth-first search method is presented. In [22], the performance of the Ford-Fulkerson maximum flow was investigated on grid and random geometric plots. In [28], the Ford-Fulkerson marking is presented for information processing networks in Japan, the boundary capacities of which are limited. In [14], combinatorial structures for weighted graphs with a low field volume were investigated by the same method. In [13], the creation of methods for calculating distances in structures with optimal space stretching is presented.

As the analysis of recent achievements and publications shows, the use of both Ford-Fulkerson and Dinitsa algorithms to maximize the formation of traffic flows has its experimental confirmation. Proceeding from this, the proposal to use this mathematical apparatus as the basis for methodological support for the maintaining and maximization of financial flows of external tourism can be considered as justified.

2   Materials and Methods

According to the Ford-Fulkerson algorithm, the network is considered as a connected digraph without loops, oriented in one direction.

With regard to the problem of maintaining and maximizing financial flows of external tourism under the constraints caused by COVID-19, the preferences of tourists in the total volume of services offered can be used as research material; graph theory using Ford-Fulkerson and Dinitz algorithms and their modifications can be used as methods. In relation to the specific conditions of external tourism in the context of COVID-19.

The formal description of Ford-Fulkerson algorithm is as follows: given a graph $G(V, E)$ with capacity $c(u, v)$ and flow $f(u, v) = 0$ for edges from u to v. It is necessary to find the maximum flow from source s to drain t. At each step of the algorithm, identical conditions are applied for all flows:

- $f(u, v) \leq c(u, v)$. i.e. the flow from u to v does not exceed the capacity;
- $f(u, v) = f(v, u)$;
- $\Sigma f(u, v) = 0 \longleftrightarrow f_{in}(u) = f_{out}(u)$ for all nodes u except s and t i.e. the flow does not change as it passes through the node;
- the flow in the network is equal to the sum of the flows of all arcs incident to the flow of the graph.

Marking is used to find a chain along which a gradually increasing flow can be sent. Each arc is assigned a weight, which is written as a fraction on the edge of the original network Fig. 2.

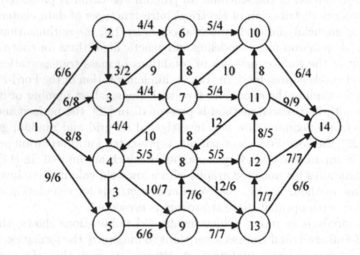

Fig. 2. Graph of the nodes interconnection within the framework of Ford-Fulkerson algorithm implementation

Initially, the residual chain is the same as the original. The algorithm starts from the zero thread and increases its value at each iteration. The amount of flow is then increased iteratively by finding a path along which more flow can be sent. For each edge on the found path, we increase the flow, and decrease the flow in the opposite one. We modify the residual network, assuming that the residual network $G_f(V, E_f)$ is a network with the capacity $c_f(u, v) = c(u, v) - f(u, v)$. For all edges, we calculate a new bandwidth by adding an edge to the residual network.

Analytically, it looks like this:

$f(u, v) := 0$ for all edges (u, v). The path p from $stottoG_f$, $c_f(u, v) > 0$ for all edges $(u < v) \in p : c_f(p) = minc_f(u, v)|(u, v) \in p$. For each edge $(u, v) \in p$, $f(u, v) := f(u, v) + c_f(p)$, $f(v, u) := f(v, u) - c_f(p)$.

The path can be found by searching both breadth and depth in $G_f(V, E_f)$.

It is possible to increase the flow along all the edges by minimizing the residual flow rates. According to the algorithm Dinitsa E.A. at each iteration of the assessment of the current situation, breadth-first search is used and the distance from the source to the vertex in the residual network is determined Fig. 3.

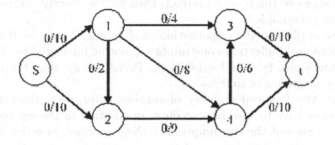

Fig. 3. Visualization of Dinitsa's algorithm

Formal description of Dinitsa's algorithm is the following.

- for each edge (u, v) of the network G we set $f(u, v) = 0$;
- construct an auxiliary net G_L from the complementary net G_f of the graph G;
- look for a blocking flow f' in G_L;
- supplement the flow f with the flow f'.

3 Methodology

With regard to the maintaining of financial flows of external tourism in the context of COVID-19, the purpose of the Ford-Fulkerson algorithm is to find such a network chain that would ensure maximum maintaining of the invested funds in the event of a forced replacement of tourist services in the structure of a tourist product for the maximum number of tourists. Maximum flow is assigned to each arc from the source s to the drain t, which is written as a fraction with the weight of the arc. In this case, the flow cannot exceed the weight of the arc, but can be equal to it. All possible chains are enumerated. These iterations are carried out until it becomes impossible to get from the source to the drain. If the flow becomes equal to the weight of the arc, then the arc is considered saturated, and it is no longer possible to pass through it. The flow in the network will be equal to the sum of the flows of all arcs incident to the flow of the graph.

Separately, we should dwell on the transformation of the services offered. If before the onset of the coronavirus, they were formed on the basis of the interests of age groups and the maximum occupancy of halls, buses, excursion groups, now the situation has changed radically. The pursuit of individualism in travel communication has fundamentally changed the essence of many travel offers. When forming a set of many tourist services, some of their types and components are either transformed or disappear altogether. In addition, the sequence of their use is gaining importance, which is determined by tastes, expediency and cognitiveness of travel. If for groups of youth tourism mountain and hiking with the use of rafting and diving brought a special flavor and made up part of the attractiveness of the tourist product, then for the elderly category such an offer is hardly acceptable.

The same applies to the organization of shopping. Young audiences facing strong financial and budgetary constraints will not be interested in visiting fashion brand boutiques, fairs and exhibitions. Perhaps only wine tourism will be welcomed by all groups of tourists.

To ensure the financial stability of tourism enterprises, the organizers of tourism services have to take into account, in addition to the age composition, the occupancy rate of the consumption of these services, in order, on the one hand, to ensure the attractiveness of these trips, on the other, the profit from the sale of these services. Under these conditions, the transition from the Ford-Fulkerson algorithm to the Dinitz algorithm becomes a necessary link in ensuring the financial stability of tourism enterprises in the context of the coronavirus.

4   Experiment

For the purposeful management of the tourist attractiveness of the proposed travel in a pandemic, it is necessary to know the characteristics, composition, conditions for the implementation of tourist offers and the necessary management tools.

Tourist trips can be divided: by geography, by the purpose of the trip, by the number of participants in the tour, by time characteristics, by mode of travel, by financial capabilities.

To evaluate the sequential operation of both the Ford-Fulkerson and Dinitsa algorithms, the most popular types of tourism were selected at the source as components of a tourism product: v1 - recreation on the sea coast, v2 - pastime in the mountains, v3 - wine and gastronomic tourism, v4 - visiting museums and various exhibitions.

These components are represented by the arcs of the corresponding digraph. The analysis of statistical reporting before the onset of COVID-19 made it possible to determine the weights of the digraph arcs of the tourist network through experimental evaluation, which are presented in Table 2.

Travel duration by days is selected as network nodes. Most often it is a week, i.e. the number of network nodes was selected to be seven.

The saturation of the network occurs along the directions of the arcs. Initialization of arcs is represented by the numbers of expert judgments. The occupancy

Table 2. Standard scores on the desirability scale

№	Type of tourism	Weight, of the arc %	Vertex of the graph
1	Rest on the seaside	48	v1
2	Pastime in the mountains	27	v2
3	Wine and gastronomic tourism	11	v3
4	Visiting museums and various exhibitions	14	v4

of the days of stay with the opportunity to participate in the services offered is represented by vertical columns 1–4, 5–8, 9–12, etc.

A fragment of the network constructed in this way is shown in Fig. 4.

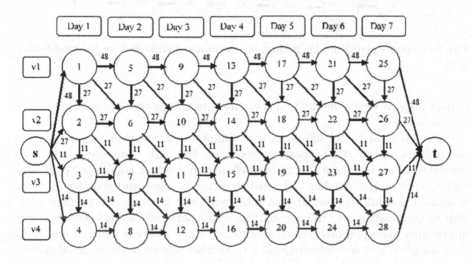

Fig. 4. Initialization of arcs in the network of the digraph of travel services

At the initial stage, all flows along each of the arcs are zero. The saturation of the network occurs along the directions of the arcs.

During the operation of the algorithm, with each step, the flow rate increases by one until the maximum possible flow in the network is found.

In each network chain, the smallest value for all edges is determined, which characterizes the minimum throughput of this network link, after which all initializations of arcs are divided by this number to identify the corresponding network labels. For each edge on the chosen path, the flow increases by C_{min}, and in the opposite direction, it decreases by the same amount. We modify the residual network taking into account the new bandwidth of the edges Fig. 5.

In the above example, due to sudden unpredictable changes, the tour operator had to urgently change the direction of tourist flows after 3 days (there is no further opportunity to relax at sea) and after 5 days (there is no further

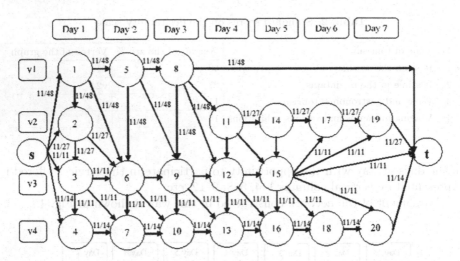

Fig. 5. Dinitsa's algorithm for finding the maximum tourist flow in the modified network

opportunity to visit wineries), and vacation in the mountains is impossible for 2–3 days tour.

Developers of travel offers have to adapt to ensure their implementation, not only based on the wishes of consumers, but also from the conditions of the external environment. So a sharp change in weather conditions (cold snap, rains), reduces the number of tourists visiting beaches and seaside, as well as mountain and hiking. But at this time, wine and gastronomic tourism with a visit to wine tasting and the peculiarities of the national cuisine becomes of great importance. The planned sequence of using tourist offers is violated and in this time iteration it is advisable to switch to another branch of the residual network, the definition of which is found using the Dinitz algorithm. Then, depending on the development of the situation, in order to preserve financial flows, it is possible either to develop the consumption of a tourist product along this branch of the network, with a return to the original branch, or to search for a new path.

The modified algorithm for managing financial flow in the context of COVID-19 is shown in Fig. 6.

Manufacturers of a tourism product incur large losses associated with the termination of the implementation of components of tourism services at any iteration of implementation. These losses of the manufacturer are not compensable. The only possible way to continue the process of implementing a tourist package is to switch to another branch of the residual network (Fig. 4). The purpose of the implementation of travel services in the proposed travel package is to maximize the preservation and compensation of manufacturers' costs while satisfying consumers. Comparing the value of these costs in terms of summing the bandwidths of the edges of the branches of the chain from the source s to the drain t in the unchanged operating conditions of the tourism industry without

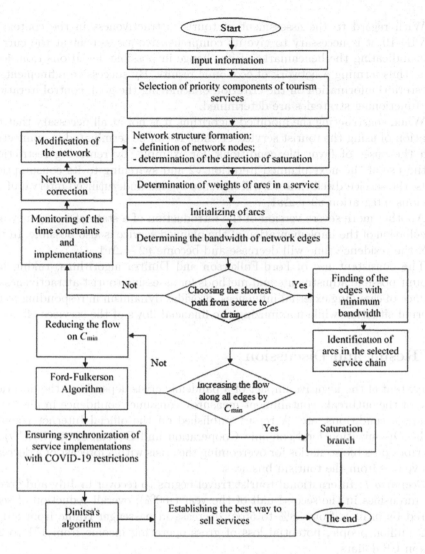

Fig. 6. Modified algorithm for maximizing financial flows of components of tourism services in the context of COVID-19 restrictions

COVID-19 with the summation of the bandwidth of the branch in the modified residual network, we determine the manufacturer's costs due to the transformation of travel services. The difference between the sum of the sequential values of the throughput of the branches of the components of tourist services involved in this transition and the sum of the components of the throughput of the paths of passing the services in the modified network represents the economic effect of implementation.

With regard to the assessment of tourist attractiveness in the context of COVID-19, it is necessary to give its comprehensive assessment at the current time, indicating the benchmarks of its change in possible deviations from forecasts, thus forming a network of economic results. By successive refinements of a posteriori information on the criterion of achieving the goal, control iterations and functioning strategies are determined.

When constructing the modified algorithm, it is not at all necessary that the iteration of using the tourist service v1 ends. It can be terminated in connection with the onset of favorable conditions, for example, by removing restrictions on the use of the next planned iteration v2 and switching to its consumption. Thus, the service dwell time v2 will increase by this underutilized interval of the previous integration $v2 + \Delta v1$.

Another more severe version of the introduction of a state of emergency and cancellation of the implementation of the planned service is also possible. In this case, the residence time will decrease and become $v2 - \Delta v1$.

The consistent use of Ford-Fulkerson and Dinitsa algorithms, taking into account possible adjustments and methods for assessing tourist attractiveness in the face of changing external influences, provides dynamism in responding to the external situation while maximizing the financial flows of the services offered.

5   Result and Discussion

The extent of the negative impact of a pandemic crisis depends on the duration, scale of the outbreak, containment measures, consumer confidence in air travel, economic conditions, etc. A report published on the official Internet resource of the Organization for Economic Cooperation and Development (OECD) [5] describes possible scenarios for overcoming the crisis with a forecast of a decrease in revenues from the tourism business.

Scenario 1: International tourist travel begins to recover in July and gradually intensifies in the second half of the year (-60%); overall reduction of seats offered by airlines from 38% to 55%; decrease in passenger traffic from 861 to 1292 million people; potential loss of gross operating income from 151 to 228 million US dollars.

Scenario 2: International tourist travel starts to recover in September and then picks up in the last quarter of the year (-75%); the overall reduction in seats offered by airlines will range from 48% to 71%; reduction in passenger traffic - from 1108 to 1524 million people; potential loss of gross operating income - from 194 to 269 million US dollars.

Against this background, methodological support for maintaining financial flows of external tourism in the face of restrictions caused by COVID-19 becomes even more urgent.

In the context of the extraordinary onset of COVID-19, for quantitative assessments of the attractiveness of tourism products, a comprehensive analysis of the various characteristics of the proposed tourism product is required. The identification and prediction of the purchase of travel products is associated with a more complete set of offered services, their characteristics and the possibilities of transformation, sale and refund in the event of an emergency travel interruption.

Depending on the a priori information about consumer preferences of a tourist product, the methods of its assessment acquire the character of certainty, therefore, the arrival of new information significantly increases the process of identifying financial flow management in the context of COVID-19.

The choice of the optimal criterion is based on the coincidence of consumer preferences and the interests of manufacturers of the tourist product. However, the constantly changing external conditions associated with restrictions on movement between countries force to replace the relations of preference with analytical evaluations of utility functions.

Based on the results of observations of the proposals of tourist services and their consumption, a formalized model of the non-stationarity of the situation can be built.

6 Conclusions

The effectiveness of management of company in the tourism industry under the constraints caused by COVID-19 is based on constant innovations, dynamic transformation of the services offered, changes in the range and conditions of sale.

A modified algorithm for determining the structure of a tourist product in a COVID-19 environment based on the Ford-Fulkerson and Dinitz algorithms ensures that the manufacturer's losses are minimized and the maximum financial flow is achieved by optimizing the residual capacity of poorly implemented tourist offers from the sources, representing the components of manufacturers before the emergence of COVID-19, to the drains, representing consumer preferences in a COVID-19 environment.

The novelty of using the proposed modified algorithm is the synchronization of technologies for using the methodology for determining the throughput of the branches of the implementation of tourism services from the moment COVID-19 restrictions were lifted and introduced.

The attractiveness of tourism products is ensured by transforming services and changing the sequence of their implementation by taking into account changes in external conditions.

References

1. Effects of novel coronavirus (COVID-19) on civil aviation: Economic impact analysis (2020). https://www.icao.int/sustainability/Documents/COVID-19/
2. Full data for OECD countries (2020). http://dx.doi.org/10.1787/888934076134
3. OECD tourism statistics (2020). https://www.oecd.org/cfe/tourism/tourism-statistics.htm

4. Tourism policy responses to the coronavirus (COVID-19) (2020). https://read. oecd-ilibrary.org/view/?ref=124_124984-7uf8nm95se&title=Covid-19_Tourism_ Policy_Responses

5. Tourism trends and policies 2020 (2020). https://www.oecd.org/cfe/tourism/oecd-tourism-trends-and-policies-20767773.htm

6. Alford, P., Jones, R.: The lone digital tourism entrepreneur: knowledge acquisition and collaborative transfer. Tourism Manag. **81**, art. no. 104139 (2020). https:// doi.org/10.1016/j.tourman.2020.104139

7. Babichev, S., Korobchynskyi, M., Mieshkov, S., Korchomnyi, O.: An effectiveness evaluation of information technology of gene expression profiles processing for gene networks reconstruction. Int. J. Intell. Syst. Appl. **10**(7), 1–10 (2018). https://doi. org/10.5815/ijisa.2018.07.01

8. Babichev, S., Škvor, J., FišÂier, J., Lytvynenko, V.: Technology of gene expression profiles filtering based on wavelet analysis, vol. 10, pp. 1–7 (2018). https://doi.org/ 10.5815/ijisa.2018.04.01

9. Bartysh, M., Dudziany, I.: Operations Research. Part 2. Optimization algorithms on graphs: Textbook. Lviv: Ivan Franko Lviv National University Publishing Center (2007)

10. Chatkaewnapanon, Y., Kelly, J.: Community arts as an inclusive methodology for sustainable tourism development. J. Place Manag. Dev. **12**(3), 365–390 (2019)

11. Cheriyan, A., Tamilarasi, S.: Block chain technology: the future of tourism. Stud. Syst. Decis. Control **295**, 481–490 (2021). https://doi.org/10.1007/978-3-030-47411-9_26

12. Dash, P., Rahman, M., Zohora, F.: An alternate simple approach to obtain the maximum flow in a network flow problem. J. Eng. Appl. Sci. **13**(Specialissue10), 8270–8276 (2018). https://doi.org/10.3923/jeasci.2018.8270.8276

13. Dinitz, M., Nazari, Y.: Brief announcement: Massively parallel approximate distance sketches. Leibniz International Proceedings in Informatics, LIPIcs 146, art. no. 42 (2019). https://doi.org/10.4230/LIPIcs.DISC.2019.42

14. Dinitz, M., Nazari, Y.: Massively parallel approximate distance sketches. Leibniz International Proceedings in Informatics, LIPIcs 153, art. no. 35 (2020). https:// doi.org/10.4230/LIPIcs.OPODIS.2019.35

15. Dolgopolov, P., Konstantinov, D., Rybalchenko, L., et al.: Optimization of train routes based on neuro-fuzzy modeling and genetic algorithms. Procedia Comput. Sci. **6149**, 11–18 (2019)

16. Ferreira, J., Callou, G., MacIel, P., et al.: An algorithm to optimise the energy distribution of data centre electrical infrastructures. Int. J. Grid Utility Comput. **11**(3), 419–433 (2020). https://doi.org/10.1504/IJGUC.2020.107625

17. Fong, S., Dey, N., Chaki, J.: AI-Empowered Data Analytics for Coronavirus Epidemic Monitoring and Control (2021). https://doi.org/10.1007/978-981-15-5936-5_3

18. Fong, S., Dey, N., Chaki, J.: An Introduction to COVID-19 (2021). https://doi. org/10.1007/978-981-15-5936-5_1

19. Ghalehkhonbadi, I., Ardjmand, E., Young, W., et al.: A review of demand forecasting models and methodological developments within tourism and passenger transportation industry. J. Tourism Futures **5**(1), 75–93 (2019). https://doi.org/ 10.1108/JTF-10-2018-0061

20. Goffman, E.: In the wake of COVID-19, is glocalization our sustainability future? Sustain.: Sci. Practice Policy **16**(1), 48–52 (2020). https://doi.org/10.1080/ 15487733.2020.1765678

21. Grilli, G., Tyllianakis, E., Luisetti, T., et al.: Prospective tourist preferences for sustainable tourism development in small island developing states. Tourism Manag. **82**, art. no. 104178 (2021). https://doi.org/10.1016/j.tourman.2020.104178
22. Laube, U., Nebel, M.E.: Maximum likelihood analysis of the Ford–Fulkerson method on special graphs. Algorithmica **74**(4), 1224–1266 (2015). https://doi.org/ 10.1007/s00453-015-9998-5
23. Qu, Q.K., Chen, F.J., Zhou, X.J.: Road traffic bottleneck analysis for expressway for safety under disaster events using blockchain machine learning. Saf. Sci. **118**, 925–932 (2019). https://doi.org/10.1016/j.ssci.2019.06.030
24. Sharko, M., Gusarina, N., Petrushenko, N.: Information-entropy model of making management decisions in the economic development of the enterprises. In: Advances in Intelligent Systems and Computing, pp. 304–314 (2019). https://doi. org/10.1007/978-3-030-26474-1
25. Sharko, M., Lopushynskyi, I., Petrushenko, N., et al.: Management of tourists' enterprises adaptation strategies for identifying and predicting multidimensional non-stationary data flows in the face of uncertainties. In: Advances in Intelligent Systems and Computing, pp. 135–151 (2020). https://doi.org/10.1007/978-3-030-54215-3
26. Solentsova, E., Krzyzewski, M., Kapitonov, A.: Analysis of ethnic tourism resources and content placement on a digital platform. Lect. Notes Netw. Syst. **133**, 219–234 (2021). https://doi.org/10.1007/978-3-030-47458-4_26
27. Sun, J., Zhang, J.H., Zhang, H., et al.: Development and validation of a tourism fatigue scale. Tourism Manag. **81**, art. no. 104121 (2020). https://doi.org/10.1016/ j.tourman.2020.104121
28. Takahashi, T.: The simplest and smallest network on which the Ford-Fulkerson maximum flow procedure may fail to terminate. J. Inf. Process. **24**(2), 390–394 (2016). https://doi.org/10.2197/ipsjjip.24.390
29. Wichmann, J., Wibotzki, M., Sandkuhl, K.: Toward a smart town: digital innovation and transformation process in a public sector environment. Smart Innov. Syst. Technol. **189**, 89–99 (2021). https://doi.org/10.1007/978-981-15-5784-2_8
30. Winarsih, Indriastuti, M., Fuad, K.: Impact of COVID-19 on digital transformation and sustainability in small and medium enterprises (SMEs): a conceptual framework. In: Advances in Intelligent Systems and Computing, vol. 1194, pp. 471–476 (2021). https://doi.org/10.1007/978-3-030-50454-0_48
31. Zang, B., Pu, Y., Wang, Y., et al.: Forecasting hotel accommodation demand based on LSTM model incorporating internet search index. Sustainability (Switzerland) **11**(17), art. no. 4708 (2019). https://doi.org/10.1108/JPMD-09-2-17-0094
32. Zenker, S., Kock, F.: The coronavirus pandemic - a critical discussion of a tourism research agenda. Tourism Manag. **81**, art. no. 104164 (2020). https://doi.org/10. 1016/j.tourman.2020.104164
33. Zwick, U.: The smallest networks on which the Ford-Fulkerson maximum flow procedure may fail to terminate. Theoret. Comput. Sci. **148**(1), 165–170 (1995). https://doi.org/10.1016/0304-3975(95)00022-O

Technology for Determining the Residual Life of Metal Structures Under Conditions of Combined Loading According to Acoustic Emission Measurements

Volodymyr Marasanov[1] , Dmitry Stepanchikov[1](✉) , Artem Sharko[1] , and Oleksandr Sharko[2]

[1] Kherson National Technical University, Kherson, Ukraine
volodymyr.marasanov@gmail.com, {dmitro_step75,sharko_artem}@ukr.net
[2] Kherson State Maritime Academy, Kherson, Ukraine
avsharko@ukr.net

Abstract. A methodology for determining the residual life of metal samples under conditions of combined deformation based on the data of acoustic emission measurements is presented. It has been established that the cause of many accidents occurring during the operation of equipment are not stresses from external loads, but residual stresses. The possibility of using the acoustic emission method for identifying the parameters of the state of metal structures under the conditions of combined loads of axial tension and transverse four-point bending by the nature of the acoustic emission signal under loading is investigated. Discrete representations of the acoustic signal are represented by their polynomial or power-law approximation. Graphic surfaces of the bearing capacity of operating states and failures are constructed in the form of a set of loads leading to destruction of the material. The values of the safety margin in the coordinates of mechanical tension and density of acoustic emission signals for metal samples made of steel St3sp have been quantitatively determined.

Keywords: Residual life · Forecasting · Acoustic emission · State identification

1 Introduction

During operation, metal structures are exposed to compressive, bending, stretching, static and cyclic loads that create a complex inhomogeneous state of the material. The intensity of the use of equipment, violation of operating rules, cyclic alternating thermal and other influences, which cannot be taken into account, lead to uncertainty in the nature and magnitude of the loads. Many accidents occurring during the operation of metal structures are caused not by

© Springer Nature Switzerland AG 2020
S. Babichev et al. (Eds.): DSMP 2020, CCIS 1158, pp. 202–217, 2020.
https://doi.org/10.1007/978-3-030-61656-4_13

stresses from external loads, but by residual stresses. Residual stresses are often present in a structure that is free from external loads. They are often formed in machining processes such as casting, welding, plate rolling and bulk rolling. They are dangerous because they are difficult to measure and add up to voltages from external loads.

Residual life of equipment is the total operating time of the equipment from the moment of monitoring the technical condition to the transition to the limit state. The problem of identifying the state and determining the residual life of metal structures during operation involves monitoring the change in the mechanical properties of materials with the accumulation of damage.

The use of acoustic emission methods for monitoring the state of metal structures makes it possible to use it as a promising area of technical diagnostics of materials in real time. Modern hardware and software for technical means for monitoring and diagnosing the state of materials in metal structures is not intended to study changes in mechanical properties due to the lack of methodological developments and practical recommendations for determining the degree of deformation, strength and residual life of materials under different types of loading.

Stretching, compression, bending and shear tests are the most common types of tests that obtain important mechanical properties of materials. In this paper, we consider the issues related to the calculation of the strength and residual life characteristics of metal samples under tension and bending, since it is these characteristics that are most often determined in practice.

The aim of this work is to develop a method for determining the residual life of metal samples made of steel St3sp, with a simultaneous combined deformation of longitudinal tension and transverse bending based on measuring the parameters of acoustic emission signals.

2 Relative Works

The interest in determining the residual life of structures during their operation has stimulated the development of modern tools and many technical applications. So, in [8] it is shown that residual stresses in workpieces have a great influence on fatigue life. The influence of residual stresses during ultrasonic turning in the cutting zone has been studied. In [22], the results of fatigue tests at a high high-cycle load of compressor blades made of titanium alloy are presented. In [17], estimates of the stress-strain state of rails under loading are presented. In [23], experimental and analytical studies of thermal barrier coatings operating under conditions of chemical-thermomechanical loading in the process of destruction are presented. It has been established that the development of residual stresses is linearly correlated with system failures.

The method for evaluating residual stresses and determining on their basis the residual life in [10] was used to assess the quality of adhesion of rods made of a polymer reinforced with basalt fiber in concrete. To study the bond behavior under cyclic loading, the relationship between stress levels and the number of cycles was investigated. For cyclic loads, an equation for predicting fatigue life is proposed. In [16], the estimation of residual stresses is used to predict the dynamic modulus of the hot mix of asphalt in the study of roads and design of road surfaces. In [9], an equation was obtained for predicting the maximum stress of concrete drainage pipelines subject to various damages and difficult operating conditions. In [12], methods for assessing the residual life were used to study the compressive strength of cement composites with a phase transition, in [18] – to predict the energy efficiency and productivity of a solar distiller. In [6], monitoring of the state of structures during penetration of metal into glass and ceramics during thermal cycling using a femto-laser sensor on a fiber Bragg grating is presented.

In recent years, there has been a significant increase in the number of works demonstrating the capabilities of acoustic emission in nondestructive testing, monitoring, detection of wear and tear faults and failures of structural states. The analysis of various principles of acoustic emission and their applicability to the assessment of residual stresses is presented in [7]. In [11], the modeling of acoustic emission caused by the dynamic shear of fluids in the lubrication mode and the influence of surface roughness under operating conditions is presented. In [14], an online localization of the acoustic emission source in concrete structures is presented using iterative and evolutionary algorithms. In [21], the diagnostics and prediction of malfunctions of bearings of wheelsets of high-speed trains using vibration and acoustic emission methods with continuous monitoring of the condition of bearings are described. A classification of malfunctions at low, medium and high speeds has been compiled to create an appropriate database and knowledge base. In [19], the results of the use of non-destructive testing of the strength of structural elements of deep-water structures based on the use of the phenomenon of acoustic emission are presented. In [24], the results of predicting the destruction of metal structures on the basis of complex acoustic emission and magnetic control of metals are presented. In [13], a model for observing the dynamic process of deformation of materials using acoustic emission is presented.

In [20], the results of acoustic emission monitoring of the fracture process of composite structures with a corrugated carbon fiber core during tests for compression and four-point bending are presented.

The analysis of the existing methods and diagnostic tools and determination of the residual life in real time without stopping the equipment showed that since the magnitude of the loading is uncertain, with intensive operation of equipment and peak loads, fully use the existing experience for the technology of determining the residual life of metal structures in a combined loading according to the data of acoustic emission measurements is not possible [4, 5].

To assess the mechanical tension under load, it is necessary to simultaneously measure the applied force and deformation, which requires several types of sensors, the information from which must be promptly processed. If the deformation is combined (for example, simultaneous stretching and bending), then the diagnosis is even more complicated. It is proposed to estimate the resource

of a sample under a combined dynamic load based on acoustic emission measurements. This approach will allow us to limit ourselves to one type of sensors
and significantly simplify the assessment of the state of the sample.

The most difficult stage in determining the residual life of metal samples
under conditions of combined deformation according to the data of acoustic
emission measurements is to solve the problem of identifying the operating conditions of diagnostic objects during operation. Under these conditions, a real
physical experiment is essential.

3   Materials, Technology and Methods

One of the most common structural carbon steels St3sp was chosen as the material. Samples for uniaxial tensile tests were cut from rolled sheet $223 \times 37 \times 3$ mm
in size, for four-point bending tests – from rolled sheet $300 \times 20 \times 4$ mm in size.
The dimensions of the samples were chosen from the conditions of ensuring the
possibility of placing acoustic sensors on non-deformable areas of the samples.

The measuring setup used broadband sensors for the AE (acoustic-emission)
device AF15 with a bandwidth of $0.2 \div 0.5$ and $0.2 \div 2.0$ MHz. The information-
measuring system provided indication, registration and preprocessing of AE signals with its further storage in the computer memory [1–3].

The parameters of AE signals: signal density, energy, frequency distribution,
etc., are in unambiguous dependence on the degree of deformation of the sample
[1–3,13]. Through the measured current parameters of the AE signals, it is possible to determine the mechanical tension or relative deformation for a specific
load.

The strength of a structure is assessed by analyzing the strength of its constituent parts – elements. In the normative documents for assessing the strength,
the design cases are formulated, the design loading conditions corresponding to
them and the safety margins are set.

The division of the structure into elements is carried out in accordance with
the design schemes of structural mechanics, for elements that are a beam, plate,
shell, ring, cylinder, etc. Various types of connections are considered separately:
welded, riveted, bolted, adhesive, etc. A structural element is a part of it for
which the design schemes of structural mechanics are applicable and the destruction or failure of which means the failure of the structure as a whole. In this case,
the structure is divided into elements connected in series, due to which the failure
of the element coincides with the failure of the entire system as a whole. Parts of
a structure connected in parallel are combined into one element. There are well-
developed estimates of strength characteristics outlined in works on resistance
of materials and structural mechanics [15].

The most important characteristic of an individual element is its bearing
capacity, which is understood as a set of loads leading to destruction of the
element. The strength condition is the failure of the loading trajectory to go
beyond the strength region of the states.

The strength of the structure material is characterized by the ultimate
resistance σ_B and the yield stress $\sigma_{0.2}$. For steel St3sp, these parameters are

respectively equal to $\sigma_B = 490.3$ MPa, $\sigma_{0.2} = 240$ MPa [2,3]. When diagnosing the state of the comparison specimen, it is necessary to know the current value of mechanical stress for tension σ_s and for bending σ_b. If the inequalities $\sigma_s < \sigma_B$ for tensile deformation and $\sigma_b < \sigma_{0.2}$ for bending deformation are satisfied, then the state of the sample can be considered serviceable. Otherwise, the state of the sample is critical for further operation. This information represents the physical nature of the method used.

4   Experiment

The parameters necessary for the further description of the experimental data are given in Table 1.

Table 1. Experimental values of the main characteristics in stretching and four-point bending of specimens from steel St3sp [2,3]

Load P, kg	Elongation (deflection) Δl, mm	Tension σ, MPa	Relative deformation ε, %	Density of AE signal N, $10^8 s^{-1}$
Stretching				
1720	0.375	281.1	0.17	0.47
1880	0.463	307.3	0.20	0.40
1920	0.477	313.8	0.21	0.19
2010	0.577	328.5	0.26	0.16
2050	0.591	335.1	0.27	0.55
2090	0.705	341.6	0.32	0.41
2130	0.737	348.1	0.33	0.33
2160	1.923	353.0	0.86	0.65
2170	4.189	354.7	1.88	0.44
2400	11.022	392.3	4.94	0.29
2600	13.330	424.9	5.98	0.25
3000	17.390	490.3	7.80	0.22
Bend				
17	6.511	93.8	1.13	1.39
20	6.815	110.4	1.19	1.02
27	8.011	149.0	1.39	1.37
38	14.011	209.7	2.44	1,92
38.5	14.312	212.4	2.49	1.88
39.4	14.823	217.4	2.59	1.86
40	15.418	218.7	2.69	1.54
47	23.901	234.5	4.17	1.66
47.5	24.030	235.3	4.19	1.73

To illustrate the proposed method, we chose the AE signal density N. This parameter for St3sp steel under tensile deformation differs by an order of magnitude from that under bending deformation. With the complex nature of longitudinal tension and transverse bending, this property will make it possible to clearly determine the type of mechanical tension in the sample – σ_s or σ_b for stretching and bending, respectively.

The general trend in the dependences of the mechanical characteristics of the material on the parameters of the AE signals arising during deformations remains for different samples made of the same material. Therefore, it is advisable to move from discrete data presentation in Table 1 to continuous. With this representation, two methods of data processing are possible: interpolation and approximation. When interpolating, tabular data is represented by a curve that passes through all the nodal points of the analyzed dependence. When approximating, the resulting smoothing curve does not necessarily pass through all the nodal points, but represents a general trend and pattern. This levels down all the random jamming of table functions. Therefore, when analyzing the experimental data of AE signals, it is the approximation against the background of a large number of statistical random noises caused, in addition to instrumental errors, also caused by the physical nature of the studied process of measuring the material structure under loading, that is of interest.

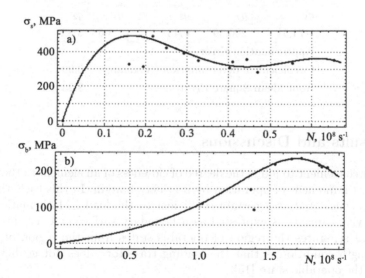

Fig. 1. Approximation of the dependence of the mechanical tension on the density of the AE signal for stretching (a) and bending (b) in specimens of steel St3sp (the points show the experimental values)

For the data presented in Table 1, the dependences of the mechanical tension on the density of the AE signals $\sigma_s(N)$ for stretching and $\sigma_b(N)$ for bending were approximated, respectively. The form of mathematical functions used for approximation is shown in Fig. 1 and it is described by formulas (1, 2). The numerical values of the approximation coefficients and errors are given in Table 2.

$$\sigma_s(N) = p_1 N^4 + p_2 N^3 + p_3 N^2 + p_4 N + p_5, \tag{1}$$

$$\sigma_b(N) = \frac{g_1 N^2 + g_2 N + g_3}{N^2 + q_1 N + q_2}, \tag{2}$$

where p_i, g_i, q_i are the approximation coefficients, N is the density of the AE signal.

Table 2. Numerical parameters of approximating functions $\sigma_s(N_s)$ and $\sigma_b(N_b)$

Stretching deformation				
p_1	p_2	p_3	p_4	p_5
$-4.00 \cdot 10^4$	$6.54 \cdot 10^4$	$-3.61 \cdot 10^4$	7313	0.86
Approximation Error				
Coefficient of determination (R-square)			0.97	
Root Mean Square Error			28.30	
Bending deformation				
g_1	g_2	g_3	q_1	q_2
-74.51	200.30	0.43	-3.63	3.82
Approximation Error				
Coefficient of determination (R-square)			0.99	
Root Mean Square Error			3.23	

5   Results and Discussions

It is most convenient to judge the degree of closeness of an element to the limiting state at each moment of operation by its safety margin. In this case, the safety margin is considered as a certain coefficient to the loads. Mathematically, the load-carrying capacity is expressed as a boundary surface or curve in the load space that separates the region of operable states from the region of failures. The strength condition is that the loading trajectory does not go beyond the range of the operable state [15].

A structural element made of steel St3sp is considered, which is subject to the simultaneous action of longitudinal tensile and transverse bending forces. The construction of the boundary curve of the bearing capacity of the structure in the load space is carried out according to the data in Table 1 (Fig. 2).

The equation of the boundary curve in Fig. 2 has the form [15]:

$$\left(\frac{\sigma_b}{\sigma_{0.2}}\right)^2 + \frac{\sigma_s}{\sigma_B} = 1. \tag{3}$$

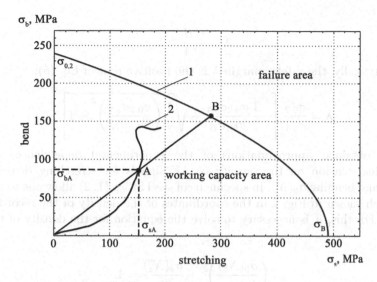

Fig. 2. Graphical interpretation of the safety factor in coordinates of mechanical tension: 1 – boundary curve 2 – loading trajectory

If the element is loaded with one load, the boundary curve degenerates into a dot. If one of the coordinates of the point is equal to zero, the bearing capacity means the loss of stability of equilibrium.

The loading path in the operability area can be any. For example, in a car engine cylinder, loads can approach the boundary surface arbitrarily close and move away from it until, one day, they cross the boundary surface, which will lead to destruction. Such a failure model in the theory of reliability is called an instantaneous destruction scheme.

Consider the scheme for calculating the safety margin for an arbitrary point A located on the loading path (curve 2 in Fig. 2). For point A, the static stability condition has the form:

$$\left(\frac{\sigma_{bA}}{\sigma_{0.2}}\right)^2 + \frac{\sigma_{sA}}{\sigma_B} \leq 1. \tag{4}$$

We multiply both terms of Eq. (3) by some coefficient λ, the value of which is chosen so that inequation (4) turns into equation [15]:

$$\left(\lambda\frac{\sigma_{bA}}{\sigma_{0.2}}\right)^2 + \lambda\frac{\sigma_{sA}}{\sigma_B} = 1. \tag{5}$$

Coefficient λ is the safety margin at the moment of time when the load corresponds to point A. Geometrically, the safety margin is equal to the ratio of the OB segment to the OA segment (see Fig. 2). Therefore, the condition for an operable state can be formulated as follows:

$$\lambda = \frac{OB}{OA} \geq 1. \tag{6}$$

Analytically, the safety margin λ is the positive root of Eq. (5):

$$\lambda = \frac{\sigma_{0.2}}{\sigma_{bA}} \left[-\frac{1}{2} \frac{\sigma_{0.2}\sigma_{sA}}{\sigma_{bA}\sigma_B} + \sqrt{\frac{1}{4} \left(\frac{\sigma_{0.2}\sigma_{sA}}{\sigma_{bA}\sigma_B} \right)^2 + 1} \right]. \tag{7}$$

The obtained approximations of the experimental dependences of the mechanical tension on the density of AE signals for stretching deformation $\sigma_s(N_s)$ and bending $\sigma_b(N_b)$ in specimens of steel St3sp (1, 2) allow one to present the graph shown in Fig. 2 in the coordinates of the density of the recorded AE signals. For this, it is necessary to solve the equation for the density of the AE signals:

$$\left(\frac{\sigma_b(N_b)}{\sigma_{0.2}} \right)^2 + \frac{\sigma_s(N_s)}{\sigma_B} = 1, \tag{8}$$

where N_s and N_b are the AE signal densities under stretching and bending deformations, respectively.

The following sequence of actions is proposed. We set the value of the density N_s of the AE signal during stretching. These values of N_s should be in the current interval $N_s \in [0; 0.7]$, which is determined by the experimental data and the condition of the approximation applicability (see Table 1 and Fig. 1(a)). For each selected value of N_s, the value of mechanical stress $\sigma_s(N_s)$ under tension is calculated according to the formula (1). According to which the values of $\sigma_b(N_b)$ are found, from formula (3) it follows:

$$\sigma_b(N_b) = \sigma_{0.2} \sqrt{1 - \frac{\sigma_s(N_s)}{\sigma_B}}. \tag{9}$$

The obtained value of $\sigma_b(N_b)$ allows one to solve Eq. (2) with respect to the density of the AE signals N_b during bending. The quadratic approximation used in (2) presupposes the presence of two solutions, of which it is necessary to leave the one that is in the actual range of values of $N_b \in [0; 1.9]$, determined by the experimental data and the condition of the approximation applicability (see Table 1 and Fig. 1(b)).

Thus, we obtain a graphical representation of the zones of operability and destruction for AE diagnostics of specimens from steel St3sp, shown in Fig. 3. Moreover, it should be noted that the loading trajectory in Fig. 3 (curve 2) and points A, B exactly correspond to the loading trajectory and points A, B in Fig. 2.

For the practical application of the obtained boundary strength curve in the coordinates of the density of the AE signals in the estimation of the residual life of specimens from steel St3sp, its polynomial approximation was carried out:

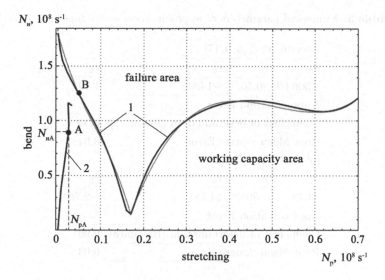

Fig. 3. Graphical interpretation of the safety margin in the coordinates of the density of the AE signals

$$N_b(N_s) = r_1 N_s^3 + r_2 N_s^2 + r_3 N_s + r_4, \qquad (10)$$

where r_i are the approximation coefficients, N_s and N_b are the densities of the AE signals under stretching and bending deformations, respectively.

To ensure high accuracy of approximation, the boundary curve was divided into two sections: the 1st section in the interval $N_s \in [0; 0.17]$, the 2nd section - in the interval $N_s \in [0.17; 0.7]$. The corresponding coefficients of approximation and error are given in Table 3.

Equation (7) is a surface $\lambda = f(\sigma_{sA}, \sigma_{bA})$, the view of which is shown in Fig. 4(a). Using relations (1, 2), Eq. (7) can also be represented as a surface $\lambda = f(N_{sA}, N_{bA})$, where N_{sA}, N_{bA} are the densities of AE signals at point A under tensile and bending deformation, respectively. The view of such a surface is shown in Fig. 4(b). It should be understood that point A, when constructing such surfaces, runs through the entire possible set of its coordinates $(\sigma_{sA}, \sigma_{bA})$ or (N_{sA}, N_{bA}) from the current range of their change.

For clarity, in Fig. 4, in addition to surfaces $\lambda = f(\sigma_{sA}, \sigma_{bA})$ and $\lambda = f(N_{sA}, N_{bA})$ (designated by number 1), planes corresponding to the ultimate safety factor $\lambda = 1$ (designated by number 2) are shown. This allows us to clearly distinguish the areas of workable states that are above the plane $\lambda = 1$ and the regions of destruction (located below the plane $\lambda = 1$). The line of intersection of both surfaces corresponds to the boundary curves, the full view of which is shown in Figs. 2, 3.

If one of the loads (longitudinal or transverse) is zero, then the solution to Eq. (5) is simplified. So, in the absence of longitudinal tension, we have:

Table 3. Numerical parameters of approximation of the function $N_b(N_s)$

interval $N_s \in [0; 0, 17]$			
r_1	r_2	r_3	r_5
-306.60	80.50	-14.53	1.79
Approximation Error			
Coefficient of determination (R-square)			0.99
Root Mean Square Error			0.04
interval $N_s \in [0.17; 0, 7]$			
r_1	r_2	r_3	r_5
33.43	-50.68	24.78	-2.76
Approximation Error			
Coefficient of determination (R-square)			0.99
Root Mean Square Error			0.03

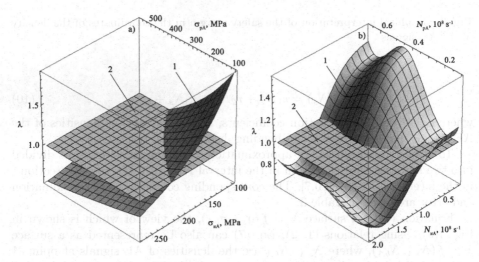

Fig. 4. The distribution of the safety margin for specimens of steel St3sp in coordinates of mechanical tension (a) and density of AE signals (b) (1 is the safety factor surface, 2 is the plane corresponding to the value $\lambda = 1$, which separates the strength region from the fracture region)

$$\lambda = \frac{\sigma_{0.2}}{\sigma_{bA}}. \tag{11}$$

In the absence of transverse bending, we have:

$$\lambda = \frac{\sigma_B}{\sigma_{sA}}. \tag{12}$$

Equations (11.12) are special cases of the problem under consideration. They can also be represented as a function of mechanical tension or as a function of the density of AE signals, which is shown in Figs. 5, 6.

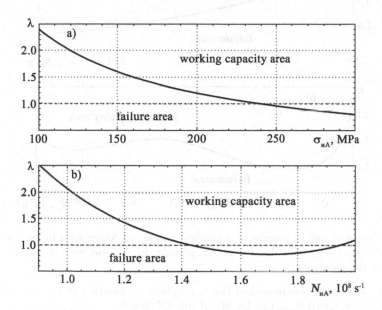

Fig. 5. Curves of the safety margin of a specimen of steel St3sp in coordinates of mechanical tension (a) and density of AE signals (b) for the case of the absence of longitudinal deformations

To determine the deformation characteristics of specimens from steel St3sp according to the density of AE signals, the following dependence was obtained:

$$\varepsilon(N) = \frac{w_1 N^2 + w_2 N + w_3}{N^2 + v_1 N + v_2}, \tag{13}$$

where w_i, v_i are the approximation coefficients, N is the density of the AE signals during stretching or bending deformations, ε is the relative deformation.

The form of dependence (13) for bending and tensile deformation of specimens made of St3sp steel is shown in Fig. 7, the numerical values of the coefficients and approximation errors are shown in Table 4.

The proposed model for determining the residual life of metal samples under conditions of combined deformation according to the data of acoustic emission measurements, in contrast to the known analogs, makes it possible to obtain the deformation and strength characteristics of structural materials, regardless of the shape and type of loading, taking into account the total effect of the stress-strain state up to the moment of failure without simplifying hypotheses of power and kinematic nature. The resulting limiting fracture surface makes it possible to estimate the residual service life of steel structures made of steel

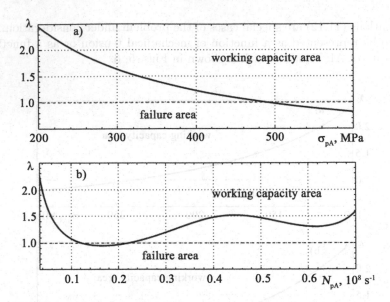

Fig. 6. Curves of safety margin of a specimen made of St3sp steel in coordinates of mechanical stress (a) and density of AE signals (b) for the case of the absence of transverse deformations

Table 4. Numerical parameters of the approximating function of the dependence of the relative deformation on the density of the AE signals

Stretching deformation				
w_1	w_2	w_3	v_1	v_2
−0.094	0.348	−0.108	−3.394	2.929
Approximation Error				
Coefficient of determination (R-square)				0.980
Root Mean Square Error				0.276
Bending deformation				
w_1	w_2	w_3	v_1	v_2
0.238	0.022	0.002	−0.436	0.049
Approximation Error				
Coefficient of determination (R-square)				0.968
Root Mean Square Error				0.715

St3sp. The high information content and accuracy of obtaining the deformation and strength characteristics of materials from the results of AE measurements makes it possible to increase the level of reliability of the condition and resource parameters of the material of structural elements during operation. The proposed

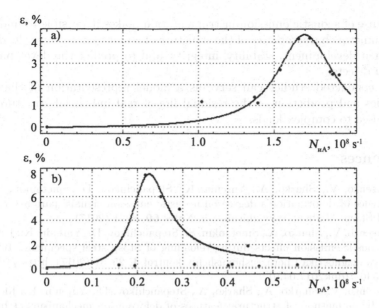

Fig. 7. Dependences of the relative deformation of the steel St3sp sample on the density of AE signals for bending (a) and (b)

method can be an alternative or addition to traditional experimental methods for determining the safety margin of the elements of metal structures.

6   Conclusions

Estimation of the residual life under conditions of combined loads during the operation of metal structures based on AE measurements makes it possible to dispense with one type of sensors, which is an undoubted advantage of the method. This approach greatly simplifies the procedure for assessing the residual life of metal structures under operating conditions, and also allows us to automate the calculation process.

The developed method for determining the residual life of metal structures with the simultaneous action of longitudinal stretching and transverse bending forces, based on calculating the safety margin at the points of the loading trajectory, makes it possible to separate the area of working capacity from the area of failures and allows us to determine the suitability of the structure for further operation.

The technology for determining the residual life of metal structures under conditions of combined loading according to the data of acoustic emission measurements makes it possible to carry out measurements at a considerable distance from the object under study. This makes it possible to use it for monitoring critical large-sized structures, extended and especially dangerous objects without taking them out of service.

The use of acoustic emission instrumentation makes it possible to find previously unknown characteristics of the structure of a material, to trace the dynamics of their development, stability, integrity, and to predict the development of material defects.

The conducted studies can serve as a model representation of changes in properties and prediction of the residual life of real industrial structures that are exposed to complex loads.

References

1. Aleksenko, V., Sharko, A., Yurenin, K., Stepanchikov, D., Smetankin, S.: The influence of deformation's degree on acoustic emission signals' parameters of the steel St3sp. Mizhvuzivsky zbirnik Sci. Notes **60**, 8–21 (2017)
2. Aleksenko, V., Sharko, A., Smetankin, S., Stepanchikov, D., Yurenin, K.: Detection of acoustic-emission effects during reloading of St3sp steel specimens. Tekhnicheskaya diagnostika i nerazrushayushchiy kontrol **4**, 25–31 (2017). https://doi.org/10.15407/tdnk2017.04.01
3. Aleksenko, V., Sharko, A., Sharko, A., Stepanchikov, D., Yurenin, K.: Identification by ae method of structural features of deformation mechanisms at bending. Tekhnicheskaya diagnostika i nerazrushayushchiy kontrol **1**, 32–39 (2019). https://doi.org/10.15407/tdnk2019.01.01
4. Babichev, S., Kornelyuk, A., Lytvynenko, V., Osypenko, V.: Computational analysis of microarray gene expression profiles of lung cancer. Biopolymers Cell **32**(1), 70–79 (2016). https://doi.org/10.7124/bc.00090F
5. Babichev, S., Škvor, J., Fišer, J., Lytvynenko, V.: Technology of gene expression profiles filtering based on wavelet analysis. Int. J. Intell. Syst. Appl. **10**(4), 1–7 (2018). https://doi.org/10.5815/ijisa.2018.04.01
6. Fan, Z., et al.: Structural health monitoring of metal-to-glass-ceramics penetration during thermal cycling aging using femto-laser inscribed FBG sensors. Sci. Rep. **10**(1), art. no. 12330 (2020). https://doi.org/10.1038/s41598-020-69282-7
7. He, Y., et al.: An overview of acoustic emission inspection and monitoring technology in the key components of renewable energy systems. Mech. Syst. Sig. Process. **148**, art. no. 107146 (2020). https://doi.org/10.1016/j.ymssp.2020.107146
8. Khajehzadeh, M., Boostanipour, O., Reza Razfar, M.: Finite element simulation and experimental investigation of residual stresses in ultrasonic assisted turning. Ultrasonics **108**, art. no. 106208 (2020). https://doi.org/10.1016/j.ultras.2020.106208
9. Li, B., et al.: Prediction equation for maximum stress of concrete drainage pipelines subjected to various damages and complex service conditions. Constr. Build. Materials **264**, art. no. 120238 (2020). https://doi.org/10.1016/j.conbuildmat.2020.120238
10. Liu, X., Wang, X., Xie, K., Wu, Z., Li, F.: Bond behavior of basalt fiber-reinforced polymer bars embedded in concrete under mono-tensile and cyclic loads. Int. J. Concrete Struct. Mater. **14**(1), 1–15 (2020). https://doi.org/10.1186/s40069-020-0394-4
11. Ma, J., Zhang, H., Shi, Z., Chu, F., Gu, F., Ball, A.: Modelling acoustic emissions induced by dynamic fluid-asperity shearing in hydrodynamic lubrication regime. Tribol. Int. **153**, art. no. 106590 (2021). https://doi.org/10.1016/j.triboint.2020.106590

12. Marani, A., Nehdi, M.: Machine learning prediction of compressive strength for phase change materials integrated cementitious composites. Const. Build. Mater. **265**, art. no. 120286 (2020). https://doi.org/10.1016/j.conbuildmat.2020.120286

13. Marasanov, V., Sharko, A., Stepanchikov, D.: Model of the operator dynamic process of acoustic emission occurrence while of materials deforming. lecture notes in computational intelligence and decision making. In: Lecture Notes in Computational Intelligence and Decision Making. ISDMCI 2019. Advances in Intelligent Systems and Computing, vol. 1020, pp. 48–64 (2020). https://doi.org/10.1007/978-3-030-26474-1_4

14. Mirgal, P., Pal, J., Banerjee, S.: Online acoustic emission source localization in concrete structures using iterative and evolutionary algorithms. Ultrasonics **108**, art. no. 106211 (2020). https://doi.org/10.1016/j.ultras.2020.106211

15. Mossakovsky, V., Makarenkov, A., Nikitin, P.: The strength of rocket structures. Vyssh. shk., Moscow (1990)

16. Moussa, G., Owais, M.: Pre-trained deep learning for hot-mix asphalt dynamic modulus prediction with laboratory effort reduction. Constr. Build. Mater. **265**, art. no. 120239 (2020). https://doi.org/10.1016/j.conbuildmat.2020.120239

17. Muravev, V., Tapkov, K.: Evaluation of strain-stress state of the rails in the production. Devices Methods Measur. **8**(3), 263–270 (2017). https://doi.org/10.21122/2220-9506-2017-8-3-263-270

18. Nazari, S., Bahiraei, M., Moayedi, H., Safarzadeh, H.: A proper model to predict energy efficiency, exergy efficiency, and water productivity of a solar still via optimized neural network. J. Clean. Prod. **277**, art. no. 123232 (2020). https://doi.org/10.1016/j.jclepro.2020.123232

19. Nosov, V.V., Zelenskii, N.A.: Estimating the strength of welded hull elements of a submersible based on the micromechanical model of temporal dependences of acoustic-emission parameters. Russian J. Nondestructive Test. **53**(2), 89–95 (2017). https://doi.org/10.1134/S1061830917020036

20. Oz, F., Calik, E., Ersoy, N.: Finite element analysis and acoustic emission monitoring of progressive failure of corrugated core composite structures. Composite Struct. **253**, art. no 112775 (2020). https://doi.org/10.1016/j.compstruct.2020.112775

21. Xu, G., Hou, D., Qi, H., Bo, L.: High-speed train wheel set bearing fault diagnosis and prognostics: a new prognostic model based on extendable useful life. Mech. Syst. Sig. Process. **146**, art. no. 107050 (2021). https://doi.org/10.1016/j.ymssp.2020.107050

22. Yang, K., et al.: Enhanced extra-long life fatigue resistance of a bimodal titanium alloy by laser shock peening. Int. J. Fatigue **141**, art. no. 105868 (2020). https://doi.org/10.1016/j.ijfatigue.2020.105868

23. Yang, S., Yuan, H., Zeng, W., Guo, H.: Chemo-thermo-mechanical modeling of EB-PVD TBC failure subjected to isothermal and cyclic thermal exposures. Int. J. Fatigue **141**, art. no. 105817 (2020). https://doi.org/10.1016/j.ijfatigue.2020.105817

24. Zagidulin, T., Zagidulin, R., Osipov, K.: On prediction of metal structure destruction on the basis of complex acoustic-emission and magnetic study. Bull. Bashkir Univ. Math. Mech. Phys. **22**(2), 350–358 (2017)

Expansion of the Capabilities
of Chromatography-Mass Spectrometry
Due to the Numerical Decomposition
of the Signal with the Mutual
Superposition of Mass Spectra

Serge Olszewski[1,2] , Yeva Zajets[2] , Violetta Demchenko[2] , Oleg Boskin[3] ,
Mariia Voronenko[3] , Volodymyr Lytvynenko[3(✉)] , Iryna Perova[4] ,
and Dmitry Stepanchikov[3]

[1] Taras Shevchenko National University of Kyiv, Kyiv, Ukraine
olszewski.serge@gmail.com
[2] Laboratory of Analytical Chemistry and Monitoring of Toxic Substances State
Institution "Kundiiev Institute of Occupational Health of the National Academy
of Medical Sciences of Ukraine", Kyiv, Ukraine
eva512@gmail.com, chemioh@ukr.net
[3] Department of Informatics and Computing Technology, Kherson National
Technical University, Kherson, Ukraine
aandre.lenoge@gmail.com, mary_voronenko@i.ua, immun56@gmail.com,
dmitro_step75@ukr.net
[4] Kharkiv National University of Radio Electronics, Kharkiv, Ukraine
rikywenok@gmail.com

Abstract. Numerical methods for expanding the field of applicability
of chromatography-mass spectrometry in the case of poorly separated
signals are considered. We found that the existence of additive noise in
the initial mixed mass spectrum gives rise to the noise component of the
weight coefficients of its components with an undetermined probability
distribution law. The power of the generated noise is higher than the
power of the additive noise of the output signal. It is shown that the
condition of orthogonality of the components of the mixed mass spectrum
makes it possible to determine their weight coefficients with a relative
error of less than 4% when the ratio of the power of additive noise to
the power of the useful signal is not more than three times. The main
result of the work, which is new compared to the one published earlier,
is that for real mass spectra it was shown that decomposition of a linear
combination of orthogonal functions by the optimal linear associative
memory (OLAM) method gives a satisfactory result even if the noise level
is three times higher than the useful signal level. The area of satisfactory
application of OLAM for the decomposition of non-orthogonal functions,
on the contrary, is limited by the condition that the signal level exceeds
the noise level by about 2.5 times.

© Springer Nature Switzerland AG 2020
S. Babichev et al. (Eds.): DSMP 2020, CCIS 1158, pp. 218–237, 2020.
https://doi.org/10.1007/978-3-030-61656-4_14

Keywords: Decomposition problem · Chromatography · Mass spectrometry · Additive noise

1   Introduction

The assortment of pesticides used in Ukraine's agriculture totals about 270 items. Their preparatory weight reaches 36,000 tons with a demand of about 40,000 tons. The area of their application is approximately 50 million hectares of agricultural land. A number of drugs according to the criterion of toxicity, persistence in the environment, migration, bioconcentration and actual pollution of environmental objects belong to hazard class 1–2 [1, 2, 7, 9, 10, 13, 14, 16, 19, 24, 27]. In this regard, the need to implement effective and accurate methods for determining the content of residual contaminants in food raw materials, food products and feed for farm animals, as well as the use of the latest technologies for cleaning products from harmful substances and preventing poisoning by them is obvious and undeniable.

The most sensitive and accurate modern methods for identifying harmful substances and determining their residual amounts, as a rule, are based on chromato-mass spectrometric measurements. However, their use in this area is complicated by the fact that most modern plant protection products used in agriculture, as a rule, contain excipients, for example, antidotes or several active substances, along with the active agent. Among the studied drugs, there are also those that contain components that are poorly separated in the column of a gas chromatograph. Their joint presence in the analyte significantly distorts the mass spectrum and reduces the reliability of identification. This is especially true for those compounds whose retention time in the column differs little, or in cases where fragments of chromatographic peaks overlap each other. In these cases, the distortion of the individual mass spectra as a result of the overlay is significant.

In chromatography, the problems associated with the application of chromatographic peaks are usually removed due to the hardware complexity of the devices. This approach does allow you to split many parametric signals into individual components, but there is a significant increase in the cost of analytical equipment, which is not cheap. On the other hand, there are a number of digital methods of signal decomposition [3–5, 8, 11, 12, 15, 17, 18, 20–23, 25, 26] which can be applied. A method for resolving an existing problem through the use of specialized methods of numerical processing of a mass spectrometric signal is considered. In particular, if there is a database of reference mass spectra of the studied substances, the mixed OLAM mass spectrum can be decomposed by the method [6] into components to obtain weight coefficients of superposition.

The purpose of the work is to experimentally verify the applicability of the decomposition of real mass spectra of an undivided mixture of polyatomic molecules by the OLAM method to increase the reliability of the individual components' identification of the mixture in the case of their individual mass spectra overlapping.

2   Related Works

In the spectral analysis, it is constantly necessary to establish the quantitative element of the mixture components based on mixed mass spectra of heterogeneous components of the molecules mixture. In other words, many sources are mixed into the signal being measured. The goal of the such signals analysis is to analyze one or more of them separately. In the case of multi-channel measurements, several methods are available to decompose the signal into its components - for example, independent component analysis (ICA). However, only a few methods are known for the single-channel records analysis. Examples are single-channel ICA (SCICA) and wavelet ICA (WICA), which all have certain limitations. The authors of [15] propose to divide a single-channel signal into independent components by combining decomposition mode with ICA using empirical modes. Empirical mode decomposition (EMD) is a signal representation division method in time into separate components. It can be compared to other analysis methods such as Fourier transform and wavelet decomposition. EMD is best suited for analyzing signals that are often non-linear and non-stationary. The EMD filters out functions that form the complete and almost orthogonal basis for the output signal. The completeness of the EMD method is an important condition for determining the method. In fact, behind empirical modes, certain functions are chosen a priori, which are called internal mode functions (IMF). An IMF set must be sufficient to describe a signal, although IMFs themselves need not be orthogonal. The fact that the functions that decompose a signal are time-dependent and have the same dimensionality as the output signal allows you to save the different frequency ranges modes in time. Receiving IMFs from real signals is important because natural processes often have several causes that are not synchronized in time. The presence of such mixed-signal components separate sources is obvious in EMD analysis but is quite hidden in Fourier images or wavelet coefficients. However, all the adequacy of the proposed method specifically for the mixed signals decomposition into separate components, it assumes the components differentiation by a certain parameter. Most often it is either frequency or phase shift between IMF packages that reproduce individual components of a mixed signal. However, based on the nature of mutually superimposed optical spectra or mass spectra of molecular mixtures, it is rather difficult to meet the conditions for reliable operation of the method presented in [15] for such signals.

A known constraint to EMD is the sensitivity to noise and sample size. These constraints could be partially eliminated by other mathematical methods aimed at solving the decomposition problem. For example, synchronous compaction, empirical wavelets, or recursive variable decomposition. In [8], the authors propose a quite non-recursive algorithm of variational mode decomposition (VMD), which performs simultaneous mode extraction. The algorithm is aimed at finding such an modes ensemble and their corresponding center frequencies, that the collective action of these modes reproduced the input signal action. In this case, after demodulation to the baseband, each mode must be smooth. In the Fourier analysis, this corresponds to a narrowband approximation. The authors emphasize the importance of applying Wiener filtering to suppress noise. In fact, the proposed method is a generalization of the classic Wiener filter for the many adaptive bands case. The presented model offers a theoretically grounded and easy to understand the decomposition problem solution. A variation model is effectively optimized using a variation method with multiple theoretical approaches. The preliminary results show attractive indices of existing models of fashion decomposition. As evidenced by the results of practical decomposition, which were obtained on a number of artificial and real data, the proposed algorithm is much more reliable for signals with noise. However, its essential disadvantage is the necessary condition for separating empirical modes. The latter makes the proposed algorithm unsuitable for the correct decomposition of signals superposition, which are mutually overlapping.

An algorithm for generating an Ensemble Empirical Mode Decomposition (EEMD) is proposed in [25, 26]. This algorithm includes sifting the ensemble of signals with additive white noise and considers such an averaging as the final true result. When using a finite, rather than infinitely small, level of white noise that is necessary to make the ensemble exhaust all possible solutions in the sifting process. In this approach, signals of different scales tend to the corresponding intrinsic mode functions (IMF) dictated by the dyadic filter basis. Since EEMD is a space-time analysis method, additive white noise is averaged when there are enough samples. The only stable part regarding averaging are the signal components, which are then treated as true physical algorithm results. The effect of artificially adding white noise is to create a uniform reference area in time-frequency space. That is, additive noise minimizes part of a signal of comparable scale into one of the IMFs. With the help of such an averaged ensemble, it is possible to divide the scale naturally without any a priori subjective selection criterion that takes place when checking for continuity in the original EMD algorithm. This approach has a significant advantage over the initial EMD because it uses the statistical characteristics of white noise for the initial signal perturbation with its subsequent relaxation to the IMF and noise component suppression when the result is achieved. So, such an improvement makes the EMD method suitable for noise data analysis. However, this approach, for all its attractiveness, does not remove the mutual overlap problem of the source signal components.

The paper [22] presents a new approach to the analysis and signals synthesis in the frequency-time space, using the decomposition methods by their own values. It is based on the S-method, which is applied to the frequency-time representation of signals for which individual components distribution is the same or close to the sum of Wigner distributions. The new method of decomposition of frequency-time signal representation was tested on the model and experimental data from Surface-Wave Radar (HFSWR). The results show that it provides an effective way to analyze and detect air targets, show significant changes in speed. The algorithm allows us to separate the single target signal from the total signal of a strong other target accumulation. The analysis shows that when processing radar signals, this method provides additional information regarding traditional FFT-based methods. However, the necessary conditions for the distribution of own decomposition task modes make this method unsuitable for the decomposition of mutually superimposed molecular emission spectra, or mass spectra of multi-atomic molecules.

In [23], the method of singular-spectrum analysis (SSA) was used, which was developed on the basis of empirical data presented in time series. This paper shows that SSA provides a strong but reliable approximation of strange attractors with toroidal surfaces in the presence of noise. This method works well for short, noisy time sequences. SSA is based on a lagged-covariance matrix. The method consists of choosing a subset of its own elements and related principal components (PCs) to implement a noise reduction algorithm, a detrending algorithm, and an algorithm to identify oscillating components. The components (RCs) are designed to provide an optimal reconstruction of a dynamic process in exact epochs rather than an averaged analysis window length. The SSA is combined with advanced spectral analysis methods such as maximum entropy (MEM) and multitaper method (MTM) - to clarify the interpretation of oscillatory behavior. The SSA-MEM combined method is also used to predict the final phase for selected RCs subsets. The performance of all method components has been tested on time sequences generated by known quasi-periodic or chaotic processes. At the same time, its application to the decomposition of aperiodic sequences is questionable. In addition, the specificity of PCs narrows down the types of time sequences that are to be reliably decomposed into their own elements inherent to this method.

For signals containing components, change at different times statistical moments may depend on the time scale in which the signal is recorded. For the identification and quantification of such signals, it is necessary to carry out a time-frequency analysis. The dependence of statistical properties of signal fluctuations on the spatial and temporal scale is characterized by the specifics of systems with non-linear links between different modes. Therefore, estimating how the statistics of oscillating signal modes depend on the scale is useful for understanding the corresponding multiscale statistics of such dynamics. The authors of [18] propose a multiscale data analysis method called Adaptive Local Iterative Filtering (ALIF). The method presented in this paper allows us to describe the multiscale nature better than with the Fourier transform. In addition, the proposed method gives better scale resolution than the classical discrete wavelet transform (DWT). ALIF is a basic measure method, focused on the allocation of mixed signals small-scale structures, such as radio flash ionospheric disturbances. However, the molecular bands or γ-spectra of radioactive isotopes contain sufficiently long, slightly variable fragments, the shape of which is important for identifying sources. So, it is quite difficult to make a reliable mixed signals decomposition consisting of such components by the ALIF method.

As an alternative to EMD, the [4] considers the approach called Iterative Filtering (IF). To ensure sufficient convergence conditions for an arbitrary IF signal, the authors propose an IF strategy together with an adaptive and controllable filter length selection to achieve decomposition. In fact, this is a special case of ALIF, which is based on the authors' work on smooth filters with compact support for solutions to the Fokker-Planck equations (FP filters). These filters fully comply with sufficient convergence conditions of the IF algorithm. Experimental testing of FP filters suitability for IF and ALIF methods demonstrates their high performance and stability. And in [3] there are two original methods The method of iterative filtering represents a method developed for decomposition and analysis of non-stationary and nonlinear signals. In this paper we offer two alternative formulations of the original algorithm, which allows us to turn an iterative filtering method into a direct reception, making the algorithm close to the online algorithm.

In [5], the authors proposed a method for using hyperspectral images to identify chemical plumes. The authors argue that for a chemical plume photographed using a hyperspectral sensor with a priori known frequency spectrum and a correctly selected threshold value, the adaptive cosine estimator allows reliable tracking of this chemical plume. However, due to the presence of noise and inadequate sensing, accurate identification of chemical pixels is not easy even in this seemingly simple situation. In this paper, the authors propose a post-processing tool that, when externally controlled, or fully adaptive, makes it possible to improve the efficiency of any classification methods in determining the loop boundaries. The authors consider this tool to be multi-dimensional iterative filtering (MIF) algorithm, which is a non-stationary signal decomposition method. The authors position the proposed approach as an innovative empirical decomposition method. Moreover, based on the MIF technique, they also propose a pre-processing method, which allows the decorrelation and centering of a hyperspectral data set. An indicator of cosine similarity, which often fails in practice, becomes a successful and superior classifier if it is equipped with the pre-processing method proposed in [5]. However, this method fundamentally requires no mutual overlay of frequency components of the studied signals. Otherwise, the high probability of bifurcation points in an iterative process of IF formation determines the algorithm instability.

For many decades there has been a general perception in the literature that Fourier methods are not suitable for analyzing nonlinear and non-stationary data. In [21], a new and adaptive Fourier decomposition method (FDM) based on the Fourier theory is proposed. This method demonstrates its effectiveness in analyzing nonlinear and non-stationary time sequences. The FDM method breaks down any data set into a small number of "Fourier internal band functions" (FIBF). FDM presents a generalized Fourier extension with variable amplitudes and variable frequencies of time sequence using the Fourier method. This work suggests the idea of a multifactor FDM (MFDM) based on zero-phase filters for analyzing multivariate non-linear and non-stationary time series using FDM. This paper also presents an algorithm for obtaining cutoff frequencies for MFDM. The proposed MFDM generates a finite number of multidimensional bands FIBF (MFIBF). MFDM preserves some internal physical properties of multivariate data such as scale alignment, trend, and instantaneous frequency. The proposed methods provide frequency energy time distribution (TFE) that reveals the internal data structure. However, the use of the decomposition method of complex signals, proposed by the authors [21], due to the mutual overlapping of components has the same disadvantages as in [5]. In [20], continues to study the problem of asymmetries concerning the Hilbert transform of native functions that can be used in frequency analysis. The systematic study of such eigenfunctions was carried out by a number of authors for a specific case of Mebius transformation. In fact, in [20] is devoted to the development of a method for building an IMF family identical to a special class of star-like functions of one complex variable. Such IMFs are called circular H-atoms. Work [20] is interesting from the point of view of concretizing the general EMD decomposition method for a specific class of signals. But the use of precisely circular H-atoms for the application of EMD in the problems of decomposition of the mixed mass spectrum does not eliminate the general problems of decomposition of mixed signals with mutual superposition in the time and frequency domains inherent in this method.

One of the directions for solving the decomposition problem can be the direct calculation of mixed mass spectra elements weight indices based on the assumption that the superposition principle is fair when forming complex mixture mass spectra. We call the vector of the obtained weights the decomposition problem exact solution. The many correct systems construction of heterogeneous linear equations provides an ensemble of exact solution implementations and requires preliminary determination of the qualitative elementary composition of the mixture under study. In the case of chromatographic analysis, these are, as a rule, a priori data. In order to build equations systems, they provide an ensemble of implementations of decomposition problem exact solution, mass spectral structures accumulated in numerous databases, such as NIST-2011, can be used. The strong sensitivity of the precise solution to the decomposition problem to the noise element, which is every time represent in the signal, requires further use of mathematical methods to suppress the noise element of the exact solution.

The peculiarity of the exact solution to the decomposition problem lies in the fact that when finding a solution to systems of heterogeneous linear equations with respect to the weight indexes of the elements of the mixed spectrum with additive noise, the additive noise in the solution grows rapidly. Moreover, the structure of the precise solution does not allow to install the form of the probability distribution law of the noise element. This means that in order to eliminate problems associated with this element, it is necessary either to use methods of preliminary noise suppression that are not based on its statistical specification, or to use the conversion of the initial signals and reference spectra, eliminating the effect of noise on the final result of the decomposition problem.

3   Materials and Methods

3.1   Preliminary Data Preparation

The mass spectrum of a complex mixture in itself is complex. As a rule, it is not very selective and does not allow for direct identification and quantification of substances in the mixture. This happens firstly, due to the mutual overlap of the mass spectra of the starting components, and secondly, due to the uncertainty of the analytical features that are different for different components of the mixture.

Gas chromatography-mass spectrometry mainly solves this problem. However, chromatography-mass spectrometry, in particular, gas chromatography-mass spectrometry, is not a universal method. This is because since for those compounds whose retention times in chromatographic columns are close to each other or fragments of chromatographic peaks overlap each other, the distortion of individual mass spectra as a result of overlapping remains significant. For such cases, it is necessary to use more complex methods of preliminary preparation and data analysis.

One of such methods may be the method of converting the initial mass spectra into the so-called "group mass spectra" developed in [26]. Such group mass spectra reflect the general characteristics of the whole system (or group of compounds), leveling the individual differences in the mass spectra of individual elements of the system. For such a group mass spectrum take the envelope curve of the intensity of the peaks of the group of ions of the homologous series.

As a rule, the maximum of such an envelope curve corresponds to the most characteristic ions of this group, and the distribution of the peak intensities of these ions is determined by the set of individual compounds in the mixture. Each type of compound has a characteristic set of fragments and, therefore, a certain set of characteristic groups of ions. As in the case of the initial mass spectra of individual compounds, the set of structural fragments of the group mass spectrum can be a descriptor of the molecule under consideration for further use in the algorithms of mathematical methods for identifying molecules.

We selected the envelope curve from the initial mass spectrum using the Fourier filtering algorithm. To do this, using the discrete Fourier transform (DFT), we obtained an array of spectral harmonic components of the original signal:

$$W[k] = \sum_{n=0}^{N-1} w[n] e^{-j\frac{2\pi}{N}kn}. \tag{1}$$

All elements of the array $W[k]$ for all $k \leq 0.001N$ were replaced by zeros to form an array, $\widehat{W}[k]$ and the inverse discrete Fourier transform of the resulting array was performed:

$$\widehat{w}[k] = \frac{1}{N} \sum_{n=0}^{N-1} \widehat{W}[n] e^{-j\frac{2\pi}{N}kn}. \tag{2}$$

The arrays $\widehat{w}[k]$ thus was obtained for the experimental and reference mass spectra were discrete group mass spectra for which further decomposition was performed.

Based on the assumption that the group mass spectrum of a mixture of molecules is a apposition of the mass spectra of the elements, then:

$$F[w] = \sum_{i=0}^{M} a_i f_i [w], \tag{3}$$

where a_i is the unknown weight coefficient of each component of the mixture, which in the future will be called the weight coefficient of decomposition. For a uniformly discretized mass spectrum, the same will take the form:

$$F[n] = \sum_{i=0}^{M} a_i f_i [n], \tag{4}$$

As a rule, for group mass spectra, the total amount of examples N of a discrete signal surpasses the amount M of mixture elements. Since the unknown coefficients a_i, which are the subject of solving the decomposition problem, are the same for $\forall n$ there is a finite set Ω of systems of heterogeneous linear algebraic equations with M unknowns, which relates the numerical values of the samples of the reference spectra $f_i[n]$, the spectrum of the mixture $F[n]$ and decomposition weights a_i:

$$\begin{pmatrix} f_1[n+1] & \dots & f_i[n+1] & \dots & f_M[n+1] \\ f_1[n+2] & \dots & f_i[n+2] & \dots & f_M[n+2] \\ \dots & \dots & \dots & \dots & \dots \\ f_1[n+M] & \dots & f_i[n+M] & \dots & f_M[n+M] \end{pmatrix} \times \begin{pmatrix} a_1 \\ a_2 \\ \dots \\ a_M \end{pmatrix} = \begin{pmatrix} F[n+1] \\ F[n+2] \\ \dots \\ F[n+M] \end{pmatrix}. \tag{5}$$

For each of these systems of equations, the solution vector $a = (a_1, a_2, ..., a_M)^T$ is the same. We call this solution the exact solution to the decomposition problem.

Finding the weighting indexes of a mixture of substances or the weighting indexes of decomposition, based on the known reference mass spectra of each individual element and the true mass spectrum of the mixture, has an precise solution.

For practical use, it is more appropriate to use the OLAM method [8,15] for finding weight coefficients. It is based on the matrix form of the principle of superposition. We write Eq. (5) in matrix form:

$$S \times a = F, \tag{6}$$

here **S** is matrix composed of $f_i[n]$ samples of the reference mass spectra, **a** is the exact solution to the decomposition problem, **F** is the vector of samples $F[n]$ of the experimental group mass spectrum. The exact solution to the decomposition problem can be obtained in matrix form:

$$a = W \times F, \tag{7}$$

where $W = S^{-1}$.

Based on the fact that the same exact solution can be obtained for all fragments of length M of group mass spectra, the matrix **W** does not have to be square. It is important that the number of columns of this matrix corresponds to the number of samples of a fragment of the experimental group mass spectrum **F**. The OLAM method consists in providing an exact formula for finding the matrix **W**:

$$W = I \times \left(S^T \times S\right)^{-1} \times S^T, \tag{8}$$

where **I** is the unit matrix dimension M.

An application of this approach for practical goales, if we take group mass spectra as a basis, has fundamental complications.

One of them is that group mass spectra do not coincide with true mass spectra due to the loss of high-frequency harmonics. However, the linearity of the direct and inverse DFT operators suggests that the use of group mass spectra instead of true masses makes the precise solution to the decomposition problem correct. Another complication is that any real signal contains an integral element of additive noise. This complication is more fundamental, since arithmetic operations on realizations of random variables do not map to similar operations on their probability distributions. Thus, the nature of the influence of the noise element on the solution of the decomposition problem requires a more detailed study.

3.2   Effect of Additive Gaussian Noise

The mathematical model for a discrete signal that is as close as possible to the reality of the observed mass spectrum will take the form:

$$Q\left[n\right] + \zeta\left[n\right] = \sum_{i=0}^{M} a_i \left(q_i\left[n\right] + \zeta_i\left[n\right]\right), \tag{9}$$

where $\zeta\left[n\right]$ is a discrete random variable corresponding to the noise element of the spectral signal of the mixture and $\zeta_i\left[n\right]$ are the noise elements of the spectral signals of the components. Generally speaking, $\zeta\left[n\right]$ and $\zeta_i\left[n\right]$ are discrete random processes. For most experimental conditions, it is sufficient to consider them as ergodic random processes.

The presented modification of the model of the observed signal transforms the exact solution of the decomposition problem into a multidimensional random variable ξ with an unknown M-dimensional probability distribution $P(\xi)$. Hypothetically, the mathematical expectation of this quantity should converge to the solution vector:

$$M\{\xi\} = \lim_{k \to \infty} \sum_{k=1}^{K} \cdots \sum_{k=1}^{K} \xi_k P\left(\xi_k\right) = a. \tag{10}$$

Hereinafter, the index k denotes the solutions of a particular system of relations from the set Ω generated by Eq. (9). To simulate the effect of additive noise on the statistical characteristics of ξ, Eq. (9) was modified into the equation:

$$\sum_{i=0}^{M} a_i q_i\,[n] = Q\,[n] + \Theta\,[n]\,, \tag{11}$$

where $\Theta\,[n]$ are examples of a discrete random process, which are given by the formula:

$$\Theta\,[n] = \zeta\,[n] - \sum_{i=0}^{M} a_i \zeta_i\,[n]\,. \tag{12}$$

With an increase in the size of the general population of the exact solution to the decomposition problem with noise, when averaging the array of implementations over the ensemble, the mathematical expectation of the noise element should tend to zero, since the initial noise is symmetric. However, the hypothesis can be confirmed only by analyzing the structure of the precise solution to the problem of decomposing a signal with noise. In addition, such an analysis will allow us to draw conclusions regarding the distribution law of a random variable, which is a solution to the problem of decomposition of a signal with noise.

4   Experiment

The study of the proposed expansion method on the mass spectra of substances such as Propiconazole, p-p' DDT and Endosulphan Sulphat.

Propiconazole – [(+/−)-1-[2-(2,4 - dichlorophenyl)-4- propyl -1,3-dioxolan-2-ylmethyl]-1H-1,2,4- triazole (IUPAC)

Isomer 1

$C_{15}H_{17}Cl_2N_3O_2$

M.m.342.22

Propiconazole is a colorless liquid. Well soluble in most organic solvents. Completely miscible with acetone, methanol and propanol. Slightly hydrolyzed. Stable up to 320 °C

Endosulphan Sulphat — 6, 7, 8, 9, 10, 10-hexachloro-1, 5, 5a, 6, 9, 9a-hexahydro-6, 9-methano-2, 4, 3-benzodioxathiepine, 3, 3-dioxide (IUPAC)

Isomer 1

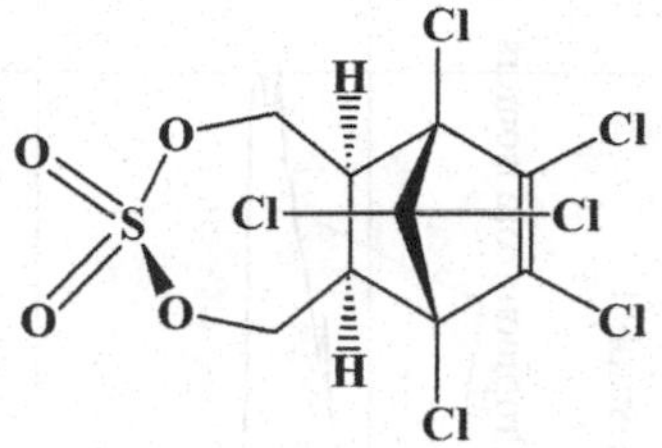

Isomer 2

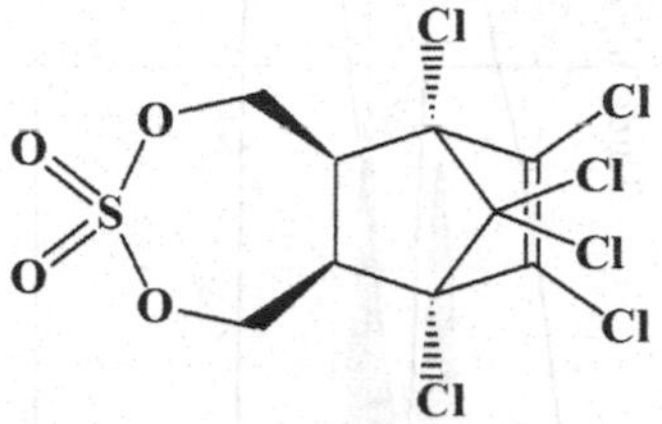

$C_9H_6Cl_6O_4S$
M.m.422.92

Endosulfan sulfate is a white, odorless, crystalline substance with a melting point of 181 °C. p-p'DDT (dichlorodiphenyltrichloroethane) - 4, 4' - dichlorodiphenyl trichloromethylmethane (IUPAC)

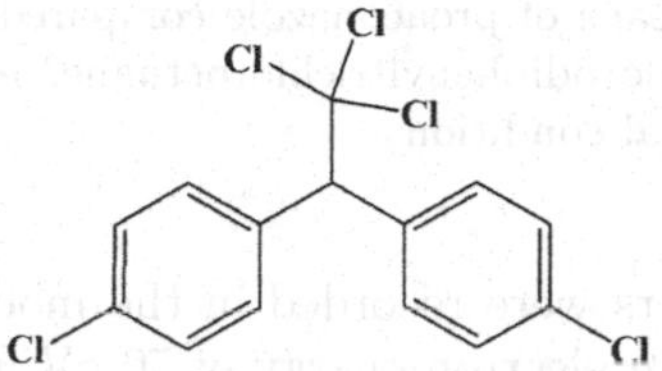

$C_{14}H_9Cl$
M.m.351.91

DDT is a white crystalline substance with a melting point $(108.5 - 109)$ °C. DDT is slightly soluble in water, it is soluble in many organic solvents, preferably in esters of lower fatty acids, ketones, aromatic hydrocarbons.

The analytical standard of propiconazole from Bayer, code No AEF 03264000 IB990012, certificate No AZ 14153, purity of the drug 99.6%, and the standard of organochlorine pesticides UMTS-CP023-7-1 were used for the research.

Chromato-mass spectrometry studies were performed on a CLARUS 600 T from Perkin Eimer (identification of propiconazole, endosulfan sulfate, and DDT).

We took the following capillary columns: No 1 - "Elite-5MS" ("Perkin Elmer"), 30 m long, 0.25 mm inner diameter. The thickness of the fixed phase layer (NF) is 0.25 μm;

No 2 - "Zebron" ZB-WAX with a stationary phase of 100 % polyethylene glycol, length 30 m (layer thickness 0.25 μm), inner diameter 0.32 mm.

We used helium as a carrier gas. The identification of compounds was performed using an automated search engine database of mass spectra of organic molecules NIST2011.

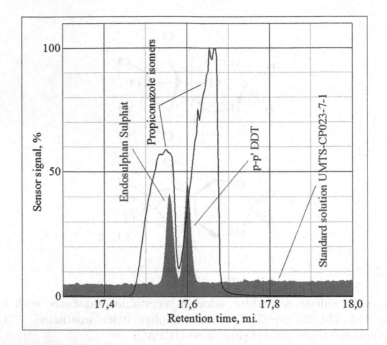

Fig. 1. Chromatographic peaks of proaconazole compared with the chromatogram of endosulfan sulfate and dichlorodiphenyltrichloroethane. All chromatographic studies were obtained under identical conditions

The mass spectrometers were recorded in the mode of molecules ionization by electron impact with an electron energy of 70 eV using the El + mode. The scan time was 0.2 s. with a pause between scans of 0.01 s. The number of scans per the averaged mass spectrum was 106. The ions of the studied molecules were fixed in the mass range from 45 to 450 m/z. The residual pressure in the ionization chamber was approximately 8.6×10^{-6}. The temperature of the ion source was 300 °C. The analyte input temperature was 280 °C.

The chromatographic method (GC-method) "QuEChERS" [16 (14)] was used to register the studied drugs components. In our opinion, it is important to analyze the method suitability of test substances identification in the presence of organochlorine pesticides, represented by a standard multicomponent solution UMTS-CP023-7-1. This is due to the fact that these substances today have a very high level of prevalence in all components of the environment and in food. In this regard, the chromatographic studies results are presented in the form of test substance combined chromatograms and standard analytical solution UMTS-CP023-7-1. Studies have shown that for propiconazole there is a mutual overlap of chromatographic peaks of its isomers with the peaks of endosulfan sulfate and DDT (Fig. 1).

The chromatographic peak of its isomer with retention time in the column 17:55 min overlaps with the peak of endosulfan sulfate (retention time

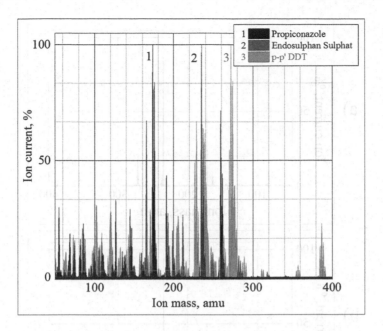

Fig. 2. Reference mass spectra of the investigated substances. Spectr 1 corresponds to Propiconazole, 2 - corresponds to Endosulphan Sulphat and 3 -corresponds to p-p 'DDT

17:56 min.), and the chromatographic peak of the isomer with a retention time of 17:65 min. With chromatographic peak DDT (retention time 17:60 min.).

Comparative analysis of test substances mass spectra indicates the fact of their significant mutual overlap in the whole range of ions charged masses. Since the ionizer conditions did not correspond to the conditions of multicharged ions formation, the numerical value of the reduced ion masses coincides with the value of the ion mass in atomic mass units (Fig. 2).

This fact makes it impossible to reliably identify some test substances in the presence of others using statistical comparison mathematical methods with their reference mass spectra. Based on this, it is proposed to use additional methods of mixed mass spectra mathematical processing aimed at their numerical decomposition. To find the decomposition weighting coefficients, we used the synthesized signal $Q[n]$ We received this signal as the sum of a linear combination of samples of the reference spectra and a random variable with a normal probability distribution law:

$$Q[n] = 5 \times q_{Prop}[n] + 10 \times q_{p-p'DDT}[n] + 1 \times q_{Endos}[n] + \Theta_G[n], \quad (13)$$

here $q_{Prop}[n]$ and $q_{Endos}[n]$ are the normalized to the maximum discrete mass spectra of Propiconazole, p-p' DDT and Endosulphan Sulphat, respectively. The term $\Theta_G[n]$ is an array of realizations of a random variable with a normal probability distribution. The selected synthesized signal satisfies all the requirements

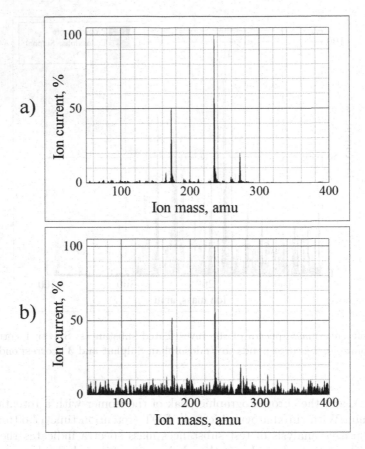

Fig. 3. Synthesized mass spectrum of a mixture of test substances. Graph a) corresponds to a useful signal in the absence of noise. Graph b) is the mass spectrum of a mixture with additive Gaussian noise, the average power of which is three times higher than the average power of the useful signal

of the model of a continuous Gaussian channel for transmitting information and adequately reproduces the properties of most spectral devices (Fig. 3).

We have obtained the general set of realizations of the precise solution to the problem of decomposing a signal with noise by successive application of the OLAM method to matched fragments of the studied mass spectra of dimension 10. In addition, we separately calculated the weighting coefficients for the complete signal consisting of 410 samples by the OLAM method. We performed the described procedure at different values of the noise power. Noise power, normalized to the full power of the synthesized signal with additive noise, we changed in the range from 0.01 to 99.01%.

5   Results and Discussions

As was established in [6], where the decomposition of molecular IR spectra was considered, even a slight signal perturbation by the noise element leads to strong scattering of the decomposition problem solutions and an increase in the error in determining the corresponding weight coefficients.

For example, an increase by one order of noise power leads to an increase in the standard error of determining the decomposition indexes by about three orders of magnitude. In particular, the error of the exact solution to the problem of decomposition of the signal with noise is satisfactory for practical use. However, for group mass spectra the situation is fundamentally different. The dependence of the variance of the weighting indexes of decomposition on the relative noise power is shown in Fig. 2.

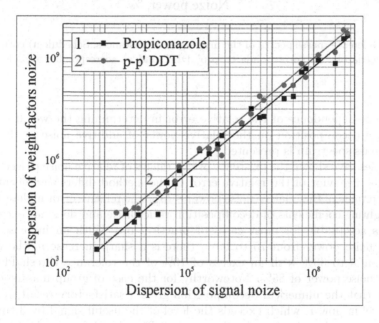

Fig. 4. The dependence of the variance of the precise solution of the decomposition problem on the variance of the additive noise of the initial mass spectrum. Curve 1 corresponds to Propiconazole, curve 2 corresponds to p-p' DDT

Studies have shown that with an increase in the power of additive noise in the signal by one order of magnitude, the variance of the total set of realizations of the exact solution to the decomposition problem for individual fragments of the studied mass spectra with a dimension of 10 samples is also increased by one order of magnitude, in contrast to the case with molecular spectra.

Even more, promising for practical application is the solution of the OLAM decomposition problem using the full data array with group mass spectra. In

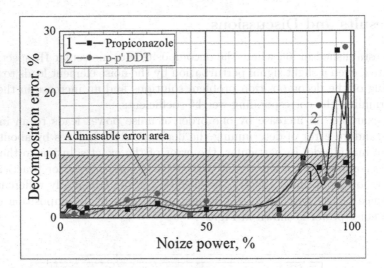

Fig. 5. Reference mass spectra of the investigated substances. Schedule a) corresponds to Propiconazole, b) corresponds to p-p' DDT and c) corresponds to Endosulphan Sulphat

Fig. 3. The dependence of the relative error in determining the weighting coefficients of decomposition on the relative power of additive noise in the initial mixed mass spectrum is presented.

Studies have shown the existence of two ranges of relative noise power, within which the behavior of the relative error of the method differs significantly. So, when the value of the relative noise power ≤75%, the relative error in determining the weighting coefficients of decomposition varies little and does not exceed 4%, which is acceptable for most cases of practical use. With an increase in the relative noise power from 75 to 99%, there is a sharp increase in the relative error from 4 to 30% with an excess of 10% of the tolerance threshold with a relative noise power of 85%. Noteworthy for the case of group mass spectra is the fact that the numerical decomposition gives a satisfactory result up to the noise level in power, which exceeds the level of the useful signal by 3 times. At the same time, the case of molecular spectra allowed satisfactory decomposition to be carried out only at a signal-to-noise ratio of at least 3.

The fundamental difference between the studied mass spectra and the case with molecular IR spectra is the fact that the selected signals are close to orthogonal functions. If for the measure of orthogonality of signals take their mutual power normalized to their Average Geometric total power:

$$\eta = \frac{\sum_n^N \left(q_1\,[n] \times q_2\,[n] \right)}{\sqrt{\sum_n^N \left(q_1\,[n] \right)^2 \times \sum_n^N \left(q_2\,[n] \right)^2}} \times 100\%, \tag{14}$$

then mutual power of all listed mass spectra does not exceed 1% of their average full power.

This difference allows us to hypothesize that the orthogonalization of the reference spectra significantly expands the range of applicability of the OLAM method for solving the problem of decomposition of a mixed signal with noise in the case when the noise power level is higher than the useful signal power level. However, verification of the validity of the hypothesis requires more detailed further research.

6 Conclusions

The paper proposes a non-iterative method for mixed signals decomposition in the additive Gaussian noise presence, which is applicable for the case of an overlapping component linear combination. The indisputable advantage of the proposed method in relation to EMD is that the sought-for components of the analyzed signal can mutually overlap in both the time and frequency domains.

The proposed method disadvantage in relation to EMD is its applicability only for the case of the nonlinear interaction absence between the mixed signal components.

The study results of additive noise level influence on the area of method applicability for practical use are obtained. It is shown that the relative error in determining the weighting coefficients of mass spectra superposition with additive noise does not exceed 4% at a noise power level three times higher than the signal power level.

It has been established that the method application to the mixed mass spectra decomposition makes it possible to expand the possibilities of the qualitative and quantitative chromatography-mass spectrometric analysis of mixed preparations in the case of using substances that are not separated by the chromatographic method.

References

1. Alford-Stevens, A., Budde, W., Bellar, T.: Interlaboratory study on determination of polychlorinated biphenyls in environmentally contaminated sediments. Anal. Chem. **57**, 2452–2457 (1985). https://doi.org/10.1021/ac00290a007
2. Ayris, S., Currado, S., Smith, D., Harrad, S.: GC/MS procedures for the determination of PCBS in environmental matrices. Chemosphere **35**(5), 905–917 (2016). https://doi.org/10.1016/S0045-6535(97)00187-2
3. Cicone, A.: Iterative filtering as a direct method for the decomposition of nonstationary signals. Numer. Algorithms 1–17 (2020). https://doi.org/10.1007/s11075-019-00838-z
4. Cicone, A., Liu, J., Zhou, H.: Adaptive local iterative filtering for signal decomposition and instantaneous frequency analysis. Appl. Comput. Harmon. Anal. **41**(2), 384–411 (2016). https://doi.org/10.1016/j.acha.2016.03.001d
5. Cicone, A., Liu, J., Zhou, H.: Hyperspectral chemical plume detection algorithms based on multidimensional iterative filtering decomposition. Phil. Trans. R. Soc. A **374**, art. no. 20160871 (2016). https://doi.org/10.1098/rspa.2016.0871

6. Coombes, K., Baggerly, K., Morris, J.: Pre-processing mass spectrometry data. In: Dubitzky, W., Granzow, M., Berrar, D. (eds.) Fundamentals of Data Mining in Genomics and Proteomics, pp. 79–102. Springer, Boston (2007). https://doi.org/10.1007/978-0-387-47509-7_4

7. Donato, F., Magoni, M., Bergonzi, R., et al.: Exposure to polychlorinated biphenyls in residents near a chemical factory in Italy: the food chain as main source of contamination. Chemosphere **64**(9), 1562–1572 (2006). https://doi.org/10.1021/es0258091

8. Dragomiretskiy, K., Zosso, D.: Variational mode decomposition. IEEE Trans. Signal Process. **62**(3), 531–544 (2014). https://doi.org/10.1109/TSP.2013.2288675

9. Gomara, B., Herrero, I., Pacepavicius, G., et al.: Occurrence of co-planar polybrominated/chlorinated biphenyls (PXBS), polybrominated diphenyl ethers (PBDES) and polychlorinated biphenyls (PCBS) in breast milk of women from Spain. Chemosphere **83**(6), 799–805 (2011). https://doi.org/10.1016/j.chemosphere.2011.02.080

10. Karlson, K., Ishaq, R., Becker, G., et al.: PCBs, DDTs and methyl sulphone metabolites in various tissues of harbour porpoises from Swedish waters. Environ. Pollut. **110**(1), 29–46 (2000). https://doi.org/10.1016/s0269-7491(99)00283-3

11. Keller, P., Kangas, L., Troyer, G., et al.: Nuclear spectral analysis via artificial neural networks for waste handling. IEEE Trans. Nucl. Sci. **42**(4), 709–715 (1995). https://doi.org/10.1109/23.467888

12. Kohonen, T., Ruohonen, M.: Representation of associated data by matrix operators. IEEE Trans. Comput. **C–22**, 701–702 (1973). https://doi.org/10.1109/TC.1973.5009138

13. Martínez-Vidal, J., González-Rodríguez, M., et al.: Selective extraction and determination of multiclass pesticide residues in post-harvest French beans by low-pressure gas chromatography/tandem mass spectrometry. J. AOAC Int. **1**, 856–867 (2003). https://doi.org/10.1093/jaoac/86.4.856

14. Meijer, S., Ockenden, W., Sweetman, A., et al.: Global distribution and budget of PCBs and HCB in background surface soils: implications for sources and environmental processes. Environ. Sci. Technol. **37**(4), 667–672 (2003). https://doi.org/10.1021/es0258091

15. Mijović, B., De Vos, M., Gligorijević, I., et al.: Huffel source separation from single-channel recordings by combining empirical-mode decomposition and independent component analysis. IEEE Trans. Biomed. Eng. **57**(9), 2188–2196 (2010). https://doi.org/10.1109/tbme.2010.2051440

16. Montory, M., Habit, E., Fernandez, P., et al.: PCBs and PBDEs in wild Chinook salmon (Oncorhynchus tshawytscha) in the Northern Patagonia. Chile. Chemosphere **78**(10), 1193–1199 (2010). https://doi.org/10.1016/j.chemosphere.2009.12.072

17. Olszewski, S., et al.: Some features of the numerical deconvolution of mixed molecular spectra. In: Lytvynenko, V., Babichev, S., Wójcik, W., Vynokurova, O., Vyshemyrskaya, S., Radetskaya, S. (eds.) ISDMCI 2019. AISC, vol. 1020, pp. 20–34. Springer, Cham (2020). https://doi.org/10.1007/978-3-030-26474-1_2

18. Piersanti, M., Materassi, M., Cicone, A., et al.: Adaptive local iterative filtering: a promising technique for the analysis of nonstationary signals. J. Geophys. Res.: Space Phys. **123**(1), 1031–1046 (2018). https://doi.org/10.1002/2017JA024153

19. Poster, D., Kucklick, J., Schantz, M., et al.: Determination of polychlorinated biphenyl congeners and chlorinated pesticides in a fish tissue standard reference material. Anal. Bioanal. Chem. **375**(2), 223–241 (2003). https://doi.org/10.1007/s00216-002-1680-5

20. Qian, T.: Mono-components for decomposition of signals. Math. Meth. Appl. Sci. **29**, 1187–1198 (2006). https://doi.org/10.1002/mma.721

21. Singh, P., Joshi1, S., Patney, R., Saha, K.: The fourier decomposition method for nonlinear and non-stationary time series analysis. Proc. R. Soc. A **473**, art. no. 20160871 (2017). https://doi.org/10.1098/rspa.2016.0871

22. Stanković, L., Thayaparan, T., Daković, M., et al.: Signal decomposition by using the S-method with application to the analysis of HF radar signals in sea-clutter. IEEE Trans. Signal Process. **54**(11), 318–336 (2006). https://doi.org/10.1109/TSP.2006.880248

23. Vautard, R., Yiou, P., Ghil, M.: Singular-spectrum analysis: a toolkit for short, noisy chaotic signals. Physica D **58**, 95–126 (1992). https://doi.org/10.1016/0167-2789(92)90103-T

24. Vetter, W., Weichbrodt, M., Scholz, E., et al.: Levels of organochlorines (DDT, PCBs, Toxaphene, Chlordane, Dieldrin, and HCHs) in blubber of south African Fur seals (Arctocephalus pusillus pusillus) from Cape Cross/Namibia. Mar. Pollut. Bull. **38**(9), 830–836 (1999). https://doi.org/10.1016/S0025-326X(99)00071-5

25. Wu, Z., Huang, N.: Ensemble empirical mode decomposition: a noise-assisted data analysis method. Adv. Adapt. Data Anal. **1**(1), 1–41 (2009). https://doi.org/10.1142/S1793536909000047

26. Wu, Z., Huang, N., Chen, X.: The multi-dimensional ensemble empirical mode decomposition method. Adv. Adapt. Data Anal. **1**(1), 339–372 (2009). https://doi.org/10.1142/S1793536909000187

27. Zhang, S., Zhang, Q., Darisaw, S., et al.: Simultaneous quantification of polycyclic aromatic hydrocarbons (PAHs), polychlorinated biphenyls (PCBs), and pharmaceuticals and personal care products (PPCPs) in Mississippi river water, in new Orleans, Louisiana, USA. Chemosphere **66**(6), 1057–1069 (2007). https://doi.org/10.1016/j.chemosphere.2006.06.067

Machine Vision and Pattern Recognition

Statistical Methods for Analyzing and Processing Data Components When Recognizing Visual Objects in the Space of Key Point Descriptors

Volodymyr Gorokhovatskyi[1], Svitlana Gadetska[2]([⊠]),
Oleksii Gorokhovatskyi[3], and Roman Ponomarenko[1]

[1] Kharkiv National University of Radio Electronics, Kharkiv, Ukraine
gorohovatsky.vl@gmail.com, roman.ponomarenko@nure.ua
[2] Kharkiv National Automobile and Highway University, Kharkiv, Ukraine
svgadetska@ukr.net
[3] Simon Kuznets Kharkiv National University of Economics, Kharkiv, Ukraine
oleksii.gorokhovatskyi@gmail.com

Abstract. In this paper, we propose the improvement of structural pattern recognition techniques in computer vision systems. We performed the transformation of the key point descriptors space into the space of the data statistical distributions to increase the speed of data processing. These distributions are based on the set of component values obtained by partitioning descriptors into non-intersecting fragments. The compression of data into the fixed set of bits allows to simplify processing and to reduce the quantity of computation operations. BRISK or ORB are suggested to be used as key point detectors, because they form binary descriptors which greatly simplifies processing and analysis. A number of traditional and up-to-date statistical approaches have been proposed and analyzed to determine the relevance of object descriptions by their distribution values and according to the significance level: the chi-square criterion, Renyi divergence, the non-parametric criterion and z-criterion. Additionally, the usage of Manhattan distance between the values of the distribution matrices was tested. The experimental part of the investigations presents the results of calculations and software modeling of the proposed methods for the icons dataset. It is shown, that the statistical distribution models are able to separate set of features effectively even in the case of a small number of bits in the data fragment. An improvement of distinguishing level is confirmed when increasing the size of the fragment in the description structure. The implementation of statistical distributions reduced processing time by hundreds of times preserving sufficient recognition quality.

Keywords: Computer vision · Object recognition · Key point ·
BRISK detector · Descriptor · Data fragment · Statistical
distribution · Relevance of descriptions · Relevance measure of
distributions · Processing time

© Springer Nature Switzerland AG 2020
S. Babichev et al. (Eds.): DSMP 2020, CCIS 1158, pp. 241–252, 2020.
https://doi.org/10.1007/978-3-030-61656-4_15

1   Introduction and Literature Review

Implementation of effective classification solutions in modern computer vision systems requires a number of problems connected with the multidimensional nature of the data to be solved. The application of structural classification methods are based on descriptions of visual objects in the form of descriptor sets of key points (KPs), where KPs are high-dimensional numerical vectors [7,11,12,18]. For example, binary representations obtained by a BRISK detector contain up to 512 components [17]. An image of an object in a data space in the form of multiple KP descriptors provides effective recognition in visual analysis applications [3,16,20,22].

A lot of different papers contain the comparative review of different features [14] or investigations about invariance and robustness [4]. But the question about the effective feature matching is still being discussed because the typical comparison of descriptors is based on nearest neighbor approaches (though comparison of bit values of description is pretty fast with Hamming or Manhattan distances). Different hashing approaches [25] and building of trees [20] were proposed earlier. The cascade comparison of binary descriptors (FREAK) was proposed in [2]. But all these approaches still require a lot of computations to match sets of descriptors.

Transformation with representing structural description data in the form of a system of smaller dimension fragments allows to simplify the implementation significantly [9,11,12]. For example, building a cluster system based on the descriptor set simplifies processing and reduces the amount of computations by ten times when implementing methods [13]. The main tool for improving data analysis procedures is the statistical investigation of descriptions which is intended to reflect the generalized properties of an object as a collection of its fragments at recognition [10,12,23].

The analysis of the KP descriptor set in the space of binary vectors enables processing and statistical analysis in the form of ordered numerical data chains. The block data structure allows to use intellectual analysis based on probabilistic estimations of values to classify the object with the description in the form of descriptor set to a specified class [8,15].

Applying the block-bit representation model and statistical analysis of the non-intersecting fragment system for the sets of descriptors [11,12] aims at improving the efficiency of the classification process in terms of reducing computational costs while providing the required level of image differentiation.

Powerful mathematical and software apparatus for statistical data analysis has been developed so far [1,5,6,19,24]. This is generally used in computer vision applications as a metric approach to the investigation of the feature space [3,7, 8,10,15–18,20,22,23]. However, the statistical grounding of the metric approach for fragment data presenting and deep connection between applied methods and traditional statistical tools is still not given enough attention.

The contribution is the investigation of the improvement and statistical justification of the classification decision-making models based on the calculation of the object description relevance with the block representation of the set of key point descriptors.

2   Materials and Methods

2.1   Statistical Model of Component Representation of Image Descriptors

We will analyze the description as an image of a visual object in the form of a finite set $Z = \{z_v\}_{v=1}^s$, where $z_v \in B^n$ – KP descriptors, B^n – the binary vector space of dimension n [10–12].

As the parameter descriptor size up to several hundred (for the BRISK descriptor), the proposed way for reduction of the data dimension is to part the KP descriptor into a sequence of m fragments ($m \ll n$) that completely cover it. In this case, the BRISK descriptor of 512 bits may be represented, for example, by a sequence of 512 fragments of one bit with values 0 and 1, or a sequence of 256 fragments of 2 bits with values 00, 01, 10, 11, or a sequence of 128 fragments of 4 elements, where each element has the form of a binary element tuple in the range from 0000 to 1111 (the number of such values is $2^4 = 16$) etc. Therefore, the description has a form of a matrix of s rows and m columns with elements belonging to certain fragment of size $k = \frac{n}{m}$ [10,12].

We introduce the mapping $Z \rightarrow Q$ from the set of binary vectors (KP descriptors) into the set Q of distributions of their block component values. This makes it possible to distinguish visual objects based on fragments of smaller dimension [12]. The distribution according to a fixed fragment with a number $j, j = 1, \ldots m$, is represented as a vector of integers $q_j = (q_1 \ldots q_w)_j$, where $q_{ij}, i = 1 \ldots w$ are the frequencies of the i-th type of fragment located in the j- th place of the chain among all descriptors, the total amount of which is equal to $s = \sum_{i=1}^w q_i$ for any number j.

Values $p_i = \frac{q_i}{s}$, $i = 1 \ldots w$ are relative frequencies (probabilistic estimates). Sometimes they can be called "posterior probabilities" [5]. In addition, $w = 2^k, \sum_{i=1}^w p_i = 1$. Generally, the set Q is described by the system:

$$Q = \{q_j = (q_1, \ldots, q_w)_j\}_{j=1}^m \tag{1}$$

for each of m fragments, therefore, can be represented by a matrix of m rows and w columns. For the normalized case, we have a system of distributions:

$$Q_{norm} = \{p_j = (p_1, \ldots, p_w)_j\}_{j=1}^m \tag{2}$$

For example, if you use the BRISK descriptor when partitioning by bytes in case $n = 512$, we have $m = 64$, $w = 256$. Thus, for the set Z, the matrix $Q(Q_{norm})$ contains the relative frequencies of all acceptable values of fragments by size in byte.

2.2   Mathematical Apparatus of Statistical Analysis for Calculating the Image Relevance

We determine the relevance of object descriptions by elementally comparing the values of matrices $Q^l = \left\{ q_{ij}^{(l)} \right\}$, $i = 1, \ldots, w$, $j = 1, \ldots, m$, $l = 1, 2$ (l- object number) of the form (1), (2). We focus analytical studies on comparing the corresponding rows of matrices Q^l.

Comparison of two distributions can be done by matching their histograms and using the modified chi-square criterion for empirical distributions [1]. We define the empirical value of the criterion for fragments with number j as:

$$\chi_{emp,j}^2 = \sum_{i=1}^{w} \frac{(q_{i,j}^{(1)} - q_{i,j}^{(2)})^2}{q_{i,j}^{(1)} + q_{i,j}^{(2)}} \tag{3}$$

Critical value of criterion (3) is found according to the chosen level of significance α and the degree of freedom s', which does not exceed $s - 1$ (s is a number of observations). The area of acceptance of the null hypothesis of the homogeneity of the analyzed histograms is determined by inequality $\chi_{emp,j}^2 < \chi_{cr,j}^2 (a, s')$, and the area of acceptance of the alternative hypothesis of significant difference between them at the level of significance α is a right-handed critical area determined by inequality $\chi_{emp,j}^2 > \chi_{cr,j}^2 (a, s')$. The next step is to calculate the proportion of the significantly different distributions, and then we make a conclusion about the level of relevance.

Another way of matching distributions is to use the Renyi α-divergence [10,24], which can be considered as information of order $\alpha\,(\alpha > 0, \alpha \neq 1)$ about their differences. We calculate the Renyi α-divergence $D_{\alpha j} \left(p_j^{(1)} \parallel p_j^{(2)} \right)$, $j = 1, \ldots, m$ for two distributions $p_j^{(1)} = (p_1, \ldots, p_w)_j^{(1)}$, $p_j^{(2)} = (p_1, \ldots, p_w)_j^{(2)}$ (for fixed number $j = 1, \ldots, m$), based on the rows of matrices $Q_{norm}^l = \left\{ p_{ij}^{(l)} \right\}$, $i = 1, \ldots, w$, $j = 1, \ldots, m$, $l = 1, 2$:

$$D_{\alpha j} \left(p_j^{(1)} \parallel p_j^{(2)} \right) = \frac{1}{\alpha - 1} \ln \sum_{i=1}^{w} \frac{\left(p_{ij}^{(1)} \right)^{\alpha}}{\left(p_{ij}^{(2)} \right)^{\alpha - 1}} \tag{4}$$

The measure (4) is a non-decreasing function of argument α, which takes non-negative values and a value of zero is reached only when $p_j^1 = p_j^2$. It is proposed to introduce measure (4) at the parameter value $\alpha = 0.5$:

$$D_{0,5;j} \left(p_j^{(1)} \parallel p_j^{(2)} \right) = -2 \ln \sum_{i=1}^{w} \sqrt{p_{ij}^{(1)} p_{ij}^{(2)}}, j = 1, \ldots, m \tag{5}$$

Note that measure (5) is a metric as well as the only case of symmetry of the Renyi divergence with respect to its arguments. It was proved [24] that the value $(\alpha - 1) D_\alpha \left(O \parallel Z^j \right)$ as $\alpha = 0.5$ takes the largest value, which corresponds to the lower limit of the probability of recognition error. From this point of view, value $\alpha = 0.5$ is best for distinguishing between structural descriptions.

We now apply the transition from block description to coding of structure by averages of fragment code values. In the case of a 2-bit BRISK descriptor partition, we encode the fragment elements 00, 01, 10, 11 with numbers from 1 to 4. According to (2) we have the distribution $p_j = (p_1, p_2, p_3, p_4)_j$ within the fragment with the number j. According to the code values, the mathematical expectation of the distribution is:

$$M_j = \sum_{i=1}^{4} i p_{i,j}, j = 1, \ldots, 256 \tag{6}$$

Then representation (2) turns into a sequence of 256 averages:

$$M = (M_1, \ldots, M_{256}) \tag{7}$$

In the general case, expressions (6), (7) take the form

$$M_j^{(l)} = \sum_{i=1}^{w} i p_{i,j}^{(l)}, j = 1, \ldots, m \tag{8}$$

$$M^{(l)} = (M_1, \ldots, M_m)^{(l)} \tag{9}$$

Comparison of two descriptions is performed by the matching of two tuples of the form (9). Comparison of sequences $M^{(1)}, M^{(2)}$ is possible using a non-parametric signs criterion [5,19], which at a given level of significance shows how the differences

$$M_i^{(2)} - M_i^{(1)}, i = 1, \ldots, w \tag{10}$$

are sign unidirectional.

According to the signs criterion, we calculate separately the sums of positive and negative differences (10), the greater of them is assigned to the typical shift, the smaller of them is assigned to the atypical one. Using the statistical tables [1], we find the critical value corresponding to the typical shift. If the atypical value does not exceed the critical value, then we conclude the significant difference between the samples (according to the level of significance).

Another way of matching sequences $M^{(1)}, M^{(2)}$ can be pairwise comparison of $M_j^{(1)}, M_j^{(2)}, j = 1, \ldots, m$ as two averages for arbitrarily distributed sets using the z-criterion, which is correct in the case of sufficiently big sample. We can calculate the empirical value of the criterion as:

$$z_{emp,j} = \frac{|M_j^{(1)} - M_j^{(2)}|}{\sqrt{\left(D_j^{(1)} + D_j^{(2)}\right)/s}}, j = 1, \ldots, m \tag{11}$$

where $D_j^{(l)} = \sum_{i=1}^{w} p_{ij}^{(l)} \left(i - M_j^{(l)}\right)^2, l = 1, 2$, is a sample variance of the distribution $p_j^{(l)} = (p_1, \ldots, p_w)_j^{(l)}, l = 1, 2$, with the corresponding code values $i = 1, \ldots, w$.

The critical value $z_{cr,j}(a)$ of the criterion $z_{cr,j}(a)$ can be found by the Laplace function table according to the significance level a : $\Phi(z_{cr,j}(a)) = (1 - 2a)/2$. The null hypothesis area of equality of averaged code values is determined by the inequality $z_{emp,j} < z_{cr,j}(a)$, the alternative hypothesis area is determined by the inequality $z_{emp,j} > z_{cr,j}(a)$. The next step is to calculate the proportion of such fragment distributions whose corresponding numbers for both objects have significantly different averaged values. Based on the results of calculation, we conclude the relevance level. It seems natural to expect a large value of such proportion for different objects, and also an increase of this value as the size of the fragment increases. The experimental part of the study includes the results of corresponding testing

3   Experimental Evaluation of Differences in Descriptions by Distributions of Data Components

We have tested the proposed approaches using the example of icon images ("Sistine Madonna", "Mother-of-God of Kazan" etc.) of size 400×540 using library tools Open CV [10,11,21]. The illustration of the image with KP coordinates is shown in Fig. 1. 700 BRISK descriptors of 512 bits in each description were taken for the experiment. An example of the distribution of description for bit pairs is given in Table 1.

Fig. 1. Picture of icon with KP coordinates

Table 1. Example of distributions for 2-bit partitioning

Fragment	Links of Icon 1				Links of Icon 2			
	00	01	10	11	00	01	10	11
1	468	21	22	189	459	47	25	169
2	213	101	236	150	175	102	263	160
...	...	...	...	...	...	...	...	...
256	357	90	58	195	351	62	64	223

As we can see from the Table 1, the distributions of fragments with the same numbers for both objects are significantly different, which is confirmed by the calculations.

We will analyze the distributions in pairs for 2, 4 and 8 bit partitions testing the hypothesis of their homogeneity by the chi-square criterion (3). In the Table 2 the results of applying the criterion (at the level of 0.05) are shown.

Table 2. The number of inhomogeneous distributions by the chi-square criterion

	The number of partition bit		
	2	4	8
Number of fragments with significant inhomogeneity of distributions	167 from 256 (64, 45%)	109 from 128 (85,16%)	64 from 64 (100%)

As we can see, the inhomogeneity of the distributions naturally becomes more visible as the size of the fragment increases. Increasing the level of object differentiation by lengthening the fragment in the descriptor structure also demonstrates the calculation of the Renyi divergence between distributions according to (5). Table 3 presents the ranges of relevance measure, where the indicators increase significantly as the number of bits in the fragment increases.

Table 3. Renyi α-divergence values based on the number of bits

Values of Renyi α-divergence	Number of bits		
	2	4	8
Minimum	0.00008	0.0039	0.05111
Maximum	0.02112	0.03248	0.18575

We now calculate mathematical expectation for each fragment distribution, reducing the dimension of the description structure. In the case of 2-bit partition we have distributions for the first fragment of the 1st and 2nd objects

$(0.669; 0.030; 0.031; 0.270)$ and $(0.656; 0.067; 0.036; 0.241)$ respectively with the mathematical expectations $M_1^{(1)} = 1.903$, $M_1^{(2)} = 1.862$. The statistical representations (2) have the form of sequences of 256 elements:

$$M^{(1)} = (1.903; 2.461; \ldots; 2.130), M^{(2)} = (1.862; 2.583; \ldots; 2.227) \qquad (12)$$

A homogeneity study based on the sign criterion leads to the conclusion about a significant difference (at the level of 0.05) at different lengths of fragments. In the Table 4 the results of applying the criterion are shown.

Table 4. Results of applying the sign criterion

The size of the fragment	Number of typical shifts	Number of atypical shifts	Critical value (0.05 significance)	Conclusion
2	197	59	87	Significant (59 < 87)
4	100	27	41	Significant (27 < 41)
8	48	16	17	Significant (16 < 17)

According to the last approach we consider the sequences of the form (9) composed of the fragment code mathematical expectations and perform pairwise comparison of $M_j^{(1)}$ and $M_j^{(2)}$, $j = 1, \ldots, m$, applying z-criterion. The empirical value of the criterion for the fragment with the number j was calculated by the formula (10). The critical value of the criterion at the significance level 0.05 is equal to 1.64 [15]. For example, the values $M_1^{(1)} = 1.903$, $M_1^{(2)} = 1.862$ for sequences (12) do not differ significantly, but values $M_2^{(1)} = 2.461$, $M_2^{(2)} = 2.583$ are significantly different (at the level 0.05). Table 5 summarizes the main results of applying the criterion.

Table 5. The number of significant differences by z-criterion

	The number of bits in a fragment		
	2	4	8
Number of fragments with significant differences (0.05 level)	148 from 256 (57, 81%)	84 from 128 (65, 63%)	44 from 64 (68, 75%)

Relevance can also be defined as a measure of the difference between matrices $Q = \{q_{i,j}\}$, $i = \overline{1, w}$, $j = \overline{1, m}$ for the distribution of object images. We calculate relevance r for descriptions a and b as the Manhattan distance between matrices $Q(a)$, $Q(b)$:

$$r\left[Q(a), Q(b)\right] = \sum_{i=1}^{w} \sum_{j=1}^{m} |q_{i,j}(a) - q_{i,j}(b)| \qquad (13)$$

To estimate the weightiness of value (13) within the defined range, we also introduce a normalized distance:

$$r^* = \frac{r}{r_{max}} \tag{14}$$

where r_{max} is maximum acceptable distance with fixed s number of descriptors, descriptor size n and number of bits in the distribution.

The modeling results obtained in experimental Table 6 contain the values of the normalized Manhattan distance r^* for descriptions of icon images, depending on the number of descriptors (16...700) of the description and the number of bits (1...8) in the distribution blocks. The similarity measure by the voting method (counting the number of similar descriptors with an equivalence threshold 20% of the Hamming distance maximum value) for these two icons equals 0.12.

Table 6. Distance values (14) depending on the number of bits

Number of descriptors	Number of bits			
	1	2	4	8
700	0.059	0.084	0.143	0.319
500	0.061	0.086	0.149	0.326
100	0.071	0.110	0.204	0.450
50	0.106	0.165	0.290	0.570
30	0.108	0.175	0.320	0.600
16	0.127	0.210	0.402	0.699

We estimate the available computational costs for implementing the considered methods in comparison with traditional approaches. The computation time using software models is fixed in Table 7 (in seconds).

Table 7. Time estimates (in seconds) for computer simulation

Number of descriptors	Measure (14)	The number of distribution bits			
		1	2	4	8
700	10.7	0.008	0.011	0.028	11
500	6.4	0.006	0.01	0.017	6.2
100	0.48	0.002	0.002	0.007	1
50	0.11	0.001	0.002	0.004	0.915
30	0.08	0.001	0.001	0.003	0.527
16	0.045	<0.001	<0.001	0.002	0.315

4 Discussion

The data in Table 3 show a significant improvement in the quality of distinction when comparing descriptions of different objects. For example, the smallest value 0.051 of similarity measure for 8-bit partition exceeds maximum value 0.032 for 4-bit partition.

Analysis of the calculation Table 4 shows that for different number of bits in the fragment we get a significant statistical difference between the descriptions of different objects in the space of statistical images. It confirms the effectiveness of using block representation for set of descriptors. As we can see from Table 4, even reducing the lengths of the sequences (9) by increasing the length of the fragments demonstrates their significant difference. It confirms the effective differentiation of the studied objects and the efficiency of the approach.

We also get from the data in Table 5 that z-criterion calculation results became the further evidence of significant differences between the objects which are actually different. In addition, the quality of distinguishing improves as the number of fragment bits increases. The results of study confirm that there is sufficient ability to distinguish objects using applied distribution model, even in the case of a small number of bits in a fragment. It is also important in terms of processing speed.

As we can see from the results of estimating the processing time in Table 7, the proposed approach has significant computational advantages over traditional voting procedures for image description, since the value of estimating time to determine relevance is less than about 1300 times for 1-bit representation and 400 times for 4-bit one. Additionally, the computation time for 8-bit case is almost equal to the computation time for the traditional method (measure (9)), but the main efforts are directed to the formation of distributions, not to the calculation of relevance.

5 Conclusions

The use of statistical criteria for the analysis of empirical data in the form of structural descriptions of images as sets of key point descriptors makes it possible to determine the quality of the constructed feature space in order to classify visual objects in computer vision systems. The implementation of block-bit model and statistical analysis for fragment values in the set of descriptors generally contributes to the improvement of object recognition, which confirmed by the increased level of differentiation as the fragment size increases in the description structure.

The application of a variety of statistical criteria yielded identical conclusions about the significance of differences of the descriptions of the compared objects, which underlines the objectivity of the study.

Generalizing statistical analysis of a fragment system for a set of descriptors is a promising direction for reducing of recognition computational costs. Probabilistic presentation of data not only significantly accelerates the processing procedures (more than a thousand times), but also provides a sufficient level of image distinguishing. It is clear, however, that the time costs for all models considered for calculating relevance are proportional to the number of descriptors and depend on the modes of input generation and program execution.

The practical importance of the work is to confirm the advisability of implementing a block structure and a statistical representation for the object description as an effective approach for solving recognition problems in computer vision. Models for determining relevancy without forming distributions for the analyzed image can be considered promising, based on the generated etalon distributions which calculated at the pre-processing stage.

The prospects for the study are also associated with the use of a mining apparatus to detect hidden patterns or knowledge in the available descriptions of visual objects, on the basis of which further facilitation of recognition procedures can be achieved.

References

1. Aivazyan, S., Yenyukov, I., Meshalkin, L.: Applied statistics: bases of modeling and initial data processing. Finansy i Statistica (1983)
2. Alahi, A., Ortiz, R., Vandergheynst, P.: Freak: fast retina keypoint. In: IEEE Conference on Computer Vision and Pattern Recognition (2012). https://doi.org/10.1109/CVPR.2012.6247715
3. Amit, Y.: Object Detection and Recognition: Models Algorithms and Networks. The MIT Press, Cambridge (2002). https://doi.org/10.1007/978-0-387-31439-6_660
4. Chatoux, H., Lecellier, F., Fernandez-Maloigne, C.: Comparative study of descriptors with dense key points. In: 23rd International Conference on Pattern Recognition 2016 (2016). https://hal.archives-ouvertes.fr/hal-01461562/document
5. Duda, R., Hart, P., Stork, D.: Pattern Classification. Wiley, Hoboken (2001)
6. Fukunaga, K.: Introduction to Statistical Pattern Recognition. Academic Press (1972)
7. Gayathiri, P., Punithavalli, M.: Partial fingerprint recognition of feature extraction and improving accelerated KAZE feature matching algorithm. Int. J. Innov. Technol. Explor. Eng. 8(10), 3685–3690 (2019). 10.35940/ijitee.J9653.0881019
8. Gorokhovatskyi, O., Peredrii, O.: Shallow convolutional neural networks for pattern recognition problems. In: IEEE International Conference on DataStream Mining and Processing (DSMP-2018), pp. 459–463 (2018). https://doi.org/10.1109/dsmp.2018.8478540
9. Gorokhovatskyi, V.: Image classification methods in the space of descriptions in the form of a set of the key point descriptors. Telecommun. Radio Eng. 77(9), 787–797 (2018)
10. Gorokhovatskyi, V., Gadetska, S.: Statistical measures for computation of the image relevance of visual objects in the structural image classification methods. Telecommun. Radio Eng. 77(12), 1041–1053 (2018)
11. Gorokhovatskyi, V., Gadetska, S., Ponomarenko, R.: Recognition of visual objects based on statistical distributions for blocks of structural description of image. In: Lytvynenko, V., Babichev, S., Wójcik, W., Vynokurova, O., Vyshemyrskaya, S., Radetskaya, S. (eds.) ISDMCI 2019. AISC, vol. 1020, pp. 501–512. Springer, Cham (2020). https://doi.org/10.1007/978-3-030-26474-1_35

12. Gorokhovatskyi, V., Gadetska, S., Stiahlyk, N.: Study of statistical properties of the block supply model for a number of decorators of key points of images. Int. J. Radio Electron. Comput. Sci. Control **2**, 100–107 (2019)
13. Gorokhovatskyi, V., Putyatin, Y., Gorokhovatskyi, O., Peredrii, O.: Quantization of the space of structural image features as a way to increase recognition performance. In: IEEE International Conference on DataStream Mining and Processing (DSMP-2018), pp. 464–467 (2018). https://doi.org/10.1109/DSMP.2018.8478434
14. Heinly, J., Dunn, E., Frahm, J.-M.: Comparative evaluation of binary features. In: Fitzgibbon, A., Lazebnik, S., Perona, P., Sato, Y., Schmid, C. (eds.) ECCV 2012. LNCS, vol. 7573, pp. 759–773. Springer, Heidelberg (2012). https://doi.org/10.1007/978-3-642-33709-3_54
15. Kamel, M., Taha, H., Salama, G., Elhalwagy, Y.: Ground target localization and recognition via descriptors fusion. In: 18th International Conference on Aerospace Sciences and Aviation Technology, pp. 1–11 (2019). https://doi.org/10.1088/1757-899X/610/1/012015
16. Karami, E., Prasad, S., Shehata, M.: Image matching using sift, surf, brief and orb: performance comparison for distorted images. In: Proceedings of the 2015 Newfoundland Electrical and Computer Engineering Conference (2015)
17. Leutenegger, S., Chli, M., Siegwart, R.: Brisk: binary robust invariant scalable keypoints. In: IEEE International Conference on Computer Vision (ICCV), pp. 2548–2555 (2011)
18. Liu, H., Tan, T., Kuo, T.: A novel shot detection approach based on orb fused with structural similarity. IEEE Access **8**, 2472–2481 (2019)
19. Mason, R., Gunst, R., James, H.: Statistical Design and Analysis of Experiments, vol. 2. Wiley, Hoboken (2003)
20. Muja, M., Lowe, D.: Fast matching of binary features. In: Conference on Computer and Robot Vision (CRV), pp. 404–410 (2012)
21. OpenCV: Open source computer vision library (2020). https://docs.opencv.org/master/index.html
22. Peters, J.F.: Foundations of Computer Vision. ISRL, vol. 124. Springer, Cham (2017). https://doi.org/10.1007/978-3-319-52483-2
23. Porter, F.: Testing consistency of two histograms (2008). https://www.researchgate.net/publication/1917663_Testing_Consistency_of_Two_Histograms
24. Renyi, A.: On measures of entropy and information. In: Fourth Berkeley Symposium on Mathematical Statistics and Probability, vol. 1, pp. 547–561 (1961). http://l.academicdirect.org/Horticulture/GAs/Refs/Renyi_1961.pdf
25. Rublee, E., Rabaud, V., Konolige, K., Bradski, G.: ORB: an efficient alternative to sift or surf. In: IEEE International Conference on Computer Vision (2011). https://doi.org/10.1109/ICCV.2011.6126544

Sewer Pipe Defects Classification Based on Deep Convolutional Network with Information-Extreme Error-Correction Decision Rules

Viacheslav Moskalenko[1](✉) (ID), Mykola Zaretskyi[1] (ID), Alona Moskalenko[1] (ID), and Viktor Lysyuk[2] (ID)

[1] Sumy State University, Sumy, Ukraine
{v.moskalenko,a.moskalenko}@cs.sumdu.edu.ua,
n.zaretskij@gmail.com
[2] Molfar.AI sp. z o.o, Gdansk, Poland
viktor.lysyuk@molfar.tech

Abstract. CCTV inspection is a modern approach for diagnosing defects in underground sewer pipes. A new deep model and multi-phase learning method for recognizing sewer pipe defects in fixed parts of video frame are proposed. The deep model is based on a convolutional feature extractor with a sigmoid output layer and information-extreme error-correction decision rules. The first phase of the proposed machine learning method includes feature extractor training on augmented data using triplet mining and softmax triplet loss with regularization term to approximate the discrete representation of data. Next phases aim to reduce intra-class dispersion of discrete data representation by computing averaged discretized representations of each class which are used as labels during training with joint binary cross-entropy loss. Last phase of the earning method is an optimization of a hyper-spherical container for each class in Hamming space based on information criterion. Shannon's measure of information expressed by logarithmic is used as an information criterion; it provides a reliable solution for the difficult case in the statistical sense. Training results on test data provided by Ace Pipe Cleaning (Kansas City, USA) confirm the efficiency of the proposed model and method and their suitability for practical application.

Keywords: Sewer pipe inspection · Convolutional neural network · Triplet mining · Triplet loss · Discrete data representation · Information-extreme learning · Classification

1 Introduction and Literature Review

Sewer pipes are critical infrastructure items which require frequent monitoring. A conventional method of analysis of sewer pipe conditions involves a CCTV

© Springer Nature Switzerland AG 2020
S. Babichev et al. (Eds.): DSMP 2020, CCIS 1158, pp. 253–263, 2020.
https://doi.org/10.1007/978-3-030-61656-4_16

sewer pipe inspection, during which the faults and defects inside the pipe identified and presented in a report with respective codes in accordance with the
applicable standards. Among the widely used standards are British MSCC5 and
US PACP6 and PACP7. Reporting on the sewer condition in accordance with
these standards requires careful examination and detailed analysis of collected
CCTV footage. Application of machine vision and machine learning methods
to CCTV inspections allows to increase the productivity and reduce inspection
costs [7].

First attempts to use machine vision toolkit for pipe inspections involved edge
detection and contour processing algorithms to identify the structural defects
[11]. This method required manual hyper-parameter tuning and did not account
for the contextual information, which reduced the reliability of such approach.
Also, in this case no detailed analysis of the region of interest for future coding
to the applicable standards of pipe inspection was undertaken. An application
of Gabor Filter for feature extraction during the CCTV sewer pipe inspections
offered a more flexible and theoretically sound approach [9]. However, the shallow
models of this type have low capacity and are unsuitable for effective analysis
of complex defects with contextual information. Besides, the automated CCTV
inspection data analysis task has many unique challenges owing to the presence
of a large number of artefacts and noise. Low visibility during inspection can
occur for many reasons – due to steam, dense gas, position of the light source,
substantial change in water level, blurring due to movement and low camera
resolution.

Deep learning is a popular contemporary choice of a tool used to improve
the performance of visual data analysis. Deep data analysis models are characterized by higher information capacity in comparison with the shallow models
[2,10] However, certain pipe features and defects appear infrequently and have
high variability, which leads to statistical imbalances in the data and insufficient
quantity of available labeled samples covering complex defects. This limits the
application of the traditional deep learning methods, which typically require vast
quantities of labeled data and substantial computational resources.

Applying information theory ideas and methods together with the principles
of decision rule synthesis in a geometric approach reduces the requirement for
training data quantity and makes the process more robust. Siamese neural networks, often used for invariant feature representation learning, are an example
of such an approach [12]. Siamese neural networks show considerable promise in
the situations where training data is limited and are often used as a base for
more complex few-shot learning algorithms. Triplet loss, applied with various
triple loss mining strategies, is the most commonly used loss function for training Siamese networks. For few-shot learning classification tasks, however, algorithms based on compact discrete data representation with model optimisation
by information criteria [2,4] offer the most promise where their ability to generalise is concerned. Error-correction output codes and information-extreme learning methods belong to the same class of algorithms. They combine the principles
of information theory with geometric approach [5,8] Combining the concepts of

Siamese neural networks, error-correction output codes and information-extreme learning thus seems the most promising direction for further enhancement of the CCTV sewer inspection footage analysis models.

To improve the efficiency of the visual classification models for sewer pipe defects models when the labeled training data is imbalanced and scarce, a deep convolutional network with information-extreme error correctiong decision rules and its new training method are proposed. The proposed algorithms are based on the ideas and methods of Siamese neural networks, error-correction output codes and information-extreme learning. The current article considers all the training stages with their corresponding results obtained on the dataset provided by Ace Pipe Cleaning (Kansas City, USA).

2 Materials and Methods

Defect recognition in frames captured by the camera turned sideways is not considered in the present work; only the forward pointed camera footage is in scope. To ease the defect localization, sewer defect analysis is not performed on the whole of the frame but only on the regions adjacent to the frame boundaries, where the distance counter value is known. Rectangular images corresponding to 20% of the image area are cut from the sides, top and bottom of the frame and subsequently resized to 160×160 pixels. A deep convolutional feature extractor based on MobileNet architecture is then used for experimentation and proof of concept. This neural network is often used as a baseline in image detection tasks under the computational capacity constraint. The capacity coefficient of such convolutional network is set to 0.25 and only a convolutional backbone without fully connected layers is used [5]. The structure of the proposed classifier model is depicted in Fig. 1 and a similar model with more classic output layers provided for evaluation of the proposed approach is presented in Fig. 2.

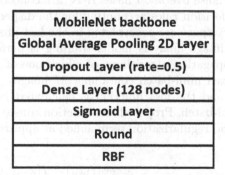

Fig. 1. Proposed image classifier model structure

Global Average Pooling is used for dimensionality reduction and regularization is achieved with a Dropout pseudo-ensemble with 50% of the input features

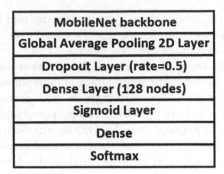

Fig. 2. Baseline image classifier model structure

dropping [5,10]. Fully connected and sigmoid layers form the output feature set. Decision rules of the proposed image classifier model's contain the rounding layer which produces the binary coded representation and radial-basis function defining the object's belonging to a certain class. The detectable classes are separated by hyperspherical containers in binary Hamming space with each hyperspherical container defined by the container radius an binary reference vector (container center) defined in Hamming distance units. In this case radial-basis membership function $\mu_z(b)$ for N-dimensional binary vector b is

$$\mu_z(b) = 1 - \frac{\sum_{i=1}^{n} b_i \oplus b_{z,i}^*}{d_z^*} \tag{1}$$

where b_z is the binary reference vector (center of optimal container) for class X_z^o; d_z^* is the radius of optimal container for class X_z^o in Hamming distance units.

The proposed method is comprised of 5 phases (Fig. 3). The first learning phase involves data augmentation, such as brightness, scale and turn variations and salt and pepper noise overlay. Phases II-IV are concerned with end-to-end learning and in the decision rules accounting for the dispersion of observations in each class in binary space are constructed in the last phase.

Second phase of image analysis model training is performed with the use of adaptive back propagation algorithms, of which one of the most popular is Adam [10,12]. A mixed mini-batch containing M images of each class is used as the model input and the loss function is calculated for M image triplets selected from the mini-batch. Proposed loss function consist of softmax function of triplet distances and regularization term aimed at approximating the discrete data representation

$$L = -log \frac{exp(\|f(x_a) - f(x_{ep})\|)}{exp(\|f(x_a) - f(x_{ep})\|) + exp(\|f(x_a) - f(x_{shn})\|)}$$
$$+ \lambda(f(x_a)^T(e - f(x_a)) + f(x_{ep})^T(e - f(x_{ep})) + f(x_{shn})^T(e - f(x_{shn}))) \tag{2}$$

where $f(x)$ is the function describing the feature extractor and establishing the dependency between the incoming image and sigmoid output layer vector; x_a is

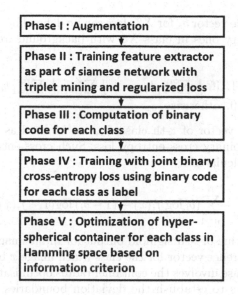

Fig. 3. Proposed classifier model training phases

the randomly chosen anchor image, selected from the mini-batch; x_{ep} is the easy positive example, consisting of the most similar image with the same label as the anchor image, e.g., $e = [1, 1, ..., 1]^T$; λ is the regularization coefficient

$$x_{ep} = arg \min_{x:C(x)=C(x_a)} \|f(x_a) - f(x)\| \tag{3}$$

where $C(x)$ is the function returning a class label for sample x, x_{shn} is the semi-hard negative example which is further from anchor than the selected positive example, which has a different label from the anchor image

$$x_{shn} = arg \min_{\substack{C(x)\neq C(x_a) \\ x:\|f(x_a)-f(x)\|>\|f(x_a)-f(x_p)\|}} \|f(x_a) - f(x)\| \tag{4}$$

The next training phase is necessary to define the binary code for each class according to error-correction output codes principle whilst accounting for both the internal class structure and relationship between the different class samples. A training sample $\{x_{z,s} | z = \overline{1, Z}, s = \overline{1, n_z}\}$ containing n_z samples of z class is coded by a discrete representation $\{b_{z,s,i} | z = \overline{1, Z}, s = \overline{1, n_z}, i = \overline{1, N}\}$ with dimensionality N, following which a reference binary vector is calculated for each class. Binary coding is performed by providing images from the set $x_{z,s}$ as model inputs and rounding of the output of the sigmoid layer to the nearest integer

$$b_{z,s,i} = \begin{cases} 1, & \text{if } f(x_{z,s,i}) > 0.5; \\ 0, & \text{otherwise.} \end{cases} \tag{5}$$

A binary reference vector b_z for X_z^o class can be defined by bitwise comparison of frequency of binary ones in class X_z^o with background frequency of ones in the training set

$$b_{z,i} = \begin{cases} 1, & \text{if } \frac{1}{n_z} \sum_{s=1}^{n_z} b_{z,s,i} > \frac{1}{Z} \sum_{c=1}^{Z} \frac{1}{n_c} \sum_{s=1}^{n_c} b_{c,s,i}; \\ 0, & \text{otherwise.} \end{cases} \tag{6}$$

Binary reference vector of z-th class, b_z, can be used as a label for further training with joint binary cross-entropy loss. Such cross-entropy loss for every input sample x is calculated as

$$L = -\sum_{n=1}^{N} (b_i \log f_i(x) + (1 - b_i) \log(1 - f_i(x))) \tag{7}$$

where $f_i(x)$ is the value of i-th sigmoid output for input image x; b_i is the value of i-th bit of the reference vector for the class which image x belongs to. The last machine learning phase involves the container radius optimisation by information criterion. This allows to establish the deviation boundaries of the observation binary representation of each class from their representative reference vectors

$$E_z^* = \max_{\{d\}} E_z(d) \tag{8}$$

where $\{d\} = \{0, 1, \ldots, (\sum_i b_{z,i} \oplus b_{c,i} - 1)\}$ is a set of container radiuses with center b_z (reference vector) of data distribution in class X_z^o, which is recomputed using rule (6); E_z is Shannon's information criterion for X_z^o class, computed as a function of accuracy characteristics [5,8].

$$E_z = 1 + \frac{1}{2}\left(\frac{\alpha_z}{\alpha_z + D_{2,z}} \log_2 \frac{\alpha_z}{\alpha_z + D_{2,z}} + \frac{\beta_z}{D_{1,z} + \beta_z} \log_2 \frac{\beta_z}{D_{1,z} + \beta_z} + \right.$$
$$\left. \frac{D_{1,z}}{D_{1,z} + \beta_z} \log_2 \frac{D_{1,z}}{D_{1,z} + \beta_z} + \frac{D_{2,z}}{\alpha_z + D_{2,z}} \log_2 \frac{D_{2,z}}{\alpha_z + D_{2,z}} \right) \tag{9}$$

where α_z is the false positive rate of decision rule for z-th class; β_z is the false negative rate; $D_{1,z}$ is the true positive rate (sensitivity); $D_{2,z}$ is the true negative rate (specificity).

Valid domain of the information criterion function is defined by inequalities:

$$\alpha_z < 0.5, \beta_z < 0.5, D_{1,z} \geq 0.5, D_{2,z} \geq 0.5.$$

The model output layer is rooted in the tenets of information theory. Binary reference class vectors are similar to Hamming error-correction codes and the maximum quantity of errors which can be corrected after the receipt of message via a noisy channel can be described by the container radius. Information criterion, in turn, defines the measure of reduction in uncertainty after the receipt of the message from a given alphabet. Thus hyper-spherical container radius optimisation allows to materially improve the decision-making efficiency when handling overlapping classes with different distributions of observations. And, should the new observations not fitting any of the existing classes appear, this also allows detecting the newness in the data. The optimisation criterion in this case is a logarithmic information measure which increases the models ability to generalise and increases its robustness in statistically complicated cases.

3   Experiment, Results and Discussion

Of many types of sewer pipe materials in existence, only Vitrified Clay and Concrete pipes are considered [7] in this study. These are amongst the most common pipe materials is use, with wide variety of characteristic defects. The class alphabet contains 9 defects encountered most frequently [9]. Class X_1^o denotes a "roots" defect, denoting tree roots penetrating the pipe. Class X_2^o corresponds to "deposits" defect, which causes a reduction in the pipe cross-section. X_3^o, X_4^o, X_5^o, X_6^o and X_7^o classes characterize various structural pipe defects such as "surface damage", "crack", "fracture", "broken" and "hole" respectively. Class X_8^o denotes "infiltration", a defect occurring when water enters the pipe from outside, either seeping through the porous area in the sewer pipe wall or entering through a structural defect or defective pipe joint. Class X_9^o corresponds to "'Obstruction" defect, indicating presence of a foreign object which substantially obstructs the free flow of water or reduces the flow rate inside the pipe. Class X_{10}^o denotes the normal pipe and is required for regularization. 100 samples were collected for each class. Although each of the chosen classes can, in turn, be broken down into further sub-classes, such extended classification image analysis is outside the scope of this research. Each of the images was used to expand the training set $4X$ by applying slight random augmentation such as turning the image up to 10% of the full range, varying brightness and scale and applying salt and pepper noise mask. The model depicted in Fig. 3 is used as a baseline used for comparison with the solutions proposed. This model differs from the proposed in only two output layers, with training based on Adam optimizer with categorical cross-entropy loss [1,10]. Figure 4 depicts the changes in model accuracy on the test and training sets at each epoch ($test_acc$ and $train_acc$). Each mini-batch contains 32 images with learning rate set to 0.0001.

Analysis of Fig. 4 shows that the incremental accuracy improvements de facto ceased after 40 epochs with maximum accuracy of the resulting model reaching 86% on test set and observed deviations between the training and test curves hinting at a presence of a slight overtraining effect. Figure 5 depicts the training results for the feature extractor with sigmoidal output layer after 60 epochs. The training is conducted with the use of loss function (2) and construction of decision rules and calculation of class-wise averaged information efficiency criterion (9) occurring every 5 epochs. After the first 30 epochs the model was saved for the subsequent experiment.

Analysis of Fig. 5 shows that from the 10th epoch onwards, growth in decision rule accuracy on test set slows down considerably. Training for 40 epochs results in the test set accuracy of 95%, 9% above the baseline. However, after the 40th

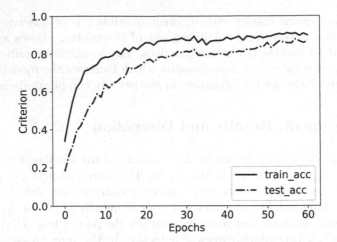

Fig. 4. Dependency of model accuracy from number of epochs on test and train sets for conventional approach

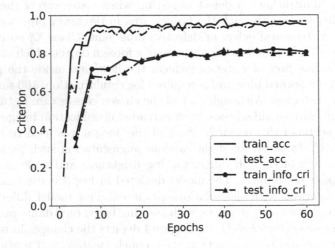

Fig. 5. Dependency of model accuracy and information criterion from number of epochs on test and train sets for proposed approach with loss function (2)

learning epoch, further improvement de-facto stops, with little deviation between the training and test accuracy curves and corresponding information criteria curves, indicating algorithm's high generalisation capacity. Multiclass average information criteria peaks at 0.815 and average distance between centres of the hyper-spherical containers is 19 units of Hamming distance whilst the average radius of containers is 8 units. This is indicative of information-extreme decision rules being highly robust to noise [3,6].

Figure 6 illustrates the subsequent training results for the model obtained after the 30 epochs in the course of previous experiment. Subsequent training was performed for further 30 epochs but with the loss function (7) aimed at reducing intra-class observations dispersion in Hamming space.

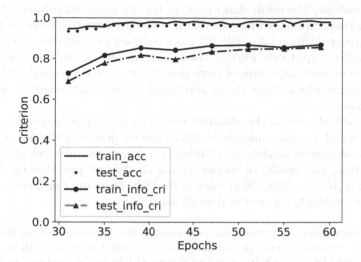

Fig. 6. Dependency of model accuracy and information criterion from number of epochs on test and train sets for proposed approach with loss function (7)

Analysis of Fig. 6 shows that using joint binary cross-entropy loss (7) generated an additional 3% accuracy improvement multiclass average information criteria maximum reached 0.856 and the average distance between centres of the hyper-spherical containers is 19 units of Hamming distance whilst the average radius of containers is 6 units. This is characteristic of high generalization capacity and noise immunity [3,6]. Thus a multi-phase learning process with information-extreme decisions rules allows to obtain a model with 11% more accuracy in comparison with the conventional approach in the same number of learning epochs.

4   Conclusions

1. The scientific novelty of the results is as follows:
   - the original deep model for visual classification of sewer pipe defects based on multilayer convolutional feature extractor with a sigmoid output layer and information-extreme error-correction decision rules. The model is characterized by better generalisation abilities;
   - the novel multi-phase training method, incorporating feature extractor training with regularized softmax triplet loss, binary coded labels computation for each class, feature extractor training with joint binary cross-entropy loss and optimisation of radial-basis error-correction decision rules based on information criterion. The proposed method allows to

increase generalization abilities and noise immunity in case of limited size of training set;

– the effectiveness of the proposed approach is compared with the conventional one. The result shows that the use of regularized softmax triplet loss for convolutional feature extractor training allows to obtain information-extreme decision rules with 9% more accuracy in comparison with the conventional approach. Further training using joint binary cross-entropy loss also reduces dispersion of intra-class observations described by extracted features which leads to an additional 3% increase accuracy and noise immunity.

2. The practical value of the obtained results for sewer pipe inspection is in the formation of a modern methodological basis for designing the defect detector in case of limited availability of labeled training examples per class. At the same time, the results of model testing on dataset provided by Ace Pipe Cleaning (Kansas City, USA) confirm the high efficiency of proposed approach and its suitability for practical application.

Acknowledgments. The work was performed in the laboratory of intellectual systems of the computer science department at Sumy State University with the financial support of the Ministry of Education and Science of Ukraine in the framework of state budget scientific and research work of DR No. 0117U003934.

References

1. Cheng, J.C., Wang, M.: Automated detection of sewer pipe defects in closed-circuit television images using deep learning techniques. Autom. Constr. **95**, 155–171 (2018). https://doi.org/10.1016/j.autcon.2018.08.006
2. Dai, Q., Li, J., Wang, J., Jiang, Y.G.: Binary optimized hashing. In: Proceedings of the 24th ACM International Conference on Multimedia, pp. 1247–1256. Association for Computing Machinery (2016). https://doi.org/10.1145/2964284.2964331
3. Dovbysh, A., Shelehov, I., Prylepa, D., Golub, I.: Information synthesis of adaptive system for visual diagnostics of emotional and mental state of a person. East.-Eur. J. Enterp. Technol. **4**(9(82)), 11–17 (2016). 10.15587/1729-4061.2016.75683
4. Hu, W., Miyato, T., Tokui, S., Matsumoto, E.: Learning discrete representations via information maximizing self augmented training. In: Precup, D., Teh, Y.W. (eds.) Proceedings of International Conference on Machine Learning, vol. 70, pp. 1558–1567, 06–11 August 2017
5. Joutsijoki, H., Haponen, M., Rasku, J., Aalto-Setala, Juhola, M.: Error-correcting output codes in classification of human induced pluripotent stem cell colony images. Biomed. Res. Int. 1–13 (2016). https://doi.org/10.1155/2016/3025057
6. Michele, A., Colin, V., Santika, D.D.: MobileNet convolutional neural networks and support vector machines for palmprint recognition. Procedia Comput. Sci. **157**, 110–117 (2019). https://doi.org/10.1016/j.procs.2019.08.147
7. Moradi, S., Zayedand, T., Golkhoo, F.: Review on computer aided sewer pipeline defect detection and condition assessment. Infrastructures **4**, 1–15 (2019). https://doi.org/10.3390/infrastructures4010010

8. Moskalenko, V., Moskalenko, A., Korobov, A., Semashko, V.: The model and training algorithm of compact drone autonomous visual navigation system. Data **4**(1), 1–14 (2019). https://doi.org/10.3390/data4010004

9. Myrans, J., Everson, R., Kapelan, Z.: Automated detection of fault types in CCTV sewer surveys. J. Hydroinform. **21**(1), 153–163 (2018). https://doi.org/10.2166/hydro.2018.073

10. Panella, F., Boehm, J., Loo, Y., Kaushik, A.: Deep learning and image processing for automated crack detection and defect measurement in underground structures. Int. Arch. Photogram. Remote Sens. Spat. Inf. Sci. **XLII-2**, 829–835 (2018). https://doi.org/10.5194/isprs-archives-xlii-2-829-2018

11. Syahrian, N.M., Risma, P., Dewi, T.: Vision-based pipe monitoring robot for crack detection using canny edge detection method as an image processing technique. Univ. Muhammadiyah Malang **2**(4), 243–250 (2017). https://doi.org/10.22219/kinetik.v2i4.243

12. Zhan, H., Shi, B., Duan, L.Y., Kot, A.: DeepShoe: an improved multi-task view-invariant CNN for street-to-shop shoe retrieval. Comput. Vis. Image Underst. **180**, 23–33 (2019). https://doi.org/10.1016/j.cviu.2019.01.001

Critical Modes of Photography: Light Sensitivity and Resolution

Maksym Korobchynskyi$^{(\boxtimes)}$ (ID), Mykhailo Slonov(ID), Myhailo Rudenko(ID),
Oleksandr Maryliv(ID), and Valentyn Pylypchuk(ID)

Military-Diplomatic Academy named after Eugene Bereznyak, Kyiv, Ukraine
{maks-kor,ruminik33}@ukr.net, slonovmu@gmail.com, olserg1982@gmail.com,
delavar65000@gmail.com

Abstract. In this paper, we present the concept of critical modes of observation of an object by discrete visual means and their influence on the quality of a digital image. A feature of such modes is the impossibility of guaranteed quality of the digital image of the object of observation. This is typical during photography of a significant change in the level of external irradiation of the subject, the possible distance of photography, the operational shift of the image and other factors. However, the observation in these conditions increases the activity, completeness and timeliness of documenting the image of the object. In the article, we offers a formalized description of the successful observation of the object. It contains the concept of a given probability of recognition of the object by observation of its image. There are offered the parameters of the camera which can provide the predicted qualitative image. Such parameters of the camera are its light sensitivity and resolution. The algorithmic relationship between the limit values of light sensitivity and resolution is determined. It allows assessing the degree of achievement of the highest perfection of a discrete iconic tool by taking into account the specified depth of recognition of the object by its image. An algorithmic assessment of the influence of photographic noise on image quality is proposed. The algorithms developed in the article are verified by a computational experiment. It allowed to estimate the rational ranges of light sensitivity, which willn't affect the resolution of the digital image of the observed object.

Keywords: Observation · Discrete visual means · Photographic equipment · Photography · Light sensitivity · Resolution · Object of observation

1 Introduction and Literature Review

Observation of the object and documentation of its image is needful for solution problems in ecological monitoring, geodesy, mapping, agriculture, etc. One of the requirements for the successful solution of such problems is the ability to conduct observations with minimal influence of external conditions to its results.

© Springer Nature Switzerland AG 2020
S. Babichev et al. (Eds.): DSMP 2020, CCIS 1158, pp. 264–274, 2020.
https://doi.org/10.1007/978-3-030-61656-4_17

Typically, there are the conditions in which automatic systems for adjusting the parameters of discrete species surveillance operate without taking into account the quality of the digital image. Under such conditions it isn't possible to guarantee the receipt of information about objects with a given depth of recognition of its image. As a result, it is impossible to predict the results of observation [15]. Such restrictions are typical in the case of changes in the level of external lighting of the subject, the possible distance of photography, the operational shift of the image and other factors that affect the image quality.

For example, when observations need to be made at dusk, the image quality decreases sharply due to its pixelation. This is a consequence of a significant increase in photographic noise [5]. Photography from the maximum possible distance requires the use of maximum optical zoom. In this case, the minimum resolution and angle of view of the lens limit the ability to control the quality of the digital image on its image on the display. The ability to take high-quality photos at dusk from the maximum possible distance increases the activity and timeliness of documenting the image of the object. Photography with predicted image shift will allow to observed from the car and other vehicles without losing the specified image quality. Thus, the task of predicting image quality when photographing in its atypical conditions is relevant.

In [1, 2, 6, 13, 17], the authors discussed general issues of increasing the ability to recognize the image of the object during photography. Functional limitations on the possible quality of the photographic image are estimated. But in these works consideration of the functionality of photographic equipment (PE) isn't tied to photography in critical modes. In [7, 8] are described an algorithm for predicting the recognizable properties of PE with taking into account the operational shift of the image and the results of checking its adequacy for photographing objects in real conditions. Note that the peculiarities of the relationship between light sensitivity and resolution of PE in critical conditions of photography are not considered.

Regarding photography in conditions of insufficient natural or artificial lighting, the hardware recommendations are the same [9]: to increase the light sensitivity of the receiver, which is programmatically implemented in the PE for the shooting mode "Auto". Adherence to the above recommendations makes some sense but only in a limited range of image pixelation intensity. Nowadays this effect hasn't been evaluated. Although it is known that visual pixelization of the image significantly reduces its quality.

Modern PE is a perfect software and hardware complex. It allows you to document the appearance of objects in almost any environment. Adaptation of PE to the object and conditions of observation is carried out by adjusting the parameters of PE. The rational values of the parameters according to the selected documentation mode are set automatically. A formalized description of the successful observation of the j-th object ($j = 1, \ldots, J$) from the distance S_j and the given credibility of its results (the probability P of the image recognition isn't less than its setpoint P_s) will look like this [15]:

$$\begin{cases} P_s \geq P, \\ P = P\left[S_j; d_{PE}; f; l_j = \min; j = 1, J\right], \end{cases} \tag{1}$$

where d_{PE} is the linear size of the PE distinguishing element (matrix pixel); f is the focal length of the PE lens; l_j is the linear size of the recognition feature of the object.

In Eq. (1) the requirements to the rational image quality (P), the conditions of photography (S), the features of the object of photography (L) and the desired values of the influential parameters of PE (d_{PE}, f) are combined. Observance (1) will allow predicting the observation of an object with a given level of image quality.

An unsolved part of the problem, of obtaining predicted image quality, is to determine the features of the relationship between light sensitivity and resolution of the PE receiver in critical shooting modes.

The aim of the paper is to determine the relationship between the limits of light sensitivity and resolution in photography to perform tasks and identify ways to expand the capabilities of photography of the object in atypical conditions.

2   Materials and Methods

The modes of automatic operation of the PE in atypical conditions are critical. In it the photographic image in the PE is remembered but its expected quality (according to the set pixel size of the image) isn't guaranteed. For such cases, the household PE provides manual control of photography parameters.

The photographer in this case must have sufficient personal experience of such a setting. It is also necessary to be guided in the circumstances that translate the normal mode of operation of the PE to a critical one. In addition, manual adjustment is provided only in professional cameras and in some cameras with a classic manual structure. In PE in which the function of photography is secondary there isn't such possibility. In professional species equipment critical operating modes are usually also not distinguished.

Therefore, it is important to determine the limits of PE parameters that can provide the predicted image quality as well as the relationship between them. Such parameters of PE are its light sensitivity S_{ISO} and resolution d. The distinction of PE d is considered to be the linear size $d_{PE} = d$ of the element of the light-sensitive matrix (matrix pixel). These are the current value of the resolution, which remembers the image according to the line of values in a particular sample. Light sensitivity S_{ISO} is characterizes the intensity of the receiver's response to the input signal. While taking photo the input signal is the light level of the receiver with light reflected or emitted from the subject. The output signal is the magnitude of the receiver's response in the form of an image on the PE display.

At the limit of detection of the image segment E, the output signal i and from m pixels (elementary receivers of the light-sensitive matrix - photo detector) will be equal to:

$$i = \frac{m_1}{m}i_1, \tag{2}$$

where m_1 is the number of elementary receivers with the output signal from them i_1.

In $m_i < m_1$ the segment isn't recognized, in $m_i > m_1$ the segment is recognized more confidently. When $m_i = m_1$ the value of i will be the criterion and $i = i_{cr}$. The value of m_i is determined by the difference in photography or its dependent value - the resolution. The maximum possible resolution R of the light-sensitive matrix with an elementary receiver with side d will be:

$$R = \frac{1}{2d}. \tag{3}$$

The number of m elementary receivers in the segment E in its square configuration with side $l_j = l$ will be equal to:

$$m = \left(\frac{l}{d}\right)^2 = 4l^2R^2. \tag{4}$$

The minimum signal from each elementary receiver i_1 depends on its area Q, material of manufacture β and technological efficiency of production and operation η:

$$i_1 = \beta\eta Q = \beta\eta d^2. \tag{5}$$

Given the relations (4, 5) of Eq. (2) can be reduced to the following form:

$$m_1 = \frac{i}{i_1}m = \frac{i}{\beta\eta d^2} = \frac{l^2}{d^2} = \frac{il^2}{\beta\eta d^4}. \tag{6}$$

The exposure H of the segment E will be sufficient if the signal from m_1 receivers exceeds the criterion value H_{cr} which determines the light sensitivity of the S_{ISO} photo detector. If the exposure of the segment has acquired a criterion value (the criterion value has acquired a signal $i = i_{cr}$ from segment E) the proportion is:

$$H_{cr} \equiv m_1 = \frac{i_{cr}l^2}{\beta\eta d^4}. \tag{7}$$

The light sensitivity of S_{ISO} is determined as follows:

$$S_{ISO} = \frac{k}{H_{cr}}. \tag{8}$$

The coefficient k is a constant value and is given in the regulatory documentation. Combine (7) and (8) and bring to the form:

$$\begin{cases} \dfrac{S_{ISO}}{d^4} = \dfrac{k\beta\eta}{i_{cr}l^2} = const, \\ S_{ISO}R^4 = \dfrac{k\beta\eta}{i_{cr}l^2} = const. \end{cases} \tag{9}$$

Equation (9) proves that the image of the distinguishing feature l of the object will be detected at the current level of perfection of PE (i_{cr}, β, η, k) and shooting conditions (η, k) only when the ratio between the light sensitivity of the photo detector and its resolution of a certain value. This once again confirms the previous conclusion about the inexpediency of an infinite increase in light sensitivity when photographing at dusk. A rational way may be to increase the size d of the elementary receiver. For PE this will correspond to the transition to a smaller pixel size of the light-sensitive matrix.

According to (9) the condition of photography can be presented as follows:

$$\frac{S_{ISO}}{d^4} \geq \frac{k\beta\eta}{i_{cr}l^2}. \tag{10}$$

In the right part of (10) there are indicators of perfection: perfection of the chosen light-sensitive material β; perfection of manufacturing technology η ; detection i_{cr} and standard coefficient k. All of them, as well as the size of the distinguishing feature l, for each individual case of photography are constant values. So the entire right part is a constant of the object and the level is a perfection of the PE. In the left part there are parameters of PE which change for each type of PE and for each sample of PE. Therefore, according to (10), a smaller resolution d in the image can be achieved only by proportionally reducing the light sensitivity of the S_{ISO}.

Thus, (10) characterizes the practical possibility of achieving the highest perfection of the iconic means, in this case - the PE sample. If the equality between the left and right parts of Eq. (10) is preserved for a specific PE sample, the limit values of resolution and light sensitivity are reached. Further studies on the possibility of achieving greater S_{ISO} light sensitivity when the resolution d is achieved may not be successful. It is necessary to move to fundamentally different light-sensitive materials, technologies, methods of obtaining and processing images.

Consider the effect on the image quality of photographic noise which increases significantly with decreasing illumination of the object of observation. This is due by increasing influence of its photonic component. The photographic noise of the PE changes the contrast between the object (reflection coefficient ρ_{ob}) and the background (reflection coefficient ρ_r) in the digital image. Let's evaluate the nature of such a change. If the luminance is sufficient there is no effect of photographic noise. In the dynamic range of the PE contrast K coincides with the contrast of the image K_{im} and is determined as follows [12]:

$$K = \frac{\rho_{ob} - \rho_r}{\rho_{ob} + \rho_r} = \frac{n_{ob} - n_r}{n_{ob} + n_r} = K_{im}, \tag{11}$$

where n_{ob} and n_r are the results of measuring the brightness of the object and the background in PE (the magnitude of the signal from the light-sensitive matrix - voltage, current, electric charge from the area of the light-sensitive matrix with the image of the object or background).

As the light decreases, the effect of photographic noise increases. It is numerically estimated by the standard deviation of σ_n in the brightness of the image of a uniformly illuminated area of the object or background (σ_n can be estimated as the standard deviation of the brightness of such area). Then (11) will be:

$$K_{im} = \frac{(n_{ob} + \sigma_n) - (n_r + \sigma_n)}{n_{ob} + \sigma_n + n_r + \sigma_n} = \frac{n_{ob} - n_r}{n_{ob} + n_r + 2\sigma_n}. \tag{12}$$

According to expressions (11, 12), the contrast in the digital image stored in the PE is a value inversely proportional to the photographic noise. The ratio of the contrasts of the same object on the same background under the condition of normal K_n and dusk K_d of lighting is written as follows:

$$\frac{K_n}{K_d} = \frac{n_{ob} + n_r + 2\sigma_{nd}}{n_{ob} + n_r + 2\sigma_n}. \tag{13}$$

where σ_{nd} is the standard deviation of the brightness in the dusk.

The value of the standard deviation σ_n in the digital image is proportional to the coefficient in the electronic path G [3]. This together with the light sensitivity of the elementary receiver determines the light sensitivity of the PE:

$$\sigma_n = GNt_e f(\triangle\lambda), \tag{14}$$

where N is the number of exposing photons during the exposure time t_e; $f(\triangle\lambda)$ is a dimensionless function of the spectral sensitivity of the photo detector $f(\triangle\lambda) = 1$, $\lambda \in \triangle\lambda$, $f(\triangle\lambda) = 0$, $\lambda \notin \triangle\lambda$; $\triangle\lambda$ is the range of spectral sensitivity of the photo detector.

To form a high-quality image, the exposure H must acquire the criterion value of N_{cr} at any level of illumination. In this case, the exposure is a constant value:

$$GNt_e = const = H_{cr}. \tag{15}$$

Equation (15) is achieved by controlling the values of N, t_e and G. This problem is automatically solved in each PE exposure system. With increasing luminance, the number of photons N during time t_e increases. Decreasing luminance leads to a decrease N. In PE provides compensation for changes in the value of N initially due to the inversely proportional change in shutter speed t_e and aperture number. If such a change affects the image quality, the change N is compensated by the light sensitivity. According to (15) it is a coefficient G in the electronic path.

3 Experiment, Results and Discussion

According to (10), there will be the following limit between the limit values of light sensitivity and PE resolution:

$$S_{ISO} \geq d^4 \frac{k\beta\eta}{i_{cr}l^2}. \tag{16}$$

Let's understand the possible values of photography parameters in the right part of (16). The coefficient of proportionality k for household photo cameras is equal to 1 [16]. The material of elementary receivers determines the quantum efficiency of the exposure process, namely the ratio between the number of photons that hit the light-sensitive surface and the number of photoelectrons β created by them. In the best case, each photon initiates the emergence of one photoelectron (β = 1). The coefficient η characterizes the technological efficiency of manufacture and operation of PE, in fact is its efficiency. At best, it is also equal to one.

The value i_{cr} can be accessed through the contrast sensitivity of the human eye. It will be 0.02. The image length of the recognition feature l will generally be nd, where n is the number of pixels in the image. When detected it will be $3d$, when recognized $6d$ and when identified it will be $12d$. Thus, from (11) we proceed to the following:

$$S_{ISO} \geq \frac{d^4}{0.02n^2d^2} = \frac{d^2}{0.02n^2}. \tag{17}$$

Estimates will be made for the Canon Power Shot SX420 IS Black [4]. Its light sensitivity will fluctuate in the range of $S_{ISO} = 100 \ldots 1600$ units ISO, the pixel size of the light-sensitive matrix will be 20 Mpx, the pixel size of the image will be $5152 \times 3864 \ px$. Accordingly, the smallest value of the resolution will be equal to $2\,\mu m = 2 \times 10^{-6}$ m. The results of calculations of the limit light sensitivity when photographing with different depth of recognition illustrates Fig. 1.

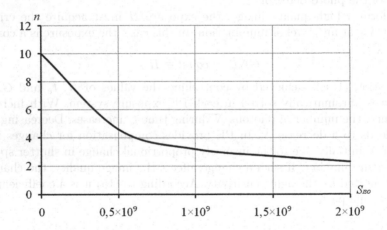

Fig. 1. The relationship between the possible light sensitivity and the specified depth of recognition of the object by its photographic image

The graph shows that as the task changes to the depth of recognition of the object by its image, the requirements for the limit value of light sensitivity of the PE change. Thus, when changing the detection task for identification the limit light sensitivity will change more than an order of magnitude.

Let us estimate the influence on the image quality of the quantity σ_n for which we use (13). Given that according to (14) $\sigma_{nd} \gg \sigma_n$, it can be presented as follows:

$$K_d \approx K_n \frac{\rho_{ob} + \rho_r}{\rho_{ob} + \rho_r + 2\sigma_{nd}} = K_n \frac{1}{1 + \dfrac{2\sigma_{nd}}{\rho_{ob} + \rho_r}}. \tag{18}$$

Analysis of the results of calculations by (18) for high-, medium- and low-contrast image of a person as an object of observation (Table 1, Fig. 2) shows that for high-contrast images already at $\sigma_{nd} > 9$ the contrast in the image becomes less than 0.02 namely less than the contrast sensitivity of the human eye. Such contrasts a person doesn't distinguish, human eye doesn't perceive the image, so accordingly there will be only photographic noise. The results of calculations on the limit light sensitivity don't match the passport data for this type of photo camera. This is due to the far from optimal technology of manufacture and operation of the PE, opportunities for further improvement of the light-sensitive receiver, the influence of operational factors especially in critical modes of operation of the PE.

Table 1. Influence of photographic noise on image contrast of human ($\rho_{ob} = 0.35$) in the conditions of photography at dusk

σ_{nd}	$K_n = 1.0$	$K_n = 0.5$	$K_n = 0.2$
0	1.000	0.500	0.200
0.2	0.461	0.184	0.045
0.4	0.305	0.113	0.025
0.6	0.226	0.081	0.018
0.8	0.180	0.063	0.014
1.0	0.149	0.052	0.011
3.0	0.055	0.019	0.004
5.0	0.034	0.012	0.002
7.0	0.024	0.008	0.002
9.0	0.019	0.006	0.001

It's important to change the requirements for light sensitivity, which can be considered rational in terms of its relationship with the distinction and opportunities offered by manufacturers of PE. Depending on the object's depth of field recognition of the object's photographic image the limit light sensitivity requirements vary slightly more than an order of magnitude. Approximately such possibilities for change of light sensitivity are provided also in the Canon Power Shot SX420 IS photo camera. The same applies to the PE installed in the Galaxy A50 Smartphone [14].

Another situation is in the Coolpix AW100 [10], Panasonic TZ18 Lumix [11] photo cameras, where this figure varies by two or more orders of magnitude.

Therefore, for predicted high-quality photographs, it is important to observe the range of calculated changes in the limit values of light sensitivity when photographing.

Thus, the generally accepted approach to exposure management in PE allows changing its value within 3...4 orders of magnitude, namely to ensure the efficiency of PE to the level of illumination in 20...30 lx. For the summer season it corresponds to 19...20 o'clock in the evening and 6...7 o'clock in the morning. This illumination of the object is provided by a table lamp installed at a distance of 1.0...1.5 m from it. It is clear that it is often necessary to take photos in the darker hours of the day and with a given or predicted image quality.

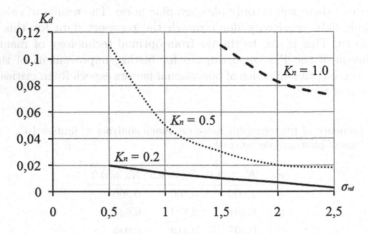

Fig. 2. The influence of photographic noise on the contrast of the image of a person at dusk

Small contrast in the image will be more appropriate to the real conditions of photography. For example, the statistically determined average contrast value of a picture that is in the corner of the lens field of view in PE "Landscape" photography is 0.18. For those images, the standard deviation σ_{nd} of 0.5 units is already critical. According to expression (14), the increase in the value of the standard deviation σ_n corresponds to an increase in the coefficient G in the electronic path, namely the light sensitivity of the PE. According to the results of calculations for high-contrast images the multiplicity of change in light sensitivity can't exceed 9, for medium-contrast - 2, for low-contrast - 0.5.

You can compare the required range of changes in light sensitivity in the PE with the actual possible value. The illumination of the Earth's surface on a sunny summer day varies from $E_{max} = 100000$ lx (12–13 h) to $E_{min} = 0.2...0.3$ lux on a lunar cloudless night. The dynamic luminance range of the E_{max}/E_{min} object will be 300000...500000 it's about five orders of magnitude. Accordingly, the parameters of the PE that determine the exposure of the image must be changed the same number of times. Approximately 1 order in exposure control can be provided by changing the shutter speed t_e (from 1/500 s to 1/50 s).

Larger shutter speeds are possible in the PE but for shooting conditions their use will result in a significant image shift. By changing the aperture number in the range of 2.4...32.0 and taking into account the quadratic effect on the exposure value it can be controlled within at least two orders of magnitude. The last exposure parameter that controls the exposure is the light sensitivity of the receiver. According to Table 1, Fig. 1 and (15), which indicates a linear relationship between the coefficient in the electronic path G and the light sensitivity of the PE, the frequency of change of light sensitivity even for high-contrast images should not exceed 9 (approximately one order).

4   Conclusions

Thus, the article defines the relationship between the values of light sensitivity and resolution when observing an object by photography. This allows to get a guaranteed and planned level of information about the object of observation by photography. The algorithmic relationship between the limit values of light sensitivity and resolution is determined. It allows assessing the degree of achievement of the highest perfection of a discrete iconic tool, taking into account the specified depth of recognition of the object by its image. An algorithmic assessment of the influence of photographic noise on image quality is proposed. The algorithms developed in the article are verified by a computational experiment. It allowed estimating the rational ranges of light sensitivity, which will not affect the resolution of the digital image of the observed object. The effect on the depth of recognition of an object by its image of the photosensitivity of the camera is estimated in order to keep its minimum possible value. The effect of photon noise on image quality in this case will be the smallest. The range of change of sensitivity of the camera by the order provided in photo cameras of the leading firms-manufacturers of the photo cameras can be considered recommended. The multiplicity of light sensitivity change for images of different contrast is estimated. For high-contrast images, the multiplicity of change in light sensitivity may not exceed 9, for medium-contrast - 2, for low-contrast - 0.5. To solve the problem of observation by photography at dusk, we can offer the following:

- search for more light-sensitive substances for matrix receivers;
- development of algorithms for finding compromise modes of operation of photographic equipment in the conditions of photography at dusk with minimal impact on the quality of the photographic image;
- use of packages of a posteriori processing of photographic images like ImageJ and Imatest to increase the recognizable properties of images, etc.

Further research in this area should focus on the development of hardware and software algorithms that are adapted to the causes of each case of critical circumstances, increase the accuracy of determining the relationship between the limit values of light sensitivity and resolution of the photo camera.

References

1. Babichev, S., Korobchynskyi, M., Mieshkov, S., Korchomnyi, O.: An effectiveness evaluation of information technology of gene expression profiles processing for gene networks reconstruction. Int. J. Intell. Syst. Appl. **10**(7), 1–10 (2018). https://doi.org/10.5815/ijisa.2018.07.01
2. Babichev, S., Kornelyuk, A., Lytvynenko, V., Osypenko, V.: Computational analysis of microarray gene expression profiles of lung cancer. Biopolym. Cell **32**(1), 70–79 (2016). https://doi.org/10.7124/bc.00090F
3. Born, M., Volf, E.: Electromagnetic theory of propagation, interference and diffraction of light. Princ. Opt. **6**, 327–329 (1980)
4. C. Canon: Digital photo canon powershot sx420 is. Manuel, pp. 20–21 (2018)
5. Jarvis, J., Wathes, C.: Mechanistic modeling of vertebrate spatial contrast sensitivity and acuity at low luminance. Vis. Neurosci. **3**, 169–181 (2012)
6. Korobchynskyi, M., Mariliv, A., Bohuslavets, A., Tsybulskyi, S., Sablina, E., Nechepurenko, V.: Algorithmic model of the cyclic changes in the temperature of the solid under the effect of convective heat exchanges with the environment. In: 15th International Conference "The Experience of Designing and Application of CAD Systems" (2019). https://doi.org/10.1109/CADSM.2019.8779332
7. Korobchynskyi, M., Slonov, M., Rudenko, M., Maryliv, O.: Assessment of the effect of image shift on the results of photo-video recording. In: 2020 IEEE 40th International Conference on Electronies and Nanotechnology (ELNANO), pp. 641–645 (2020)
8. Lytvyn, V., Peleshchak, I., Vysotska, V., Peleshchak, R.: Satellite spectral information recognition based on the synthesis of modified dynamic neural networks and holographic data processing techniques. In: 2018 IEEE 13th International Scientific and Technical Conference on Computer Sciences and Information Technologies (CSIT) (2018). https://doi.org/10.1109/STC-CSIT.2018.8526595
9. Mitchell, E.: Photographic Science. The University of North Carolina at Chapel Hill, Wiley, Chapel Hill (1984)
10. C. Nicon: Digital photo coolpix aw100. Manuel, pp. 20–21 (2011)
11. C. Panasonic: Digital photo panasonic tz18 lumix. Manuel, pp. 33–35 (2015)
12. Reulke, R.: Design and application of high-resolution imaging systems. GIS GeoInformationsSystem **3**, 30–37 (2003)
13. Rudenko, M., Slonov, M., Khamula, S.: Recognitional possibilities of results of special observation of the environmental monitoring object. Environ. Sci. **4**(27), 115–119 (2019). https://doi.org/10.32846/2306-9716-2019-4-27-16
14. C. Samsung: Smartphone galaxy a50. Manuel, pp. 57–60 (2019)
15. Slonov, M., Moldovan, V., Khamula, S., Korobchynskyi, M., Maryliv, O.: A method for determining of the maximum possible pixel format of object image memorizing during its photography. In: 9th International Youth Science Forum "Litteris Et Artibus", pp. 46–53 (2019)
16. Standard: Photography - Color reversal camera films - Determination of ISO speed. Published Standard ISO 2240:2003 (2003)
17. Vasiliev, V., Mashkov, O., Frolov, V.: Methods and technical measures of the ecological monitoring. Environ. Sci. **1**(5), 57–67 (2014)

Multiclass Image Classification Explanation with the Complement Perturbation Images

Oleksii Gorokhovatskyi(✉) and Olena Peredrii

Simon Kuznets Kharkiv National University of Economics, Kharkiv, Ukraine
oleksii.gorokhovatskyi@gmail.com, elena_peredriy@ukr.net

Abstract. The paper describes the investigation of a possibility to explain the result of the black box neural network image classifier with the pair of images we call complement. We generate them from the initial image being recognized with the hiding of some parts of it. The first image in the pair should be classified correctly, while another one should have another class label. Searching for the parts to hide may be based on the clustering of an image or just its geometrical division. The iterative division of an image was tested as a way to form parts and compared with well-known clustering methods. Different hiding methods that include the replacing with fixed black or white color or the blurring of part with various distortion levels were investigated. The chances to find the explanation in a form of explanation success rate were estimated for different methods and conditions. It was shown that the recursive division may be successful in this task.

Keywords: Image classification · Explanation · Black box · Interpretation · Recursive division · Complement images

1 Introduction

The plenty of various classification, recognition, and prediction practical problems in image processing, computer vision, and pattern recognition fields using the different artificial neural networking approaches are resolved and already embedded into our everyday life. The application of deep neural networks often allows us to achieve the state-of-the-art or at least very good results. The main bottleneck of the usage of neural networks is theirs natural black box structure, which means that the motivation of decisions being made by automatic artificial systems is not known and clear for humans. Such understanding may be critical for humans in the solution of sensitive problems like medical and health care, security, person identification, etc. The lack of decision reasoning leads to the development of different methods that help to understand the "logic" of the decision process by black box models last years to create explainable, interpretable, or transparent artificial intelligence tool [13,14] humans can trust to.

© Springer Nature Switzerland AG 2020
S. Babichev et al. (Eds.): DSMP 2020, CCIS 1158, pp. 275–287, 2020.
https://doi.org/10.1007/978-3-030-61656-4_18

2   Related Works

Different methods to get explanations [15] are known. Backpropagation (measures the influence of each pixel on the common result exploring backpropagation of a signal) and perturbation (creates some modification of initial signal and measures how classification result changes) are the most common ones. There are three main classes of methods to search for the explanations [20]. Backpropagation based methods measure the importance of each pixel in the initial image at the common result with the investigation of the backpropagation of signal processing. Activation based methods explore a linear combination of activations from convolutional layers to search for the explanation. Finally, the perturbation methods are based on the change of the initial image (typically, by the hiding of some parts) and the investigation of how this change influences the classification result. Each of the abovementioned methods has its own advantages and disadvantages like the quality of explanation, the performance of the method, the level of dependence on the model.

We will focus on the perturbation methods family, which allows to find agnostic (model-independent) explanations of the particular input image easily but has poor performance and the coarse explanation quality. We will not utilize the backpropagation of the signal or analysis of the architecture of neural network model. One of the most famous methods is LIME (Local Interpretable Model-Agnostic Explanations) [16,17] that is based on the hiding of superpixels of an input image with some color to build the set of perturbation images. After that, the well interpretable surrogate model (e.g. decision trees) is trained on these perturbation images like training set and allows to explain the classification result. This method has some issues with performance and stability.

The occlusion of input image parts with the grey square is used for the researching and visualizing of the activity in the intermediate layers of the deep neural network [22]. The generation of random occlusion masks to measure the importance of each pixel in the overall decision is proposed in [15]. The creation of perturbations with the replacing with constant color, blurring, and noising is proposed in [11]. The comparison of hiding the image parts with superpixels versus grid masks as well as the benefit of superpixels in terms of intersection over union are shown in [18]. The generation of superpixel score map visualization along with the interactive building of explanations when the user selects the superpixel is proposed in [21].

The researches of occlusion strategies are limited with hiding of superpixels or rectangular parts of images with black/grey colors or blurring them. The performance of these approaches is not very high or unclear. Additionally, it is also unknown whether the process of searching the explanations via brute force hiding of parts may fail, the probability of success is uncertain. The contributions of the paper include:

- the research of different image segmentation methods to form parts (clusters) which may be hidden and used to search for explanations of black-box neural network model;

– the competition research of different distortions in forming the perturbation images including blurring with different scales, replacing the parts of images with black/white.

3   Recursive Division (RD)

Perturbation based searching explanation methods assume the change of the initial image in different ways, classification of these perturbation images with the black box classifier following the analysis of classification results. The result of this analysis is typically the single image that shows important/unimportant regions during the classification of the particular initial image. Our explanation will consist of two complement images. We call the pair of images complement if some regions of the first image are covered with distortions (filling with color, blurring, etc.) and in the second image these distortions appear in other regions expect those if the first image. Examples of complement images are shown in Fig. 1.

Fig. 1. The examples of complement images: hiding of K-means clusters with black color and Gaussian blur with kernel (21 × 21)

Let's assume, that we have some black box classifier and we used it to predict the class for some initial image, the classification result has the label of class L. Having this, our goal is to find such complement images (created with perturbations from the initial one), first one of which is still classified as L, but the second one is classified as not L. We will use the geometric division of an image into square parts without analysis of content. The common algorithm follows:

1. Classify initial image to search explanation for and get its class label L.
2. Split initial image into square non-intersecting parts, distort parts one by one in initial image, generating in such a way perturbation images.
3. Classify each generated image searching for label of another class $L \neq L$.
   3.1 If there are no images with different label Ll then choose one of generated images as initial and return to step 2.
   3.2 For each image with label $L \neq L$: generate complement image to it and verify whether it is classified as class with label L. If it is true, complement pair is found, processing might be stopped or continued to find another complement pairs. If complement pair is not found then choose one of generated images as initial and return to step 2.
4. If all generated images are processed and no successful complement pair was found, algorithm fails.

The initial parameters of recursive division (RD) algorithm may be set up a sequence of parts $RD = (v_1, h_1, v_2, h_2, ...)$ in each stage, where v_1 is the quantity of vertical parts at the first partition stage, h_1 - is the quantity of horizontal parts in first partition stage etc. E.g $RD = (1, 2, 2, 2)$ means that image at the first stage is split just into two horizontal pieces and at all next stages it will be split into 2 vertical and 2 horizontal parts.

4   Network Structure, Training, Quality

We tried to solve the multiclass Image Scene Classification problem [5], the goal of which was to recognize the class image belongs to. There are six such classes: building, forest, glacier, mountain, sea, and street. The training set contains 14 034 images (from nearly 2100 to 3500 images per class), the testing set contains 3 000 images with a nearly close number of images representing different classes. All images are 150 by 150 pixels. The feature selection stage of our model includes the VGG16 network [19], pretrained on the ImageNet dataset. On top of it, we used two fully connected layers: the first one contains 50 RELU neurons and the last output layer contains 6 neurons with a sigmoid activation function. The additional dropout layer that ignores 50% of random neurons was added in between of these two fully connected layers.

The training of the net was done with Adam optimizer according to the following partial procedure. The image size was reduced to 128×128 pixels, the initial training set was split into parts with 2000 images in each, each such part was trained over 15 epochs with 32 images in a batch. The overall training time is about 50 min, the accuracy of this network was 0.9230 for the training set and 0.8697 for the testing one. The entire confusion matrix is shown in Fig. 2.

			Classification result				
		buildings	forest	glacier	mountain	sea	street
Real class	buildings	389	2	2	1	5	38
	forest	1	459	4	8	0	2
	glacier	2	3	441	89	15	3
	mountain	1	4	61	446	12	1
	sea	7	3	45	41	413	1
	street	28	5	2	1	4	461

Fig. 2. The confusion matrix

5   Experimental Results and Discussion

There is a summary of the whole explanation searching process:

- classify initial image;
- apply various clustering/segmentation approaches in order to split image into parts;
- hide each cluster/part one by one in turn with black/white/blur and check for the classification result;
- search for complement pair of images with different class labels.

5.1   Comparison Methods

K-means is a clustering algorithm that splits N feature vectors into K clusters in which each vector belongs to the cluster with the nearest mean (cluster centers). The OpenCV implementation of the K-means algorithm [1] was used. The algorithm was stopped if it reached 0.2 epsilon or 100 iterations. 10 clustering attempts with random centers were performed, the attempt with the best compactness (the least sum of squared distance from cluster centers to items in this cluster) was returned. Color RGB values were used as feature vectors. We varied the K value from 2 to 7.

Mean shift [9,12] is an iterative clustering method, that searches for the density blobs in the data. The implementation [6] of the algorithm requires a bandwidth of the neighborhood to be set up and estimates the number of clusters automatically. We used 100 samples and varied quantile parameter from $q = 0.4$ to $q = 0.1$ values according to [3].

SLIC [8] is the segmentation based on superpixels and the only parameter it requires is the approximate quantity of superpixels S [7]. This method is popular when searching for explanations that allows to replace the analysis of separate pixels with the analysis of superpixels and reduce processing time.

Density-Based Spatial Clustering of Applications with Noise (DBSCAN) [10] finds core samples of high density and expands clusters from them. We used $E = 35$ and $E = 25$ as a maximum distance between two color points in the scope of color and geometric manhattan distance and 50 sample points as a minimum quantity to form a cluster for implementation [4].

We also tested the **triangulation** of an image as a partition following examples and code from [2].

5.2 Success Rate

The explanation success rate is calculated according to: $ESR = N_s/N$, where N is the total quantity of correctly classified test images ($N = 2609$), N_s – is the quantity of correctly classified test images we successfully found the pair of complement explanation images for. We will calculate ESR value for all the abovementioned methods, trying to find explanations in a form of complement images. We consider only hiding or changing just one part of the image, not a combination of them. E.g. if there are 5 clusters in an image we take into account 5 perturbation images, in each, some cluster is hidden or replaced, but not all combinations of tuples, triples, etc. of hidden clusters.

5.3 Accuracy and Performance

Let's compare how successful are all the methods. We performed a lot of experiments with varying parameters for each method. While comparing ESR values we should control the real quantity of clusters for those methods, that estimate this value themselves: SLIC, mean shift, DBSCAN, because the explanation makes no sense when cluster count is equal to 1, this is the same that hiding the whole image instead of hiding the part of it. According to this, we didn't take into account all such cases and the appropriate choice of clusters number for SLIC is 4 and greater.

The results which show ESR for different methods when parts were hidden with black color are presented in Fig. 3. As one can see, the method that forms parts from triangles is not effective as well as a recursive division with a small size of parts at the first stage. SLIC seems to be the most successful, but it is difficult to control it with the number of superpixels, e.g. for $S = 4$ only 327 images had exactly 4 superpixels, 750 contained 3 superpixels, and more than 1500 contained 1 or 2 superpixels. It's worth noting that the recursive division

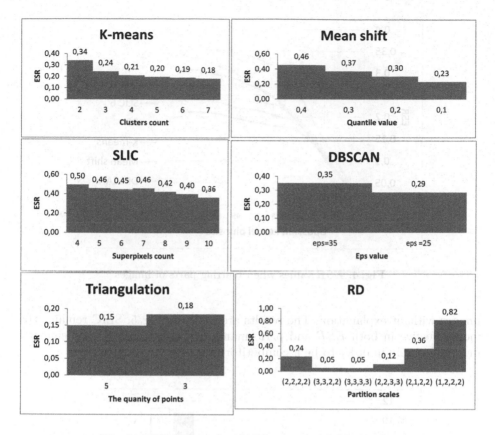

Fig. 3. ESR values when hiding parts with black color

approach shows a very different ESR value when the image is split vertically (0.36) and horizontally (0.82) at the first stage.

Similar experimental results when parts of images were hidden with white color are shown in Figure 8 in Appendix. Generally, they are a bit worse compared to hiding with black. Let's look at the accuracy when parts of the images are blurred instead of replaced (Fig. 4). We used Gaussian blurring with square kernels from 3×3 to 61×61. The following parameters were selected for clustering methods: 2 clusters count for K-means, $q = 0.25$ for mean shift, 4 and 6 superpixels for SLIC, $E = 35$ for DBSCAN and $(2, 2, 2, 2)$ partitioning for RD. So, SLIC method with $S = 4$ allows to find such partition of an image, that guarantees the best ESR value. But after verification we found, that the average quantity of superpixels was only 2.28, so we added the curve with $S = 6$ (the average number of superpixels, in this case, was 3.07). For the significant level of blur, RD outperforms all methods except for SLIC for 4 superpixels.

Let's compare the performance of all the above methods. We measured the time that is required to process the image searching for the explanation. Results are averaged separately for the images the explanation was found for and for the

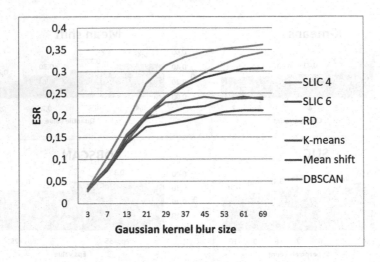

Fig. 4. *ESR* values when blurring parts of images

images without explanation. The results are shown in Fig. 5. SLIC remains the most effective in both *ESR* and performance and RD should be implemented more effectively in order to be a competitor to it.

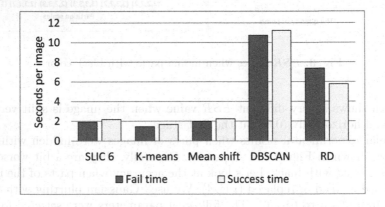

Fig. 5. Performance for different methods

5.4   Quality

Now we will compare the visual difference between explanation and speed for various methods (Fig. 6). At this example, all images in the first row were classified as "sea", all images in the second row - as "building", the correct class for this sample (20064.jpg) is "building".

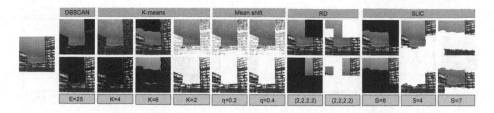

Fig. 6. Explanation examples for different methods

The first column contains an explanation result, based on the DBSCAN partition with the initial setting of $E = 25$ and hiding clusters with black color. 8 clusters were formed, this seems to be a lot for this image, but all other attempts of DBSCAN application with different initial options and blurring were unsuccessful at all. The next three columns show the all explanation results based on K-means split with a different quantity of clusters and black and white hiding. As you can see, two examples are very interesting, in the second column we see, that only yellow windows in this image are classified as "building" as well as the only blue region of the sky in the next column. Two following columns show the result about the application of mean shift clustering with different quantile parameters and the result are pretty the same as for previous 2-means hiding with white.

The results of the explanation found after RD partition are shown in the next two columns and again something interesting appears here. The top right part of the image seems to be very important to classify it as"building, additionally, the results when hiding parts with black and white are different. There are results of searching for explanations after hiding of clusters formed by SLIC method with different expected superpixels quantity $S = 4$, $S = 7$, and $S = 8$ in the last three columns. But in reality, only 3 or 4 superpixels were found in this image. All experiments with the blurring of parts of this image for all methods and options were unsuccessful.

The results of processing of images representing other classes: "forest" (Fig. 9) and "street" (Fig. 10) are shown in Appendix. The explanation results, found in this way depend on the model. We trained additionally the same model, described in paragraph 4 but with different initial random training seed. The accuracy of this net was 0.90 for the training set and 0.85 for the testing one. Then we applied the partitioning with the same methods (Fig. 6) and compare results, which are presented in Fig. 7. As one can see, three methods were unable to generate the partitions suitable for successful search of the explanations (they are marked with the red crosses). The explanations found by RD split are different that confirms that even small part of image may matter. The explanations, based on the partition of image into bigger fragments are the same.

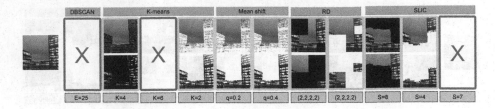

Fig. 7. Explanation examples for another net with same architecture

6 Conclusions

The key idea of the paper relates to the search for the explanation of the particular black box classification result via the pair of perturbation images, generated from the initial one. The method consists of the multiple classifications of the perturbation images, achieved from the image being classified with the blurring and replacing some parts of it with black/white colors. We stop the process when the pair of perturbed images is found, the first of which should be classified correctly, the second one - not. Various methods to split image to parts (clusters), as well as different distortion (hiding with black and white, blur with different kernel size) methods, were tested. The explanation success rate was calculated for all of them, it was shown, that simple recursive division of image may be successful in solving this task but the current implementation requires some performance boost.

A Appendix

The *ESR* values calculated for different clustering methods with the following hiding with white color are shown in Fig. 8. The examples of complement images explaining "forest" and "street" images are shown in Fig. 9 and Fig. 10 respectively.

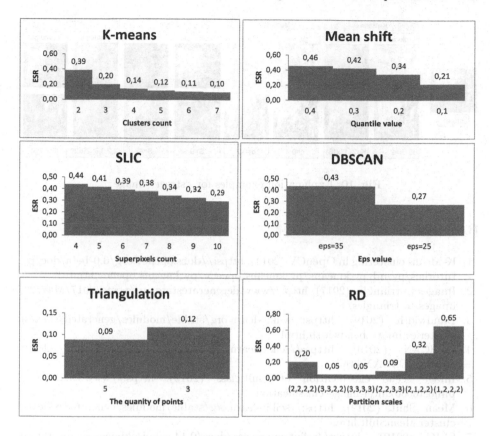

Fig. 8. *ESR* values when hiding parts with white color

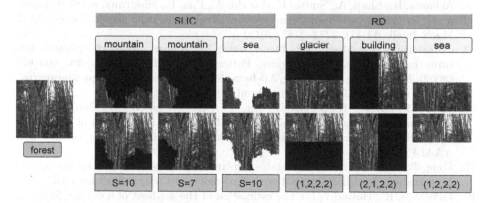

Fig. 9. Explanation examples for "forest" image

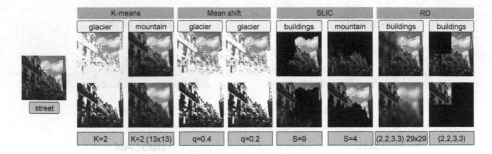

Fig. 10. Explanation examples for "street" image

References

1. K-Means clustering in OpenCV (2014). https://docs.opencv.org/3.0-beta/doc/py_tutorials/py_ml/py_kmeans/py_kmeans_opencv/py_kmeans_opencv.html
2. Images to triangles (2017). http://www.degeneratestate.org/posts/2017/May/24/images-to-triangles/
3. Bandwidth (2019). https://scikit-learn.org/stable/modules/generated/sklearn.cluster.estimate_bandwidth.html
4. DBSCAN (2019). https://scikit-learn.org/stable/modules/generated/sklearn.cluster.DBSCAN.html
5. Image scene classification of multiclass (2019). https://www.kaggle.com/puneet6060/intel-image-classification
6. Mean Shift (2019). https://scikit-learn.org/stable/modules/generated/sklearn.cluster.MeanShift.html
7. SLIC (2019). https://scikit-image.org/docs/0.14.x/api/skimage.segmentation.html#skimage.segmentation.slic
8. Achanta, R., Shaji, A., Smith, K., Lucchi, A., Fua, P., Süsstrunk, S.: SLIC superpixels compared to state-of-the-art superpixel methods. IEEE Trans. Pattern Anal. Mach. Intell. **34**(11), 2274–2282 (2012)
9. Comaniciu, D., Meer, P.: Mean shift: a robust approach toward feature space analysis. IEEE Trans. Pattern Anal. Mach. Intell. **24**, 603–619 (2002). https://docs.opencv.org/3.0-beta/doc/py_tutorials/py_ml/py_kmeans/py_kmeans_opencv/py_kmeans_opencv.html
10. Ester, M., Kriegel, H., Sander, J., Xu, X.: A density-based algorithm for discovering clusters in large spatial databases with noise. In: Proceedings of the Second International Conference on Knowledge Discovery and Data Mining, pp. 226–231. AAAI Press (1996)
11. Fong, R., Vedaldi, A.: Interpretable explanations of black boxes by meaningful perturbation. In: IEEE International Conference on Computer Vision (2017)
12. Fukunaga, K., Hostetler, L.: The estimation of the gradient of a density function, with applications in pattern recognition. IEEE Trans. Inf. Theory **21**(1), 32–40 (1975)
13. Gunning, D.: Explainable artificial intelligence (XAI) (2017). https://www.darpa.mil/attachments/XAIProgramUpdate.pdf
14. Molnar, C.: Interpretable machine learning. A guide for making black box models explainable (2020). https://christophm.github.io/interpretable-ml-book

15. Petsiuk, V., Das, A., Saenko, K.: Randomized input sampling for explanation of black-box models. In: British Machine Vision Conference (BMVC) (2018)
16. Ribeiro, M.: Lime - Local interpretable model-agnostic explanations (2016). https://homes.cs.washington.edu/~marcotcr/blog/lime/
17. Ribeiro, M., Singh, S., Guestrin, C.: Why should i trust you? Explaining the predictions of any classifier. In: 2016 Conference of the North American Chapter of the Association for Computational Linguistics (2016). https://doi.org/10.18653/v1/N16-3020
18. Seo, D., Oh, K., Oh, I.: Regional multi-scale approach for visually pleasing explanations of deep neural networks. IEEE Access **8**, 8572–8582 (2020)
19. Simonyan, K., Zisserman, A.: Very deep convolutional networks for large-scale image recognition. In: International Conference on Learning Representations (ICLR) (2015)
20. Wagner, J., Köhler, J.M., Gindele, T., Hetzel, L., Wiedemer, J.T., Behnke, S.: Interpretable and fine-grained visual explanations for convolutional neural networks. In: 2019 IEEE/CVF Conference on Computer Vision and Pattern Recognition (CVPR), pp. 9089–9100 (2019). https://doi.org/10.1109/CVPR.2019.00931
21. Wei, Y., Chang, M., Ying, Y., Lim, S., Lyu, S.: Explain black-box image classifications using superpixel-based interpretation. In: 2018 24th International Conference on Pattern Recognition (ICPR), pp. 1640–1645 (2018)
22. Zeiler, M.D., Fergus, R.: Visualizing and understanding convolutional networks. In: Fleet, D., Pajdla, T., Schiele, B., Tuytelaars, T. (eds.) ECCV 2014. LNCS, vol. 8689, pp. 818–833. Springer, Cham (2014). https://doi.org/10.1007/978-3-319-10590-1_53

Image Enhancement in Automatic Mode by Recursive Mean-Separate Contrast Stretching

Sergei Yelmanov[1]([✉])[iD] and Yuriy Romanyshyn[2,3][iD]

[1] Special Design Office of Television Systems, Lviv, Ukraine
sergei.yelmanov@gmail.com
[2] Lviv Polytechnic National University, Lviv, Ukraine
[3] University of Warmia and Mazury, Olsztyn, Poland
yuriy.romanyshyn1@gmail.com

Abstract. In this paper, the problem of improving the efficiency of transforming the intensity of complex images by piecewise linear contrast stretching in an automatic mode was considered. A new technique of intensity transformation by recursive mean-separate contrast stretching (RMSCS) was proposed. Our proposed technique of RMSCS allows us to improve the image by piecewise-linear contrast stretching in automatic mode using an arbitrary number of mean-separate intervals. The proposed approach to defining the gain factors allows more evenly distributed the average brightness of objects in the image based on the analysis of the number of pixels and their cumulative sum in chosen intervals. The proposed technique provides an effective enhance the images without the appearance of unwanted artifacts through a more evenly distributes the average brightness of objects in an image. The results of the research confirm the effectiveness of the proposed approach to enhance images in automatic mode.

Keywords: Image enhancement · Intensity transformation · Recursive mean-separate contrast stretching

1 Introduction

Fusion and joint analysis of the video and the information from other sensors is one of the major trends in smart technology. The analysis of video on-line can significantly improve situational awareness and effectively increase the reliability and accuracy of solving a wide range of various complex tasks in different applications.

Widespread use of video in on-line requires solving the task of effectively real-time improving the quality of the source raw images [1, 4, 13, 17, 18]. The need to improve raw images is due to some objective reasons, the main of which are the not high enough technical characteristics of the image sensor, the unfavorable conditions of shooting, the shortcomings of the observed objects and scenes

© Springer Nature Switzerland AG 2020
S. Babichev et al. (Eds.): DSMP 2020, CCIS 1158, pp. 288–306, 2020.
https://doi.org/10.1007/978-3-030-61656-4_19

[2, 4, 13, 19]. These shortcomings lead to a significant reduction in the quality of images being formed. At the same time, the effectiveness of perception, analysis, and recognition of the image depends critically on its quality [2, 4, 13].

There is a large amount of research dedicated to solving the problem of improving images in automatic mode, but this task is still very far from its final solutions [8–10, 15, 16]. Most of the existing methods of image pre-processing have significant flaws that limit their use to enhance images on-line [13, 18]. These disadvantages include the low inefficiency of transforming images with full dynamic range, the appearance of unwanted artifacts, an excessive increase in the contrast of large extended objects, a reduction in the contrast of objects with small sizes, the need to adjust parameters of processing in interactive mode, high level of computational cost.

The problem of creating new, computationally simple, but effective technologies for improving images on-line in real-time and mobile applications is now particularly urgent [1, 2, 4, 18]. This paper looks at the issue of real-time enhancing the images in mobile and wireless apps.

The purpose of this work is to improve the efficiency of improving the image by adaptively transforming its intensity in automatic mode. To meet this challenge in this work proposes a new approach to enhance the image by adaptively transforming its intensity based on mean-separate contrast stretching.

2   Fundamentals

There are many different approaches to improving the quality of images [2, 4, 13, 19]. The techniques based on transformations in the spatial domain are most often used to enhance images in real-time because of the simplicity in their implementation [2, 15, 17].

The simplest way to process an image in a spatial domain is to transform its intensity, in which the neighborhood is 1×1 pixel, i.e., the result of transformation for the current pixel depends only on the brightness value in that pixel. Intensity transformations are quite efficient, have low computational costs, and are simple to implement in real-time. The various techniques based on the non-inertial statistical transformations of image intensity are very widely used to enhance images in real-time applications.

There are different approaches to transforming image intensity.

2.1   Image Intensity Transformation

Intensity transformation is the easiest and quite effective way to improve images and is extremely widely used in various applications for image preprocessing in real-time [17, 18].

A generalized description of the transformation of image intensity is generally represented as [13]:

$$y = y_{low} + (y_{upp} - y_{low}) \cdot F(x), \tag{1}$$

$$0 \leq x_{min} \leq x \leq x_{max} \leq 1, \text{ and } 0 \leq y_{low} < y_{upp} \leq 1, \tag{2}$$

where x is the brightness for the current pixel in the source image X, $x \in X$, $0 \leq x \leq 1$; $F(x)$ is the intensity transformation function; y is the result of transforming for current pixel; Y is the transformed image, $y \in Y$, $0 \leq y \leq 1$; y_{low} and y_{upp} are the set boundaries for the dynamic range $[y_{low}, y_{upp}]$ of possible brightness values for Y, $0 \leq y_{low} < y_{upp} \leq 1$.

If one assumes that the dynamic range of the transformed image coincides with the interval of possible brightness values (i.e., it is normalized in the interval $[0, 1]$), then y_{low} is 0 and y_{upp} is 1. In this case, the definition (1) takes the form $y = T(x)$ [13]. In (1) it is assumed that the transformation function $F(x)$ is unambiguously and well-defined in the entire range of $[0, 1]$ of possible brightness values and the range of possible values for $F(x)$ coincides with its domain of definition:

$$F : X \mapsto Y, \ F : y = F(x), \ x \in X, y \in Y, \ 0 \leq x, y \leq 1, \tag{3}$$

$$0 \leq F(x) \leq 1, \ \forall x \in X \ : \ 0 \leq x_{min} \leq x \leq x_{max} \leq 1, \tag{4}$$

where x_{min} and x_{max} are minimal and maximal values of brightness.

It is also assumed that $F(x)$ is the non-descending function in the entire range of brightness values:

$$\forall x_i, x_j \in X \ : \ \text{if } x_i > x_j \Rightarrow F(x_i) \geq F(x_j), \tag{5}$$

and takes extreme values at extreme brightness:

$$F(x_{min}) = 0, \text{ and } F(x_{max}) = 1, \tag{6}$$

Conditions (2)–(6) describe the basic mandatory requirements for $F(x)$ [13]. There are now a lot of different ways to transforming image intensity [2, 4, 13]. Various techniques of intensity transformation are widely used to solve a wide range of problems in different applications [2, 19]. Intensity transformations are most widely used to normalize the initial raw images and increase their overall contrast [8–10, 15, 16].

In accordance with generally accepted classification, existing methods of intensity transformation are most often subdivided into three main groups [2, 4, 13]:

- basic transformations of image intensity [2, 4, 13, 17];
- contrast stretching based techniques [11, 13, 14];
- histogram equalization technique and its modifications [3, 5–7, 13].

A large number of studies are devoted to the analysis of these methods, and their capabilities and main limitations ones are carefully explored [6, 8, 10, 16]. The main drawbacks of existing methods of intensity transformation are their inefficiency in processing complex images with the uneven multimode distribution of brightness, the appearance of distortions and artifacts, an excessive increase in contrast for extended objects and a decrease in the contrast of objects with small sizes, the need to adjust the values of transformation parameters in an interactive mode, etc [13,17]. Methods based on the technique of linear contrast stretching are of great interest to use in automatic mode. This technique potentially allows improved the quality of the source image while maintaining the ratio of the increments of the contrast of its objects with a scalable change in the average brightness of the image, which largely avoids the appearance of unwanted artifacts and distortions [11,13,14].

2.2   Linear Contrast Stretching

Contrast stretching (CS) is the easiest technique for intensity transformation and, in certain cases, when used correctly, can be very effective [11,13]. The technique of contrast stretching is based on linear transformation (stretching) of selected sub-intervals of the image brightness scale [4,14].

In the simplest case, only one interval is considered, which is linearly stretched to the full scale of brightness (i.e., to the range of [0, 1]) [13]. Such an approach to CS is commonly referred to as partial linear stretching at which the transformation function $F(x)$ (1) has the form [13]:

$$y = F_1(x) = \begin{cases} 0, & \text{if } x \le a \\ \dfrac{1}{b-a} \cdot (x-a), & \text{if } a < x < b \\ 1, & \text{if } x \ge b \end{cases} \tag{7}$$

where a and b are the lower and upper boundaries for the interval $[a, b]$ of linear stretching, the parameters of transformation, $0 \le a < b \le 1$.

The most known CS technique is min-max contrast stretching, in which the dynamic range $[x_{min}, x_{max}]$ of the source image stretched to the range [0, 1] of possible values of brightness, and at which $a = x_{min}$ and $b = x_{max}$ [13,14]. Another popular technique is percentile contrast stretching [4,11], in which the boundaries of the interval $[a, b]$ of linear stretching are determined from the equations $\mathrm{CDF}(a) = \delta$ and $\mathrm{CDF}(b) = 1 - \delta$, where CDF is the cumulative distribution function, δ is the threshold value, parameter. Threshold value δ most often takes a values from the range [0,005–0,03].

Partial linear stretching is a standard "lassic" procedure of image preprocessing that is quite effective under certain conditions. The techniques of min-max and percentile stretching are widely used to normalize the source raw images with a narrow range of brightness values and enhance them in automatic mode [13,14]. However, these methods are ineffective in processing complex images with full dynamic range and uneven distribution of brightness [13].

Methods based on piecewise linear stretching technology [11,13,14], which is a generalization of the technique of partial stretching for the case of multiple intervals, allow us to address these shortcomings.

The most popular technique of piecewise linear stretching is a method based on the use of two intervals, which can be represented as [4, 13, 14]:

$$
y = F_2(x) = \begin{cases} 0, & \text{if } x \le a \\ \dfrac{k}{b-a} \cdot (x-a), & \text{if } a < x \le b \\ k + \dfrac{1-k}{c-b} \cdot (x-b), & \text{if } b < x \le c \\ 1, & \text{if } x > c \end{cases} \tag{8}
$$

where a, b, c are the boundaries for the interval $[a, b]$ and $[b, c]$ of linear stretching, $0 \le a < b < c \le 1$; k is the gain factor, $0 < k < 1$.

Based on the requirement (6), it is usually assumed that $a = x_{min}$ and $c = x_{max}$ and transformation (7) essentially has only two parameters, namely the central threshold b and the gain factor k. The values of the central threshold b and the gain factor k determine the transformation (10). When choosing the parameters for transformation (10), the most often proceed from the assumption that the best in terms of perception and subsequent analysis is the image with full dynamic range $[0, 1]$ and average brightness that is equal to $1/2$:

$$
y_{mean} = \text{mean}(Y) = \int_0^1 y \cdot h(y) \, dy = \int_0^1 F(x) \cdot f(x) \, dx = 1/2. \tag{9}
$$

where y_{mean} is the average brightness of transformed image; $f(x)$ is the probability density functions (pdf) of source image X; $h(y)$ is the pdf of transformed image Y. Based on this assumption, it is often assumed that $b = x_{mean}$ and $k = 1/2$. A piecewise linear stretch (10) with such parameters allows us to change the mean of brightness by shifting it into the range of average values of brightness (i.e., up to $1/2$). There are also other approaches to defining the central threshold b. As the central threshold b, the median of the brightness distribution and the optimal threshold by the Otsu's method are also often used.

In general, however, transformation (8) with such parameters does not ensure strict fulfillment of condition (9) [20]. In [20], it has been shown that the value of the gain factor k at which the exact fulfillment of condition (9) is ensured has a more complicated dependence on the statistical characteristics of the source image. In [20], it was also shown that strict compliance with the condition (9) could lead to unwanted artifacts at the processing of complex images with a wide range of brightness and a uneven multimodal distribution due to excessive enhance the contrast and loss of information in the black and white areas of the brightness scale. This drawback can be addressed by increasing the number of intervals for stretching, but this approach significantly increases the number of parameters of a piecewise linear transformation (boundaries for the interval and gain factor), and the task of selecting their values is much more complicated. Therefore, the values of these parameters are usually chosen in an interactive mode. These disadvantages substantially limit the practical use of exiting techniques of piecewise linear stretching for enhancing images in real-time applications.

To address these disadvantages, we propose a new technique of piecewise linear contrast stretching in an automatic mode based on the use of an arbitrary number of intervals and their adaptive stretching given the distribution of brightness in these intervals.

3 Proposed Technique

In this paper, we propose a new technique of adaptive transformation of image intensity in automatic mode by **recursive mean-separate contrast stretching (RMSCS)**.

This technique is based on a piecewise linear transformation of the dynamic range of the source image, which has the following form:

$$
y = F_n(x) = \begin{cases} 0, & \text{if } x \leq t_0 \\ \sum_{j=1}^{i-1} k_j \cdot (t_j - t_{j-1}) + k_i \cdot (x - t_{i-1}), & \text{if } t_{i-1} < x \leq t_i \quad (10) \\ 1, & \text{if } x > t_n \end{cases}
$$

$$
0 \leq t_0 < t_1 < t_2 < \ldots < t_{n-1} < t_n \leq 1, \tag{11}
$$

where F_n is the piecewise linear transformation for n intervals of stretching; n is the number of intervals that are linearly stretched; t_i are the boundaries for the intervals of linear stretching ($i = \overline{0, n}$), where $t_0 = x_{min}$ and $t_n = x_{max}$; k_j are the gain factors ($j = \overline{1, n}$).

There are different approaches to divide the dynamic range of the image into sub-interfaces. Suppose that the choice of the boundaries of the intervals is based on a well-known method of recursively mean-based separation of the image range into parts (sub-intervals), at which each new interval further recursively separates into two parts relative to the mean of its brightness. A key issue in implementing the proposed technique to piecewise linear stretching is choosing to determine the gain factors $k_i, (1 < i < n)$. Various approaches to defining gain factors k_i are possible. As an example, it can be assumed that the average brightness in recursively mean-separated intervals should be evenly distributed in a transformed image, i.e., that there are in the converted image these mean-separated intervals should have the same length. In this case (based on this assumption), the gain factors k_i is defined as:

$$
k = \frac{1}{n} \cdot \frac{1}{t_i - t_{i-1}}, \quad i = \overline{1, n}. \tag{12}
$$

Transformation (10), (12) allows us a more evenly distribute the brightness of objects in the image. However, with such transformation analyzes only the lengths of the mean-separated sub-intervals, and does not take into account the features of the distribution of brightness at these intervals, in particular the number and cumulative sum of their elements. To address these disadvantages, we propose new definitions for gain based on the solution of a system of equations:

$$k_i \cdot \int_{t_{i-1}}^{t_i} x \cdot f(x)\, dx - \gamma_i \cdot \int_{t_{i-1}}^{t_i} f(x)\, dx = 0, \quad i = \overline{1,n}. \tag{13}$$

where γ_i are the normalizing factors, which are equal to:

$$\gamma_i = \int_{t_{i-1}}^{t_i} u\, du \ / \int_0^n u\, du, \quad i = \overline{1,n}. \tag{14}$$

From (15) it follows that:

$$k_i = \gamma_i \cdot \int_{t_{i-1}}^{t_i} f(x)\, dx \ / \int_{t_{i-1}}^{t_i} x \cdot f(x)\, dx. \tag{15}$$

Expressions (10), (11), (14) and (15) defined of the proposed approach to enhancing images by **recursive mean-separate contrast stretching (RMSCS)**. Our proposed technique of RMSCS allows us to improve the image in automatic mode by piecewise-linear contrast stretching using an arbitrary number of mean-separate intervals. The proposed approach (10), (15) for defining the gain factors allows us more evenly distributed the average brightness of objects in the image based on the analysis of the number of pixels and their cumulative sum in chosen intervals.

4   Research

Research is carried out by a comparative analysis of the results of quantifying the overall contrast for six groups of test images. Each from these six groups is formed by processing the appropriate source raw image using the chosen (known and proposed) techniques of intensity transformation in automatic mode. For image processing, the following well-known and proposed techniques of intensity transformation were used, namely:

1) min-max linear stretching [13,14];
2) percentile linear stretching [11,13];
3) adaptive gamma correction to mean for the case where $y_{mean} = 1/2$ [13];
4) piecewise linear stretching for the case where $T(x_{mean}) = 1/2$ [20];
5) exact stretching the average brightness of an image to 1/2 relative to the mean value ($T(x_{mean}) = 1/2$) for the case where $n = 2$ [20];
6) exact stretching the average brightness of an image to 1/2 relative to the median ($T(x_{med}) = 1/2$) for the case where $n = 2$ [20];

7) exact stretching the average brightness of an image to $1/2$ relative to the Otsu threshold value $(T(x_{otsu}) = 1/2)$ for the case where $n = 2$ [20];

8) histogram equalization (HE) technique [5];

9) BBHE technique [7];

10) RSMHE technique [3];

11) piecewise linear contrast stretching (10), (12) for $n = 4$;

12) proposed technique of RMSCS (10), (15) for $n = 4$.

The six source images and their histograms are presented in Fig. 1 and the results of their processing using the above methods are shown in Figs. 2, 3, 4, 5, 6, 7, 8 and 9.

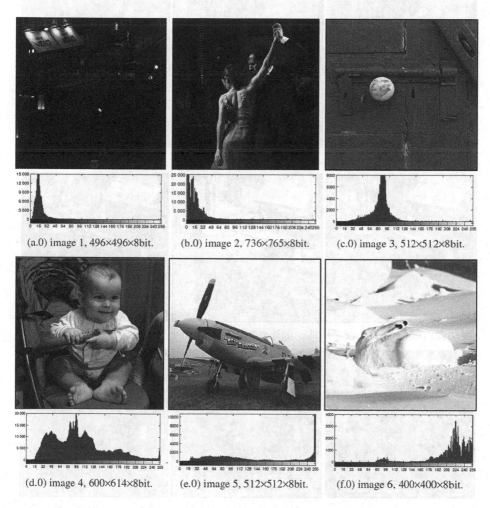

(a.0) image 1, 496×496×8bit.   (b.0) image 2, 736×765×8bit.   (c.0) image 3, 512×512×8bit.

(d.0) image 4, 600×614×8bit.   (e.0) image 5, 512×512×8bit.   (f.0) image 6, 400×400×8bit.

Fig. 1. Test images and their histograms.

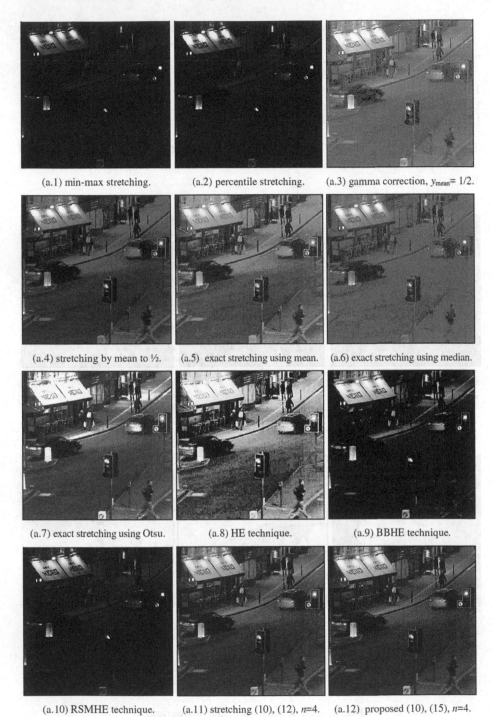

(a.1) min-max stretching.   (a.2) percentile stretching.   (a.3) gamma correction, $y_{mean}= 1/2$.

(a.4) stretching by mean to ½.   (a.5) exact stretching using mean.   (a.6) exact stretching using median.

(a.7) exact stretching using Otsu.   (a.8) HE technique.   (a.9) BBHE technique.

(a.10) RSMHE technique.   (a.11) stretching (10), (12), $n=4$.   (a.12) proposed (10), (15), $n=4$.

Fig. 2. The results of processing for test image a.0.

(b.1) min-max stretching.   (b.2) percentile stretching.   (b.3) gamma correction, $y_{mean}= 1/2$.

(b.4) stretching by mean to ½   (b.5) exact stretching using mean.   (b.6) exact stretching using median

(b.7) exact stretching using Otsu.   (b.8) HE technique   (b.9) BBHE technique.

(b.10) RSMHE technique.   (b.11) stretching (10), (12), n=4.   (b.12) proposed (10), (15), n=4.

Fig. 3. The results of processing for test image b.0.

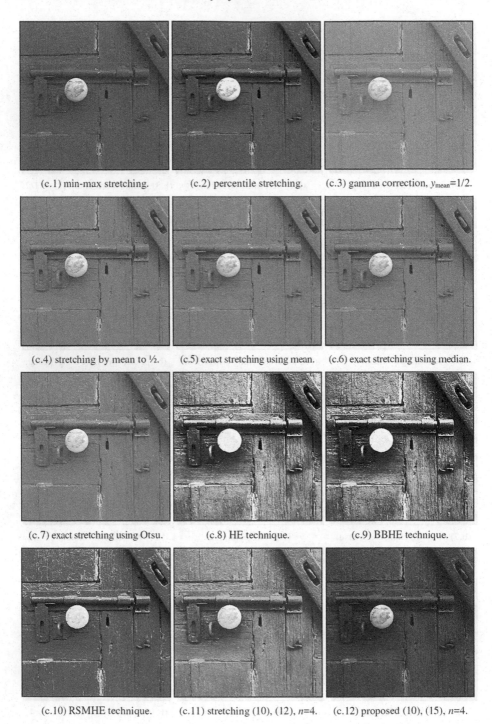

(c.1) min-max stretching.   (c.2) percentile stretching.   (c.3) gamma correction, $y_{mean}=1/2$.

(c.4) stretching by mean to ½.   (c.5) exact stretching using mean.   (c.6) exact stretching using median.

(c.7) exact stretching using Otsu.   (c.8) HE technique.   (c.9) BBHE technique.

(c.10) RSMHE technique.   (c.11) stretching (10), (12), $n=4$.   (c.12) proposed (10), (15), $n=4$.

Fig. 4. The results of processing for test image c.0.

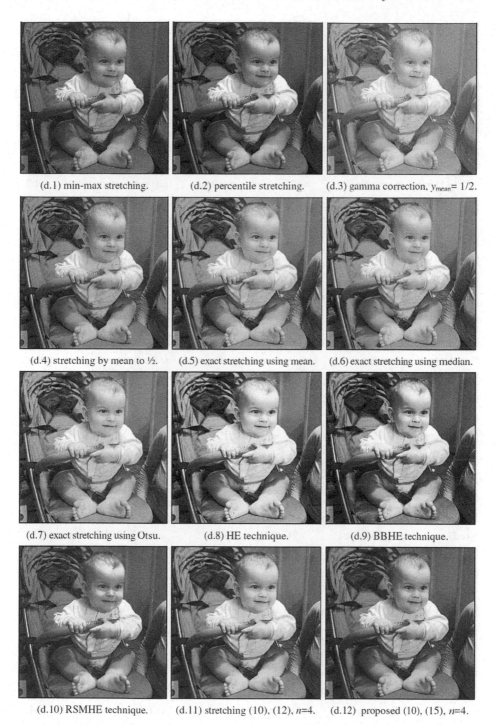

(d.1) min-max stretching.   (d.2) percentile stretching.   (d.3) gamma correction, $y_{mean} = 1/2$.

(d.4) stretching by mean to ½.   (d.5) exact stretching using mean.   (d.6) exact stretching using median.

(d.7) exact stretching using Otsu. (d.8) HE technique.   (d.9) BBHE technique.

(d.10) RSMHE technique.   (d.11) stretching (10), (12), $n=4$. (d.12) proposed (10), (15), $n=4$.

Fig. 5. The results of processing for test image d.0.

(e.1) min-max stretching.   (e.2) percentile stretching.   (e.3) gamma correction, y_{mean}= 1/2.

(e.4) stretching by mean to ½.   (e.5) exact stretching using mean.   (e.6) exact stretching using median.

(e.7) exact stretching using Otsu.   (e.8) HE technique.   (e.9) BBHE technique.

(e.10) RSMHE technique.   (e.11) stretching (10), (12), n=4.   (e.12) proposed (10), (15), n=4.

Fig. 6. The results of processing for test image e.0.

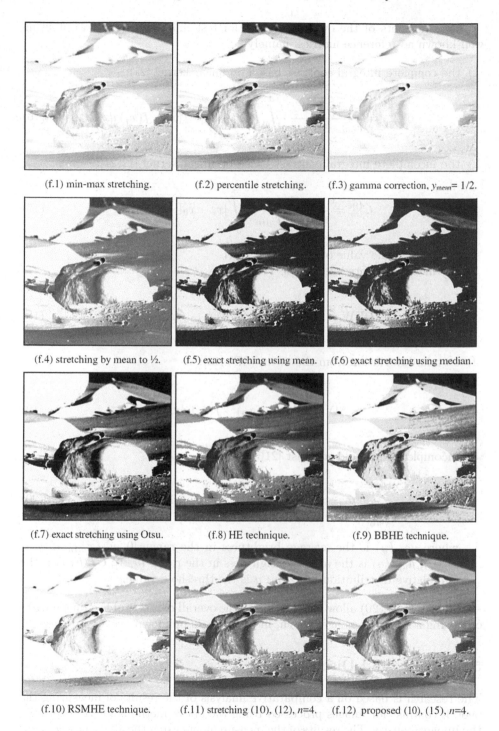

(f.1) min-max stretching.   (f.2) percentile stretching.   (f.3) gamma correction, $y_{mean}= 1/2$.

(f.4) stretching by mean to ½.   (f.5) exact stretching using mean.   (f.6) exact stretching using median.

(f.7) exact stretching using Otsu.   (f.8) HE technique.   (f.9) BBHE technique.

(f.10) RSMHE technique.   (f.11) stretching (10), (12), $n=4$.   (f.12) proposed (10), (15), $n=4$.

Fig. 7. The results of processing for test image f.0.

Measurements of the overall contrast for test images are carried out using well-known no-reference metrics, namely:

1) the complete integral contrast based on linear kernel [21]:

$$C_{com}^{lin} = \frac{1}{x_{max} - x_{min}} \cdot \int_0^1 \int_0^1 |x_i - x_j| \cdot f(x_i) \cdot f(x_j) \, dx_i dx_j, \qquad (16)$$

2) the incomplete integral contrast based on linear kernel [12,21]:

$$C_{inc}^{lin} = \frac{1}{x_{max} - x_{min}} \cdot \int_0^1 |x_i - x_0| \cdot f(x_i) \, dx_i, \qquad (17)$$

where x_0 is the value of adaptation level.

3) the mean of squared deviations (DEW):

$$DEW = \int_0^1 \int_0^1 (x_i - x_j)^2 \cdot f(x_i) \cdot f(x_j) \, dx_i dx_j, \qquad (18)$$

4) standard deviation from the mean (SD) [13]:

$$SD = \left[\int_0^1 (x_i - x_0)^2 \cdot f(x_i) \, dx_i \right]^{1/2}, \qquad (19)$$

5) incomplete threshold contrast [21]:

$$C_{inc}^{thr} = \int_{x_{min}}^{x_{max}} |\mu_{upp}(u) - \mu_{low}(u)| \cdot CDF(u) \cdot (1 - CDF(u)) \, du, \qquad (20)$$

where $\mu_{low}(u)$ is the average brightness in the range $[0, u]$ ($x_{min} < u < x_{max}$); $\mu_{upp}(u)$ is the average brightness in the range $[u, 1]$; $CDF(u)$ is the cumulative distribution function; u is the threshold value.

Metrics (16)–(20) allow us to estimate the overall contrast of the image without using a reference image, which, in our case, is unknown.

5   Results and Discussion

The research is based on a comparative analysis of the results of measuring the overall contrast for images processed using the above methods for transforming the image intensity. The results of the measurements using the above no-reference metrics (16)–(20) are shown in Figures 8, 9, 10, 11, 12 and 13.

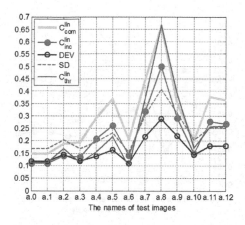

Fig. 8. The estimates of contrast for a.0–a.12.

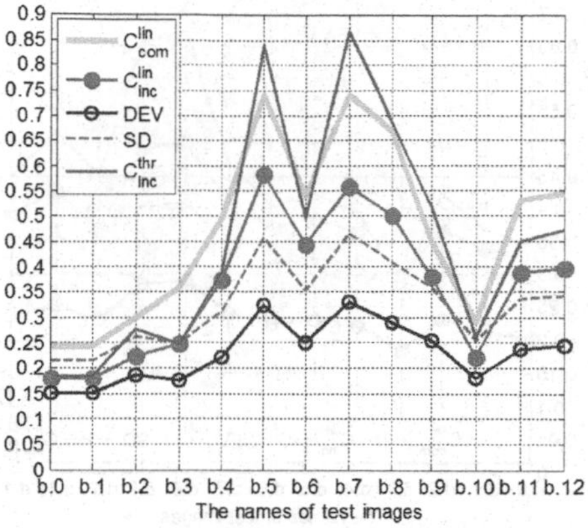

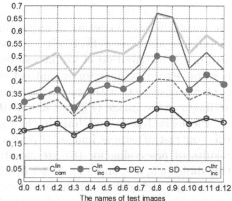

Fig. 9. The estimates of contrast for b.0–b.12.

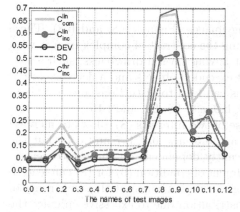

Fig. 10. The estimates of contrast for c.0–c.12.

Fig. 11. The estimates of contrast for d.0–d.12.

The results of the study research the well-known fact that the methods of min-max and percentile contrast stretching can significantly enhance images with a narrow range of brightness values (Figures c.2, e.2), but they are ineffective in processing images with a full dynamic range (Figures a.1, a.2, b.1, b.2, c.1, e.1, and f.1).

The results of a power-law transformation (or the gamma correction) are determined by the brightness distribution and the values of transformation parameters (Figures a.3, c.3, e3 and f.3). In some cases, this technique can be very effective (Figures b.3 and d.3), but the problem of choosing the parameters of correction is very acute. Histogram equalization and its modifications

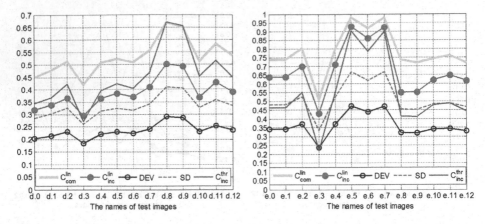

Fig. 12. The estimates of contrast for e.0–e.12.

Fig. 13. The estimates of contrast for f.0–f.12.

are most effective in terms of enhancing images (Figures a.8, and b.8). These techniques allow very effectively improving the contrast of complex images with an uneven distribution of brightness but having several drawbacks, such as the possible excessive increase in contrast of extended objects and a decrease in the contrast of objects with small sizes. This can lead to distortions and unwanted artifacts in the image (Figures a.9, a.10, b.9, e.8, f.8, f.9, and f.10).

Piecewise linear stretching in the case of two intervals (8) allows to increase the contrast of simple images (Figures a.4, a.5, a.7, b.4, b.7 and e.4), but the results of processing for (8) are significantly dependent on the choice central threshold (a.5, a.6, and a.7). Strict fulfillment of condition (9) for (8) can lead to distortions and artifacts at the processing of complex images with a wide range of brightness and an uneven multimodal distribution due to excessive enhance the contrast and loss of information in black and white areas of the brightness scale (Figures f.5, f.6, f.7, e.5 and e.6, e.7). Research shows that existing methods of piecewise linear stretching in the case of a small number of intervals ($n \leq 3$) are ineffective for processing complex images with uneven distribution brightness.

Improving the efficiency of enhancing complex images is possible by increasing the number of stretch intervals. The proposed technique of RMSCS allows us to realize piecewise linear stretching of contrast in the automatic mode for an arbitrary given number of intervals. The RMSCS technique provides a more uniform distribution of the contrast of objects in the image, thereby reducing the risk of appearance of unwanted artifacts. Research shows that the proposed techniques (10), (12), and (10), (15) of RMSCS for case $n = 4$ allow us to improve all test images without the appearance of unwanted artifacts.

6 Conclusions

The purpose of this work was to improve the efficiency of transforming the intensity of complex images by piecewise-linear contrast stretching in automatic mode. For this purpose, a new technique of intensity transformation by recursive mean-separate contrast stretching (RMSCS) was proposed.

The RMSCS technique performs a piecewise-linear contrast stretching for an arbitrary set number of intervals. The proposed RMSCS technique is grounded on determining the gain factors based on the analysis of the number of pixels and the sum of their brightness in chosen intervals. The proposed approach to defining gain factors provides a more evenly distributes the average brightness of objects in an image compared to traditional piecewise-linear stretching.

The proposed RMSCS technique provides an effective enhance the images without the appearance of unwanted artifacts for all test images.

The results of the research confirm the effectiveness of the proposed technique of RMSCS. The proposed technique of RMSCS is highly effective, parameter-free, simple to implement, least computationally costly, and can be recommended for real-time enhance images in mobile apps.

References

1. Bovik, A.C.: Handbook of Image and Video Processing, 2nd edn. Academic Press, A Harcourt Science and Technology Company, San Diego (2005)
2. Burger, W., Burge, M.J.: Point Operations. In: Burger, W., Burge, M.J. (eds.) Principles of Digital Image Processing. Undergraduate Topics in Computer Science. Springer, London (2009). https://doi.org/10.1007/978-1-84800-191-6_4
3. Chen, S.D., Ramli, A.: Contrast enhancement using recursive mean separate histogram equalization for scalable brightness preservation. IEEE Trans. Consum. Electron. 49(4), 1301–1309 (2003). https://doi.org/10.1109/TCE.2003.1261233
4. Gonzalez, R., Woods, R.: Digital Image Processing, 4th edn. Pearson Education, New Jersey (2018)
5. Hummel, R.: Histogram modification techniques. Comput. Graph. Image Process. 4(3), 209–224 (1975). https://doi.org/10.1016/0146-664X(75)90009-X
6. Kaur, M., Kaur, J., Kaur, J.: A survey on image enhancement by histogram equalization methods. Int. Res. J. Eng. Technol. IRJET 3(4), 1047–1052 (2016)
7. Kim, Y.T.: Contrast enhancement using brightness preserving bi-histogram equalization. IEEE Trans. Consum. Electron. 43(1), 1–8 (1997). https://doi.org/10.1109/30.580378
8. Kotkar, V., Gharde, S.: Review of various image contrast enhancement techniques. Int. J. Innov. Res. Sci. Eng. Technol. 2(7), 2786–2793 (2013)
9. Maini, R., Aggarwal, H.: A comprehensive review of image enhancement techniques. J. Comput. 2(3), 8–13 (2010)
10. Maragatham, G., Roomi, M.: A review of image contrast enhancement methods and technique. Res. J. Appl. Sci. Eng. Technol. 9(5), 309–326 (2015). https://doi.org/10.19026/rjaset.9.1409
11. Mokhtar, N., Harun, N., Mashor, M.Y.: Image enhancement techniques using local, global, bright, dark and partial contrast stretching for acute leukemia images. In: Proceedings of the World Congress on Engineering WCE, vol. 1, pp. 807–812 (2009)

12. Nesteruk, V., Sokolova, V.: Questions of the theory of perception of subject images and a quantitative assessment of their contrast. Optiko-Electr. Ind. **5**, 11–13 (1980)
13. Pratt, W.K.: Digital Image Processing PIKS Scientific Inside, 4th edn. PixelSoft Inc., Los Altos (2017). https://doi.org/10.7551/mitpress/2946.001.0001
14. Radha, N., Tech, M.: Comparison of contrast stretching methods of image enhancement techniques for acute leukemia images. Int. J. Eng. Res. Technol. IJERT **1**(6), 1–7 (2012)
15. Rahman, S., Rahman, M., Hussain, K., Khaled, S., Shoyaib, M.: Image enhancement in spatial domain: A comprehensive study. In: 17th International Conference on Computer and Information Technology ICCIT, pp. 368–373 (2014). https://doi.org/10.1109/ICCITechn.2014.7073123
16. Rao, Y., Chen, L.: A survey of video enhancement techniques. J. Inf. Hiding Multimed. Signal Process. **3**(1), 71–99 (2012)
17. Woods, R.E., Gonzalez, R.C.: Real-time digital image enhancement. Proc. IEEE **69**(5), 643–654 (1981). https://doi.org/10.1109/PROC.1981.12031
18. Xu, L., Doermann, D.: Computer vision and image processing techniques for mobile application. Center for Automation Research, University of Maryland LAMP-TR-151 (2008)
19. Yaroslavsky, L.: Digital Holography and Digital Image Processing. Springer, New York (2004). https://doi.org/10.1007/978-1-4757-4988-5
20. Yelmanov, S., Romanyshyn, Y.: Image contrast enhancement in automatic mode by nonlinear stretching. In: Proceedings of 2018 XIV-th International Conference on Perspective Technologies and Methods in MEMS Design (MEMSTECH), pp. 104–108. IEEE (2018). https://doi.org/10.1109/MEMSTECH.2018.8365712
21. Yelmanov, S., Romanyshyn, Y.: Rapid no-reference contrast assessment for wireless based smart video applications. In: Proceedings of 2018 IEEE 4th International Symposium on Wireless Systems within the International Conferences on Intelligent Data Acquisition and Advanced Computing Systems (IDAACS-SWS), pp. 171–174. IEEE (2018). https://doi.org/10.1109/IDAACS-SWS.2018.8525682

Method of Speech Signal Structuring and Transforming for Biometric Personality Identification

Eugene Fedorov$^{(\boxtimes)}$ ⓘ, Tetyana Utkinaⓘ, Olga Nechyporenkoⓘ, and Yaroslav Korpanⓘ

Cherkasy State Technological University, Cherkasy, Ukraine
{fedorovee75,olne}@ukr.net,
t.utkina@chdtu.edu.ua,
populusdocti@gmail.co

Abstract. This paper proposes a method for structuring and transforming a speech signal. For this, segmentation method, methods for determining the fundamental tone of the vocal segment and determining on its basis the boundaries of the quasiperiodic oscillations of the vocal segment, the geometric transformation of quasiperiodic oscillations of the vocal segment were suggested. The proposed segmentation of the speech signal uses statistical estimation of short-term energies, which allows the use of an adaptive threshold, thus increasing the vocal segments determination accuracy. The proposed definition of fundamental tone of the vocal segment uses bandpass filtering and statistical estimation of local extremum, which reduces computational complexity, and also reduces noise dependency and allows the use of an adaptive threshold, thus increasing the accuracy of determining the fundamental tone and the boundaries of quasiperiodic oscillations of the vocal segment. The proposed geometric transformation of quasiperiodic oscillations of the vocal segment allows you to transform quasiperiodic oscillations to a single amplitude-time window, which allows you to form patterns of the vocal segment, taking into account its structure. A method for determining a model structure for transforming speech signal patterns is proposed, which is based on a statistical evaluation of the quality of the transforming, which provides a high degree of compression and the speech signal identification.

Keywords: Biometric identification of a person · Speech signal · Segmentation structuring · Calculating the fundamental tone · Dividing segments into quasiperiodic oscillations · Geometric transformation of quasiperiodic oscillations

1 Introduction and Literature Review

Automated biometric identification of a person implies making decisions based on acoustic and visual information, which improves the recognition quality of

© Springer Nature Switzerland AG 2020
S. Babichev et al. (Eds.): DSMP 2020, CCIS 1158, pp. 307–322, 2020.
https://doi.org/10.1007/978-3-030-61656-4_20

the studied person [4,8,13]. Unlike the traditional approach, computer-assisted biometric identification speeds up and improves the accuracy of the recognition process, which is especially crucial in a limited time conditions.

Methods based on the analysis of acoustic information form a special class of biometric identification of a person [5,12,15,17,24]. Known methods for biometric voice identification, such as

- dynamic programming [2,25];
- vector quantization [16,22];
- artificial neural networks [23,26] and decision tree [14], Gaussian mixture models (GMM) [6,9,19,21];
- combination of these methods [10],

when analyzing the signal, divide the signal into frames (sections of equal length) without taking into account its structure, which reduces the effectiveness of biometric identification. Speech signal structuring is based on the segmentation and partitioning of segments of vocal sounds into quasiperiodic oscillations based on the fundamental tone.

The following features are usually used for segmentation [20]: the number of transitions through zero, energy. Hereinbefore listed methods do not use an adaptive threshold, thus reducing the segmentation accuracy.

Methods which are used to calculate the fundamental tone are based on the analysis of the following representations of the signal [18,20]: amplitude-time, spectral (amplitude-frequency), cepstral (amplitude-random), wavelet spectral (amplitude-frequency-time). These methods have one or more of the following disadvantages: have high computational complexity; depend on the noise level, which reduces the accuracy of determining the fundamental tone; do not use an adaptive threshold, which reduces the accuracy of determining the fundamental tone.

Thereby, it is the current interest to create a method for speech signal structuring, which will eliminate these drawbacks. The following features can be used to increase the efficiency of structured signal identification: eigenvalues [1,3,7], eigenvectors [1,3,7], singular values [11], singular vectors [11]. The following techniques are usually used to extract features of a speech signal: principal component analysis (PCA) [7], independent component analysis (ICA) [1], linear discriminant analysis (LDA) [3], singular value decomposition (SVD) [11]. These methods have a high degree of information compression. The SVD method provides the highest identification probability. They have one or more of the following disadvantages: high computational complexity, not automated determination of the coding model structure, exact number of classes is required. Thereby, the creation of a speech signal structuring and transforming method, which will eliminate these drawbacks, is relevant.

Thus, the lack of effectiveness of biometric identification is an unsolved problem, caused by the lack of consideration of the signal structure, insufficient segmentation and determination of the fundamental tone, and high computational complexity of the conversion.

The aim of the work is to increase the efficiency of biometric identification of a person using preliminary speech signal structuring and transformation. To achieve this goal it is necessary to solve the following tasks:

- vocal speech signal segments determination based on short-term statistical evaluation of energies;
- fundamental tone of the vocal segment determination based on bandpass filtering and statistical estimation of local extremum;
- determination of the boundaries of quasiperiodic oscillations of the vocal segment based on the fundamental tone;
- geometric transformation of quasiperiodic oscillations of the vocal segment to a single amplitude-time window;
- the speech signal structuring quality criteria determination;
- development of a method for determining the structure of a model for transforming speech signal patterns;
- determination of the quality criterion for transforming the speech signal patterns.

2 Materials and Methods

2.1 Vocal Speech Signal Segments Determination Based on Short-Term Statistical Evaluation of Energies

This subsection describes a method for determining vocal segments of a speech signal based on statistical estimation of short-term energies, which includes the following steps:

1. Determination of the speech signal with one vocal sound $y(n)$, $n \in \overline{1, N^f}$. Set the number of quantization levels of a speech signal L (for an 8-bit sound sample $L = 256$). Specify the length of the frame N, on which the momentary energy is calculated, $N = 2^b + 1$, wherein an integer parameter b is selected from the inequality $b - 1 < \log_2 \left(\frac{f_d}{f_{\min}} \right) < b$, f_d is a speech signal sampling rate in Hz, $8000 \leq f_d \leq 22050$, $f_{\min}$ is the minimum frequency of the person's fundamental tone in Hz, $f_{\min} = 50$. Set a parameter for the adaptive threshold β, $0 < \beta < 1$.
2. Calculation of the short-term energies:

$$E(n) = \sum_{m=-N/2}^{N/2} y^2(m+n), n \in \overline{N/2+1, N^f - N/2 - 1}.$$

3. Calculation of the mathematical expectation of short-term energies:

$$\mu = \frac{1}{N^f - N - 1} \sum_{n=N/2+1}^{N^f - N/2 - 1} E(n).$$

4. Calculation of the standard deviation of short-term energies:

$$\sigma = \sqrt{\frac{1}{N^f - N - 1} \sum_{n=N/2+1}^{N^f - N/2 - 1} E^2(n) - \mu^2}.$$

5. Calculation of the adaptive threshold:

$$T = \mu - \beta\sigma.$$

6. Determination of the left and right boundaries of the vocal segment:
   (a) Set the reference number $n = 1$.
   (b) If $E(n) < T \wedge E(n+1) \geq T$, then $N^l = n + 1$ go to step (f).iv.
   (c) If $E(n) \geq T \wedge E(n+1) < T$, then $N^r = n$, complete.
   (d) If $n < N^f - N - 1$, then go to the next sample, i.e. $n = n + 1$, go to step (f).ii, otherwise $N^r = n$, complete.

As a result, the left and right boundaries of the vocal segment are determined.

2.2   Fundamental Tone of the Vocal Segment Determination Based on Bandpass Filtering and Statistical Estimation of Local Extremum

Here, we present a method for determining the fundamental tone of the vocal segment based on bandpass filtering and statistical estimation of local extremum, which includes the following steps:

1. Define a speech signal with vocal sound $y(n)$, $n \in \overline{1, N^f}$. Set filter parameter α, $0 < \alpha < 1$. Set the left and right boundaries N^l, N^r of the vocal segment in the signal $y(n)$. Set the minimum frequency of the person's fundamental tone in Hz, $f1$, $f1 = 85$. Set the maximum frequency of the person's fundamental tone in Hz, $f2$, $f2 = 255$. Set the number of frames $I = [N^f/N]$ of length N. $N = 2^b$, wherein an integer parameter b is selected from the inequality $b - 1 < \log_2\left(\frac{f_d}{f_{\min}}\right) < b$, f_d is a speech signal sampling rate in Hz, $8000 \leq f_d \leq 22050$, $f_{\min}$ is the minimum frequency of the person's fundamental tone in Hz, $f_{\min} = 50$, $[]$ is getting the integer part of the number.

2. Break the speech signal into frames

$$s_i(n) = y((i-1) * N + n + 1), n \in \overline{0, N-1}, i \in \overline{1, I}.$$

3. Balance frames spectrums, that have a steep decline in the high frequency region, using LPF

$$\check{s}_i(n) = s_i(n+1) - \alpha s_i(n), n \in \overline{0, N-1}, i \in \overline{1, I}.$$

4. Calculate suspended frames spectrums, using a direct discrete Fourier transform and the Hamming window

$$\widehat{s}_i(n) = \check{s}_i(n)\ w(n), w(n) = 0.54 + 0.46\ \cos\frac{2\pi n}{N},$$

$$n \in \overline{0, N-1}, i \in \overline{1, I},$$

$$\widehat{S}_i(k) = \sum_{n=0}^{N-1} \widehat{s}_i(n)\ e^{-j\,(2\pi/N)\,kn}, k \in \overline{0, N-1}, i \in \overline{1, I},$$

where $w(n)$ is the Hamming window.

$$\tilde{S}_i(k) = \begin{cases} \widehat{S}_i(k), & f1 * N/f_d \le k \le f2 * N/f \\ 0, & f1 * N/f_d > k \vee k > f2 * N/f \end{cases}$$

$$k \in \overline{0, N-1}, i \in \overline{1, I}$$

5. Calculate the inverse discrete Fourier transform of the filtered frames

$$\tilde{s}_i(n) = Re\left(\frac{1}{N}\sum_{n=0}^{N-1}\tilde{S}_i(k)\ e^{j\,(2\pi/N)\,kn}\right), n \in \overline{0, N-1}, i \in \overline{1, I}.$$

6. Combine the filtered frames into a speech signal

$$\tilde{y}((i-1)*N+n+1) = \tilde{s}_i(n), n \in \overline{0, N-1}, i \in \overline{1, I}.$$

7. Calculate the position of local extremum in the filtered vocal segment.
   (a) Set the reference number $n = N^l + 1$. Set the number of local extremum $Q = 0$.
   (b) If $\tilde{y}(n) > \tilde{y}(n-1) \wedge \tilde{y}(n) > \tilde{y}(n+1) \wedge \tilde{y}(n) > 0$, then fixate the position of the local extrema, i.e. $e_{Q+1} = n$, increase the number of local extremum, i.e. $Q = Q + 1$.
   (c) If $n < N^r - 1$, then go to the next sample, i.e. $n = n + 1$, go to step (g).ii.
8. Calculate the distances between local extremum in the filtered vocal segment

$$\Delta_m = e_{m+1} - e_m, m \in \overline{1, Q-1}.$$

9. Calculate the mathematical expectations of the distances

$$\mu = \frac{1}{Q-1}\sum_{m=1}^{Q-1}\Delta_m.$$

10. Calculate the standard deviation of the distances

$$\sigma = \sqrt{\frac{1}{Q-1}\sum_{m=1}^{Q-1}(\Delta_m)^2 - \mu^2}.$$

11. Exclude random outliers from the distances
    (a) Set distance number $m = 1$. Set the number of new distances $\tilde{Q} = 0$.
    (b) If $\mu - \sigma \le \Delta_m \le \mu + \sigma$, then fixate a new distance, i.e. $\tilde{\Delta}_{\tilde{Q}+1} = \Delta_m$, increase the number of new distances, i.e. $\tilde{Q} = \tilde{Q} + 1$.
    (c) If $m < Q-1$, then go to the next distance, i.e. $m = m+1$, go to step (k).ii.
12. Calculate the length of the fundamental tone as the mathematical expectation of new distances

$$N^{FT} = \frac{1}{\tilde{Q}} \sum_{m=1}^{\tilde{Q}} \tilde{\Delta}_m.$$

As a result, the length of the fundamental tone of the vocal segment is determined.

2.3 Determination of Quasiperiodic Oscillations of the Vocal Segment

The author's method for determining the boundaries of quasiperiodic oscillations of the vocal segment include the following steps:

1. Define the speech signal $y(n)$, $n \in \overline{1, N^f}$. Set the left and right boundaries of the vocal segment N^l, N^r in the signal $y(n)$. Set the length of the fundamental tone of the vocal segment N^{FT}. Set parameter γ for determining the boundaries of quasiperiodic oscillations of the vocal segment, $0 < \gamma < 1$.
2. Initialize variables for determining the boundaries of quasiperiodic oscillations of the vocal segment as

$$N_0^{max} = \arg\max_n y(n),$$

$$n \in \left\{ N^l - \gamma \cdot N_0^{FT}, \dots, N^l + \gamma \cdot N_0^{FT} \right\}, N_0^{FT} = N^{FT}.$$

3. Set the quasiperiodic vocal segment oscillations number $I = 1$.
4. Determine the boundaries of quasiperiodic oscillation of a segment of vocal speech sound in the form of

$$N_I^{min} = N_{I-1}^{max}, N_I^{max} = \arg\max_n y(n),$$

$$n \in \left\{ N_I^{min} + (1-\alpha) \cdot N_{I-1}^{FT}, \dots, N_I^{min} + (1-\alpha) \cdot N_{I-1}^{FT} \right\},$$

$$N_I^{FT} = N_I^{max} - N_I^{min}.$$

5. If $N_I^{max} \le N^r$, then increase the number of quasiperiodic oscillations, i.e. $I = I + 1$, go to step (d).

As a result, the set of boundaries of the quasiperiodic oscillations of the segment is formed.

2.4   Geometric Transformation of Quasiperiodic Oscillations of the Vocal Segment to a Single Amplitude-Time Window

Method for geometric transformation of quasiperiodic oscillations of the vocal segment to a single amplitude-time window proposed in this work consists of the following steps:

1. Define the speech signal $y(n)$, $n \in \overline{1, N^f}$. Set the number of quantization levels of a speech signal L (for an 8-bit sound sample $L = 256$). Define the set of boundaries of the quasiperiodic oscillations of the vocal segment $\left\{ \left(N_i^{\min}, N_i^{\max} \right) \right\}$. Set the length of the amplitude-time window N, $N = 2^b$, where the integer parameter b is selected from the inequality $b - 1 < \log_2 \left(\frac{f_d}{f_{\min}} \right) < b$, f_d is a speech signal sampling frequency in Hz, $8000 \leq f_d \leq 22050$, $f_{\min}$ is the minimum frequency of the person's fundamental tone in Hz, $f_{\min} = 50$.

2. Determine the minimum and maximum values of the quasiperiodic oscillations of the vocal segment as

$$A_i^{\min} = \min_n y(n), n \in \left\{ N_i^{\min}, \dots, N_i^{\max} \right\},$$

$$A_i^{\max} = \max_n y(n), n \in \left\{ N_i^{\min}, \dots, N_i^{\max} \right\}.$$

3. Determine the finite set of discrete samples shifted in time and amplitude, described as finite family of integer bounded finite discrete functions $X^s = \left\{ x_i^s | i \in \{1, \dots, I\} \right\}$, as

$$x_i^s(n) = \begin{cases} y\left(n + N_i^{\min} - 1 \right) - A_i^{\min}, & n \in \{ 1, \dots, N_i + 1 \} \\ 0, & n \notin \{ 1, \dots, N_i + 1 \} \end{cases},$$

$$N_i = N_i^{\max} - N_i^{\min}, A_i = A_i^{\max} - A_i^{\min}.$$

4. Determine a finite set of continuous samples obtained as a result of linear interpolation and described by a finite family of real-valued bounded finite continuous functions $\Psi = \left\{ \psi_i | i \in \{ 1, \dots, I \} \right\}$, in the form of

$$\forall t \in \left[\breve{T}^{\min}, \breve{T}^{\max} \right]$$

$$\psi_i(t) = \sum_{n=1}^{N_i} \chi_{(t_n, t_{n+1})}(t) \left(x_i^s(n) + \frac{x_i^s(n+1) - x_i^s(n)}{\Delta t} (t - t_n) \right)$$

$$+ \sum_{n=1}^{N_i+1} \chi_{\{t_n\}}(t) x_i^s(n),$$

$$\forall t \notin \left[\breve{T}^{\min}, \breve{T}^{\max} \right] \psi_i(t) = 0, \breve{T}^{\min} = \Delta t, \breve{T}^{\max} = 2^b \Delta t,$$

$$t_n = n \, \Delta t, \chi_B(t) = \begin{cases} 1, t \in B \\ 0, t \notin B \end{cases},$$

where Δt is the time quantization step of the speech signal, $\chi_B(t)$ is the indicator function.

5. Define a finite set of shifted and time-scaled continuous samples described by a finite family of real-valued bounded finite continuous functions $\Psi^s = \{ \psi_i^s | i \in \{ 1, \dots ,I \} \}$, in the form of

$$\forall t \in \left[\, \check{T}^{\min}, \check{T}^{\max} \right] \psi_i^s(t) = \psi_i \left(T_i \frac{t - \check{T}^{\min}}{\check{T}^{\max} - \check{T}^{\min}} \right),$$

$$\forall t \notin \left[\, \check{T}^{\min}, \check{T}^{\max} \right] \psi_i^s(t) = 0, \check{T}^{\min} = \Delta t, \check{T}^{\max} = 2^b \Delta t.$$

6. Determine the finite set of shifted and amplitude-scaled continuous samples described by a finite family of real-valued bounded finite continuous functions $\Psi^{ss} = \{ \psi_i^{ss} | i \in \{ 1, \dots ,I \} \}$, in the form of

$$\forall t \in \left[\, \check{T}^{\min}, \check{T}^{\max} \right] \psi_i^{ss}(t) = \check{A}^{\min} + \frac{\check{A}^{\max} - \check{A}^{\min}}{\tilde{A}_i^{\max} - \tilde{A}_i^{\min}} \psi_i^s(t),$$

$$\forall t \notin \left[\, \check{T}^{\min}, \check{T}^{\max} \right] \psi_i^{ss}(t) = 0,$$

$$\tilde{A}_i^{\max} = \max_t \psi_i^s(t), t \in \left[\, \check{T}^{\min}, \check{T}^{\max} \right],$$

$$\tilde{A}_i^{\min} = \min_t \psi_i^s(t), t \in \left[\, \check{T}^{\min}, \check{T}^{\max} \right], \check{A}^{\min} = 1, \check{A}^{\max} = L.$$

7. Determine a finite set of discrete samples obtained from continuous ones using time discretization and described by a finite family of integer bounded finite discrete functions $S = \{ s_i | i \in \{ 1, \dots , I \} \}$ as

$$s_i(n) = round \, (\psi_i^{ss}(n \, \Delta t)), n \in \left\{ \, \check{N}^{\min}, \dots , \check{N}^{\max} \right\},$$

$$\check{N}^{\min} = \check{T}^{\min} / \Delta t, \check{N}^{\max} = \check{T}^{\max} / \Delta t,$$

where $round \, ()$ is the function that rounds the number to the nearest integer.

As a result, the set of samples is formed, all of which are in a single amplitude-time window.

2.5   The Speech Signal Structuring Quality Criteria Determination

This subsection formulates the speech signal structuring quality criteria as selection of such parameters β and γ, that deliver a minimum of standard error

$$F = \frac{1}{2 \, I} \sum_{i=1}^{I} \left(\tilde{N}_i^{\min} - N_i^{\min} \right)^2 + \left(\tilde{N}_i^{\max} - N_i^{\max} \right)^2 \to \max_{\beta, \gamma}, \qquad (1)$$

where $\tilde{N}_i^{\min}$, $\tilde{N}_i^{\max}$ are the boundaries of quasiperiodic oscillations of the vocal segment, defined by an expert, $N_i^{\min}$, $N_i^{\max}$ are the calculated boundaries of quasiperiodic oscillations of the vocal segment.

2.6 Development of a Method for Determining the Model Structure for Transforming Speech Signal Patterns

The method for determining the model structure for transforming speech signal patterns is based on a statistical evaluation of the transformation quality.

The singular value decomposition (SVD) method has the highest identification probability, therefore, in the work the SVD transform model was selected as a model for transforming speech signal patterns, which in this paper is proposed to be defined in the following way

$$\check{s}_{\check{n}_1}(\check{n}_2) = \sum_{n_2=1}^{N_2} \left(\sum_{n_1=1}^{N_1} u_{\check{n}_1 n_1} s_{n_1}(n_2) \right) v_{n_2 \check{n}_2}, \check{n}_1 \in \overline{1, \check{N}_1}, \check{n}_2 \in \overline{1, \check{N}_2},$$

where $U = [u_{\check{n}_1 n_1}]$ is the matrix containing the principal components of the matrix $\tilde{C} = SS^T$, $V = [v_{n_2 \check{n}_2}]$ is the matrix containing the principal components of the matrix $C = S^T S$, $\check{N}_1$ is the number of principal components of the matrix $\tilde{C} = SS^T$, $\check{N}_2$ is the number of principal components of the matrix $C = S^T S$.

Determining the structure of the model for speech signal patterns transformation reduces to determining the number of principal components, which is not automated and is performed by the operator based on his empirical experience. Therefore, in the work, to determine the number of principal components, a method is proposed based on statistical evaluation of the transformation quality, which includes the following steps:

1. Define the set of speech patterns $\{s_{n_1}(n_2)\}$, $n_1 \in \overline{1, N_1}, n_2 \in \overline{1, N_2}$. Set the minimum acceptable probability of personal identification by voice $P^{\min}$. Define the initial fraction of the explained variance α_0, which controls the number of principal components. Set the increment step of the fraction of the explained variance δ.

2. Calculate the matrix

$$\tilde{C} = [\tilde{c}_{lm}], \tilde{c}_{lm} = \sum_{n_2=1}^{N_2} s_l(n_2) s_m(n_2), l, m \in \overline{1, N_1}.$$

3. Find the set of eigenvalues $\left\{ \tilde{\lambda}_{n_1} \right\}$ and the set of eigenvectors $\{\tilde{e}_{n_1}\}$ of the matrix $\tilde{C}$.

4. Sort the set of eigenvalues $\left\{ \tilde{\lambda}_{n_1} \right\}$ and the set of eigenvectors $\{\tilde{e}_{n_1}\}$ in descending order of eigenvalues, i.e. $\tilde{\lambda}_{n_1} > \tilde{\lambda}_{n_1+1}$.

5. Calculate the matrix

$$C = [c_{lm}], c_{lm} = \sum_{n_1=1}^{N_1} s_{n_1}(l) s_{n_1}(m), l, m \in \overline{1, N_2}.$$

6. Find the set of eigenvalues $\left\{ \tilde{\lambda}_{n_2} \right\}$ and the set of eigenvectors $\{\tilde{e}_{n_2}\}$ of the matrix C.

7. Sort the set of eigenvalues $\left\{\tilde{\lambda}_{n_2}\right\}$ and the set of eigenvectors $\left\{\tilde{e}_{n_2}\right\}$ in descending order of eigenvalues, i.e. $\lambda_{n_2} > \lambda_{n_2+1}$.
8. Set the fraction of the explained variance $\alpha = \alpha_0$.
9. Determine the number of principal components based on the explained and sample variance

$$\check{N}_1 = \arg\min_m \left(\sum_{n_1=1}^m \tilde{\lambda}_{n_1} - \alpha \sum_{n_1=1}^{N_1} \tilde{\lambda}_{n_1} \right), m \in \overline{1, N_1 - 1},$$

$$\check{N}_2 = \arg\min_m \left(\sum_{n_2=1}^m \lambda_{n_2} - \alpha \sum_{n_2=1}^{N_2} \lambda_{n_2} \right), m \in \overline{1, N_2 - 1}.$$

10. From the subset of eigenvectors $\left\{\tilde{e}_1, ..., \tilde{e}_{\check{N}_1}\right\}$ form a matrix containing the principal components of the matrix $\tilde{C}$

$$U = [u_{\check{n}_1 n_1}], u_{\check{n}_1 n_1} = \frac{\tilde{e}_{\check{n}_1 n_1}}{\|\tilde{e}_{\check{n}_1}\|}, \check{n}_1 \in \overline{1, \check{N}_1}, n_1 \in \overline{1, N_1}.$$

11. From the subset of eigenvectors form a matrix, containing the principal components of the matrix C

$$V = [v_{n_2 \check{n}_2}], v_{n_2 \check{n}_2} = \frac{e_{n_2 \check{n}_2}}{\|e_{n_2}\|}, n_2 \in \overline{1, N_2}, \check{n}_2 \in \overline{1, \check{N}_2}.$$

12. Perform SVD speech patterns transformation

$$\check{s}_{\check{n}_1}(\check{n}_2) = \sum_{n_2=1}^{N_2} \left(\sum_{n_1=1}^{N_1} u_{\check{n}_1 n_1} s_{n_1}(n_2) \right) v_{n_2 \check{n}_2}, \check{n}_1 \in \overline{1, \check{N}_1}, \check{n}_2 \in \overline{1, \check{N}_2}.$$

13. Calculate the voice recognition probability based on a Gaussian mixture model (GMM)

$$P = \frac{1}{\check{N}_1} \sum_{i=1}^{\check{N}_1} \chi_{\{0\}} \left(\arg\max_z \ln P_{\check{n}_1 z}(\check{s}_{\check{n}_1}) - d \right), z \in \overline{1, Z},$$

$$\chi_{\{0\}}(x) = \begin{cases} 1, x = 0 \\ 0, x \neq 0 \end{cases},$$

where d is the identifier of a particular person represented by a speech signal, Z is the number of persons, $\ln P_{\check{n}_1 z}(\check{s}_{\check{n}_1})$ is the GMM calculated logarithm of the probability of occurrence of the $n_1{}^{th}$ pattern of the speech signal of the zth person,
$$\check{s}_{\check{n}_1} = \left(\check{s}_{\check{n}_1}(1), ..., \check{s}_{\check{n}_1}(\check{N}_2) \right).$$

14. If $P^{\min} > P \wedge \alpha < 1$, then increase the fraction of the explained variance, i.e. $\alpha = \alpha + \delta$, go to step (i).

As a result, the number of principal components is determined.

2.7   Determination of Characteristics and Quality Criteria of Methods for Transforming Speech Signal Patterns

To evaluate the quality of speech patterns transformation methods, the following characteristics are proposed:

The probability of person identification by voice

$$P = \frac{1}{\check{N}_1} \sum_{i=1}^{\check{N}_1} \chi_{\{0\}} \left(\arg\max_z \ln P_{\check{n}_1 z} \left(\check{s}_{\check{n}_1} \right) - d \right), z \in \overline{1, Z},$$

$$\chi_{\{0\}} (x) = \begin{cases} 1, x = 0 \\ 0, x \neq 0 \end{cases},$$

where d is the identifier of a particular person represented by a speech signal, Z is the number of persons, $\ln P_{\check{n}_1 z} (\check{s}_{\check{n}_1})$ is the GMM calculated logarithm of the probability of occurrence of the $n_1{}^{th}$ pattern of the speech signal of the zth person, $\check{s}_{\check{n}_1} = \left(\check{s}_{\check{n}_1} (1), ..., \check{s}_{\check{n}_1} \left(\check{N}_2 \right) \right)$.

Compression ratio of speech signal patterns

$$C = \frac{N_1 \times N_2}{\check{N}_1 \times \check{N}_2},$$

where N_1 is the number of patterns, N_2 is the pattern length, $\check{N}_1$ is the number of patterns after transformation (for PCA and ICA $\check{N}_1 = N_1$), $\check{N}_2$ is the pattern length after transformation. The computational complexity of determining GMM parameters is inversely proportional to the compression ratio.

The following criterion of the quality of the speech signal patterns transformation is formulated in the work, which means the choice of such a fraction of the explained variance α, which controls the number of principal components and delivers a minimum to the sum of the probability of an erroneous identification of a person by voice and value inversed to the compression ratio

$$F = (1 - P) + \frac{1}{C} \underset{\alpha}{\to} \min. \tag{2}$$

3   Experiment

For speech signals containing vocal sounds, the sampling frequency is established at $f_d = 8$ kHz and the number of quantization levels is $L = 256$. Frame length is $N = 256$. For the speech signal structuring method, the parameters $\beta = 0.4, \gamma = 0.1$ were used. Human speech signals were selected from the TIMIT database.

Figures 1, 2, 3 and 4 shows an example of structuring the initial speech signal (Figure 1) with segmentation of the speech signal based on statistical estimation of short-term energies based on mathematical expectation and standard deviation (Fig. 2); determination of the boundaries of quasiperiodic vibrations of the vocal segment based on the fundamental tone of the vocal segment, which was calculated by bandpass filtering based on the discrete Fourier transform and statistical estimation of local extrema based on mathematical expectation and standard deviation (Fig. 3); geometric transformation of quasiperiodic vibrations of the vocal segment to a single amplitude-time window based on linear interpolation, shift and scaling in time and amplitude, and discretization in time (Fig. 4).

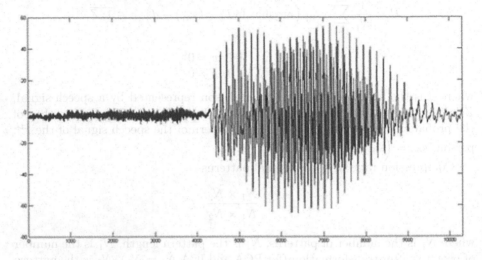

Fig. 1. The initial speech signal (8-bit, 22050 Hz, length 10304)

4   Results and Discussion

The speech signal segmentation (Fig. 2) shows that the automatically determined boundaries of the segment (highlighted by vertical lines) correspond to the natural boundaries of the segment of vocal sound. The determination of the boundaries of quasiperiodic oscillations of the vocal segment (Fig. 3) shows that the automatically determined boundaries of quasiperiodic oscillations (highlighted by vertical lines) correspond to the natural boundaries of quasiperiodic oscillations. The geometric transformation of the quasiperiodic vibrations of the vocal segment (Fig. 4) shows that all quasiperiodic vibrations (highlighted by vertical lines) are in the amplitude-time window of the same size.

As a result of a numerical study of the speech signal structuring method according to criterion (1), the mean squared error of 0.02 was obtained. Thus, the selected parameter values $\beta = 0.4$, $\gamma = 0.1$ provide high accuracy of structuring the speech signal.

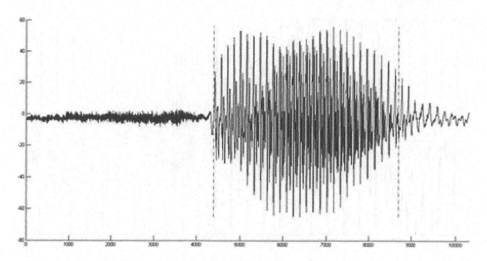

Fig. 2. Speech signal after segmentation, which distinguishes the boundaries of the vocal segment (parameter β = 0.4)

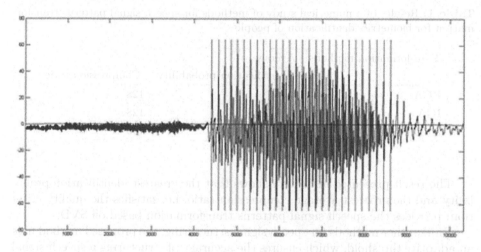

Fig. 3. The speech signal after marking the boundaries of the sound oscillations of the vocal segment (parameter γ = 0.1)

The results of a numerical study of the transformation methods used for biometric identification of people from the TIMIT database by speech signals using GMM are presented in Table 1. In this case, the method proposed by the authors was used to determine the structure of the transformation model. For speech signal patterns transformation methods, the fraction of explained variance α = 0.97.

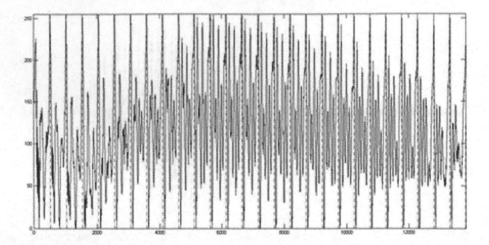

Fig. 4. Vocal sound after geometric transformations of sound oscillations to a single amplitude-time window

Table 1. Results of a numerical study of methods for speech signal patterns transformation for biometric identification of people

Transformation methods	Average	
	Identification probability	Compression ratio
PCA	0.96	128
ICA	0.95	128
SVD	0.98	128

The result presented in Table 1 shows that the greatest identification probability and the greatest average compression ratio, i.e. satisfies the quality criterion, provides the speech signal patterns transformation based on SVD.

Unlike other methods for speech signal structuring, the proposed method uses an adaptive threshold, which ensures the accuracy of structuring a speech signal of 0.02 and converts quasiperiodic vibrations to a single amplitude-time window, which makes it possible to form vocal segment patterns taking into account its structure, which ensures the probability of identifying a speech signal of 0.98 (Table 1).

Unlike other methods for determining the model structure for transforming speech patterns, the proposed method uses the SVD method in combination with the proposed quality criterion, which provides a compression ratio of 128 (Table 1).

5   Conclusions

In this paper, the problem of improving the quality of biometric identification by voice was solved. For its solution were proposed:

- a speech signal structuring method, which includes determining the vocal segments of a speech signal based on statistical estimation of short-term energies;
- determination of the fundamental tone of the vocal segment based on bandpass filtering and statistical estimation of local extremum;
- geometric transformation of sound vibrations of the vocal segment;
- a method for determining the model structure for transforming speech signal patterns, which is based on a statistical assessment of the quality of the transformation.

The use of an adaptive threshold in the speech signal structuring method ensures the accuracy of speech signal structuring of 0.02. The conversion of quasiperiodic oscillations to a single amplitude-time window in the speech signal structuring method allows to generate patterns of the vocal segment taking into account its structure, which ensures the probability of the speech signal identification of 0.98. Using the SVD method in combination with the proposed quality criterion in the method for determining the model structure for transforming speech patterns provides a compression ratio of 128.

Thus, the proposed methods provide high accuracy of speech signal structuring, a high probability of speech signal identification, a high degree of the speech signal compression, which increases the efficiency of biometric identification of a person by voice.

The advantage of the proposed approach is its adaptability to the structure of the speech signal. The proposed methods allow posing and solving the problems of preliminary processing of a speech signal, which is used for analysis and storage of biometric information.

References

1. Bartlett, M., Movellan, J., Sejnowski, T.: Face recognition by independent component analysis. IEEE Trans. Neural Netw. **13**(6), 1450–1464 (2002). https://doi.org/10.1109/TNN.2002.804287
2. Beigi, H.: Fundamentals of Speaker Recognition. Springer, New York (2011). https://doi.org/10.1007/978-0-387-77592-0
3. Belhumeur, P., Hespanha, J., Kriegman, D.: Eigenfaces vs fisherfaces: recognition using class specific linear projection. IEEE Trans. Pattern Anal. Mach. Intell. **19**, 711–720 (1997). https://doi.org/10.1109/34.598228
4. Bolle, R., Connell, J., Pankanti, S., Ratha, N., Senior, A.: Guide to Biometrics. Springer, New York (2004). https://doi.org/10.1007/978-1-4757-4036-3
5. Campbell, J.: Speaker recognition: a tutorial. IEEE **85**, 1437–1462 (1997). https://doi.org/10.1109/5.628714
6. Chauhan, V., Dwivedi, S., Karale, P., Potdar, S.: Speech to text converter using gaussian mixture model (gmm). Int. Res. J. Eng. Technol. (IRJET) **3**, 160–164 (2016)
7. Draper, B., Baek, K., Bartlett, M., Beveridge, J.: Recognizing faces with PCA and ICA. Comput. Vis. Image Understand. (Special Issue Face Recognit.) **91**(1–2), 115–137 (2003). https://doi.org/10.1016/S1077-3142(03)00077-8

8. Dunstone, T., Yager, N.: Biometric System and Data Analysis Design, Evaluation, and Data Mining. Springer, New York (2009). https://doi.org/10.1007/978-0-387-77627-9

9. Fedorov, E., Lukashenko, V., Utkina, T., Lukashenko, A., Rudakov, K.: Method for parametric identification of gaussian mixture model based on clonal selection algorithm. In: CEUR Workshop Proceedings, vol. 2353, pp. 41–55 (2019). https://doi.org/10.15588/1607-3274-2019-2-10

10. Larin, V.J., Fedorov, E.E.: Combination of PNN network and DTW method for identification of reserved words, used in aviation during radio negotiation. Radioelectron. Commun. Syst. **57**(8), 362–368 (2014). https://doi.org/10.3103/S0735272714080044

11. He, J., Zhang, D.: Face recognition using uniform eigen-space svd on enhanced image for single training sample. J. Comput. Inf. Syst. **7**(5), 1655–1662 (2011)

12. Herbig, T., Gerl, F., Minker, W.: Self-Learning Speaker Identification a System for Enhanced Speech Recognition. Springer, Heidelberg (2011). https://doi.org/10.1007/978-3-642-19899-1

13. Jain, A., Flynn, P., Ross, A.: Handbook of Biometrics. Springer, New York (2008). https://doi.org/10.1007/978-0-387-71041-9

14. Jeyalakshmi, C., Krishnamurthi, V., Revathi, A.: Speech recognition of deaf and hard of hearing people using hybrid neural network. In: Mechanical and Electronic Engineering (ICMEE 2010), vol. 1, pp. 83–87. (2010). https://doi.org/10.1109/ICMEE.2010.5558589

15. Keshet, J., Bengio, S.: Automatic Speech and Speaker Recognition: Large Margin and Kernel Methods. John Wiley, Chichester, West Sussex (2009)

16. Kinnunen, T., Li, H.: An overview of text-independent speaker recognition: from features to supervectors. Elsevier Speech Commun. **52**, 12–40 (2010). https://doi.org/10.1016/j.specom.2009.08.009

17. Li, Q.: Speaker Authentication. Springer, Heidelberg (2012). https://doi.org/10.1007/978-3-642-23731-7

18. Markel, J., Gray, A.: Linear Prediction of Speech. Springer, Berlin (1976). https://doi.org/10.1007/978-3-642-66286-7

19. Nayana, P., Mathew, D., Thomas, A.: Comparison of text independent speaker identification systems using gmm and i-vector methods. Proc. Comput. Sci. **115**, 47–54 (2017). https://doi.org/10.1016/j.procs.2017.09.075

20. Rabiner, L., Jang, B.: Fundamentals of Speech Recognition. Prentice Hall PTR, Englewood Cliffs (1993)

21. Reynolds, D.: Automatic speaker recognition using gaussian mixture speaker models. IEEE Trans. Speech Audio Process. **3**, 1738–1752 (1995)

22. Reynolds, D.: An overview of automatic speaker recognition technology. In: IEEE International Conference on Acoustics, Speech, and Signal Processing (ICASSP), vol. 4, pp. 4072–4075 (2002)

23. Reynolds, D., Rose, R.: Robust text-independent speaker identification using gaussian mixture speaker models. IEEE Trans. Speech Audio Process. **3**, 72–83 (1995)

24. Singh, N., Khan, R., Shree, R.: Applications of speaker recognition. Proc. Eng. **38**, 3122–3126 (2012). https://doi.org/10.1016/j.proeng.2012.06.363

25. Togneri, R., Pullela, D.: An overview of speaker identification: accuracy and robustness issues. IEEE Circ. Syst. Mag. **11**, 23–61 (2011). https://doi.org/10.1109/MCAS.2011.941079

26. Zeng, F.Z., Zhou, H.: Speaker recognition based on a novel hybrid algorithm. Proc. Eng. **61**, 220–226 (2013). https://doi.org/10.1016/j.proeng.2013.08.007

Method of Improving Instance Segmentation for Very High Resolution Remote Sensing Imagery Using Deep Learning

Volodymyr Hnatushenko[1]([✉]) [iD] and Vadym Zhernovyi[2] [iD]

[1] Dnipro University of Technology, Dnipro, Ukraine
vvgnat@ukr.net
[2] Oles Honchar Dnipro National University, Dnipro, Ukraine
vadym.zhernovyi@gmail.com

Abstract. In current work a complex solution for very high resolution remote sensing data processing is suggested. The approach is based on modern deep learning techniques such as fully convolutional neural networks and solves multiple significant remote sensing problems such as detection and instance segmenetation of manmade land objects on very high resolution hyperspectral map scenes and taking an advantage of non-visible bandwidths. The solution consists of three parts: dataset development, neural network development, neural network fine-tuning. The first part of the solution suggests a semi-automated method of rapid dataset development using modern tools and keeping the advantages of remote sensing imagery such as very high resolution and using the variety of hyperspectral imagery bandwidths, both - visual and thermal. In order to prove application of a dataset, current article suggests an approach to the problem of remote sensing imagery segmentation using deep fully convolutional neural networks. The best deep learning architectures for instance segmentation are considered and investigated, and the binary classifier for a dataset is built based on Mask RCNN. The final neural network architecture with the new classifier is fine-tuned using alternative configurations and optimizers, and altered to benefit more from the developed hyperspectral remote sensing dataset.

Keywords: Remote sensing · Instance segmentation · Neural network fine-tuning · Adam optimizer · Dice coefficient

1 Introduction

Problem Statement. Remote sensing data processing is the process of performing operations on aerial images, which includes their correction, transformation and improvement, decoding, visualization, etc. The main stages of processing of data of space pictures: preliminary and thematic processing. Pre-processing is the correction and improvement of satellite images. However, some

© Springer Nature Switzerland AG 2020
S. Babichev et al. (Eds.): DSMP 2020, CCIS 1158, pp. 323–333, 2020.
https://doi.org/10.1007/978-3-030-61656-4_21

methods of image enhancement (filtering, changing the contrast) cause a change in the spectral characteristics of the image, so after their application can not use thematic processing methods based on the analysis of spectral brightness of pixels (classifications, arithmetic channel transformations, etc.).

Currently, in the conditions high growth and rapid development of digital technologies, there is a need for quality and timely processing of huge amounts of data. In particular, this includes the need for a compact representation of images. This problem is especially actual in remote sensing imagery of the Earth during transmission and storage of the received objective information about environment. Terabytes of such imagery is transferred to the Earth and needed to be processed as fast as possible.

Remote sensing technology is based on the observation of the Earth's surface from aboard a satellite vehicle, obtaining images of certain geographical areas and objects, and their subsequent analysis and interpretation are opportunities to solve the thematic problem. Few of such thematic problems are surveillance, land object measurements, microplastic detection in the world ocean, etc.

Today there are many algorithms for image processing and image compression. Processing parameters directly depend on the scope of this information.

A promising direction in the development of these algorithms is a set of approaches which are based on artificial neural networks.

2   Latest Research Papers and Article Review

Currently a large number of processing methods and algorithms multispectral aerospace images are developed [23,25], which can be divided into two major groups: classic algorithms for which the classifier and classification algorithm are rigidly formulated, and flexible algorithms that adapt to changing conditions of observation of search objects. Algorithms of the first group have a very narrow application, primarily due to the difficulty of correctly adjusting the classifier for each available type of multispectral data [4,17]. To overcome these problems flexible algorithms are used, among which recently more and more application acquire neural networks [10,15,19].

With the advent of modern electronics, the first attempts at hardware reproduction of the human thinking process began. The first step was taken in 1943 with the publication of an article by neurophysiologist Warren McCulloch and mathematician Walter Pitts on the work of artificial neurons and the representation of a neural network model in electrical circuits [22]. In parallel with advances in neuroanatomy and neurophysiology, psychologists have created models of human learning. In the 1950s and 1960s, a group of researchers combined these biological and psychophysiological approaches to create the first artificial neural networks under the direction of Nathaniel Rochester [24].

The first successes caused an explosion of activity and optimism. Minsky, Rosenblatt, Vidrow, and other scientists developed networks consisting of a single layer of artificial neurons called perceptrons. These networks have been used to solve a wide range of problems: weather forecasting, electrocardiogram analysis, and artificial vision. For a while, it seemed that the key to intelligence had been found, and the reproduction of the human brain was only a matter of constructing a fairly large network. But this illusion soon dissipated. Networks could not solve all the problems that can be solved by humans. From these failures began a period of intensive analysis.

Between the 1980s, interest in artificial neural networks grew rapidly. Specialists from such distant fields as technical design, philosophy, physiology and psychology were intrigued by the possibilities offered by this technology and actively sought its application within their disciplines. In 2007, Jeffrey Hinton of the University of Toronto developed algorithms for deep learning of multilayer neural networks [12]. This marked the beginning of the active use of artificial neural networks in various fields of human activity and gave impetus to the development of artificial intelligence technology.

Lately many deep learning solutions based on artificial neural networks are applied to solve pattern recognition tasks on modern satellite remote sensing data. The most success is achieved with the use of convolutional neural networks (CNN) and fully convolutional neural networks [16,26].

The purpose of current article is to develop an approach for pattern recognition and measurements in commercial remote sensing data using convolutional neural networks and techniques and frameworks for working with very high resolution data.

3 Materials and Methods

Artificial Neural Networks. Selection of neural networks, specifically convolutional neural networks (CNN) (see Fig. 1) to solve the problem of recognition is associated with the ability of these networks, in conditions of correct training approach, to detect objects in difficult conditions of observation and at deformation of the observed object which happens often with very high resolution multispectral data.

With the advent of large amounts of data and large computations opportunities neural networks have become actively used. Convolutional neural networks are especially popular. Architecture was proposed by Jan LeCun [20] and aimed for an effective image recognition. The network architecture got its name from the presence of a convolution operation (1), the essence of which is that each fragment of the image is multiplied by convolution matrix (core) element by element, and the result is summed and recorded in a similar position of the original image. A prior knowledge of the computer vision subject area is laid in a network architecture: an image pixel is strongly related to the neighboring pixels (local correlation) and the object in the image can be found in any part of the image [7].

$$g(x,y) = \omega * f(x,y) = \sum_{dx=-a}^{a} \sum_{dx=-b}^{b} \omega(dx,dy)f(x+dx,y+dy) \tag{1}$$

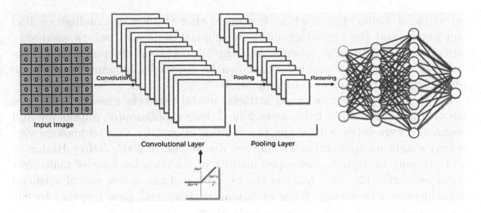

Fig. 1. Convolution neural network

The convolutional neural networks received special attention after the ImageNet competition, which took place in October 2012 and was devoted to the classification of objects in photographs. The competition required pattern recognition in 1000 categories. The winner of this competition - Alex Krizhevsky, using a convolutional neural network, significantly outperformed other participants [18]. The success of the application of convolutional neural networks to the classification of images has led to many attempts to use this method for other missions.

A convolutional neural network is usually an alternation of convolution layers, subsampling layers, and fully-connected layers at the output. All three types of layers can alternate in any order [20].

Data Annotation and the Problem of Small Data. In this paper, data annotation is considered and used as one of the main tools for development of pre-processing methods in the context of deep learning tasks for pattern recognition targeting remote sensing data.

There are many tools for annotating graphical three-channel data (RGB images). One of the most common such tools is VIA - VGG Image Annotator [8]. This annotator is used in particular to prepare datasets for State-of-the-Art (SotA) models of neural networks for image segmentation.

The main drawback of all such annotators is the specification on monochrome images or on three-channel RGB images. Using such tools, it is impossible to benefit from non-visible bands and biogeophysical information, which is often provided accompanied by remote sensing data in the form of metadata files. It was found that today, one of the best ways to avoid these shortcomings is to use modern versions of GIS products that provide the ability to adapt remote sensing data to work on in-depth learning tasks. One such GIS is Arcmap from the ESRI Arcgis product package. In recent years, ESRI has been developing plug-ins for in-depth learning at various stages [1], for the preparation and annotation of data including. Arcmap provides tools for data annotation and, most importantly, implements the export interfaces of these annotations in a form that is suitable for direct use with modern frameworks for deep learning, such as Keras, PyTorch, etc. [2]. These frameworks are often the core for the vast majority of modern deep learning network architects.

Often, in order to provide recognition results comparable to the human eye, deep learning as a method requires huge data sets. Data collection and annotation is a time consuming process.

In remote sensing, the data collection process is almost always automatic, thanks to mobile aircraft and artificial satellites of the Earth. The collection process is often referred to as data registration. This process is physically affected by the laws of optics. As a result, raw data from aircraft are not always correct in terms of representing the relevant ground objects on the surfaces. Such data is still subject to the process of stitching and some other transformations (such as orthonormalization, etc) due to specific tasks.

Despite the fact that deep training demonstrates impressive results in the field of remote sensing digital data processing, development of a universal image recognition system is almost impossible due to the variety of satellite imagery registration methods and, of course, the diversity of land cover, namely buildings, seas, forests, etc. Furthermore, it can be concluded that a significant amount of success in constructing a neural pattern recognition model depends on the size of the data set for deep learning. The current work uses tools and methods that are applicable even to small data sets. Most of them are also successfully used for large datasets.

4   Experiment

One of the most actual problems of processing remote sensing data using deep learning solutions is taking an advantage of satellite imagery multi spectrality and very high resolution of images. Virtually all state-of-the-art (SotA) solutions, like ResNet or DeepLabV3, are designed and tested to work with usual RGB images from mobile devices and cameras which often are of lower resolution in comparison to remote sensing imagery. In current work, this problem is approached in multiple steps:

- dataset development;
- neural network development;
- neural network fine-tuning.

Dataset Development. Initial imagery for a dataset development is a very high resolution (VHR) capture of Donetsk region (Ukraine) from a WorldView-3 commercial satellite engine. WorldView-3 is a commercial satellite designed for Earth observation. At launch, WorldView-3 had the highest spatial resolution of all commercial remote sensing satellites: up to 31 cm in the panchromatic range, 1.24 m in the multispectral range, and 3.7 m in the mid-infrared range.

The scene was captured in two modes: panchromatic and multispectral. The panchromatic image is a grayscale image of the highest resolution possible. And, a multispectral image is an image which contains multiple bands of different waves length including visible and not visible (thermal).

In order to increase an amount of initial data for a dataset development, both panchromatic and multispectral images was fused so the resulting image contained all bandwidths of a multispectral image and a resolution of a panchromatic image. This approach is called pansharpening which involves upscaling of a multispectral to a scale of a panchromatic one using interpolation with a smoothing filter [13]. Later, the resulting image is referenced as a pansharpened image.

In previous work [14], images are tiled using GDAL software library and then smaller images are annotated. In current work, more effective tool is discovered. Using the latest versions of ArcMap from ArcGIS software package it is possible to annotate the whole scene by adding an additional layer/band which represents annotations. In current work annotations are represented by polygons which described a shape of land objects. Also, ArcMap suggests tools for exporting the annotations in different formats suitable for neural network training using the most of modern deep learning frameworks such as Tensorflow or PyTorch. Before exporting, polygons must be converted in raster form. This is accomplished by ArcMap Python API so the resulting polygons are described by an array of numbers which represent a pixel coordinates of points which describe polygons.

In order to take an advantage of not visible bands of a multispectral image, the dataset is augmented with band combination described in [14].

Neural Network Development. In current work, the problem of constructing a neural network is approached from the perspective of instance segmentation since classified objects are often located close to each other and must be distinguished. Currently, the best deep learning solutions for instance segmentation remain still Mask R-CNN [3,9]. UNet is often compared with Mask R-CNN in research papers [5]. In current work a neural network is built based on Mask R-CNN neural network architecture implemented in Keras [6].

In the original solution, Mask R-CNN is designed and trained on MS COCO (Common Objects in Context) dataset [21] to recognize 80 classes of manmade objects. In current work, a binary classifier was developed to recognize a single class - buildings. The new classifier for our dataset replaces head layers of Mask R-CNN to suit a task of detection and recognition of land objects on WorldView-3 remote sensing imagery.

Mask R-CNN configuration is also changed for this task. Since the scene contained a lot of small building objects of similar size and shape, the task was considered similar to a task of nuclei detection [11]. The configuration for nuclei detection was used with a little of adjustments. Minimum detection confidence was changed from 0.5 to 0 since we have the only one class to detect. Backbone network was changed from ResNet50 to ResNet101. ResNet50 demostrated worse resutls in comparison to ResNet101 in all experiments. A number of training and validation steps were adjusted for our dataset.

For measuring a performance of Mask R-CNN, MS COCO metrics are used and are not suitable for our dataset since it is implemented in a different way.

In current work, multiple metrics are implemented and used to measure and demonstrate a performance of the neural network on our dataset:

- accuracy;
- precision;
- recall;
- Dice coefficient (F1-score).

Accuracy and precision demonstrate how accurate masks which are generated for true positive detections and are based on Intersection-over-Union (metric) calculated for a mask generated by the neural network and an annotated mask. As true positive detections considered all mask with IoU more than 0.5. Recall is calculated to demonstrate a completeness of detection and represents how much annotated building are found in annotated data. Dice coefficient (2) is a complex metric which considers both precision and recall and often used in research made for remote sensing data [5].

$$DSC = \frac{2TP}{2TP + FP + FN} \tag{2}$$

Initial training was performed on Google Colaboratory virtual machine with 12GB GPU. 80:20 split is used for training and validation data respectively. The network is trained for 40 epochs: first 20 epochs only our classifier is trained and then 20 epochs all layers are trained for better generalization. For initial weights, MS COCO weights are often used and demonstrate good results for training on RGB images. Since in current work not only RGB images are used, weights are initialized randomly. The basic augmentation were used which involved Gaussian blur, random horizontal and vertical flipping, affine transformations (less than 15o). Results are demonstrated in Table 1.

Table 1. Initial training results

Metric	Value
Accuracy	0.927615746303340
Precision	0.927615746303340
Recall	0.773446754846146
F1-score	0.8435443037974676

Neural Network Fine-Tuning. Additional research was done to discover ways to improve detection results with the same amount of data. The goal of fine-tuning was to improve recall rate to a level of accuracy and precision. Multiple changes were considered to the original Mask R-CNN architecture:

- Stronger weight decay;
- Resnet50 backbone;

- Adam optimizer;
- Intensive classifier training;
- More complex augmentation;
- Increase maximum image dimension.

Stronger weight decay was investigated and implemented in Mask R-CNN but didn't show any different to detection results.

ResNet50 were claimed to work better on smaller datasets but in all experiments ResNet101 performed better than ResNet50.

In original Mask R-CNN implementation SGD optimized is used. We replaced SGD optimizer with Adam and obtained better results with it. The configuration from previous training was not changed. Results are in Table 2.

Intensive classifier training stood for more epochs for training a classifier layers than for the other layers. More complex augmentation and increased maximum image dimension were purposed for artificial increase of a size of the dataset. The last 3 approaches are not covered by current research since they were not tested enough to make a conclusion on them if training of the neural network benefits from it.

Table 2. Results with Adam optimizer

Metric	With SGD	With Adam
Accuracy	0.890909090909090	0.8326539677398763
Precision	0.927615746303340	0.8612048477479264
Recall	0.773446754846146	0.9653233726573571
F1-score	0.8435443037974676	0.9102965493655825

5   Results and Discussion

In current work a complex problem of land cover objects detection was approached with multiple methods using deep learning.

The specific dataset was developed from one whole scene remote sensing imagery of Donetsk region in order to benefit from remote sensing data very high image resolution and hyperspectral image bandwidths. The dataset is mainly purposed for training the neural network using modern deep learning frameworks.

The neural network classifier was built for use with Mask RCNN. This modification of Mask RCNN was trained and then fine-tuned for the dataset developed in current work.

Fine-tuning was planned and based on the best fine-tuning techniques ever used for research in different areas - not only remote sensing, but medicine, robotics, etc.

The vast majority of fine-tuned training results were very close to the original results which are not statistically significant. However, changing an optimizer from SGD to Adam provided significantly different results. Although, the accuracy and precision were decreased by 6%, this loss is barely noticable looking at actual generated masks. Furthermore, the recall rate was increased by hefty 19% which is huge difference in comparison to the initial results and any results using fine-tuning techniques. The recall rate of total 96.5% demonstrates an ability to spot almost every annotated building in a validation dataset. In order to understand if such improvement in the recall rate costs the mentioned loss in accuracy and precision, the dice coefficient is calculated which considers both precision and recall and it still shows a 7% increase. Such increase in Dice coefficient is considered as an overall improvement of the neural network performance.

6 Conclusions

Deep learning still remains the most promising approach in computer vision research and remote sensing imagery processing in particular. Due to unpredictability and technical complexity, both development of new datasets and neural networks architecture development and alteration contribute in research of remote sensing data processing. Current work demonstrates minor but yet significant improvement that can be made for improving land cover object detection. Suggested techniques and approaches can be successfully applied for different satellite imagery, datasets, neural network architecture, or even in different are of research. The latter is proven by applying fine-tuning techniques that were discovered in research done for Healthcare.

Due to mentioned above, the focus of future work is to perform more research on fine-tuning techniques which were not covered in current research, determine the best configuration for training the neural network, adjust these techniques to one of the main Mask R-CNN competitors - UNet.

References

1. Deep learning in ArcGIS Pro–ArcGIS Pro | Documentation. https://pro.arcgis.com/en/pro-app/help/analysis/image-analyst/deep-learning-in-arcgis-pro.htm
2. Export Training Data For Deep Learning (Spatial Analyst)–ArcGIS Pro | Documentation. https://pro.arcgis.com/en/pro-app/tool-reference/spatial-analyst/export-training-data-for-deep-learning.htm
3. Papers with Code - Instance Segmentation. https://paperswithcode.com/task/instance-segmentation
4. The use of geometrical methods in multispectral image processing. https://doi.org/10.1615/JAutomatInfScien.v35.i12.10
5. Satellite Images Segmentation and Sustainable Farming, July 2018. https://devblogs.microsoft.com/cse/2018/07/05/satellite-images-segmentation-sustainable-farming/
6. Abdulla, W.: Mask R-CNN for object detection and instance segmentation on keras and tensorflow (2017). https://github.com/matterport/Mask_RCNN

7. Chen, L., Papandreou, G., Kokkinos, I., Murphy, K., Yuille, A.L.: Deeplab: semantic image segmentation with deep convolutional nets, atrous convolution, and fully connected crfs. IEEE Trans. Pattern Anal. Mach. Intell. **40**(4), 834–848 (2018). https://doi.org/10.1109/TPAMI.2017.2699184
8. Dutta, A., Zisserman, A.: The VIA annotation software for images, audio and video. In: Proceedings of the 27th ACM International Conference on Multimedia, pp. 2276–2279. ACM, Nice France, October 2019. https://dl.acm.org/doi/10.1145/3343031.3350535
9. He, K., Gkioxari, G., Dollár, P., Girshick, R.: Mask R-CNN (2017)
10. Heermann, P.D., Khazenie, N.: Classification of multispectral remote sensing data using a back-propagation neural network. IEEE Trans. Geosci. Remote Sensing **30**(1), 81–88 (1992). https://doi.org/10.1109/36.124218
11. Höfener, H., Homeyer, A., Weiss, N., Molin, J., Lundström, C.F., Hahn, H.K.: Deep learning nuclei detection: a simple approach can deliver state-of-the-art results. Comput. Med. Imaging Graph. **70**, 43–52 (2018). https://doi.org/10.1016/j.compmedimag.2018.08.010, http://www.sciencedirect.com/science/article/pii/S0895611118300806
12. Hinton, G.E., Osindero, S., Teh, Y.W.: A fast learning algorithm for deep belief nets. Neural Comput. **18**(7), 1527–1554 (2006)
13. Hnatushenko, V.V., Kavats, O.O., Shevchenko, V.Y.: Improvement the spatial resolution of multichannel aerospace high spatial resolution images on the base of hyperspherical transform. Radio Electron. Comput. Sci. Control (2014). https://doi.org/10.15588/1607-3274-2015-1-10
14. Hnatushenko, V., Zhernovyi, V.: Complex approach of high-resolution multispectral data engineering for deep neural network processing. In: Lytvynenko, V., Babichev, S., Wójcik, W., Vynokurova, O., Vyshemyrskaya, S., Radetskaya, S. (eds.) ISDMCI 2019. AISC, vol. 1020, pp. 659–672. Springer, Cham (2020). https://doi.org/10.1007/978-3-030-26474-1_46
15. Hordiiuk, D.M., Hnatushenko, V.V.: Neural network and local laplace filter methods applied to very high resolution remote sensing imagery in urban damage detection. In: 2017 IEEE International Young Scientists Forum on Applied Physics and Engineering (YSF), pp. 363–366 (2017). https://doi.org/10.1109/ysf.2017.8126648
16. Hordiiuk, D., Oliinyk, I., Hnatushenko, V., Maksymov, K.: Semantic segmentation for ships detection from satellite imagery. In: 2019 IEEE 39th International Conference on Electronics and Nanotechnology (ELNANO), pp. 454–457. IEEE (2019). https://doi.org/10.1109/elnano.2019.87838220
17. Kashtan, V., Hnatushenko, V., Shedlovska, Y.: Processing technology of multispectral remote sensing images. In: 2017 IEEE International Young Scientists Forum on Applied Physics and Engineering (YSF), pp. 355–358. IEEE (2017). https://doi.org/10.1109/ysf.2017.8126647
18. Krizhevsky, A., Sutskever, I., Hinton, G.E.: Imagenet classification with deep convolutional neural networks. In: Pereira, F., Burges, C.J.C., Bottou, L., Weinberger, K.Q. (eds.) Advances in Neural Information Processing Systems 25, pp. 1097–1105. Curran Associates, Inc. (2012). http://papers.nips.cc/paper/4824-imagenet-classification-with-deep-convolutional-neural-networks.pdf
19. Kuchuk, H., Podorozhniak, A., Hlavcheva, D., Yaloveha, V.: Application of deep learning in the processing of the aerospace system's multispectral images. In: Handbook of Research on Artificial Intelligence Applications in the Aviation and Aerospace Industries, pp. 134–147. IGI Global (2020). https://doi.org/10.4018/978-1-7998-1415-3.ch005

20. Lecun, Y., Bottou, L., Bengio, Y., Haffner, P.: Gradient-based learning applied to document recognition. Proc. IEEE **86**(11), 2278–2324 (1998). https://doi.org/10.1109/5.726791
21. Lin, T.Y., et al. Microsoft coco: common objects in context (2014)
22. McCulloch, W.S.: From logical neurons to poetic embodiments of mind: Warrens. mcculloch's project in neuroscience. Sci. Context **14**(4), 591–614 (2001)
23. Paola, J.D., Schowengerdt, R.A.: A review and analysis of backpropagation neural networks for classification of remotely-sensed multi-spectral imagery. Int. J. Remote Sensing **16**(16), 3033–3058 (1995). https://doi.org/10.1080/01431169508954607
24. Strachnyi, K.: Brief history of neural networks, January 2019. https://medium.com/analytics-vidhya/brief-history-of-neural-networks-44c2bf72eec
25. Yokoya, N., Grohnfeldt, C., Chanussot, J.: Hyperspectral and multispectral data fusion: a comparative review of the recent literature. IEEE Geosci. Remote Sensing Mag. **5**(2), 29–56 (2017). https://doi.org/10.1109/MGRS.2016.2637824
26. Zhang, C.W.: EagleView Super-High-Resolution Image Segmentation with Deeplabv3+/Mask-RCNN using Keras/ArcGIS, August 2020. https://towardsdatascience.com/eagleview-super-high-resolution-image-segmentation-with-deeplabv3-mask-rcnn

Computer Vision System for Recognizing the Coordinates Location and Ripeness of Strawberries

Dmitry Khort[1] , Alexey Kutyrev[1] , Igor Smirnov[1] ,
Volodymyr Osypenko[2] , and Nikolay Kiktev[3](✉)

[1] Federal Scientific Agroengineering Center VIM, Moscow, Russian Federation
dmitriyhort@mail.ru, alexeykutyrev@gmail.com, rashn-smirnov@yandex.ru
[2] Kyiv National University of Technologies and Design, Kyiv, Ukraine
vvo7@ukr.net
[3] National University of Life and Environmental Sciences of Ukraine, Kyiv, Ukraine
nkiktev@ukr.net

Abstract. Increasing the efficiency of using the technological capabilities of agricultural aggregates is achieved by extensive computerization and robotization of production and their individual stages, the development of automated systems. In recent years, a new direction has been actively developing - robotic harvesting of fruits and vegetables, as well as other agricultural robots. The automatic manipulator control algorithm, implemented in the high-level object-oriented language Python 3.7.2, includes operations to determine the x and Y coordinates of the berry, its degree of maturity, as well as to calculate the distance from the manipulator to the berry. It was found that the efficiency of detecting berries, their area and borders using the camera and the OpenCV library 300 Lux illumination reaches 94.6 of percent. An algorithm for harvesting strawberries using a robotic manipulator located on a moving car has been developed.

Keywords: Actuator · Software · Algorithm · Computer vision · Recognition · Garden strawberry · Agricultural automation

1 Introduction

There are many methods for identifying both weeds and cultivated plants. When recognizing plants, various algorithms for the operation of vision systems are used [1,2,10]. Morphological characteristics of plants are used, which are obtained during their linear measurements [5,13]. The operation of existing recognition systems in the production of agricultural products in the field is complicated by the variety of climatic and lighting conditions from day to evening. Within the field during the growing season, a wide variety of appearance of the same plant variety can be observed, which also significantly complicates the process of their recognition. Scientists have found that it is possible to qualitatively determine

© Springer Nature Switzerland AG 2020
S. Babichev et al. (Eds.): DSMP 2020, CCIS 1158, pp. 334–343, 2020.
https://doi.org/10.1007/978-3-030-61656-4_22

the coordinates of berries by color tone using computer vision systems [3,14]. Increasing productivity, using the full range of possibilities in the operation of machines and mechanisms for harvesting is accompanied by comprehensive computerization and robotization of production processes and the introduction of advanced automation systems on technological equipment. The application of computer vision technologies in agricultural production has great prospects in computer control systems. They can be used for robotic harvesting of berries, fruits and vegetables, watering, planting seedlings, pruning trees and other technological processes in agriculture. To establish optimal operating modes and successfully implement the system being developed on an industrial scale, research is needed to improve the efficiency of the technology and expand its application to other crops. The results will become the basis for the transition of agricultural sectors to a new technological level of production. Pattern recognition is one of the common modern practical tasks of artificial intelligence. This task, in its capabilities, approaches the capabilities of a person or any living creature whose life consists of the continuous execution of an algorithm: "isolate and classify an image - make a decision - act" [9]. There are several approaches to optical image recognition: the method of searching the object's view when changing the viewing angle, scales, and offsets; determining the shape contour and investigating its properties (connectivity, presence of angles, etc.); the use of artificial neural networks (multilayer perceptrons, quantization networks, Kohonen maps, recurrent networks) [8,9]. The first approach is more suitable for text recognition. In more complex tasks (for example, face recognition), artificial neural networks (ordinary fully connected and convolutional ones) are used. Convolutional neural networks are considered the best for solving the image recognition problem [7]. For the task of recognizing strawberries on a bush, the use of the second group of methods with determining the contour and color separation is suitable [8]. The theoretical justifications for image recognition during data clustering are described in [11,12]. The use of recognition in agriculture for assessing the state of soil from photographs taken from a quadrocopter is described in [4]. This task is a continuation of the project to develop a self-propelled robotic platform for harvesting strawberry garden [6].

The aim of the research is to develop an algorithm for recognizing the coordinates of the location and ripeness of strawberries in various lighting conditions.

2   Materials and Methods

The system's ability to process sensory data is one of the essential components for successful robotic harvesting. At the same time, it is necessary to evaluate and recognize the input video information. When picking strawberries, you first need to determine the ripeness of the berry by its color, as well as its location in the space of the farm. A special feature is the need for recognition from a certain distance (30–200 mm). Technical means for recognition are: Basler acA1920-155uc video camera, GigE Vision-interface, Sony IMX174 CMOS matrix. Video shooting parameters - 164 frames per second. For further processing and analysis of the obtained data, we will use the Open Source Computer Vision Library (OpenCV) [3,13]. Camera Matrix has a resolution of 1920 × 1200p, an interpolated resolution of 2.3 MP. For conducting experiments, measuring illumination, A Radex Lupin luxmeter (Quarta Rad, manufactured in Russia) was used, with a relative measurement error of 10%. The text of the software product was created in the environment of the Sublime Text 3 editor. As a result of the research conducted in the object-oriented language Python 3.7.2, an algorithm was created and used that includes operations to determine the location of the collected object, the degree of maturity, and calculating the distance from the manipulator to the strawberry itself. The video camera is used to capture streaming video and transmit it via USB 3.0. The resulting video frames are saved and processed in the PC RAM. For all found objects, the XYZ location is determined. The calculated coordinates are written to the data array for subsequent computing operations. To recognize the ripeness of wild strawberry berries, a size factor was used:

```
def get_frame(cap, scaling_factor):
ret, frame = cap.read()
# Apply the size factor using the RGB segment.
frame = cv2.resize(frame, None, f x = scaling_factor,
fy = scaling_factor, interpolation = cv2.INTER_AREA)
return frame
```

The size factor allows you to change the resolution obtained from the camera, which makes it possible to adjust image detail and increase the speed of the implemented computer vision algorithm. Footage from the footage is translated into the HSV color palette:

```
frame = get_frame (cap, scaling_factor)
# Transfer frames from footage to the HSV color model.
hsv = cv2.cvtColor(frame, cv2.COLOR_BGR2HSV)
```

To calibrate colors in the HSV palette (Hue, Saturation, Value - hue, saturation, value), the function of displaying color in coordinates is implemented:

```
def on_mouse_click (event, x, y, flags, frame):
if event = cv2.EVENT_LBUTTONUP:
# Color determination function in coordinates [y, x].
colors.append(frame[y,x].tolist())
```

The red color in the HSV palette is located at the borders of two color tones $H = 5/6$ and $H = 1/6$. To determine the degree of ripeness of wild strawberries by color tone, the color ranges of ripe and unripe berries are indicated (Fig. 1).

After specifying the color ranges, a mask is created for overlaying on the images (Fig. 1):

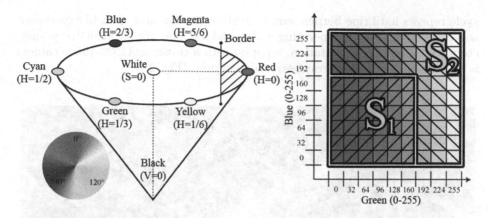

Fig. 1. The selection of the color range to determine the degree of ripeness of strawberries (Color figure online)

```
lower_red = np.array([0, 150, 60])
upper_red = np.array([10, 255, 255])
# Search mask for a given range of colors in the image.
mask0 = cv2.inRange(hsv, lower_red, upper_red)
lower_red = np.array([170, 165, 50])
upper_red = np.array([180, 255, 255])
# Applying a mask to a color image.
mask1 = cv2.inRange(hsv, lower_red, upper_red)
mask = mask0+mask1
```

When determining the degree of ripeness of the berry due to the high pixel density and high ISO sensitivity, noise appears on the images (randomly scattered pixels of random color and brightness that do not correspond to the registered light). To level them to the image, Morphological Transformations of the OpenCV library of open and closed type are applied. A normally open filter allows you to remove noise from the image, while a normally closed filter removes holes in recognized objects. After creating filters, masks are superimposed on the main image and remove unnecessary colors, leaving only the established ranges of color tones that correspond to ripe strawberries. To smooth the contour, the contour blur function is applied:

```
kernelOpen = np.ones((15,15))
kernelClosse = np.ones((20,20))
# Applying morphological transformations to an image.
maskOpen = cv2.morphologyEx(mask,cv2.MORPH_OPEN, kernelOpen)
maskClose = cv2.morphologyEx(maskOpen, cv2.MORPH_CLOSE, kernelClosse)
```

From all the found contours, an array is created containing the contour itself and its coordinates. In the loop for each contour its coordinates X, Y and Z are determined, after which the algorithm proceeds to the next found berry and the cycle repeats until ripe berries remain in the collection area. A field experiment was carried out to set up operating modes and software, check calculated parameters. On a industrial plantation, a tripod with a Basler acA1920-155uc camera is installed in the row of strawberry horticultural (Fig. 2).

Fig. 2. Conducting a field experiment (Color figure online)

3   Experiment

The results of the experiment are presented in Table 1. Statistical processing of the obtained experimental data showed that the berries of wild strawberries can be distinguished from bushes (background) using their color characteristics.

In different lighting conditions, at different times of the day (from 9:00 AM to 6:00 PM), using the developed algorithm, we measured the area of berries in a row. Using the developed algorithm of the computer vision system, 6,000 images were processed (Figs. 3, 4). The area of berries for the triplicate experiment is determined in pixels (elements of a two-dimensional digital image). The found area, knowing the focal length of the camera, is converted to square centimeters. It was established that successful segmentation of berries and background significantly depends on climatic conditions and lighting (Fig. 5).

Table 1. Results of the experimental determination of the area of the berry of the participant in the row of garden strawberry

Indicators	The found area of strawberry berries in various lighting conditions, cm^2					
	AM 9:00	AM 10:00	AM 12:00	PM 2:00	PM 4:00	AM 6:00
Measurement 1	106,4	115,5	129,2	95,8	92,1	81,5
Measurement 2	105,6	115,3	130,1	95,9	91,6	80,2
Measurement 3	107,1	114,9	128,9	94,6	92,5	81,3
The average value, cm^2	106,4	115,2	129.4	95,4	92,1	81,0
Standard deviation, cm	0,51	0,22	0,47	0,56	0,31	0,53
Dispersion, cm^2	0,56	0,09	0,39	0,52	0,20	0,49

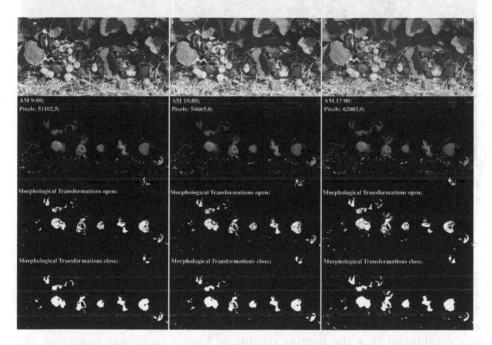

Fig. 3. Graph of the determination of the area of berries on the speed of movement of the robotic platform and lighting conditions (AM 9:00, 10:00, 12:00)

The variation range of the obtained experimental data on the area of berries from 9:00 AM to 6:00 PM was 48.4 cm^2. The detection efficiency of berries of their area and borders using the Basler acA1920-155uc camera and the OpenCV library with an illumination of 72,600 lux reaches 95.6%. The discovered berry area at 12:00 PM was 129.4 cm^2 with a real berry area of 135.3 cm^2 (out of 64731 pixels, strawberries were detected by the garden camera in 62003 pixels). With a decrease in illumination to 56300 lux at 6:00 PM, the average area of the found berries decreased to 81 cm^2 by 62.6% (out of 64731 pixels, strawberries were found by the garden camera to 39141.5 pixels).

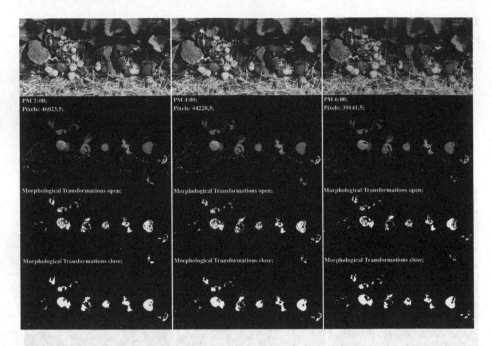

Fig. 4. Graph of the determination of the area of berries on the speed of movement of the robotic platform and lighting conditions (PM 2:00, 4:00, 6:00)

4   Results and Discussion

The conducted experimental studies showed that the developed computer vision system and the algorithm for processing input video data, searching for garden strawberry berries and determining their degree of ripeness are workable, they allow strawberry berries to be recognized with a high degree of accuracy. It was established that the lighting conditions have a significant impact on the detection of strawberry, garden, their area and borders, which ultimately has a significant impact on the efficiency of harvesting strawberry garden berries in an automated mode. Studies have been conducted to assess the feasibility of using an automated device with a developed computer vision system for the selective collection of strawberries. In particular, a prototype installation was created with the proposed computer vision module for practicing recognition of the degree of maturity of strawberries and their coordinates at various degrees of illumination. This model consisted of a self-propelled chassis, a mobile manipulator with 6 degrees of freedom, a coaxial grip, servos, a controller, computer vision cameras, a control computing device, laser sensors, a voltage regulator, and a lithium-polymer battery. In the Python 3.7.2 programming language, a control program for the movement of an automatic manipulator has been compiled and debugged (Fig. 6).

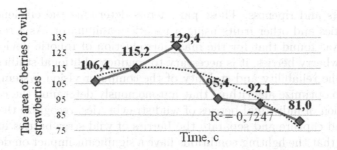

Fig. 5. Graph of the determination of the area of berries on the speed of movement of the robotic platform and lighting conditions

Fig. 6. Experimental model of an automated platform with a manipulator and a computer vision system

5   Conclusions

In this paper, we have developed an algorithm for determining the coordinates of the location and degree of maturity of garden strawberries at different times of the day. The technology of berry picking in industrial conditions using a robotic device based on a moving vehicle is presented. The conducted research has shown the efficiency of the developed system of technical vision for searching and determining strawberry berries. Algorithms for processing input video data and the operation of an intelligent automated computer vision system allow you to recognize strawberries with a high degree of accuracy (up to 94.6%). Light conditions significantly affect the detection of strawberry berries, their area, borders and ripeness. These parameters determine the efficiency of harvesting berries and other fruits using a robotic manipulator. As a result of the studies, it was found that for the mass introduction of robotic devices for collecting strawberry berries, it is necessary to conduct additional studies aimed at improving the reliability and stability of the computer vision system. It is also necessary to optimize algorithms that autonomously determine the coordinates of the location of individual berries of wild strawberries, recognize the degree of ripeness, and capture and separate the berries of wild strawberries in the field. It is proved that the lighting conditions have a significant impact on determining the area, borders and ripeness of strawberries using a computer vision camera. In the future, it is necessary to investigate and establish optimal operating modes for the implementation of the developed system in the production process, as well as for the application of this technology in a wide range of conditions for the production of garden crops. The use of computer vision systems in agricultural aggregates represents a huge potential in solving problems of automation, robotics, decision-making, accounting and control of products. In the future, it is possible to use other methods for recognizing collected products – artificial neural networks (fully connected and convolutional). This will allow you to more accurately recognize berries, fruits, and vegetables. To evaluate, it is necessary to conduct research on fruit recognition using various methods and compare the results.

References

1. Arima, S., Monta, M., Namba, K., Yoshida, Y., Kondo, N.: Harvesting robot for strawberry grown on table top culture **3**(15), 162–168 (2003). https://doi.org/10.3182/20101206-3-JP-3009.00016
2. Cui, Y., Nagata, M., Guo, F., Hiyoshi, K., Kinoshita, O., Mitarai, M.: Study on strawberry harvesting robot using machine vision for strawberry grown on annual hill top (part 2). J. Jpn. Soc. Agric. Mach. **2**(69), 60–68 (2007). https://doi.org/10.11357/jsam1937.69.2-60
3. Dimeas, F., Sako, D.V., Moulianitis, V.C., Aspragathos, N.A.: Design and fuzzy control of a robotic gripper for efficient strawberry harvesting. Robotica (33), 1085–1098 (2015). https://doi.org/10.1017/S0263574714001155
4. Dolia, M., et al.: Information technology for remote evaluation of after effects of residues of herbicides on winter crop rape. In: 3rd International Conference on Advanced Information and Communications Technologies (AICT), pp. 469–473 (2019). https://doi.org/10.1109/AIACT.2019.8847850
5. Hayashi, S., et al.: Evaluation of a strawberry-harvesting robot in a field test. Biosyst. Eng. **105**, 160–171 (2010). https://doi.org/10.1016/j.biosystemseng.2009.09.011
6. Khort, D., Kutyrev, A., Filippov, R., Kiktev, N., Komarchuk, D.: Robotized platform for picking of strawberry berries. In: IEEE International Scientific-Practical Conference Problems of Infocommunications, Science and Technology (PIC SandT), vol. 2, pp. 873–876 (2019). https://doi.org/10.1109/PICST47496.2019.9061448

7. Krizhevsky, A., Sutskever, I., Hinton, G.: ImageNet classification with deep convolutional neural networks. Int. J. Pattern Recogn. Artif. Intell. **6**(60), 84–90 (2012). https://doi.org/10.1145/3065386
8. LeCun, Y., Boser, B., Denker., J.: Backpropagation applied to handwritten zip code recognition. Neural Comput. **1**(4), 151–160 (1989). https://doi.org/10.1162/neco.1989.1.4.541
9. Mazurov, V.: Mathematical methods for pattern recognition (Matematicheskie metody raspoznavaniya obrazov). Ural State University, Yekaterinburg (2010)
10. Mu, L., Cui, G., Liu, Y., Cui, Y., Fu, L., Gejima, Y.: Design and simulation of an integrated end-effector for picking kiwifruit by robot. Inf. Process. Agric. **7**(1), 58–71 (2019). https://doi.org/10.1016/j.inpa.2019.05.004
11. Osypenko, V., Lurie, I., Yakobchuk, M., Savina, N., Boskin, O., Lytvynenko, V.: About innovation-investment designing of complex systems by inductive technology of system information-analytical research. In: 10th IEEE International Conference on Intelligent Data Acquisition and Advanced Computing Systems IDAACS, pp. 424–430 (2019). https://doi.org/10.1109/IDAACS.2019.8924434
12. Osypenko, V.: Two approaches to solving the problem of clustering in a broad sense from the standpoint of inductive edeling (dva pidxody' do rozv'yazannya zadachi klasteryzaciyi u shyrokomu sensi z pozycij induktyvnogo modelyuvannya). Energetyka i avtomatyka **1**, 84–97 (2014)
13. Xiong, Y., Grimstad, L., Peng, C., From, P., Volkan, I.: Development and field evaluation of a strawberry harvesting robot with a cable-driven gripper. Exp. Tech. **157**, 392–400 (2019). https://doi.org/10.1016/j.compag.2019.01.009
14. Yamamoto, S., Hayashi, S., Yoshida, H., Kobayashi, K.: Development of a stationary robotic strawberry harvester with picking mechanism that approaches target fruit from below. Jpn. Agric. Res. Q. **48**, 261–269 (2014). https://doi.org/10.6090/jarq.48.261

Dynamic Data Mining and Data Stream Mining

Novel Nonparametric Test for Homogeneity and Change-Point Detection in Data Stream

Dmitriy Klyushin[1]([✉])(iD) and Irina Martynenko[2](iD)

[1] Taras Shevchenko National University of Kyiv, Kyiv, Ukraine
dokmed5@gmail.com
[2] Academy of Labour, Social Relations and Tourism, Kyiv, Ukraine
martia@rambler.ru

Abstract. In the paper, a new nonparametric algorithm for the homogeneity and change-point detection in random sequences is proposed. This algorithm is based on Klyushin–Petunin test for samples heterogeneity which allows us both absolutely continuous distributions and distributions with ties. The implementation of the algorithm may be both online and offline. It allows us to analyze small chunks of data stream for comparison providing the significance level less than 0.05. The comparisons show that proposed algorithm is more sensitive and robust than their counterparts. Opposite to the counterpart tests (Kolmogorov–Smirnov and Wilcoxon), the proposed algorithm well detect the homogeneity of samples from both distributions which differ in means and it has the same variance and distributions with the same mean but different variances. The algorithm has also wide field of applications from the detection of drift concept in texts to tracking the healthy parameters and coordinates of patients obtained from wearable gadgets.

1 Introduction and Literature Review

At every time moment in various fields huge amounts of information is been measured. Data analysts obtain coordinates of numerous mobile phone users, health data provided by wearable devices, telemetric data from space objects etc. The changes in these data may be markers of important events. For example, adverse changing in health state of a patient, outage of software or hardware etc. Therefore, the development of precise and sensitive methods for heterogeneity and change-point detection in random sequences is an urgent and important problem.

The problem of the random sequences heterogeneity is posed as follows: whether the random sequence consists of the segments with the same distribution or not. In the problem of change-point detection it is necessary to test whether contiguous segments of the random sequences have the same distribution or not. If the distributions of the contiguous segments are different the boundary point between these segments is a change-point.

S. Babichev et al. (Eds.): DSMP 2020, CCIS 1158, pp. 347–356, 2020.
https://doi.org/10.1007/978-3-030-61656-4_23

Usually, methods of change-point detection are classified as offline and online. Offine methods allow detecting the change-points analyzing all samples. Meanwhile online methods detect change-points based on current data in real-time mode. Selective survey of offline change-point detection methods was made in [26]. In the paper, we restrict ourselves to consideration only univariate random while there are many papers devoted to offline methods for detection homogeneity and change-points in multivariate time series [27]. The multivariate case is the future scope of our researches. Statistical tests for homogeneity and changepoint detection in random series are divided on parametric and non-parametric. Parametric methods use the assumption that data have some given distribution (for instance, normal distribution) or have some form with unknown parameters [9–12,15,28]. Non-parametric tests does not use any information about distribution functions besides of most common ones, for instance, absolutely continuous etc. (see [1–4,6–8,14,21,29,30]).

Online or sequential algorithms for detection change-point were considered in [5,20,23–25]. The specificity of these papers is that the algorithms for changepoint detection do not use complete information about sequence and must to give an answer using only partial data. Also, they do not store large amount of data as far as they analyze only short segments of a random sequence. It is very important aspect in the context of big data when storing of huge amounts of information is a hard problem.

The purpose of the paper is development a new online algorithm to test homogeneity of a random sequence and detect its change-points. The novelty of the proposed algorithm consists of the use of Klyushin–Petunin test [17] but not the standard tests having wide application in the field of random sequences analysis (Kolmogorov–Snirnov test, Wilcoxon test etc.). In many cases, Klyushin–Petunin test has advantages over its counterparts. This algorithm may be a useful tool for application in various areas regarding monitoring of signals.

2   Homogeneity and Change-Point Detection Test

The problem of random sequence homogeneity test could be reduced to the twosample problem of homogeneity of contiguous segments. There is wide range of different tests to resolve this problem, in particular, Kolmogorov–Smirnov test, Wilcoxon test, Klyushin–Petunin test [17] etc.

Let $x = (x_1, x_2, \ldots, x_n)$ and $y' = (y_1, y_2, \ldots, y_m)$ be two samples drawn from the general populations G_1 and G_2 with distribution functions F_1 and F_2 respectively. The null hypothesis of samples homogeneity states that these samples belong to the same general population, i.e. $F_1 = F_2$. The alternative hypothesis states that $F_1 \neq F_2$.

This problem can be resolved with the help of nonparametric two-sample tests, for example Kolmogorov-Smirnov test, Wilcoxon test etc. However, these tests can cause the statistical uncertainty because they use one-sided tolerance limits. For instance, Kolmogorov-Smirnov test is based on Kolmogorov-Smirnov statistics D_n for which we need to find the confidence limit $t_\beta(n)$ corresponding to the given significance level β and the sample size n. If $D_n \geq t_\beta(n)$ we consider samples to be homogeneous, else the statistical uncertainty occurs and we cannot to accept any decision. Wilcoxon test has the same drawback.

In order to fix such difficulties there the homogeneity measure based on Matveychuk-Petunin model [16,18,19] and two-sample Klyushin–Petunin test of homogeneity was proposed [17] which makes possible to compute two-sided confidence interval (p_l, p_2) corresponding to the given significance level regardless of whether the null hypothesis H be true or false. Also,it allows estimating the probability of the first and second kind errors.

Let $x = (x_1, x_2, \ldots, x_n) \in G_1$ and $y = (y_1, y_2, \ldots, y_m) \in G_2$, and $x_{(1)} \leq \cdots \leq x_{(n)}, y_{(1)} \leq \cdots \leq y_{(n)}$ be respective order statistics. The null hypothesis H_0 states that $F_1 = F_2$. Suppose that H_0 is true. Then, by the Hill's assumption [13]

$$p_{ij} = p(x_k \in (x_{(i)}, x_{(j)})) = \frac{j - i}{n + 1}, \ i < j. \tag{1}$$

Find the relative frequency h_{ij} of the random event $A_{ij} = \{y_k \in (x_{(i)}, x_{(j)})\}$ and confidence limits $p_{ij}^{(1)}, p_{ij}^{(2)}$ for the binomial proportion p_{ij} corresponding to given significance level β: $B = \{p_{ij} \in (p_{ij}^{(1)}, p_{ij}^{(2)})\}$, $p(B) = 1 - \beta$. These limits have been calculated by various formulas [22], for instance, for the Wald confidence interval we have the following:

$$p_{ij}^{(1)} = \frac{h_{ij}m + g^2/2 - g\sqrt{h_{ij}(1 - h_{ij})m + g^2/4}}{m + g^2} \tag{2}$$

$$p_{ij}^{(2)} = \frac{h_{ij}m + g^2/2 + g\sqrt{h_{ij}(1 - h_{ij})m + g^2/4}}{m + g^2} \tag{3}$$

Here, the parameter g we may put be equal to 3.

Denote by N the number of all confidence intervals $I_{ij} = (p_{ij}^{(1)}, p_{ij}^{(2)})$, $(N = n(n - 1)/2)$ and L the number of those intervals I_{ij} which contain the binomial proportions p_{ij}; then $\rho(x, y) = \frac{L}{N}$ is the relative frequency of the random event $B = \{p_{ij} \in I_{ij}\}$ having the probability $p(B) = 1 - \beta$. Putting $h_{ij} = h$, $m = N$ and $g = 3$ in formulae (2), (3) we get a confidence interval $I = (p^{(1)}, p^{(2)})$ for the probability $p(B)$ with the confidence level which approximately equals 0.95. A decision rule for the test of hypothesis H_0 with significance level which approximately equals to 0.05 may be formulated in the following way: if the confidence interval I contains the probability $p(B)$, (for example, $p(B) \approx 0.95$) then hypothesis H_0 is accepted, otherwise it is rejected. The statistics $\rho(x, y)$ is a heterogeneous measure of the samples x and y.

It should be noted that the confidence limits (2), (3) are not exact confidence limits corresponding to the given significance level even for the Bernoulli model but they are only the asymptotic confidence limits; in our case calculation of the exact confidence intervals is based on the investigation of the so-called generalized Bernoulli model (Matveychuk-Petunin model [18,19], or MP model by terminology Johnson and Kotz [16]). In addition, the statistics $d(x, y)$ is not metrics as far as it does not satisfy any axiom of the distance in the metric space.

The useful feature of the above described test in contrast to its counterparts consists in the fact that the confidence interval I contains the mathematical expectation $m(d)$ with the significance level which approximately equals to 0.05 in the case where the hypothesis H_0 is false too. However, to justify this statement and obtain the suitable interpretation of the value $m(d)$ we should carry out the additional random experiment (randomizing procedure) which is random sampling of the events $B_{ij} = \{p_{ij} \in (p_{ij}^{(1)}, p_{ij}^{(2)})\}$. Denote by $\tilde{B}$ the random event consisting in the random sampling of the event B_{ij} with the probability $\frac{1}{N}$ from the general populations of the random events $B^* = \{B_{ij} = \{p_{ij} \in (p_{ij}^{(1)}, p_{ij}^{(2)})\}, i < j\}$. Then, due to the formula of total probability

$$p(\tilde{B}) = \frac{1}{N} \sum_{i<j} p(B_{ij})$$

(if hypothesis H is false then $p(B_{ij}) \neq 1 - \beta$ and can be depending on i and j). Thus, after carring out the randomized procedure we obtain the formula

$$m(\rho) = p(\tilde{B}) = \frac{1}{N} \sum_{i<j} p(B_{ij}),$$

so that ρ is the frequency of the random event $\tilde{B}$ which has the probability $p(\tilde{B})$. Consequently, the confidence interval I for the binomial proportion $p(\tilde{B})$ (or, that is the same, for the mathematical expectation $m(h)$) by vertue of 3σ rule has the significance level ≈ 0.05. In the case when the hypotheses H is true the event $\tilde{B}$ coincides with the event B and carring out of the additional random experiment does not give any new results as far as $p(\tilde{B}_{ij}) = p(B) = 1 - \beta$.

For the sake of objectivity it should be noted that the previous reasoning about the confidence level of the interval I was not correct enough because the events B_{ij} are dependent ones and $D(h) \neq \frac{\sigma^2}{N}$, where σ^2 is variance of the random variable h_{ij}. To fix this drawback let us consider in more detail the problem of correctness of the formulae (2), (3) when $g = 3$ for construction of the confidence intervals for the probability p_{ij} in computation of the proximity measure $h = p(x, x')$ between two samples $x = (x_1, x_2, \ldots, x_n)$ and $y = (y_1, y_2, \ldots, y_m)$. Let $x_{(i)}, x_{(j)}$ $(i < j)$ be the order statistics generated by the sample x and γ_{ij}^k be the random variable which is defined by the formula

$$\gamma_{ij}^{(k)} = \begin{cases} 1, & \text{if } y_k \in (x_{(i)}, x_{(j)}), 1 \leq k \leq m \\ 0, & \text{if } y_k \notin (x_{(i)}, x_{(j)}), 1 \leq k \leq m \end{cases}$$

Evidently, the frequency h_{ij} of the random event

$$A_{ij} = \{y_k \in (x_{(i)}, x_{(j)})\}$$

is equal to

$$h_{ij} = \frac{1}{m} \sum_{k=1}^{m} \gamma_{ij}^{(k)}.$$

Unfortunately, the random variables $\gamma_{ij}^{(k)}, k = 1, \ldots, m$, obtained as a results of the using the MP-model in contrast to the Bernoulli model are dependent on each other. In addition, as it has been proved in [18, 19], in spite of

$$m(h_{ij}) = p_{ij} = \frac{j-i}{n+1}$$

in the case when the hypothesis H_0 is true, its variance do not equals to

$$\sigma_{ij,B} = \frac{p_{ij}(1-p_{ij})}{m},$$

as in the Bernoulli model, but it is calculated by the formula

$$D(h_{ij}) = \frac{p_{ij}(1-p_{ij})}{m} \cdot \frac{m+n+1}{n+2} = \alpha_{n,m}\sigma_{ij,B}^2,$$

where $\alpha_{n,m} = \dfrac{m+n+1}{n+2}$.

For the samples x and y of equal size n we have

$$\alpha_{n,m} = \frac{2 + \dfrac{1}{n}}{1 + \dfrac{2}{n}} \approx 2.$$

If $n \gg m$, then

$$\alpha_{n,m} = \frac{\dfrac{m}{n} + 1 + \dfrac{1}{n}}{1 + \dfrac{2}{n}} \approx 1.$$

Hence, for the samples of equal size

$$D(h_{ij}) \approx 2\sigma_{ij,B}^2$$

$$\sigma_{ij} = \sqrt{D(h_{ij})} \approx \sqrt{2}\sigma_{ij,B},$$

and provided that $n \gg m$

$$\sigma_{ij} \approx \sigma_{ij,B}.$$

When deriving the formulae (2), (3) for the confidence limits $p_{ij}^{(1)}$ and $p_{ij}^{(2)}$ containing the probability p_{ij} with the confidence level $1 - \beta$ it is not hard to see the significance level of the interval $I = (p^{(1)}, p^{(2)})$ exactly coincide with the significance level of the confidence interval

$$\hat{I} = (h_{ij} - g\sigma(h_{ij}), h_{ij} + g\sigma(h_{ij})) = (h_{ij} - g\sigma_{ij}, h_{ij} + g\sigma_{ij})$$

for p_{ij}. It is well known that in Bernoulli model for the 5% significance level, we have $\beta = 0.05$ and $g \approx 1.96$. To define the significance level of the confidence interval $I^* = (h_{ij} - 3\sigma_{ij,B}, h_{ij} - 3\sigma_{ij,B})$ constructed by 3σ rule in MP model we transform it to the following form

$$I^* = (h_{ij} - 3\sigma_{ij,B}, h_{ij} + 3\sigma_{ij,B}) = (h_{ij} - \frac{3}{\sqrt{2}}\sqrt{2}\sigma_{ij,B}, h_{ij} + \frac{3}{\sqrt{2}}\sqrt{2}\sigma_{ij,B}) \approx$$

$$\approx (h_{ij} - 2.1213\sigma_{ij,B}, h_{ij} + 2.1213\sigma_{ij,B}) \supset (h_{ij} - 1.96\sigma_{ij}, h_{ij} + 1.96\sigma_{ij}).$$

As far as the relative frequency h_{ij} in the MP model as well as in the Bernoulli model is the asymptotically normal random variable [18,19] then the confidence level of the interval $(h_{ij} - 1.96\sigma_{ij}, h_{ij} + 1.96\sigma_{ij})$ is approximately equal to 0.95, that is why the significance level of the interval I^* in the MP-model is some below 0.05. Hence, the confidence interval $I = (p_{ij}^{(1)}, p_{ij}^{(2)})$ constructed by the 3σ-rule in the MP model in the case when $n = m$ or $n \gg m$ has the significance level β not exceeding 0.05. If the hypothesis H_0 about the equivalence of the hypothetical distribution functions F_1 and F_2 is false then

$$p(A_{ij}) = p(x_k' \in (x_{(i)}, x_{(j)})) = \bar{p}_{ij} \neq p_{ij} = \frac{j-i}{n+1},$$

but all previous reasonings remain true if we substitute p_{ij} by $\bar{p}_{ij}$. That is why the conclusion about the significance level of the confidence interval $I = (\bar{p}_{ij}^{(1)}, \bar{p}_{ij}^{(2)})$ for the binomial proportion $\bar{p}_{ij}$ constructed by the 3σ-rule in the MP model remains valid. Thus, we can formulate the following theorem [17].

Theorem 1. *If $x = (x_1, x_2, \ldots, x_n)$ and $y = (y_1, y_2, \ldots, y_m)$ are sample of independently distributed continuous random values, $0 < \lim_{n \to \infty} p_{ij}^{(n)} = p_0 < 1$, and $0 < \lim_{n \to \infty} P(A_{ij}| H_0) = p^* < 1$, then the asymptotic significance level β of a sequence of confidence intervals $I_{ij}^{(n)}$ for the probabilities $p(A_{ij}^{(n)})$ does not exceed 0.05.*

Corollary 1. *If $x = (x_1, x_2, \ldots, x_n)$ and $y = (x_{n+1}, x_{n+2}, \ldots, x_{2m})$ are the contiguous segments of the random sequence of independently distributed continuous random values, than the Klyushin–Petunin test for heterogeneity provides the significance level which is less than 0.05.*

3 Comparison of Klyushin–Petunin Test with Kolmogorov-Smirnov and Wilcoxon Tests

To estimate the effectiveness of the Klyushin–Petunin test, let us to compare it with the well-known statistics which are widely used for construction of tests for homogeneity and change-point detection (for example, Kolmogorov-Smirnov statistics and Wilcoxon statistics). To compare the effectiveness of the above mentioned statistics, we considered the samples ($n = 40$) for the distributions which have the same mathematical expectation and the different variance, the same variance and the different mathematical expectations, the different variance and the different mathematical expectations, and the same variance and the same mathematical expectation.

Here, we will use the following notation: Normal(a, b) is the normal distribution, where a is the mean and b is the standard deviation, Uniform(a, b) is the uniform distribution on an interval (a, b), Lognormal(a, b) is the lognormal distribution, where a is the mean and b is the standard deviation, Poisson(a) is the Poisson distribution with the parameter a, Exponential(a) is the exponential distribution with the parameter a, Gamma(a, b) is the gamma distribution with parameters a and b.

Consider the segment of the random sequence $(x_1, x_2, \ldots, x_n)$. The change-point of this sequence is the point x_m such that $(x_1, x_2, \ldots, x_m)$, $m < n$ has the distribution F_1 and $(x_{m+1}, x_{m+2}, \ldots, x_n)$ has the distribution F_2 and $F_1 \neq F_2$. The problem of the change-point detection could be formulated as follows. Consider a random sequence $x = (x_1, x_2, \ldots)$ and the segments $(x_1, x_2, \ldots, x_n) \in G_1$ and $(x_{n+1}, x_{n+2}, \ldots, x_{2m}) \in G_2$ where G_1 and G_2 are different general populations. Let us freeze the segment $(x_1, x_2, \ldots, x_n)$ and consider the sliding segment $(x_i, x_{(i+1)}, \ldots, x_{(i+n)})$ where $i = 1, \ldots, n$. Thus, we obtain the series of two samples where the first sample is the frozen segment and the second sample is sliding and when i increases this sample becomes "contaminated" by the values from the second sample. By construction, when i is small the first and second samples are homogeneous, but when i is large the first and second samples are heterogeneous.

In Table 1, the order numbers of the change points detected by Klyushin Petunin, Kolmogorov–Smirnov and Wilcoxon tests with 5% significance level for various distributions are represented. The change-point in Table 1 is such point x_m that the test accepts the hypothesis H_0 for samples $(x_1, x_2, \ldots, x_n) \in G_1$ and $(x_1, x_2, \ldots, x_k, x_{k+1}, \ldots, x_n)$, $k \leq m$ such that the values $x_1, x_2, \ldots, x_k \in G_1$ and the values $x_{k+1}, x_{k+2}, \ldots, x_n \in G_2$. For instance, when the first segment $(x_1, x_2, \ldots, x_{40})$ has the distribution Normal(0,1) and the second segment $(x_{41}, x_{42}, \ldots, x_{80})$ has the distribution Normal(3,1) the samples $(x_1, x_2, \ldots, x_{40})$ and $(x_m, \ldots, x_{40}, x_{41} \ldots, x_{m+39})$ are considered homogeneous for $m < 16$ and for $m \geq 16$ the samples are considered heterogeneous (see Table 1). The numbers indicated in the parentheses are the numbers that are false-positive responses. These numbers are evidences of instability of the test. It is easy to see, that the Klyushin–Petunin test is more stable than its counterparts in all considered cases. If the entry of Table 1 is 40 then the corresponding test did nor reject the null hypothesis H_0.

The sensitivity of the test may be estimated by the comparison of the order number of the change-points. The less the order number of the change-point the more sensitive test (it's reacting faster on the changes in the samples). Table 1 shows that Wilcoxon test is more sensitive for shifted distributions with the different means and the same standard deviation (Normal(0,1) vs Normal(1,1),

Table 1. Order numbers of change-points

Test	Tests		
	Klyushin–Petunin	Kolmogorov–Smirnov	Wilcoxon
Normal(0,1)–Normal(3,1)	16	15	10
Normal(0,1)–Normal(2,1)	15	17	12
Normal(0,1)–Normal(1,1)	23	25	6
Normal(0,1)–Normal(0,4)	24	25	33
Normal(0,1)–Normal(0,3)	20	35	34 (39)
Normal(0,1)–Normal(0,4)	22	40	40
Lognormal(0,1)–Lognormal(3,1)	11	11	7
Lognormal(0,1)–Lognormal(2,1)	14	17	5
Lognormal(0,1)–Lognormal(1,1)	40	27 (24)	9
Lognormal(0,1)–Lognormal(0,4)	23	19	28
Lognormal(0,1)–Lognormal(0,3)	18	29	40
Lognormal(0,1)–Lognormal(0,2)	28	34	40
Uniform(0,1)–Uniforml(2,3)	12	11	7
Uniform(0,1)–Uniform(1,2)	12	11	9
Uniform(0,1)–Uniform(0.5,1.5)	21	15	23
Poisson(1)–Poisson(4)	40	13	40 (37)
Poissin(1)–Poisson(3)	40	31	40
Poisson(1)–Poisson(2)	40	30 (27)	40
Exponential(1)–Exponential(4)	20	19	24
Exponential(1)–Exponential(3)	31	32	28
Exponential(1)–Exponential(2)	29	29	37
Gamma(1,2)–Gamma(4,1)	13	12	9
Gamma(1,2)–Gamma(4,2)	16	19	12
Gamma(1,2)–Gamma(2,2)	19	22	25 (29)

Normal(2,1), and Normal(3,1), Lognormal(0,1) vs Lognogmal(1,1), Lognormal(2,1), and Lognormal(3,1), Uniform(0,1) vs Uniform(2,3), Uniform(1,2), and Uniform(0.5,1.5)) than its counterparts. For Poisson test, Klyushin–Petunin and Wilcoxon tests were not detected any change-points in opposite to Kolmogorov–Smirnov test. For exponential and gamma distributions, Klyushin–Petunin test is in average more sensitive.

The analysis of Table 1 shows also, that the Klyushin–Petunin test is more sensitive for distributions with the the means and the different standard deviation (Normal(0,1) vs Normal(0,4), Normal(0,3), and Normal(0,2), Lognormal(0,1) vs Lognogmal(0,4), Lognormal(0,3), and Lognormal(0,2) than its counterparts. The second important result shown in Table 1 is the fact that Klyushin–Petunin test is more stable than both Kolmogorov–Smirnov and Wilcoxon tests in all cases. The conjunction of the good sensitivity (excepting Poisson distribution) and stability (for all distributions) makes the Klyushin–Petunin test the effective tool for test heterogeneity and change-point detection.

4 Conclusions

The proposed test for heterogeneity and change-point detection has the following advantages in contrast to Kolmogorov–Smirnov and Wilcoxon statistics:

1. In opposite to other tests the confidence interval I of Klyushin–Petunin test contains the mathematical expectation of the heterogeneity measure with the significance level which approximately equals to 0.05 regardless of whether the hypothesis H_0 be true or false.
2. Klyushin–Petunin test is more stable for all considered distributions.
3. Klyushin–Petunin test is more accurate for the distributions with the same or close mathematical expectations and different standard deviations.
4. Klyushin–Petunin test has the high sensitivity in all analyzed cases of the samples from the different general populations with difference mathematical expectations and the same standard deviations.

References

1. Brodsky, B.: Change-Point Analysis in Nonstationary Stochastic Models. CRC Press, Boca Raton (2017). https://doi.org/10.1201/9781315367989
2. Brodsky, B., Darkhovsky, B.: Extrapolation, Interpolation, and Smoothing of Stationary Time Series. Kluwer Academin Press, Dordrecht/Boston (1993). https://doi.org/10.1007/978-94-015-8163-9
3. Brodsky, B., Darkhovsky, B.: Non-Parametric Statistical Diagnosis: Problems and Methods. Springer, Heidelberg (2010). https://doi.org/10.1007/978-94-015-9530-8
4. Chen, J., Gupta, A.: Parametric Statistical Change Point Analysis With Applications to Genetics, Medicine, and Finance. Birkhauser, Basel (2012). https://doi.org/10.1007/978-0-8176-4801-5
5. Fearnhead, P., Liu, Z.: On line inference for multiple change point problems. J. Roy. Stat. Soc. Ser. B **69**, 203–213 (2007). https://doi.org/10.1111/j.1467-9868.2007.00601.x
6. Ferger, D.: On the power of nonparametric changepoint-tests. Metrika **41**, 277–292 (1994). https://doi.org/10.1007/BF01895324
7. Gombay, E.: U-statistics for sequential change detection. Metrika **52**, 113–145 (2000). https://doi.org/10.1007/PL00003980
8. Gombay, E.: U-statistics for change under alternatives. J. Multivar. Anal. **78**, 139–158 (2001). https://doi.org/10.1006/jmva.2000.1945
9. Gombay, E., Horvath, L.: An application of the maximum likelihood test to the change-point problem. Stoch. Process. Appl. **50**, 161–171 (1994). https://doi.org/10.1016/0304-4149(94)90154-6
10. Gombay, E., Horvath, L.: On the rate of approximations for maximum likelihoodtests in change-point models. J. Multivar. Anal. **56**, 120–152 (1996). https://doi.org/10.1006/jmva.1996.0007
11. Gurevich, G.: Retrospective parametric tests for homogeneity of data. Commun. Stat. Theor. Methods **36**, 2841–2862 (2007). https://doi.org/10.1080/03610920701386968

12. Gurevich, G., Vexler, A.: Retrospective change point detection: from parametric to distribution free policies. Commun. Stat. Simul. Comput. **39**, 1–22 (2010). https://doi.org/10.1080/03610911003663881

13. Hill, B.: Posterior distribution of percentiles: Bayes' theorem for sampling from a population. J. Am. Stat. Assoc. **63**, 677–691 (1968). https://doi.org/10.1080/01621459.1968.11009286

14. Holmes, M., Kojadinovic, I., Quessy, J.: Nonparametric tests for change-point detection a la Gomabay and Hovath. J. Multivar. Anal. **115**, 16–32 (2013). https://doi.org/10.1016/j.jmva.2012.10.004

15. James, B., James, K., Siegmund, D.: Tests for a change-point. Biometrika **74**, 71–83 (1987). https://doi.org/10.1093/biomet/74.1.71

16. Johnson, N., Kotz, S.: Some generalizations of Bernoulli and Polya-Eggenberger contagion models. Stat. Pap. **32**, 1–17 (1991). https://doi.org/10.1007/BF02925473

17. Klyushin, D., Petunin, Y.: A nonparametric test for the equivalence of populations based on a measure of proximity of samples. Ukrainian Math. J. **55**(2), 181–198 (2003)

18. Matveichuk, S., Petunin, Y.: A generalization of the Bernoulli model occurring in order statistics. I. Ukrainian Math. J. **42**(4), 459–466 (1990)

19. Matveichuk, S., Petunin, Y.: A generalization of the Bernoulli model occurring in order statistics. II. Ukrainian Math. J. **43**(6), 728–734 (1991)

20. Mei, Y.: Sequential change-point detection when unknown parameters are present in the pre-change distribution. Ann. Stat. **34**, 92–122 (2006). https://doi.org/10.1214/009053605000000859

21. Pettitt, A.: A non-parametric approach to the change-point problem. Appl. Stat. **28**, 126–135 (1979). https://doi.org/10.2307/2346729

22. Pires, A., Amado, C.: Interval estimators for a binomial proportion: comparison of twenty methods. REVSTAT-Stat. J. **6**, 165–197 (2008). https://doi.org/10.1080/01621459.1968.11009286

23. Poor, H., Hadjiliadis, O.: Quickest Detection. Cambridge University Press, Cambridge (2009). https://doi.org/10.1017/CBO9780511754678

24. Siegmund, D.: Sequential Analysis. Springer Series in Statistics. Springer, New York (1985). https://doi.org/10.1007/978-1-4757-1862-1

25. Tartakovsky, A., Rozovskii, B., et al.: A novel approach to detection of intrusions in computer networks via adaptive sequential and batch-sequential change-point detection methods. IEEE Trans. Sig. Process **54**(9), 3372–3382 (2006)

26. Truong, C., Oudre, L., Vayatis, N.: A review of change point detection methods. CoRR, abs/1801.00718 (2018), http://arxiv.org/abs/1801.00718

27. Truong, C., Oudre, L., Vayatis, N.: Selective review of offline changepoint detection methods. Sig. Process. **167**, 107299 (2020). https://doi.org/10.1016/j.sigpro.2019.107299

28. Vexler, A., Gurevich, G.: Average most powerful tests for a segmented regression. Commun. Stat. Theor. Methods **38**, 2214–2231 (2009). https://doi.org/10.1080/03610920802521208

29. Wolfe, D., Schechtman, E.: Nonparametric statistical procedures for the change point problem. J. Stat. Plann. Infer. **9**, 389–396 (1984). https://doi.org/10.1016/0378-3758(84)90013-2

30. Zou, C., Liu, Y., Qin, P., Wang, Z.: Empirical likelihood ratio test for the change-point problem. Stat. Prob. Lett. **77**, 374–382 (2007). https://doi.org/10.1016/j.spl.2006.08.003

Modeling of Animator Studio Control Service Functionality Using Data Mining Tools

Olga Smotr[1](✉) ⓘ, Romanna Malets[2] ⓘ, Solomija Ljaskovska[3] ⓘ,
and Oksana Karabyn[1] ⓘ

[1] Lviv State University of Life Safety, Lviv, Ukraine
olgasmotr@gmail.com, karabynoks@gmail.com
[2] Ivan Franko National University of Lviv, Lviv, Ukraine
romashkaandko@gmail.com
[3] Lviv Polytechnic National University, Lviv, Ukraine
solomiam@gmail.com

Abstract. The research addresses to the animation studio services issues, advantages and disadvantages of their functioning, both for the ordinary user and the developer. It makes sense to provide the client with information about two areas: pricing policy and content of services. The services automation methods within animation studios are researched using modern methods of Data Mining. It is proposed to create the work logic using data mining methods, Decision Trees methods, for the animation studio management services effective functioning. It is determined that in case of client priority search criteria choice is related to pricing policy, it makes sense to organize the operation of the animation studio management service based on the backtracking algorithm. In the case of client's search criteria choice priority are content-related topics of services, apply algorithms for constructing decision-making tree. It is proposed to solve the problem of comparing the services of different animation studios, their pricing policy, location, etc. by building a composite web application - data mashup of children's animation studios.

Keywords: Information technology · Data Mining · Decision Trees · Mashup · Animation studio · Entertainment

1 Introduction

Recently, there has been a rapid development of the entertainment industry worldwide. This is the entry into a post-industrial stage of development, for most of the developed countries in the world, a characteristic feature is the significant growth of services and service industries. After all, quality of life is a priority of post-industrial society. In addition, the crazy rhythm of the modern world requires constant recreation of the psychophysiological state of the individual, ie requires rest and change of activities. That is why today, the leisure and

© Springer Nature Switzerland AG 2020
S. Babichev et al. (Eds.): DSMP 2020, CCIS 1158, pp. 357–371, 2020.
https://doi.org/10.1007/978-3-030-61656-4_24

entertainment industry, which provides us with space for our leisure, is one of the most important areas of everyday life. The entertainment industry allows members of society not only to meet their spiritual needs, but also to form an idea of their well-being and social status. Given the complexity and diversity of services provided by the industry, it is able to reach different segments of the population, with different needs, interests and different social status. Despite the fact that the entertainment industry is one of the youngest sectors of the socio-cultural sphere, it accounts for about 6% of the world's capital [23].

In today's conditions of informatization and computerization of the society [21] and the rapid increase in demand for services of the entertainment industry [19,22]. Business development in this area requires new approaches to information processing and decision-making. The most notable change can be observed in the travel companies that actively involve organizations to process activities, advanced digital technology [1,2,7,8,20]. These include global computer reservation systems, integrated communications networks, multimedia systems, smart cards, management information systems, and more.

The demand for the children's animation studios services is constantly growing. Modern animation is the activity of developing and implementing special leisure programs [11]. With a data web - site for parents Britain Netmum, parents spend on children's holiday from $200 to several thousands of dollars, and in general, the market value of children's parties is over $1.5 billion [10]. Similarly, in Ukraine, on average, the organization of children's holidays costs about $200 [22].

Given the high demand, the number of children's animation studios and the variety of services they provide are steadily increasing. It is quite difficult for the average consumer to navigate this diversity. It takes a long time to analyze all the information provided by animation studios and their clients (customer feedback) and to choose exactly the suggestions that addresses his/her needs and capabilities. Providing quality service without rapid response to user requests and needs is impossible for animation studios, without modern informational systems and technologies [14].

2 Problem Statement

As of today, most animation studio, event-agency etc. have their own web sites, where the highlight information about their services and show potential customers their own successful experiences conducting their activities, etc. However, this is not enough. The client (animation customer) needs the ability to quickly and conveniently view the offerings of different animation studios with the ability to compare their services, pricing, quality of service and the ability to provide these services in the right location and time range, etc.

Analyzing typical for the Ukrainian market, web services animation studio "Children's Planet" [16], "Igroland" [17], "Papashon" [15], event - agency "Empire holidays" [18] it is difficult not to notice, that the data the services are not convenient and do not meet the above requirements. Obviously, all four main

Fig. 1. View of the main pages of services of children's animation studios: a) children's animation studio "Igroland"; b) children's animation studio "Children's Planet"; c) the PAPASHON entertainment complex; d) "Empire of the Holiday" event-agency

pages of web services (Fig. 1) are not very different and do not display information regarding the choice of possible services. They do not have an intuitive or adapted interface. After pressing certain buttons and selecting menus, which, by the way, are not easy to find, the information doesn't get much more clear. So, for example, to find the list of services of the children's animation studio "Children's Planet", you must use the page scrolling, on the website of the children's animation studio "Igroland" you need to find the "Menu" button, and click on the "Details" button on the main page of the entertainment complex PAPASHON. However, even after that, not much more information is displayed. None of these services are immediately accessible to the complex of services that can be obtained based on a certain budget. Also, none of these services has the opportunity to introduce, for example, topics that are interesting for the child to get information about the range of services that the company can provide and the price range of these services, it is difficult to find differentiation of services by age categories and so on.

In addition to imperfect client-side work, these services are not functional enough to meet the needs of animation studio staff. Here are some of the main unsolved problems:

- does not have a cumulative database of customer preferences and needs;
- there is no service of forming comparative characteristics (cost, duration in time, age restrictions and number of participants, etc.) of different offers;

- when the client posts an order the administrator receives a notification about this event, which is not processed by the service itself, respectively, with a large influx of people who want to order the same service, the service will not help the administrator with this problem;
- there is no dynamic selection of the set of possible offers for the client according to the criteria he/she has set;
- there is no dynamic selection of possible offers for the client, taking into account time and quantitative parameters, the possibilities of the studios themselves, etc.

Survey questions introducing information technology in the entertainment industry dedicated work of many domestic and foreign researchers, scientific publications is Pauline J. Sheldon and P. Benckendorff [3] Rob Law and Ulrike Gretzel [5,9], R. Egger and D. Buhalis [4], M. M. Skopen [13], S. Melnichenko [12].

However, they are mostly dedicated to addressing the digitization of tourism animation services and, unfortunately, very little attention has been paid to digitizing the children's animation studio segment.

3   The Method of Improving the Work of Children's Animation Studio Services with the Use of Data Mining Technique

The problem of comparing different animation studios services, their pricing policy, the convenience of their location for the client and the quality of services, in our opinion, can be solved by building a composite web application - mashup data of children's animation studios [7]. Travature, which is a popular portal about tourism. Mashup Travature integrates flight search, hotel reviews and acts as a travel guide. Graphic, text, formal, etc. can be used to specify web services and their compositions ways. The main difference between a composite web application and web services that use dynamic server-side content generation with Java, CGI, PHP, or ASP technologies is that mashup content can be generated on the client browser side through client scripts. The logic of generating content on the client side is a combination of code embedded directly in the mashup web page.

To solve the problem of fast and high-quality data sampling, according to certain criteria set by the client (customer of animation services), it is necessary to use modern methods of intellectual data analysis. We believe that it is most appropriate for the organization of the effective operation of a service for managing the work of animation studios to use the Decision Trees methods, such as to enable, step by step, based on the client's request, to form from the existing set of services, the set of the most client-friendly solutions.

To construct Decision Trees most widely used in practice: algorithms binary search tree (BST), returning search algorithm (backtracking algorithm) and algorithms decision tree.

Obviously, the most effective way to search is to view all the data consistently. In fact, if you don't have the data you need, then you need to look through the entire list to find out. The binary search tree avoids this. The only requirement is the introduction of some linear order for the data [6], However, this way of organizing a children's animation studio service is not efficient, since many services providing these services are quite diverse in many aspects (age, price, preference, etc.) and arranging many of these different types of elements into a clear linear sequence is quite difficult and makes no sense. To our opinion, to sample a variety of possible services, it is advised to use the backtracking algorithm when choosing a client as a priority, the direction of pricing.

The main idea behind the backtracking algorithm is that the solution is built up gradually, starting with an empty sequence $\varnothing$ (length 0). In general, if there is a partial (incomplete) solution $(x_1, ..., x_i)$, where i< n, then we try to find such an admissible value of x_{i+1} that can be continued $(x_1, ..., x_i, x_{i+1})$ pending full resolution. If such a valid but not yet used value of x_{i+1} exists, then we add this new component to the partial solution and continue the process for the sequence $(x_1, ..., x_i, x_{i+1})$. If there is no such value of x_{i+1} , then we go back to the previous sequence $(x_1, ..., x_{i-1})$ and continue the process, looking for a new, not yet used value of x_i' [6].

The operation of this algorithm can be interpreted as a process of bypassing a tree. Each peak corresponds to it a sequence $(x_1, ..., x_i)$, with peaks that correspond to sequences of the form $(x_1, ..., x_i, y)$, sons of the summit. The root of the tree corresponds to an empty sequence. This tree is being traversed by searching deep. In addition, a predicate P is specified on all tree vertices. If $P(v) = False$, then the subtree vertices with root at vertex v are not considered, and the volume of the bust decreases. The predicate $P(v)$ acquires the value $False$ when it becomes clear that the sequence $(x_1, ..., x_i)$, corresponding to vertex v cannot be added to the complete solution. To apply this method, the solution of the problem must look like a finite sequence of elements $(x_1, ..., x_n)$.

In our case, the elements $(x_1, ..., x_n)$ of this sequence are the cost of the services that can be provided to the client within the budget that he or she determines (predicate P). This is exactly what a client wants, based on a specific budget. Initially, the client is offered a set of services that can be provided within a given budget, the client is able to remove/add certain of them, then the budget for other services increases/decreases. The algorithm returns the customer to the previous selection step, with the other set of service elements until the desired set of services within the client's budget is formed.

3.1   Description of the Backtracking Algorithm

After entering in the search window the "budget" of the amount that the client focuses on, the logic of the system employs a backtracking algorithm, which allows to form the set of services that can be provided within the specified budget.

Let us illustrate the algorithm for generating multiple offers (search with returns) in case the client chooses as a priority, the direction of the pricing policy, that is, according to the criteria "budget", in a specific example. Suppose that Table 1 sets the sets of services $(p_1, ..., p_n)$.

Table 1. Set of existing services

Code	Service	Cost	Duration
p1	Costume photoshoot	50 USD	1 h
p2	Rolledrome	30 USD	1 h
p3	Birthday greetings with cake	27 USD	30 min
p4	Weaving of African pigtails	25 USD	1 h
p5	Soap bubbles show	25 USD	1 h
p6	Trampoline arena	6 USD	1 h
p7	Aqua makeup	5 USD	30 min
p8	Trampoline "Treasure Island"	4 USD	30 min
p9	Maze	3 USD	unlimited

Each service is matched by its cost. You need to find a subset of which the cost of the elements does not exceed the client's criterion "budget" (CB). If the sum is so large that the addition of any new number exceeds CB then we go back and change the last addition of the sum. Let CB = 50 USD. Figure 2 illustrates part of the backtracking algorithm for the problem of finding a subset of a set of services $(p_1, ..., p_n)$ with the criterion "budget" equal to 50 USD. In

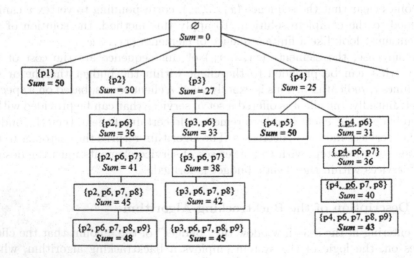

Fig. 2. Part of the backtracking algorithm for problem of finding the subset of a set of services $(p_1, ..., p_n)$ with the CB = 50 USD

general, when a subset of the set of services $(p_1, ..., p_n)$, given in Table 1 from the criterion "budget" is equal to 50 USD. The client may be offered 6 possible service options. Formed variants of subsets of possible services are given in Tables 2, 3, 4, 5, 6 and 7, respectively. And it should be noted that these options are provided, with information on the possible duration of the organized holiday.

Table 2. Set of existing services

Code	Service	Cost	Duration
p1	Costume photoshoot	50 USD	1 h
	Sum	**50 USD**	**1 h**

Table 3. Set of existing services

Code	Service	Cost	Duration
p2	Rolledrome	30 USD	1 h
p6	Trampoline arena	6 USD	1 h
p7	Aqua makeup	5 USD	30 min
p8	Trampoline "Treasure Island"	4 USD	30 min
p9	Maze	3 USD	unlimited
	Sum	**48 USD**	**unlimited**

Table 4. Set of existing services

Code	Service	Cost	Duration
p3	Birthday greetings with cake	27 USD	30 min
p6	Trampoline arena	6 USD	1 h
p7	Aqua makeup	5 USD	30 min
p8	Trampoline "Treasure Island"	4 USD	30 min
p9	Maze	3 USD	unlimited
	Sum	**45 USD**	**unlimited**

Once the client selected, a subset of the solutions that are most appropriate for him/her, he/she can make changes by removing/adding certain services (this will result in a certain budget change) and place an order.

If the client chooses as a priority, the content area of services, the most appropriate is to use the algorithm of building a decision tree. In this case, we need to solve the typical classification problem.

Table 5. Set of existing services

Code	Service	Cost	Duration
p4	Weaving of African pigtails	25 USD	1 h
p5	Soap bubbles show	25 USD	1 h
	Sum	**50 USD**	**2 h**

Table 6. Set of existing services

Code	Service	Cost	Duration
p4	Weaving of African pigtails	25 USD	1 h
p6	Trampoline arena	6 USD	1 h
p7	Aqua makeup	5 USD	30 min
p8	Trampoline "Treasure Island"	4 USD	30 min
p9	Maze	3 USD	unlimited
	Sum	**43 USD**	**unlimited**

Table 7. Set of existing services

Code	Service	Cost	Duration
p5	Soap bubbles show	25 USD	1 h
p6	Trampoline arena	6 USD	1 h
p7	Aqua makeup	5 USD	30 min
p8	Trampoline "Treasure Island"	4 USD	30 min
p9	Maze	3 USD	unlimited
	Sum	**43 USD**	**unlimited**

After all, when we consider a client's request in terms of the content topics of animation studio services, we need to make decisions about the set of existing objects (animation studio services), assigning them to certain thematic classes, that is, providing these objects with classification features. So we need to solve a typical classification problem whose set of conditional attributes A will be made up by the client's requirements. The set W is an active animation studio service; the set d is a decision attribute - two elements { "good luck", "bad luck" }.

3.2 Description of the Algorithm for Building a Decision Tree

After selecting a search box of your request priority area "subject", the customer will be asked to answer a few questions that are conditional attributes and accordingly help shape due to the algorithm for constructing Decision Tree, the set of possible proposals for a client under given his attributes.

Let's use one of the algorithms for building a Decision Tree, namely the algorithm ID3 (Iterative Dichotomiser-3 algorithm) [6]. To illustrate the algorithm for generating set of proposals using the algorithm for constructing Decision Tree to a specific example.

Let Table 8 provide information on options for a children's holiday. We construct Decision Tree for given Table 8.

A holiday is a decision-making attribute. The set of all conditional attributes $A = \{$ "age", "gender", "number of participants", "subject matter", "type of entertainment", "duration of entertainment", "budget"$\}$ corresponds to the root node. Select the attribute "age" and mark it the root vertex. The set of values of this attribute consists of three elements: up to 5 years, 5–10 years, more than 10 years. Put the root vertex in correspondence with three edges, each of which is attributed to the value of the attribute "age". Set examples will be divided into three subsets that correspond to the values of the attribute "age"; these subsets correspond to each of the vertices 2, 3, 4 of the tree shown in Figs. 3 We remove the attribute "age" from the set A and get the set $A = \{$ "gender", "number of participants", "subject matter", "type of entertainment", "duration of entertainment", "budget"$\}$.

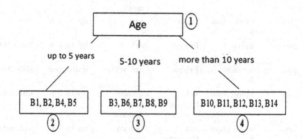

Fig. 3. The first step of the ID3 algorithm (removing the "age" attribute)

Consider the vertex number 3. It is matched by the subset of examples {B3, B7} that have the value of the decision attribute "Yes" and the subset of examples {B6, B8, B9} that have the value of the attribute of the decision "No". We select the following attribute from the set A; let it "gender". Denote by vertex 3, construct two edges with the values of this attribute, and divide the set of examples in vertex 3 into two subsets, in each of which the values of gender are the same (Fig. 4).

Consider the vertex number 6. It corresponds to the subset {B3}, which has the value of the decision attribute "Yes", and the subset of examples {B8, B9}, which have the value of the decision attribute "No". We select the following attribute from the set A; let it be the "number of participants". Denote by vertex 6, construct three edges with values of this attribute and divide the set of examples in vertex 3 into two subsets, in each of which the values of the number of participants are the same.

Table 8. Set of options for organizing holidays

Version	Age	Gender	Number of participants	Subject	Type of entertainment	Duration of entertainment	Budget	Holiday
1	up to 5 years	boy	up to 4	not thematic	are active	unlimited	unlimited	Yes
2	up to 5 years	boy	up to 4	ninja	science	30 min – 1 h	100–200	No
3	5–10 years	boy	4–8	ninja	science	30 min – 1 h	100–200	Yes
4	up to 5 years	boy	more than 8	Peppa	art	up to 2 h	unlimited	No
5	up to 5 years	girl	more than 8	Peppa	art	unlimited	100–200	Yes
6	5–10 years	girl	4–8	ninja	team entertainment	unlimited	100–200	No
7	5–10 years	girl	4–8	Lady Bug	team entertainment	unlimited	100–200	Yes
8	5–10 years	boy	more than 8	Lady Bug	team entertainment	unlimited	100–200	No
9	5–10 years	boy	more than 8	pirates	team entertainment	unlimited	up to 100	No
10	10 years	girl	more than 8	Peppa	art	up to 2 h	100–200	No
11	10 years	girl	up to 4	Peppa	art	up to 2 h	100–200	Yes
12	10 years	girl	more than 8	Peppa	are active	unlimited	100–200	No
13	10 years	girl	more than 8	not thematic	beauty and fashion	up to 2 h	unlimited	Yes
14	10 years	boy	more than 8	not thematic	beauty and fashion	up to 2 h	unlimited	No

In Fig. 5 in verse 7 we have an empty set, which indicates that under such criteria given by the client, we will not be able to offer him anything, that means that the holiday cannot be organized, so we will mark this vertex "no" and it will become a leaf. In verse 9, examples B8 and B9 have the same attributes of the game attribute - "No". Therefore, we denote this vertex by "No" and it will become a leaf. Similarly, we denote vertex 8 as "Yes" and it will also become a leaf.

Based on the decision tree we can define many rules. For example, the set of rules for the tree shown in Fig. 6 would look like this:

1) if (age = 5–10 years) and (gender = boy) and (number of participants = up to 4), then (holiday = no);
2) if (age = 5–10 years) and (gender = boy) and (number of participants = 4–8), then (holiday = yes);
3) if (age = 5–10 years) and (gender = boy) and (number of participants = over 8), then (holiday = no);

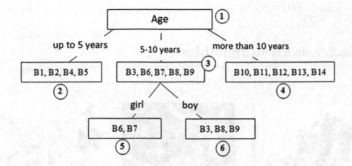

Fig. 4. The second step of the ID3 algorithm (removing the "gender" attribute)

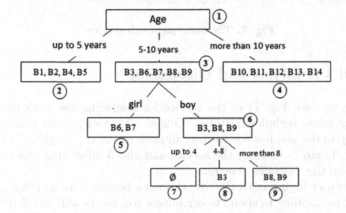

Fig. 5. The third step of the ID3 algorithm (removing the "number of participants" attribute)

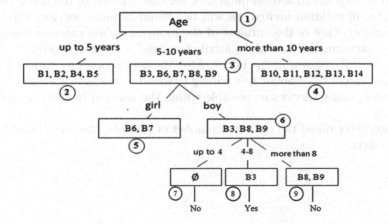

Fig. 6. The fourth step of the ID3 algorithm

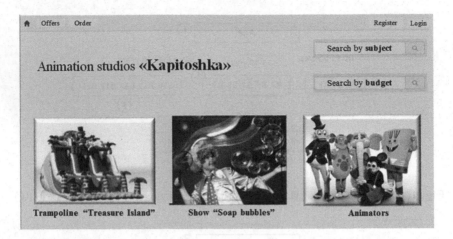

Fig. 7. The main page web service

4   Results Analysis and Discussion

The main page (see Fig. 7) of the service for managing the work of children's animation studios, includes buttons: "Offers" - for viewing, all available offers, "Order" - go to the window where you can place an order, "Register" - to register for service, "Login" - to enter the service and also 3 offers that can be accessed by clicking on the "Details" button.

After the user logged in to the site, chooses a budget search option and enters the amount he's willing to spend to organize a holiday, he will be offered as many services as possible within the selected budget, as shown in the Fig. 8.

If someone at the login page of the site selects the "search offers" option the direction of "subjects" and introduce the desired subjects of the holiday, he will be asked to respond to several questions, such as: the age of the child; budget, the number of children invited, he will be offered as many services within the chosen subject. One of the variants of the proposals when choosing the theme "Active entertainment" and given attributes: "age" - 11 years; "gender" - boy", budget - 50 USD, shown in the Fig. 9. After the user chooses a "budget search" option and enters the amount he's willing to spend to organize a holiday, he will be offered as many services as possible within the selected budget, as shown in the Fig. 8.

Having determined the optimum number of services, the user can order the selected offers.

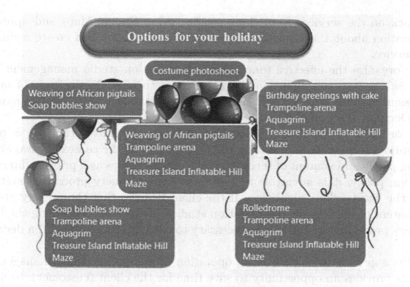

Fig. 8. A list of suggested holiday options

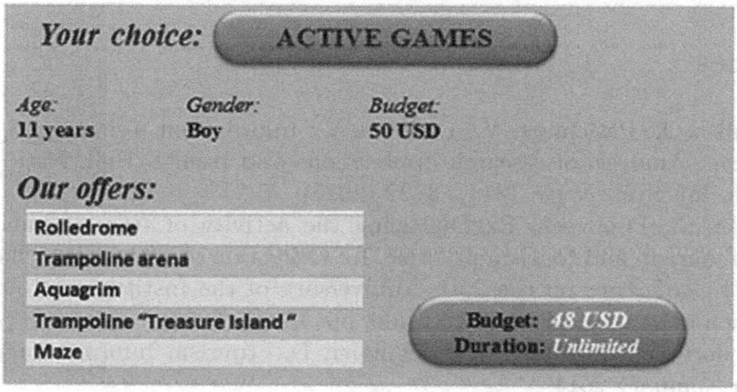

Fig. 9. A list of the proposed "Active Entertainment" holiday option

5   Conclusions

The demand for the services of children's animation studios is constantly growing. The number of children's animation studios and the variety of their services
is growing in direct proportion to the growth in demand. Accordingly, the search
for the best option for organizing a children's holiday, with a set of acceptable
(thematically/financially) services takes a long time. Building a composite web
application for animation studios will allow you to solve several tasks at once,
such as processing data from several sources, analyzing them, comparing them
and, as a result, choosing the suitable one. By combining various data (photos, videos, text information) about animation studios services, with people's

feedback on the services from these studios using Google Maps and applying information about the location of animation studios, you can create a unique web service.

To organize the effective functioning of animation studio management services, taking into consideration the specifics of their work, the logic of query processing systems must be built using modern methods of Data Mining, namely the "Decision Tree" methods.

In order to provide quality services, in a user-friendly format, it is most appropriate to provide information to the customer in the context of two areas: pricing policy and content of services. If the client chooses as a priority direction - pricing policy, it is advisable to build the logic of query processing systems using the backtracking algorithm. If the client believes that the priority area is the content of the services of animation studios, then when developing the logic of query processing systems, it is necessary to use algorithms to build a decision tree.

This approach to modeling the operation of animation studio management services provides an opportunity to save time for the client (customer), to make the optimal selection of services for each client from a set of possible services and reduce the burden on administrators of animation studios.

References

1. Artemenko, O., Pasichnyk, V., Egorova, V.: Information technologies in the field of tourism. Analysis of research applications and results. Bull. Natl. Univ. Lviv Polytech. Inf. Syst. Netw. (814), 3–22 (2015)
2. Babushko, S., Popovych, S.: Digitizing the activity of travel agencies. Topical issues of tourism and tourism practice. In: Collection of Materials of the Scientific-Practical Conference on the 25th Anniversary of the Institute of Tourism of the Federation of Trade Unions of Ukraine, pp. 13–15 (2019)
3. Benckendorff, P., Sheldon, P., Fesenmaier, D.: Tourism Information Technology, 2nd edn., January 2014
4. Buhalis, D., Egger, R. (eds.): eTourism case studies: management & marketing issues in eTourism, Butterworth Heinemann Oxford, February 2008. ISBN 0750686677, http://goo.gl/oavpD1, https://doi.org/10.13140/2.1.1225.5048
5. Buhalis, D., Leung, D., Law, R.: eTourism: critical information and communication technologies for tourism destinations. In: Destination Marketing and Management: Theories and Applications, pp. 205–224, August 2011. https://doi.org/10.1079/9781845937621.0205
6. Corman, T.: Algorithms: Construction and Analysis, 3rd edn. (2013). Trans. with English. M.: LLC "I. D. Williams"
7. Dumich, N., Smotr, O.: Construction composite web application animation studio. In: Abstracts of the Third All-Ukrainian Scientific and Practical Conference of Young Scientists, Students and Cadets "Information Protection in Information and Communication Systems", Lviv, 28 November 2019, pp. 268–269 (2019). https://ldubgd.edu.ua/sites/default/files/8_konferezii/zbirnyk_zakhystinformatsii.pdf
8. Gelter, H.: Digital tourism - an analysis of digital trends in tourism and customer digital mobile behavior for the Visit Arctic Europe project, May 2017

9. Gretzel, U., Law, R., Fuchs, M.: Information and Communication Technologies in Tourism. Springer, New York (2010). https://doi.org/10.1007/978-3-030-36737-4

10. Khoup, K.: The adult price for a children's holiday: how much do children's parties have? BBC News (2015). https://www.bbc.com/ukrainian/entertainment/2015/04/150407_children_party_dt

11. Kylymystyj, S.: Classification of animation activities. Int. Bull. Cult. Stud. Philol. Musicol. (II (5)), 77–83 (2015)

12. Melnichenko, S.: Information Technologies in Tourism: Theory, Methodology, Practice. KNTEU, Kyiv (2007)

13. Skopen, M., Sukach, M.: Information Systems and Technologies of Marketing in Tourism. Lira, Kyiv (2017). https://doi.org/10.26884/mks.t1627

14. VASYuK, K.: Digitization vs imitation: why technology progress in Ukraine is impaired (2017). https://eba.com.ua/didzhytalizatsiya-vs-imitatsiya-chomu-v-ukrayini-galmuye-tehnologichnyj-progres/

15. Website: The official website of Papashon entertainment complex. https://papashon.com/

16. Website: The official website of the children's animation studio "children's planet". http://dityacha-planeta.com/

17. Website: The official website of the children's animation studio "igroland". http://igroland.com.ua/ua

18. Website: The official website of the event-agency "empire of the holiday". http://isvyata.org/

19. Website: Theme parks business (part 1): how much money do they make? The parks database (2016). http://www.theparkdb.com/blog/the-business-of-theme-parks-part-i-how-much-money-do-they-make/

20. Website: Theme parks business (part 2): how much do they cost? And earn? The parks database (2016). http://www.theparkdb.com/blog/the-business-of-theme-parks-part-ii-how-much-do-they-cost-and-earn/

21. Website: Top 10 digital trends in 2018. Idea Digital Agency (2018). https://ideadigital.agency/10-golovne-digital-trendiv-u-2018-rotsi/

22. Website: State statistics service of Ukraine (2019). http://www.ukrstat.gov.ua/

23. Website: Why Tourism? World Tourism Organisation UNWTO (2019). https://www.unwto.org/global/press-release/2019-01-21/international-tourist-arrivals-reach-14-billion-two-years-ahead-forecasts

On-Line Data Processing, Simulation and Forecasting of the Coronavirus Disease (COVID-19) Propagation in Ukraine Based on Machine Learning Approach

Dmytro Chumachenko[1]([✉]) [iD], Tetyana Chumachenko[2] [iD], Ievgen Meniailov[1] [iD],
Pavlo Pyrohov[1] [iD], Ihor Kuzin[3] [iD], and Roman Rodyna[3] [iD]

[1] National Aerospace University "Kharkiv Aviation Institute", Kharkiv, Ukraine
dichumachenko@gmail.com, evgenii.menyailov@gmail.com,
pavel.vogorip@gmail.com
[2] Kharkiv National Medical University, Kharkiv, Ukraine
tatalchum@gmail.com
[3] State Institution "Public Health Center of the Ministry of Health of Ukraine",
Kyiv, Ukraine
ihorkuzin@gmail.com, r.rodyna@phc.org.ua

Abstract. The article analyzes the epidemic process of a new coronavirus infection. The influence of COVID-19 on society, education, healthcare and other areas is analyzed. The analysis of restrictive measures that are implemented in different countries is carried out. Based on machine learning methods, a model for the spread of the incidence of COVID-19 has been developed. The forecast of incidence in Ukraine is calculated. The accuracy of the forecast is 97.6%. For automatic calculation of predicted morbidity, a web service has been developed for processing data in real time. The developed model enables to conduct prospective monitoring of the epidemic situation, redistribute limited resources between different regions of the country that need them more at the forecast time, introduce new control methods or, on the contrary, weaken restrictive measures, and adjust measures depending on the forecast situation on the simulated territory.

Keywords: Machine learning · COVID-19 · Epidemic process simulation · Logistic growth · Coronavirus forecasting

1 Introduction and Current Research Analysis

Despite on the efforts of WHO to develop measures to prevent significant damage to the population from the emergence of a new previously unknown pathogen, the creation of programs and documents that highlight the main algorithms for action in the event of the emergence of such a new, previously unknown pathogen (IMSC), the medical community was unable to predict the emergence of a new

© Springer Nature Switzerland AG 2020
S. Babichev et al. (Eds.): DSMP 2020, CCIS 1158, pp. 372–382, 2020.
https://doi.org/10.1007/978-3-030-61656-4_25

pathogen and prevent its spread across countries and territories of the world. A new pathogen appeared at the end of 2019, and on December 31, 2019, WHO became aware of it, after receiving reports from China about the occurrence of a cluster of cases of pneumonia associ-ated with a previously unknown type of coronavirus, which was later called SARS-CoV-2, and the disease they cause is COVID-19 [37]. SARS-CoV-2 virus belongs to the Coronaviridae family, represented by more than 40 species that infect mammals and birds. It was found that the virus passed to humans from bats, however, as it happened, who is the intermediate host of the pathogen has not yet been established.

Scientists quickly deciphered the genetic structure of the pathogen [26], however, the features of its epidemiology required study. An important characteristic for assessing the spread of the virus is its contagiousness. The base reproductive number (R_0) was estimated at 2.2 (95% CI, 1.4 to 3.9) [20], i.e. one person can infect 2–3 susceptible individuals. Later, after the spread of COVID-19 in Europe, the average R_0 was estimated as 3.28, with a median of 2.79 [46]. The introduction of mitigation measures, the frequency of transmission of the pathogen from one person, the calculated effective reproductive number (R_e) was lower than the initial R_0 and amounted to 2.76 and 3.25 in all regions of Italy [9], especially after the national level comprehensive measures of physical distance have been introduced [21].

The complete lack of immunity in the population to a suddenly emerged new pathogen [30], the easily implemented aerosol transmission mechanism, the presence of mild and asymptomatic forms of the disease, and a rather high contagiousness were the main biological factors contributing to the wide spread of the virus among people. High migration activity of the population, its increased density, socio-economic characteristics of the development of regions, the lack of vaccines and specific treatment have become the main socio economic drivers that contributed to the coverage of COVID-19 large territories in a short time [38].

On 30 January 2020, WHO declared a global public health emergency - the highest level of anxiety that has persisted so far [36]. On March 11, 2020, when the virus spread to almost all continents of the world, WHO announced the COVID-19 pandemic [7].

As previously established, any biological threat causes not only medical damage, but also causes significant economic, social, cultural and humanitarian damage. Thus, the consequences of an anthrax attack in 2001 in the USA were diseases in 22 people, death of 5 and more than 1 billion dollars to climinate the consequences of using a biological agent [16]. In 2003, the financial loss from SARS was 30 billion in just 4 months [19]. In 2009, during the H1N1 pandemic, 284,000 people died in the first year alone [35].

The current COVID-19 pandemic claimed the lives of more than 302 thousand people, and more than 4.5 million people worldwide fell ill. In countries affected by the pandemic, the economy is suffering; business, primarily related to the service sector - closed restaurants, cafes, hairdressers, beauty salons, etc. [27]. There is a general loss of jobs, especially where work cannot be done remotely, and unemployment is growing [18]. Workers working in other countries cannot get to the place of work because of closed borders and discontinued work of transport, therefore they suffer significant losses and cannot support their families [42]. In general, the social standard of living of the population is declining, and there is a threat of hunger and poverty [17]. This situation not only directly affects the well-being of people who experience it, but can also indirectly affect society, leading to unpredictable consequences and a social crisis [40].

In the field of health, threats are not only related to COVID-19. People do not receive routine medical care, which can lead to exacerbation and progression of chronic diseases [22], chronicity of acute processes (diseases) [11]. There are difficulties in providing medical supplies, equipment, supplies due to the reduction or termination of supplies.

There are also problems in education [8]. Closing kindergartens slows the development of children, their cognitive abilities and communication skills [45], the absence of fresh air, and the sun worsens the physical condition of children, reduces the body's resistance, weakens the immune system [10]. Closed schools, the transfer of distance learning reduces the level of basic education, children are deprived of face-to-face communication, lose their non-verbal communication skills, teamwork skills [41]. The transfer of universities to distance education does not provide an opportunity to master practical skills [43], and for some specialties, for example, medical [12], this can be critical or even catastrophic [34].

People are deprived of their usual way of life, cannot travel, carry out religious functions, are forced to spend a long time in a confined space with their family members. This can cause psychological discomfort, mental disorders [32]. There are reports of an increase in the frequency of suicides during quarantine [15], an increase in the number of cases of domestic violence [39], especially in relation to women [33] and children [13]. The quarantine exerts a destabilizing pressure on cultural and religious traditions [31], a person's social status, and people's connection with society. Thus, the consequences of the COVID-19 pandemic can be serious and even catastrophic [1].

Each country independently chooses its own way of combating the SARS-CoV-2 coronavirus. But the society and government of each country faces a difficult choice - to impose strict restrictions on the population, or vice versa, it is possible to carry out soft restrictive measures or even completely abandon them [28]. When to start easing restrictions? How to establish, without a significant increase in the number of cases and deaths, that the lifting of restrictions was premature? Which managerial decision to adjust public health measures and social activities should be chosen? How to reduce the impact of existing risks on the health and life of a person and society? How to establish a reasonable balance between the level of security and the prevention of financial, socio-economic, humanitarian, cultural damage?

The COVID-19 pandemic has become a challenge for healthcare systems, and forecasting the dynamics of cases has become an indispensable tool for calculating the required capacities of medical institutions, the supply of personal protective equipment, medicines, ICU ventilators, etc. [4]. Forecasting helps to implement rational measures to mitigate the spread of the virus so that the health system could handle the flow of patients [23]. A forecast is also necessary so that governments, having assessed the situation, can implement measures to preserve both the health and lives of the population and the country's economy [2].

This article proposes a tool for high-precision short-term prediction of the spread of SARS-CoV-2, which can be used to assess the dynamics and extent of the spread of SARS-CoV-2 and make decisions on adjusting public health measures to reflect the changing epidemiological situation as the pandemic develops.

2   Materials and Methods

2.1   Data and Sources

At the first stage, a model of the epidemic process was built on the basis of machine learning methods. For this, we used the data of the State Institution "Public Health Center of the Ministry of Health of Ukraine" on the daily incidence of coronavirus infection (COVID-19), distributed across the regions of Ukraine.

The second stage included the translation of the model online to calculate the forecast of the dynamics of coronavirus infection (COVID-19) in Ukraine in real time. For this, we used the statistics of new cases of coronavirus infection (COVID-19) published on the official website of the National Security and Defense Council of Ukraine.

2.2   Simulation Method

We have built a mathematical model of spreading of coronavirus infection based on machine learning and evaluated its effectiveness.

The machine learning methods of epidemic process simulation have shown the best performance in this study [6]. The method used to simulate population dynamics was used - the model of logistic growth, or the Verhulst model [29]. The model has the form of a differential equation

$$\frac{dP}{dt} = rP(1 - \frac{P}{K}), \tag{1}$$

where P is the population size, t is time, r is the virus propagation speed, K is the medium capacity, or the maximum population size.

The exact solution to Eq. (1) is the logistic function, which has the following form:

$$P(t) = \frac{KP_0e^{rt}}{(K + P_0(e^{rt} - 1)}, \lim_{t\to\infty} P(t) = K. \tag{2}$$

Polynomial regression [44] was used to predict the number of patients with coronavirus. The polynomial is selected by dividing the samples into the ones by which the model will be trained and tested. An experimental study showed that the most accurate prediction of the incidence of coronavirus in Ukraine is achieved using a polynomial of the 6th degree. The accuracy of the forecast was evaluated by comparing the forecast of incidence for the last week with actual data on incidence, and it was equal to 97.9 % (Fig. 1).

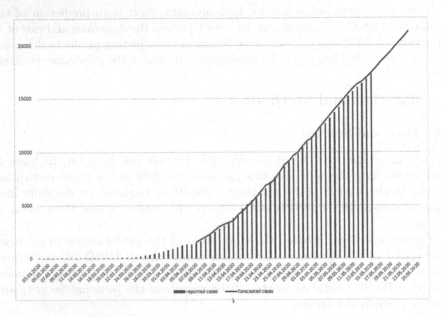

Fig. 1. Validation of simulation model (example of new COVID-19 cases in Ukraine)

3   Results and Discussion

3.1   Forecasting Results

The model allows to build a short-term forecast for 10 days with high accuracy. This allows to assess the real situation in the country and shows the prospects of control and preventive measures.

The forecast obtained as a result of simulation shows an exponential increase in the incidence of coronavirus in Ukraine (Fig. 2).

3.2   Web-Service Development

Web services enable interoperability of software systems regardless of platform. There are many ways to organize a web service that will process HTTP requests from users and return the desired result. Python was used for data processing, therefore, for easier organization of the web service, Python libraries were also chosen.

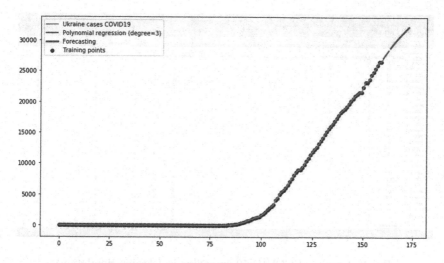

Fig. 2. Results of COVID-19 spreading in Ukraine simulation

Flask [14] is a framework for creating web applications in the Python programming language, using the Werkzeug toolkit, as well as the Jinja2 template engine. It belongs to the category of so-called microframes - minimalistic frameworks of web applications with an integrated web server. The Requests [5] library was also used for: creating HTTP requests; analysis of data requests and responses; Creation of authorized requests; query settings to pre-vent crashes and slow down the application.

You also need to select a tool to collect data from html pages and save them to the database. For these purposes, the open-source Scrapy [3] - framework library was selected for retrieving data from web pages. Features are: the ability to export data in such formats as JSON, CSV and XML; has built-in support for selecting and retrieving data from sources using XPath or CSS expressions. XPath is a query lan-guage for xml and xhtml documents. XPath selectors are used when working with the lxml library.

After parsing the necessary data for the regions of Ukraine per day, the data is saved in a csv file using the Pandas library. The view of this file is shown in Fig. 3. Pandas [24] is a Python program library for data processing and analysis. Pandas data work is built on top of the NumPy library, which is a lower-level tool. Provides special data structures and operations for manipulating numerical tables and time series. Randas is licensed under the BSD.

To create interactive graphs, the Plotly library [25] was used. Plotly was built using Python and the Djang framework, with an external interface using JavaScript and the D3.js visualization library, HTML and CSS. With Plotly, you can easily create interactive charts to visualize data. Any chart created using the library is equipped with features such as zooming, panning, auto-scaling, etc. These functions are very useful when you have to visualize a large amount of

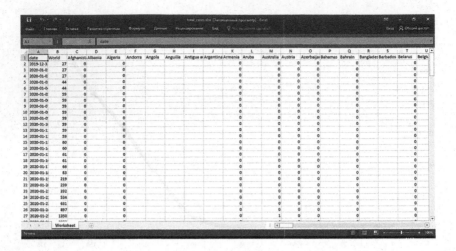

Fig. 3. Results of COVID-19 spreading in Ukraine simulation)

data. All events during operation are displayed in the API, so it is possible to create scripts to perform your own actions when processing any event.

The general structure of the developed Web service is shown in Fig. 4.

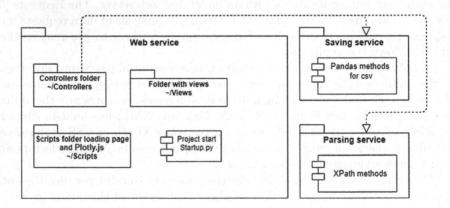

Fig. 4. Web-service structure

The developed web service consists of 4 components. The main component is the Startup.py file - it serves to launch a web project using the Flask library. The Views folder contains views for displaying the user interface. The Scripts folder contains the main scripts for the Plotly.js library. The Controllers folder contains scripts for organ-izing page transitions and the main dependency functionality of the two Saving and Parsing services. Saving service is used to update, save, read data. Parsing service for working with parsing sites with the necessary data and their processing.

Figure 5 presents the visualization of data on the number of cases in each of the region of Ukraine.

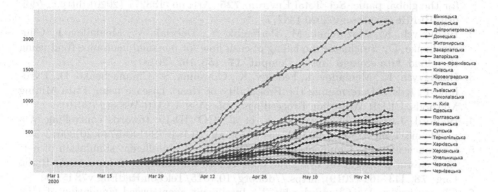

Fig. 5. Interactive graph of COVID-19 incidence

4 Conclusions

COVID-19 pandemie is an unpredictable threat to public health, national economies and the development of society, which can have uncontrolled consequences and cascading effects on all aspects of society. In order to successfully cope with the threat that has arisen, reduce the impact on the health systems and economies of the countries, and overcome the unintended consequences of public health measures taken to combat the COVID-19 pandemic, it is necessary to respond in a timely manner to the changing epidemic situation, introducing effective, scientifically based, adequate to the existing situations, rational measures. An effective tool has been developed for this.

We proposed a method for estimating and short-term forecasting of the incidence of COVID-19, which is based on machine learning. The model shows high accuracy and can be applied both in different countries and different regions of one country, which was verified by experiments on actual incidence data in Ukraine.

Despite on the fact that the method has certain limitations, such as neglection of the influence of factors on the spread of the pathogen, the presence of asymptomatic and low-symptom cases that are not included in the statistics, and the fact that the introduction of new methods to curb the spread of the virus can affect the accuracy of the forecast, the possibility of daily forecasting for the next 10 days allows to miti-gate these shortcomings.

We consider the developed model enables to conduct prospective monitoring of the epidemic situation, redistribute limited resources between different regions of the country that need them more at the forecast time, introduce new control methods or, on the contrary, weaken restrictive measures, and adjust measures depending on the forecast situation on the simulated territory.

References

1. Balachandar, V., Kaavya, J., Mahalaxmi, I., et al.: COVID-19: a promising cure for the global panic. Sci. Total Environ. **725**, Art. no. 138277 (2020). https://doi.org/10.1016/j.scitotenv.2020.138277
2. Bazilevych, K., Mazorchuk, M., Parfeniuk, Y., Dobriak, V., Meniailov, I., Chumachenko, D.: Stochastic modelling of cash flow for personal insurance fund using the cloud data storage. Int. J. Comput. **17**, 153–162 (2018)
3. Bazilevych, K., Meniailov, I., Fedulov, K., Goranina, S., Chumachenko, D., Pyrohov, P. (eds.): Determining the Probability of Heart Disease using Data Mining Methods, CEUR Workshop Proceedings, vol. 2488. CEUR-WS.org (2019)
4. Bedford, J., Enria, D., Giesecke, J., et al.: COVID-19: towards controlling of a pandemic. Lancet **395** (2020). https://doi.org/10.1016/S0140-6736(20)30673-5
5. Chumachenko, D., Chumachenko, K., Yakovlev, S.: Intelligent simulation of network worm propagation using the code red as an example. Telecommun. Radio Eng. **78**, 443–464 (2019). https://doi.org/10.1615/TelecomRadEng.v78.i5.60
6. Chumachenko, D., Chumachenko, T.: Intelligent agent-based simulation of HIV epidemic process. In: Lytvynenko, V., Babichev, S., Wójcik, W., Vynokurova, O., Vyshemyrskaya, S., Radetskaya, S. (eds.) ISDMCI 2019. AISC, vol. 1020, pp. 175–188. Springer, Cham (2020). https://doi.org/10.1007/978-3-030-26474-1_13
7. Cucinotta, D., Vanelli, M.: WHO declares COVID-19 a pandemic. Acta BioMedica: Atenei Parmensis **91**, 157–160 (2020). https://doi.org/10.23750/abm.v91i1.9397
8. Daniel, J.: Education and the COVID-19 pandemic. PROSPECTS **49**, 1–6 (2020). https://doi.org/10.1007/s11125-020-09464-3
9. D'Arienzo, M., Coniglio, A.: Assessment of the SARS-CoV-2 basic reproduction number, R0, based on the early phase of COVID-19 outbreak in Italy. Biosaf. Health **2**(2), 57–59 (2020). https://doi.org/10.1016/j.bsheal.2020.03.004
10. Dong, Y., Mo, X., Hu, Y., Qi, X., Jiang, F., Jiang, Z., Tong, S.: Epidemiology of COVID-19 among children in China. Pediatrics **145**(6) (2020). https://doi.org/10.1542/peds.2020-0702
11. Extance, A.: COVID-19 and long term conditions: what if you have cancer, diabetes, or chronic kidney disease? (2020). https://doi.org/10.1136/bmj.m1174
12. Ferrel, M., Ryan, J.: The impact of COVID-19 on medical education. Cureus **12** (2020). https://doi.org/10.7759/cureus.7492
13. Green, P.: Risks to children and young people during COVID-19 pandemic. BMJ **369**, Art. no. m1669 (2020). https://doi.org/10.1136/bmj.m1669
14. Grinberg, M.: Flask Web Development: Developing Web Applications with Python, 1st edn. O'Reilly Media Inc., Newton (2014)
15. Gunnell, D., Appleby, L., Arensman, E., et al.: Suicide risk and prevention during the COVID-19 pandemic. Lancet Psychiatry **7** (2020). https://doi.org/10.1016/S2215-0366(20)30171-1
16. Joshi, S., Cymet, H., Kerkvliet, G., Cymet, T.: Anthrax in America 2001–2003. J. Natl. Med. Assoc. **96**, 344–50 (2004)
17. Kalu, B.: COVID-19 in Nigeria: a disease of hunger. Lancet Respir. Med. **8**(6), 556–557 (2020). https://doi.org/10.1016/s2213-2600(20)30220-4
18. Kawohl, W., Nordt, C.: COVID-19, unemployment, and suicide. Lancet Psychiatry **7**, 389–390 (2020). https://doi.org/10.1016/S2215-0366(20)30141-3
19. Lee, J.W., Mckibbin, W.: Estimating the global economic costs of SARS. In: Learning from SARS: Preparing for the Next Disease Outbreak - Workshop Summary, pp. 92–109 (2004)

20. Li, Q., Guan, X., Wu, P., et al.: Early transmission dynamics in Wuhan, China, of novel coronavirus-infected pneumonia. New Engl. J. Med. **382**(13), 1199–1207 (2020). https://doi.org/10.1056/NEJMoa2001316
21. Liu, Y., Gayle, A.A., Wilder-Smith, A., Rocklöv, J.: The reproductive number of COVID-19 is higher compared to SARS coronavirus. J. Travel Med. **27**(2) (2020). https://doi.org/10.1093/jtm/taaa021
22. Martini, N., Piccinni, C., Pedrini, A., Maggioni, A.: COVID-19 and chronic diseases: current knowledge, future steps and the MaCroScopio project. Recenti progressi in medicina **111**, 198–201 (2020). https://doi.org/10.1701/3347.33180
23. Mazorchuck, M., Dobriak, V., Chumachenko, D.: Web-application development for tasks of prediction in medical domain, pp. 5–8 (2018). https://doi.org/10.1109/STC-CSIT.2018.8526684
24. McKinney, W.: Python for Data Analysis. Data Wrangling with Pandas, NumPy, and IPython, 2nd edn. OReilly Media Inc., Newton (2017)
25. Meniailov, I., Bazilevych, K., Fedulov, K., Goranina, S., Chumachenko, D.: Using the K-means method for diagnosing cancer stage using the pandas library. In: MoMLeT (2019)
26. Mousavizadeh, L., Ghasemi, S.: Genotype and phenotype of COVID-19: their roles in pathogenesis. J. Microbiol. Immunol. Infect. (2020). https://doi.org/10.1016/j.jmii.2020.03.022
27. Nicola, M., Alsafi, Z., Sohrabi, C., et al.: The socio-economic implications of the coronavirus and COVID-19 pandemic: a review. Int. J. Surg. **78** (2020). https://doi.org/10.1016/j.ijsu.2020.04.018
28. Nussbaumer-Streit, B., Mayr, V., Dobrescu, A., et al.: Quarantine alone or in combination with other public health measures to control COVID-19: a rapid review. Cochrane Database Syst. Rev. **4** (2020). https://doi.org/10.1002/14651858.CD013574
29. Polyvianna, Y., Chumachenko, D., Chumachenko, T.: Computer aided system of time series analysis methods for forecasting the epidemics outbreaks, pp. 1–4 (2019). https://doi.org/10.1100/CADSM.2019.8779344
30. Prompetchara, E., Ketloy, C., Palaga, T.: Immune responses in COVID-19 and potential vaccines: lessons learned from SARS and MERS epidemic. Asian Pac. J. Allergy Immunol. **38** (2020). https://doi.org/10.12932/AP-200220-0772
31. Quadri, S.A.: COVID-19 and religious congregations: implications for spread of novel pathogens. Int. J. Infect. Dis. **96** (2020). https://doi.org/10.1016/j.ijid.2020.05.007
32. Rajkumar, R.: COVID-19 and mental health: a review of the existing literature. Asian J. Psychiatry **52**, Art. no. 102066 (2020). https://doi.org/10.1016/j.ajp.2020.102066
33. Roesch, E., Amin, A., Gupta, J., García-Moreno, C.: Violence against women during COVID-19 pandemic restrictions. BMJ **369**, Art. no. m1712 (2020). https://doi.org/10.1136/bmj.m1712
34. Rose, S.: Medical student education in the time of COVID-19. JAMA **323** (2020). https://doi.org/10.1001/jama.2020.5227
35. Shrestha, S., Swerdlow, D., Borse, R., et al.: Estimating the burden of 2009 pandemic influenza a (H1N1) in the United States (April 2009–April 2010). Clinical infectious diseases: an official publication of the Infectious Diseases Society of America **52**(1), S75–82 (2011). https://doi.org/10.1093/cid/ciq012
36. Sohrabi, C., Alsafi, Z., O'Neill, N., et al.: World health organization declares global emergency: a review of the 2019 novel coronavirus (COVID-19). Int. J. Surg. **76**, 71–76 (2020). https://doi.org/10.1016/j.ijsu.2020.02.034

37. Steffens, I.: A hundred days into the coronavirus disease (COVID-19) pandemic. Euro. Surveill. Bull. Europeen sur les maladies transmissibles = Euro. Commun. Disease Bull. **25**(14), art. no. 2000550 (2020). https://doi.org/10.2807/1560-7917. ES.2020.25.14.2000550

38. Trilla, A.: One world, one health: the novel coronavirus COVID-19 epidemic. Medicina Clínica (English Edition) **154**(5), 175–177 (2020). https://doi.org/10. 1016/j.medcle.2020.02.001

39. Usher, K., Bhullar, N., Durkinet, J., et al.: Family violence and COVID-19: Increased vulnerability and reduced options for support. Int. J. Mental Health Nurs. **29**(4), 549–552 (2020). https://doi.org/10.1111/inm.12735

40. Van Lancker, W., Parolin, Z.: COVID-19, school closures, and child poverty: a social crisis in the making. Lancet Pub. Health **5** (2020). https://doi.org/10.1016/ S2468-2667(20)30084-0

41. Viner, R., Russell, S., Croker, H., et al.: School closure and management practices during coronavirus outbreaks including COVID-19, a rapid systematic review. Lancet Child Adolesc. Health **4** (2020). https://doi.org/10.1016/S2352-4642(20)30095-X

42. Wells, C., Sah, P., Moghadas, S., et al.: Impact of international travel and border control measures on the global spread of the novel 2019 coronavirus outbreak. Proc. Natl. Acad. Sci. **117**, art. no. 2002616 (2020). https://doi.org/10.1073/pnas. 2002616117

43. Wendelboe, A., Drevets, D., Miller, E., Jackson, D., et al.: Article: tabletop exercise to prepare institutions of higher education for an outbreak of COVID-19. J. Emerg. Manag. **18**, 183–184 (2020). https://doi.org/10.5055/jem.2020.0463

44. Xue, H., Bai, Y., Hu, H., Ldfs, H.: Influenza activity surveillance based on multiple regression model and artificial neural network. IEEE Access (2017). https://doi. org/10.1109/ACCESS.2017.2771798

45. Zhen-Dong, Y., Gao-Jun, Z., Run-Ming, J., et al.: Clinical and transmission dynamics characteristics of 406 children with coronavirus disease 2019 in China: a review. J. Infect. (2020). https://doi.org/10.1016/j.jinf.2020.04.030

46. Zhu, N., Zhang, D., Wang, W., et al.: A novel coronavirus from patients with pneumonia in China, 2019. New Engl. J. Med. **382**(8), 727–733 (2020). https:// doi.org/10.1056/NEJMoa2001017

Detecting Items with the Biggest Weight Based on Neural Network and Machine Learning Methods

Vitaliy Danylyk[1] , Victoria Vysotska[1](✉) , Vasyl Lytvyn[1] ,
Svitlana Vyshemyrska[2] , Iryna Lurie[2] , and Mykhailo Luchkevych[3]

[1] Lviv Polytechnic National University, Lviv, Ukraine
webdvitaly@gmail.com, {Victoria.A.Vysotska,vasyl.v.lytvyn}@lpnu.ua
[2] Kherson National Technical University, Kherson, Ukraine
printvvs@gmail.com, lurieira@gmail.com
[3] Drohobych Ivan Franko State Pedagogical University, Drohobych, Ukraine
luchkevychmm@gmail.com

Abstract. The article considers the development of a program for predicting areas on the design of the graphical interface, where users' attention will be greatest. Current methods of improving graphic design in accordance with UX and software for getting UX information are considered. In this project the problem in complexity of creation of the graphic user interface for modern programs, web resources, and applications is considered. Namely, the problem is related to UX design, with errors that occur at the stage of product launch. Also considered methods to help avoid errors, software, using which, will help avoid difficulties and errors. The concept of developing a program for recognizing areas to which the user is most likely to pay attention in the first place is considered. This program aims to help designers to create a modern graphical user interface design that will guide the user to the right places and the user will spend a minimum of time and effort to interact and use the program. A method has developed to collect data on the behavior of the user's eyes when using the program, during user interaction with the program interface. This method will create a database on the basis of which the program to predict the most visible areas will return the result.

Keywords: UX design · Tolkit · Web design · User experience ·
User statistic · Neural network · User information · Predict
information · GUI · Prediction · MachinelLearning · Visual weight ·
Detecting item · Biggest weight · Graphical interface ·
IntelligentsSystem · Program

1 Introduction

In today's world, more and more programs are appearing to make people's lives easier. Because people use them, developers make a graphical interface for human

© Springer Nature Switzerland AG 2020
S. Babichev et al. (Eds.): DSMP 2020, CCIS 1158, pp. 383–396, 2020.
https://doi.org/10.1007/978-3-030-61656-4_26

interaction with the program. Now, there are many useful applications that are used by many people, but not all of them are perfect [2,3,13]. Comparing programs with similar functionality, you can find many disadvantages and many advantages. Since modern programs have a lot of functionality, there are many disadvantages that due to the difficulty of finding the right information [1,18,19]. Today, users do not want to spend time and effort searching for the right information or function provided by the program, and if the copied program is easier to perceive, it usually replaces the existing one. In the field of digital technologies, there is a tendency to simplicity. The simpler the website or interface of the program, the more understandable it is to the user and the easier it is to use. In this regard, it will be useful to create a program to facilitate the work of designers, which can be used anywhere where there is access to the Internet. To facilitate the work of designers, they would be very useful information about their analyzed design prototype, according to which they would immediately make appropriate changes.

The aim of the work is to develop a system for predicting areas with the greatest visual weight, and its implementation in the WEB. The object of the study is the user's actions on different types of graphical program interfaces, as well as their feelings when using different programs with different visual interfaces.

The subject of the research is the methods and means by which it is possible to predict the details of the design to which the user will pay attention in the first place.

As a result of the study, a system was created, the functionality of which allows you to predict the areas that will attract the user's attention in the first place.

2   Related Works

One of the first concepts of the graphical interface is web representation [13]. The web, originally invented by programmers for their own needs, did not long remain an uncomfortable realm of randomly selected fonts on a grey background [3]. Already in the mid-nineties, business came to him, and after him, feeling the demand, and designers came up. Initially, they were natives of printing, primarily advertising. A little later, they were joined by printers - specialists in the correct placement of text. They provide it with greater readability and quality of perception.

But by the end of the nineties - the beginning of zero, it became clear that the sites are much more complex than printed products: the whole thing was in their interactivity. How to place a button so that it is noticed? Why do my users not want to fill out the feedback form and the competitor is fine with it? How, after all, to force the person to remain on a site longer if only one click on an oblique cross separates it from care? Every year the urgency of these questions grew, and those who could answer them became more and more popular. It occurred to them that ease of use is more important than the beauty of the product [2].

These people called their new discipline usability. Later, usability began to call themselves designers of user interfaces - UI-designers [1,18,19].

The path from creating just user-friendly interfaces to the work of UX designers, to the full design of the user experience - this is how you can most fully explain the meaning of the abbreviation UX - took about ten years.

UX (user experience) designers are responsible for the simplicity and ease of perception of information [2,3,13]. Specialists in this area in IT create interfaces that greatly facilitate the interaction of people with any computer system [4, 5,14,15,22]. They keep the TA (Target Audience) in the application or on the pages of the virtual portal, promote attachment to the product. For example, user interest quickly disappears if:

- The user has to be nervous because of the inconvenient search for settings on the smartphone [7,20,21];
- Spend a lot of time on useless clicks in the online store to make a purchase [12,23];
- Go through all the navigation functions in the application for use an easy action.

Lightness, conciseness and instant solution of the target task - this is what the modern public on the Internet and owners of mobile devices need. The main purpose of integrated design for one or a team of specialists in the direction of UX and UI design is to bring the guest of the web resource or application user to a specific logical point by the shortest path [8–11,16,17]. Actions must be performed in the most understandable interface for him. The aesthetic design of the shell and the hidden functionality behind it should make it easier for the user to achieve his goals, and, at the same time, lead to the purchase or order of the service. This is the main difficulty, and many beginners make many mistakes.

3   Materials and Methods

The "<canvas>" tag is used to visualize the program on the web page. It is controlled from JS and displays the entire program. The Brain.JS library is used to work with the neural network. With the help of this library, a neural network is created and the result calculations are performed.

This library implements the main functions responsible for the operation of the neural network. They are all well optimized. There are two main ones:

- "Feedforward" algorithm,
- "Backpropagation" algorithm.

3.1   "Feedforward" Algorithm

This algorithm is used to calculate the value of each neuron in the neural network (Fig. 1). At the entrance to the network comes the initial data, i.e. the initial layer of neurons is filled. Since neurons are connected, these connections have their own weight, which determines what will be at the output of the system [22]. This algorithm runs on each neuron and calculates the value according to the formula: $x = \sum_{i=0}^{n} \omega_{ji} * x_{ji}$, where j - is the number of the neuron's layer, ω - is the weight of the connection between the neurons, x - is the value of the neuron of the previous layer. After that, the value is overwritten by the value that has passed through the activation function. The activation function looks like this: $(x) = \dfrac{1}{1 + e^{-x}}$.

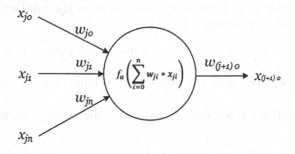

Fig. 1. "Feedforward" algorithm

It is used in the main program to process input data and obtain output.

3.2 "Backpropagation" Algorithm

This algorithm is used to train the neural network (Fig. 2), i.e. to determine the weights of the connections of neurons. For it to work, you need to have an actual and correct answer. Accordingly, to obtain the actual response of the network, you need to skip the input data using a direct propagation algorithm with which all the values of neurons will obtained. Subtracting the correct answer from the actual, we get a mistake on the original neuron or neurons [22]. Next, having an error, the new weight of the connection of neurons is determined by the formula: $\omega_{new} = \omega_{old} + \eta\delta\dfrac{df_a(x)}{dx}x$, where ω – is the weight, η – is learning speed ratio, δ – is right neuron error, x – is the value of the left neuron, f_a – is activation function. To find the error on all other neurons except the original you need to use the formula: $\delta_{(j-1)0} = \sum_{i=0}^{n} \omega_{ji} * \delta_{ji}$, where ω - is all the weight of the connection coming from the neuron for which the error is sought, δ – is the error.

It is used to form connections between neurons (Fig. 3). After starting this algorithm, a file is created which is used in the main program to form a neural network in the client's computer.

The neural network consists of an input layer, four hidden layers, and an output layer. The input layer takes the value of pixels, one pixel - one neuron. Hidden layers contain 800, 700, 600, 500 neurons, respectively. The source layer contains two neurons, which have the value of the position of the point showing the area with the highest visual weight (X and Y coordinates). Such a large number of neurons are because the more neurons there are in the neural network,

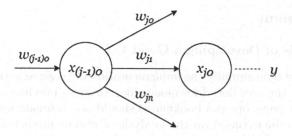

Fig. 2. "Backpropagation" algorithm

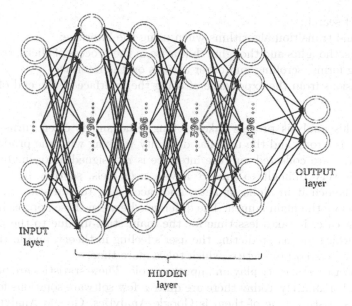

Fig. 3. View of the neural network

the better it can determine the hidden patterns. Since the input images can have different sizes, which mean different numbers of pixels, it was necessary to convert the image to a fixed, defined size to use one neural network with a given number of input neurons. Therefore, any image is cropped, and reduced or enlarged to 64 by 64 pixels. In addition, the pixel consists of 3 colors and this means that the number of input neurons should increase threefold, but we can convert the image to black and white image. This means that the value of the three colors in a pixel will be the same and it is enough to transmit only the value of one color and the neural network.

4   Experiment

4.1   Methods of Developing a Good UX

The structure should simplify the implementation of targeted actions as much as possible. What the user does (downloads files, makes a purchase, answers a poll, goes to another page, opens a bookmark) should also resonate with the business goals of the product. Based on the analysis of real or predicted actions of the TA, the concept of UX is created in the early stages of development. Thus, all way and sequence of actions of the target client is investigated [2, 3, 13]:

- Product search;
- Click and transition algorithms when using the interface;
- Feelings, thoughts and thoughts that arise in the process of clicks, transitions, sending forms, scrolling and other actions on the interface;
- Impressions from the experience of using the interface at the end of the process.

Usually, this analysis process takes a long time and it often turns out that something is wrong and the user has difficulty working with the product. Then the statistics are collected and the interface is redesigned accordingly. In some cases, it is very difficult to predict how a user feels, so they first create an interface, launch it in alpha or beta, and, according to statistics, make many changes before the main launch. The difference between these approaches is that in the first case, it takes less time for the main start-up due to the performed research, which means predicting the user's feeling in theory, and in the second case, it is all tested in practice, which takes more time.

In two cases, statistics play an important role. These statistics are not so easy to collect. Fortunately, today there are quite a few software solutions for collecting these statistics. One of them is Google Analytics. Google Analytics easily integrates into the code and allows you to collect the necessary information:

- The number of clicks in the area;
- How long the user has been on a page;
- How much time the user spent searching for the required information.

It is also easy to export data in various forms for use in other data analysis programs. Still, like in all other programs, you need not only to draw the design, but also to program it for the interface to work properly, because to collect information it needs to published, and users must be able to interact with it. This takes a lot of time from the developers and because of this, a large audience is lost.

4.2   A Program that Will Help us to Develop a Good UX

Since in current approaches the audience plays an important role for statistics and, accordingly, it takes a lot of time, so, it was necessary to do it, to obtain information about the design of the interface, without its programming and publication, at the drawing stage. This would give maximum time optimization. It becomes clear that the answer is a program, the entrance to which comes the picture, and the output will be information, predictions about user actions.

We can try many approaches to program development, but the most optimistic is to use an artificial neural network [5,6,14]. Having large statistics of user actions on various graphical interfaces it is possible to transfer this data to a neural network that it will have trained by this information. The network will give very accurate results according to these statistics for new GUI designs, i.e. will predict a user experience according to statistics. For convenience, the information provided by the design program (Fig. 4) will displayed directly on the initial image of the design. The first version of the program includes the ability to predict the area that attracts the most attention. This feature will describe below.

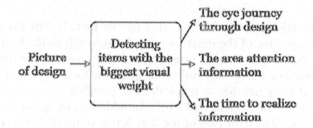

Fig. 4. Diagram of the program working

The source information will be:

- Travel the user's gaze on the design
- The area that attracts the most attention
- The time required to understand the information

You can make design changes to this information. The program does not require large system requirements, so for ease of use it is better to do on the web [4,15,22]. Users will be able to use it without unnecessary installations [7,12,20,21,23]. At the beginning, a prototype of the program was developed (Fig. 5).

It shows the placement of the program logo and the program itself in the form of a squared box. This box will display the loaded design image. Thus, the designer will need to analyze the information coming from the program in accordance with the input design and in accordance with the analysis to make corrections.

The program should provide a sense of user, respectively; you need to have a lot of data, a large database. There is a lot of data on the Internet, but not in the form we need, so first we had to somehow collect this data. The way out was a copy of the main program, but with some differences. This data collection

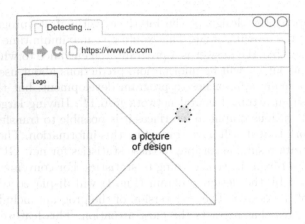

Fig. 5. Prototype of the program

program allows the user to select the area he saw first. It will already contain a database with pictures of the design on which users will walk. As a result, there will be two programs: the main program and the program for data collection. It is very important for a data collection program to involve as many users as possible so that they provide as much data as possible, because the more data, the more accurate the system will work. In addition, programs do not require large system capacity, so for ease of use it is better to do them on the web. Users will be able to use them without unnecessary installations and difficulties, as well as on various devices, which will attract as many users as possible. In addition, the implementation on the web provides several opportunities. This program for collecting information could be made as a simple website and a plug-in for the browser, as well as in the form of advertising, i.e. users visiting various websites could interact with the program through a frame.

As for the methods of operation of the program, the best option is to use a neural network. Having large statistics of user actions on various graphical interfaces, it is possible to transfer this data to a neural network that it learned on them. The network will give very accurate results according to these statistics for new GUI designs, i.e. it will provide a user experience according to the statistics.

For the operation of the main program will need only the algorithm "feed forward" as the neural network will already have the correct weight, the value of connections between neurons. Accordingly, before running the program, you will need to train the network using the algorithm "backpropagation" with a sample for training which will be received from the program for data collection.

The prototype also shows a circle with a dotted frame [8–11]. This is the visualization of the data, namely, the area with the greatest visual weight. Visual weight is a measure of how boldly visible an object is. Since the program will use in a browser, the following technologies must used for programming:

– HTML, CSS, JS are for the graphical interface of the program;
– JS is to work with the neural network.

5 Results

To give more accurate data, a contrast filter is applied before sending the image to the neural network (Fig. 6). This allows the program to see the edges of the figure better (Fig. 7). After transforming the image, the original image is transmitted to the neural network and the algorithm of feedforward, the program returns the result. In addition, the result is visualized in the picture.

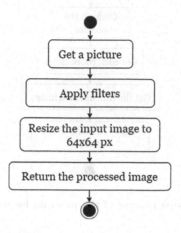

Fig. 6. The process of image transformation

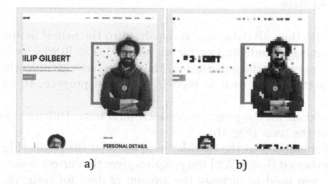

a)   b)

Fig. 7. Program. a) how a person sees; b) how a program sees

To work with the program, you must first teach it. Before launching the program, it is trained by the backpropagation algorithm. However, before that it was necessary to find the necessary data. There is a lot data on the Internet, but not in such a form, as it is needed, so this main program was copied with some changes. It collected user data. Pictures were already set inside the program and users used it to provide information. This information was stored in a database and then this data is used to train the neural network. To develop a data collection program, the already created main program was copied and it was possible to select the area with the greatest visual weight yourself (Fig. 8).

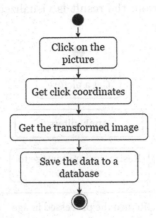

Fig. 8. Working process of the program for data collection

PHP is used to work with the data. With its help storage, loading, data processing are performed.

6   Discussions

After data collection, all data were transmitted to the neural network for training. After training, a configuration file was created (Fig. 9) which contained data on the neural network, the neurons and the connections between them. This file plays an important role, as it is used by the main program to form a neural network.

After development, the program passed several tests. Different design options are chosen for the tests (Fig. 10).

They are submitted to the entrance and received the result (Fig. 11).

The tests showed that 87% of the program gives the correct result. To increase this number, you need to increase the amount of data for training, and retrain the network. Also, the data storage program was tested. During the testing process, no problems were noticed in the operation of the program, the database file (Fig. 12) was filled with data according to the purpose.

Having done program on the web, it gave several opportunities. This program for collecting information could make both as a simple website and as a plug-in for the browser and even in the form of advertising, i.e. users visiting various websites could interact with the program through an iframe. All this made it

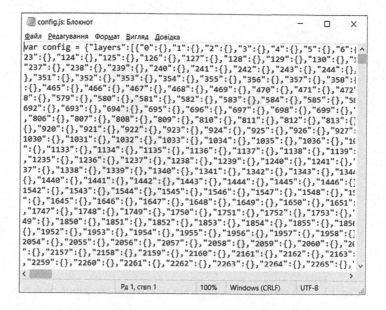

Fig. 9. Configuration file

Fig. 10. Website design

possible to attract as many users as possible and accordingly benefited, because the more users, the more data, and the more data was on the training stage, the more accurately the program works. After data collection, all data are transmitted to the neural network for training. After the training, a configuration file is created which contained data about the neural network, about neurons and connections between them. This file plays an important role, as the main program to form a neural network uses it.

Fig. 11. The result of the program relative to the input design

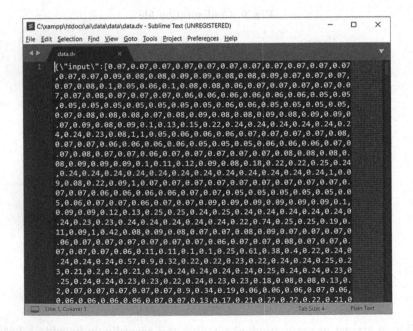

Fig. 12. User action data

7   Conclusions

Today there are many programs and many more are being developed. To create competition in the market you need to attract as many people as possible, to have the largest TA. To do this, you need to make a good graphic design according to UX. To know whether it is convenient for people to use the program, you need to collect and analyze statistics. In addition, to run the program closest to the ideal, you need to predict user behavior. To do this, a program is developed to identify the areas with the greatest visual weight. With this program, you can create designs that will direct the user to the right places, to the places they need. This will allow you to not lose users at the beginning of the program working. After development, the program passed several tests. Different design options were chosen for the tests. They applied to the entrance and received the result. The tests showed that 87% of the program gives a relevant result. To increase this number, you need to increase the amount of data for training, and retrain the network. Further experimental trials for different audiences will significantly improve the accuracy of the result. In the future, it is necessary to conduct research for thematic training of the site by site profile, age and gender of the potential audience, features of the content, regionality of the potential user, etc. Software implementation is a crucial part of creating a product. Solutions for web applications occupy a very important place among the areas of development, although they are more often components of more complex enterprise-level systems than stand-alone applications. So in the future, this program will be added as a plugin to other programs, such as: Photoshop, Scetch and others.

References

1. Usability of the site. http://www.sembook.ru/book/povyshenie-konversii-sayta/yuzabiliti-sayta/
2. Ux. https://skillbox.ru/media/design/srochno_uchi_ux/
3. Ux/ui design. https://branchup.pro/blog/chto-takoye-ui-ux-design
4. Almeida, F.M., Ribeiro, A., Ordonez, E.D., Montesco, C.A.: Performance evaluation of an artificial neural network multilayer perceptron with limited weights for detecting denial of service attack on Internet of Things. Traininge **11**, 12 (2016)
5. Babichev, S., Škvor, J., Fišer, J., Lytvynenko, V.: Technology of gene expression profiles filtering based on wavelet analysis. Int. J. Intell. Syst. Appl. **10**(4), 1–7 (2018). https://doi.org/10.5815/ijisa.2018.04.01
6. Babichev, S., Taif, M., Lytvynenko, V.: Inductive model of data clustering based on the agglomerative hierarchical algorithm. In: Proceedings of the 2016 IEEE 1st International Conference on Data Stream Mining and Processing, DSMP, pp. 19–22 (2068). https://doi.org/10.1109/DSMP.2016.7583499
7. Batiuk, T., Vysotska, V., Lytvyn, V.: Intelligent system for socialization by personal interests on the basis of SEO-technologies and methods of machine learning. In: CEUR Workshop Proceedings, vol. 2604, pp. 1237–1250 (2020)
8. Borovska, T., Vernigora, I., Severilov, V., Kolesnik, I., Shestakevych, T.: Model of innovative development of production systems based on the methodology of optimal aggregation. In: Shakhovska, N., Medykovskyy, M.O. (eds.) CSIT 2018. AISC, vol. 871, pp. 171–181. Springer, Cham (2019). https://doi.org/10.1007/978-3-030-01069-0_12

9. Cherednichenko, O., Vovk, M., Kanishcheva, O., Godlevskyi, M.: Studying items similarity for dependable buying on electronic marketplaces. In: CEUR Workshop Proceedings, vol. 2136, pp. 78–89 (2018)
10. Cherednichenko, O., Yanholenko, O., Vovk, M., Sharonova, N.: Towards structuring of electronic marketplaces contents: items normalization technology. In: Computational Linguistics and Intelligent Systems, COLINS. CEUR Workshop Proceedings, vol. 2604, pp. 44–55 (2020)
11. Chyrun, L., et al.: Web resource changes monitoring system development. In: CEUR Workshop Proceedings, vol. 2386, pp. 255–273 (2019)
12. Chyrun, L., et al.: Heterogeneous data with agreed content aggregation system development. In: CEUR Workshop Proceedings, vol. 2386, pp. 35–54 (2019)
13. Dumas, J.S., Redish, J.C.: A Practical Guide to Usability Testing. Intellect Books, Exeter (1999)
14. Feng, S., Cao, J.: Improving group recommendations via detecting comprehensive correlative information. Multimedia Tools Appl. **76**(1), 1355–1377 (2015). https://doi.org/10.1007/s11042-015-3135-y
15. Hu, Y.: Clustering-based hot topic detecting in Chinese microblog. TELKOMNIKA Indonesian J. Electr. Eng. **12**(3), 2096–2103 (2014). https://doi.org/10.11591/telkomnika.v12i3.4283
16. Lipyanina, H., Sachenko, A., Lendyuk, T., Nadvynychny, S., Grodskyi, S.: Decision tree based targeting model of customer interaction with business page. In: CEUR Workshop, Proceedings of the Third International Workshop on Computer Modeling and Intelligent Systems (CMIS-2020), Zaporizhzhia, Ukraine, pp. 1001–1012 (2020)
17. Shestakevych, T., Pasichnyk, V., Nazaruk, M., Medykovskiy, M., Antonyuk, N.: Web-products, actual for inclusive school graduates: evaluating the accessibility. In: Shakhovska, N., Medykovskyy, M.O. (eds.) CSIT 2018. AISC, vol. 871, pp. 350–363. Springer, Cham (2019). https://doi.org/10.1007/978-3-030-01069-0_25
18. Shinkarenko, V.S.: Audience analysis and forecasting the attendance of the internet resource. http://www.masters.donntu.org/2006/fvti/shynkarenko/diss/
19. Tidwell, J.: User Interface Design. Peter (2007)
20. Varetskyy, Y., Rusyn, B., Molga, A., Ignatovych, A.: A new method of fingerprint key protection of grid credential. In: Choraś, R.S. (ed.) Image Processing and Communications Challenges 2. AINSC, vol. 84, pp. 99–103. Springer, Heidelberg (2010). https://doi.org/10.1007/978-3-642-16295-4_11
21. Veres, O., Rusyn, B., Sachenko, A., Rishnyak, I.: Choosing the method of finding similar images in the reverse search system. In: CEUR Workshop Proceedings, vol. 2136, pp. 99–107 (2018)
22. Yu, D., Zhang, P., Yang, J., Chen, Z., Liu, C., Chen, J.: Efficiently detecting structural design pattern instances based on ordered sequences. J. Syst. Softw. **142**, 35–56 (2018). https://doi.org/10.1016/j.jss.2018.04.015
23. Zdebskyi, P., Vysotska, V., Peleshchak, R., Peleshchak, I., Demchuk, A., Krylyshyn, M.: An application development for recognizing of view in order to control the mouse pointer. In: CEUR Workshop Proceedings, vol. 2386, pp. 55–74 (2019)

Big Data and Data Science Using Intelligent Approaches

Product Development of Start-up Through Modeling of Customer Interaction Based on Data Mining

Viktor Morozov$^{(\boxtimes)}$ ⓘ, Olga Mezentseva ⓘ, Grigory Steshenko ⓘ,
and Maksym Proskurin ⓘ

Taras Shevchenko National University of Kyiv, Kyiv, Ukraine
knumvv@gmail.com, olga.mezentseva.fit@gmail.com, gmsteshenko@gmail.com,
proskuryn69@gmail.com

Abstract. The article deals with issues related to the development of
start-ups in the tech industry. Start-ups in the form of small enterprises
create a good environment for innovation development. The activities of
such companies are aimed at meeting market needs by developing a business model around an innovative idea. At the same time, such projects
are very risky, and up to 90% of start-ups fail. For the reduction of these
problems, the conclusion is made on the necessity to consider the efficiency of interaction of users with IT product of a start-up project. We
propose to use the Customer Journey Map method to analyse the customer's "journey". In this case, the product development of the project
start-up should be done in terms of the quality of interaction at each
point of contact through several channels and for a certain time. Also,
it's necessary to combine millions of events, which will provide the necessary analysis of the impact on the customers' journeys and will determine
the direction of further development. The article proposes a mathematical description of data mining techniques for analysis of information
about such interaction. This allows the construction of appropriate formal graphs (maps), which are analysed using Markov chain theory. For
testing presented models, the heuristic algorithm with the function of
optimisation is proposed. For chain training, the Python functionality
is applied, using user activity data sets. We carried out an analysis and
conclusions about the effectiveness of the proposed approach.

Keywords: Projects · Startup · Information interaction · Customer
journey map · Data mining · Markov chains

1 Introduction

Today's experience in the development and implementation of IT systems in
various industries shows numerous developments in the form of start-ups, the
amount of which is constantly growing around the world. Start-ups in the form of

© Springer Nature Switzerland AG 2020
S. Babichev et al. (Eds.): DSMP 2020, CCIS 1158, pp. 399–415, 2020.
https://doi.org/10.1007/978-3-030-61656-4_27

small enterprises create a good environment for innovation development. Because "Start-up" is a newly emerged and fast-growing business used to search for a repeatable and scalable business model in conditions of extreme uncertainty that aims to meet a marketplace need by developing an innovative product, service, process or a platform [4]. But the survival rate of projects implemented by startups is quite low, because they are quite risky. Small Biz Trends [24] showed in a recent research study that 90% of new startups fail.

To help IT entrepreneurs achieve greater success, Eric Ries, based on his personal experience, defined the Lean Start-up methodology [22] in 2008. He combined client development, agile software development methodologies and Lean Manufacturing methods (based on productivity improvements) into an integrated base for fast and efficient development of project activity products.

Startups with the SaaS (Software as a Service) [16] and B2B (Business to Business) [25] business model have problems with long sales cycles because the client's decision is collective, depends on many factors. Client experience means numerous information interactions with the company before the purchase and a wide range of touchpoints both in the IT product itself (user experience) and outside it (emails, calls, video calls, personal meetings, etc.).

To solve these problems, the method of analysis of the "journey" (interaction with an IT product) of a future client (Customer Journey Map - CJM) can be used [3,15]. In this case, the product development of the start-up project should be done in terms of the quality of interaction in each point of contact through several channels and for a certain time. Also, it's necessary to combine millions of events, which will provide the necessary analysis of the impact on the customers' journeys and will determine the future content of projects to develop such IT products.

According to the IBM Institute for Business Value, 71% of organizations use big data and analytics to develop innovative products or services [11]. Customer journey analytics gives marketers, sales and product managers a powerful tool to understand and engage with individual customers at a personal level and on a scale. By analysing millions of data points in realtime, they can find the most important customer trips and prioritise those opportunities that have a significant impact on business goals, such as increasing revenue, reducing customer churn, improving customer service and developing innovation within the company.

In the beginning, it is necessary to receive datasets about the interaction of all clients (users) with a system (IT product) to carry out the analytical research of interactions. The most appropriate way is to use data mining [2] with the construction of the graph of interaction states [30]. In this case, the sequence of client's transitions can be transformed into a sequence of events and reflects the Markov chain [9]. The Markov property of user behaviour is confirmed by the fact that in both CJM models and Markov chains performed at time t, the system is transferred to a new state; new tasks correspond to the stages of the interaction process; the execution of each interaction transfers the information system to a new state; the sum of probabilities of all interactions at each step is equal to one; the transition probabilities depend only on the state from which and to which the transition occurs.

Thus, it is relevant to create an effective model of customer journey analysis to better understand customer behaviour, which will allow startups to reduce the sales cycle and loyalty loop [7], as well as create a source of competitive advantage and the key to success.

2 Literature Review

In today's conditions of development of the tech industry, the use of the project management approach is an undoubted advantage. At the same time, the innovative nature of modern technologies is performed through the creation of start-ups with their further growth. The issue of characteristics and parameters of the IT product provided by the start-up is important enough. Besides, variety of publications has been devoted to a combination of the project approach with a start-up product development [4,7,9,17,19,20,22,24,27,30]. For example, in [20] the use of technological processes in the creation of innovative products in medium and large projects is investigated. At the same time, it is proposed to use an agile approach based on Lean methodology for startups [22]. Though methods of lean production of IT products are offered here, methods of both development and promotion of startups are not given. One of the possible approaches to the solution of development problems of IT of start-ups products can be the use of the proactive approach which is effective for the management of complex projects based on forecasting of project conditions and described in [17,19,27]. This can be applied to determining the directions of product development to increase the level of customer interaction with the system on the terms of loyalty.

The results of the modelling of the potential rules of interactions in active databases are analysed in [30], but the specifics of the development of start-up projects are not considered. Often, it is difficult to determine a suitable methodology for managing the development of innovative projects due to frequent changes and the impact of a turbulent business environment. For example, in [9] innovation management models based on methods of convergence of different project management methodologies are investigated. However, methods of management of interactions of clients with IT product are not given.

It was noted that innovative start-ups are often connected with the development of a certain business, which is formed using the B2B (Business to Business) [25] or SaaS (Software-as-a-Service) models [16]. In this case, the directions of product development can be based on the acquisition and retention of a large number of subscribed customers.

Switching to review of modern, well-proven methods of the analysis of the interaction with clients, it is possible to note the following works [7,12,21]. As it is noted in these researches, for the decision of the specified problems it is possible to use effective models of the customers' journeys [12]. At the same time, it is possible to estimate the value of interaction, however, large volumes of data are formed [7,21], but how to analyze them in the conditions of the project approach these works are not specified.

To carry out effective analysis of customer interaction with an IT system with large volumes of data, it is necessary to use modern techniques of intelligent data analysis. Such basic papers are devoted to the use of such techniques [2,5,11, 16,29]. These papers analyse the use of analytics for the large volumes of data in the development of similar SaaS products at the state level, but at the level of development of start-ups there will be less data and simpler methods can be used.

Since our system of interaction with the client is an event-driven one, the use of the Markov chains method may be suggested as the primary method of modelling and research in this paper. Applied aspects of using this method have been demonstrated in [9,23]. This approach may well be applied to these studies, but in our system, the interaction processes have a more complex structure to be represented by a single graph.

Thus, the analysis of information sources [1–30] has shown that for working out and management of projects of the development of innovative IT products there is no single approach, models and methods. Such models should allow reacting quickly to results of interaction with clients in an automated mode, to carry out the predicted functions based on technologies of the intellectual analysis of the data [7,21]. Such an approach will allow effective analysis of these interactions data and quick determination of directions for further IT product improvement.

3   Purpose Formulation

The main goal of the research carried out by the authors is the development of new models for evaluating the interaction of clients with the components of innovative IT products of start-up projects in the creation and development of information systems. This will mean higher quality development management with cost optimization for the development of startups, increase their commercial attractiveness and allow them to acquire more customers to the product.

Thus, the main tasks of the research were defined as follows:

- to analyse examples of the use of customer journey maps during interaction with the product of the project and to form groups of key metrics to manage the development of such product;
- to build a scheme of interaction of the main key stakeholders of the development project of the creation of complex IT products of start-up projects;
- to offer a mathematical description of the process of creating complex IT products and build a modelling algorithm;
- to use special software required to perform modelling based on Markov chains;
- to analyse statistical experimental data and obtained results concerning commercial results of the development project.

4   Materials and Methods

4.1   Build Customer Interaction Models with IT Product Based on Customer Journey Maps

As mentioned above, we suggest using the customer journey map (CJM) models to obtain data about user interaction with the IT system. It is a tool for visualizing the interaction of the consumer with a product or service. When analysing information sources, in this study these models combine two approaches: the process of analysing the interaction and the process of generating ideas to improve this interaction.

CJM displays a time-bound interaction broken down into small components. The constitutive interactions refer both to the process (consumers' goals and objectives, their actions, expected results, problems and barriers preventing the transition to the next step, touchpoints, materials, tools, equipment, KPI from the business point of view, etc.) and to the psycho-emotional state of the consumer (thoughts, feelings, emotions).

In addition to the above, CJM usually contains recommendations for product improvements and the removal of barriers that may exist:

- technical (for example, absence or incorrect work of some function in the interface);
- organisational (e.g., low motivation of employees working with clients and, as a result, lack of attention to their requests);
- others.

This approach to development is particularly useful for products which are characterised by multi-channel interaction, i.e. when the consumer and the product "touch" at several points. The customer always has a sum of impressions of the interaction with the product through all available channels, so that even one negative experience is able to vilify the entire product in the eyes of the client and force him to cancel the subscription.

As an example, we can consider the CJM shown in Fig. 1, which displays the interaction in the environment of the web service "client-bank", where the user can perform transactions with his account and bank cards through the mobile application "client-bank".

In this way, CJM can be represented as an oriented graph, on which the path of the consumer of the provided service or the interaction with the product is displayed through contact points. When we consider in more depth the scheme of interaction between users and the start-up information system, we can identify several groups of key participants in the interaction process. The *first* and main group includes many different classes of clients who are business representatives. These are a novice, advanced and loyal customers who have linked their business with this IT product for a long time. Their interaction contributes to the more efficient development of their own business (for example, logistics, transportation). The *second* significant group consists of representatives of the developer

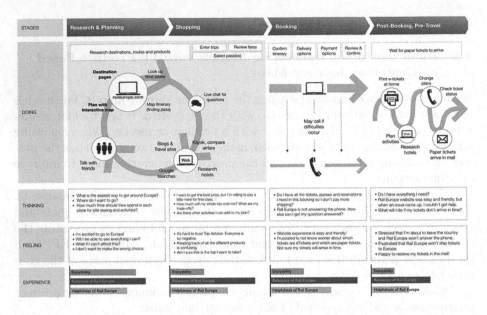

Fig. 1. Example of a client IT product interaction card [12]

of this information system. They will perform the tasks concerning the development of the product. The *third* group of specialists are representatives of the customer or the IT product owner. It was this group who initiated this launch, raised funds and introduced the first version of the product to the market.

The essence of such interaction of various groups with the IT product under consideration is shown in Fig. 2. As you can see from Fig. 2, the client can interact with each point through different channels. For example, the site of a liquor store can be opened on a laptop, tablet, smartphone; you can communicate with the courier by phone or in person, etc.

4.2   Building a Mathematical Model to Evaluate Customer Interaction with IT Product Using Data Mining Tools

For the construction of the analytical model of research CJM, it is possible to take advantage of Process Mining applied to reports of work of information systems as a result of interaction with clients. This will automate the construction of a model of business processes by extracting from the protocols of the site most commonly used templates. The mathematical model of this process looks like sequential construction and optimisation of directed graphs. First, the graphs are built based on a complete formal business process Workflow-chart - a scheme that describes in what sequence the client should direct their attention and do conversion actions on the site (planned CJM). However, depending on the customer behaviour, the values of the process variables may be different, the transitions at the routing nodes will be different or even stop. At the same time,

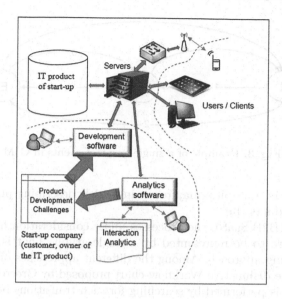

Fig. 2. The scheme of stakeholder engagement with the IT product of the start-up project

the actual execution of the process will not cover all nodes of the circuit. The parts of the scheme covered by the clients are called *instances*.

Logs (numeric records of all events on the site in chronological order) in the form of tables are submitted to the model input. To reproduce all interaction flows, i.e., the cause-effect relationship between the events specified in the log, we rely on the theory of Markov's discrete random processes [23]. That is, it is a question of a finding of the most probable sequences of events of the interaction of users with IT product of a start-up project. The algorithm used in this case converts these probabilities into states and transitions between states. As a result, he builds a state graph in the form of a finite deterministic state automaton of a client and IT product interactions. While executing the specified algorithm, tables of probabilities for sequences of interaction events are created by counting the number of appearances of identical sequences in the flow of events.

A directed graph is created based on the generated probability tables in the following way: for each type of events there corresponds its vertex, then for each sequence of events, the probability and number of appearances of which exceed the specified threshold, a uniquely named edge is created from one element of the sequence directly to the element following it in that sequence (Fig. 3).

R, C, E are the tops of the event graph in which the event type is compared. $1, 2, 3, 4, 5, 6$ is a sequence of more defined limits to which an event type label is assigned. For example, applying process mining to the audit trails of a work-flow management system, enterprise resource planning system logs, or electronic

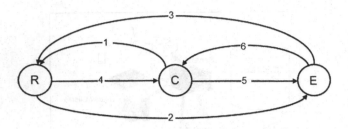

Fig. 3. Example of a single graph of events in CJM

medical records in a hospital may result in models describing processes, organizations and products [14].

In our case (B2B SaaS), the processes under consideration have too complicated a structure to be represented by a single graph. That is, it is advisable to use a clustering approach. Among the different approaches of such partitioning, we chose the disjunctive Workflow-chart proposed by Greco and others [10]. Clustering in it is performed by searching for such transitions between states in the model, at obligatory triggering or not triggering, which can be concluded that a significant part of the model is unattainable. This is what makes it possible to divide the model into parts.

Summing up above told, it is possible to offer a method of analytical processing of data flows from interactions of clients with IT product which is constructed on the formal model describing processes and protocols [1]. The existing set of different tasks from the instances, of which the process P consists (Fig. 1), and the set of different possible *sequences*, in which they should be performed, is modelled using the following marked graph. This graph will be called - the graph of PCJM process data flow control. So, we have a tuple set:

$$PCJM = (A, E, a_0, F), \tag{1}$$

where A is the limited set of tasks (according to the instance); $E \subseteq (A - F) \times (A - \{a_0\})$ is the ratio of order among tasks; $a_0 \in A$ is the initial task; $F \subseteq A$ is the set of end tasks (possibly completed or stopped).

Any related subgraph $I = (A_1, E_1)$, which is also a flow control graph, such as this:

$$a_0 \in A_1; A_1 \in F \neq \varnothing \tag{2}$$

corresponds to one of the possible instances of the P process recorded in the site's logs. To prevent the model from generating multiple copies, the following restrictions will be imposed. Let us define the concept of local constraints with the help of three functions, each of which puts a natural number in correspondence to the *node*:

$$ACJM \rightarrow: N : IN, OUT_{min}; OUT_{max}, \tag{3}$$

Assign the input peak as:

$$InDegree(a) = |\{(b, a)|(b, a) \in E\}|, \tag{4}$$

and the output peak:

$$OutDegree(a) = |\{(a,b)|(a,b) \in E\}|. \tag{5}$$

The constraint is this: task a may not start until at least $IN(a)$ of the previous tasks have been completed.

$$\forall a \in A - \{a_0\}, 0 < IN(a) \leq InDegree(a), \tag{6}$$

$$\forall a \in A - F, 0 < OUT_{min}(a) \leq OUT_{max}(a) \leq InDegree(a), \tag{7}$$

$$IN(a_0) = 0; \forall a \in F, OUT_{min}(a) = OUT_{max}(a) = 0 \tag{8}$$

where OUT_{min} and OUT_{max} is an output arc power (cardinality) at the completion of the process.

Let A_p is the process task identifier set P. There are also cases where the actual $WS(P)$ Workflow-chart for process P is unknown. Then the problem is to determine the correct scheme from the $WS(P)$ set, for which A_p is a set of nodes. With this approach, a set of limitations is presented in the form of different variants of performance, often found in the log. As a result, the Workflow-chart is con-sidered as a union of several schemes of simpler variants of data flows without global restrictions.

Let WS^V be the disjunctive Workflow-scheme, and L_p be process log P, then the following formula determines the correctness of the model:

$$soundness(WS^V, L_p) = \frac{|\{I|I| = WS^V \Lambda \exists s \in L_p s.t. s| =^1 WS^V\}|}{|\{I|I| = WS^V\}|} \tag{9}$$

The percentage of instances of the P process that do not have corresponding traces in the log or the completeness of the data modelling (have any compatible traces in the log) is determined in this way:

$$soundness(WS^V, L_p) = \frac{|\{s|s \in L_p \Lambda s| =^1 WS^V\}|}{|\{s|s \in L_p\}|} \tag{10}$$

The Process Discovery algorithm gets WS^V, using the method of hierarchical clustering, which begins (step 1) with the detection of the flow control graph CF_σ, using the procedure $minePrecedences$. Each Workflow-chart, which is ultimately attached to WS^V, has the number i - the number of optimisation steps required, and the number j - is used to distinguish schemes at one optimisation level; $L(WS_i^j)$ – a certain set of traces in the cluster. In step 2, an initial schema containing all traces from the set is inserted into WS^V. In step 3, the model is optimised by identifying local constraints.

Input: Problem $PD(P, \sigma, m)$, natural number $maxFeatures$
Output: Process model
Algorithm: Follow the steps:

1. $CF\sigma(WS_0^1) := minePrecedences\ (L_p)$

2. let WS_0^1
3. mineLocalConstraints (WS_0^1)
4. $WS^V := WS_0^1$/Start clustering with only a dependency graph
5. While $|WS^A| \leq m$ do
   5.1 $WS_i^j := leastSoundWS^A)$
   5.2 $WS^V := WS^V - \{WS_i^j\}$
   5.3 refineWorkflow (i,j)
6. return WS^V

The refineWorkflow function is the following:

1. $F: =$ identifyRelevantFeatures $(L\ (WS_i^j, \sigma, maxFeatures, CF\sigma))$
2. $R(\ WS_i^j)\ = project\ L(WS_i^j),\ F)$
3. $k := |F|$
4. If $k > 1$ then
   4.1 $j =: max\{j|WS_{i+1}^j \in WS^V\}$
   4.2 $\langle WS_{i+1}^{j+1}, ... , WS_{i+k}^{j+k} \rangle := k - means(R(WS_i^j))$
   4.3 For each WS_{i+1}^h do
      4.3.1 $WS^V = WS^V \cup \{WS_{i+1}^h\}$
      4.3.2 $CF\sigma(WS_{i+1}^h) := minePrecedences(L(WS_{i+1}^h))$
      4.3.3 mineLocalConstraints (WS_{i+1}^h)
5. else // leave the tree
   5.1 $WS^V = WS^V \cup \{WS_i^j\}$

The algorithm is "greedy" heuristics, every step of the way he chooses a scheme. $WS_i^j \in WS^V$ to optimise the $refineWorkflow$ function based on which of them is the most profitable to optimize.

For chain training, the *Python* functionality was used on these log files of user activity. This is a CSV file containing a table of three columns: *user id*, *event name*, *time* when it happened. These three fields are enough to trace the client's movements, build a map and eventually get the Markov chain. The graph of the received matrix was built by the NetworkX library. To visualise the matrix, you can use the Graphviz package in Fig. 4.

Markov chains were algorithmized using the Python language. A fragment of Markov chain modelling code for CJM:

```
1 import os
2 import numpy as np #For matrix multiplication
3 import networkx as nx # For the chain building
4
5 wd - 'C://PythonCode' #your working directory with the data
      set file in it
6 os.chdir(wd)
7 filename = 'worklist.csv' #file name
8 sep1 = ';' #separator in the file
9 start_state = 'Start General Course' #name of the Start
      node
```

```
10  end_states = ['Finished course', 'Dropped Course', 'fell
        asleep'] #list of end nodes
11  steps = 1000 #number of steps n the random walk in the
        chain

12
13  fhand = open(filename, 'r')
14  i = 0
15  data01 = []
16  states = []

17
18  def sort_key (line):
19      result = int(line[0]) * 100000 + float(line[1])
20      return(result)

21
22  for line in fhand:
23      data01.append(line.rstrip().replace(',', '.').split(dep
            = dep1))
24      states.append(line.rstrip().replace(',', '.').split(dep
            = dep1)[1])
25  fhand.close()

26
27  data01.sort(key = sort_key)
28  states = list(set(states))

29
30  calc_matrix = []
31  for i in range(len(states)):
32      calc_matrix.append([])
33      for i in range(len(states)):
34          calc_matrix[i].append(0)

35
36  for i in range(len(data01) - 1):
37      if data01[i][0] == data01[i-1][0]:
38          calc_matrix0states.index(data01[i][1]))[states.
            index(data01[i=1][i])]
```

5   Experiment, Results and Discussion

The results of the research on the interaction of clients with current versions of IT product were formed into monthly data sets for two years starting from 2018. Before that, the considered innovative product had already existed on the market for about two years. Using the Markov chains modelling approach, we have obtained data sets of predicted targets for the growth of the value of the product. Every 3–4 days, we held meetings to manage the progress of the product development using the Scrum methodology [6, 8, 28], evaluated the results achieved and formed new tasks. In this way, the realization of the program of works on improvement of a product, based on the analysis of the data of the clients' interaction was carried out.

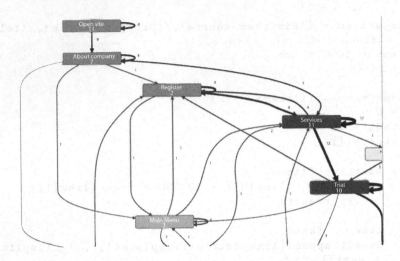

Fig. 4. Fragment of the obtained computer model CJM

Filter B = Budget / A = Actual		Jan-18	Feb-18	Mar-18	Apr-18	May-18	Jun-18	Jul-18	Aug-18	Sep-18
Customer & Revenue Development										
B	Total Revenue	60,000 €	60,300 €	60,414 €	60,367 €	60,182 €	59,878 €	59,472 €	95,029 €	136,554 €
B	Basic	15,000 €	13,200 €	11,616 €	10,222 €	8,995 €	7,916 €	6,966 €	20,830 €	36,643 €
B	Pro	20,000 €	22,600 €	24,788 €	26,615 €	28,128 €	29,364 €	30,360 €	43,746 €	59,427 €
B	Enterprise	25,000 €	24,500 €	24,010 €	23,530 €	23,059 €	22,598 €	22,146 €	30,453 €	40,484 €
A	Total Revenue	60,000 €	60,300 €	60,414 €	60,367 €	60,182 €	59,878 €	59,472 €	95,029 €	136,554 €
A	Basic	15,000 €	13,200 €	11,616 €	10,222 €	8,995 €	7,916 €	6,966 €	20,830 €	36,643 €
A	Pro	20,000 €	22,600 €	24,788 €	26,615 €	28,128 €	29,364 €	30,360 €	43,746 €	59,427 €
A	Enterprise	25,000 €	24,500 €	24,010 €	23,530 €	23,059 €	22,598 €	22,146 €	30,453 €	40,484 €
B	MRR	60,000 €	60,300 €	60,414 €	60,367 €	60,182 €	59,878 €	59,472 €	64,929 €	76,354 €
B	Basic	15,000 €	13,200 €	11,616 €	10,222 €	8,995 €	7,916 €	6,966 €	8,230 €	11,443 €
B	Pro	20,000 €	22,600 €	24,788 €	26,615 €	28,128 €	29,364 €	30,360 €	33,246 €	38,427 €
B	Enterprise	25,000 €	24,500 €	24,010 €	23,530 €	23,059 €	22,598 €	22,146 €	23,453 €	26,484 €
B	MoM Growth Rate		0%	0%	0%	0%	-1%	-1%	9%	18%
A	MRR	60,000 €	60,300 €	60,414 €	60,367 €	60,182 €	59,878 €	59,472 €	64,929 €	76,354 €
A	Basic	15,000 €	13,200 €	11,616 €	10,222 €	8,995 €	7,916 €	6,966 €	8,230 €	11,443 €
A	Pro	20,000 €	22,600 €	24,788 €	26,615 €	28,128 €	29,364 €	30,360 €	33,246 €	38,427 €
A	Enterprise	25,000 €	24,500 €	24,010 €	23,530 €	23,059 €	22,598 €	22,146 €	23,453 €	26,484 €
A	MoM Growth Rate		0%	0%	0%	0%	-1%	-1%	9%	18%
B	Total Customers	60	59	58	56	55	54	53	59	72
B	Basic	30	26	23	20	18	16	14	16	23
B	Pro	20	23	25	27	28	29	30	33	38
B	Enterprise	10	10	10	9	9	9	9	9	11
A	Total Customers	60	59	58	56	55	54	53	59	72
A	Basic	30	26	23	20	18	16	14	16	23
A	Pro	20	23	25	27	28	29	30	33	38
A	Enterprise	10	10	10	9	9	9	9	9	11
Customer Acquisition										
B	Lead Quota per Sales Rep	40	40	40	40	40	40	40	40	40

Fig. 5. Dataset of growth in the value of the product based on forecast targets and actual data

The dataset formed in this way is presented in Fig. 5, where values of predicted planned indicators of success and obtained indicators based on interaction with clients of the system are indicated. In general, such dataset includes tariff payments for the growing number of online service clients, the cost of refining the software and functional component (Fig. 2), advertising campaigns and others.

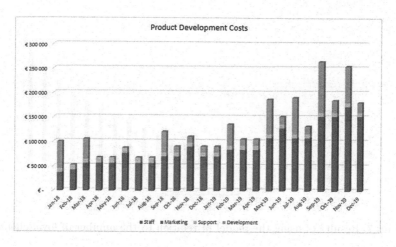

Fig. 6. Cost of IT product improvement

Analyzing in more detail the expenses connected with the development of a software component, the perfection of an IT product of similar start-up projects, personnel expenses, development and other expenses it is possible to show in Fig. 8. Thus, consolidated actual expenses for product development were considered based on the data presented also in Fig. 6.

Thus monthly the analysis of clients at interaction with system was spent. *Three types* of such clients were defined: their total number, the number of clients who did not fit the proposed composition of services regarding their business and who left the system, and the number of loyal users. They were the clients who were able to propose improvements and concluded long-term contracts. The results of this assessment are shown in Fig. 7.

As it has been told in the introduction, the given processes of the development of products of IT projects should be seen in the direction of the development of the companies with B2B business models. It is not possible to obtain data on the commercial performance of such clients. However, it was still profitable for loyal customers. The customer or the owner of the start-up project with a SaaS business model who used the given approach with the offered models and methods of modelling, could during two years of research build the graph of profitability of the project of development of a product which is shown in Fig. 8. It indicates the planned and actual profitability of such a development project.

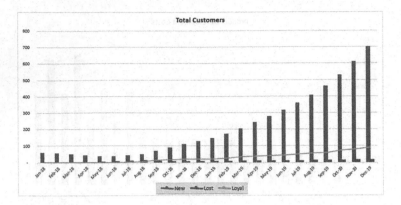

Fig. 7. Results of using the model in relation to the number of loyal clients

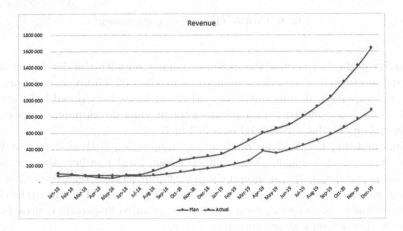

Fig. 8. Results of using the model by income received

6   Conclusions

To solve the problems of determining the directions of development and the work program for improving the IT products of innovative projects, an approach based on the CJM model was used, based on the analysis of interactions between clients and the IT system. Our research has confirmed the fact that this approach helps to identify IT product functionality bottlenecks in the dynamics of customer interactions and the often-changing development project environment. This, in turn, makes it possible to quickly concentrate resources on the development of product functions and adapt the system to the changing needs of customers in the shortest possible time. In the course of two years of product development, we managed to create unique data sets that were used for analysis and subsequent forecasting of the project's metrics.

And each of the data sets included 125 positions on the project budget, 142 positions on actual data on the interaction with clients, 153 positions on combined financial indicators, 125 indicators of the trading platform budget, 232 positions on SaaS budget, the level of customer churn was taken into account and a number of groups of specific indicators. All this was calculated on a monthly basis within 24 months. The resulting large number of data sets of user interaction (client interaction) of the system resulted in the need to use methods of intelligent data analysis. There was also a need to combine millions of events in the journey preferences from a client's perspective to get a more complete picture and provide the necessary analysis of the impact on customer travel. To this end, the authors proposed a scheme of interaction between stakeholders and the IT product startup project. Based on its decomposition, we were able to propose and implement a number of models.

For the construction of the analytical model of research, it has been offered to use means Process Mining, applied to reports of work of information systems as a result of their interaction with clients. It has allowed automating the construction of the model of business processes by a method of extraction of the most frequently applied templates from reports of work of a site. The mathematical model of this process looks at consecutive construction and optimization of the directed graphs.

In this case, it was proved that the use of Markov chains as a result of the analysis of the schedule of events and transitions between the interaction events allowed to solve the set tasks, to build and conduct computer modelling of our models. Software using Python was developed and modelling was carried out, which in its turn allowed to get unique data sets about perspective system states.

The financial results of the two-year research history presented in this document showed a gradual increase in the number of loyal customers who had long term subscriptions from 80 per month in the first year to 145, in the third half of the year to 300 and at the end of the second year to 700 contracts. At the same time, the outflow of clients was kept low, with an average of up to 100 clients per month during the first year and up to 180 clients during the second year. However, such a tendency also took place to increase. All trends, as shown in the respective graphical interpretations of data sets, showed that startups were profitable based on the proposed approach and the effectiveness of the implemented tools.

References

1. van der Aalst, W.M.P., de Medeiros, A.K.A., Weijters, A.J.M.M.: Genetic process mining. In: Ciardo, G., Darondeau, P. (eds.) ICATPN 2005. LNCS, vol. 3536, pp. 48–69. Springer, Heidelberg (2005). https://doi.org/10.1007/11494744_5
2. Anderson, S.: Seductive Interaction Design: Creating Playful, Fun, and Effective User Experiences (Voices That Matter). New Riders, Indianapolis (2011)
3. Andreev, A.: Customer journey map: how to understand what the consumer needs (2018). https://www.uplab.ru/blog/customer-journey-map/

4. Blank, S., Dorf, B.: The Startup Owner's Manual: The Step By Step Guide for Building a Great Company. K&S Ranch (2018)
5. Chatfield, A., Reddick, C.: Customer agility and responsiveness through big data analytics for public value creation: a case study of Houston 311 on-demand services. Gov. Inf. Q. **35**(2), 336–347 (2017). https://doi.org/10.1016/j.giq.2017.11.002
6. Conforto, E., Amaral, D.: Evaluating an agile method for planning and controlling innovative projects. Proj. Manag. J. **41**(2), 73–80 (2010). https://doi.org/10.1002/pmj.20089
7. Edelman, D., Singer, M.: Competing on customer journeys you have to create new value at every step (2015). https://hbr.org
8. Garaedagi, D.: Systems Thinking How to Manage Chaos Complex Processes Framework for Modeling Business Architecture. Grevtsov Buks, Minsk (2010)
9. Gogunskii, V., Kolesnikov, O., Oborska, G., et al.: Representation of project systems using the Markov chain. Eastern-Eur. J. Enterp. Technol. **1/3**(85), 25–32 (2017). https://doi.org/10.15587/1729-4061.2017.97883
10. Greco, G., Guzzo, A., Pontieri, L., Saccà, D.: Mining expressive process models by clustering workflow traces. In: Dai, H., Srikant, R., Zhang, C. (eds.) PAKDD 2004. LNCS (LNAI), vol. 3056, pp. 52–62. Springer, Heidelberg (2004). https://doi.org/10.1007/978-3-540-24775-3_8
11. Hearn, J., Debicki, B., Shockley, R.: Analytics: the real-world use of big data in consumer products. Technical report, IBM Institute for Business Value (2013)
12. Herhausen, D., Kleinkercher, K., Verhoef, P.C., et al.: Loyalty formation for different customer journey segments. J. Retail. **95**, 9–29 (2019). https://doi.org/10.1016/j.jretai.2019.05.001
13. Hu, J., Wellman, M.: Multiagent reinforcement learning: theoretical framework and an algorithm. In: ICML, pp. 242–250 (1998). https://doi.org/10.1.1.138.2589
14. Kirchmer, M., Laengle, S., Masías, V.: Transparency-driven business process management in healthcare settings [leading edge]. IEEE Technol. Soc. Mag. **32**(4), 14–16 (2013). https://doi.org/10.1109/MTS.2013.2286427
15. Linoff, G., Berry, M.: Data Mining Techniques: For Marketing, Sales, and Customer Relationship Management. Wiley, Hoboken (2011)
16. Loukis, E., Janssen, M., Mintchev, I.: Determinants of software-as-a-service benefits and impact on firm performance. Decis. Support Syst. **117**, 38–47 (2019). https://doi.org/10.1016/j.dss.2018.12.005
17. Morozov, V., Kalnichenko, O., Bronin, S.: Development of the model of the proactive approach in creation of distributed information systems. Eastern-Eur. J. Enterp. Technol. **43/2**(94), 6–15 (2018)
18. Morozov, V., Kalnichenko, O., Mezentseva, O.: The method of interaction modeling on basis of deep learning of neural networks in complex IT-projects. Int. J. Comput. **19**(1), 88–96 (2020)
19. Morozov, V., Kalnichenko, O., Proskurin, M., Mezentseva, O.: Investigation of forecasting methods of the state of complex IT-projects with the use of deep learning neural networks. In: Lytvynenko, V., Babichev, S., Wójcik, W., Vynokurova, O., Vyshemyrskaya, S., Radetskaya, S. (eds.) ISDMCI 2019. AISC, vol. 1020, pp. 261–280. Springer, Cham (2020). https://doi.org/10.1007/978-3-030-26474-1_19
20. PMI: A Guide to the Project Management Body of Knowledge (PMBOK® Guide), 6th edn. Project Management Institute (2017)
21. Polaine, A.: Service Design: From Insight to Implementation. Rosenfeld Media, New York (2013)
22. Ries, E.: The Lean Startup: How Today's Entrepreneurs Use Continuous Innovation to Create Radically Successful Businesses. Currency (2011)

23. Sherstyuk, O., Olekh, T., Kolesnikova, K.: The research on role differentiation as a method of forming the project team. Eastern-Eur. J. Enterp. Technol. **2/3**(80), 63–68 (2016). https://doi.org/10.15587/1729-4061.2016.65681
24. SmallBusinessTrends: Startup statistics - the numbers you need to know (2020). https://smallbiztrends.com/2019/03/startup-statistics-small-business.html
25. Swani, K., Brown, P., Mudambi, M.: The untapped potential of B2B advertising: a literature review and future agenda. Ind. Mark. Manag. (2019). https://doi.org/10.1016/j.indmarman.2019.05.010
26. Tesauro, G.: Extending Q-learning to general adaptive multi agent reinforcement learning: theoretical framework and an algorithm. In: Advances in Neural Information Processing Systems 16, pp. 871–878. NIPS (2003). https://doi.org/10.5555/2981345.2981454
27. Timinsky, A., Voitenko, O., Achkasov, I.: Competence-based knowledge management in project oriented organisations in bi-adaptive context. In: Proceedings of the IEEE 14th International Scientific and Technical Conference on Computer Sciences and Information Technologies (CSIT-2019), vol. 1, pp. 17–20. IEEE (2019). https://doi.org/10.1109/STC-CSIT.2019.8929806
28. Turner, R.: The Handbook of Project-based Management: Leading Strategic Change in Organizations. McGraw-Hill Professional, New York (2008)
29. Zhang, H., Xiao, Y.: Customer involvement in big data analytics and its impact on B2B innovation. Ind. Mark. Manag. **86**, 99–108 (2019). https://doi.org/10.1016/j.indmarman.2019.02.020
30. Zudov, A.: Modeling of potential rule interactions in active databases systems. Mod. Probl. Sci. Educ. **1**(1) (2015)

Developing a Simulation Model of the Information Gathering System Within the "Smart Packaging" Concept

Iryna Biskub[1] and Lyubov Krestyanpol[2]

[1] Lesya Ukrainka Eastern European Nationa University, Lutsk, Ukraine
ibiskub@eenu.edu.ua
[2] Lutsk National Technical University, Lutsk, Ukraine
lkrestyanpol@gmail.com

Abstract. The article presents the process of developing the model of the information gathering system. The authors suggest the possibility of designing the product monitoring system working on the wireless data transmission methods. RFID technology is viewed as an instrument for gathering information about the condition of particular products. Three main stages of system functioning have been singled out. At the first stage, the programming and product marking-up is carried on. Corresponding product conditions and the systems for their coding are defined. The performance principles of the product monitoring system are described. The second stage presupposes defining the mechanisms of reading the coding system from RFID tags. At the third stage, the information is gathered from the customers. For this, the authors suggest to integrate into the developed system an additional element – a web framework. For the developed system, the authors have constructed a simulation model of gathering information from the customers, and the adequacy of the model has been checked experimentally. The developed system enables gathering and processing information in the real time mode, and the decision-making process concerning product utilization depends on the input data. Thus, the authors suggest the possibility of applying the developed system for resolving global food waste and food shortage issues.

Keywords: Simulation model · Web framework · Radio frequency identification · Automated information system · Smart packaging

1 Introduction

Within the recent twenty years packaging recycling and disposal have one of the most often discussed topics. Therefore, new packaging methods, packaging recycling technologies and ecological ways of packaging emerge [5]. However, the humanity has always been concerned about the problem of the rational use of natural resources, which has become a global issue, and requires a careful scientific discussion [10]. According to the research of the influential international organizations (The United Nations, FAO, and UNEP), food waste has become the world's main source of the environmental pollution. Every year more than four billion tons of food products is produced by the food industries, one third of which turns into food waste (1.3 billion tons) [1]. Trying to resolve the problem at the global level, The UN developed a special "Save Food" program which aims at finding the effective ways of decreasing the level of food waste and food loss, the preservation and the rational use of the natural resources owned by the humanity, minimizing man's destructive impact on nature. Global prevention of malnutrition and starvation has long ago become an urgent topic, which is being constantly discussed by many international organizations. These facts predetermined the urgency of the present article, the authors of which have developed a concept of the "smart packaging" providing the relevant conditions for preserving food products and preventing food wastage [6, 7]. One of the basic elements of developing the concept of "smart packaging" is the creation of the specific information gathering system. Below we will consider three main stages of' developing such a system which include new technical solutions, as well as social and communicative aspects of processing information.

2   Literature Review

"Smart packaging" could be used a general term referring both to "active" and "smart packaging", as well as to the specific functional components intended for the "smart packaging" design. This definition covers all the aspects of packaging design, the use of the new packaging materials. It also presupposes including mechanical, chemical, electrical and electronic components, or their combinations into the packaging design. Packaging approaches and technologies used in the packaging procedure are predetermined by the final application of the "smart packaging", namely in logistic operations [3], in the technologies for the prolongation of the expiration date, in preventing robberies, or product identification procedures [9].

"Smart packaging" enables receiving and providing information about the functions and properties of food products. It confirms and guarantees packaging integrity, safety and quality of the products. In this paper, the authors suggest the possibility of creating "smart packaging" that will help to prevent food loss by means of combing two basic components: technical solutions and social engineering. The problem of food loss has been the focus of attention of I. Miroshnyk [10], who in her works raises public awareness about this important issue of modern world and calls for spreading more information about food damage. Food and Agriculture Organization of the United Nations [1], has offered a global strategy of the rational use of food products.

Some organizational foundations of creating "smart packaging" are offered in the works of A. Butrin [2], K. Finkenzeller [4]. C. Scholz [17] highlighted essential technical aspects of a RFID system, in particular its spacial localization.

A group of authours [6] developed the structure of "smart packaging", which makes it possible to control the information on all the stages of the logistic chain.

They also consider a possibility of applying the achievements of modern science for creating a "smart" packaging within a RFID system, which would prevent food loss.

3   Materials and Methods

At first stage, we will discuss the process of developing automated information system the using RFID technologies. It should be noted, that modern food manufacturing market is characterized by a strong tendency towards increasing food wastage. Food waste emerges even before food products reach the customers. The reasons for food losses and food waste are different in different corners of the globe. Food products manufacturing consists of a definite set of technological operations it shown in Fig. 1. This set presupposes some basic stages similar for all type of products. Food loss and wastage occur at all stages of the food supply chain.

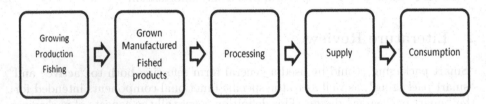

Fig. 1. Life cycle of food products

If we compare the percentage ratio of the reasons for food loss and the emerging of food waste, research has shown that food loss constitutes 20 and 30 per cent at the stages of retailing and consuming correspondingly [7]. One of the possible ways to reduce global food loss and waste is to develop new automated systems for monitoring all the stages of food producing, manufacturing, retailing and consuming. In the present paper, we suggest developing a new concept of "smart packaging" integrated into a RFID system that will be permanently processing the input data from the consumers.

RFID (Radio Frequency Identification) is a wireless control system using electromagnetic induction as the main method of communication tranmitting data transmission. It differs from other known wireless technologies such as Wi-Fi, Bluetooth, 3G that are based on radio transmitters [2,4]. Object identification is performed according to the unique digital code recorded on a special electronic tag (RFID-tag) and is later read from it with the help of special RFID-tag readers. Radio frequency tags are attached to the identified object enabling the product quality control and making product movement in space possible [14]. Standard RFID System consists of the RFID-tag reader with an antenna, and RFID-tags with the corresponding information. RFID-tag reader, in its turn, consists of the transceiver and an antenna sending and receiving back a signal from the RFID-tag, a microprocessor for data checking and decoding, and memory for data storage [11]. A RFID-tag consists of an integrated circuit governing the connection to the tag reader and an antenna it shown in Fig. 2. The tag reader's antenna sends the radio signal that is caught by RFID-tag antenna. It activates the RFID-tag with the subsequent exchange of radio signals for self-identification and data transmission between the RFID-tag and RFID-tag reader. The information from the RFID-tag is sent by the RFID-tag reader to the main computer for processing and administering. There is no visible contact between the tag and the reader. Figure 3 shows the general scheme of the RFID scheme [14, 16, 17].

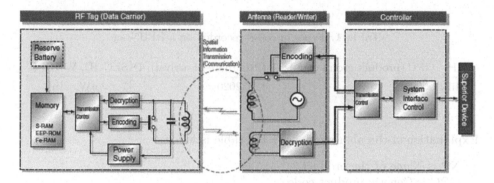

Fig. 2. The construction of the RFID-tag [11]

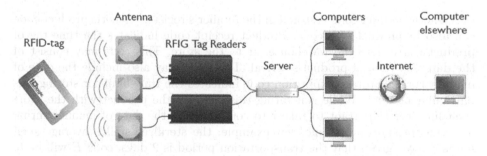

Fig. 3. The construction of the RFID system [11] (Color figure online)

The work of the Automated information system consists in three main stages where at which particular operations are performed. The first stage of the Automated information system presupposes programming and marking the arrived consignment of the homogeneous products by the specific tags. At this stage each product item is marked by the RFID-tag. The tag, in its turn, has the recordings of the three types of codes. Tag activity algorithm is predetermined by the type of code and allows for the three possible states. These states are related to the product's expiry date information.

- The green state indicates meeting-adhreing to the terms and conditions of the product shelf life. For the consumer it means that the product is ready for consumption.
- The yellow state indicates warning about the approaching of the expiry date. For the retailer it means urgent sale. The product is still ready for consumption, but the expiry date approaches very soon (in 3–4 days).
- The red state indicates the end of consumption. The retailer should extract the product (Table 1).

Table 1. Types of codes recorded on a RFID-tag

NP	GPC (product group code), G	PRC (date of arrival), D	SEC	ID, W	ID, R
Milk	00001	12032020	7	nW	nR

Explanation of the abbreviations in the table is follows:

- NP is Name of the product.
- GPC is Generic product code.
- PRC is Product receipt code.
- SEC is Storage expiration code.
- ID, W is ID Warning.
- ID, R is ID Recycling.

Generic product code is stored in the retailer's register. Generic product code can also be product's barcode. Product receipt code indicates the time tag of product's arrival to the warehouse, or to the store. This code may consist of the date and time of product's arrival. This code may also include the date of manufacturing. Storage expiration code indicates the time limit for storing this particular product. While generating this code for the product with the short shelf life, it is important to take into consideration the date of manufacturing and the transportation time. For example, the sterilized milk's average shelf life is 7 days; given that the transportation period is 2 days, code E will be 5. Therefore, the code recorded on the RFID-tag will have no identification data: 00001120320205. The second stage of the automated information system consists in reading the information from the RFID-tag on the required period of time. The algorithm of the tag's performance is shown in Fig. 4.

The first recording on the tag is the hardware recording of the product identification code 00001120320205. Every day RFID-tag reader's antenna sends a radio signal with the confirmation code. The cycle of antenna's radio signals depends on E. The expiry date code E indicates the number of the input signals sent by the antenna to identify the state of the tag. Once the required cycle of

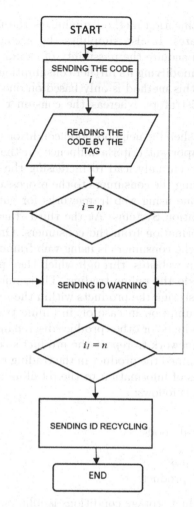

Fig. 4. Flowchart of the algorithm of sending information to AIS using web frameworks

signals is completed and the tag is activated, tag-reader's antenna sends an ID
Warning code $00001120320207nW$. Once ID Warning is received, the tag sends
a code that indicates the tag's transition to the yellow state. The duration of the
yellow state is predetermined by the product's expiry date. Every day of RFID-
tag's yellow state, the RFID tag-reader's antenna sends a radio signal with ID
Warning code. The cycle of the signals depends on the nW parameter, where is
the number of possible shelf life days. After the ID Recycling $00001120320207nR$
is sent, the tag moves to the red state. Thus, after the ID Recycling code is sent
again, the tag will send the code to the tag-reader. And this will be the direct
instruction for the retailing administrator to extract the product.

The suggested identification method minimizes the time spent on checking products' expiration dates. It also simplifies the accounting procedures. The retailing administrators acquire the possibility of examining the product's condition just on time and modifying its further consumption procedure. Regardless of its obvious benefits, this method is only based on one-side control performed by the retailing administrators, whereas the consumer in not involved in the control procedure at all.

The violation of the shelf life neighborhood conditions, ignoring temperature, humidity, and other important criteria influence on the quality and product's expiry date. This will eventually lead to increasing the amount of food waste. Thus, we suggest involving the consumers to the process of the product's quality control. This can be done using web frameworks for gathering information for the Automated Information Systems. At the third stage of AIS's functioning, the system gathers information from the consumers. One of the effective ways of gathering data from the consumers is using web frameworks. All big retailing networks have their own websites, through which they provide the information for the consumers and do the online trading. Thus, information gathering can be done at the stage of storing the products within the retailing network, as well as at the stage of consumption in case of, in online trading. In case of defect detection, damaged products, or other product discrepancies, the consumer may fill-in a special web framework to report the product's condition.

Having visually examined the product in the trading room, the consumer may send the following types of information to the retailing administrator. Information about the product is follows:

- lack of product;
- mechanically damaged goods;
- contaminated goods;
- the signs of product use;
- the signs the spoiled product.

Information about product storage conditions is follows:

- violation of the commodity neighborhood rules;
- violation of the storage conditions (temperature, humidity, direct sunlight);
- lack of price tags.

The retailing administrator may gather all the above-mentioned types of information using a web framework. The main purpose of using web frameworks is sending the information from the user to the mainframe computer. As a rule, the result of the information exchange is the new HTML-document generated by the mainframe for the user, based on the previously sent information [13]. Web frameworks can be created using programming codes, Google forms, plugins [8, 15]. The user can fill in a web framework using websites or mobile applications.

In this paper, we introduce a sample web framework for gathering information for the AIS, based on the algorithm presented in Fig. 4. The first action of the user is signing up at the website, or logging in with the previously created login and password to create an account. While signing up, the user has to provide an email address and his/her user name/login. To protect account's privacy, the user has to create a password to log in. This is a common registration method. The user can also log in using his social networks accounts (Facebook, VK, Twitter). In this case, the user does not have to fill in his personal information fields. Social network, however, shares user's personal data with the website. With his next action, the user opens the web framework's dialog box and fills in the requested fields. Once all the fields are completed, the web framework checks the fields. If the some field needs correction, the framework informs the user about it. Having completed the web framework, the user receives the confirmation message. The results of our research have shown that developing a relevant algorithm of the user's activity while completing the web framework helps improving the framework's structure for its further optimization.

4   Experiment

Developing a web framework and integrating it into the simulation model of AIS. The experimental part of oue research was based on developing typical form for gathering information comprises the following five components:

1. Structure. This component predefines the succession of the fields, framework's outlook, cross-referencing between particular fields.
2. Input. This component includes text fields, password fields, flag tags, radio-buttons, moving fields, and all other types of fields for the user's input information.
3. Labels. They provide the explanation of the input fields.
4. Action buttons. When the user presses this button, the action is performed by the system (e.g. sending a form).
5. Feedback. This component informs the user about the effectiveness of the action. Most websites and mobile applications use text messages as a feedback response. The message informs the user about the result of the action. The result can be positive (the message sent), or negative (sending error).

Web frameworks may also have some additional components:

- Help is instructions about completing a form. It is realized by using an attribute placeholderfor the $<input>$ tag.
- Check is checking data to make sure the input data is correct. It is realized by using an attribute patternfor the $<input>$ tag.

Figure 5 shows the developed web framework for gathering information in the AIS with the representation of all the components required [18].

After all fields are completed, the form is double-checked. If something is wrong, the user receives a warning message pointing to the field that needs correction. The correction procedure is not applied to the user's name field, since this field presents a unique and confidential information that is not meant to be corrected. Having sent the form, the user receives a confirmation message.

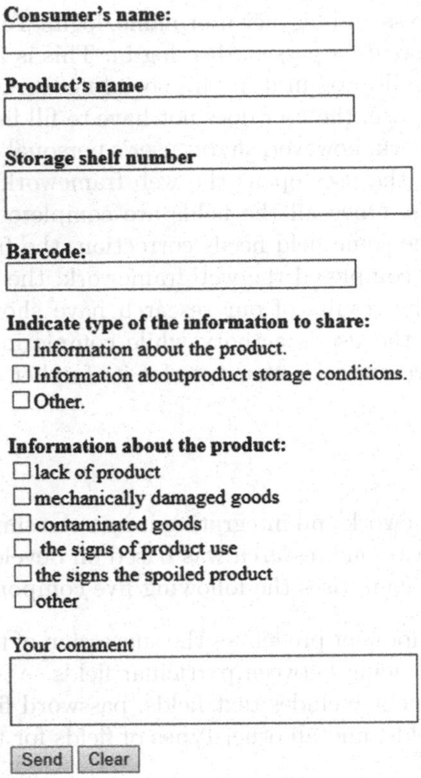

Consumer's name:

Product's name

Storage shelf number

Barcode:

Indicate type of the information to share:
☐ Information about the product.
☐ Information aboutproduct storage conditions.
☐ Other.

Information about the product:
☐ lack of product
☐ mechanically damaged goods
☐ contaminated goods
☐ the signs of product use
☐ the signs the spoiled product
☐ other

Your comment

Send Clear

Fig. 5. The developed web framework for gathering information in the AIS

In order to specify the process of gathering information about the products, the authors of this paper have developed a simulation model of the process. Our simulation model defines the process of sending the information from the user (i.e. a consumer) to the retailing administrator. This model makes it possible to prognose the behavior of the system as a whole. The suggested simulation model aims at simulating the process of visiting a store by the consumer, finding violations of product quality, and informing retailing administrators about them. The construction of the model presupposes the following set of actions.

Creating the plan of the trading room and virtual marking of the operation zones. Figure 6 presents a 2-D model of the trading room plan. The dotted line highlights and marks six (1–6) zones where the consumer is supposed to stay and perform some preconditioned algorithm of actions. These zones correspond to the shelvings with goods. The plan also indicates consumer's entrance and exit points. To make the model more realistic, we have added 3-D images of the cashiers at the exit, trading machines, and boxes with goods. Developing the Action Part of the Model shows in Fig. 7.

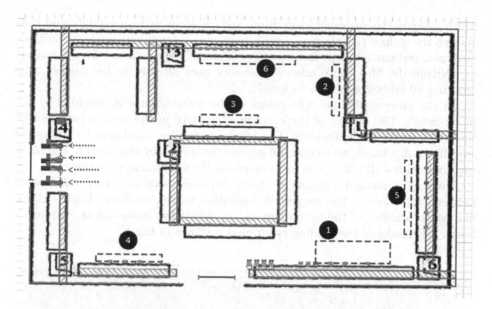

Fig. 6. 2-D model of the trading room plan with the virtually marked zones

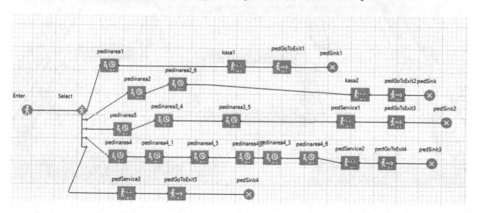

Fig. 7. Action diagram of modeling the process of gathering information from the consumers

Constructing the algorithm of the model's performance consists in creating the blocks related to one another with the help of connectors. The PedSourse (Enter) block creates the flow of agents (in our case – the consumers). It is used as a starting block of the process diagram [12]. In our model, we suggest five route schemes that cover all possible movements of the customers in the trading room according to the suggested market zones. Within the first route scheme, the customer visits one zone and then goes to the cashier (Blocks:pedinarea1). Within the second route scheme the customer visits two zones and then goes to the cashier (Blocks: pedinarea2, pedinarea2–6). Within the third and the fourth route schemes the customer visits three and six zones correspondingly and then goes to the cashier (Blocks:pedinarea3, pedinarea3–4, pedinarea3–5), (Blockspedinarea4, pedinarea4–1, pedinarea4–2, pedinarea4–3, pedinarea4–5, pedinarea4–6). Within the fifth route scheme customer goes directly to the cashier zone ignoring all other zones (Blocks:kasa5).

In the process diagram, the choice of the route scheme is provided by the block Select. The timing of the customers' activity in the zone is provided by the block pedWait (pedinarea). The block pedService simulates the process of standing and waiting in the line and getting the service by the cashier. The block pedSink deletes all the agents and completes the simulation procedure.

Having monitored customers' route schemes showing their movements between the zones of the suggested simulation model, we have clearly defined five route schemes of the customers and modelled five independent customer's flows. 2-D model of the trading room plan is shown in Fig. 8.

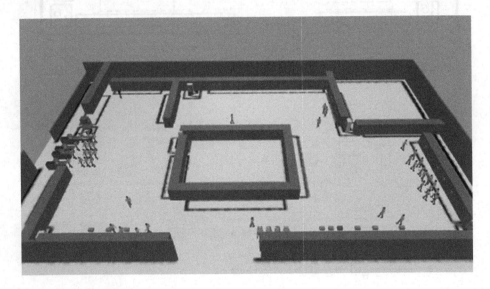

Fig. 8. 3-D model of the trading room showing the simulation of the information gathering process

While analyzing the above presented simulation model, we have also designed customer's behavior in the zones marked by the deviations in the product conditions.

5   Results and Discussion

The presented research resulted in the development of the concept of an automated information system for gathering information. The developed simulation model is based on modern technical requirements, as well as it takes into consideration the existing patterns of customers' social interactions. Technical requirements include RFID-tags, RFID-tag readers, computer frameworks for processing and retrieving the input data, and some additional computer equipment for the system functioning.

Having analyzed the developed simulation model, we suggest the following action algorithm:

- Indicating products expiration date. The type of products (meat, fish, vegetables, dairy products etc.) predetermines the storage conditions for every stage of production, and the choice of the "smart packaging" for every particular type of product.
- Marking the packaging by the RFID-tags, and the programming of these tags.
- Reading RFID-tags and initiating product search.
- Gathering information from the customers to control the quality of the products.

The whole simulation procedure, that will be replicated in the real world context, consists of the following stages:

- At the first stage, the final expiry date is indicated due to the regulated conditions.
- At the second stage, the packaging is marked by the RFID-tags. Each tag is programmed due to the type of the product and its expiration date. Each day and hour have their own unique ID keys.

The next stage is characterized by the procedure of tag reading and product search, the results of which predetermine the algorithm of the tag codes classification. The stage of gathering information from the customers is represented by the simulation model mentioned above. While analyzing the specifications of the suggested simulation model, we have concluded that customer's behavior may be simulated by two stages depending on the indicated deviations in the condition of the goods. The customer may perform two possible actions regarding the particular specifications within the zone of his location:

1. The customer finds deviations in the product condition (changes in the storage conditions, signs of the spoiled products) and fills in the suggested web framework to inform the retailer about the deviations.
2. The customer ignores the web framework and follows the indicated route scheme. In this case he stays in the particular zone for about 1 min.

The first option is, obviously, more desirable, since both sides – the customer and the retailer – will benefit from the indicated and reported deviations. Thus, another important aspect in developing our simulation model is finding the mechanisms of encouraging the customers to fill in the web framework. For this, we suggest to apply some specific communication strategies to facilitate the communication between the customer and the retailer via web framework. In modern sphere of Human-Computer Interaction, communication strategies predetermine the choice of language means to be represented in the web framework. The appropriate choice of the names of the fields will make web framework's interface user-friendly. A well-designed user-friendly interface will encourage the customer to inform the store administrators about the indicated problems. Communication strategy used in the web framework's interface can be viewed as:

- global strategy (i.e. being polite, being positive, being honest);
- local strategy (i.e. greetings, request for the personal information, detailed description, appreciation of the customer's help).

Communication strategy is a powerful means of modeling the communication between the customer and the automated information gathering system. While filling the web framework, the customer will be involved in a sort of dialogue with the system. The more rational and user-friendly is the interface, the more resultative will be the process of gathering the information. The choice of language means for the framework's interface has two aims:

1. Planning the structure of the communicative act (dividing communication into parts, establishing logical relations between these parts).
2. Prognosing customer's behavior (simulating customer's decisions, communicative choices and verbal responses.

Following the specifications described above, we suggest the sample communication model simulating the conversation between the customer and the automated information gathering system (Fig. 9).

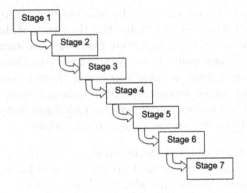

Fig. 9. Scheme of the process of gathering information from the consumers .

Stage 1. Greetings – "Hello! You are about to send your product quality control feedback.
Stage 2. Entering personal data – "Please, enter your name (product name, storage shelf number, barcode)".
Stage 3. Identifying type of the product – "Please, indicate the name of the product", "Please, indicate product storage conditions".

Stage 4. Gathering information about the deviations in product condition/quality – "Please, choose one or more of the following problems: lack of product; mechanically damaged goods; contaminated goods; the signs of product use; the signs the spoiled product; other).

Stage 5. Customer's evaluation of product condition – "Please, leave your comment and let us know about the indicated problem".

Stage 6. Appreciation – "Thank you for your help! Together we can minimize the amount of food loss and food waste. Together we can make the world a better place".

Stage 7. Completing the procedure – "Send your feedback"/"Clear the form".

It should be mentioned that the customer must have the full information about the procedure he is involved in. He should understand the importance of his feedback and should be motivated to provide as much information as possible in order to minimize the amount of food loss. At the same time, the process of gathering information should not last for too long, otherwise the customer will simply give up, or will break up in the middle of the information gathering process while filling in the web form. The average timing of filling in the web framework is calculated according to the triangular distribution of probabilities. It is rarely an accurate representation of a data set. However, it is employed as a functional form of control for fuzzy logic due to its ease of use. The triangular distribution can take on very skewed forms including negative skewness. For the exceptional cases where the mode is either the min or max, the triangular distribution becomes a right triangle. The triangular distribution of probabilitie is shown in Fig. 10.

Given: min - x value - 1 min
max - the maximum x value - 5 min.
mode - the most likely x value - 3 min.

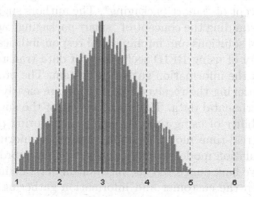

Fig. 10. Triangular distribution of probabilities for the agents staying in the zones with the indicated deviations in product conditions

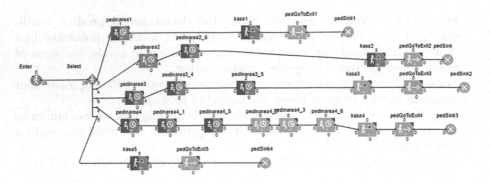

Fig. 11. Probabilities of the agents stay represented on the agent diagram modeling the process of gathering information from the customers

The developed simulation model, shown in Fig. 11, enabled deeper understanding of the information gathering process, which is an essential part of the concept of "smart packaging". The visualization of the results obtained within the procedure of modeling helps to clarify the interaction between all parts of the project. The suggested time control management reduces the simulated time of the procedure. All this has an important analytical and optimization potential for the development of "smart packaging" concept in order to essentially reduce food loss and food waste. In addition, the results of the application of the developed simulation model will make an important contribution into the creation of Decision Support Systems.

6   Conclusions

The article presents the analysis of a new information gathering system aimed at refining the concept of "smart packaging". The authors suggest an innovative approach to understanding the concept of "smart packaging" as an integral unity of modern technical solutions and human social responsibilities. The paper highlights the possibility of using RFID technology of data transmission to support the performance of the information gathering system. The procedures of coding RFID tags and retrieving the received information are clearly defined and illustrated by the experimental data. The main benefit of the suggested simulation model is the possibility of using time ID-tags in monitoring product expiration date limits in the real-time mode. Just like any other information technology, the developed simulation model strongly depends on an appropriate input data.

In this paper, we have suggested the mechanism of modeling automatic communication between the customer and information gathering system by means of using specific communication strategies. Therefore, the authors suggest using web frameworks to gather the requested information directly from the customers in the real-time mode. This will help preventing modern retailing networks from unnecessary food loss and food waste, which is a very disturbing issue in modern world. The suggested simulation model for "smart packaging" will enable companies, countries, cities to predict and quantify the unnecessary food loss, as well as to develop relevant strategies to benefit from "smart packaging" technologies.

References

1. Official website of the food and agriculture organization of the united nations. http://www.fao.org/savefood/resources/keyfindings/infographics/fruit/en/
2. Butrin, A.: Use of radiofrequency identification technology in the warehouse of temporary storage. Actual Probl. Aviat. Cosmonautics **2**(11), 847–849 (2015)
3. Cujan, Z.: Packaging technique and identification. Vysoka skola logistiky, Prerov (2012)
4. Finkenzeller, K.: RFID Handbook: Radiofrequency Identification Fundamentals and Applications. Wiley, Hoboken (2003). https://doi.org/10.1002/0470868023
5. Gavva, O., Tokarchuk, S., Kokhan, O.: Smart packing for food. Packaging **2**, 36–40 (2013)
6. Krestyanpol, L.: The developing of "smart packaging". Technol. Complexes **1**(13), 70–74 (2016)
7. Krestyanpol, L.: Economic feasibility of smart packaging under the global initiative "save food". Technol. Complexes **1**(14), 68–74 (2017)
8. Krestyanpol, L., Bisub, I.: Web forms as a tool for automated information collection. Vega-Druk, Lutsk (2020)
9. Krestyanpol, L., Palchevskyi, B.: Comparative analysis model of liquor product pricing with consideration of costs of the protection against falsification. Actual Probl. Econ. **184**, 444–452 (2016)
10. Miroshnyk, I.: Why save food is important for Ukraine. http://savefood-ua.com/blog/92/
11. Palchevskyi, B., Krestyanpol, O., Krestyanpol, L.: Information technologies in the design of the system of protection of packaged products. Vega-Druk, Lutsk (2015)
12. Palchevskyi, B., Krestyanpol, O., Krestyanpol, L.: The use of Anylogic system for modelling a flexible automated packing system in training engineering students. Inf. Technol. Learn. Tools **75**(1), 225–236 (2020). https://doi.org/10.33407/itlt.v75i1.2714
13. Pavlenko, A.: UX review: developing the right forms of information input. https://medium.com/@pavljenko/ux-viewdevelopment-right-form-introduction-information-3844211d1e17
14. Plugina, T., Reut, O.: Design models of radio frequency identification systems. Bull. Kharkov Natl. Automob. Highw. Univ. **55**, 23–28 (2011)
15. Romaniuk, O.: Web Design and Computer Graphics: A Textbook for Students of Software Engineering in All Specialties. Vinnytsia National Technical University (2007)
16. Scharfeldt, T.: Low cost RFID systems, Moscow (2006)
17. Scholz, C., Doerfel, S., Atzmueller, M., Hotho, A., Stumme, G.: Resource-aware on-line RFID localization using proximity data. Mach. Learn. Knowl. Discov. Databases **6931**, 129–144 (2011). https://doi.org/10.1007/978-3-64223808-69_17
18. Zavyalets, Y.: Web-technologies and web-design, Chernivtsi (2014)

The Use of the "Digital Twin" Concept for Proactive Diagnosis of Technological Packaging Systems

Bogdan Palchevskyi[1] and Lyubov Krestyanpol[2]([✉])

[1] Eastern European Scientific Society, Lutsk, Ukraine
bogdan-pal@ukr.net
[2] Lutsk National Technical University, Lutsk, Ukraine
lkrestyanpol@gmail.com

Abstract. An important issue to produce the technological equipment including the equipment for packaging is the up-grading of production automation systems, which involves improving the control and monitoring over the industrial equipment, providing its self-test. Technological equipment is used in many branches of industry. Its malfunction leads to a significant decline in the economic efficiency of production. To eliminate material losses directly during the equipment operation, there shall be carried out its predictive (proactive) maintenance and repair. To solve this issue, the methods of Big data analysis, artificial intelligence principles, digital technologies are being applied more widely in the industry, which make it possible to create Digital Twins of technological equipment and use them for self-test of manufacturing systems. These Digital Twins model the internal processes, technical specifications and behavior of the technological equipment under the conditions of interference and environmental effect, which makes it possible to perform data analysis in order to identify the sources of efficiency loss. At the stage of operation, the Digital Twin model of the technological equipment can be used to provide feedback in order to adjust the diagnostics and forecast malfunctions and to increase the operating efficiency of the technological equipment. There has been proposed a method of using digital models of the technological equipment condition, based on the measurement and comparison of the parameters that characterize the equipment operability, which promotes to the early detection of malfunctions and their elimination.

Keywords: Digital twin · Big data · Diagnostics · Malfunction matrix · Expectation value · System analysis · Additive evaluation indicators · Parameter

1 Introduction

In these days, it has become possible to take production automation processes to a significantly new level due to the increasing use of artificial intelligence

© Springer Nature Switzerland AG 2020
S. Babichev et al. (Eds.): DSMP 2020, CCIS 1158, pp. 432–444, 2020.
https://doi.org/10.1007/978-3-030-61656-4_29

in manufacturing systems. It is the consolidation of integrated manufacturing systems with intelligent control systems which has become the main feature in creation of the modern intellectual manufacture that has begun to develop in all branches of industrial production. This development has been called the fourth industrial revolution by experts. Typical changes in the modern packaging manufacture include, first of all, the intellectualization of technological equipment management system. The effect of this change is also the appearance of Intelligent maintenance systems. One of the advanced types of manufacturing equipment maintenance is predictive (proactive) maintenance (PdM). It allows repairing not according to a pre-arranged plan, but when it is required. It means not elimination but prevention of the equipment failures by means of interactive evaluation of its technical condition based on the data set received from the sensors, and determining the optimal terms of repair works. Predictive (expected or proactive) maintenance is applied in cases when the degree of mechanism use in the workflow is estimated as high and its malfunction leads to the long downtime and significantly lost productivity.

The effectiveness of predictive technical equipment maintenance is achieved by means of:

- collecting data on the technical condition of the equipment and its pre-processing,
- early detection of malfunctions,
- predicting the time of failure.

The Digital Twin concept of technological equipment, Big Data technology, which make it possible to predict the time of failure with high accuracy, are used for practical implementation of intelligent maintenance. The combination of these technologies in the Intelligent technological equipment makes it possible to implement modern advanced methods of maintenance. This concept is used at all stages of the product life cycle, including design, production, operation and utilization. Depending on the scale of operational modeling, the following levels of Digital Twins of manufacturing system are distinguished:

- digital twin of a manufacturing system;
- digital twin of a manufacturing line;
- digital twin of a separate technological equipment of the manufacturing line.

An important task of the operation model of manufacturing system Digital Twin is to minimize possible malfunctions of the technological equipment by its timely maintenance and repair. To solve this issue, the information from sensors of a real operating device is used as an input for the Digital Twin. It provides comparing the information of the virtual sensors of the Digital Twin with the sensors of the real device, and detecting anomalies and their causes. At the equipment is various sensors, the data on its technical condition can be collected continuously, even during its operation. Timely detection of even small deviations in operating parameters makes it possible to take prompt measures to ensure the correct operation of the equipment by its maintenance.

Big Data Technology (Big Data) allows identifying hidden patterns, that elude from limited human perception by the detection from data of previously unknown, non-trivial, practically useful knowledge, which is necessary for decision making. For this purpose, there are used such special data processing methods as, for example, application of associative rules, classifications to break down into categories, cluster analysis, regression analysis, detection and analysis of deviations, etc.

The aim of the research is development of the digital twin principles of technological systems, methods of big data for creation of conditions for their predictive (proactive) technical support.

2   Literature Review

Specialists on production automation argue has already become a notable presence of a common approach to structure of intelligent manufacturing system (IMS) [1,3,4,6]. Implementation of efficiency in the creation of intellectual production is based on automated procedures for collecting and storing production information needed to track the deliveries of raw materials, finished goods, equipment and human resources [17,19].

The historical experience of industry development objectively shows that the traditional system of industrial production is not capable to ensure sustainable and harmonious development of the national and world economy [10,13,15]. Nowadays, it becomes evident that mass production, directed to a stable production of a narrow range of products, is disappering in conditions of growing competition. The experience of using the production systems for machine-building, instrument-making, food and packing industries shows that the one of their minuses is the low efficiency of the basic equipment use. The indicators of the machines exploitation definitely influence to stoppages because of organizational and technical reasons, as well as the seasonality of the lines exploitation, for example, as it has place in packaging production [14].

Therefore, recently there are three key sources that have led to the creation and development of intellectual or "smart" production:

- necessity of increasing of the flexibility of production, which will allow the efficient exploitation of equipment throughout the year;
- providing of complex automation of integrated production, use of control systems in the technological lines, which implement the direct control functions of the equipment, planning and dispatching of its loading, monitoring and diagnosing the state of equipment by collecting and analyzing of information about its reliability;
- implementation of the artificial intelligence principles into production systems.

Increasing the Modern Production Systems Flexibility. Since the initial stage in the development of intellectual production was the creation of flexible production systems (FPS) [12,16], further development of the intelligent manufacturing system (IMS) is based on the well-developed concept of flexible production systems (FPS), which allow to produce a wide range of products at a cost close to the cost of mass production within the technological capabilities united in the machine system [6,8,17].

Providing of the Complexity of Production Automation. When creating an IMS, there is the transition from increasing efficiency at each stage of production separately to the optimization of the production process in general [4,6,18]. It should be noted that during the automation of production systems there was a range of visible tendencies, namely:

- reducing human participation in production processes, up to providing the solitude of technology, which allows to increase the speed of machinery, to apply special environments and to increase the sterility and stability of products;
- reducing human participation in processes of displacement, manipulating, stacking and re-formating of products through the wider use of industrial robots that increases the speed of products and semi-finished products movement.

Implementation of Artificial Intelligence Principles in Production Systems. The main task of artificial intelligence is usually interpreted as the property of an automatic production system to assume the individual functions of human intelligence. Expert systems embedded in the IMS play here an important role [7]. The use of intelligent control systems, the expansion of the number of their feedbacks increases the controllability of processes that occur in machines and provides autonomy of their operation [2,7,15].

3   Materials and Methods

As the experience of operating technological systems made by different manufactures shows, one of the most significant disadvantages is the low efficiency of the main equipment [5,6]. The key influence on the equipment operating indicator is carried by the idle time because of organizational and technical reasons, or by the idle time due to the time adjustment of the technological lines in processing and packaging production caused by their seasonal use [13,14].

Nearly always the operation of the manufacturing system is accompanied by the constant need to reduce its operating costs. The modern way to solve this issue is to create intelligent manufacturing system based on the applying of advanced information technology to optimize operating costs [3,7,19]. Summarizing the arguments of many researchers [2,4,9], we can state that the intelligent manufacturing system adapts to work in external conditions which are changing over time, basing on the appropriate adaptation algorithm. The basis for making management decisions to optimize operating costs in terms of maintenance of intelligent technological systems is to create and apply digital models that describe the condition of the manufacturing system.

Thus, in these days, there are two key sources for improving the efficiency of integrated intelligent manufacturing systems:

- high flexibility of production that allows efficient use of the equipment all year round is based on a sufficiently developed concept of flexible manufacturing systems (FMS), which make it possible within the technological capabilities of the integrated machines to produce a wide range of products at a cost close to cost of mass production [6,13];
- complex automation of technological systems, when the transition from efficiency improvement at each stage of production separately to optimization of the manufacturing process as a whole is made. Here with it is monitored the use of planning and scheduling functions of technological equipment loading, its control and diagnostics of its condition to provide the proactive (predictive) maintenance [15]. The applying of the intelligent systems of control, the increasing quantity of feedbacks in the technological equipment, help to increase the machine processes control and give the independence in their functioning [9,13].

To form a managed maintenance program for a technological system, it is necessary to consider possible manufacturing situations by making certain changes to the control algorithm [3,9,11]. Obviously, first of all, it is required to evaluate the external conditions to make necessary changes in the maintenance algorithm and be provided with a digital model that describes the technological system condition in the given time intervals [1].

The efficiency of such use of digital models for forming a managed maintenance program for a technological system, has its disadvantage, despite the possibility of manufacture analyses and identifying the necessary reasons for correction, has the disadvantage. Since the equipment is being operated day and night at many manufacturing facilities, its unexpected stoppage can cause considerable losses [1,8]. To prevent this problem, we have developed a mathematical model to determine the controlled parameters and features that describe functioning of the technological automated machine, which make it possible to determine the current state of the machine and to predict the necessary preventive maintenance actions.

The digital model of the manufacturing system is based on data collection regards the duration time of the equipment being in different states. Information about the technological equipment in the state of downtime is obtained based on the analysis of the functioning and downtime of the technological equipment, which is put in the standard equipment malfunctions and downtime log that is carried out at every modern enterprise. Ranking of the malfunction and downtime reasons in units of time, for example, in minutes, is performed by digital data processing for the main aggregate of the manufacturing system over the long observation time. To solve the issue (to improve the manufacturing system) means to eliminate the reasons that lead to a decrease of its efficiency. Obviously, there are many of such reasons and it is very difficult and expensive to eliminate each of them. Therefore, to identify the parameters that for the greater part affect the unsatisfactory values of the target property of the system, we use a method of data aggregation, which is known from the system analysis. While creating aggregative test objects, you can determine the efficiency of the equipment as a fraction of the effective time of its operation. It is the improvement and stabilization of these generalized technical equipment parameters that shall be focused on during the following planning steps for maintenance. Such aggregative parameters are often found among the target properties of the system. The system analysis logic provides identifying the most significant causes that lead to the problem and concentrating all efforts on them.

To determine the probability of diagnoses by the Bayesian method it is necessary to make a diagnostic matrix, which is formed on the basis of previous statistical material. This table shows the probabilities of the signs categories and their corresponding probabilities of predicted diagnoses for different combinations of signs. The size of the studied values is determined by the number of possible (potential) signs of failures and malfunctions.

Ideally, to fill in this matrix, it is necessary to keep a continuous record of the technical condition of the equipment during its every regular maintenance with the condition of its systems and mechanisms being recorded.

The term "technical diagnostics" means recognition of the control object state in the conditions of incomplete information [6,18]. In this case, it is assumed that those states are the most known, which are often met. It follows from the definition that the primary is the choice of a states set, which is very large for a complex object.

Diagnostic operation, as a rule, shall answer the question:

- What is the malfunction?
- What item of equipment is down?
- What is the prognosis for further course of the process?
- What is the effect of the malfunction on the control object characteristics and the quality of the technological process?

Let's consider an example how to create the diagnostic matrix by Bayes algorithm for a technological machine for packing paste into polymer bags [8].

To determine the group of downtime caused by malfunctions of the separate machine mechanisms, let's consider its workflow. Packing automatic machine performs the following technological transitions: unwinding the laminate from the roll, forming a pipe from it, longitudinal welding of the sides to form a pack, cutting it off from the pipe, cutting the corner of the package and welding cork into it, filling the pack and its pressurization with welding Fig. 1.

We select five main machine states and three main diagnostic characteristics (parameters) of various malfunctions:

- malfunctions in the system of laminate supply – state D_1;
- malfunctions in the system of cork supply – state D_2;
- malfunctions in the system of supply and dosage of paste – a product – state D_3;
- malfunctions in the system of welding mechanisms – state D_4;
- machine state in working order – D_0.

We shll accept that the basis for the proactive maintenance of the machine is the boundary state of the machine in terms of its productivity, product quality

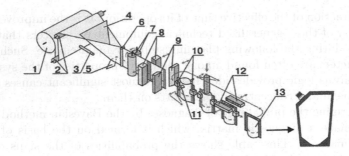

Fig. 1. Technological scheme of paste packing in the doy-pack bags and doy-pack bag with a cork. 1-laminate roll, 2-laminate unwinding, 3-puncher, 4-pipe forming, 5-photodetector, 6, 7-rolls, 8-longitudinal welding, 9-cutting, 10- opening of a pack, 12-pressurization of pack, 13-pack

and material consumption. We shall choose the intensity of changes in these indicators as a diagnostic characteristic. Each characteristic has three levels of state: good, satisfactory, and unsatisfactory, corresponding to a system malfunction:

- the intensity of downtime and efficiency changes – k_1;
- the intensity of quality product change – k_2;
- the intensity of material consumption change – k_3.

If the diagnosis D_j exists and there is simple characteristic k_j, that is met with this diagnosis, so the probability of the combination of these two occurrences, that is the presence in object of the D_j state and characteristic k_j will be defined as:

$$P(D_j k_j) = P(D_j) \times P(\frac{k_j}{D_j}) = P(k_j) \times P(\frac{D_j}{k_j}) \tag{1}$$

From this equation, we get the probability of a D_j diagnosis after the appearance of k_j characteristic in objects, the so-named posterior probability of a diagnosis $P(\frac{k_j}{D_j})$:

$$P(\frac{D_j}{k_j}) = P(D_j) \times \frac{P(\frac{k_j}{D_j})}{P(k_j)} \tag{2}$$

where:

$$P(D_j) - D_j \tag{3}$$

diagnosis probability, which is which is determined by statistics, the so-called a priori probability of diagnosis; $P(\frac{k_j}{D_j})$ - probability of characteristic k_j appearance in objects with state D_j; $P(k_j)$ - probability of characteristic k_j appearance in objects, regardless of their state(namely, diagnosis).

Table 1. Packing machine malfunction matrix

Diagnosis of machine	Marking	k_1	k_2	k_3	$P(D_i)$
MSLS	D_1	$P(\frac{k_1}{D_1})$	$P(\frac{k_2}{D_1})$	$P(\frac{k_3}{D_1})$	$P(D_1)$
MSCS	D_2	$P(\frac{k_1}{D_2})$	$P(\frac{k_2}{D_2})$	$P(\frac{k_3}{D_2})$	$P(D_2)$
MSDP	D_3	$P(\frac{k_1}{D_3})$	$P(\frac{k_2}{D_3})$	$P(\frac{k_3}{D_3})$	$P(D_3)$
MSWM	D_4	$P(\frac{k_1}{D_4})$	$P(\frac{k_2}{D_4})$	$P(\frac{k_3}{D_4})$	$P(D_4)$
MWO	D_0	$P(\frac{k_1}{D_0})$	$P(\frac{k_2}{D_5})$	$P(\frac{k_3}{D_5})$	$P(D_0)$

The explanations for abbreviations in Table 1:

- MSLS is Malfunctions in the System of Laminate Supply.
- MSCS is Malfunctions in the System of Cork Supply.
- MSDP is Malfunctions in the System of Supply and Dosage of Product.
- MSWM is Malfunctions in the System of Welding Mechanisms.
- MWO is Machine in Working Order.
- k_1 is the idle time and efficiency loss.
- k_2 is the defective products.
- k_3 is the material overconsumption.

The occurrence (Characteristic appearance) k_1, k_2 occurs in conjunction with one of the mutually exclusive occurrence-diagnoses D_1, D_2 (for example, the object's malfunctioning or working state). D_j occurrencess are called hypotheses $P(D_j)$ is the apriori probabilities of hypotheses, and $P(\frac{k_j}{D_j})$ probabilities is the posteriori of these hypotheses, under condition that the occurrence k_j took place. Probabilities of the states, when several characteristics appeared, is defined by the expression:

$$P(\frac{D_j}{k_1 \times k_2 \times k_3}) = \frac{P(D_j) \times P(\frac{k_1}{D_j}) \times P(\frac{k_2}{D_j}) \times P(\frac{k_3}{D_j})}{\sum_j P(D_j) \times P(\frac{k_1}{D_j}) \times P(\frac{k_2}{D_j}) \times P(\frac{k_3}{D_j})} \quad (4)$$

The range of characteristic changes from good to unsatisfactory is determined by the corresponding values of these characteristics in terms of prolonged operation of the machine. These data must be obtained in the manufacturing environment and they serve to determine the boundary conditions in diagnostic operation of the machine state and to determine the moments of predictive maintenance and repair.

4   Experiment

The development of a digital model of the technological line was done in Any-Logic. AnyLogic simulation environment is based on an object-oriented concept and has a number of benefits. Some of them are: the existence of all modeling paradigms (high choice of approach flexibility); the possibility to decide between paradigms or apply an integrated approach; it has all the properties necessary to develop simulation models [11]. AnyLogic environment is developed in a universal Java programming language, which allows it not to depend on the type of operating system. Simulation modeling consists of two major stages: the creation of a model and the analysis of the data obtained with the help of a decision model.

The elements of the system, their relations, parameters and variables, as well as their relationships and the laws of their changes, must be expressed by means of the simulation environment, that is, in this environment, variables and parameters of the model must be defined, procedures for calculating the variables changes and model characteristics in time are constructed in this environment. First of all, it is required to define the input parameters for the simulation model. The input parameters of the model are:

- type of product;
- speed of the conveyor;
- parameters of packing machines (weight of packed products);
- breakage of conveyors.

This model will be done in a discrete-abstraction event.

5   Results and Discussion

Data for processing the digital model of the packing machine functioning are placed in a database – a log of equipment malfunctions and downtime. Causes ranking is done through digital data processing. Figure 2 shows the results of downtime ranking in minutes of the main aggregates of the manufacturing system during the year. The manufacturing system model is based on the collected data as to the duration time of the equipment being in different states.

An explanation of the numerals in Fig. 2:

- 1 is the drag mechanism;
- 2, 3 are the capture mechanism;
- 5, 6 are the mechanism of supply and insertion of the closure;
- 7, 8 are the mechanism of soldering the crust;
- 9 is the soldering mechanism;
- 10 is the dispenser with nozzle;
- 11 is the cooling mechanism with thermal sensor;
- 12 is the vacuum pump;
- 13, 15 are the heating element and temperature sensor;
- 14 is the photodetector;
- 16 is the vibrocontainer.

The data aggregation method known from the system analysis is used to determine the efficiency of the equipment and its maintenance plan as a fraction of the effective time of its operation. The aggregation ends when critical machine

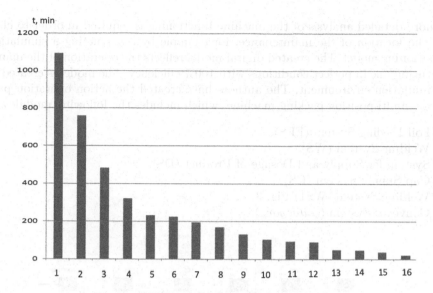

Fig. 2. Idle time types by machine mechanisms

Table 2. Malfunctions packing machine matrix

Diagnosis of machine	Marking	$P(\frac{D_j}{k_1 \times k_2 \times k_3})$	k_1	k_2	k_3	$P(D_i)$
MSLS	D_1	0,05353	1,0	0,2	0,2	0,0387
MSCS	D_2	0,27670	1,0	1,0	1,0	0,0080
MSDP	D_3	0,10956	0,2	1,0	0,6	0,0264
MSWM	D_4	0,56024	0,6	1,0	1,0	0,0270
MWO	D_0	0	0	0,05	0,07	0,9000

maintenance periods are identified, that is the parameters that most affect the unsatisfactory value of the performance target of the machine. It is the improvement and stabilization of these parameters that shall be focused on while planning the stages of proactive (predictive) maintenance.

In the normal state of the machine (state D_j) the characteristic k_1 is not observed, the characteristic k_2 is observed in 5% of the time, and the characteristic k_3 is observed in 7% of the time. Based on statistic data, it is known that the characteristic k_1 in the state D_1 occurs in 100% of the time, and the characteristics k_2 and k_3 occur in 20% of the time. In the state D_2, the values of all characteristics are 100 % of the time, and in the state D_3, respectively, 20%, 100% and 60% respectively. In the state D_4, the characteristics are 60%, 100% and 20%, respectively.

It can be stated from the calculations that under the presence of three characteristics with probability 0,56, the machine is in the state D_4, that is with a malfunctioning system of welding mechanisms. In the absence of these characteristics, the machine will be in its normal state D_0. In the intermediate cases, a more detailed analysis of the machine functioning is required in order to clarify the location of the maintenance, for example by constructing a simulation functioning model. The created digital model reflects the operation of the manufacturing line in perfect conditions with 100% efficiency. The model is created in a simulation environment. The authors have created the action operation part of the multi-position packing machine, which includes the following modules:

- Foil Feeding System (FFS).
- Welding System (WS).
- System for Supply and Dosage of Product (DS).
- Cap Supply System (CS).
- Welding System (WS1) Fig. 3.
- Conveyor System ($conveyor_n$).

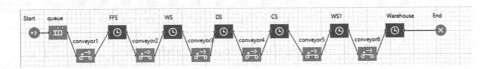

Fig. 3. Action diagram of the technological line operation account for mechanisms malfunctions

To reflect the adequate functioning of the technological system under the conditions of malfunctions of its constituent elements, there has been introduced a block for its maintenance in case of malfunctionsd. The created model in the further researches gives an opportunity to predict the characteristics of malfunctions, and optimize the process of under other operating conditions, the normal state of the machine (state D_0) is characterized by other values of the diagnostic characteristics k_1, k_2, k_3, which can be determined statistically. A significant reduction in experimental studies is achieved with the help of a simulation model (Fig. 4).

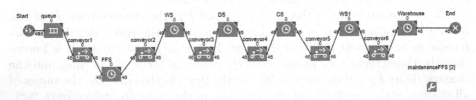

Fig. 4. Action diagram of technological line operation with account for mechanism malfunctions

6 Conclusions

It becomes clear for manufacturers of modern technological equipment that more functional, flexible and productive machines, which are connected to the information network of the enterprise, are required to increase the production efficiency. In recent years, more and more enterprises in the area of packing equipment manufacture, in order to achieve that, are expanding production automation systems, which already anticipate improving not only the control and operation of industrial equipment, but also the introduction of methods of its self-test and predictive (proactive) maintenance. For this purpose, a number of solutions have already been developed based on the applying of digital twins of technological systems in machine-building, packing and other manufactures in terms of the use of big data analysis methods.

Taking into account that digital twin technologies enable for product manufacturers to make proactive decisions based on big data, the efficiency increase in the applying of industrial equipment is achieved. High-productive manufactures, which include the machine-building, packaging, pharmacological and food industries are the areas of the highest growth in the digital twin application.

Two areas of building intellectual manufacturing systems shall be determined: first, top-down, that is by attaching a new component to the existing intellectual system, and, secondly, from the bottom to the top, that is by providing intellectual properties to the bottom components. It is typical for mechanic units. Any production task, the solution algorithm of which is unknown in advance or which is created on the basis of incomplete data, as well as systems, programs, which perform the actions to solve this problem, can be attributed to artificial intelligence if the Result of their operation will be similar to the result of human activities in terms of solving the same issue.

The concept of artificial intelligence can be applied to technological systems in their using of the subsystems which change their operation algorithm depending on changes in external or internal conditions. Obviously, to solve the issues how to increase efficiency of the industrial equipment by means of the digital twin principles of technological systems, methods of big data for creation of conditions for their predictive (proactive) maintenance is a relevant scientific and practical task.

References

1. Boschert, S., Fisher, J., Rosen, R.: Next generation digital twin: an ecosystem for mechatronic systems. IFAC-PapersOnLine **52**(15), 265–270 (2019). https://doi.org/10.1016/j.ifacol.2019.11.685
2. Camarinha-Matos, L.M., Afsarmanesh, H., Marik, V. (eds.): Intelligent Systems for Manufacturing. ITIFIP, vol. 1. Springer, Boston, MA (1998). https://doi.org/10.1007/978-0-387-35390-6
3. Gaines, B., Norrie, D.: Knowledge systematization in the international ims research program. In: 1995 IEEE International Conference on Systems, Man and Cybernetics Intelligent Systems for 21st Century. **1**, pp. 958–963. IEEE (1995). https://doi.org/10.1109/ICSMC.1995.537891

4. Gola, A., Swic, A., Kramar, V.: A multiple-criteria approach to machine-tool selection for focused flexible manufacturing systems. Manage Prod. Eng. Rev. **2**(4), 21–32 (2011)
5. Goldman, S., Nagel, R., Preiss, K.: Agile Competitors and Virtual Organizations: Strategies for Enriching the Customer. Van Nostrand Reinhold, New York (1995)
6. Groover, M., Zimmers, E.: CAD/CAM: Computer-Aided Design and Manufacturing. Prentice-Hall, New Jersey (1984). https://doi.org/10.1109/ICSMC.1995.537891
7. Guldentops, E.: Board Brefing on IT Governance. Rolling Meadows, IL (2003)
8. Nilsson, N.J.: Principles of Artificial Intelligence. Artificial Intelligence. Springer-Verlag, Berlin Heidelberg (1982)
9. Palchevskyi, B.: Application of digital models in intelligent packaging systems. In: TC-2018 International Conference Progressive directions of technological complexes development. **1**, pp. 3–5 (2018)
10. Palchevskyi, B., Krestyanpol, O., Krestyanpol, L.: Principles of designing and developing intelligent manufacturing systems of packaging. Int. J. Sci. Tech. Innovations Ind. **11**, 515–519 (2017)
11. Palchevskyi, B., Krestyanpol, O., Krestyanpol, L.: The use of anylogic system for modelling a flexible automated packing system in training engineering students. Inf. Technol. Learn. Tool. **75**(1), 225–236 (2020). https://doi.org/10.33407/itlt.v75i1.2714
12. Palchevskyi, B., Swic, A., Krestianpol, H.: Computer Integrated Designing of Flexible Manufacturing Systems. Lublin University of Technology, Lublin (2015)
13. Palchevskyi, B., Swic, A., Krestyanpol, H.: Increasing efficiency of flexible manufacturing systems based on computer product grouping. Adv. Sci. Technol. Res. J. **12**(2), 6–10 (2018). https://doi.org/10.12913/22998624/92093
14. Russell, S., Norvig, P.: Artificial intelligence: a modern approach. NJ: Prentice-Hall, Englewood Cliffs (1995)
15. Schwaninger, M.: Intelligent Organizations. Powerful Models for Systemic Management. Springer-Verlag Berlin, Heidelberg (2009). https://doi.org/10.1007/978-3-540-85162-2
16. Tarasenkov, F.: Applied systems analysis: science and the art of problem solving: a textbook. Tomsk: TSU (2004)
17. Tolio, T.: Design of Flexible Production Systems. Methodologies and Tools. Springer-Verlag, Berlin Heidelberg (2009). https://doi.org/10.1007/978-3-540-85414-2
18. Waterman, D.A.: Design of Flexible Production Systems. Mir, Methodologies and Tools (1989)
19. Yampolsky, L., Melnychuk, P., Ostapchenko, K., Lisovichenko, O.: Flexible computer-integrated systems: planning, modeling, verification, control. Zhytomyr (2010)

Identification of Predictors of Burnout Among Employees of Socially Significant Professions

Igor Zavgorodnii[1] , Olha Lalymenko[1] , Iryna Perova[2](✉) ,
Polina Zhernova[2] , and Anastasiia Kiriak[2]

[1] Kharkiv National Medical University, Kharkiv, Ukraine
zavnikua@gmail.com, yaloposta@gmail.com
[2] Kharkiv National University of Radio Electronics, Kharkiv, Ukraine
rikywenok@gmail.com, polina.zhernova@gmail.com, anastasiia.kiriak@nure.ua

Abstract. The article presents theoretical and practical aspects of study of professional burnout formation among representatives of socially significant professions. The issues of establishing the relationship between work-related behaviors using the Work-related Behavior and Experience Pattern (AVEM) and professional burnout predictors based on the Maslach Burnout Inventory questionnaire among medical workers, medical university teachers and bank employees are studied. It was established the most informative subscales of Maslach Burnout Inventory questionnaire that correspond to initial burnout level for each profession. It has been established that critically significant questions of the MBI questionnaire are the affirmations of the "cynicism" subscale for all three groups of respondents (medical workers of the emergency medical service, university teachers and bank employees); at the same time, significant results on the "personal achievement reduction" scale were obtained in the group of medical worker and university workers teachers.

Keywords: Professional burnout · Work-related behavior · Mental health · Regression model · Questionnaire

1 Introduction

The definition of "health" by the WHO encompasses the state of physical, mental and social well-being in absence of diseases as well as dysfunctions of organs and systems of the body [1]. According to the guidelines of the National Institute for Health and Care Excellence (NICE) (2017), health covers a person's physical and mental favourable condition and well-being. Well-being is a subjective health state, including happiness, comfort and satisfaction with the quality of life. At the same time, mental health is not only the absence of mental disorders, but also the positive state of psychological health of workers in general [3]. Mental well-being concerns the emotional and psychological state of a person, including self-esteem and the ability to communicate with colleagues and cope with difficulties

© Springer Nature Switzerland AG 2020
S. Babichev et al. (Eds.): DSMP 2020, CCIS 1158, pp. 445–456, 2020.
https://doi.org/10.1007/978-3-030-61656-4_30

as well as the ability to develop and broaden potential, work productively and creatively, build strong and positive relationships with other people, and make a contribution to the community [12, 23]. One of necessary conditions for achieving a high degree of professionalism is the improvement of professional skills along with the psychological characteristics of the person, depending on the type of activity. But the specifics of a particular profession can lead to the emergence of various negative phenomena in the psychological structure of the personality, complicating the adaptive behavior of a specialist and effective implementation of their professional tasks. The path of formation and development of a professional requires exertion of energy, activation of physical and psychosocial resources of the individual. One of the results of such a destructive effect of professional activity on a person is the phenomenon of professional (emotional) burnout [16, 24].

A wide range of negative consequences of professional burnout has been identified. Thus, interpersonal consequences are manifested in social, family relationships, as well as in labor conflicts or destructive stress when communicating with colleagues, business partners, clients, etc. Workers who are excessively absorbed by work problems and cannot even get rid of them in the family circle or with friends are most susceptible to the development of psychological deformation due to so-called professional burnout. The consequences of professional burnout manifest in the development of negative attitudes towards clients, work, organization or yourself as well as in alienation from work and, as a result, in a significant decrease in loyalty and attractiveness of the work in this company. Behavioral consequences manifest both at the individual employee level and at the level of the whole company. Such workers resort to unconstructive or ineffective behaviors, exacerbating their own feelings of distress and increasing tension, which undoubtedly leads to the decrease in the quality of work and communications [7].

Scientific and practical interest of professional burnout syndrome is due to the fact that such a condition is a direct manifestation of ever-growing problems associated with the well-being of employees, their labor efficiency and the company's progression. The concern of employers and managers about the burnout of employees could be explained by the fact that it is unnoticed at the beginning; but its consequences manifest in the form of "economic losses" are known to be very expensive for companies [9, 19].

Study of the characteristics of professional burnout, determination of its emotional and personal prerequisites as well as its effects within the framework of individual specializations will help better understand the specifics of the destructive influence of professional activity on the personality as well as develop directions for improving the conditions of professional activity and means to ensure professional longevity and health of specialists.

2   Review of the Literature

Professional burnout is known to be a syndrome that is characterized by emotional exhaustion, depersonalization and low personal self-esteem, leading to the development of psychological deformation of the personality and subsequently the formation of psychosomatic pathology. The term "professional burnout" was firstly mentioned as a condition that arises among employees of "assisting professions". The authors of such a term were Bradley in 1969, Herbert Freudenberg in 1974 and Christina Maslach in 1976 [11,17]. On May 27, 2019, occupational burnout was recognized in the 11th revision of the International Classification of Diseases by the World Health Organization as an occupational phenomenon. It is described in the chapter: "Factors influencing health status or contact with health services" - which includes reasons for which people contact health services but that are not classed as illnesses or health conditions [27].

An estimated number of 30–50% of health workers worldwide experience symptoms of burnout. At the same time, the formation of professional burnout among medical workers can lead to deterioration of their attitude to patients, a decrease in professionalism, the development of depressive and suicidal thoughts, and professional errors, affecting patients . In addition, healthcare providers who experience burnout symptoms may develop sleep disturbances, alcoholism, musculoskeletal disorders, hypertension, and coronary heart disease [8,21]. The characteristic feature of the professional activity of teachers of higher educational institutions is known to be hard work associated with increased emotional tension, the complexity of interpersonal communication, great intellectual, sensory, emotional stress as well as unfavorable mode of work. Teachers of higher educational institutions, in addition to teaching and research, have significant voice and psycho-emotional stress and are exposed to constant background noise while performing administrative, organizational and methodological work [26]. According to studies conducted in a number of countries, it has been shown that about 30% of teachers at various departments of medical universities in Germany and Austria show pronounced signs of professional burnout syndrome, manifesting in a decrease in ability to constructively solve professional tasks, a tendency to refuse in situations of failure, and a feeling of dissatisfaction with the results of their activities [14].

At the same time, employees of financial institutions work in constant contact with a large number of people in a tight schedule and time limit in compliance with instructions and regulations; what is more, they work with financial documents, thus constant high concentration of attention is highly required. As a result, specialists form a specific behavior model aimed to maintain internal psychological comfort; long-term work under such conditions is accompanied by signs of internal accumulation of negative emotions and gradually leads to professional burnout [13].

A number of authors consider professional burnout as a consequence of the influence of individual and organizational factors when there is a mismatch between the individual and the working environment. Numerous recent studies have proved psychosocial production factors to be important in the violation of both mental and physical health. According to the International Labor Organization (1998), factors affecting the occurrence of professional burnout include such aspects of work and the working environment as the organizational climate or culture, work roles, interpersonal relationships at work, the structure and content of tasks, as well as the organizational environment (internal needs) and aspects of personality [4]. The organizational factor of emotional burnout is associated with hours of work that is not properly evaluated, requiring exceptional productivity and appropriate training. Professional experience and the time spent in a stressful environment play an important role as well [5].

In order to identify symptoms of professional burnout, a three-factor model of K. Maslach and S. Jackson is used, which includes emotional exhaustion, depersonalization and reduction of personal achievements, manifesting usually among employees of "assisting professions". Emotional exhaustion is considered as the main component of emotional burnout and manifests in a reduced emotional state, indifference, or emotional glut. The second component (depersonalization) manifests in the deformation of relations with other people. In some cases, this may lead to an increase in dependence on others. In other cases, there is an increase in negativity, cynicism of attitudes and feelings towards recipients: patients, clients, etc. The third component of emotional burnout - the reduction of personal achievements - can manifest either in a tendency to negative self-assessment, underestimation of one's professional achievements and successes, negative attitude to labor dignities and opportunities or to downplay their own dignity, limiting their capabilities, duties in relation to others [15].

According to K. Maslach and C. Jackson, burnout is considered in general as a stressful reaction and as structural formation, which is largely determined by individual and personal properties, which allows simultaneously considering this phenomenon in the aspect of the phenomenon of professional deformation. Questionnaire for the diagnosis of professional burnout by K. Maslach MBI-GS contains three subscales that evaluate emotional exhaustion (EE), depersonalization (DP) and a sense of low personal achievement (LPA) [20]. This is the most commonly used and proven tool for detecting burnout among healthcare professionals, and is therefore considered the gold standard, as shown in Fig. 1. The definition of burnout using MBI-GS is such that the higher the scores in the area of exhaustion and cynicism and the lower the score for professional performance, the higher the degree of burnout. The reliability of MBI-GS was confirmed in studies conducted in various European countries.

According to procedural models of burnout, burnout is considered as a dynamic process that develops over time and has certain phases or stages. Procedural models consider the dynamics of burnout development as a process of increasing in emotional exhaustion, which results in negative attitudes towards subjects of professional activity. A burned out specialist is trying to create an emotional distance with their colleagues as a way to overcome exhaustion. At the same time, a negative attitude is developing in relation to their own professional achievements (reduction of professional accomplishments) [10].

Stress experienced by workers can be caused by various factors, generally caused by external factors and internal factors of the individual themselves. Existing studies tend to focus on the influence of external factors on stress conditions experienced by workers, such as environment and work situation.

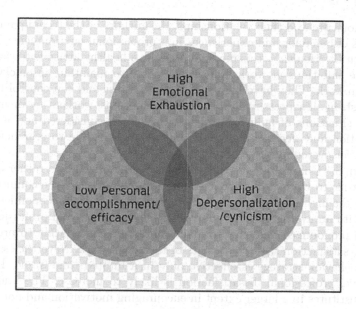

Fig. 1. Three subscales of Maslach Burnout Inventory

Meanwhile, studies focusing on internal factors as a cause of worker stress are still not widely practiced, particularly with regard to experience patterns and work-related behavior. Measurements used to measure experience patterns and work-related behavior are also newly adapted in some countries, using the AVEM test.

Questionnaire "Work-related behaviors and experiences" Arbeitsbezogenes Verhaltens- und Erlebensmuster (AVEM) was developed by W. Schaarschmidt and A. Fisher and reflects human reactions to the requirements of the professional environment and behaviors formed on the basis of these reactions, as well as the severity of manifestations of emotional burnout. The AVEM questionnaire is a 66-point diagnostic tool that allows determining the characteristics of the behavior and feelings of employees when their professional requirements are presented to them. The questionnaire includes 11 scales, each containing 6 questions, with answer options presented in the form of a five-point Likert scale ranging from 1 ("I completely disagree") to 5 ("I completely agree"). The questionnaire encompasses three areas of human behavior and experience that are associated with professional activities. The first one describes the readiness for energy costs, the degree of involvement into the work, the subjective significance of the activity and professional ambitions. The second area characterizes the psycho-emotional stability in situations of failure, as well as the willingness to overcome them. The third area reflects the emotional attitude to the activity, the possibility to obtain social support, as well as the experience of own professional success [25]. Based on the analysis of indicators of individual scales of the questionnaire and their relationships, the authors of the technique identified four types of behavior and experiences in a professional environment:

Pattern G: "Health" - this model represents a healthy attitude towards work. People are ambitious at work, but are also able to maintain an emotional distance from work. They have high resistance to stress and can control their own energy costs in all aspects related to positive emotions; workers are mentioned to overcome situations of failure and defeat, which are considered not as a source of frustration and negative emotions, but as an incentive to search for active strategies for overcoming them.

Pattern S: "Unambitious" - this model is characterized by a rather unpretentious attitude to work, while the lowest ratings characterize the commitment to work and the highest ones - rates of detachment. This is an economical, thrifty pattern with an average level of motivation, energy costs and professional aspirations, a pronounced tendency to maintain distance in relation to professional activities, satisfaction with the results of their own work. Nevertheless, an economical behavior strategy is effective only in a limited time frame. In further perspective, professional dissatisfaction is likely to increase. The issue of this model constitutes in a larger extent in encouraging motivation and not to health as.

Risk pattern A: "Overexertion" - this model is characterized by excessive commitment to work and difficulties in emotional suspension from work, excessively high subjective importance of professional activity, a high degree of readiness for energy costs, and low resistance to frustration and stress. The high level of negative emotions resulting from mental overload, the pursuit of excellence and the resulting dissatisfaction with the effectiveness of one's activities and the violated mechanisms to overcome stress and negative emotions also characterize such debilitating pattern.

Risk pattern B: "Burnout" - People with such a model show low ratings for parameters related to professional commitment. They achieve high scores for retirement tendencies and, accordingly, low scores for emotional distance and active overcoming difficulties. Their emotional status is characterized by low scores in balance and mental stability, job satisfaction, life satisfaction and limited experience of social support. Low subjective value of activity, low stress resistance, limited ability to relax and constructive problem solving, a tendency to refuse in difficult situations, a constant sense of anxiety and pointless fear are widely developed. It should be noted that, there is a similarity between types B and S related to a low subjective value of activity, however, the difference between them is that type B is not capable of maintaining the necessary distance with respect to work. This leads to additional mental stress, constant dissatisfaction with oneself, a decrease in the overall mental stability of the body, apathy and unwillingness to perform professional tasks [22]. This model presents the main symptoms of burnout.

The study of the internal psychological characteristics of an individual contributing to the development of professional burnout allows considering the type of behavior in the work environment as a conscious strategy of employee behavior, responsible for its implementation both in a successful situation and in failure [18].

The results of many studies of recent years allow concluding that the leading role in the emergence and development of factors of emotional burnout belongs to the personal factor, which is a combination of individual psychological characteristics. Individual psychological characteristics are understood as private psychological properties and qualities (such as rigidity - mobility, emotional reactivity, etc.), as well as holistic personality formations (interests, character, lifestyle, etc.). On the one hand, individual psychological characteristics undergo changes due to age, as a result of continuous training; on the other hand, a single lifestyle of the personality, subordinating all private qualities and characteristics to one direction, remains quite stable throughout life [6].

3   Problem Statement

It is obvious that the study of the formation of professional burnout among employees of socially significant professions, by identifying the relationship between the nature, degree of individual psychological characteristics of a person in relation to their professional activity and the level of burnout, is not well understood and is of great interest nowadays. Identification of the most significant relationships between the risk of professional burnout and the behavior and experiences associated with work, taking into account specific issues of MBI-GS and AVEM, combined with identification of the most significant statements, can significantly improve and speed up the procedure for diagnosing professional burnout in employees.

4   Experiment, Results and Discussion

The study was conducted by questioning 360 employees (emergency medical center employees - 120, teachers of university departments - 120, bank employees - 120). In order to identify symptoms of professional burnout, a survey was conducted using the standardized Maslach Burnout Inventory - General Survey (MBI-GS). The risk of developing professional burnout is determined on the basis of three subscales: "emotional exhaustion", "cynicism" (depersonalization) and "reduction of personal achievements".

For all employees standard calculation of burnout level was provided. After that we should identifier an employees in each of three professions with initial burnout level. It gives us possibilities defining the most significant statements that correspond to beginning of a burnout process. Using standard approach for calculation burnout level by MBI questionnaire (Fig. 2) we have summarized results of three scales: "emotional exhaustion" (cell "SumA" in Fig. 2), "cynicism" (cell "SumB" in Fig. 2) and "reduction of personal achievements" (cell "SumC" in Fig. 2). Further, we have converted these amounts to point (cells "RezA", "RezB" and "RezC" in Fig. 2) and summarized them (cell "Result" in Fig. 2). As a group with the initial burnout level was taken a group with

ID	GENDER	AGE	A_1	A_2	A_3	A_4	A_5	A_6	A_7	A_8	A_9	A_10	A_11	A_12	A_13	A_14	A_15	A_16	sumA	sumB	sumC	RezA	RezB	RezC	Result
418001	0	46	0	0	0	0	0	0	6	0	0	6	6	6	0	0	0	6	0	0	30	0	0	0	0
418002	0	65	1	3	1	1	6	3	6	0	0	5	6	5	5	1	0	5	9	6	33	0	1	0	1
418003	0	58	1	3	1	0	6	0	6	1	1	6	6	5	5	1	1	6	5	9	35	0	1	0	1
418004	0	68	0	0	0	0	6	0	6	0	0	6	6	6	0	0	0	6	0	6	36	0	1	0	1
418005	1	35	0	0	0	0	6	0	6	0	0	6	6	6	0	0	0	6	0	0	36	0	0	0	0
418006	1	35	6	6	6	6	5	5	5	1	2	6	6	6	3	0	0	6	29	6	34	2	1	0	3
418007	1	65	3	2	1	0	2	1	6	0	0	6	5	6	1	3	0	6	7	4	31	0	1	0	1
418008	1	45	0	0	0	0	6	0	6	0	0	6	6	6	0	0	0	6	6	0	36	0	0	0	0
418009	1	31	3	6	5	3	6	4	6	1	1	6	6	6	5	6	2	6	21	15	36	2	2	0	4
418010	1	43	6	6	6	0	6	6	2	0	5	6	6	6	6	2	6	4	24	19	30	2	2	0	4
418011	1	65	0	0	0	0	1	0	6	0	0	3	4	6	0	0	0	6	0	0	26	0	0	0	0
418012	0	78	2	0	3	6	6	0	6	0	0	6	6	1	6	0	0	6	11	6	31	0	1	0	1
418013	0	38	3	4	4	2	5	2	5	3	3	5	5	5	5	1	5	5	15	17	30	1	2	0	3
418014	1	37	0	0	1	0	6	1	5	0	0	6	6	5	0	1	0	6	2	1	34	0	0	0	0
418015	1	37	4	5	5	1	6	4	6	0	3	6	6	6	4	0	0	6	19	7	36	1	1	0	2
418016	0	73	0	0	0	0	6	1	6	0	0	6	6	6	1	0	0	4	1	1	34	0	0	0	0

Fig. 2. MBI questionnaire answers

value less than 3 in "Result" cell and values less than 2 in "RezA", "RezB" and "RezC" cells. So, from university department's teachers number of objects in the group with initial burnout level is equal to 29, emergency medical center employees - 22, bank employees - 31.

For best understanding of mutual position of clusters, which corresponds to different burnout levels, visualization using principal component analysis (PCA) method was provided. PCA data visualizations for different professions are presented on Figs. 3, 4 and Fig. 5. On each figure a group with the initial burnout level marked by yellow color, a group with the high burnout level - by red color, a group without burnout symptoms - by blue color. It is easy to see that group without burnout symptoms forms a compact cluster while a groups of initial and high burnout level form clusters with low density because professional burnout can be shown in three different subscales.

Defining the most significant statements that correspond to beginning of a burnout process cab be done using regression analysis and eli5 Python library. This library allows to visualize results of logistic regression model, it provides a way to explain black-box models results [2]. So, logistic regression model was trained on data of MBI questionnaire, accuracy is from 88% to 92% for different professions using cross-validation. Result of eli5's processing for three professions is presented on Fig. 6.

For each profession numbers of most informative questions from MBI questionnaire are different. For teachers and emergency medical center employees the most informative questions belong to subscales of "cynicism" and "reduction of personal achievements", for bank employees - to subscales of "cynicism".

Work-related characteristics and models of behavior using the AVEM questionnaire were studied. AVEM questionnaire and MBI questionnaire describe different parts of total professional burnout. For all three professions employees without burnout symptoms correspond to pattern G ("Health") of AVEM questionnaire by 84,7%. Using logistic regression and eli5 Python library the most informative questions from AVEM questionnaire were established. We have to note the need of additional studying for best understanding this approach.

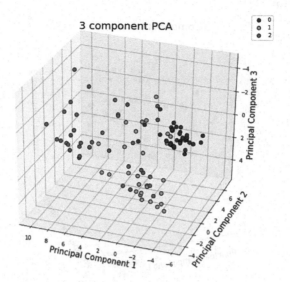

Fig. 3. Data visualization for teacher's group

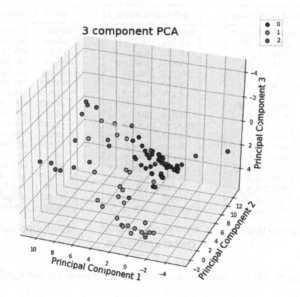

Fig. 4. Data visualization for bank employee's group

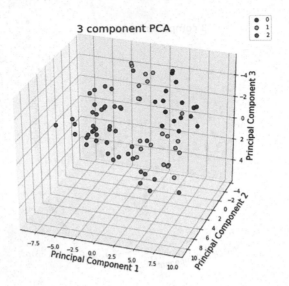

Fig. 5. Data visualization for group of emergency medical center employees

y=1.0 top features		y=1.0 top features		y=1.0 top features	
Weight?	Feature	Weight?	Feature	Weight?	Feature
+2.089	A_13	+0.745	MBI_11_lf	+1.841	MBI_13_zy
+0.365	A_1	+0.607	MBI_13_zy	+0.581	MBI_15_zy
+0.241	A_2	+0.575	MBI_07_lf	+0.434	MBI_02_ee
+0.144	A_5	+0.322	MBI_10_lf	+0.192	MBI_16_ef
+0.085	A_10	+0.299	MBI_04_ee	+0.183	MBI_14_zy
-0.013	A_7	-0.031	MBI_12_lf	+0.160	MBI_07_ef
-0.019	<BIAS>	-0.103	MBI_09_zy	+0.157	MBI_05_ef
-0.027	A_11	-0.172	MBI_08_zy	+0.103	MBI_10_ef
-0.270	A_3	-0.200	MBI_01_ee	+0.051	MBI_01_ee
-0.309	A_6	-0.267	MBI_03_ee	+0.013	MBI_12_ef
-0.448	A_12	-0.290	MBI_05_lf	-0.017	MBI_09_zy
-0.640	A_15	-0.345	MBI_02_ee	-0.041	MBI_03_ee
-0.743	A_14	-0.354	MBI_06_ee	-0.055	MBI_11_ef
-0.929	A_4	-0.384	<BIAS>	-0.122	MBI_04_ee
-1.184	A_9	-0.396	MBI_16_lf	-0.344	MBI_08_zy
-1.186	A_16	-0.421	MBI_14_zy	-0.492	MBI_06_ee
-1.299	A_8	-0.526	MBI_15_zy	-0.801	<BIAS>
university teachers		**emergency medical center employees**		**bank employees**	

Fig. 6. Eli5's visualizing of logistic regression model results

5   Conclusions

This paper is dedicated to the first in Ukraine study of professional burnout among employees of socially significant professions: emergency medical center employees, teachers of university departments, bank employees. For each professions the most informative questions of MBI and AVEM questionnaire were established. It was also revealed that a pronounced feature of bank employees according to the AVEM questionnaire was the decrease in motivation for professional attachments, energy costs in relation to work, a decrease in the quality of performed work and ability to hold distance from professional activities, as well as a decrease in satisfaction with their professional achievements marked against the background of low mental stability of the respondents. In university teachers, the AVEM questionnaire revealed a decrease in the active strategy of solving problems, a decrease in the feeling of social well-being and a sense of success in the professional activity. At the same time, medical workers were distinguished by a high inability to maintain distance in relation to work and excessive dissatisfaction with life circumstances.

Acknowledgments. Research on the topic "Establishing early criteria for the diagnosis of burnout in workers of socially significant occupations", state registration number 0118U000946, was financed by the Ministry of Health of Ukraine at the expense of the state budget.

References

1. Official Records Constitution of the health organization, vol. 2. World Health Organization (2006)
2. Welcome to eli5's documentation! (2016). https://eli5.readthedocs.io/en/latest/
3. Healthy workplaces: improving employee mental and physical health and wellbeing (qs147) (2017). http://nice.org.uk/guidance/qs147
4. Aronsson, G., et al.: A systematic review including meta-analysis of work environment and burnout symptoms. BMC Publ. Health **17**, 264 (2017). https://doi.org/10.1186/s12889-017-4153-7
5. Bhui, K., Dinos, S., Galant-Miecznikowska, M., Jongh, B., Stansfeld, S.: Perceptions of work stress causes and effective interventions in employees working in public, private and non-governmental organisations: a qualitative study. BJPsych Bull. **40**(6), 318–325 (2016). https://doi.org/10.1192/pb.bp.115.050823
6. Briaa, M., Spânua, F., Băbana, A., Dumitras, D.: Maslach burnout inventory - general survey: factorial validity and invariance among romanian healthcare professionals. Burnout Res. **1**, 103–111 (2014). https://doi.org/10.1016/j.burn.2014.09.001
7. Bridgeman, P., Bridgeman, M., Barone, J.: Burnout syndrome among healthcare professionals. Am. J. Health Syst. Pharms. **75**(3), 147–152 (2018). https://doi.org/10.2146/ajhp170460
8. Castanelli, D., Wickramaarachchi, S., Wallis, S.: Burnout and the learning environment of anaesthetic trainees. Anaesth. Intensive Care **45**(6), 744–751 (2017). https://doi.org/10.1177/0310057X1704500615
9. Connolly, D., Anderson, M., Colgan, M., Montgomery, J., Clarke, J., Kinsella, M.: The impact of a primary care stress management and wellbeing programme (renew) on occupational participation: a pilot study. Br. J. Occup. Therapy **82**(2), 112–121 (2018). https://doi.org/10.1177/0308022618793323
10. Dunford, B., Shipp, A., Boss, R., Angermeier, I., Boss, A.: Is burnout staticor dynamic? A career transition perspective of employee burnout trajectories. J. Appl. Psychol. **97**(3), 637 (2012)
11. Freudenberger, H.: Staff burn-out. J. Soc. Issues **30**(1), 159–165 (1974)

12. Funk, M.: Mental health and work : impact, issues and good practices, p. 67. World Health Organization, Geneva (2005)
13. Giorgi, G., Arcangeli, G., Ariza-Montes, A., Rapisarda, V., Mucci, N.: Work-related stress in the italian banking population and its association with recovery experience. Int. J. Occup. Med. Environ. Health **32**(2), 255–265 (2019). https://doi.org/10.13075/ijomeh.1896.01333
14. Klingbeil, D., Renshaw, T.: Mindfulness-based interventions for teachers: a meta-analysis of the emerging evidence base. Sch. Psychol. Q. **33**(4), 501–511 (2018). https://doi.org/10.1037/spq0000291
15. Lim, W., et al.: The abbreviated maslach burnout inventory can overestimate burnout: a study of anesthesiology residents. J. Clin. Med. **9**, 61–75 (2020). https://doi.org/10.3390/jcm9010061
16. Luken, M., Sammons, A.: Systematic review of mindfulness practice for reducing job burnout. Am. J. Occup. Therapy **70**(2), 7002250020 (2016). https://doi.org/10.5014/ajot.2016.016956
17. Maslach, C., Jackson, S., Leiter, M., Schaufeli, W., Schwab, R.: Maslach burnout inventory, vol. 21, pp. 3463–3464. Consulting Psychologists Press (1986)
18. Maslach, C., Leiter, M.: Understanding the burnout experience: recent research and its implications for psychiatry. World Psychiatry **15**(2), 103–111 (2016). https://doi.org/10.1002/wps.20311
19. Neckel, S., Schaffner, A.,K., Wagner, G. (eds.): Burnout, Fatigue, Exhaustion. Palgrave Macmillan(2017). https://doi.org/10.1007/978-3-319-52887-8
20. Parola, V., Coelho, A., Cardoso, D., Sandgren, A., Apóstolo, J.: Prevalence of burnout in health professionals working in palliative care: a systematicreview. JBI Database Syst. Rev. Implement Rep. **15**(7), 1905–1933 (2017)
21. Poulsen, A., Meredith, P., Khan, A., Henderson, J., Castrisos, V., Khan, S.: Burnout and work engagement in occupational therapists. Br. J. Occup. Therapy **77**(3), 156–168 (2014). https://doi.org/10.4276/030802214X13941036266621
22. Qudsyi, Q., et al.: Adaptation of avem (arbeitsbezogenes vehaltens-und erlebens-muster) test to measure work-related behavior and experience patterns. Int. J. Sci. Technol. Res. **8**(6), 62–69 (2019)
23. Rajgopal, T.: Mental well-being at the workplace. Ind. J. Occup. Environ. **14**(3), 63–65 (2010). https://doi.org/10.4103/0019-5278.75691
24. Scanlan, J., Hazelton, T.: Relationships between job satisfaction, burnout, professional identity and meaningfulness of work activities for occupational therapists working in mental health. Aust. Occup. Therapy J. **66**(5), 581–590 (2019)
25. Schaarschmidt, U.: Avem: Ein instrument zur interventionsbezogenen diagnostik beruflichen bewaltigungsverhaltens. In: Arbeitskreis Klinische Psychologie in der Rehabilitation BDP (Hrsg.). Psychologische Diagnostik - Weichenstellung fur den Reha-Verlauf. Deutscher Psychologen Verlag GmbH, Bonn, pp. 59–82 (2006)
26. Voltmer, E., Spahn, C., Schaarschmidt, U., Kieschke, U.: Work-related behavior and experience patterns of entrepreneurs compared to teachers and physicians. Int. Arch. Occup. Environ. Health **85**(5), 479–490 (2011). https://doi.org/10.1007/s00420-011-0632-9
27. WHO: Cd-11 for mortality and morbidity statistics. qd85 burn-out (2019). https://icd.who.int/browse11/l-m/en#/id.who.int/icd/entity/129180281

Software for Shelter's Fire Safety and Comfort Levels Evaluation

Yevgen Martyn⬤, Olga Smotr⬤, Nazarii Burak(✉)⬤, Oleksandr Prydatko⬤, and Igor Malets⬤

Lviv State University of Life Safety, Lviv, Ukraine
evmartyn@gmail.com, olgasmotr@gmail.com, nazar.burak.ac@gmail.com,
olexandrprydatko@gmail.com, igor.malets@gmail.com

Abstract. The article deals with the problem of public awareness about existing special purpose buildings such as protective buildings and shelters that can be used to protect against emergencies. The status update on the problem is considered. The recent scientific papers in the field of modern information technologies integration into civil protection system were analyzed during research. The necessity of the use of modern informational graphic technologies for fire safety level evaluation in such type of shelters was substantiated. The features of actual data visualization with the involvement of mathematical transformations and methods of visual information graphing are investigated based on the offered methods of visualization graphics information. The software emulator "Fireware Emulator" has been developed. It can be used for fire safety level evaluation in buildings of such type.

Keywords: Informational technologies · Software · Emulator · Shelter · Civil protection · Room plan

1 Introduction

The current integration state of modern information technologies for human life environment initiate appearance of new natural threats which can be serious risks for its normal and safety life. Military conflicts and the risks for using mass destruction weapon forced us to make protective purpose buildings - safety places such as housing units and shelters where peoples could stay and live during emergency situation.

Based on the daily facts of human life process both society and its individual members, we observe a progressive tendency towards increasing potential threats to humanity. The amount of the increasing anthropogenic and natural character risks is proportional to the number of tasks to be undertaken for ensure the safety of human life. Among these problems, we could highlight the problems of peoples safe staying in protective purpose buildings: housing units and shelters.

The process of necessary building choosing is based on own human's preferences, its geographic location, type of emergency situation and other additional

© Springer Nature Switzerland AG 2020
S. Babichev et al. (Eds.): DSMP 2020, CCIS 1158, pp. 457–469, 2020.
https://doi.org/10.1007/978-3-030-61656-4_31

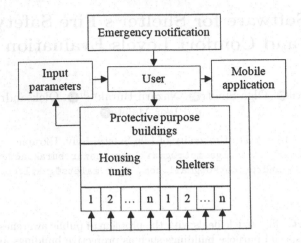

Fig. 1. Flowchart of necessary protective purpose buildings choosing process

factors. But, the most important among them is security (Fig. 1). First, in such protective building, user should to determine the state of fire safety, the possibility of safe evacuation from the rooms and the comfortableness level of staying. After it, on the basis of visualized data about protective building, human should to analyze the possible deterioration causes of the situation in the shelter and to identify ways to better its planning. All upgrades must be produced by taking into account the position of ensuring proper level of fire safety. If the emergency situation will appear and it is necessary to use protective building or air raid shelter, user should know in advance all important data including comfortableness level and safety stay within them.

The main requirements that applies to protective buildings and shelters are regulated by the relevant state documents and the Civil Protection Code of Ukraine. These documents specify the external and internal parameters of the protective buildings. External includes geographical location and distance from neighboring homes, and internal includes buildings configuration and planning of elements for safe staying users indoors. However, it is also important for users to have actual information about such buildings.

2   Literature Review and Problem Statement

Review of recent international research shows numbers of existing developments in the fire safety field, particularly about uses of information technologies to improve human's life safety. The complete process of modeling protective environment in buildings for different purpose including shelters has been describing in detail by scientists. In [6] the authors explored some aspects and approaches for creation of user-oriented mobile information technologies. This software is developing for individual use to help people in choosing suitable fire protective building where they could hide during emergency situation. In accordance with

[7], the authors analyzed the fire safety requirements to information technology for implementation in selected commercial building. The main practical requirements to information technologies for fire safety providing in different types of buildings are highlighted and analyzed in [4,11,12].

Researches [1–3,8,9] refer the evaluation system of building fire emergency response capability maturity (FE-CMM) that based on the capability maturity model (CMM). Mostly, they considered the acceptable ways for emergency situations response. Authors declared that the proposed module could preliminarily realize the intelligent evaluation of building fire emergency response capability. Moreover, it able to improve the practice and intelligence of the fire emergency response capability evaluation, especially in smart cities. Studies [5,10] analyzed the main features of developing, improvement and uses of modern information technologies in the field of civil protection, particularly during implementation of safety-oriented emergency response projects.

However, there are still little number of studies that related to software development for protective buildings safety evaluation, as well as for situation comparing capability in different buildings during best option choosing process. Today, there are also not enough information about qualitative evaluation of information technology impact to decision making process of choosing particular building type.

Current state regulatory documents determine all requirements to protective structures, buildings and shelters arrangement, particularly, from the point of safe stay in them. But, due to requirements universality and generality, shelters are objectively limited in ability of getting attention to each ones. The reason of it – lack of a real possibility to create completely safe building for a long stay. As a result, people must make choice of protective building and carry out its arrangement by themselves. This can be possible only in the cases, when the following conditions will be performed:

– the choice of each protective building or shelter is based on both its level of comfortableness and fire protection;
– all possible ways of getting to the protective building or shelter are analyzed depend on humans' location during an emergency;
– information technologies are used as a helping tool to make choice of protective building;
– preliminary prediction is made to determine unforeseen occasions appearance possibility during humans' stay in shelter;
– it is possible to make own additions to the contingency plan.

Therefore, according to previously outlined problems, developing of graphic information technology for fire safety evaluation of protective purpose buildings is one of the most important and urgent task in nowadays moving world.

3   Substantiation of the Use of Data Visualization Methods in Protective Buildings Fire Safety Evaluation Process

In general, users informational content I concerning protective buildings or shelters includes two components: visual (presence component) and virtual (technological component) object review. Some users can get necessary information directly by observing selected object without using any information technology (IT), while others can use special software. Bases on this and according to [8], informational content I could be determine by the following equation:

$$I = u + iv = (x + iy)^3 \tag{1}$$

where u and v are the components of information content without and with the use of information technology respectively; x is the presence component parameter that indicate the level of knowledge about object without using IT; y is the technological component parameter that indicate the level of knowledge about object with using IT.

Parameter y also takes into account both the level x' of knowledge about the object(building) and f - the use of developed application:

$$y = x' + f \tag{2}$$

In most cases, x' does not always equal to x, but for simplifying research, we accept that $x = x'$. According to this, (1) takes the following form:

$$I = u + iv = x \cdot ((4x^2 + 6xf + 3f^2) + i \cdot (x^2 - 3f^2)) \tag{3}$$

The working range of variables x and f in information content I level determining process is within the range from 0 to 1. Equation (3) determines information contents value I as a direct numerical dependence to the parameter x: for each level of information support f, the value of information content is equal to zero if $x = 0$. As result, information content components u and v define functions x and f. Thus, if we take these conditions into account, components values will determine like (4) and (5):

$$u = 4x^2 + 6xf + 3f^2 \tag{4}$$

$$v = x^3 - 3xf^2 \tag{5}$$

If user does not use software for help in choosing suitable shelter and condition (2) is fulfilled, the value of components u and v will determine (6) and (7):

$$u = 4x^3 \tag{6}$$

$$v = x^3 \tag{7}$$

Component v has value change restriction (8) of x and f. In our research, we use only positive values that fits condition $x > 3f = a$ and belongs to zone **A** (Fig. 2).

$$v = x \cdot (x^2 - 3f^2) = x \cdot (x - \sqrt{3f}) \cdot (x + \sqrt{3f}) \tag{8}$$

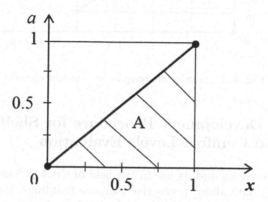

Fig. 2. Restriction zones of parameters

Now, let us to determine the influence of parameters x and f for component u (4) values change. Even if x gets small values, such as $x = 0.1$, the values of component u increases extremely fast (Fig. 3). This proves the efficiency of using information technologies f.

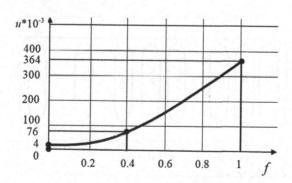

Fig. 3. Dynamics of component u values change

The information contents' component v is determined by the amount of knowledge set $(x' = x)$ about buildings fire safety state according to which IT is used for help. The main condition that applies to v it is $x' = x > \sqrt{3f}$ (Fig. 4).

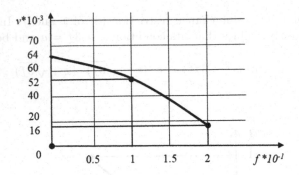

Fig. 4. Dynamics of component v values change

4   Software Development Procedure for Shelter's Fire Safety and Comfort Levels Evaluation

Information technologies and its use in the field of Civil Defense can solve problem of visualizing data about protective purpose buildings. Basically, proposed emulator will work with graphical parameters of the buildings, which are used during its floors plan creation. Also, there will be possibility to add another data, such as temperature of the shelter environment, the presence of fire extinguishers, etc. If we take into account all this conditions, it becomes possible to build model of data visualisation process in emulator (Fig. 5).

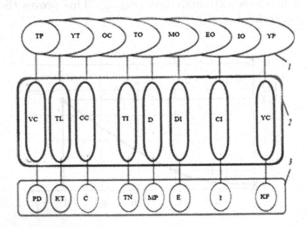

Fig. 5. Information model of data visualization process about protective purpose buildings with use of emulator

Here, **1** is the emulator software operation block: TP is the technological process of emulator creation; YT is control units; OC is the provision by programmers; TO is the level of equipment provision; MO is the material resources;

EO is the energy resources; IO is the financial value of technology; YP is the software resources; **2** is the functional parameters of providing data visualization processes: VC is the emulator implementation environment; TL is the involved information technologies to the emulator creation process; CC is the level of performers provision; TI is the level of information provision; D is the level of GPS monitoring technologies involvement; DI is the level of easy getting to the building; CI is the transport infrastructure near buildings location; YC is the basic standards for program creation; **3** is the visualization resources: PD is the output product of emulator; KT is the programmers team; C is the product of created program; TN is the technical means; MP is the material resources; E is the energy resources; I is the information resources; KP is the IT project team.

A flowchart of proposed software development stages was designed to facilitate the process of its programming (Fig. 6). The emulator has friendly user interface, is quite reliable and provides high speed of safety evaluate algorithm calculation.

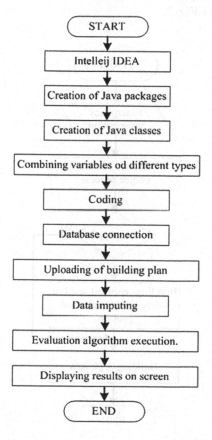

Fig. 6. The flowchart of the "Fireware Emulator" development process

Software is designed as an emulator program "Fireware Emulator". For its development were chosen Java software. "Fireware Emulator" allows users to evaluate protective buildings or shelters safety level.

Java is an object oriented language which gives a clear structure to programs. There are some major advantages of this language. Java is straightforward to use, write, compile, debug, and learn than alternative programming languages. Object oriented programming is associated with concepts like class, object, inheritance, etc. which allows you to create modular programs and reusable code. Java code runs on any machine that doesn't need any special software to be installed. Those advantages are essential in developing secure, powerful device or computer system that gives you possibility for quick use of the right class and method. Software emulator "Fireware Emulator" was developed using Intellij IDEA 2019.1 Community Edition.

Designed sofware as an emulator program allows users evaluate the security level of shelters independently. The software supports different types of protective buildings and their plans. An algorithm for the process of choosing a safe building is presented in Fig. 7.

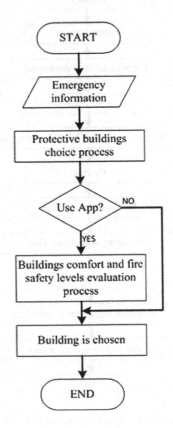

Fig. 7. The flowchart of protective building choosing process

User obtains actual information about buildings fire safety level and it can check its reliability and evaluate his own protection in emergencies. This is possible by integrating buildings plan into emulator's database. When buildings or shelters plans are importing into software database, the following parameters must be specified: inner temperature, height and width of the room, a wall material, the number of persons who may present at the same time. Lighting and air filtration settings are also available. Based on all this data, the program makes analyze and outputs the result of security level evaluation.

Software adaptation to the real conditions of the shelters and protective buildings was provided by changes of their plans. They are made based on additional perimeter measurements. Emulator "Fireware Emulator" stores visualized data of plan in its database which makes them acceptable for changes up to different conditions.

The emulator interface for the school building is shown in Fig. 8.

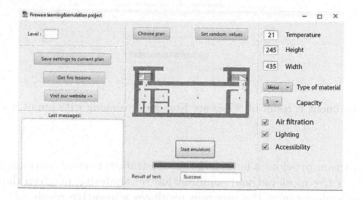

Fig. 8. Initial parameters values setting in software "Fireware Emulator"

Input parameters are the following: two hundred sixty-three students and four teachers will be staying in building at the same time and each of them had passed a fire safety courses; there are four floors, three emergency exits and fifteen fire extinguishers; all-day water supply.

Developed software is open for updates. There is an opportunity to quickly add plans of buildings, functionality, providing reliability, accessibility and multiplatform. A high level of protection against unauthorized changes to the code was used.

5   The Use of the Developed Software for Fire Safety Evaluation Procedure

The next stage of the research is analyzing correctness of the software algorithms. There were 4 practical experiments conducted using different input parameters, protective building plans and squares.

Experiment 1. Input parameters used in experiment: storage temperature - 21 °C, height - 2.45 m, width - 4.35 m, wall material - metal construction, number of persons - 5. The result of emulation (Fig. 9) demonstrates that such protective building complies to all standards and regulations and is completely safe to stay in an emergency.

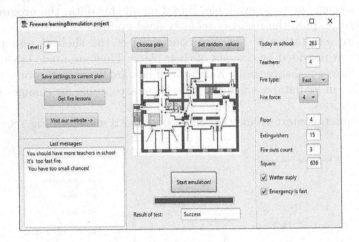

Fig. 9. Experiment 1: result of "Fireware Emulator" running with imput paramemters

The program provides a large number of parameters combinations. The algorithm selects the most optimal combination by analysing of given data [8]. In the case of inconsistency, the program produces a negative result.

Experiment 2. Were used parameters which are not complies to standards or regulatory documents. Due to input parameters, this shelter is uncomfortable for staying and the result of fire safety evaluation is negative (Fig. 10).

This is because there is no ability to avoid the danger: the building has a large square and only one spare exit, the number of people is too big, the fire ignites quickly and there are only eight fire extinguishers.

Experiment 3. A shelter with small square were analysed. Also, there were a low wall height and inside temperature (8 °C), the number of staying persons - 6. According to the normative documents, such protective building is not suitable for a comfortable staying despite positive level of fire safety evaluation. The result of the program demonstrates a similar conclusion (Fig. 11).

Experiment 4. A graphic information window for displaying problems which must be solved to increase both fire safety and comfortability levels is predicted in developed software "Fireware Emulator". Figure 12 presents the result of evaluation process in accordance with the input parameters. The text message with recommendations is displayed in the information window.

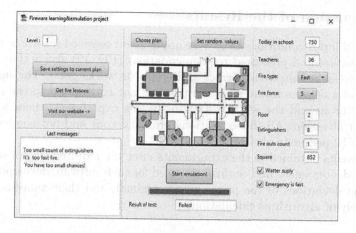

Fig. 10. Experiment 2: the result of buildings fire safety evaluation with many people inside

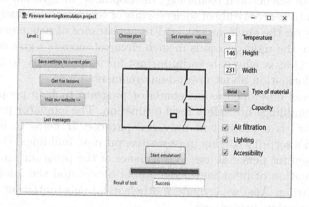

Fig. 11. Experiment 3: negative result of shelter staying comfortability

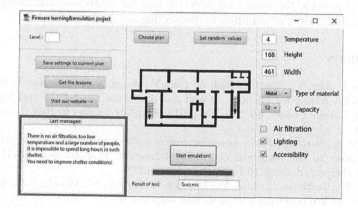

Fig. 12. The result of evaluation process with generated recommendations

6   Discussion of the Results

Analyses of input conditions that were applied and received results of fire safety level evaluation and presented recommendations (Fig. 12) shows that the algorithm of message output is correct and emulator works good. The inside temperature of 4 degrees above zero storage does not correspond to the norm, the height - 1.68 m and the width - 4.61 m. In this experiment, there is lighting, but no air filtration. All this conditions are dangerous and not comfortable for staying of 52 people in shelter.

The results obtained in the experiments meet the requirements of state standards for shelter safety and confirm the need for such software development. The errors and deviations of the program are minimal, and their analysis indicates correctively of algorithms calculations.

7   Conclusions

Current rates of science and technology development, integration of information technologies into everyday life of society, state of ecology and influence of anthropogenic factor on the environment lead to appearance of new emergencies. The ability to make the right decisions in such circumstances is a guarantee of safety human's life. That is why it is so important for human today to have as much as possible information about around environment.

Software was developed as an emulator program to help people in process of protective buildings fire safety level evaluation. The emulator program "Fireware Emulator" is a product of universal purpose. It helps to determine the level of person's security staying in protective purpose buildings. Developed software is designed for personal use. Performance of the program can be enhanced by the combination of prior knowledge about object and the information component comparing. Also were made mathematical substantiation of evaluation algorithms execution correctness.

Integration of the latest information technologies in the field of civil protection will provide to society an effective tool for analyzing and using data to explore possible ways of avoiding or protecting against emergencies.

References

1. Cheng, J., Tan, Y., Song, Y., Mei, Z., Gan, V., Wang, X.: Developing an evacuation evaluation model for offshore oil and gas platforms using BIM and agent-based model. Autom. Constr. **89**, 214–224 (2018). https://doi.org/10.1016/j.autcon.2018.02.011
2. Granda, S., Ferreira, T.M.: Assessing vulnerability and fire risk in old urban areas: application to the historical centre of Guimarães. Fire Technol. **55**(1), 105–127 (2018). https://doi.org/10.1007/s10694-018-0778-z
3. Kwok, N., Bratiotis, C., Luu, M., Lauster, N., Kysow, K., Woody, S.R.: Examining the role of fire prevention on hoarding response teams: Vancouver fire and rescue services as a case study. Fire Technol. **54**(1), 57–73 (2017). https://doi.org/10.1007/s10694-017-0672-0

4. Ma, G., Tan, S., Shang, S.: The evaluation of building fire emergency response capability based on the CMM. Int. J. Environ. Res. Public Health **16**(11), 1962 (2019). https://doi.org/10.3390/ijerph16111962
5. Malets, I., Popovych, V., Prydatko, O., Dominik, A.: Interactive computer simulators in rescuer training and research of their optimal use indicator. In: Proceedings of the 2018 IEEE Second International Conference on Data Stream Mining and Processing (DSMP), pp. 558–562 (2018). https://doi.org/10.1109/DSMP.2018. 8478486
6. Martyn, Y., Ljaskovska, S., Tarapata, N.: Emulator of analysis of bombshelters. Sci. Bull. Tavria Agrotechnological State Univ. **1**(9) (2019). https://doi.org/10. 31388/2220-8674-2019-1-62
7. Mishra, A., Shrestha, A.: Assessment of exit requirements for fire safety of commercial buildings, Kathmandu, Nepalemulator of analysis of bombshelters. Int. J. Emerg. Technol. Innov. Res. **4**(10), 248–255 (2017). https://doi.org/10.1717/ JETIR.17074
8. Ratushnyi, R., Khmel, P., Tryhuba, A., Martyn, E., Prydatko, O.: Substantiating the effectiveness of projects for the construction of dual systems of fire suppression. Eastern-Euro. J. Enterp. Technol. **4**, 46–53 (2019). https://doi.org/10.15587/1729-4061.2019.175275
9. Rego, A., Garcia, L., Sendra, S., Lloret, J.: Software defined network-based control system for an efficient traffic management for emergency situations in smart cities. Future Gener. Comput. Syst. **88**, 243–253 (2018). https://doi.org/10.1016/j.future. 2018.05.054
10. Smotr, O., Borzov, Y., Burak, N., Ljaskovska, S.: Implementation of information technologies in the organization of forest fire suppression process. In: Proceedings of the 2018 IEEE Second International Conference on Data Stream Mining and Processing (DSMP), pp. 157–161 (2018). https://doi.org/10.1109/DSMP.2018. 8478416
11. The Hong Kong Buildings Department: Code of practice for fire safety in buildings (2011). https://www.bd.gov.hk/doc/en/resources/codes-and-references/ code-and-design-manuals/fs2011/fs2011-full.pdf
12. U.S. Department of Labor, Occupational Safety and Health Administration: Emergency exit routes fact sheet (2018). https://www.osha.gov/OshDoc/data-Genera-Facts/emergency-exit-routes-factsheet.pdf

Methods for Forecasting Nonlinear Non-stationary Processes in Machine Learning

Peter Bidyuk[1]([✉])[ID], Aleksandr Gozhyj[2][ID], Irina Kalinina[2][ID],
and Victoria Vysotska[3][ID]

[1] National Technical University of Ukraine
"Igor Sikorsky Kyiv Polytechnic Institute", Kyiv, Ukraine
`pbidyke@gmail.com`
[2] Petro Mohyla Black Sea National University, Nikolaev, Ukraine
`alex.gozhyj@gmail.com`, `irina.kalinina1612@gmail.com`
[3] National University "Lvivska politechnika", Lviv, Ukraine
`Victoria.A.Vysotska@lpnu.ua`

Abstract. The article discusses the methodology for solving forecasting problems using machine learning methods. The issues of accounting and correct processing of nonlinear non-stationary processes in the problems of modeling and forecasting time series in various fields are considered. The stages and methods of solving machine learning problems are analyzed. A comparative analysis of normalization methods in data clustering is given. A technique is proposed for solving forecasting problems, taking into account testing the initial data for linearity. As an example, the problem of forecasting currency pairs based on historical data is considered. According to the proposed methodology, a short-term forecast was developed for six currency pairs.

Keywords: Nonlinear non-stationary processes · Data preprocessing · Model selection · Testing for linearity · Short term forecasting · Financial processes

1 Introduction

The main forecasting problem solved by many applied sciences, such as economics, finance, ecology, etc., is to obtain the correct forecasts affecting the behavior of complex systems based on data on their past behavior. However, many problems that arise in practical applications cannot be solved by known methods and corresponding algorithms. This is due to the fact that the mechanisms for generating the source data are not exactly known or there are not enough statistical data to build a predictive model. At the same time, it is necessary to comprehensively study the initial sequence of the source data and try to make forecasts, constantly improving this scheme of processing the source data

© Springer Nature Switzerland AG 2020
S. Babichev et al. (Eds.): DSMP 2020, CCIS 1158, pp. 470–485, 2020.
https://doi.org/10.1007/978-3-030-61656-4_32

in the process of evaluating forecasts. An approach in which past data or examples are used to formulate and improve a forecasting scheme is one of the tasks of machine learning. Machine learning is an extremely broad and dynamically developing field of research, which uses a huge number of theoretical and practical methods. Most models and forecasting methods in machine learning problems use the methods of probability theory and estimation, as well as mathematical statistics [9,10,14,18]. As part of this approach, we consider the problems of classification and regression analysis. The learning process consists of selecting a classification or regression function from a predetermined wide class of possible functions.

The article discusses the methodology for solving the problem of forecasting non-linear non-stationary data (processes) using machine learning methods in which the questions of testing the initial data for linearity are studied in more detail. To build forecasts, historical exchange rate data is accepted as non-linear and time-dependent data.

Problem Statement. The purpose of this study is to develop a general methodology for constructing forecasts of non-linear non-stationary financial processes based on methods and technologies of machine learning. The methodology will be based on modern principles of system analysis, including the identification and accounting of possible characteristic uncertainties, the hierarchical structure of the entire data processing procedure, the application of optimization and adaptation methods, ensuring the correctness and completeness of data processing procedures, linearity testing, and application of relevant statistical quality criteria at each stage data analysis, which guarantee high quality of intermediate and final data processing results.

2   Materials and Methods

2.1   Features of Nonlinear and Non-stationary Data

In various fields, such as finance, ecology, social systems, management related to data processing, first of all, it is necessary to determine and classify what information and with what type of process we will have to work with and on this basis to determine data processing methods [3–7,17,19]. However, usually there are known features of the process, such as linearity / non-linearity and stationary / non-stationary, which can be quickly determined and classified in order to select the appropriate modeling and forecasting methods [2,5]. Figure 1 shows the classification of processes, from which it is possible to determine and classify the structure of mathematical models that are used to describe dynamic processes in solving the forecasting problem.

Linear processes can be stationary without a trend and unsteady when they include a component in the form of a first-order trend. If the variance (or covariance) of a stochastic linear process depends on time, then it is classified as heteroskedastic and requires the use of nonlinear models to describe the variance

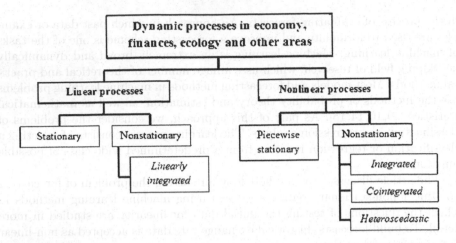

Fig. 1. Classification of the processes being studied

of the process and the process itself [6,8,15]. There is also a wide range of non-linear processes (types of non-linearity), although for the analysis of economic processes only some of them that are more common in economics and finance will be important. These processes can be classified as non-linear in parameters and non-linear in variables. The first type is more complex in terms of modeling and parameter estimation and usually requires more effort and time to develop their models. For example, when constructing logistic regression. Some non-linear processes may exhibit linear behavior in their stable or long-term mode of operation. This function allows you to linearly describe the process near the operating point. This type of non-linearity is very common in economic problems and is used to solve them using machine learning methods. Typically, complex processes include integrated processes (IP) that contain a trend of a second or higher order, as well as co-integrated processes with trends of the same order and heteroskedastic processes with time-varying dispersion. A significant part of the financial processes related to the dynamics of prices for stock exchange instruments belong to this class [11,15]. In engineering applications, such processes are studied and used in diagnostic systems, where an appropriate decision is made regarding the current state of the system. Since there are always elements of non-stationary and non-linearity in financial processes, the subject of research will be the solution of the problem of forecasting exchange rates using machine learning methods.

2.2   Features Forecasting in Problems of Machine Learning

The methodology for solving forecasting problems using machine learning methods consists of the following stages: the stage of data preprocessing, data normalization, testing normalized data for linearity, using classification methods, clustering, data aggregation and forecasting.

Preliminary Data Processing. Preliminary data processing and purification is an important task that must be performed before a data set can be used to train a model. Raw data is often distorted and unreliable, and some values may be omitted. The use of such data in modeling can lead to incorrect results. Actual data is collected for further processing from various sources. At the initial stage of data preparing, preliminary processing (preprocessing) and data filtering are necessary. Data preprocessing and filtering are tasks that must be completed before the data set can be used to train the model selected. Raw data is often distorted, there may be missing data in it. The use of such data in modeling and forecasting can lead to inaccurate and incorrect results. These tasks are part of the data processing and analysis process and are usually used in the initial review of the data set required during preprocessing. They may contain errors and damage that adversely affect data quality. The main problems that may arise:

- incompleteness (data do not contain attributes, or they lack knowledge);
- noise (data contains erroneous records or omissions);
- independence (data contains conflicting records or extensions).

High quality of source data is necessary condition for creating high quality forecasting models.

Data Nomalization. The purpose of normalization is to change the values of the numeric columns in the data-set to a common scale without distorting differences in the ranges of values. To perform machine learning, each data set needs normalization. Consider the two most popular: *min-max normalization* and *mean normalization.*

Min-max Normalization, also known as minimum scaling or normalization of the minimum maximum, is the simplest method and is applied to scale the range of functions to the range of $[0,1]$ or $[-1,1]$. The choice of target range depends on the nature of the data available. The general formula for min-max $[0,1]$ is given as:

$$x' = \frac{x - min(x)}{max(x) - min(x)},$$

where x is original observation value, x' is the normalized value. To zoom between an arbitrary set of values $[a,b]$, the formula becomes as follows:

$$x' = a + \frac{(x - min(x))(b - a)}{max(x) - min(x)},$$

where a, b are the minimum and maximum values.

Mean Based Nomalization:

$$x' = a + \frac{x - average(x)}{max(x) - min(x)},$$

where x is initial value, and x' is the normalized value.

Testing for Linearity. The main task of the data linearity testing phase is to determine what type of data needs to be processed after normalization. Consider the possibility of testing data for linearity using Lagrange multipliers. Since estimating the parameters and structure of nonlinear models is a more difficult task than for linear models, it is more convenient to use methods that do not require an assessment of the structures of nonlinear models. In cases where a particular model is not identified with the formulation of the null hypothesis regarding the linearity of the process, tests based on the assessment of some non-linear alternative, as a rule, do not exist. That is why the use of Lagrange multipliers is advisable when creating and applying linearity tests. It should also be noted that some other testing approaches can be successfully used.

Consider nonlinear model of the following structure:

$$y(k) = \beta^T \mathbf{w}(k) + f(\theta, \mathbf{w}(k), \mathbf{v}(k)) + u(k), \tag{1}$$

where, $\mathbf{w}(k) = [1, y(k-1), ..., y(k-p); x_1(k), ..., x_l(k)]^T$ is measurement vector for the principal variable and possible independent variables; $\mathbf{v}(k) = [u(k-1), ..., u(k-q)]^T$ is a random process vector characterizing influence of stochastic disturbances $u(k) = g(\beta, \theta, \mathbf{v}(k)) \cdot \varepsilon(k)$; $\varepsilon(k)$ is a martingale difference process with the following statistical characteristics: $E[\varepsilon(k)|\mathbf{I}(k)] = 0$, cov $[\varepsilon(k)|\mathbf{I}(k)] = \sigma_\varepsilon^2$; $\mathbf{I}(k) = \{y(k-j), j > 0; \mathbf{x}(k-j), j \geq 0\}$ represents measurement information. In the process of model constructing it is necessary to find such approximating function, $f(\mathbf{w}(k))$, that $E[y(k)|\mathbf{I}(k)] = \beta^T \mathbf{w}(k) + f(\theta, \mathbf{w}(k), \mathbf{v}(k))$.

Thus, on the basis of the suggestions accepted we can write that:

$$E[u(k)|\mathbf{I}(k)] = 0; \quad \text{cov}[u(k)|\mathbf{I}(k)] = \sigma_\varepsilon^2 g^2(\beta, \theta, \mathbf{w}(k), \mathbf{v}(k)).$$

Suppose that the function $f(\cdot)$ is at least two times differentiable regarding parameters, $\theta = [\theta_1, ..., \theta_m]^T$, and that $f(0, \mathbf{w}(k), \mathbf{v}(k)) = 0$. Thus, the hypothesis regarding linearity can be formulated as follows: $H_0 : \theta = 0$.

In a case when, $g \equiv 1$, we have: $\varepsilon(k) = u(k)$. To perform the linearity hypothesis testing write conditional (pseudo-) logarithmic likelihood function of the form:

$$L[\theta, \beta, y(N), \mathbf{w}(N), \mathbf{w}(N-1), ..., \mathbf{w}(1), \mathbf{v}(N), \mathbf{v}(N-1), ..., \mathbf{v}(1)|\mathbf{W}(0), \mathbf{U}(0)] =$$

$$= \sum_{k=1}^{N} L[k, \theta, \beta, y(k)|\mathbf{w}(k), ..., \mathbf{w}(1), \mathbf{v}(k), ..., \mathbf{v}(1), \mathbf{W}(0), \mathbf{U}(0)] =$$

$$= c - \frac{N}{2} \log \sigma_u^2 - \frac{1}{2\sigma_u^2} \sum_{k=1}^{N} u^2(k).$$

The corresponding scoring vector normalized by $1/\sqrt{N}$ is as follows [20]:

$$\frac{1}{\sqrt{N}} \frac{\partial L}{\partial \theta} = \frac{1}{\sqrt{N}\sigma_u^2} \sum_{k=1}^{N} u(k)\mathbf{h}(k); \quad \mathbf{h}(k) = \left(\frac{\partial u(1)}{\partial \theta_1}, ..., \frac{\partial u(k)}{\partial \theta_m} \right).$$

This expression will not have zero value under accepted zero hypothesis. The information matrix has a block diagonal form with each diagonal element multiplied by, σ_u^2. Thus, an inverse for each block is related to θ and can be represented as follows:

$$\mathbf{I}_\theta = \left(N\sigma_u^2\right)^{-1} \sum_{k=1}^{N} \tilde{\mathbf{h}}(k)\tilde{\mathbf{h}}^T(k)-$$

$$-\sum_{k=1}^{N} \tilde{\mathbf{h}}(k)\mathbf{w}^T(k) \left(\sum_{k=1}^{N} \mathbf{w}(k)\mathbf{w}^T(k)\right)^{-1} \sum_{k=1}^{N} \mathbf{w}(k)\tilde{\mathbf{h}}^T(k),$$

where, $\tilde{\mathbf{h}}(k)$ is $\mathbf{h}(k)$, estimated under formulated hypothesis H_0. Setting, $\tilde{\mathbf{u}} = [\tilde{u}(1), ..., \tilde{u}(N)]^T$, we will get the following expression for the test statistics:

$$LM = \tilde{\sigma}^{-2}\tilde{\mathbf{u}}^T\mathbf{H}\left(\mathbf{H}^T\mathbf{M}_w\mathbf{H}\right)^{-1}\mathbf{H}^T\tilde{\mathbf{u}}, \tag{2}$$

where $\mathbf{M}_w = \mathbf{I} - \mathbf{W}(\mathbf{W}^T\mathbf{W})^{-1}\mathbf{W}^T$; $\tilde{\sigma}^2 = N^{-1}\sum_{k=1}^{N}\tilde{u}^2(k)$; and elements of the vector, $\tilde{\mathbf{u}}$, are residuals of the equation (1), that is consistently estimated under formulated, H_0, and with $g \equiv 1$. The value computed via expression (2), asymptotically has distribution of, $\chi^2(m)$, under formulated hypothesis, H_0.

In practice the test statistic is often computed via simplified procedure using the ordinary LS parameter estimates in the following way:

- construct linear regression for principal variable $y(k)$ on $\mathbf{w}(k)$: $y(k) = \beta^T\mathbf{w}(k) + u(k)$;
- compute residuals of the model, $\tilde{u}(k)$, and the residuals square sum, SSR_0;
- construct regression of $\tilde{u}(k)$ on $\mathbf{w}(k)$, and compute the residuals square sum for the model, SSR_1;
- compute the test statistic:

$$F_s(m, N - n - m) = \frac{(SSR_0 - SSR_1)/m}{SSR_1/(N - n - m)},$$

where, $n = l + p + 1$; $m = \dim[\theta]$; the test statistic computed this way has F – distribution for $\theta = 0$. The statistic, F_s, is preferably used instead of χ^2 – test for analyzing relatively short samples [13].

Clustering. Normalization is a technique that is often used as part of preparing data for machine learning. The purpose of normalization is to change the values of the numeric columns in the data set to a common scale without distorting the differences in the ranges of values. For machine learning, each data set does not require normalization.

Clustering is the task of dividing a population of data points into a number of groups (clusters), so that data points in the same groups where more like other data points of the same group than other groups.

Clustering can be divided into two subgroups:

- Rigid clustering: in hard clustering, each data point either belongs to the cluster completely or not.
- Soft clustering: in soft clustering, instead of putting each data point in a separate cluster, the probability or probability that this data point will belong to these clusters is assigned.

Since clustering tasks are subjective, there are many tools that can be used to achieve this goal. Each methodology adheres to a different set of rules for determining similarity among data points. In fact, more than 100 clustering algorithms are known [1,11,12,16,21,22].

Aggregation of Data. Time series aggregation can be seen as a process of "data reduction" in the sense that it summarizes a set of time series. In practice, this process is widely used, especially in clustering or classification procedures.

During clustering, most algorithms repeat 2 main steps: the assignment step and the centering or recalculation step. During the assignment phase, the algorithm calculates the distances between each observation and each centroid (also called the representative or prototype that represents the best representative of the cluster). The observation is then distributed to its nearest cluster (minimum distance from the centroid). During the centering phase, the centroids are updated according to their assigned data points. In some algorithms, such as known KNNs or hierarchical clustering algorithms, centroids are obtained by aggregating observations from the same cluster.

In the classification, data reduction is used to reduce the training set to a smaller one and this is really advantageous when using KNN-like algorithms. On the one hand, a smaller training set can gain accuracy if noisy specimens are filtered correctly. On the other hand, computational complexity decreases as the number of examples in the training set decreases. Finally, the third goal of time series aggregation is a quick and easy way to visualize the main trend of several time series, because it generalizes several curves into one generalized one.

Most averaging algorithms proposed in the literature are based on pair averaging methods. Such strategies really depend on the order in which the series are taken into account, without any guarantee of obtaining the same accuracy with another order. Due to this limitation, two types of global approaches have recently been developed: *DTW Barycenter Averaging* and *Soft-DTW*.

DBA. This approach aims to calculate an average sequence called the barycenter, such as the sum of the square DTW between the barycenter and the set of considered sequences is minimal. This is done iteratively and coordinated by coordinate: in other words, each coordinate of the averaged sequence is the barycenter of the associated coordinates of the set of series. Therefore, the sum of the squares is minimized locally, which minimizes the total similarity of the square DTWs.

Soft-DTW. In this approach, the mean sequence is determined by at least the weighted sum of the distances of the soft DTWs between the set of rows and the mean. The weights depend on a set of coefficients, which may be different for each sequence in the set (but normalized so that their sum is equal to 1) and is divided by the product of the lengths of the considered sequence and the average.

The results of both approaches on one data sample are shown below (Fig. 2). In blue – the middle series with the DBA approach, and in orange and green – the aver-age sequence calculated by averaging the barycenters of soft DTW.

Forecasting. Forecasting can be done on the basis of the variety of known methods including visual.

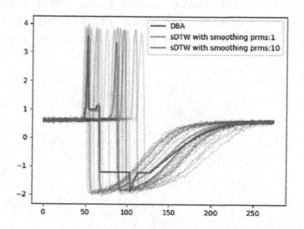

Fig. 2. Results of DBA and Soft-DTW algorithms

3   Example of Exchange Rate Forecasting

As an example of application of the machine learning methods consider forecasting exchange rates. As initial data, historical data of 6 currency pairs were used: AUDUSD, CHFJPY, EURUSD, GBPUSD, NZDUSD, USDJPY from 1990 to 2020 with an interval of 1 day. The data source for forecasting was the service Investing.com. Table 1 shows the values of descriptive statistics for the studied pairs.

Normalization. At the data prepossessing stage, the normalization was applied. As a normalization method, the method based on the average value is used. Normalization results based on the average method are presented in Fig. 3.

Table 1. Descriptive statistics for the studied currency pairs

Descriptive Statistics	AUD USD	CHF JPY	EUR USD	GBP USD	NZD USD	USD JPY
Quantity	6890	6940	7709	6881	6693	7718
Mean	0.761	91.8777	1.2065	1.5865	0.6594	110.5596
Std	0.1358	15.4668	0.1480	0.182	0.1123	15.3731
Min	0.4786	59.2300	0.8267	1.2023	0.3907	75.7800
25%	0.6778	81.7475	1.1155	1.4827	0.5896	102.5200
50%	0.7494	88.3300	1.2077	1.5790	0.6773	110.3500
75%	0.8264	104.2725	1.3144	1.6578	0.7295	119.8500
Max	1.1023	138.3200	1.5997	2.1065	0.8819	159.850

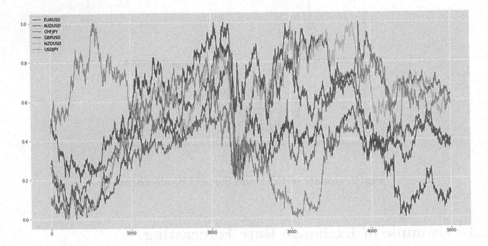

Fig. 3. Normalization results for various currency pairs

Clustering. In this example, the clustering procedure is used to perform search for price patterns and mark time series according to the similarity of patterns. For clustering the time series, the KNN method with the accuracy metric DTW is used. This approach allows one to accurately group time series into clusters by similarity even if there is a certain time shift. The training data was divided into 100 clusters due to the large amount of data and for greater accuracy in forecasting the price of currency pairs. In Fig. 4 examples of time series clustering are shown.

Table 2. Descriptive statistics of the studied currency pairs

Algorithm	Mean distance DTW
Euclidean barycenter	2.201
DTW	1.603
Soft DTW ($\gamma = 1$)	1.861
Soft DTW ($\gamma = 0.1$)	1.605
Soft DTW ($\gamma = 0.01$)	1.600

To study the effectiveness of various machine learning methods in the task of classifying price patterns, we used the historical data of the closing prices of GBPUSD and AUDUSD currency pairs with an interval of 1 day from 1990 to 2020. The data were divided into training and test (validation) sets. The training set contains data for 7437 days, and the test set – 281. Further on, the data were combined into time series of 15 days long (3 weeks without days off) for marking DTW-KNN data and 10 days long for forecasting. All time series were normalized to mean. The result of data marking by the DTW-KNN method is shown in the form of distribution in Fig. 6.

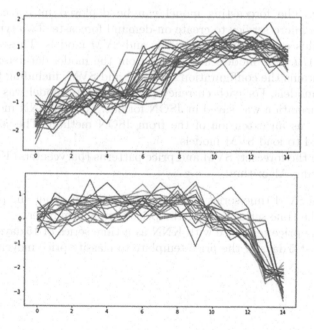

Fig. 4. Examples of clustering the time series selected for the cluster 0 and 2

The results of using the algorithms to solve the problem of classifying time series are shown in Table 3.

Table 3. The results of algorithms for classification problems

Algorithms	Template classification accuracy, %	Accuracy of classification price direction,%	Area ROCAUC
Decision tree	22.22	68.52	0.69
Logistic regression	25.93	74.07	0.75
Multilayer perceptron	35.19	72.2	0.73
Support vector machine (SVM)	38.89	75.93	0.76
Naive Bayesian classifier	37.03	70.37	0.71
Gradient Boosting	27.78	64.81	0.65

Aggregation of the time series selected is performed by a search for a barycenter. Various methods were used to search for the barycenter, and the average DTW distance for the accuracy metric. The results of the study are presented in Table 2, and their corresponding graphical comparison in Fig. 5.

Forecasting. The forecasting model can be deployed into a container and launched as a micro service to create on-demand forecasts. Two types of models are used in this container: KNN models and SVM models. These models have the *sklearn API*. The models are loaded from the model database. The model database contains the configuration for KNN and SVM, including the basic settings of the models. For each currency pair a separate model was trained. The resulting information was saved in JSON format. To load KNN models, use the *sklearn API* as an extension of the from JSON method. The *joblib* Python library is used to load SVM models.

To obtain the forecast, SVM and price patterns (barycenters) KNN are used. The Forecasting Algorithm:

1. Submit an SVM time series containing information about the past 10 days.
2. Classify the time series and get the price template number.
3. Export the price template with KNN as a time series of 15 days.
4. Use the last 5 days of the price template to classify price movements.

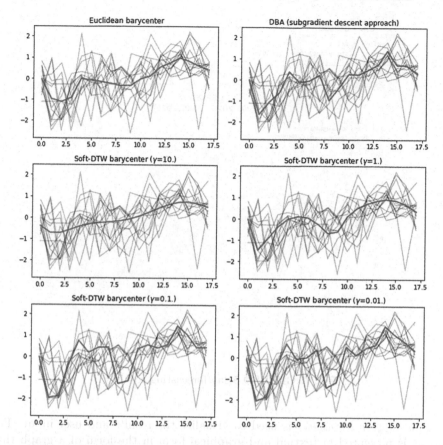

Fig. 5. Results of estimating the barycenter for different algorithms

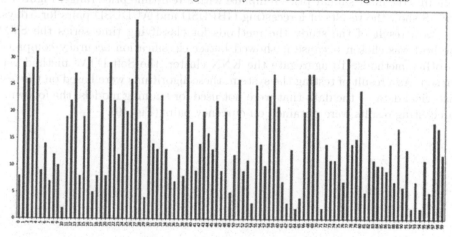

Fig. 6. Distribution of test case marks

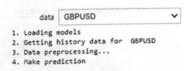

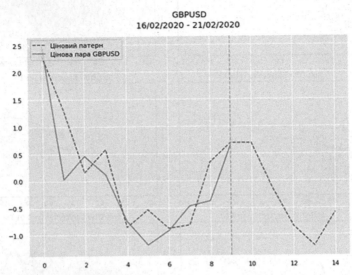

Fig. 7. GBPUSD 5 day forecasting results

The *Jupyter Notebook* is used to visualize the results and user input. The output is presented in textual and graphical form in the form of a graph that contains the most similar price template with a real-time price range. Figures 7 and 8 show the results of forecasting GBPUSD and AUDUSD pairs for 5 days.

As a result of the study the methods for classifying time series the SVM method was chosen because it showed better classification accuracy compared to other methods. To aggregate the KNN cluster, the Soft-DTW method was chosen. As a result of testing the system, these algorithms were based on the test historical data — the data that were not used for training models, the following forecasting results were obtained on currency pairs (Fig. 9).

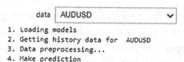

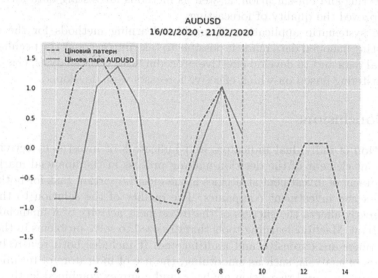

Fig. 8. GBPUSD 5 day forecasting AUDUSD 5 day forecasting results

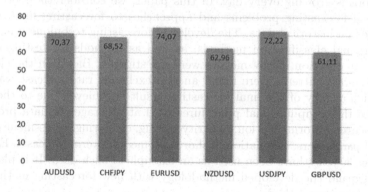

Fig. 9. Forecasting results of currency pairs based on historical data for 2019–2020

4   Discussion

The results achieved in modeling and forecasting showed that the proposed systematic approach is useful for developing modeling techniques and forecasting investment performance indicators. The developed methodology for solving forecasting problems and approaches to forecasting financial market indicators is based on machine learning methods. Computational experiments conducted with the use of evidence for nonlinear non-stationary processes showed the usefulness of the approach for its practical application for modeling and forecasting, as well as the need for further refinement in future studies. In addition, it is important to note that the application of the developed methods for predicting the methods of clustering and classification, as well as methods for testing data for linearity, has improved the quality of forecasting.

The systematic application of machine learning methods for the tasks of forecasting financial data made it possible to take into account the peculiarities of financial data and to develop effective procedures for data analysis, classification and clustering based on which effective forecasts were developed.

5   Conclusions

Prediction of individual indicators and indicators of investment activity is an important element of the decision-making process in the financial market. The development of investment strategies is the most important task for both private investors and investment companies. The quality of the solution to this problem directly affects the success of the investment activity of a financial market participant. Machine learning tools that are used to solve problems in the investment sphere are extensive and multifaceted. It includes both relatively simple methods of analysis, such as smoothing, the use of indicators of technical analysis, correlation and regression analysis, and complex combined methods. With the development of computer technology and artificial intelligence, the accuracy of methods is growing every day. In this paper, we consider the methodology for solving forecasting problems and approaches to forecasting financial markets based on historical data. The developed forecasting technique used various clustering and classification methods, as well as methods for testing data for linearity. In addition, DTW metrics were investigated. Based on the clustering methods, price patterns were found and an exchange rate forecast was developed. High quality of the final forecasting result is achieved due to the proper control of the computational procedures used at all stages of data processing: data processing, normalization, linearity testing, clustering, assessment of structure and parameters, calculation of short and medium-term forecasts. Exchange rates over 30 years have been used as an example of such data. It is planned to further expand the developed methodology with new forecasting methods and machine learning methods.

References

1. Andersen, T.T., Bollerslev, T., Lange, S.: Forecasting financial market volatility: sample frequency visa-vis forecast horizon. J. Empirical Finance **6**(5), 457–477 (1999)
2. Asai, M., McAleer, M.: The structure of dynamic correlations in multivariate stochastic volatility models. J. Econometrics **150**, 182–192 (2009)
3. Bidyuk, P., Gozhyj, A., Kalinina, I.: The methods bayesian analysis of the threshold stochastic volatility model. In: Proceedings of the 2018 IEEE 2nd International Conference on Data Stream Mining and Processing, pp. 70–75 (2018)

4. Bidyuk, P., Gozhyj, A., Kalinina, I., Gozhyj, V.: Analysis of uncertainty types for model building and forecasting dynamic processes. In: Advances in Intelligent Systems and Computing II, vol. 689, pp. 66–78. Springer-Verlag (2018). https://doi.org/10.1007/978-3-319-70581-1

5. Bidyuk, P.I., Romanenko, V.D., Timoshchuk, O.L.: Time Series Analysis. Polytechnika NTU Igor Sikorsky KPI, Kyiv (2013)

6. Bollerslev, T.: Generalized autoregressive conditional heteroskedasticity. J. Econometrics 31(3), 307–327 (1986)

7. Bollerslev, T.: A conditionally heteroskedastic time series model forspeculative prices and rates of return. Rev. Econ. Stat. 69(3), 542–547 (1987)

8. Bollerslev, T., Chou, R., Kroner, K.: Arch modeling in finance : a review of the theory and empirical evidence. J. Econometrics 52(1–2), 5–59 (1992). https://doi.org/10.1016/0304-4076(92)90064-X

9. Engle, R.: Autoregressive conditional heteroscedasticity with estimates of variance of United Kingdom inflation. Econometrica 50, 987–1008 (1982)

10. Engle, R., Bollerslev, T.: Modelling the persistence of conditional variances. Econometric Rev. 5(1), 1–50 (1986)

11. Fulcher, B.D., Jones, N.S.: Highly comparative feature-based time-series classification. In: IEEE Transactions on Knowledge and Data Engineering, vol. 26, pp. 3026–3037 (2014). https://doi.org/10.1109/TKDE.2014.2316504

12. Fulcher, B.D., Little, M.A., Jones, N.S.: Highly comparative time-series analysis: the empirical structure of time series and their methods. J. Royal Soc. Interface 10(83), 20130048 (2013). https://doi.org/10.1098/rsif.2013.0048

13. Harvey, A.C.: Econometric Analysis of Time Series. John Wiley and Sons Ltd, New York (1990)

14. Harvey, A.C.: Forecasting, Structural Time Series Models and The Kalman Filter. The MIT Press, Cambridge (Massachusetts) (1990)

15. Hyndman, R.J., Wang, E., Laptev, N.: Large-scale unusual time series detection. In: Proceedings of 15th IEEE International Conference on Data Mining Workshop, ICDMW 2015, pp. 1616–1619 (2016). https://doi.org/10.1109/ICDMW.2015.104

16. Pesaran, M.H., Pick, A.: Optimal forecasts in the presence of structural breaks. J. Econometrics 177(3), 134–152 (2013). https://doi.org/10.1016/j.jeconom.2013.04.002

17. Pretis, F., Reade, J.J., Succarat, G.: Automated general-to-specific (GETS) regression modeling and indicator saturation for outliers and structural breaks. Stat. Softw. 86(3), 1–44 (2018). https://doi.org/10.18637/jss.v086.i03

18. Rasmussen, C.E., Williams, C.I.: Gaussian Processes for Machine Learning. The MIT Press, Cambridge (Massachusetts) (2006)

19. Succarat, G., Escribano, A.: Automated model selection in finance: general-to-specific modeling of the mean, variance and density. Oxford Bull. Econ. Stat. 74(5), 716–735 (2012). https://doi.org/10.1111/j.1468-0084.2011.00669.x

20. Terasvirta, T., Tjostheim, D., Granger, C.J.: Aspects of modeling nonlinear time series. Handb. Econometrics 4, 2919–2957 (1994)

21. Watsham, T.J., Parramore, K.: Quantitative Methods in Finance. International Thomson Business Press, London (1997)

22. Xekalaki, E., Degiannakis, S.: ARCH Models for Financial Applications. The MIT Press, Cambridge (Massachusetts) (2010)

Bayesian Regression Approach for Building and Stacking Predictive Models in Time Series Analytics

Bohdan Pavlyshenko[✉] [iD]

Ivan Franko National University of Lviv, Lviv, Ukraine
b.pavlyshenko@gmail.com

Abstract. The paper describes the use of Bayesian regression for building time series models and stacking different predictive models for time series. Using Bayesian regression for time series modeling with nonlinear trend was analyzed. This approach makes it possible to estimate an uncertainty of time series prediction and calculate value at risk characteristics. A hierarchical model for time series using Bayesian regression has been considered. In this approach, one set of parameters is the same for all data samples, other parameters can be different for different groups of data samples. Such an approach allows using this model in the case of short historical data for specified time series, e.g. in the case of new stores or new products in the sales prediction problem. In the study of predictive models stacking, the models ARIMA, Neural Network, Random Forest, Extra Tree were used for the prediction on the first level of model ensemble. On the second level, time series predictions of these models on the validation set were used for stacking by Bayesian regression. This approach gives distributions for regression coefficients of these models. It makes it possible to estimate the uncertainty contributed by each model to stacking result. The information about these distributions allows us to select an optimal set of stacking models, taking into account the domain knowledge. The probabilistic approach for stacking predictive models allows us to make risk assessment for the predictions that are important in a decision-making process.

Keywords: Time series · Bayesian regression · Machine learning · Stacking · Forecasting · Sales

1 Introduction

Time series analytics is an important part of modern data science. The examples of different time series approaches are in [2,3,5,10,11,21,22]. In [6,9,18–20,23], a range of ensemble-based methods for classification problems is considered. In [14], the authors studied a lagged variable selection, hyperparameter optimization, as well as compared classical and machine learning based algorithms for time series. Sales prediction is an important part of modern business intelligence

© Springer Nature Switzerland AG 2020
S. Babichev et al. (Eds.): DSMP 2020, CCIS 1158, pp. 486–500, 2020.
https://doi.org/10.1007/978-3-030-61656-4_33

[7, 13, 24]. Sales can be regarded as a time series. However, time series approaches have some limitations for sales forecasting. For instance, to study seasonality, historical data for large time period are required. But it frequently happens that there are no historical data for a target variable, e.g. when a new product is launched. Furthermore, we must take into consideration many exogenous factors influencing sales. We can consider time series forecasting as a regression problem in many cases, especially for sales time series. In [16], we considered linear models, machine learning and probabilistic models for time series modeling. In [15], we regarded the logistic regression with Bayesian inference for analysing manufacturing failures. In [17], we study the use of machine learning models for sales predictive analytics. We researched the main approaches and case studies of implementing machine learning to sales forecasting. The effect of machine learning generalization has been studied. This effect can be used for predicting sales in case of a small number of historical data for specific sales time series in case when a new product or store is launched [17]. A stacking approach for building ensemble of single models using Lasso regression has also been studied. The obtained results show that using stacking techniques, we can improve the efficiency of predictive models for sales time series forecasting [17].

In this paper, we consider the use of Bayesian regression for building time series predictive models and for stacking time series predictive models on the second level of the predictive model which is the ensemble of the models of the first level.

2   Bayesian Regression Approach

Probabilistic regression models can be based on Bayesian theorem [4, 8, 12]. This approach allows us to receive a posterior distribution of model parameters using conditional likelihood and prior distribution. Probabilistic approach is more natural for stochastic variables such as sales time series. The difference between Bayesian approach and conventional Ordinary Least Squares (OLS) method is that in the Bayesian approach, uncertainty comes from parameters of model, as opposed to OLS method where the parameters are constant and uncertainty comes from data. In the Bayesian inference, we can use informative prior distributions which can be set up by an expert. So, the result can be considered as a compromise between historical data and expert opinion. It is important in the cases when we have a small number of historical data. In the Bayesian model, we can consider the target variable with non Gaussian distribution, e.g. Student's t-distribution. Probabilistic approach enables us an ability to receive probability density function for the target variable. Having such function, we can make risk assessment and calculate value at risk (VaR) which is 5% quantile. For solving Bayesian models, the numerical Monte-Carlo methods are used. Gibbs and Hamiltonian sampling are the popular methods of finding posterior distributions for the parameters of probabilistic model [4, 8, 12].

Bayesian inference makes it possible to do nonlinear regression. If we need to fit trend with saturation, we can use logistic curve model for nonlinear trend and find its parameters using Bayesian inference. Let us consider the case of nonlinear regression for time series which have the trend with saturation. For modeling we consider sales time series. The model can be described as:

$$log(Sales) \sim \mathcal{N}(\mu_{Sales}, \sigma^2)$$
$$\mu_{Sales} = \frac{a}{1 + exp(bt + c)} + \beta_{Promo}Promo+$$
$$\beta_{Time}Time + \sum_j \beta_j^{wd}WeekDay_j, \tag{1}$$

where $WeekDay_j$ are binary variables, which is 1 in the case of sales on an appropriate day of week and 0 otherwise. We can also build hierarchical models using Bayesian inference. In this approach, one set of parameters is the same for all data samples, other parameters can be different for different groups of data samples. In the case of sales data, we can consider trends, promo impact and seasonality as the same for all stores. But the impact of a specific store on sales can be described by an intersect parameter, so this coefficient for this variable will be different for different stores. The hierarchical model can be described as:

$$Sales \sim \mathcal{N}(\mu_{Sales}, \sigma^2)$$
$$\mu_{Sales} = \alpha(Store) + \beta_{Promo}Promo+$$
$$\beta_{Time}Time + \sum_j \beta_j^{wd}WeekDay_j, \tag{2}$$

where intersect parameters $\alpha(Store)$ are different for different stores.

Predictive models can be combined into ensemble model using stacking approach [6,9,18–20,23]. In this approach, prediction results of predictive models on the validation set are treated as covariates for stacking regression. These predictive models are considered as a first level of predictive model ensemble. Stacking model forms the second level of model ensemble. Using Bayesian inference for stacking regression gives distributions for stacking regression coefficients. It enables us to estimate the uncertainty of the first level predictive models. As predictive models for first level of ensemble, we used the following models: 'ARIMA', 'ExtraTree', 'RandomForest', 'Lasso', 'NeuralNetowrk'. The use of these models for stacking by Lasso regression was described in [17]. For stacking, we have chosen the robust regression with Student's t-distribution for the target variable as

$$y \sim Student_t(\nu, \mu, \sigma) \tag{3}$$

where

$$\mu = \alpha + \sum_i \beta_i x_i, \tag{4}$$

ν is a distribution parameter, called as degrees of freedom, i is an index of the predictive model in the stacking regression, $i \in \{$ 'ARIMA', 'ExtraTree', 'RandomForest', 'Lasso', 'NeuralNetowrk' $\}$.

3   Numerical Modeling

The data for our analysis are based on store sales historical data from the "Ross-mann Store Sales" Kaggle competition [1]. For Bayesian regression, we used Stan platform for statistical modeling [4]. The analysis was conducted in Jupyter Notebook environment using Python programming language and the following main Python packages *pandas, sklearn, pystan, numpy, scipy, statsmodels, keras, matplotlib, seaborn*. For numerical analysis we modeled time series with multi-plicative trend with saturation. Figure 1 shows results of this modeling where mean values and Value at Risk (VaR) characteristics are given. VaR was calcu-lated as 5% percentile. Figure 2 shows probability density function of regression coefficients for Promo factor. Figure 3 shows box plots for probability density function of seasonality coefficients.

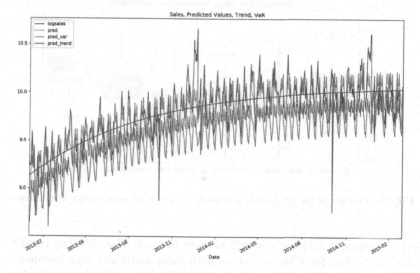

Fig. 1. Time series and trend forecasting

Let us consider Bayersian hierarchical model for time series. Intersect param-eters $\alpha(Store)$ in the model (2) are different for different stores. We have con-sidered a case with five different stores. Figure 4 shows the boxplots for the probability density functions of intersect parameters. The dispersion of these dsitributions describes an uncertainty of influence of specified store on sales. Hierarchical approach makes it possible to use such a model in the case with short historical data for specific stores, e.g. in the case of new stores. Figure 5 shows the results of the forecasting on the validation set in the two cases, the fisrt case is when we use 2 year historical data and the second case is with his-torical data for 5 days. We can see that such short historical data allow us to estimate sales dynamics correctly. Figure 6 shows box plots for probability den-sity function of intersect parameters of different time series in case of short time

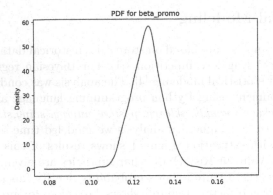

Fig. 2. Probability density function of regression coefficients for Promo factor

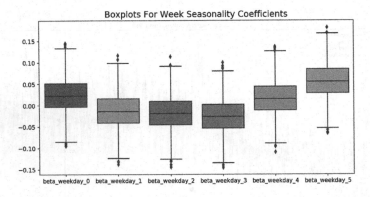

Fig. 3. Box plots for probability density function of seasonality coefficients

period of historical data for a specified store *Store_4*. The obtained results show that the dispersion for a specific store with short historical data becomes larger due to uncertainty caused by very short historical data for the specified store.

Let us consider the results of Bayesian regression approach for stacking predictive models. We trained different predictive models and made the predictions on the validation set. The ARIMA model was evaluated using *statsmodels* package, Neural Network was evaluated using *keras* package, Random Forest and Extra Tree was evaluated using *sklearn* package. In these calculations, we used the approaches described in [17]. Figure 7 shows the time series forecasts on the validation sets obtained using different models.

The results of prediction of these models on the validation sets are considered as the covariates for the regression on the second stacking level of the ensemble of models. For stacking predictive models we split the validation set on the training and testing sets. For stacking regression, we normalized the covariates and target variable using z-scores:

$$z_i = \frac{x_i - \mu_i}{\sigma_i}, \tag{5}$$

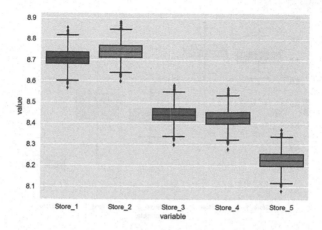

Fig. 4. Boxplots for probability density functions of intersect parameters

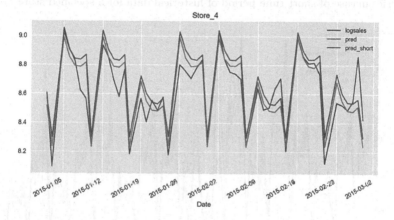

Fig. 5. Forecasting on the validation set for specified time series in cases with different size of historical data

where μ_i is the mean value, σ_i is the standard deviation. The prior distributions for parameters α, β, σ in the Bayesian regression model (3)–(4) are considered as Gaussian with mean values equal to 0, and standard deviation equal to 1. We split the validation set on the training and testing sets by time factor. The parameters for prior distributions can be adjusted using prediction scores on testing sets or using expert opinions in the case of small data amount. To estimate uncertainty of regression coefficients, we used the coefficient of variation which is defined as a ratio between the standard deviation and mean value for model coefficient distributions:

$$v_i = \frac{\sigma_i}{\mu_i}, \tag{6}$$

where v_i is the coefficient of variation, σ_i is a standard deviation, μ_i is the mean value for the distribution of the regression coefficient of the model i. Taking

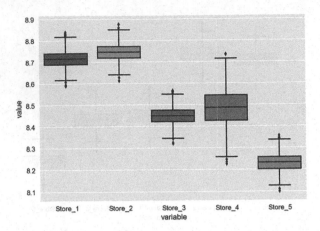

Fig. 6. Box plots for probability density function of intersect parameters of diferent time series in case of short time period of historical data for a specified store *Store_4*.

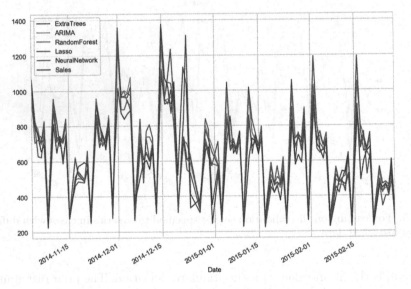

Fig. 7. Forecasting of different models on the validation set

into account that μ_i can be negative, we will analyze the absolute value of the coefficient of variation $|v_i|$. For the results evaluations, we used a relative mean absolute error (RMAE) and root mean square error (RMSE). Relative mean absolute error (RMAE) was considered as a ratio between the mean absolute error (MAE) and mean values of target variable:

$$RMAE = \frac{E(|y_{pred} - y|)}{E(y)} 100\% \qquad (7)$$

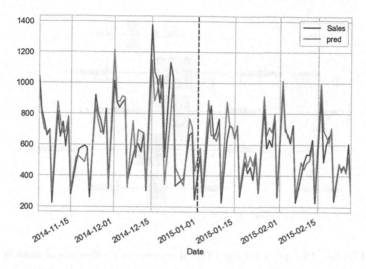

Fig. 8. Time series of mean values for real and forecasted sales on validation and testing sets

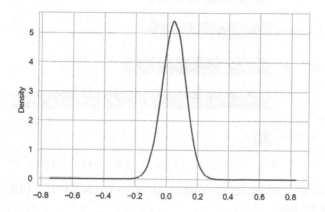

Fig. 9. The PDF for intersect parameter of stacking regression

Root mean square error (RMSE) was considered as:

$$RMSE = \sqrt{\frac{\sum_i^n (y_{pred} - y)^2}{n}} \tag{8}$$

The data with predictions of different models on the validation set were split on the training set (48 samples) and testing set (50 samples) by date. We used the robust regression with Student's t-distribution for the target variable. As a result of calculations, we received the following scores: RMAE(train) = 12.4%, RMAE(test) = 9.8%, RMSE(train) = 113.7, RMSE(test) = 74.7. Figure 8 shows mean values time series for real and forecasted sales on the validation and testing sets. The vertical dotted line separates the training and testing

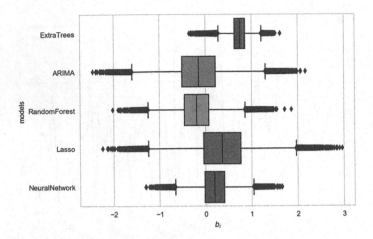

Fig. 10. Box plots for the PDF of regression coefficients of models

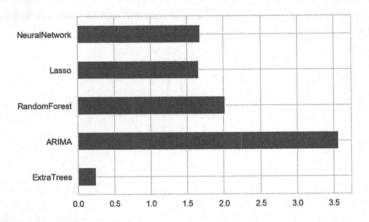

Fig. 11. Absolute values of the coefficient of variation for the PDF of regression coefficients of models

sets. Figure 9 shows the probability density function (PDF) for the intersect parameter. One can observe a positive bias of this (PDF). It is caused by the fact that we applied machine learning algorithms to nonstationary time series. If a nonstationary trend is small, it can be compensated on the validation set using stacking regression.

Figure 10 shows the box plots for the PDF of coefficients of models. Figure 11 shows the coefficient of variation for the PDF of regression coefficients of models.

We considered the case with the restraints to regression coefficient of models that they should be positive. We received the similar results: RMAE(train) = 12.9%, RMAE(test) = 9.7%, RMSE(train) = 117.3, RMSE(test) = 76.1. Figure 12 shows the box plots for the PDF of model regression coefficients for this case.

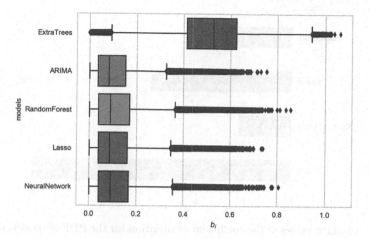

Fig. 12. Box plots for the PDF of regression coefficients of models in case with the restraints to regression coefficient to be positive

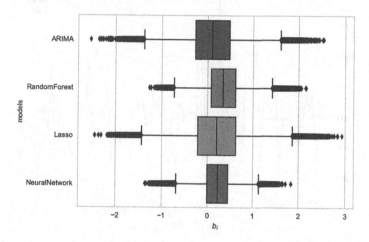

Fig. 13. Box plots for the PDF of regression coefficients of models in case without ExtraTree model

All models have a similar mean value and variation coefficients. We can observe that errors characteristics RMAE and RMSE on the validation set can be similar with respect to these errors on the training set. It tells us about the fact that Bayesian regression does not overfit on the training set comparing to the machine learning algorithms which can demonstrate essential overfitting on training sets, especially in the cases of small amount of training data. We have chosen the best ExtraTree stacking model and conducted Bayesian regression with this one model only. We received the following scores: RMAE(train) = 12.9%, RMAE(test) = 11.1%, RMSE(train) = 117.1, RMSE(test) = 84.7. We also tried to exclude the best model ExtraTree from the stacking regression and

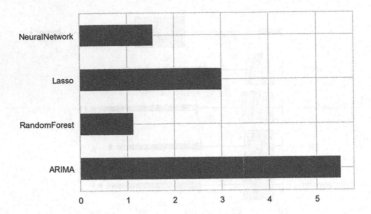

Fig. 14. Absolute values of the coefficient of variation for the PDF of models regression coefficients in case without ExtraTree model

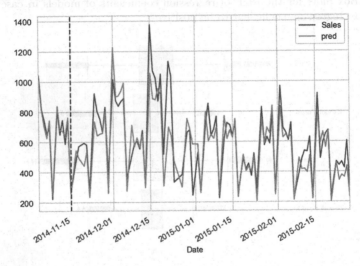

Fig. 15. Mean values time series for real and forecasted sales on the validation and testing sets in the case of small training set

conducted Bayesian regression with the rest of models without ExtraTree. In this case we received the following scores: RMAE(train) = 14.1%, RMAE(test) = 10.2%, RMSE(train) = 139.1, RMSE(test) = 75.3. Figure 13 shows the box plots for the PDF of model regression coefficients, Fig. 14 shows the coefficient of variation for the PDF of regression coefficients of models for this case study. We received worse results on the testing set. At the same time these models have the similar influence and thus they can potentially provide more stable results in the future due to possible changing of the quality of features. Noisy models can decrease accuracy on large training data sets, at the same time they contribute to sufficient results in the case of small data sets.

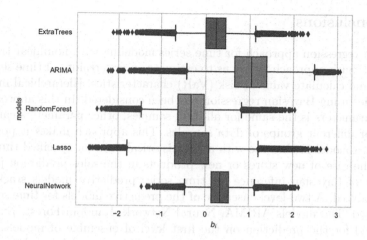

Fig. 16. Box plots for the PDF of regression coefficients of models in the case of small training set

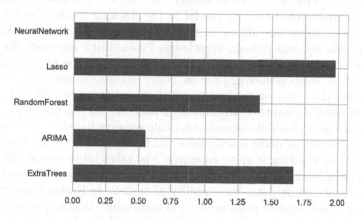

Fig. 17. Absolute values of the coefficient of variation for the PDF of regression coefficients of models in the case of small training set

We considered the case with a small number of training data, 12 samples. To get stable results, we fixed the ν parameter of Student's t-distribution in Bayesian regression model (3)–(4) equal to 10. We received the following scores: RMAE(train) = 5.0%, RMAE(test) = 14.2%, RMSE(train) = 37.5, RMSE(test) = 121.3. Figure 15 shows mean values time series for real and forecasted sales on the validation and testing sets. Figure 16 shows the box plots for the PDF of regression coefficients of models. Figure 17 shows the coefficient of variation for the PDF of regression coefficients of models. In this case, we can see that an other model starts playing an important role comparing with the previous cases and ExtraTree model does not dominate.

The obtained results show that optimizing informative prior distributions of stacking model parameters can improve the scores of prediction results on the testing set.

4   Conclusions

Bayesian regression approach for time series modeling with nonlinear trend was analyzed. Such approach allows us to estimate an uncertainty of time series prediction and calculate value at risk (VaR) characteristics. Hierarchical model for time series using Bayesian regression has been considered. In this approach, one set of parameters is the same for all data samples, other parameters can be different for different groups of data samples. This approach makes it possible to use such a model in the case with short historical data for specified time series, e.g. in the case of new stores or new products in the sales prediction problem. The use of Bayesian inference for time series predictive models stacking has been analyzed. A two-level ensemble of the predictive models for time series was considered. The models ARIMA, Neural Network, Random Forest, Extra Tree were used for the prediction on the first level of ensemble of models. On the second stacking level, time series predictions of these models on the validation set were conducted by Bayesian regression. Such an approach gives distributions for regression coefficients of these models. It makes it possible to estimate the uncertainty contributed by each model to the stacking result. The information about these distributions allows us to select an optimal set of stacking models, taking into account domain knowledge. Probabilistic approach for stacking predictive models allows us to make risk assessment for the predictions that is important in a decision-making process. Noisy models can decrease accuracy on large training data sets, at the same time they contribute to sufficient results in the case of small data sets. Using Bayesian inference for stacking regression can be useful in cases of small datasets and help experts to select a set of models for stacking as well as make assessments of different kinds of risks. Choosing the final models for stacking is up to an expert who takes into account different factors such as uncertainty of each model on the stacking regression level, amount of training and testing data, the stability of models. In Bayesian regression, we can receive a quantitative measure for the uncertainty that can be a very useful information for experts in model selection and stacking. An expert can also set up informative prior distributions for stacking regression coefficients of models, taking into account the domain knowledge information. So, Bayesian approach for stacking regression can give us the information about uncertainty of predictive models. Using this information and domain knowledge, an expert can select models to get stable stacking ensemble of predictive models.

References

1. Rossmann Store Sales. Forecast sales using store, promotion, and competitor data. Kaggle. Com. Available online: http://www.kaggle.com/c/rossmann-store-sales
2. Box, G.E., Jenkins, G.M., Reinsel, G.C., Ljung, G.M.: Time Series Analysis: Forecasting and Control. John Wiley & Sons, Hoboken (2015). https://doi.org/10.1111/jtsa.12194
3. Brockwell, P.J., Davis, R.A., Calder, M.V.: Introduction to Time Series and Forecasting, vol. 2. Springer, Berlin (2002)

4. Carpenter, B., et al.: Stan: a probabilistic programming language. J. Stat. Softw. **76**(1) (2017). https://doi.org/10.18637/jss.v076.i01
5. Chatfield, C.: Time-Series Forecasting. Chapman and Hall/CRC, United Kingdom (2000). https://doi.org/10.1201/9781420036206
6. Dietterich, T.G.: Ensemble methods in machine learning. In: Kittler, J., Roli, F. (eds.) MCS 2000. LNCS, vol. 1857, pp. 1–15. Springer, Heidelberg (2000). https://doi.org/10.1007/3-540-45014-9_1
7. Efendigil, T., Önüt, S., Kahraman, C.: A decision support system for demand forecasting with artificial neural networks and neuro-fuzzy models: a comparative analysis. Expert Syst. Appl. **36**(3), 6697–6707 (2009). https://doi.org/10.1016/j.eswa.2008.08.058
8. Gelman, A., Carlin, J.B., Stern, H.S., Dunson, D.B., Vehtari, A., Rubin, D.B.: Bayesian Data Analysis. Chapman and Hall/CRC, United Kingdom (2013). https://doi.org/10.1201/b1601
9. Gomes, H.M., Barddal, J.P., Enembreck, F., Bifet, A.: A survey on ensemble learning for data stream classification. ACM Comput. Surv. (CSUR) **50**(2), 1–36 (2017). https://doi.org/10.1145/3054925
10. Hyndman, R.J., Athanasopoulos, G.: Forecasting: Principles and Practice. OTexts, Melbourne (2018)
11. Hyndman, R.J., Khandakar, Y., et al.: Automatic Time Series for Forecasting: The Forecast Package for R, vol. 6. Monash University, Department of Econometrics and Business Statistics, Melbourne (2007)
12. Kruschke, J.: Doing Bayesian Data Analysis: A Tutorial with R, JAGS, and Stan. Academic Press, United States (2014)
13. Mentzer, J.T., Moon, M.A.: Sales Forecasting Management: A Demand Management Approach. Sage, United States (2005). https://doi.org/10.4135/9781452204444
14. Papacharalampous, G., Tyralis, H., Koutsoyiannis, D.: Univariate time series forecasting of temperature and precipitation with a focus on machine learning algorithms: a multiple-case study from Greece. Water Res. Manage. **32**(15), 5207–5239 (2018). https://doi.org/10.1007/s11269-018-2155-6
15. Pavlyshenko, B.: Machine learning, linear and bayesian models for logistic regression in failure detection problems. In: Big Data (Big Data), 2016 IEEE International Conference on, pp. 2046–2050. IEEE (2016). https://doi.org/10.1109/bigdata.2016.7840828
16. Pavlyshenko, B.M.: Linear, machine learning and probabilistic approaches for time series analysis. In: Data Stream Mining & Processing (DSMP), IEEE First International Conference on, pp. 377–381. IEEE (2016). https://doi.org/10.1109/dsmp.2016.7583582
17. Pavlyshenko, B.M.: Machine-learning models for sales time series forecasting. Data **4**(1), 15 (2019). https://doi.org/10.3390/data4010015
18. Rokach, L.: Ensemble methods for classifiers. Data Mining and Knowledge Discovery Handbook, pp. 957–980. Springer, Berlin (2005). https://doi.org/10.1007/0-387-25465-x_45
19. Rokach, L.: Ensemble-based classifiers. Artif. Intell. Rev. **33**(1–2), 1–39 (2010). https://doi.org/10.1007/s10462-009-9124-7
20. Sagi, O., Rokach, L.: Ensemble learning: a survey. Wiley Interdisc. Rev. Data Min. Knowl. Discov. **8**(4), e1249 (2018). https://doi.org/10.1002/widm.1249
21. Tsay, R.S.: Analysis of Financial Time Series, vol. 543. John Wiley & Sons, Hoboken (2005). https://doi.org/10.1002/0471746193

500   B. Pavlyshenko

22. Wei, W.W.: Time series analysis. In: The Oxford Handbook of Quantitative Methods in Psychology, Vol. 2 (2006)
23. Wolpert, D.H.: Stacked generalization. Neural Netw. **5**(2), 241–259 (1992). https://doi.org/10.1016/s0893-6080(05)80023-1
24. Zhang, G.P.: Neural Networks in Business Forecasting. IGI Global, United States (2004). https://doi.org/10.4018/978-1-59140-176-6

Forest Cover Type Classification Based on Environment Characteristics and Machine Learning Technology

Vasyl Kiyko[1] , Vasyl Lytvyn[1(✉)] , Lubomyr Chyrun[2] ,
Svitlana Vyshemyrska[3] , Iryna Lurie[3] , and Mykhailo Hrubel[4]

[1] Lviv Polytechnic National University, Lviv, Ukraine
{vasyl.kiiko.sa.2017,Victoria.A.Vysotska,vasyl.v.lytvyn}@lpnu.ua
[2] Ivan Franko National University of Lviv, Lviv, Ukraine
Lyubomyr.Chyrun@lnu.edu.ua
[3] Kherson National Technical University, Kherson, Ukraine
printvvs@gmail.com, lurieira@gmail.com
[4] Hetman Petro Sahaidachnyi National Army Academy, Lviv, Ukraine
m.g.grybel@gmail.com

Abstract. Today, one of lot global problems is forest deforestation and monitoring. The article describes the system creation for forests control and monitoring. This work aims is to develop a model for the forest cover type determination based on environmental characteristics and machine learning as the currently developing project part "Monitoring the trees condition using drones". The project aims is to simplify and partially automate the control and monitoring of trees using drones and machine learning to improve the forest situation. The task is to create a model for predict what trees types grow in the area based on environmental characteristics. Therefore, the main system will able to compare the existing values/characteristics with the predicted ones (which tree should normally there) to find discrepancies. Eventually, the main system will able to use this information to report and inform relevant staff and authorities. This work is based on a data set for learning system that includes observations of trees from four areas of Roosevelt National Forest in Colorado. All observations are cartographic variables (without remote sensing) from 30 × 30-m forest areas. In total, there are more than half a million measurements. The work aim is the development of a forest cover types classification model depending on the environment and its characteristics.

Keywords: Drone monitoring · k-NN algorithm · Machine learning ·
Forest cover · Scenario RUP · Forest cover type ·
Cover type classification · Data analysis · Cover type ·
Intelligent system · Certain area

S. Babichev et al. (Eds.): DSMP 2020, CCIS 1158, pp. 501–524, 2020.
https://doi.org/10.1007/978-3-030-61656-4_34

1   Introduction

It is difficult to overestimate the role of plants in people's lives, especially trees [5]. The forests disappear in different ways: from fires and diseases to human activities, mass deforestation [13]. Therefore, the system creation for forests and certain tree species control and monitoring is relevant today [14,22,23,25]. The work aim is forest cover type's classification model creation depending on the environment and its characteristics. Respectively, the object of the study are different forest types and standard natural environmental conditions in which they grow. According to the purpose, the main task of this work is to investigate the subject area and develop a model of machine learning, which could determine the environment characteristics. This model could determine what trees type should grow in the study area, and check the area for discrepancies and various deviations. Automatic detection of anomalies in different parts of the forest will greatly facilitate the work of scientists and other workers whose task is to monitor the condition of surrounding forests and individual tree species. Therefore, by integrating the developed system with various projects aimed at protecting and controlling the condition of trees, it is possible to achieve the preservation of more trees and better monitoring of the situation with the environment. The project aims to simplify and partially automate the control and monitoring of trees using drones and machine learning to improve the forest situation. The task is to create a model that could predict what trees types grow in the area based on environmental characteristics. Therefore, the main system will able to compare the existing values/characteristics with the predicted ones (which tree should normally there) to find discrepancies. Eventually, the main system will able to use this information to report and inform relevant staff and authorities.

2   Related Works

The World Bank estimates that about 3.9 million square miles (10 million square kilometres) of forest have lost since the early 20th century [5,13]. Over the past 25 years, forests have shrunk by 502,000 square miles (1.3 million square kilometres), an area larger than South Africa. In 2018, The Guardian reported that a forest piece corresponding to the size football field is lost every second [14,22,23,25]. Thus, from the above factors, it becomes clear that any assistance to workers and persons responsible for forest conservation and environmental monitoring is necessary. For example, should create a model that can identify inconsistencies in the vegetation of a certain area or, conversely, changes in the environment [11,19,24,26,27]. An environment that does not match the vegetation on it will a great help in the fight against deforestation [12,12,16,32].

The Open Foris (OF) initiative is led by FAO Forestry to support multi-purpose forest inventories, data processing and dissemination of results [5]. OF provides a set of free, open source software to facilitate flexible and efficient collection, analysis, and reporting for field and satellite data. The initiative is a joint effort of numerous public and private institutions run by the FAO Department of

Forestry. Open Foris offers ideal tools for fast, accurate and cost-effective assessments. It is customized to the specific needs and methods of data collection. Open Foris tools are used in the forest sector, especially in NFIs in more than 20 countries, including NFIs in Tanzania, Zambia, Bhutan, Sri Lanka, Vietnam and Argentina. In addition, OF tools are used, for example, for socio-economic inventory in Mongolia and dairy industry research in Kazakhstan. The suite of software includes:

- OF Collect, which is used to determine the hierarchical structure of the survey and to determine the attributes to be collected and their parameters;
- OF Collect Mobile is a tablet tool that allows you to enter data directly into the field, thereby significantly improving the quality of the collected data;
- OF Calc, which supports data analysis and reporting across different sampling design approaches.

Earth Collection, which is part of Open Foris, is a tool that allows collect data using Google Earth software. Data collected through Collect Earth can exported to commonly used formats, and can export to Saiku, a tool that facilitates data analysis. Together with Google Earth, Bing Maps and Google Earth Engine, users can analyse high and very high-resolution satellite imagery for a variety of purposes, including [5]:

- collection of spatially explicit socio-economic data;
- checking existing maps;
- monitoring of agricultural lands and urban areas;
- land use assessment, land use change and forestry;
- supporting multiphase NFI;
- quantitative assessment of deforestation, reforestation and desertification.

This project is already a powerful tool. However, we also found a project "Monitoring the trees condition using drones" that is at the stage of creation, in addition to domestic [14,22,23,25]. Its essence is to create a system for monitoring the condition of trees using drones. Accordingly, since the system will automatic, there will algorithms and models of machine learning. The project itself offers hope, because unlike Open Foris, it uses drones, which will provide automatic information collection, while the previously considered option requires manual data entry. Drones also provide a wider opportunity: coverage of a large area, the ability to work in urban areas, they are cheaper to maintain than other aircraft and others. Since this project is open [14,22,23,25], we decided to join its creation, namely the part concerning the creation of a model that will classify trees according to the taken measurements.

3   Materials and Methods

There are many different Machine Learning algorithms for satisfy the problem. Among them are the following:

- algorithm k-NN - k nearest neighbours [15];
- decision trees [3].

The KNN algorithm assumes that such things exist in the immediate vicinity [15]. KNN captures the idea of similarity by calculating the distance between points. KNN algorithm [3, 15, 30]:

1. Upload data;
2. Initialize K to the number of neighbours you selected;
3. For each example in the data;
   a. Calculate the distance between the query example and the current example from the data;
   b. Add the distance and index of the example to the ordered collection;
4. Sort an ordered collection of distances and indicators from smallest to largest (in ascending order) by distance;
5. Select the first K records from the sorted collection;
6. Get the labels of the selected K records;
7. If regression, return the average value of the K marks;
8. If classification, return the K label mode.

For select the K that matches data, should run the KNN algorithm several times with different K values and select K, which reduces the number of errors encounter while maintaining the algorithm's ability to make accurate predictions when given data that it does not seen before. Here are some things to keep in mind [3, 15, 30]:

- if reduce the value of K to one then predictions become less stable;
- conversely, as K increases, predictions become more stable due to voting/voting averaging, and thus are more likely to make more accurate predictions (until a certain point). Eventually must start to see more and more mistakes. It is at this point that know that have pushed the value of K too far;
- in cases where accept the majority of votes (for example, the choice of mode in the classification problem) among the labels, usually make K an odd number to have an interrupt.

KNN algorithm disadvantage: this algorithm becomes much slower as the number of examples and/or predicted/independent variables increases. KNN algorithm advantages [3, 15, 30]:

- the algorithm is universal. It can use for search, regression and classification;
- do not need to create a model, adjust several parameters or make additional assumptions;
- the algorithm is easy and simple to implement.

Decision trees are a method that is suitable not only for solving classification problems but also for calculations, and is therefore widely used in the fields of finance, business and medicine. Because of applying this method to the training data sample, a hierarchical structure of classification rules such as "IF ...,

THAT ..." is created, which looks like a tree. To decide which class an object or situation belongs to, we answer the questions that are at the top of this tree, starting from its root. If the answer is positive, then we go to the left vertex of the next level, if negative - to the right vertex; then we again answer the question related to the corresponding vertex. In this way, we reach one of the end vertices, a leaflet, which contains an indication of which class the object being analysed should assigned. The advantages of this method are that such a representation of the rules is clear and easy to understand [3].

The popularity of the approach is associated not only with the clarity and clarity of the presentation, but also with the ease of implementation. The disadvantage of this method is that decision trees are fundamentally incapable of finding "better" rules in the data. However, using them, you can more or less accurately classify the object depending on the number of known features. Decision trees can considered as the most efficient structured data warehouse. As proven in graph theory, binary tree search is the most efficient search algorithm available.

The decision tree is the most powerful and popular tool for classification and forecasting [3, 9, 17, 18, 28, 30]. The decision tree is a tree-type structure, where each internal node represents an attribute test, each branch is a test result, and each leaf node (end node) contains a class label. The tree can "taught" by dividing the set of sources into subsets based on a test of attribute values. This process is repeated on each subset in a recursive manner, called a recursive division. Recursion ends when all subsets in the node have the same value of the target variable or when splitting no longer add value to the predictions. Building a decision tree classifier does not require any domain knowledge or parameter settings, and is therefore suitable for intelligence knowledge. Solution trees can process large data. In general, the decision tree classifier has good accuracy. Decision tree induction is a typical inductive approach to mastering classification knowledge. Decision trees classify specimens by sorting them by tree from root to some leaf node, which provides specimen classification. An instance is classified starting at the root node of the tree, testing the attribute defined by that node, and then moving down the branch of the tree that corresponds to the value of the attribute, as shown in the figure above. This process is repeated for under a tree rooted in a new node. Strengths of the decision trees [3, 9, 17, 18, 28, 30]:

- provide clear information about which fields are most important for forecasting or classification;
- it is able to handle both continuous and categorical variables;
- perform classification without requiring large calculations;
- it is able to generate clear rules.

Weaknesses of decision trees are [3, 9, 17, 18, 28, 30]:

- prone to errors in classification problems with many classes and a relatively small number of learning examples;
- less suitable for evaluation tasks when the goal is to predict the value of a continuous attribute;

– learning can be computationally expensive. The process of growing a decision tree is computationally expensive. At each node, each candidate partition field must sort before its best split can found. Some algorithms use combinations of fields and you should look for the optimal combination of weights. Trimming algorithms can also be expensive, as need to create and compare many candidates.

Today there are a large number of algorithms for implement the decision trees construction. Which the following are the most widely used and popular [3, 9, 17, 18, 28, 30]:

– C4.5 is an algorithm for constructing a decision tree with an unlimited number of descendants at the top, developed by R. Quinlan (Fig. 1); not suitable for working with a continuous target field, so it solves only the classification problem [29].

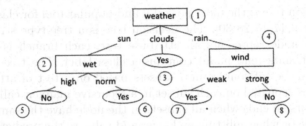

Fig. 1. Solution tree for step 5 of C4.5 algorithm execution.

– CART (Classification and Regression Tree) -is an algorithm developed by L. Breiman (Fig. 2); is an algorithm for constructing a binary decision tree - a dichotomous classification model; each apex of a tree at splitting has only two descendants; as its name implies, the algorithm solves the problems of both classification and regression [10].

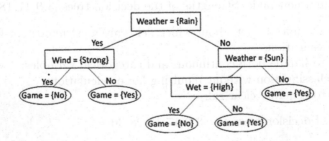

Fig. 2. Decision tree in the 3rd stage of execution of CART algorithm.

- QUEST (Quick, Unbiased, Efficient Statistical Trees) is an algorithm developed by Wei-Yin Loh and Yu-Shan Shih, which uses improved variants of the method of recursive quadratic discriminate analysis, which allows to realize multidimensional branching of linear combinations of ordinal predicates; contains a number of new tools to increase the reliability and efficiency of the induction tree [21].

4   Experiment

The system analyses the obtained environmental data and creates forecasts based on the obtained data on what type of tree should grow in the area. The main processes that the system will perform [11,14,19,27]:

- Model training on database data.
- Obtaining data for analysis.
- Tree type forecasting.
- Generating and sending reports.

The best way to describe system requirements is RUP:

Standard precedent scenario RUP:

1. Stakeholders of the precedent and their requirements:
   - Researcher: wants to get the result of the model forecast.
   - Drone: collects data and transmits it to the system.
   - Database: provides data for model learning and gets the result of the system to update its own data.
2. User PS (main actor) is a researcher who receives the results of automated system analysis.
3. Prerequisites for precedent: the drone takes a picture of the environment of a certain area.
4. The main successful scenario:
   - The system starts training the mathematical model of machine learning on the data available in the database.
   - The drone provides measurements taken from the environment of a certain area into the system.
   - The system transmits data to the model.
   - The model creates a forecast and returns the result to the system.
   - The system sends the result to the database to update the data in the database.
   - The system generates a record and adds it to the general report.
   - The system sends a report to the researcher.
5. Baseline extensions or alternate threads:
   - The researcher chooses not to generate a report, but to send each value.
   - The system starts training the mathematical model of machine learning on the data available in the database.
   - The drone provides measurements taken from the environment of a certain area into the system.

508   V. Kiyko et al.

- The system transmits data to the model.
- The model creates a forecast and returns it to the system.
- The system sends the result to the database to update the data in the database.
- The system generates a record.
- The system sends the record to the researcher.

6. Post-conditions:
   - Forecast data are stored in a common database for further analysis;
   - The researcher receives a report on the analysis and forecasts.
7. Special SR:
   - The system must be connected to the drone system;
   - Need to ensure the security of data transmission;
   - Need to ensure a constant reliable connection with the database with training data.
8. List of necessary technologies and additional devices:
   - The aircraft should be developed as an additional system to assist the drone system that collects site measurements;
   - Database with data on trees and the environment and conditions of their stay in nature.

   The functional purpose of the system is best assessed using a use cases diagram (Fig. 3). This diagram shows the main and alternative scenarios for using the designed system. The main actors are "Drone", "Database" and "Researcher". The "drone" provides data for forecasting and analysis, and the "researcher" receives the result of this system forecast, the "Database" provides data for training and receives new measured data for storage. First, the database provides data for training the forecasting model.

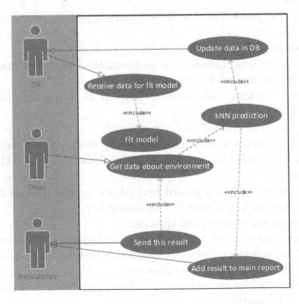

Fig. 3. Use case diagram.

This is information about trees and their living conditions in nature. Then the model is trained. At that time, the Drone analyses the area and sends the data to the system for further forecasting. The system processes the input data and passes it to the model to create a forecast. The created forecast is brought to the reporting form, and is sent to the database and the researcher. The next step is create an activity diagram; it is essentially a description of the behaviour in the form of an activity graph (Fig. 4).

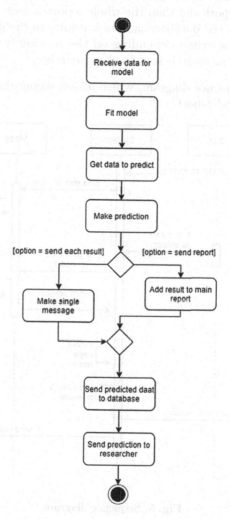

Fig. 4. Activity diagram

It depicts the following activities [12, 16, 24, 26, 31, 32]:

1. Get data for model training: the system receives data from the database to train the forecasting model.

2. Teach the model: the model is trained based on the obtained data.
3. Get data for research: the drone provides taken measurements to create a forecast for a specific area.
4. Form a prediction of the result: with the help of the model and the obtained data a forecast is formed.
5. Next, depending on the selected option:
   - Formation of a single message - 1 result is formed.
   - Adding the result to the general report - a specific forecast is attached to the general report and then the whole report is sent.
6. Send the result to the database: add new results to the database.
7. Send result to researcher: depending on the previously generated result, a report or a single message is sent to the researcher.

The Fig. 5 shows sequence diagram, which allows seeing the components interaction in the temporal aspect.

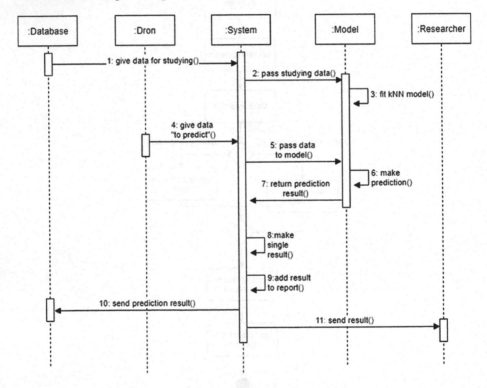

Fig. 5. Sequence diagram

:Database provides data for training, :system transfers this data to :Model for training.

Then the system waits until :Drone will provide data for research. System transmits this data to :Model, where :model generates a forecast by a given machine learning algorithm. Next :Model returns the result to the system.

:System processes the return value, and generates a single report or adds an entry to the overall report. After that :System sends data to :Database to store the results of forecasts and sends a report to :Researcher.

:Model learns at system start-up and exists as long as :System exists.

The last diagram is the deployment diagram (Fig. 6).

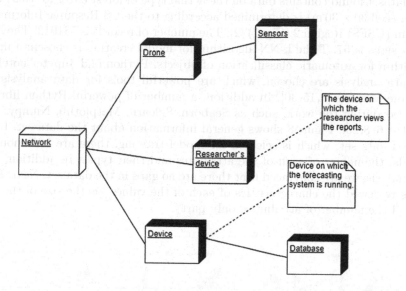

Fig. 6. Deployment diagram

The deployment diagram shows five processors and one device. Processors:

1. Device - it runs a program, can on a personal computer, the following connections: Network and Database nodes.
2. Researcher device is devices for data perception by the researcher. Has a connection to the Network node.
3. Database - a processor that contains a program database. The device is connected to a node.
4. A drone is an unmanned aerial vehicle that will scan an area.
5. Sensors - are located on the drone and collect measurements from the environment.

Device — Network is a closed network through which data is sent between the drone and the device, and the device and the researcher's device connects to Drone, Explorer Device, and Device.

5   Results

5.1   Data for Training

The dataset found contains data on the actual type of forest cover for this observation (cell 30 × 30 m) is determined according to the US Resource Information System (USFS) Region 2 (Fig. 7) [2]. The number of records is 581012. The number of signs is 57. TThe k-NN algorithm for model creation is chosen: a metric algorithm for automatic classification of objects. Python and Jupyter notebook for data analysis are chosen, which are powerful tools for data analysis and machine learning [3,15,30]. In addition, a number of powerful Python libraries are used during the work, such as Seaborn, Sklearn, Matplotlib, Numpy, Pandas [1,4,6–8,20]. Figure 8 shows general information about the data set. In the studied data set, which is selected for model training, there are 581 thousand records, the names of each of the attributes and their types. In addition, after the analysis, we are convinced that there are no gaps in the data set. Next, Fig. 9 shows reviewed the characteristics of each of the values (as the size of the data set and the number of attributes, only part).

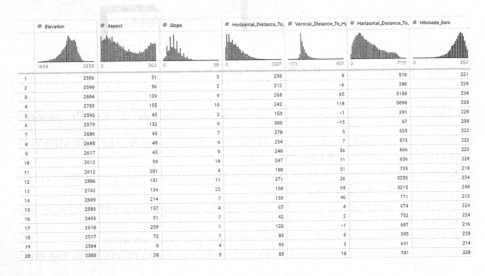

Fig. 7. Part of dataset

```
Data columns (total 55 columns):
 #   Column                              Non-Null Count     Dtype
---  ------                              --------------     -----
 0   Elevation                           581012 non-null    int64
 1   Aspect                              581012 non-null    int64
 2   Slope                               581012 non-null    int64
 3   Horizontal_Distance_To_Hydrology    581012 non-null    int64
 4   Vertical_Distance_To_Hydrology      581012 non-null    int64
 5   Horizontal_Distance_To_Roadways     581012 non-null    int64
 6   Hillshade_9am                       581012 non-null    int64
 7   Hillshade_Noon                      581012 non-null    int64
 8   Hillshade_3pm                       581012 non-null    int64
 9   Horizontal_Distance_To_Fire_Points  581012 non-null    int64
10   Wilderness_Area1                    581012 non-null    int64
11   Wilderness_Area2                    581012 non-null    int64
12   Wilderness_Area3                    581012 non-null    int64
13   Wilderness_Area4                    581012 non-null    int64
14   Soil_Type1                          581012 non-null    int64
15   Soil_Type2                          581012 non-null    int64
16   Soil_Type3                          581012 non-null    int64
17   Soil_Type4                          581012 non-null    int64
18   Soil_Type5                          581012 non-null    int64
19   Soil_Type6                          581012 non-null    int64
20   Soil_Type7                          581012 non-null    int64
21   Soil_Type8                          581012 non-null    int64
22   Soil_Type9                          581012 non-null    int64
23   Soil_Type10                         581012 non-null    int64
24   Soil_Type11                         581012 non-null    int64
25   Soil_Type12                         581012 non-null    int64
26   Soil_Type13                         581012 non-null    int64
27   Soil_Type14                         581012 non-null    int64
28   Soil_Type15                         581012 non-null    int64
```

Fig. 8. Data information

```
data.describe()
```

	Elevation	Aspect	Slope	Horizontal_Distance_To_Hydrology	Vertical_Distance_To_Hydrology	Horizontal_Distance_To_Roadways	Hills
count	581012.000000	581012.000000	581012.000000	581012.000000	581012.000000	581012.000000	581(
mean	2959.365301	155.656807	14.103704	269.428217	46.418855	2350.146611	:
std	279.984734	111.913721	7.488242	212.549356	58.295232	1559.254870	
min	1859.000000	0.000000	0.000000	0.000000	-173.000000	0.000000	
25%	2809.000000	58.000000	9.000000	108.000000	7.000000	1106.000000	
50%	2996.000000	127.000000	13.000000	218.000000	30.000000	1997.000000	:
75%	3163.000000	260.000000	18.000000	384.000000	69.000000	3328.000000	:
max	3858.000000	360.000000	66.000000	1397.000000	601.000000	7117.000000	:

Fig. 9. Data description

5.2 Data Analysis and Model Creation

Figure 10 shows results after checking the asymmetry coefficient for each attributes - the numerical characteristic of the probability distribution of the actual random variable (the asymmetry coefficient for the normal distribution is close to 0). Negative values indicate that the attribute value is asymmetric to

Skewness of the below features:

Feature	Value	Feature	Value
Elevation	-0.817596	Soil_Type15	440.078023
Aspect	0.402628	Soil_Type16	14.185489
Slope	0.789273	Soil_Type17	12.914877
Horizontal_Distance_To_Hydrology	1.140437	Soil_Type18	17.405794
Vertical_Distance_To_Hydrology	1.790250	Soil_Type19	11.895466
Horizontal_Distance_To_Roadways	0.713679	Soil_Type20	7.730948
Hillshade_9am	-1.181147	Soil_Type21	26.274260
Hillshade_Noon	-1.063056	Soil_Type22	3.804032
Hillshade_3pm	-0.277053	Soil_Type23	2.677848
Horizontal_Distance_To_Fire_Points	1.288644	Soil_Type24	4.933954
Wilderness_Area1	0.205618	Soil_Type25	34.968140
Wilderness_Area2	4.061595	Soil_Type26	14.880229
Wilderness_Area3	0.257822	Soil_Type27	23.065265
Wilderness_Area4	3.575561	Soil_Type28	24.722103
Soil_Type1	13.736670	Soil_Type29	1.512910
Soil_Type2	8.615358	Soil_Type30	4.038910
Soil_Type3	10.838630	Soil_Type31	4.436636
Soil_Type4	6.625176	Soil_Type32	2.856975
Soil_Type5	18.995243	Soil_Type33	3.154625
Soil_Type6	9.240061	Soil_Type34	18.911839
Soil_Type7	74.367173	Soil_Type35	17.442936
Soil_Type8	56.946415	Soil_Type36	69.853269
Soil_Type9	22.440005	Soil_Type37	44.121596
Soil_Type10	3.855317	Soil_Type38	5.859748
Soil_Type11	6.621186	Soil_Type39	6.253684
Soil_Type12	4.054662	Soil_Type40	7.963478
Soil_Type13	5.510281	Cover_Type	2.276574
Soil_Type14	31.096237		

Fig. 10. Skewness of the features

the left (the left part of the graph is longer than the right), and positive, respectively, indicate that the value of the attribute is asymmetric right). Some values are significantly asymmetric (strongly deviate from 0). It is easier to depict it on a graph in Fig. 11.

Next, the ratio of the number of trees by class is reviewed (in digital representation and in the form of a graph) show in Fig. 12.

As can see from the results, the most common type in the study area is type 2 and type 1 (Lodz pine and spruce), the least common is Willow. After that, checked the distribution of data by attributes (visually look at the reliability of the asymmetry search results) show in Fig. 13.

As can see visually from the graphs, the results of the calculations look valid.

Next, reviewed the distribution of classes by attributes, using the scope chart to represent. Here are just a few shows in Fig. 14.

As can see from the graphs, some properties do not have much difference depending on the class. However, there are those that are well distributed, such as Elevation. Next, reviewed the number of trees for the binary data set: soil type and territory show in Fig. 15.

From the given graphs, it is possible to tell, how many trees of each of types according to value of the territory and soil are in a data set.

Then it created a correlation matrix show in Fig. 16.

As can see from the matrix, a high relationship is observed between the values of Hillshade_3pm and Hillshade_9am, Aspect and Hillshade_3pm, Horizontal_distance_to_hidrology and Vertical_distance_to_hidrology and others.

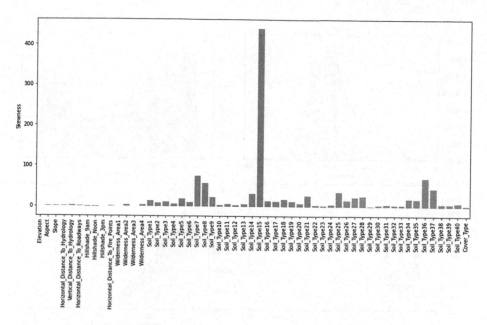

Fig. 11. Graphic representation of Fig. 10

Cover_Type 1
36.46 %
Cover_Type 2
48.76 %
Cover_Type 3
6.15 %
Cover_Type 4
0.47 %
Cover_Type 5
1.63 %
Cover_Type 6
2.99 %
Cover_Type 7
3.53 %

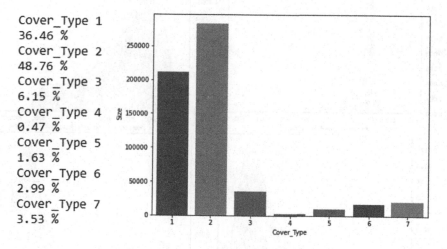

Fig. 12. Distribution of records in a set on classes

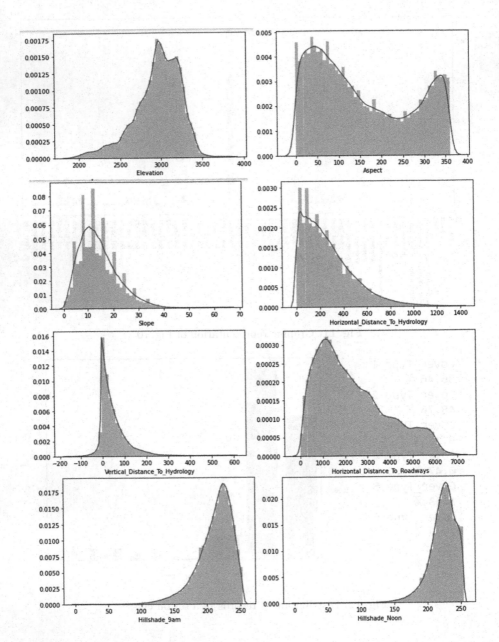

Fig. 13. Distribution of data in the set by attributes.

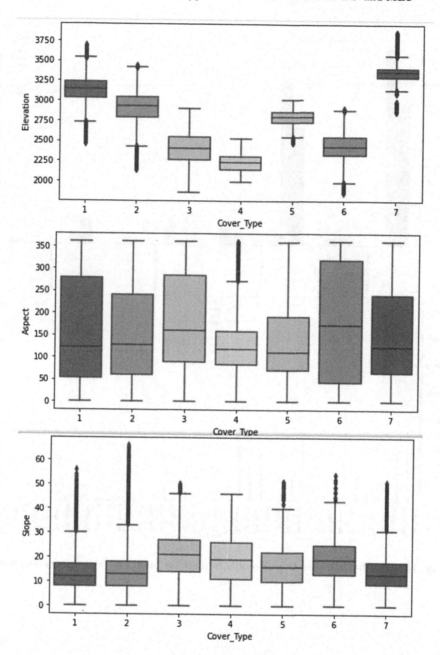

Fig. 14. Distribution of data in the set by classes

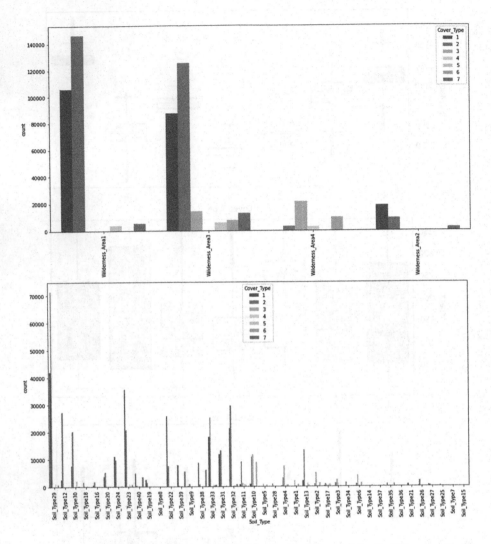

Fig. 15. Distribution of to-those records in a set on binary data (territory and soil)

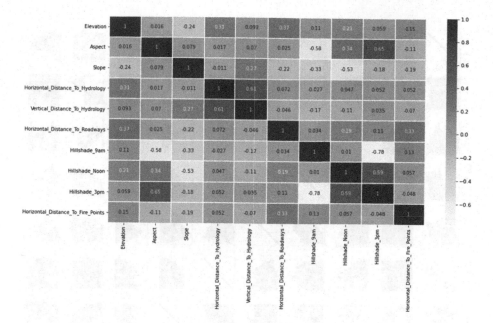

Fig. 16. Correlation matrix

6   Discussions

After analysing the data (Fig. 17), began to build a model. The algorithm that is chosen to work with the data is kNN.

Therefore, first, reviewed the results of the model with different parameters of k-neighbours. The CPU time of the Intel Core i3-3000 and 8 GB of RAM on my PC show Fig. 18.

For display the results for different k, derived the following graph of the accuracy of the results on the number of k show in Fig. 19.

After that, using $k = 5$ conducted training on the training sample and derived the results in the confusion matrix show in Fig. 20.

Correctly, classified data instances are placed diagonally. The accuracy of the trained model is 96.6%. Correctly, classified data instances are placed diagonally. Convinced of the adequacy of the sample and the high accuracy of the k-NN algorithm on the current data type, began to implement the program. Since further integration with the drone system, which will provide and measure information for analysis, is envisaged, the software implementation should look like a module to a part of the measurement system. However, to demonstrate now the work of this module, in the process of performing the work will created a minimalist graphical interface with the ability to enter data. Python is chosen for the development of the system, so the Flask library was chosen for presentation - a micro framework for web applications. It is not demanding on

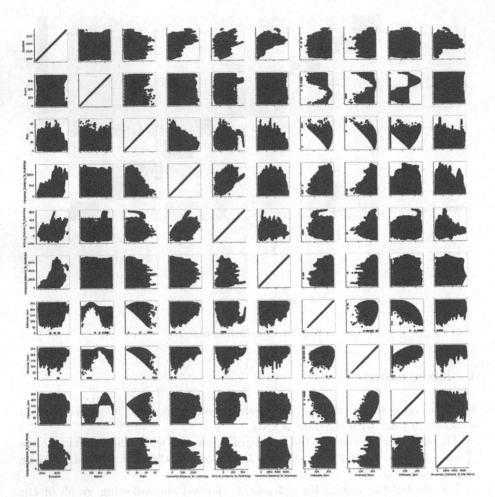

Fig. 17. Analysing the data in correlation matrix.

Wall time: 9min 48s

Fig. 18. Search k time

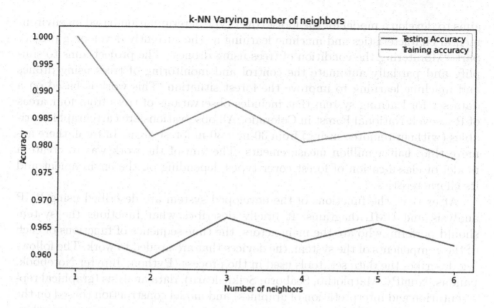

Fig. 19. The accuracy ratio depending on k

Predicted / True	1	2	3	4	5	6	7	All
1	61175	2007	4	0	26	7	180	63399
2	1789	82794	127	1	183	90	9	84993
3	3	128	10483	42	10	156	0	10822
4	0	3	129	640	0	57	0	829
5	29	292	31	0	2510	8	0	2870
6	3	139	214	23	7	4863	0	5249
7	175	30	0	0	2	0	5935	6142
All	63174	85393	10988	706	2738	5181	6124	174304

Fig. 20. Confusion matrix

the device, because it uses a web browser to display. Unlike PyQt5, which is processor demanding and consumes many resources and the same Django.

7   Conclusion

This article briefly describes the global problem of monitoring the situation of trees in nature, the role of trees in human life and the planet, their impact on nature; the main problems caused by deforestation are highlighted. This work aims to develop a model for the forest cover type determination based on environmental characteristics and machine learning as the currently developing project part "Monitoring the condition of trees using drones'. The project aims to simplify and partially automate the control and monitoring of trees using drones and machine learning to improve the forest situation. This work is based on a data set for learning system that includes observations of trees from four areas of Roosevelt National Forest in Colorado. All observations are cartographic variables (without remote sensing) from 30-m × 30-m forest areas. In total, there are more than half a million measurements. The aim of the work was to create a model of classification of forest cover types depending on the environment and its characteristics.

After that, the functions of the developed system are described using RUP analysis and UML diagrams. It briefly describes what functions the system should perform, who are the main actors, the time sequence of functions of each of the components of the system, the devices that are needed to work. The following describes the data set, tools used in the process (Python, Jupyter Notebook, pandas, NumPy, Matplotlib, Seaborn, Scikit-learn), data analysis (graphical representation and interpretation of graphics) and model construction (based on the training sample), which was taught by the selected machine learning algorithm. At the end of the article, the results of testing the trained model with part of the data that are selected for testing, and the construction of a matrix of errors and finding the accuracy of the model. Accuracy is 96.6%, which is a high figure. Correctly, classified data instances are placed diagonally. Convinced of the adequacy of the sample and the high accuracy of the k-NN algorithm on the current data type, began to implement the program. Since further integration with the drone system, which will provide and measure information for analysis, is envisaged, the software implementation should look like a module to a part of the measurement system. However, to demonstrate now the work of this module, in the process of performing the work will created a minimalist graphical interface with the ability to enter data. Therefore, the main system will able to compare the existing values/characteristics with the predicted ones (which tree should be there normally) to find discrepancies. Eventually, the main system will be able to use this information to report and inform relevant staff and authorities.

References

1. Choosing Python or R for Data Analysis? An Infographic. https://www.datacamp.com/community/tutorials/r-or-python-for-data-analysis
2. Covertype Data Set. UCI Machine Learning Repository. https://archive.ics.uci.edu/ml/datasets/Covertype
3. Decision Tree. https://www.geeksforgeeks.org/decision-tree/?ref=lbp
4. R Packages. https://rstudio.com/products/rpackages/
5. The state of the world's forests. http://www.fao.org/state-of-forests/en/
6. Top 10 python libraries for machine learning. https://light-it.net/blog/top-10-python-libraries-for-machine-learning/

7. Babichev, S., Korobchynskyi, M., Mieshkov, S., Korchomnyi, O.: An effectiveness evaluation of information technology of gene expression profiles processing for gene networks reconstruction. Int. J. Intell. Syst. Appl. **10**(7), 1–10 (2018). https://doi.org/10.5815/ijisa.2018.07.01

8. Babichev, S., Škvor, J., Fišer, J., Lytvynenko, V.: Technology of gene expression profiles filtering based on wavelet analysis. Int. J. Intell. Syst. Appl. **10**, 1–7 (2018). https://doi.org/10.5815/ijisa.2018.04.01

9. Bădulescu, L.A.: Data mining classification experiments with decision trees over the forest covertype data-base. In: 2017 21st International Conference on System Theory, Control and Computing (ICSTCC), pp. 236–241 (2017). https://doi.org/10.1109/ICSTCC.2017.8107040

10. Breiman, L., Friedman, J., Olshen, R., Stone, C.J.: Classification and Regression Trees (1983). https://doi.org/10.2307/2530946

11. Chatterjee, S., Ghosh, S., Dawn, S., Hore, S., Dey, N.: Forest type classification: a hybrid NN-GA model based approach. In: Satapathy, S.C., Mandal, J.K., Udgata, S.K., Bhateja, V. (eds.) Information Systems Design and Intelligent Applications. AISC, vol. 435, pp. 227–236. Springer, New Delhi (2016). https://doi.org/10.1007/978-81-322-2757-1_23

12. Cheng, K., Wang, J.: Forest type classification based on integrated spectral-spatial-temporal features and random forest algorithm - a case study in the Qinling mountains. Forests **10**(7), Article no. 559 (2019). https://doi.org/10.3390/f10070559

13. Derouin, S.: Deforestation: facts, causes & effects. https://www.livescience.com/27692-deforestation.html

14. Dmytriv, A., Vysotska, V., Kravets, P., Karpov, I., Emmerich, M.: Trees' condition data analysis based on drone monitoring and machine learning technology. In: CEUR Workshop Proceedings, vol. 2631, pp. 433–456 (2020)

15. Harrison, O.: Machine learning basics with the k-nearest neighbors algorithm. https://towardsdatascience.com/machine-learning-basics-with-the-k-nearest-neighbors-algorithm-6a6e71d01761

16. Hassan, M.M., Smith, A.C., Walker, K., Rahman, M.K., Southworth, J.: Rohingya refugee crisis and forest cover change in Teknaf, Bangladesh. Remote Sens. **10**(5), Article no. 689 (2018). https://doi.org/10.3390/rs10050689

17. Jiang, X., Lin, M., Zhao, J.: Woodland cover change assessment using decision trees, support vector machines and artificial neural networks classification algorithms. In: 2011 Fourth International Conference on Intelligent Computation Technology and Automation, vol. 2, pp. 312–315 (2011). https://doi.org/10.1109/ICICTA.2011.363

18. Kishore, R.R., Narayan, S.S., Lal, S., Rashid, M.A.: Comparative accuracy of different classification algorithms for forest cover type prediction. In: 2016 3rd Asia-Pacific World Congress on Computer Science and Engineering (APWC on CSE), pp. 116–123 (2016). https://doi.org/10.1109/APWC-on-CSE.2016.029

19. Li, M., Im, J., Beier, C.: Machine learning approaches for forest classification and change analysis using multi-temporal Landsat TM images over Huntington Wildlife Forest. GISci. Remote Sens. **50**(4), 361–384 (2013). https://doi.org/10.1080/15481603.2013.819161

20. Lipyanina, H., Sachenko, A., Lendyuk, T., Nadvynychny, S., Grodskyi, S.: Decision tree based targeting model of customer interaction with business page. In: CEUR Workshop, Proceedings of the Third International Workshop on Computer Modeling and Intelligent Systems (CMIS-2020), Zaporizhzhia, Ukraine, pp. 1001–1012 (2020)

21. Loh, W.Y., Shih, Y.S.: Split selection methods for classification trees. Statistica sinica (1997). http://www3.stat.sinica.edu.tw/statistica/oldpdf/A7n41.pdf

22. Lytvyn, V., et al.: Conceptual model of information system for drone monitoring of trees' condition. In: CEUR Workshop Proceedings, vol. 2604, pp. 695–714 (2020)

23. Lytvyn, V., Kowalska-Styczen, A., Peleshko, D., Rak, T., Voloshyn, V., Noennig, J.R., Vysotska, V., Nykolyshyn, L., Pryshchepa, H.: Aviation aircraft planning system project development. In: Shakhovska, N., Medykovskyy, M.O. (eds.) CSIT 2019. AISC, vol. 1080, pp. 315–348. Springer, Cham (2020). https://doi.org/10.1007/978-3-030-33695-0_23

24. Maxwell, A.E., Warner, T.A., Fang, F.: Implementation of machine-learning classification in remote sensing: an applied review. Int. J. Remote Sens. 39(9), 2784–2817 (2018). https://doi.org/10.1080/01431161.2018.1433343

25. Peleshko, D., Rak, T., Lytvyn, V., Vysotska, V., Noennig, J.: Drone monitoring system DROMOS of urban environmental dynamics. In: CEUR Workshop Proceedings, vol. 2565, pp. 178–191 (2020)

26. Pham, B.T., Khosravi, K., Prakash, I.: Application and comparison of decision tree-based machine learning methods in landside susceptibility assessment at Pauri Garhwal Area, Uttarakhand, India. Environ. Process. 4(3), 711–730 (2017). https://doi.org/10.1007/s40710-017-0248-5

27. Pham, B.T., Shirzadi, A., Bui, D.T., Prakash, I., Dholakia, M.B.: A hybrid machine learning ensemble approach based on a radial basis function neural network and rotation forest for landslide susceptibility modeling: a case study in the Himalayan area, India. Int. J. Sediment Res. 33(2), 157–170 (2018). https://doi.org/10.1016/j.ijsrc.2017.09.008

28. Qian, Y., Zhou, W., Yan, J., Li, W., Han, L.: Comparing machine learning classifiers for object-based land cover classification using very high resolution imagery. Remote Sens. 7(1), 153–168 (2015). https://doi.org/10.3990/2.376

29. Salzberg, S.L.: C4.5: programs for machine learning by J. Ross Quinlan. Mach. Learn. 16, 235–240 (1994). https://doi.org/10.1007/BF00993309

30. Thanh Noi, P., Kappas, M.: Comparison of random forest, k-nearest neighbor, and support vector machine classifiers for land cover classification using Sentinel-2 imagery. Sensors 18(1), Article no. 18 (2018). https://doi.org/10.3390/s18010018

31. Tien Bui, D., et al.: Land subsidence susceptibility mapping in South Korea using machine learning algorithms. Sensors 18(8), Article no. 2464 (2018). https://doi.org/10.3390/s18082464

32. Wu, Q., Zhong, R., Zhao, W., Fu, H., Song, K.: A comparison of pixel-based decision tree and object-based Support Vector Machine methods for land-cover classification based on aerial images and airborne lidar data. Int. J. Remote Sens. 38(23), 7176–7195 (2017). https://doi.org/10.1080/01431161.2017.1371864

Approach for Modeling Search Web-Services Based on Color Petri Nets

Aleksandr Gozhyj[1]([⊠])(iD), Irina Kalinina[1](iD), Victor Gozhyj[1](iD),
and Valeriy Danilov[2](iD)

[1] Petro Mohyla Black Sea National University, Nikolaev, Ukraine
alex.gozhyj@gmail.com, irina.kalinina1612@gmail.com, gozhyi.v@gmail.com
[2] National Technical University of Ukraine "Igor Sikorsky Kyiv Polytechnic
Institute", Kyiv, Ukraine
danilov1950@gmail.com

Abstract. The article discusses issues related to the construction and implementation of search web services. Algebra for modeling and building web services is presented. As the basic operations for algebra are used: sequence, alternative selection and cycle. In addition, combined operations are determined based on the basic ones. The operations were chosen to provide a general and extended set of operations for the implementation of web search services. After defining each construction, the formal semantics of the operator is given in terms of Petri nets. An example of modeling and development of a real estate web-service in the CPN Tools. The indexes of efficiency of the developed service.

Keywords: Search web service · Algebra · Basic operations · Combined operations · Interaction of web services · Petri nets

1 Introduction

Current trends in data processing and the development of search engines on the Internet are focused on combining data from different sources to provide new functionality for information retrieval. This creates a demand for methods of collecting and transforming data in the framework of solving specific problems. Currently, various methods of building search engines are used. One of the methods is using web services. Developers use Service Oriented Architecture (SOA) Web services [2] as building blocks for loosely coupled, distributed information gathering applications. The tasks of collecting and transforming information are called data aggregation [14].

In fact, a modern web service is created by combining various web services and their components to create a component service that offers a set of new functional services. This process is called web service composition [16]. More sophisticated applications where users can query and filter content of interest include RDF distributed search engines, indexed system services, or service providers that offer financial, demographic, and other business data, usually measured by query count or analytic.

S. Babichev et al. (Eds.): DSMP 2020, CCIS 1158, pp. 525–538, 2020.
https://doi.org/10.1007/978-3-030-61656-4_35

The main modern concept that has arisen from the processing of services for finding the necessary information is mashup-technologies [2]. These are applications that combine data from one or more existing (external) sources in order to create a new service with new functionality. When building search web services, the most critical is the interaction of web services and their components with each other, which requires a detailed formal description of the processes of functioning and research and modeling of their behavior. In this context, algebra is proposed for modeling the interaction of web services and their components based on Petri nets, as well as their modifications [1,3,4,6,7,13,15,17]. This allows for the formal description and modeling of complex compositions of web services.

Problem Statement. The purpose of this work is to research and develop a model approach for building search web services. It is necessary to investigate the operations of service algebra to build models of interaction between web services and their components in the tasks of information aggregation. And also to investigate the construction of models and the effectiveness of web search services based on Petri nets and their modifications.

2   Materials and Methods

2.1   Formally Description Aggregated Search Service

Formally description aggregated search service based interaction basic web-service is as follows:

$$SS = \langle Din, Q, WS, OI, InWS, Dout, T \rangle, \tag{1}$$

where, $Din = \{din_i | i = \overline{1, N_{Din}}\}$ is a set of input data; $Q = \{q_i | i = \overline{1, N_Q}\}$ is a set of queries; $WS = \{ws_i | i = \overline{1, N_{WS}}\}$ – a set of basic web services; OI – a set of basic operations of interaction of web services; $InWS = \{inws_i | i = \overline{1, N_{InWS}}\}$ – a set of rules for interaction between web services; $Dout = \{dout_i | i = \overline{1, N_{Dout}}\}$ – a set of output data; $T = \{t_i | i = \overline{1, N_T}\}$ – a set of temporal indicators of interaction between elements of the search engine; $SS = \{ss_i | i = \overline{1, N_{SS}}\}$ is a set of output characteristics of the aggregated search service operation.

When developing a search service taking into account the dynamic interaction of web services, an important process is to determine the composition of basic operations in the interaction of OI web services, as well as a set of rules for the interaction of $InWS$ web services. From the composition of the basic operations of the interaction of web services OI, a certain subset of those operations and the rules of interaction of web services are distinguished, on the basis of which the model of aggregation of web services will be formed, which is described by a certain scheme S.

When considering the interaction of web services in the development of search services, various mathematical models of interaction between web services are used [1,6,7,12]. To determine the type of mathematical model, it is necessary to solve the following problems:

- Selection of a set of models of web services that are most effective for solving the problems of constructing models of dynamic interaction of web services under given search conditions.
- Selection of a set of operations from the list of basic or combined ones to create models of search web services.
- Combining models into a single system for solving problems of dynamic interaction of web services during development, for the task of a multi-criteria search web service.
- Inter-model agreement in the search web-service.

In these models, the main aspects are taken into account when solving problems related to the construction of effective search web services and the selection of mathematical models, namely: determining the set of web services and determining the structure of the web service, taking into account the dynamics of information change, taking into account the main uncertainties when building the structure web service. The developed model of a search dynamic web service makes it possible to describe a web service and use it in the process of building other web services to store data about the structure of a web service.

To solve these problems, a model approach has been developed based on an algebraic-logical description of the rules for the functioning of a web service.

A model approach for solving the problems of dynamic interaction of web services consists of the following stages:

Stage 1. Preliminary determination of the structure of the WSx web service, which is put in accordance with the set of acceptable solutions $WSx_{S\beta}$, the mathematical model M_ν, within which the structure of the web service x is found:

$$M_\nu = \langle WSx \in WSx_{S\beta}, f_j(x) \rangle, j \in J_\nu,$$

where, $f_j(x)$ is a criterion that takes values in a certain measurement scale and by which service x is evaluated; $j \in J_\nu$ is the set of indices of elements of the set of criteria of the ν-th model; ν is the model number. In general, each service is evaluated according to one or more metrics within one or more models.

Stage 2. Presentation of the problem of model selection of efficient service structures. Formalization is carried out as follows:

$$WSt^M = \langle M, \left\{ r_i^{M(\alpha)} \right\}, \left\{ r_i^{M(\beta)} \right\} \rangle, i \in N^M,$$

where, M is a set of models within which the structure is determined when developing a web service, $r_i^{M(\alpha)}$ are binary relations defined on the set of elements of a service model, $r_i^{M(\beta)}$ is a relation that sets constraints overlaid on the model selection. The result of the choice in the mathematical structure WSt^M is an element M^*, that is, a subset of $M : M^* = \{m_\nu\}_{\nu \in J^*} \subseteq M$, where J^* is the set of indices of elements of the set M^*.

Stage 3. Distribution of indicators for assessing quality and efficiency. Distribution by models is represented as a mathematical structure of choice:

$$WSt^X = \langle X^{M^*}, \left\{ r_i^{X(\alpha)} \right\}, \left\{ r_i^{X(\beta)} \right\} \rangle, i \in N^X,$$

where, X is the set of indicators by which the quality is assessed, $r_i^{X(\alpha)}$ is the ratio reflecting the choice in the distribution of indicators by models, for example, the minimum number of indicators for each model, duplication of indicators in different models, $r_i^{X(\beta)}$ – a relation that sets constraints (completeness of accounting for all indicators in a complex of models, the impossibility of representing certain indicators in a particular model, the impossibility of optimizing a certain model, etc.)

The result of the choice in the structure WSt^X is a set of tuples of the form $\langle m^*, X_{m^*} \rangle$, which assigns a set of quality indicators to each model. Combining sets of quality indicators X_{m^*} for all models $m^* \subset M^*$.

Stage 4. Inter-model agreement. The union of the set M^* into a single service is represented as the following selection structure:

$$WSt^\pi = \left\langle M^*, \pi, \left\{ r_i^{\pi(\alpha)} \right\}, \left\{ r_i^{\pi(\beta)} \right\} \right\rangle, i \in N^\pi,$$

where, π is the set of possible principles of model matching for combining service models with M^* into a single service.

Stage 5. Building models of effective service. The problem of constructing models of an effective service provides for solving selection problems in the structures WSt^M, WSt^X, WSt^π. Formally, this problem is presented in the form of the following structure:

$$WSt = \left\langle WSt^M, WSt^X, WSt^\pi, \left\{ r_i^\beta \right\} \right\rangle,$$

where through r_i^β indicated by the relationships that limit the choice of effective solutions in development of dynamic web-services.

2.2 Modeling the Interaction of Web-Services

Based on the presented approach to describing the interactions of web services, an algebraic system was created to describe the interaction of basic and composite services when creating aggregating web systems, and on their basis hierarchical models of web services for various purposes were built in the *CPN Tools* environment.

The basis for this was the algebra of services [7]. The basic constructions for algebra are: sequence, alternative and iteration. In addition, combined constructs, parallelism, arbitrary sequence, discriminator and dynamic selection are defined [1,6]. The designs were chosen to provide a general and extended set of operations for a combination of web services. After the definition of each construction in Tables 1, 2 a mathematical description and formal semantics of the operator are given in terms of Petri nets. In Fig. 1 is a graphical representation of options for combinations of web service models.

Modeling the Interaction of Web Services When Building a Combined Service. For the joint use of basic and combined operations of the algebra of

Table 1. Combined constructions of web-service interaction operators. (Part 1.)

	Designation of the service	Description of the service	Mathematical description
1.	Iterative sequence $Loop(Seq(WS_1, WS_2))$	The *iterative sequence* operator simulates the execution of a combined service that is executed a certain number of times. As a combined service is meant to perform two service operations WS_1 and WS_2 sequentially	$Loop(Seq(WS_1, WS_2)) =$ $= (NameWs, Desc, Loc, URL,$ $CS, SN)$, where $- NameWs -$ is the name of the new service; $- Desc$ a description of the new service; $- Loc -$ is the location of the new service; $- URL -$ is a call to a new service; $- CS = WS_1 \cup WS_2;$ $- SN = (P, T, W, i, o, l),$ where $P = P_1 \cup P_2 \cup \{i, o\},$ $T = T_1 \cup T_2 \cup \{st_1, t_{in}, t_{out}, t_{loop}\},$ $W = W_1 \cup W_2 \cup \{(i, t_{in}), (t_{in}, i_1),$ $(o_1, st_1), (st_1, i_2), (o_2, t_{out}), (t_{out}, o),$ $(o_2, t_{loop}), (t_{loop}, i_1)\},$ and $l = l_1 \cup l_2 \cup \{(st_1, \tau), (t_{in}, \tau),$ $(t_{out}, \tau), (t_{loop}, \tau)\}$
2.	Iterative arbitrary sequence $Loop(ArbSeq(WS_1, WS_2))$	Operator *iterative sequence of arbitrary execution* models combined service that performs two services WS_1 and WS_2 random, but performs a number of times. If the service WS_1 is executed first, then the service WS_2 is executed. And if the service WS_2 is executed first, then the service WS_1 is executed after it	$Loop(ArbSeq(WS_1, WS_2)) =$ $= (NameWs, Desc, Loc, URL,$ $CS, SN)$, where $- NameWs -$ is the name of the new service; $- Desc$ a description of the new service; $- Loc -$ is the location of the new service; $- URL -$ is a call to a new service; $- CS = WS_1 \cup WS_2;$ $- SN = (P, T, W, i, o, l),$ where $P = P_1 \cup P_2 \cup \{i, o, p_{in}, p_{mult},$ $p_1, p_2, p_3, p_4, p_5\},$ $T = T_1 \cup T_2 \cup \{t_{in}, t_{out}, t_{loop}, st_1,$ $st_2, st_3, st_4, st_5, st_6\},$ $W = W_1 \cup W_2 \cup \{(i, t_{in}), (t_{in}, p_{in}),$ $(p_{in}, st_1), (st_1, p_1), (st_1, p_2), (st_1, p_3),$ $(p_1, st_2), (p_2, st_2), (p_2, st_5), (p_2, st_3)\},$ $(p_3, st_3), (st_2, i_1), (st_3, i_2), (o_1, st_4),$ $(st_4, p_2), (st_4, p_4), (p_4, st_5), (o_2, st_6),$ $(st_6, p_2), (st_6, p_5), (p_5, st_5),$ $(st_5, p_{mult}), (p_{mult}, t_{out}), (t_{out}, o),$ $(p_{mult}, t_{loop}), (t_{loop}, p_{in}),$ and $l = l_1 \cup l_2 \cup \{(st_1, \tau), (st_2, \tau),$ $(st_3, \tau), (st_4, \tau), (st_5, \tau), (st_6, \tau),$ $(t_{in}, \tau), (t_{out}, \tau), (t_{loop}, \tau)\}$

Table 2. Combined constructions of web-service interaction operators. (Part 2.)

	Designation of the service	Description of the service	Mathematical description
3.	Iterative selection $Loop(Choice(WS_1, WS_2))$	*Iterative selection* operator - is a combined service that performs a certain number of times the task of the service WS_1, or service WS_2. If one of the services is selected, then the other service is not considered	$Loop(Choice(WS_1, WS_2)) =$ $= (NameWs, Desc, Loc, URL,$ $CS, SN)$, where $- NameWs -$ is the name of the new service; $- Desc$ a description of the new service; $- Loc -$ is the location of the new service; $- URL -$ is a call to a new service; $- CS = WS_1 \cup WS_2;$ $- SN = (P, T, W, i, o, l)$, where $P = P_1 \cup P_2 \cup \{i, o, p_{in}, p_{out},$ $p_1, p_2, p_3, p_4, p_5\},$ $T = T_1 \cup T_2 \cup \{t_{in}, t_{out}, t_{loop},$ $st_1, st_2, st_3, st_4\},$ $W = W_1 \cup W_2 \cup \{(i, t_{in}), (t_{in}, p_{in}),$ $(p_{in}, st_1), (p_{in}, st_2), (st_1, i_1), (st_2, i_2),$ $(o_1, st_3), (o_2, st_4), (st_3, p_{out}),$ $(st_4, p_{out}), (p_{out}, t_{out}), (t_{out}, o),$ $(p_{out}, t_{loop}), t_{loop}p_{in})\}$, and $l = l_1 \cup l_2 \cup \{(st_1, \tau), (st_2, \tau),$ $(st_3, \tau), (st_4, \tau), (t_{in}, \tau), (t_{out}, \tau),$ $(t_{loop}, \tau)\},$
4.	Iterative dynamic selection $Loop(WS_1(p_1, q_1): : WS_n(p_n, q_n))$	The *iterative dynamic selection* operator simulates the execution of a combined service, which is performed a certain number of times and each time allows you to choose the best service provider among several competing providers	$Loop(WS_1(p_1, q_1): WS_n(p_n, q_n)) =$ $= (NameWs, Desc, Loc, URL,$ $CS, SN)$, where $- NameWs -$ is the name of the new service; $- Desc$ a description of the new service; $- Loc -$ is the location of the new service; $- URL -$ is a call to a new service; $- CS = \bigcup_{i=1}^{n} WS_i;$ $- SN = (P, T, W, i, o, l)$, where $P = \bigcup_{i=1}^{n} P_i \cup \{i, o, p, q, p_{in}, p_{out}\},$ $T = \bigcup_{i=1}^{n} T_i \cup \{t_{SendReqServ},$ $t_{SelectServ}, t_o, t_{in}, t_{out}, t_{loop}\} \cup$ $\cup \{t_i, t'_i | 1 < i < n\},$ $W = \bigcup_{i=1}^{n} W_i \cup \{(i, t_{in}), (t_{in}, p_{in}),$ $(p_{in}, t_{SendReqServ}), (p_{SelectServ}, p),$ $(q, t_o), (st_2, i_2), (t_o, p_{out}), (p_{out}, t_{out}),$ $(t_{out}, o), (p_{out}, t_{loop}), (t_{loop}, p_{in})\} \cup$ $\cup \{(t_{SendReqServ}, \tau), (q_i, t_{SelectServ}),$ $(p, t'_i), (t'_i, t_i), (o_i, t_i), (t_i, q)|$ $|1 < i < n\}$, and $l = \bigcup_{i=1}^{n} l_i \cup \{(t_{SendReqServ}, \tau),$ $(st_{SelectServ}, \tau), (t_o, \tau), (t_{in}, \tau),$ $(t_{out}, \tau), (t_{loop}, \tau)\} \cup \{(t_i, \tau), (t'_i, \tau)|$ $|1 < i < n\}$

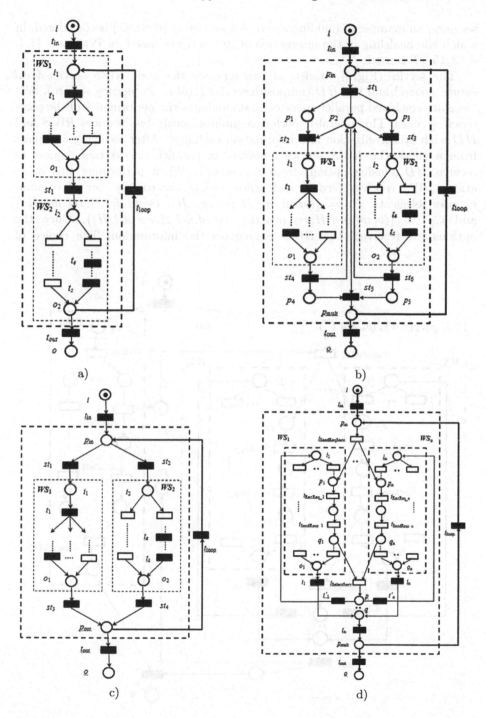

Fig. 1. Graphical representation of the combined design of operators of interaction of Web-services: a) iterative sequence, b) iterative arbitrary sequence, c) iterative selection, d) iterative dynamic selection.

services, an example of building a complex service (real estate) is considered, in which the modeling of the interaction of web services based on Petri nets [3,4, 7,13,15,17] is used.

The service (Fig. 2) consists of two services: the basic RWS service (*real estate service*) and the HD composite service (*real estate agency service*). Services are combined parallel operator that simulates the performance of the combined services. This operator performs simultaneously two services RWS and HD with synchronization and information exchange. After receiving a request from a client, the RWS service launches, in parallel, an external request to receive HD housing options from the service. When performing this operation, RWS receives Ord_H and sends Del_H accordingly. Set of communication elements: $C_1 = \{(send\_ord\_H, rec\_ord\_H), (send\_del\_H, rec\_del\_H)\}$ and $C_2 = \{(send\_ord\_H, rec\_ord\_H), (send\_del\_H, rec\_del\_H)\}$. Once the options are received, the RWS aggregates the information. The choice of

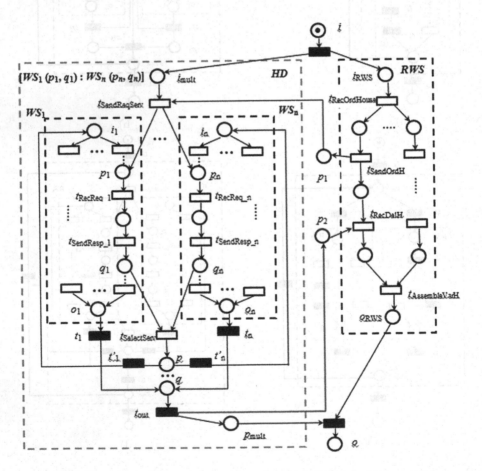

Fig. 2. Composite real estate service

housing can be dynamically obtained among several available services (for example,$WS_1...,WS_n$), which are services of various real estate agencies. Thus, replacing the service of one real estate agency with a dynamic selection structure allows the selection of the best service provider among several competing providers.

3   An Example of Building a Real Estate Service

As an example of building a service model for finding information, let's consider the process of a model for building a real estate service. The real estate web service is a software web system that organizes the provision of services for the selection of real estate options, insurance services, loan processing and payment for the selected real estate option. She works with a client via the Internet and makes it possible to find the necessary options for the best means in real estate agencies, place an order, use various services, pay for services, choose a means of payment and take out insurance.

3.1   Development of a Model of a Real Estate Web Service

Let's compose a formal description of a real estate web service using a combination of operators. At the top level of modeling for a real estate web service, the structure of the model is presented as:

$$Seq(Registering, Loop(Seq(EnerPrivateOffice, Seq(HDWS,$$
$$Choice(FWS, Seq(IWS, FWS))))))).$$

The structure of models for each external web service, which is included in the aggregated real estate web service, is presented in a similar way.

Let's represent the service model as a hierarchical Petri net. In Fig. 3 shows the main page of the hierarchical Petri net, which reflects the main processes in the functioning of a real estate web service [5,8–11,18,19]. The system consists of six main processes: finding a web service, registering, searching for a list of offers, insurance service and payment for selected services, as well as a "Private Office". Each of the presented processes can function separately, for this it is necessary to divide the main processes into networks of the second level. When analyzing the state space of a hierarchical network, a state graph was built. There are no cycles in the system, but there are two dead-end markings. These markings are web service exit states, that is, they are considered shutdown states.

Since the networks of the second level (*Registering, IWS, FWS, Enter PrivateOffice, HDWS*) are subsystems, they can be analyzed separately from the main network.

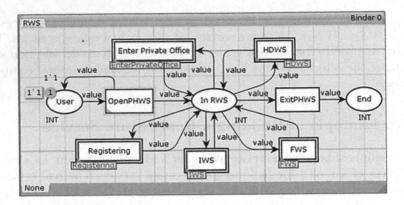

Fig. 3. The main page of the hierarchical Petri network of a real estate web service

The state space for this network looks like this:

$$V = \{m_1(1,0,0), m_2(0,1,0), m_3(0,0,1)\}$$
$$E = \{(m_1, SetFilters, m_2), (m_2, FindHousing, m_3),$$
$$(m_3, ReceiveSpecialOffers, m_3), (m_3, GetScheduleInspection, m_3),$$
$$(m_3, GetPriceList, m_3), (m_3, GetLocation, m_3),$$
$$(m_3, PageHousingToRWS, m_1)\}.$$

Analysis of the state space reveals the presence of three vertices and seven arcs with the network marking, the absence of loops, dead-end markings and the possibility of being implemented for all transitions.

The similarity of the results for all second-level nets makes it possible to simplify the Petri net. The positions of each second-level network are replaced by a single analogous entrance to the second-level network in the main network. For a simplified Petri net of a real estate web service, a state graph was built. There are two dead-end markings on the network that are associated with the logout state. Thus, these errors are ignored, there is no looping in the network, all transitions are triggered. Figure 4 shows a general view of the site of a real estate web service, which reflects links to resources, or web services that perform the main functions of a web system.

3.2   Building a Model of a Real Estate Web Service Using Interaction Operators

Let's present a model of an aggregated web service of real estate services by combining several types of interaction operators. The model is built on the basis of algebraic services and the basic model of a combined web service. Real estate web service (RWS) has the ability to collect information from several real estate agencies, in the form of a list of proposals. The real estate agency web service models interact with the dynamic selection operator

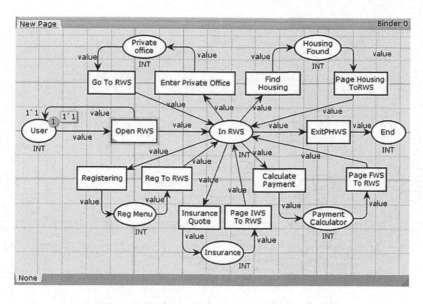

Fig. 4. Petri network of a real estate web service

$([WS_1(p_1, q_1) : WS_3(p_3, q_3)])$ because the agency web services $(WS_1, WS_2,$ and $WS_3)$ compete to complete the customer order. The web service of real estate services fulfills a complex request from the client, therefore it works in parallel with the web services of real estate agencies. But RWS has information exchange with them, and when building a model of interaction between two combined services, a parallel communication operator is used $([WS_1(p_1, q_1) : WS_3(p_3, q_3)]\|_C RWS)$. The simulation model of the real estate service (Fig. 2) implemented in CPN $Tools$ is shown in Fig. 5.

3.3 Analysis of Performance Indicators of a Real Estate Web Service

To assess the quality of the web service, we analyzed information about the operation of the web service, created using a model approach, in comparison with popular web services for real estate. The data for the analysis was information from independent sources: *Sitechecker*, *Similarweb* and *Google Analyitics* services. The following indicators were analyzed: download speed (resource: *Sitechecker*), time spent on page visits, number of pages viewed, average bounce rate (resources: *Similarweb, Google Analyitics*) and performance indicators on the Internet, such as: first display of all content, speed index, time to full service interaction, first significant reflection, overall resource speed (resource: *Similarweb*).

The analysis of performance indicators, when creating a real estate service is shown in Fig. 6, 7 shows content download speed metrics for services.

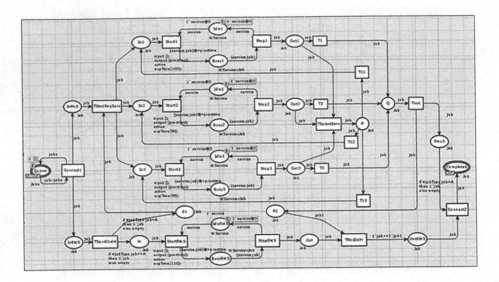

Fig. 5. Model combined the real estate service

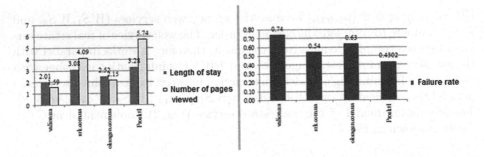

Fig. 6. Qualitative indicators for real estate services

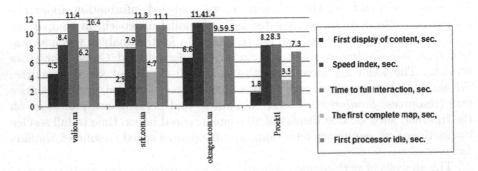

Fig. 7. Performance indicators

4   Discussion and Conclusions

The presented approach for the design of search web services based on service algebra and dynamic models of interaction between web services has the following features. The proposed algebra checks the closure property. This ensures that each result of a service operation is a service to which algebraic operators can be reapplied. And it allows you to build more complex and combined services by aggregating and reusing existing services through declarative service algebra expressions. To build complex interactions of web services, it is necessary to use constructions with wider functionality. They are designed with combined operations to perform iterative procedures. This will expand the functionality of search web services and develop web-systems with smart search elements.

The work presented a model approach for building search web services. The approach is based on the application of specialized algebra to the construction of search services. The semantics of the presented algebra can be used to prove the algebraic properties of web service constructions. This might be the case when creating a search web service by combining existing web services using algebra operators. Algebraic properties can then be used to transform and optimize the combined web services based on the following web service operational metrics such as cost and duration. The use of service algebra with the presented set of operations makes it possible to use it to model color Petri nets for search web services.

To create search web services, a system of models was built in *CPN Tools* of the first and second levels. Simulation modeling and research of the developed models were carried out. The models made it possible to study in detail the interaction of search services and their components, as well as to increase the efficiency and speed of web systems.

References

1. Chemaa, S., Bachtarzi, F., Chaoui, A.: A high-level Petri net based approach for modeling and composition of web services. Procedia Comput. Sci. **2012**(9), 469–478 (2012). International Conference on Computational Science, ICCS
2. Erl, T.: "SOA principles of Service Design. (The Pearson Service Technology Series from Thomas Erl), 1st edn. Prentice Hall (2007)
3. Feng, X., Liu, Q., Wang, Z.: A web service composition modeling and evaluation method used Petri net. In: Proceedings of the APWeb Workshops, pp. 905–911 (2006)
4. Genrich, H.J., Lautenbach, K.: System modeling with high level Petri nets. Theor. Comput. Sci. **13**, 109–136 (1981)
5. Gozhyj, A., Kalinina, I., Gozhyj, V.: Fuzzy cognitive analysis and modeling of water quality. In: 9th IEEE International Conference on Intelligent Data Acquisition and Advanced Computing Systems: Technology and Applications (IDAACS), Bucharest, pp. 289–294 (2017). https://doi.org/10.1109/IDAACS.2017.8095092

6. Gozhyj, A., Kalinina, I., Gozhyj, V., Vysotska, V.: Web service interaction modeling with colored Petri nets. In: 10th IEEE International Conference on Intelligent Data Acquisition and Advanced Computing Systems: Technology and Applications (IDAACS), Metz, pp. 319–323 (2019). https://doi.org/10.1109/IDAACS.2019.8924400

7. Hamadi, R., Benatallah, B.: A Petri net based-model for web service composition. In: Proceedings the 14th Australasian Database Conference, Adelaide, pp. 191–200. Australian Computer Society, Darlinghurst (2003)

8. Jensen, K.: Coloured Petri nets: a high level language for system design and analysis. In: Jensen, K., Rozenberg, G. (eds.) High-level Petri Nets, pp. 44–119. Springer, Heidelberg (1991). https://doi.org/10.1007/978-3-642-84524-6_2

9. Kang, H., Yang, X., Yuan, S.: Modeling and verification of web services composition based on CPN. In: 2007 IFIP International Conference on Network and Parallel Computing-Workshops, pp. 613–617. IEEE Computer Society Press (2007)

10. Kharchenko, V., Sachenko, A., Kochan, V., Fesenko, H.: Reliability and survivability models of integrated drone-based systems for post emergency monitoring of NPPs. In: Proceedings of the International Conference on Information and Digital Technologies (IDT 2016), Rzeszow, Poland, pp. 127–132 (2016)

11. Lars, M., Kristiansen, S.C., Jensen, K.: The practitioner's guide to colored Petri nets. Int. J. Softw. Tools Technol. Transfer **2**, 98–132 (1998). https://doi.org/10.1007/s100090050021

12. Liu, Z., Ranganathan, A., Riabov, A.: Modeling web services using semantic graph transformations to aid automatic composition. In: IEEE International Conference on Web Services (ICWS 2007), Salt Lake City, Utah, 13–19 July (2007)

13. Murata, T.: Petri nets: properties, analysis and applications. In: Proceedings of the IEEE, vol. 77, pp. 541–580 (1989). https://doi.org/10.1109/5.24143

14. Papazoglou, M.P.: Service-oriented computing, "concepts, characteristics and directions". In: Proceedings of the 4th International Conference on Web Information Systems Engineering (Wise 2003), pp. 3–12 (2003). https://doi.org/10.1109/WISE.2003.1254461

15. Petri, C.A.: Kommunikation mit automaten. Ph.D. dissertation. University of Bonn, Germany (1962). (in German)

16. Schuster, H., Georgakopoulos, D., Cichocki, A., Baker, D.: Modeling and composing service-based and reference process-based multi-enterprise processes. In: Wangler, B., Bergman, L. (eds.) CAiSE 2000. LNCS, vol. 1789, pp. 247–263. Springer, Heidelberg (2000). https://doi.org/10.1007/3-540-45140-4_17

17. Tan, Z., Lin, C., Yin, H., Hong, Y., Zhu, G.: Approximate performance analysis of web services flow using stochastic Petri net. In: Jin, H., Pan, Y., Xiao, N., Sun, J. (eds.) GCC 2004. LNCS, vol. 3251, pp. 193–200. Springer, Heidelberg (2004). https://doi.org/10.1007/978-3-540-30208-7_31

18. Yang, Y., Tan, Q., Xiao, Y.: Verifying web services composition based on hierarchical colored Petri nets. In: Proceedings of the First International Workshop on Interoperability of Heterogeneous Information Systems IHIS 2005, New York, NY, USA, pp. 47–54 (2005)

19. Zhang, Z., Hong, F., Xiao, H.: A colored Petri net-based model for web service composition. J. Shanghai Univ. (Engl. Ed.) **12**(4), 323–329 (2008). https://doi.org/10.1007/s11741-008-0409-2

Intelligence Information Technologies for Financial Data Processing in Risk Management

Nataliia Kuznietsova$^{(\boxtimes)}$ and Peter Bidyuk

Institute for Applied System Analysis of the National Technical University of Ukraine "Igor Sikorsky Kyiv Polytechnic Institute", Kyiv, Ukraine
natalia-kpi@ukr.net, pbidyuke_00@ukr.net

Abstract. The paper describes advanced information technology created on the basis of system methodology which uses methods and models of dynamic, probabilistic and statistical, regression assessment of financial risks, combined methods and models for missing and lost data recovery, methods of structural-parametric adaptation. Information technology is implemented in the form of client-server architecture, microservices and clouds. The main tasks in financial data analysis are research of the financial processes volatility and financial risk assessment. Proposed IT is flexible and adaptable from a practical point of view to both tasks and allows to include only the necessary resources and blocks with optimal use of the server and to integrate in the existing information system of the functioning enterprise (at the expense of the developed microservices which are connected to system if necessary, and implementing separate functions). In the paper the main stages and means for creating new information technologies for financial processes forecasting based on different regression models and dynamic financial risks modeling are discussed.

Keywords: Information technology · Decision support system · Business intelligence system · Systemic methodology · Financial data analysis · Risk management

1 Introduction

Fast changing and quick moving of the social world need new solutions and modern business technologies for evaluating important indicators and values, determining trends and waves which are not only determined by one sphere but could be also influenced by another areas, processes, companies and countries, economics and world fluctuations. Necessity of systems' finance risk assessment, financial processes' prediction and their development greatly increases. Today, financial institutions use a wide variety of software products for data analysis. These are the most famous foreign systems SAS, SAP, SPSS as well as their own

© Springer Nature Switzerland AG 2020
S. Babichev et al. (Eds.): DSMP 2020, CCIS 1158, pp. 539–558, 2020.
https://doi.org/10.1007/978-3-030-61656-4_36

developments of analysts and programmers [4,7,13,17,18]. Most of these products use the methods of logistic regression, neural networks, decision trees, fuzzy sets, Bayesian networks etc. The research analytical company Gartner [3] annually publishes reports on the situation on the information technology market, using two linearly progressive expert scales: completeness of vision and ability to execute.

Modern business intelligence (BI) platforms [4,6,15,17,18] are characterized by easy-to-use tools that support a complete analytical workflow: from data preparation and input to visual research and decision generation. They differ most from traditional BI platforms in that they do not require significant involvement of IT specialists in predefined data models or storage in traditional data warehouses. The emphasis is on self-service and speed [19]. Most modern analytics and BI platforms also have their own stand-alone memory, which provides fast performance and prototyping, but it is also possible to use existing simulated data sources. Streaming and logical data require modern analytical processing, and therefore there is a huge need for BI-platforms that can process less formalized data. Companies developing traditional BI platforms have developed their capabilities for modern data analysis based on the visual basis, which also includes data management and advanced analytics [19,22]. New companies continue to develop capabilities that previously focused on processing speed, expanding them to provide better management and scalability, as well as sharing. Advanced analytics includes machine learning, which generates an idea of the growing volumes of data, as well as natural language processing.

Therefore to describe correctly modern financial processes in the most important financial systems such as banking system, stock trading systems, market, macro-economy, and processes in insurance and investment companies the adequate models should be developed and used. They should take into account changes of financial parameters, previous states as well as disturbances that affect the states. Dynamic changes in financial and economic processes are characterized by their volatility that cannot be described by homogeneous models due to available abrupt changes in the market factors influencing the processes. At least two models are required to describe formally heteroskedastic processes (HP): a model for the process itself (amplitude model), and a model for describing dynamics of the process variance or volatility model [2,21]. As far as HPs are nonlinear according to existing definition very often the problem can be rather complicated. Both research directions are developed rapidly and it can be seen that every year new models are presented by researchers from many countries. While financial risks are unsystematic, and financial processes are nonlinear and non-stationary, so it is necessary to include into Information Technology (IT) and Information Decision Support System (IDSS) on its basis those modeling methods that allow to predict such financial processes and allow to construct the best models with minimal computational costs [13,20].

Existing financial systems significantly differ and may include different components, solve different business problems and perform different functions [9,11,14,21]. The modern information technology connects the main flows of interaction, roles, data and knowledge, determines the structure and choice of modules to solve specific set of problems. Ideal for financial systems is the information technology for integration into the existing ERP-system and therefore it is advisable to consider the technology as implementation of separate web applications for risk management and for its further imbedding.

The main objective of this research is to study the main types of possible informational technologies which are recommended for the use in modern financial systems and to find appropriate solution which provides a possibility for combining basic types of heteroskedastic models for volatility estimation of selected financial processes, dynamic risks assessment, and evaluation of the most significant indicators.

2   Background to Informational Technologies Requirements and Principles

It is important to adhere to the basic principles and requirements of DSS in general, to take into account the specific features of the complex being developed for financial systems. IDSS should comply with the basic principles of the systemic methodology and provide comprehensive, effective and adequate risk management, taking into account the specifics of financial activities [13], the need for dynamic risk estimating and forecasting [9], degree, profile and level of risk and be based on the following principles:

- *effectiveness* of financial systems risk management which allows to assess the degree and level of risk, the full range of measures to minimize losses, taking into account the criteria of quality risk management and the effectiveness of the applied set of risk management measures;
- *timeliness* assumes that IDSS should work in real time to ensure the features of identification, risk assessment at the initial stage and monitoring and timely application of precautionary measures;
- IDSS structure should consist of separate modules and applications that perform *non-duplicating functions*;
- *distribution of responsibilities* (separation of the monitoring function and decisions effectiveness evaluating from direct risk management) assumes ensuring functions distribution between individual users and providing limited authority to access and make decisions on data, criteria, models and alternative decisions [13];
- *comprehensiveness and complexity* involves the developed system should analyze, assess and monitor all types of risk (credit, financial, information, operational, currency etc.) from its detection to the application of anti-risk actions and evaluate the risk management system effectiveness;
- *functional compliance* or creating an effective risk management system, ensuring all stages of business processes in the financial system, compliance with these types of risk and processing them according to the described indicators (degree, level and time);

- *independence* from decision maker external factors and influences that may distort the results of the risk management system;
- *confidentiality* or security of personal data, compliance with legal requirements for the protection of personal or confidential information;
- *unambiguity and clarity* assumes providing results that can be interpreted only in a certain form, are clear and unambiguous for decision maker and management of the company, institution or bank;
- *transparency* is the ability to provide results for internal and external monitoring and audit of the system feasibility and effectiveness [13].

3   Online Data Processing in IT for FMCG

During the business activity a large number of various documents are collected and maintained by divisions and departments. These are sales statistics, invoices, reports, agreements with contractors, leasing agreements, services etc. The procedure of financial data analysis can be represented as a consequence of stages that summarize the main operations of financial data processing as it is shown on the Fig. 1. Complexity and accumulation of information depends on how large the company is and how much market share it occupies. For example, the company's initial sales to distributors or "key customers" (large retail chains such as Metro, Auchan) are presented in the form of large packages, boxes, which are often purchased for a month or more and for all stores at once. This is the total wholesale purchase of goods which under the contracts may contain a certain load and certain bonuses that means the mandatory purchase of a certain number of boxes, type of goods etc. [13].

All this statistical information is collected along with information from the "fields"—information from distributors, sales representatives, retail chains, markets on the volume of products sold in secondary markets. Information from the "fields" is the widespread terminology for sales, analytics, research activities and means that this information is received definitely from the final users, it contains data on real demand and gives more precise view on consumer preferences. This information is collected, for example, on a weekly basis and consolidated into a single database by region. At the end of each month it is possible to make conclusions about the implementation of the sales plan and adjust forecasts for future periods. For internal financial analysis, the volume of sold products can be presented in cash (UAH or foreign currency), to generate company reports, establish the profitability of the enterprise and adjust pricing policy for certain products. Also it makes sense to represent the volume of sales in units of supply (in boxes or packaging) which will allow to compare correctly sales in different periods. This information is sufficient for the initial analysis in the company, but it does not provide a deep understanding of causes and factors affecting fluctuations in goods demand, does not provide information on regional coverage, quantity of goods per capita and does not take into account regional and demographic factors.

For adequate analysis along with the established indicators and data, information should be collected on the population in the region, the level of sales

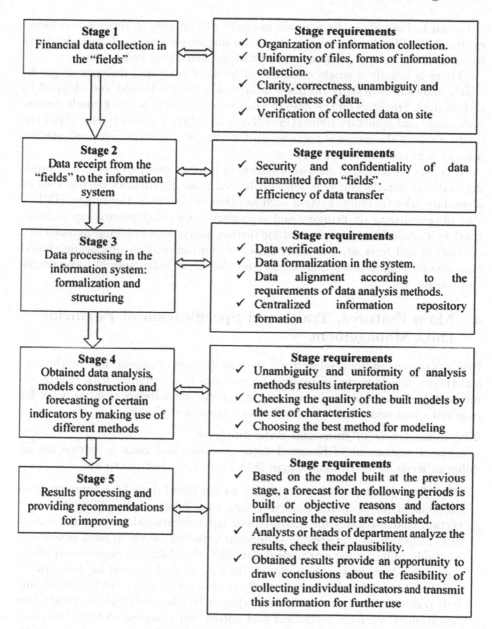

Fig. 1. Financial data collection, transformation and online analysis in large retail company

(ideally) or the number of competing products on the shelf etc. It will give the possibility not only forecast sales but also analyze how successful is the distributor, whether the marketing company is effective and how well the company is known in the region. As a result analysts will be able to provide a detailed explanation of hidden reserves existence for market saturation of these products (or even a certain type), the need for changing marketing policy, etc.

There is usually a single database of levels of sales and delivery of goods, which allows receive daily updated information on goods sold and shipped to distributors. Statistics on the level of sales are collected in units of goods (boxes, packaging) and monetary units (US dollars and UAH). For objectivity, given the fluctuations of the national currency in Ukraine, it is necessary to evaluate the data in boxes or US dollars [11].

It is possible to obtain such information by product groups, as well as by product code. In parallel, information is collected from distributors on the level of secondary sales (in online system such as Information Trade Technology (ITT)). The obtained data on primary and secondary sales using macros are summarized in a single file, which is used for further analysis and making dynamically evaluation and forecast. For other types of companies data processing should have similar stages and requirements and also needs some special technologies and means.

4   Main Features, Traits and Specification of Financial Data Management

Risk assessment in financial systems requires the use of appropriate mathematical theory, development of application methods in accordance with recognized international standards and the usage of appropriate software and hardware for required speed and relevance of indicators dynamic evaluation.

The main levels of financial data analysis

Consistent assessment of financial data, processes and risks is carried out at different levels, involves some stages (Fig. 2) from the bottom to up:

- *The first level* provides the ability to download data by importing from different file(s) (formats, sources), data consolidation, the ability to select certain characteristics for analysis and input additional information manually. Detection of statistically significant variables, usage of data processing methods, filling in gaps or missed data [10], the ability to process and eliminate redundant data, preparation of data for analysis should be done [13].
- At *the second level*, the data analysis of financial processes is carried out. It is possible visually evaluate data, identify trends, check the stationary and nonlinearity, perform statistical and correlation analysis, identify the most important variables that characterize the financial process and should be included in constructing the models based on data mining methods, integrated models and Bayesian networks.
- *The third level* provides a set of tools for creating different type candidate models, checking the models adequacy and the forecast quality.
- *The fourth level* implements the procedures of modeling financial risks, i.e. forecasting possible losses, the probability of risk or both parameters simultaneously on the basis of the best model chosen at the third level.

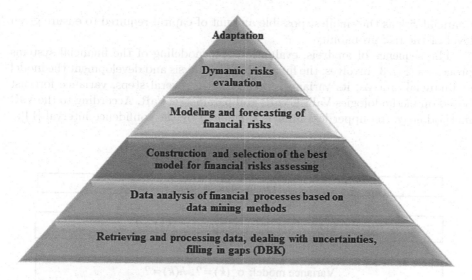

Fig. 2. Hierarchical levels of data analysis for financial enterprises

- *The fifth level* provides an opportunity to perform a dynamic risk assessment and to determine the moment of risks transition to higher level or degree based on the best dynamic model [10].
- *The sixth level* implements adaptation of the models or construction new models taking into account the received new data and knowledge, criteria, assessments [13].

Let's consider the basic methods and mathematical equations for the main financial indicators evaluation.

The method of financial risks assessment based on the probability calculations is inconvenient for usage from the financial manager point of view due to the fact that it determines the probability distribution of losses and doesn't perform a specific cost assessment of financial risk (FR). That's why for decision making it is better to give the interval for the probability and losses acceptable for financial enterprise. Usually different approaches are hired based on the causes and effects of deep analysis to perform risk management. Among known methods the Value-at-risk (VaR-method) is a method for financial risks estimating based on the analysis of the market statistical nature which offers a universal technique for assessing various types of risks (price, currency, credit and liquidity risk). VaR has become a widely accepted method of risk assessment among participants in the Western financial system and regulators. In fact, the VaR technique is currently used as the risk assessment standard [14]. Non-financial corporations can use VaR to assess cash flow risks and make hedging decisions (protecting capital from adverse price movements). The main advantages of the method are high accuracy of calculations, aggregation of separate positions risks into uniform size for the whole portfolio. The essence of the method is to determine the value of financial risk as the smallest possible amount of capital required to ensure given level of the risk probability.

The sequence of analysis, evaluation and modeling of the financial systems processes (Fig. 3) involves: the financial data analysis and development the model of financial process, its variance, forecasting in several steps, variance forecast based on methodologies VaR, CVaR, and parametric VaR. According to the VaR methodology, the upper loss limit is calculated by the confidence interval [14]:

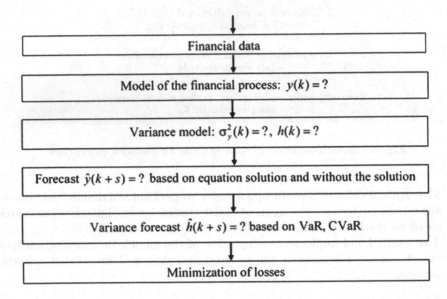

Financial data

Model of the financial process: $y(k) = ?$

Variance model: $\sigma_y^2(k) = ?$, $h(k) = ?$

Forecast $\hat{y}(k + s) = ?$ based on equation solution and without the solution

Variance forecast $\hat{h}(k + s) = ?$ based on VaR, CVaR

Minimization of losses

Fig. 3. Sequence of analysis, evaluation and modeling of the financial systems processes

$$P(Loss_t(k) < VaR_t(k)) = (100 - \alpha)\% \qquad (1)$$

where $Loss_t(k)$ are actual losses at the time t for the period of k days; VaR_t are projected losses at the period t of k days, α is confidence level.

Conditional Value at Risk (CVaR), also known as the expected deficit, determines the amount of risk or "tail thickness" for an investment portfolio. CVaR is calculated based on the weighted average value of "extreme" tail losses that exceed the VaR limit:

$$CVaR = E(X|X > VaR), \qquad (2)$$

that is

$$CVaR = \frac{1}{1 - c} \int\limits_{-1}^{VaR} xp(x)dx, \qquad (3)$$

where $p(x)$ is the density of the loss distribution; c is the cut-off point on the distribution set by the analyst as the VaR threshold; $\overline{VaR}$ is the agreed upper limit of VaR. The parametric VaR is computed as follows:

$$VaR = \alpha * \sigma * OP * \sqrt{N}, \tag{4}$$

where α is quantile of the confidence interval; σ is volatility (rate of variability); OP is the value of the open position; N is forecasting period.

The most interesting thing is that for enterprise it is needed to make such losses and probability of risk evaluation not once but actually continuously during business activities. It is important to do dynamically forecast of the main indicators as their absolute values but also their variance, to calculate the risk probability, to correct if needed appropriate models and obviously to modify decisions based on previous key indicators.

5 Client-Server Architecture for Data Processing and Financial Risks Assessment

Information technology and information decision support system for financial risk management are implemented in a three-level client-server architecture and involve obligatory set of applications, data and knowledge base server of specific financial system (DKB FS) and client parts (Fig. 4). Advanced IT includes in its applications the main methods and models, data mining methods implementation for analysis of non-stationary processes of arbitrary nature based on system analysis methods, provides and implements the possibility of financial risks hierarchical analysis, modeling and forecasting. IT takes into account structural, parametric and statistical uncertainties [13]. Some applications implement dynamic risk assessment, forecasting the time of risk transition from suitable (feasible) or acceptable to a critical or catastrophic level; adapting risk assessment and forecasting models to changes in processes and applying alternative assessment methods for finding better model structures using a variety of statistical quality criteria. Information technology ensures the successful implementation of the necessary functionality of the developed algorithms and methods in the form of separate software applications which are called when necessary and provide effective support for the financial company business activities.

Advanced information technology is available online 24 h per day for financial enterprise users through automated workstations (WS). To provide individual user groups with access only to the required applications (implementing methods, models or reporting), administrators install an application server, a financial system database and knowledge server (DKB FS), and a client application on a physical server, creating a computing environment for users. IT is also really useful for remote work while it gives the possibility for users with correctly installed configuration to receive access from their workstations with appropriate rules and requirements to the system security. If there is a group of servers, such environment on the cluster and virtualization technologies can be used [1, 5, 13].

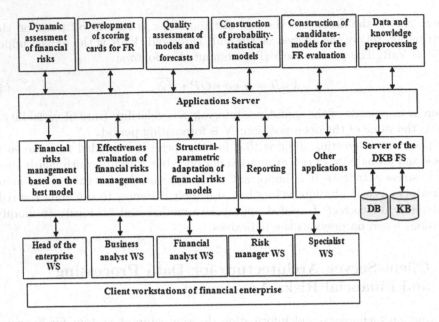

Fig. 4. Client-server architecture of advanced information technology for financial risk management

Knowledge and data base includes a database (DB) with information in the form of external and internal data, archived reports, statistical information about customers, goods and services, financial statements and more. The Knowledge Base (KB) contains regulatory documentation from national and international financial organizations on capital ratios, risk ratings etc.; legislative normative and regulatory acts for financial activity in the country; expert assessments obtained at the previous stage to implement the initial risk analysis, scenarios and algorithms of certain procedures.

In the proposed information technology based on the application server the following applications were implemented:

- preliminary processing of data and knowledge;
- development the set of candidate models for financial risk assessment;
- construction of probabilistic and statistical models for risk assessment;
- checking the models adequacy and assessing the quality of forecasts;
- development of the scoring cards for financial risk assessment;
- dynamic modeling of financial risks;
- risk management based on the best model and scoring card;
- assessing the effectiveness of financial risk management;
- structural and parametric adaptation of financial risk models;
- reporting;
- other applications.

The information technology can include as all the basic blocks shown in Fig. 4 in the applications and only some of them which are needed for a specific enterprise. The set of services and libraries that implement the most important and critical functions (basic functionality) forms the core of the application server. The peculiarity of the implementation is that one client can access on demand for many different applications, and different types of clients (respectively, different automated workstations have access to the same application, for example, with different levels of access [13]. Clients interact through the application server, sending requests and receiving answers and the necessary information from the DKB FS. For the physical design of the obtained data model, the database management system Microsoft SQL Server 2016 was chosen, which provides the construction of centralized databases using client-server technology, allows efficient organization of work with the same data to multiple users [13,16]. It is also possible to connect other applications in information technology and IDSS to perform additional functions.

6 Basic Architecture of the Information Decision Support System (IDSS)

Developed IDSS should provide decision maker with a full range of mechanisms for modeling, evaluation and forecasting of FR and criteria for assessing the quality of data and models, with the ability to respond adaptively to prevent and reduce financial risks taking into account new evidence, data and challenges in the modeling process [13]. IDSS architecture should be based on the principles of appropriate functionality, modularity, scalability, interactivity etc.

The decision support system generates a set of alternatives for making recommendations to the decision maker. IDSS should contain a set of functions and procedures for implementation of sufficient completeness of decisions. We formulate the following statement about the functional completeness of the developed IDSS.

The functional completeness of IDSS for risk management can be represented as follows:

$$IDSS = \{DKB, DP, IR(MS, MMP, FMP), RE(SRE, DRE, SC),$$
$$MR(DQ, MAQ, FQ, DE, SPA)\}, \quad (5)$$

It involves the implementation of the entire sequence of risk management procedures in the form of appropriate modules: identification, modeling, assessment and minimization of risks. Also it contains functions for data processing and accounting for uncertainties and other risks [11], static and dynamic risk assessment [9], forecasting the probabilities and consequences, building a scoring card as measures of risk, adaptation and verification of the quality and effectiveness of the proposed solutions. Here DKB is data and knowledge base; DP is a set of procedures and functions of preliminary preparation, consolidation and data processing using the proposed methods of filling in incomplete or lost data [10,12];

IR are risk identification procedures which involve development of the model that describes the change in risk, assessing its structure and parameters, forecasting the consequences and probability of risk. The procedures IR contain the following elements: MS are procedures for data preparation and evaluation of the mathematical model structure (for example, based on Bayesian networks); MMP is a unit for estimating the mathematical model parameters; FMP is a module for estimating losses forecasts (consequences) and the risk probability on the basis of the selected mathematical model. $RE(SRE, DRE, SC)$ are procedures for static SRE and dynamic DRE risk evaluation; construction the risk scoring cards SC. $MR(DQ, MAQ, FQ, DE, SPA)$ is the risk management application based on the criteria of adequacy of mathematical models MAQ, accuracy of forecasts FQ, efficiency of decisions DE and functions of structural-parametric adaptation of risk assessment models SPA.

Each module of IDSS represents its separate functional element which implements all set of procedures, functions and classes for integration with DKB, other modules and users. It is clear that IDSS must meet the general requirements for decision support systems [20]: contain modern databases, models, criteria and the necessary computational procedures. Also it should have a convenient and simple interface; the sequence of performance functions must correspond to human perception and representation. IDSS should accumulate knowledge and adapt in the process of its functioning; have the necessary speed of procedures and necessary accuracy; generate the forms and reports necessary for decision maker; provide interactive interaction with other users. Also it gives the possibility to exchange data and knowledge with other information processing systems using computer networks; able to add new procedures, functions and modules.

The extended IDSS architecture is quite complex and could be represented in understandable way as a set of applications presented in Fig. 5 as a set of sequentially combined modules, in particular:

- **Module for uncertainties processing** with such features:
  - the combined method of processing incomplete (lost and missed) data based on BN and regression models [10];
  - taking into account the information risk associated with inaccuracy, untimeliness, inconsistency and inaccuracy of the information, incompleteness, unclearness of input data and knowledge [12].
- **The scoring card development module as a measure of risk** performs:
  - construction of scoring models based on data mining methods;
  - choosing the best model based on statistical criteria;
  - a scoring card construction and establishment of scoring points;
  - neuro-fuzzy method of supplementing data with rejected applications for scoring card developing.
- **The module for financial risks dynamic assessment** carries out:
  - construction the dynamic risk models for forecasting the risk level and degree;
  - calculation of the time of risk occurrence in the dynamic method based on the degree of risk (probability);

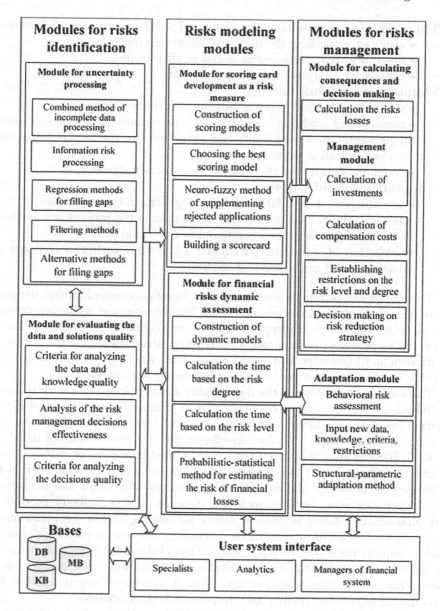

Fig. 5. Client-server architecture of advanced information technology for financial risk management

- determining the moment of risk on the basis of the risk level (acceptable, critical, catastrophic);
- probabilistic and statistical assessment of the financial losses risk (calculation the amount of losses and probabilities);

– **The module for evaluating the data and solutions quality**. It includes:
  - criteria for checking the data and knowledge quality;
  - analysis of risk management decisions effectiveness;
  - criteria for analyzing the decisions quality.
– **Management module** includes:
  - calculation the real losses of possible risk realization;
  - management modules: calculation the investments; compensatory losses for risks combat; setting limits and restrictions for the level of losses and the risk realization probability;
  - recommendations for choosing a risk reduction strategy.
– **Adaptation module** allows:
  - introduction of new data and knowledge, criteria, restrictions;
  - behavioral risk assessment (risk assessment in the process and verification of its degree and level compared to the initial state);
  - execution of structural-parametric adaptation with two contours of adaptation and use of rejected applications.

The system can be represented in different modifications and content depending on the needs of the financial enterprise. This architecture is the new type of system which reflects the concept of systemic methodology for analysis, assessment and management of financial risks. IDSS database consists of the database by its own and knowledge and model bases (MB) where the best models built to solve problems of static and dynamic risk assessment stores.

The module for evaluating the data quality and decisions related to the main modules is performed both at the stage of data transfer for modeling and initial verification of their quality, and at the stage of the quality of forecasts and models checking, testing the solutions effectiveness to reduce financial risks.

Each IDSS module is by itself the separate functional element, which implements the whole set of procedures, functions, classes for integration with databases of knowledge and models, other modules and users. The module of uncertainty processing includes such operations as data preliminary processing and consolidation, filling in gaps or recovering missing or lost data [12], information risks assessment, uncertainties processing. The scoring card development module implements statistical data analysis, model structure formation and scoring model parameters evaluation, construction the scoring cards, calculation of short-term and medium-term forecasts. Also it provides a special module for checking the input data quality and proposed solutions efficiency.

The dynamic risk assessment module is based on the use of several different types of dynamic models for risk assessment, choosing the best of them, and using algorithms for calculating the moment of risk on the basis of the degree and level of risk.

Modules for impact assessment and verification of the effectiveness of decisions allow identification of how good the risk management is carried out, and if necessary, refer to the adaptation module for improving the models quality and the effectiveness of decisions.

7   Implementation of Unformation Technology in the Form of Microservices

Based on the business requirements associated with the need for practical development and integration of the risk management information technology into existing decision support system, one can use the architecture of microservices. This approach assumes that each application is developed as a set of small services which work in their own processes and communicates with other services through data transmission protocols in computer networks, for example, with the protocol http [13]. Implementation of microservices allows to distribute separate business tasks between different developers teams, proceeding from needs of the company concerning time of tasks introduction and use (urgent, non-urgent), using the automated environment for their implementation, Processes will be parallel, therefore "easier" performing. It also greatly simplifies communication both within the application and with other applications, and there is almost no centralized management [1].

To develop own methods and approaches microservices are used and integrated into the existing system. The financial system continues to operate normally, the information system performs its normal functions. Microservices are added to the existing system upon completion of their development, providing additional features and capabilities to users as soon as possible rather than upon completion of all functions and applications simultaneously. Another key point is that financial companies operate in a fast-growing industry, and therefore need to focus and respond quickly to new challenges. Therefore, the need to "anticipate" new features, capabilities and applications for the system is quite relevant but also quite complex. Deployment of microservices and their integration with the main system is a simple and original solution that does not require stopping the existing financial processes functioning and it does not need to develop a new IDSS architecture [13]. Similarly, if you need to remove some functionality from the system with microservices, it is enough to remove the necessary microservice without having to rewrite the entire system. Microservices allow achieve architecture scalability thanks to repeated use of services in many copies, with use of various technologies and libraries. For example, for the services offered on R, which implemented the developed dynamic method and dynamic models, it is possible to integrate with already functioning services of existed information system created with Python [13,15]. For the purpose of standardization it is expedient to apply the same services and methods of development, programming languages. However, if the implemented algorithms already exist in other environments, it may be advisable to use them (at least in the early stages) to run additional features immediately.

8   Experiment Results and Discussion

Effectiveness of the mentioned approach could be shown on financial risks evaluation and forecasting (not only the absolutely value of indicators but also their variance). We proposed to use such idea in the information technology based on the microservices described above. In real enterprise we solve a variety of different tasks for online financial data processing and financial management. In this study we would like to illustrate one of the solved task such as the financial stability forecast based on the enterprise financial statistics. We illustrate clearly application of the microservices approach in our informational technology which was developed using R Studio and the main program packages are represented in the Fig. 6. It should be admitted here that the whole process of the data processing could also include such stages as preliminary data analysis and filtering which are denoted with dotted dashes. For this reason the modules with Kalman filter [8] and Holt-Winters method were used. It was experimentally proved that such preliminary data processing gives us improvement of the model accuracy and quality and also allows receive more precise data forecast. The choice of the best model is made on the basis criteria such as:

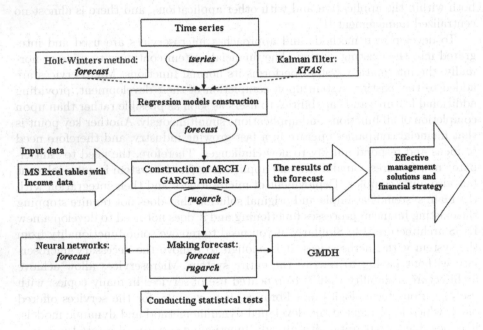

Fig. 6. Most significant R's packages in the data analysis process flow

- – Akaike Information Criterion:

$$AIC = Nln(\sum_{k=1}^{N} \varepsilon^2(k)) + 2n, \qquad (6)$$

- – Bayes-Schwartz criterion:

$$BSC = Nln(\sum_{k=1}^{N} \varepsilon^2(k)) + nln(N), \qquad (7)$$

where $n = p+q+1$ is a number of model parameters estimated using statistical data (p is the number of parameters of autoregressive component of the model; q is the number of parameters of the moving average; 1 appears when the offset a_0 is estimated).

During research we have constructed different types of regression models such as autoregressive models (AR), autoregressive moving average models (ARMA) autoregressive model with integrated moving average (ARIMA). While in time series were admitted the trend and season effects, the season ARIMA model (SARIMA) shows the best quality. The results of the analysis are shown in the Table 1. The best model defined was the model SARIMA (0,2,1) (2,0,1) [4] with such parameter values: ma1= −0.9849, sar1=0.9005, sar2=0.0506, sma1 = −0.7649. The graph of model's standardized residuals is presented on the Fig. 7. The presence of autoregressive conditional heteroskedasticity in the model residues was verified using the Ljung-Box tests and that's why such heteroskedasticity models were constructed. It appears that he best model is ARCH (2) model. The next step was using SARIMA (0,2,1) (2,0,1) (4) model for forecasting the absolute value and ARCH model for forecasting the process volatility. Then both models were used for forecasting the intervals for financial indicators. The set of models candidates for forecasting based on SARIMA (0,2,1) (2,0,1) [4] and ARCH (2) models, as well as models based on the Group Method of Data Handling (GMDH), and autoregressive neural networks were also build. The results of the experiment with actual data for forecasting the profitability of Intel Corporation for 2019 is illustrated in Table 2. As it is shown the results on the financial data of Intel Corporation for 1975–2019 were quite good by all models. The information technology for modeling and dynamic forecasting income was developed and included the set of following models: multiple regression models, integrated autoregressive model with moving average, inte-

Table 1. Comparison of the models for forecasting the absolute value

Model	AIC	BSC
ARIMA(0,1,0)	−344.0483	−344.0483
ARIMA(1,1,0)	−371.0826	−364.753
ARIMA(0,1,1)	−374.7508	−368.4212
ARIMA(1,1,1)	−373.157	−363.6626
ARIMA(2,1,1)	−371.1632	−358.5041
ARIMA(2,1,0)	−370.7163	361.222
ARIMA(0,1,2)	−373.2225	−363.7282
ARIMA(0,2,1)	−373.0245	−366.7064
ARIMA(0,2,0)	−307.1782	−304.0191
ARIMA(1,2,0)	−315.3137	−308.9956
SARIMA(0,2,1)(2,0,1) [4]	−406.4964	−390.7011

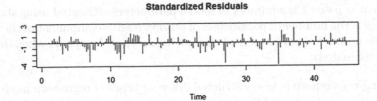

Standardized Residuals

Time

Fig. 7. Graph of standardized residuals for the SARIMA model [(0,2,1) (2,0,1) (4)]

Table 2. Comparison of the models for forecasting the enterprise profitability

Model	MSE	MAE	MAPE	THEILU
GMDH	0.0095	0.0885	0.009	0.0099
NNAR	0.0087	0.0906	0.0093	0.0095
SARIMA(0,2,1)(2,0,1) [4] + ARCH(2)	0.0041	0.0515	0.0053	0.0065

grated autoregressive model with moving average combined with conditional heteroskedasticity model, models based on Group Method of Data Handling; models based on neural networks. The IT gives the possibility for comparing the results and use the preliminary data processing and smoothing by the method of Holt-Winters and Kalman filter. In our research the input data needed preliminary processing that's why appropriate models were used and the gaps were filled by the method of the nearest neighbors. Such technology also gives the opportunity to select the best model for forecasting as well as apply the above methods for data manipulation.

9   Conclusions

To build the system for financial risk management of an enterprise, to support the adoption of adequate management decisions it is necessary to ensure the availability of appropriate analytic computational tools. The authors present the main modern practical tools and technologies for analysis and processing of financial data used by global companies, analyze their main capabilities, development trends and prospects for their use by Ukrainian financial companies. The authors revealed their own experience in creating industrial solutions and modern information technologies for specific financial institutions, banks and companies. The structure of information technology and functional composition of the expanded information DSS with complex application of the system approach to architecture development, functional scheme and procedures of the data analysis offered by probabilistic-statistical, combined, dynamic and structural-parametric methods of modeling were presented. The system provides the possibility to generate a set of complementary alternatives and objectively choose the best one of them using several sets of statistical criteria for data quality, models and estimates of forecasts. IDSS provides the dynamic assessment and forecasting the risk of losses and fulfills adaptation and construction of new adequate mathematical models for financial risks taking into account new data, criteria, requirements and information clarifications. Tools for solving applied problems of analysis and management of financial risks in the form of information technology and IDSS (client-server architecture, using microservices) are developed. Using of microservices which are connected to the system if necessary provides an opportunity to adapt proposed technologies for using in existing management systems.

Active practical applications indicate the need for further in-depth research and development of theoretical foundations for financial risk analysis, creating the new tools for processing large financial data (Big Data) and forecasting catastrophic events as well as constructing new advanced mathematical models for financial risks assessing and forecasting, taking into account data uncertainty, model structures, computational procedures and financial processes with high volatility.

References

1. Almazov:net core: how microservices in containers work. https://dou.ua/lenta/articles/microservices-net-core/. (in Russian)
2. Bidyuk, P.I., Kuznietsova, N.V.: Forecasting the volatility of financial processes with conditional variance models. J. Autom. Inf. Sci. **46**(10), 11–19 (2014)
3. Gartner. https://www.gartner.com/en
4. Hodeghatta, U.R., Nayak, U.: Business Analytics Using R – A Practical Approach. Apress, New York (2017)
5. Hyper-V: Technology overview. https://docs.microsoft.com/en us/windows-server/virtualization/hyper-v/hyper-v-technology-overview
6. IBM: Cognos business intelligence. https://www.ibm.com/support/knowledgecenter/ru/SSEP7J_10.1.1/com.ibm.swg.ba.cognos.wig_cr.10.1.1.doc/c_gtstd_c8_bi.html
7. IBM: SPSS statistics. https://www.ibm.com/ru-ru/products/spss-statistics
8. Kalman, R.E.: A new approach to linear filtering and prediction problems. J. Basic Eng. **82**(1), 35–45 (1960)
9. Kuznietsova, N.V.: Information technologies for clients' database analysis and behaviour forecasting. In: CEUR Workshop Proceeding, vol. 2067, pp. 56–62. CEUR (2017). http://ceur-ws.org/Vol-2067/
10. Kuznietsova, N.V.: Analytical technologies for clients' preferences analyzing with incomplete data recovering. In: CEUR Workshop Proceeding, vol. 2318, pp. 118–128. CEUR (2018). http://ceur-ws.org/Vol-2318/
11. Kuznietsova, N.V., Bidyuk, P.I.: Information technology for financial data analysis based on the integrated method. Syst. Res. Inf. Technol. **1**, 22–33 (2011). (in Ukrainian)
12. Kuznietsova, N.V., Bidyuk, P.I.: Business intelligence techniques for missing data imputation. Res. Bull. NTUU "KPI" **5**, 47–56 (2015). https://doi.org/10.20535/1810-0546.2015.5.60503
13. Kuznietsova, N.V., Bidyuk, P.I.: Generalization of the information technology structure for financial risk management. KPI Sci. News **3**, 33–43 (2019). https://doi.org/10.20535/kpi-sn.2019.3.176414. (in Ukrainian)

14. McNeil, A.J., Frey, R., Embrechts, P.: Quantitative Risk Management. Concepts, Techniques and Tools – Revised Edition. Princeton University Press, Princeton (2015)
15. Python. https://www.python.org/
16. Rolik, O., Telenyk, S., Zharikov, E.: The service level management in the internet of things system with microcloud-based architecture. Bull. NTUU "KPI". Inf. Comput. Intell. Syst. **65**, 110–117 (2017). (in Ukrainian)
17. SAP: Software solutions: Business applications and technology. https://www.sap.com/index.html
18. SAS: Analytics, artificial intelligence and data management. https://www.sas.com/en_gb/home
19. Solutions: Review (2020). https://solutionsreview.com/
20. Trofymchuk, O.M., Bidyuk, P.I., Gozhyj, O.P., Bidiuk, O.P.: Decision support system for implementing systemic approach to forecasting. Int. J. Comput. Technol. **14**(5), 5769–5778 (2015)
21. Tsay, R.: Analysis of Financial Time Series. Wiley, New York (2010)
22. Tuffery, S.: Data Mining and Statistics for Decision Making. Wiley, New York (2011)

Author Index

Printed in the United States
By Bookmasters